Hall

FIRE

IN THE STREETS

America in the 1960s

MILTON VIORST

SIMON AND SCHUSTER · NEW YORK

DESIGNED BY EVE METZ
PHOTO EDITOR: VINCENT VIRGA

MANUFACTURED IN THE UNITED STATES OF AMERICA
1 2 3 4 5 6 7 8 9 10
LIBRARY OF CONGRESS CATALOGING IN PUBLICATION DATA
VIORST, MILTON.
    FIRE IN THE STREETS.
    BIBLIOGRAPHY: P.
    INCLUDES INDEX.
    1. RADICALISM—UNITED STATES—CASE STUDIES. 2. CIVIL
RIGHTS—UNITED STATES—CASE STUDIES.   3. UNITED STATES
—SOCIAL CONDITIONS—1960–   —CASE STUDIES.   I. TITLE.
HN90.R3V56   309.1'73'092   79-18582

ISBN 0-671-24323-3

The author gratefully acknowledges permission to quote from the following:

Profile of James Dean by John Dos Passos. Copyright © 1960–1961 by John Dos Passos. Published in *Midcentury* by Houghton Mifflin. Reprinted by permission.

"Each Morning" (Section 4 from "Hymn for Lanie Poo") by LeRoi Jones, also known as Imamu Amiri Baraka, from *New Negro Poets: USA*, edited by Langston Hughes, copyright © 1964 by Langston Hughes. Reprinted by permission of Indiana University Press.

From *Howl and Other Poems* by Allen Ginsberg. Reprinted by permission of City Lights Books.

From *Mayor: Notes on the Sixties* by Ivan Allen, Jr., as told to Paul Hemphill. Copyright © 1971 by Ivan Allen, Jr., and Paul Hemphill. Reprinted by permission of Simon and Schuster.

From "A Novel" by Allen Ginsberg, published in *Allen Ginsberg Journals: Early Fifties–Early Sixties*. Copyright © 1977 by Allen Ginsberg. Reprinted by permission of Grove Press.

TO MY WIFE
JUDY
with whom I shared these years

CONTENTS

INTRODUCTION

THIS IS A BOOK about America in the 1960s. Whoever lived through those years will inevitably remember them as tumultuous, exalting and foreboding—but they were, I think, very bewildering as well. A nation that had prided itself on its political stability found its political system no longer equal to meeting the demands for change. A nation that had taken for granted a collective commitment to public order was suddenly stunned by the fragility of its institutions, and the assault upon the values professed by the society. In the 1960s, Americans for the first time took to the streets by the thousands, sometimes by the tens of thousands, to resolve disputes once left to the established governmental processes.

I remember the beginning, when a handful of young blacks who had tired of the deliberations of the courts, the indifference of Congress and the caution of the executive in enforcing the Constitution chose to take matters into their own hands by sitting-in at a dime store in Greensboro, North Carolina. Their gesture struck me as cavalier, and very distant from where the real decisions were being made. Though I sympathized instinctively with these young men, I was a bit dismayed by their substitution of physical for forensic confrontation. I had no idea that their act had emerged from a cal-

11

culated body of thought, whose origins dated back at least ten or twenty years, or that from it would develop a pattern of political behavior which would dominate the decade.

In 1960, the year of the sit-ins, I had turned thirty, the age conventionally cited in those days as the dividing line between the generations. In my own case, the citation was probably accurate. I had spent more than my share of time in universities, had seen much of my own country and the world. I had worked for several years as a journalist in Washington, and I thought of myself as something of an expert in politics, as well as a reasonably competent observer of society. But the 1960s were a decade commandeered by the young, and as events unfolded in dazzling succession I found myself as often as not left behind, uncomprehending. Much as I came to admire it, I could not identify myself with the generation under thirty.

Perhaps the difference was that I had never lost faith in the integrity, or the values, of the adult world. I thought of myself as sharing in the tradition of the men and women who had struggled to create the New Deal, defeat Fascism, turn back McCarthyism. It was true that my own swath of the population was called the "silent generation" for our acceptance of the stifling orthodoxy of the 1950s, but we had not surrendered our ideals, and as Eisenhower's term came to an end we foresaw a rush of vigor into the nation's political life. We knew that the machinery of American democracy was creaky, but we nonetheless considered it serviceable for enacting basic social reforms. A wave of young people, however, disputing our integrity and scoffing at our machinery, chose instead to take their politics to the streets.

Before I could grasp the meaning of the sit-ins, the Freedom Ride came along. As the Washington correspondent of the *New York Post,* I followed the buses' penetration of the South from the pressroom of Robert Kennedy's command post in the Justice Department. In my mind there was no doubt that the Freedom Riders' cause was just, and I accepted by now the contention that blacks had no obligation to wait for their rights until the political process recovered from its paralysis. Still, I wondered by what set of notions the Freedom Riders, however noble their ends, justified abandoning the means that the society had painstakingly developed for correcting injustice. I was unaware that the idea of the Freedom

Ride had been gestating for years, and that behind it stood not only deeply considered moral principles but a carefully calculated political strategy.

And so it was throughout the 1960s: one spectacular departure from the political norms that I had known cascading down upon the next. Before long, young whites replaced young blacks on center stage, and the Vietnam war replaced civil rights as the object of their demonstrations. Since I endorsed the aims of both the civil rights and antiwar movements, I gave my approval to most of these demonstrations. A few I participated in myself, though more of them I covered as a journalist. Being over thirty, however, I always felt myself an outsider, and in the last years of the decade I became increasingly estranged from the tumult by the bizarre turn that student radicalism took. Yet I never ceased being surprised by events, right until the 1960s ended in a volley of gunfire on an Ohio campus which killed four students during a protest against the invasion of Cambodia.

A few years later I started this book. I had emotions and opinions but, to the best of my knowledge, no scores to settle, no axes to grind. I had no grand theories about the 1960s to expound and, in fact, the more literature of the period I read the more skeptical I became of theories, particularly psychological ones. Someday, surely, a talented historian will sum up the 1960s in a slender, neatly sculptured volume. My objective has been more modest, and the result less succinct. I began by realizing that, though I had lived through the 1960s, I had known very little about these years. I had first to find out what happened before I could hope to understand why it did.

This book is not a history of the decade. I have tried to keep my focus on the phenomenon of social disorder, which is what made a cohesive historical unit of the period from Greensboro in 1960 to Kent State in 1970. I have gone back and traced the sequence of events, examined the range of ideas, explored the diversity of personalities that made up the richness and complexity of the period. I have not hesitated to interpret where the evidence justified it, and my duty as a writer required it. But my first objective has been to take what began for me as a jumble of sensations, and assemble the source of those sensations into a comprehensible decade. The work has made the 1960s less mystifying to me than before.

13

THE
SOURCES
1956

I
E. D. NIXON:
The New Expectations

"The third person I called was Martin Luther King. He said, 'Brother Nixon, let me think about it a while and call me back.' And when I called him back he was number nineteen. He said, 'Brother Nixon, you know I been thinking about that and I believe you got something there and I'll go along with it.' I said, 'I'm glad to hear you say that, Reverend, because I've told everybody to meet at your church this evening.'"

THE SPRING BLOOMED HOPEFULLY for American blacks in 1954. Jim Crow, the devil that had brutalized black people for so long, appeared doomed to die. After twenty years of lawsuits by the NAACP, the Supreme Court in *Brown* v. *Board of Education* had at last ruled that segregation in the nation's public schools was unconstitutional. It seemed reasonable that the courts would forthwith abolish the remaining racial barriers in American society, and that blacks would be included at last within the promise of equality before the law.

"All of us thought our problems was over with," E. D. Nixon told me. The man I spoke to was a tall, leather-skinned black whose deep voice communicated authority, a touch of humor, deep pride and perhaps even some grandeur. We talked in the living room of his little house in Montgomery, Alabama, its surfaces covered with mementos of the civil rights struggle. Nixon shook his head as we spoke, as if reproaching himself for his brief lapse into innocence. "We really thought we had it made," he remembered ruefully.

In 1954, E. D. Nixon was the acknowledged leader of the black community in Montgomery. He was head of the local organizations of both the National Association for the Advancement of Colored People and the Brotherhood of Sleeping Car Porters. Apart from the black church, these were the two strongest and most influential black institutions in the country. Already toughened by the fight against discrimination, Nixon was preparing for a new round of struggle against the racial practices of the white South.

19

E. D. Nixon, as much as any man, planted the seed of the 1960s. It was he who led the cause for civil rights from the courtroom to the streets. He conceived of the Montgomery bus boycott, the first battle that used the strategy of direct action to challenge the established practices of the society. Subsequently overshadowed by the greatness of his early subordinate, Martin Luther King, Jr., he has been largely bypassed by history. But it was Nixon who applied the spark to the tinder which blazed forth as the era of the 1960s. In the fall of 1954, he took the first tentative steps when he led a handful of black children to enroll at William Harrison, a white school a few blocks from the black neighborhood where he lived.

"We is two or three members of the NAACP," Nixon said in his rolling Southern tongue. "We met with the parents and talked about it, and everybody was ready for it. We told the parents to stay out of it, let us have the children, and all the children just followed us right on over. We thought it was wonderful but the superintendent thought it was the worst thing in the world, and the police was there and they pushed us out.

"That's when our feets hits the ground. We found out that if we really wanted to have integration, we was going to have to fight for it."

The weakness of the *Brown* decision, scarcely noticed in the euphoria of the moment, was that it contained no enforcement provisions. Nixon recalled that, shortly after the incident at the Harrison school, he received a directive from the NAACP's national office in New York. It said that the NAACP would take the desegregation issue back to the courts, and that no more challenges were to be made at the schoolhouse door.

Because he was not happy with the directive, Nixon turned his mind to finding another way, less tortuous than the lawsuit, to break down the barriers of segregation. He proposed the boycott, and fifty thousand blacks in Montgomery rallied to him. Not since the Civil War had blacks reached out so massively, or so courageously, for their own freedom.

The boycott drew not just upon Nixon's roots in the Brotherhood and the NAACP but, much more importantly, it mobilized the force of the black church in the South. It inspired blacks everywhere, and particularly the young, to a militant assertion of their rights, and it won sympathizers throughout the world. It became a popular

20

movement—in a few years, it would be known as *the* movement—
and it changed American society permanently.

Son of a sharecropper, Edgar Daniel Nixon was born in rural
Alabama just before the turn of the century. He managed to finish
a few years of school before leaving the countryside at the age of
fourteen to go off on his own to Montgomery. After holding a series
of jobs, he was hired in the baggage room at the Montgomery railroad station. In 1923, he was taken on as a Pullman porter, one of
the most prestigious jobs then available to blacks.

"Until I started working for the Pullman Company," Nixon told
me, "I'd felt that the whole world was like Montgomery. I figured
if there was segregation here, there was segregation everywhere. I
just didn't think about it.

"I first went to St. Louis, and then to Jacksonville, Florida. I went
to Atlanta and then I went to Chicago, to Detroit, to Canada, to Los
Angeles, to Texas, to New York, to Washington.

"When I first went into St. Louis, I remember I couldn't hardly
believe it. St. Louis was a Jim Crow town, yet in the station black
and white peoples sat down together. You couldn't go to one of the
hotels outside, but you could eat at the same counter in the railroad
station. Then I went out the station and I saw a black policeman. I
was talking to a friend of mine and he said they had fifty-two parks
in St. Louis, and black people could go into any of them. And we in
Montgomery didn't have any black policemans and couldn't go into
any parks. I came back here and started thinking about things."

In the late 1920s, Nixon remembered, he first met A. Philip Randolph. From the perspective of the 1970s, it is difficult to imagine
the daring required of a young man like Randolph in the era between the wars to assert the equality of blacks in America. In much
of America blacks were still lynched with impunity, and in the
North no less than the South, the Ku Klux Klan swaggered through
the streets. But the principle Randolph believed in he did not es-
pouse softly. From every rostrum he could find, he preached that a
black was any man's equal. Nixon said A. Philip Randolph was to
be forever his inspiration and ideal.

"When I heard Randolph talk the first time, I had never heard a
black man talk like that before. Let me tell you, that guy could talk!

21

Today peoples don't realize that there was no way Martin Luther King could take Randolph. Reverend King could talk, all right, don't let nobody fool you, but I don't know if any boy could talk any better than A. Philip Randolph. From the first time on, whenever I had an opportunity just to listen to him, I made every effort to go hear him.

"And let me tell you, Randolph made me see myself as a different type of man. He pointed out things that men ought to be manly enough to stand up for. He said that if you had a conviction that what you were doing was right, then you oughtn't to let nobody stop you. And when I heard how he handled Pullman officials, who were all white at that time, it changed my view about life. Randolph said that if life isn't worth dying for, then it isn't worth living for. Nobody in all my years influenced me or made me feel like A. Philip Randolph did."

Born in 1889, Phil Randolph was tall and slim, with cordovan skin and fine features, and a voice which conveyed an elegance that belied his impoverished Southern origins. In 1911, Randolph arrived in Harlem, a tempest of men and ideas, and in the ensuing decade of war and postwar reaction, he became increasingly known, and a trifle notorious, as an outspoken partisan of pacifism, Socialism and Negro power.

In those days, racial equality was a farfetched idea. Debate between blacks tended to be between the partisans of Booker T. Washington, who argued that his people should resign themselves to serving as a permanent underclass of artisans, and of W. E. B. Du Bois, who responded that the "talented tenth" of the race should be fully admitted to the nation's intellectual and professional life. Later, Marcus Garvey captured the black imagination, arguing not for equality but a doctrine of withdrawal from American life, in favor of a massive return to Africa.

Randolph rejected Garvey's separatism, as he did the submissiveness of Washington and the elitism of Du Bois. He maintained that the black masses had to organize themselves to acquire economic and political strength, and be prepared to struggle as a people until they established their rights to full equality in American society.

In 1925, Randolph set out on his lifework, to organize the Brotherhood of Sleeping Car Porters, which he saw as an opportunity "to

22

carry the gospel of unionism in the colored world." It was the chance he had dreamed of to forge black strength through unity, through the instrument of the strike, through black economic might. The union, as Randolph envisaged it, would create a new black man, vigorous, self-respecting, tough.

But the effort, begun in antiunion times and carried on during depression, was discouraging and painful. A breakthrough came in 1929, when the Brotherhood was admitted into the American Federation of Labor. The affiliation assured the Brotherhood's stability, and established its respectability. Organizing and bargaining would never be easy and, compared to other unions, it would never be very powerful. But the Brotherhood raised the banner of black economic power and, as its spokesman, Randolph became the preeminent spokesman of the black working classes. He also came to be recognized as the country's strongest black leader.

E. D. Nixon said he first encountered Randolph on a run to St. Louis, and went to hear him speak there at a Negro Y. Porters, Nixon said, were then earning $72 a month, and Randolph promised them that if they signed up with him they would soon be earning $150. Nixon said he was skeptical, but gave Randolph a dollar for dues anyhow.

Nixon remembered that when he walked up to the podium that night to shake Randolph's hand, Randolph asked him to organize a Brotherhood unit in Montgomery. Nixon said he promised to try, but as soon as he got back home his superintendent was waiting menacingly for him on the platform. With a touch of laughter, he recalled the encounter like this:

" 'They tell me you went to one of the meetings of the Brotherhood out there in St. Louis the other day,' the superintendent said, and I answered, 'Yes, I did.' And he said, 'Well, I'm going to tell you right now, we're not going to have any of our porters joining the Brotherhood.' And I said, 'Well, I was just about to tell you, after I heard Mr. Randolph talk I thought it was a good thing, and I agreed to join up with him. I also figured you was going to come out here and tell me I couldn't, so the next thing I decided is that anybody mess with my job I'm going to haul them into court, 'cause I've got the right to join any type of organization that I want and you or nobody else can't stop me.'

"Now that was nothing but a bluff. I doubt whether I knew a

lawyer's name at that time. But I bluffed him out of it, and I organized a local union here and I served as president for twenty-five
years."

Persuaded by Randolph's arguments that blacks had to organize
on a massive scale, Nixon set out at about the same time to found a
Montgomery chapter of the NAACP. Inspired by W. E. B. Du Bois,
the National Association for the Advancement of Colored People
had been established in 1909 in reaction to Booker T. Washington's
advocacy of lower-caste ranking for blacks. Its ideology was integrationist, and its leadership throughout its early decades was
largely, sometimes preponderantly, white. Its strategy was chiefly
judicial, and from its early years it regularly won important decisions in the Supreme Court. For decades it reflected Du Bois's
early elitism, and attracted the "better class" of blacks.

By the 1930s, Du Bois had moved significantly to the left in his
politics, and he regarded the NAACP as hopelessly middle class.
Randolph agreed with him. But it was the closest thing that blacks
had to a nationwide, mass-based organization of their own, and it
was a major step to have its presence established in the Southern
city of Montgomery.

Nixon said he and a postman named William G. Porter embarked
on a campaign to sign up members, and in the first years it was hard
to persuade enough people out into the open to attend meetings.
As president he finally got some preachers to join, Nixon said, then
some women, and then some socially prominent business people.
Finally the momentum picked up, he said, and by the late 1930s
the chapter had more than two thousand members, many from the
black working class, all paying dues of $1 a year.

In 1941, Nixon recalled, he led a march of 750 people to the
county courthouse to register to vote. Before the authorities closed
the doors, 42 of them actually got on the rolls. That was the year,
Nixon said, that he established his own right to vote, after a lawsuit
and a decade of persistence. But white resistance to the black vote
remained implacable, he said, and even though a few brave souls
regularly went down to the courthouse, the registration campaign
died.

Instead, the NAACP chapter turned its attention to abusive police practices, Nixon said, which were much more central to the
daily life of Montgomery's Negroes. He acquired considerable

court experience, Nixon said, trying to assure a fair trial for blacks who faced charges that were often patently trumped up. Sometimes, crosses were burned on the lawn of black houses, and with some frequency he himself received phone calls in the night threatening him with beatings and death. Whites commonly exacted economic retribution against unsubmissive blacks, Nixon said, but he noted that the Brotherhood protected his own job. Nixon acknowledged that it was the strength of the Brotherhood that permitted him to take certain stands which others could not.

Nixon offered no claim that the NAACP made much of an improvement in the life of Montgomery's blacks in those days. But it kept contact with the masses of blacks, for whom the simple act of paying $1 in dues was commitment to a cause. Whatever its failures, however, Nixon remained faithful to Randolph's ideal that blacks had to stand together against a hostile world. Nixon said the NAACP, if only by its persistent presence, helped build a sense of solidarity within the black community, which burst forth at the time of the boycott in 1955.

The day-to-day concerns of the NAACP's Montgomery chapter were far removed from the work of the NAACP's national office in New York, which was waging an antisegregation campaign through the medium of the courts. After a series of promising rulings, the NAACP resolved in 1934 to fritter away its resources no longer on efforts to attain a dubious equality for blacks under the "separate but equal" doctrine that American courts had accepted as constitutional since the 1890s. The NAACP adopted a strategy of striking at segregation directly, by persuading the Supreme Court to banish Jim Crow altogether.

Concentrating first on graduate education, NAACP lawyers won one lawsuit after another, on the grounds that equal facilities could not be assured in a segregated graduate school. By 1950, more than a thousand blacks were attending the graduate and professional schools of white Southern universities. But the ultimate test still loomed, when the NAACP would be required to persuade the Supreme Court that all segregated education was unequal, at any level, and therefore unconstitutional.

In December of 1953 Thurgood Marshall, the NAACP's legal

25

director, appeared before the Supreme Court to deliver his final argument in the *Brown* case. In his seventeen years as a lawyer for the NAACP, Marshall had pleaded before a thousand magistrates in the shabby courtrooms of the rural South. He had slept in hundreds of segregated fleabag hotels, and many times had had his life threatened by racist whites. Now he was at the pinnacle of the judicial structure, arguing before the nine judges who embodied federal justice. Marshall's long years of services, and his earlier successes before the Supreme Court, had made him "Mr. Civil Rights." Analysts considered him likely to win the *Brown* case, which would become his crowning triumph.

On an ideological level, Chief Justice Earl Warren's decision in the *Brown* case was indeed a victory for Marshall. Warren wrote that "in the field of public education the doctrine of 'separate but equal' has no place." But on a practical level the Court was less decisive.

Rather than provide for immediate relief, the justices called for further arguments on enforcement. Thurgood Marshall, of course, pleaded for immediate integration. Lawyers for the Southern states proposed a gradual transition, implemented according to local circumstances within each school district. President Dwight Eisenhower said nothing in support of *Brown*, and his attorney general quietly endorsed the South's position.

A full year after *Brown*, the Supreme Court decreed no date for the enforcement of its decision but said desegregation should be accomplished district by district "with all deliberate speed." It was the first time the Court had vindicated a constitutional right, then deferred its exercise to a more convenient time.

By the fall of 1955, Southern whites had taken courage from the faintheartedness of the federal authorities, and begun to entertain the notion that they could hold off any change indefinitely. This was still the era of witch-hunting, of McCarthyism, and of the conservative Eisenhower, when any effort, from whatever quarter, to change society was looked upon with suspicion. Most Americans probably rejected the Southern claim that the civil rights campaign was a Communist conspiracy but they were apprehensive, nonetheless, of its potential to invoke disorder. Within a few months of the Supreme Court's order to proceed, the South had made up its mind not to comply.

Senator Harry Byrd of Virginia, one of the esteemed members of the South's Old Guard, issued a call for "massive resistance" to the Court's decision. Nineteen senators and twenty-seven representatives from eleven Southern states endorsed a "Southern Manifesto" containing the same message. Alabama declared *Brown* "null, void and of no effect" and defied a court order to admit a black woman to the state university. In response to Alabama's action the federal government did nothing.

Emboldened by the message of federal indifference, working-class whites in the South swelled the ranks of a resurgent Ku Klux Klan. White violence against blacks, ranging from psychological humiliation to beatings and lynchings, had deep roots in the South, and in the mid-1950s it took on a renewed vigor. Middle-class whites founded a network they called "citizens councils," a white-collar version of the Klan. White supremacy hardly seemed in jeopardy as NAACP lawyers in places like E. D. Nixon's Montgomery filed desegregation suits, which Southern lawyers handily tied up in local courts.

Such was the treacherous atmosphere when E. D. Nixon in 1955 contemplated the available options. The *Brown* decision had made Southern whites more fearful, angrier, more resourceful, more violent than before. But it had made blacks hungrier than ever for equality. Within the country there was no discernible wave of support for civil rights, but a concern for the integrity of the Constitution was emerging. A quiet consensus was building, which held that, whatever the South's hostility to *Brown*, there could be no turning back.

What E. D. Nixon understood better than the others, however, was that the system could not be left to proceed at its own leisurely pace. Thurgood Marshall's very victory had rendered him an anachronism. Civil rights lawyers, and their liberal allies, might one day redeem the promise of *Brown*, but the legal process could have taken a half-century, or more, and blacks did not want to wait. E. D. Nixon concluded that it was time for his people to act on their own to obtain their rights, not in the courtroom but in the streets.

"We'd talked about the bus boycott all year," Nixon recounted to me with ardor. "I kept saying the only way we're going to do any

27

good is to hit these people right where it hurts, and that's in the pocketbook. I kept telling people every time we had police brutality on the bus and everything—and they would come to me about it—there ain't but one way we're going to break it up and that's we goin' to have to boycott these buses. I started telling about if we stayed off the bus, at least we could make them know we mean business."

The bus system in Montgomery, as in many Southern cities, was a particular torment to the black community. Blacks were its principal patrons, yet it had no black drivers, and the white drivers took it as their personal prerogative to abuse and degrade their black customers. Montgomery's particular version of segregation required that blacks pay their fare in the front, then get out and reenter the bus through the rear. It was an uncomfortable system in winter and in the rain, and in rush hour bus drivers sometimes pulled away before blacks, having paid their money, reached the rear door. More obnoxious were the seating practices inside. Blacks were required to seat themselves from back to front, whites from front to back, and when the bus filled, the driver was empowered to order blacks to vacate their places to whites. "Niggers, move back!" was the driver's conventional command. The humiliation of having to relinquish a seat already occupied was a special irritant to black pride, and it assured a recurrence of acrimonious incidents.

Throughout the painful months of 1955, when civil rights seemed to be everywhere in retreat, Nixon bided his time, confident that the right incident for starting the boycott would come along. "You think anybody that got arrested would be good," he said, ". . . but my training with the NAACP and the Brotherhood of Sleeping Car Porters taught me different. I've handled so many cases that I know when a man would stand up and when he wouldn't." Nixon rejected a minister's daughter because he sensed she was too weak, a schoolgirl because she had a promiscuous reputation, a woman who lived with a father who was a notorious drunk. Then, on December 1, Rosa L. Parks was arrested on a charge of violating the Alabama segregation law, and Nixon knew he had his case.

Rosa Parks has been depicted in many accounts as a chance player in the Montgomery drama, a seamstress who took it into her head to defy a white driver because she was tired from a hard day at work. Indeed, Mrs. Parks's decision that afternoon was sponta-

28

neous, but the role was one for which she had spent many years preparing. Nixon remembered Mrs. Parks as one of the first women with the courage to join the Montgomery chapter of the NAACP. Later she became the chapter secretary, and for some years she managed the office in downtown Montgomery which served as Nixon's headquarters when he was, simultaneously, state president of the NAACP and regional director of the Brotherhood. Mrs. Parks was widely known in Montgomery as a woman with a steely belief in racial equality.

On several earlier occasions Rosa Parks, without being arrested, had been evicted from Montgomery buses for refusing to obey the drivers. But now the line between the races was more tautly drawn than before. Mrs. Parks was taken off the bus by two policemen and driven to the jail, where she was charged, photographed and fingerprinted. Nixon arrived a few hours later to sign the bond for her release.

"The next morning, I called Reverend Ralph D. Abernathy," Nixon recalled, "and told him what had happened and that I expected him to support me in the boycott, and he said, 'I'll go along with you.' I called the late Reverend H. H. Hubbard and he said, 'Brother Nick'—you see, everybody called me Brother Nick in those days—'you know I'll go along with you.' Abernathy was secretary of the Baptist Ministers Alliance and the Reverend Hubbard was president.

"The third person I called was Martin Luther King. He said, 'Brother Nixon, let me think about it awhile and call me back.' And when I called him back he was number nineteen. He said, 'Brother Nixon, you know I been thinking about that and I believe you got something there and I'll go along with it.' I said, 'I'm glad to hear you say that, Reverend, because I've told everybody to meet at your church this evening.'* The reason I set it up at his church was I wanted it right downtown. Reverend King didn't even know Mrs. Parks at that time."

The Montgomery bus boycott would not have happened without the hope engendered among blacks by the Supreme Court's *Brown*

* King's account of the start of the bus boycott, published in his *Strive Toward Freedom*, differs substantially from Nixon's. It tends to emphasize his own role, though not necessarily in a self-serving way. King simply seemed to be unaware of what Nixon was doing during these days and he never bothered to find out.

decision the year before, and the despair which accompanied the recognition that desegregation would not be enforced. The boycott would surely not have happened without Nixon, who introduced to the community the ideological militancy of A. Philip Randolph and the organizational mission of the NAACP. But, having begun, it could not have endured until victory without Martin Luther King's genius for imparting to it a moral quality, which in turn mobilized the churches to sustain it. Conditions were no worse in Montgomery than they were elsewhere in the South, and they were better than in many cities. Only a unique convergence of men and ideas distinguished Montgomery from so many other places in the South and transformed it into the first major battleground in the new uprising for equality.

Martin Luther King, Jr., had arrived from Atlanta only the year before. Bearer of a reputation for erudition, he was the son of an esteemed family. His maternal grandfather had been pastor of the Ebenezer Baptist Church in Atlanta, and a charter member of the NAACP. His father, a self-taught sharecropper's son, had taken over at Ebenezer after marrying the pastor's daughter.

Raised in the secure comfort of Atlanta's black middle class, Martin Luther King, Jr., attended Morehouse, one of the well-regarded black colleges in the South, the Crozer Theological Seminary in Chester, Pennsylvania, and Boston University, where he received a doctorate in theology. At the age of twenty-five, he was invited to become the pastor of the Dexter Avenue Baptist Church in the center of Montgomery, one of the black South's most prestigious churches.

Some forty leaders of the black community, more than half of them ministers, attended the meeting that night in King's church. E. D. Nixon, off on his regular run on the railroad, was absent, but his will dominated the proceedings. There was a mood of defiance among the men, but they argued lustily until they reached a consensus that the black community was prepared to support them. Then they voted unanimously to begin the boycott on Monday, two days hence.

King and the staff of the church got out leaflets announcing the boycott the next morning. The *Montgomery Advertiser* acquired a copy and reproduced it in the Sunday editions. The publicity was indispensable to the boycott. Proof to whites of a heinous conspiracy, the leaflet was to blacks a call to act.

It was a cold winter Monday, December 5, when Montgomery's buses first rode empty, while blacks by the thousands traveled in improvised car pools, or trudged back and forth, many of them for miles, to their jobs. At police court that morning, Rosa Parks was found guilty of violating the city's Jim Crow ordinance and fined $14. Fred Gray, a young black lawyer who had worked with Nixon on NAACP cases, announced his intention to appeal. In the afternoon, the black leadership met to form an organization to keep the boycott going.

Some of the men at the meeting, out of a reflexive fear of provoking the white community, wanted to operate the organization in secret. E. D. Nixon, who was back in town now, would not hear of it. "We are acting like little boys," King's book quotes Nixon as saying. ". . . If we are afraid, we might as well fold up right now . . . The white folks are eventually going to find it out anyway. We'd better decide now if we are going to be fearless men or scared boys."

Nixon had a more pungent recollection of the episode. "Well, I was sittin' there boiling over," he told me, "so mad I didn't know what to do, so I jumped up, and I forgot about we was up in the balcony of the church. I said, 'What the hell you people talkin' 'bout?' Just like that, see, and I cussed. I said, 'How you gonna have a mass meeting, gonna boycott a city bus line without the white folks knowing it? You guys have went around here and lived off these poor washerwomen all your lives and ain't never done nothing for 'em. And now you got a chance to do something for 'em, you talkin' about you don't want the white folks to know it. Un-less'n this program is accepted and brought into the church like a decent, respectable organization, . . . I'll take the microphone and tell 'em the reason we don't have a program is 'cause you all are too scared to stand on your feet and be counted.' " *

Whichever account may be more accurate, neither left any doubt that Nixon settled the dispute, but he was not the only brave man

* This, and several other quotes from Nixon, are drawn from Howell Raines, *My Soul Is Rested.*

in the church that evening. In the atmosphere of December 1955, the act of chartering an organization to confront the power of the white majority in Montgomery, Alabama, required huge courage. It also required the daring to cast off old habits of mind, which were the accomplice of white supremacy. These black men, only a generation or two away from slavery, broke new ground in the South that day by standing up for what they believed were their rights. They called the organization they founded the Montgomery Improvement Association.

E. D. Nixon agreed to serve as treasurer of the MIA. He told me he ruled out being a candidate for the presidency because he knew that the boycott would be long and the crises recurring, and that too much of the time he would be away riding the trains. He also told me he felt the MIA needed "a man who is intelligent enough to meet with any class of people," which he said disqualified him. It was a touching, self-effacing admission from a man who had spent a lifetime defying persecution, and in whose mind the boycott had taken shape, but who doubted whether he, a Pullman porter, was equal to the more wide-ranging public responsibilities that he foresaw for the MIA.

Without debate, Martin Luther King, Jr., was elected the MIA's president. The mythology holds that King was selected because special qualities were recognized in him. It is more likely true that the choice was made, unanimously, because King, being new in town, had not been compromised by his dealing with the whites, or weakened in factional disputes during his dealing with the blacks.

"The action had caught me unawares," King wrote in *Stride Toward Freedom*. "It happened so quickly that I did not even have time to think it through. It is probable that if I had, I would have declined the nomination."

The statement is credible, and corresponds with what we know of King's character. King was not conventionally ambitious. He drew self-assurance from his social rank in the black community, from a sense of *noblesse oblige*. It is likely he would have been content to spend his life at the center of an observant and dutiful Christian congregation, a pastor recognized for his scholarship and good works, not for political leadership.

During his first year in Montgomery, King had given no evidence of great secular concern. He lingered over the final touches of his doctoral dissertation, and proceeded circumspectly to shape new pastoral programs. With civil rights a growing public preoccupation, he delivered excellent sermons on racial issues, but he made no effort to draw his congregation, the most influential in the black community of Montgomery, into social activism. A month before the boycott began, he had declined nomination to the presidency of the city's chapter of the NAACP.

Throughout his life, in fact, there was a side of King, discernible even in his finest moments, of ambiguity and self-doubt. This was not a man endowed with a feeling of God-given righteousness. He did not claim to be an oracle. Unable to summon the certainty of a fanatic, he agonized at every juncture over the morality and the prudence of the choices he faced. Instead of dogmatism, there burned in him an unquenchable faith in God, which transcended his fears and vacillation and, transmitted to his followers, gave them strength.

King would probably have been satisfied to play a lesser role in the boycott, as he would have been happy, in the years that followed, to relinquish responsibility and withdraw to lesser prominence in the civil rights struggle. King was not comfortable with leadership. He accepted it only reluctantly. And yet, without King's leadership, the civil rights movement is unlikely ever to have become the dynamic force which moved the nation.

King sat at the center of the platform in the Holt Street Baptist Church, awaiting his turn to speak, the night the boycott started. It was a mass meeting of the Montgomery Improvement Association, the kind that would be repeated twice a week throughout the year-long campaign. The hall was filled to its remotest corners. The outside world sensed that something important was happening, and television cameras whirred. Rosa Parks was introduced and received a standing ovation. A series of ministers delivered prayers and invocations.

E. D. Nixon, who also spoke, provided the following recollection:

"I told the people there, this is going to be a long-drawn-out affair. What I'm going to tell you right now is before this thing is over with, somebody is gonna die. It might be me, for all I know, but the only thing I ask is if it be me, don't let me die in vain. And nobody got up and got their hat and left that night.

"And then I said, for twenty-some-odd years I been fightin' and sayin' to myself that I didn't want the children to come along and have to suffer all the insults that I've suffered. Well, hell, I changed my mind tonight. Just like that, I decided that I wanted to enjoy some of this freedom myself. And everybody hollered when I said that.

"And the paper will tell you that forty-five hundred hymn-singing niggers were at the Holt Street Baptist Church and organized the Montgomery Improvement Association. But I'm telling you that if it weren't seventy-five hundred people down there, there weren't a single soul."

For Martin Luther King that night, the speech he was called upon to make represented a major effort at self-examination. He had never before thought seriously about the social implications of his religious beliefs. In his theological studies, he had been attracted to the activist interpretation of the church contained in the social gospel. He had been drawn by his personal religious credo to the concept of society shaped by Christian pacifism. He had acquired some familiarity with Gandhi's ideas of nonviolent direct action and Thoreau's of civil disobedience. But he had never tried to put them together in a practical program, and he was troubled by the apparent contradiction in inspiring his listeners to show courage in behalf of a just cause without engendering in them un-Christian feelings of resentment and hate.

"How could I make a speech," he later wrote, "that would be militant enough to keep my people aroused to positive action and yet moderate enough to keep this fervor within controllable Christian bounds?"

What King articulated was a dilemma he would never permanently resolve, nor were his successive formulations to resolve it ever completely accepted by those who followed him. Still, in Montgomery, King forged the ideas of nonviolent direct action into a powerful weapon. With this weapon, he was able to mobilize Christian morality and apply its force to the cause of racial equality. It was a weapon he would work to refine, but from which he never turned, throughout the remainder of his life. It was his transcendent achievement that he was able to harness the latent dynamism of the black church, as a religious and social force, and put it to the service of civil rights.

In a large sense, this dynamism had always lain concealed beneath the surface of the black man's Christianity, waiting to be tapped. For many years, the black church had been a passive force in Southern society, even an accomplice of Jim Crow. King himself attributed this complicity to the Fundamentalist doctrine imbedded in the black church which held that "ministers are not supposed to get mixed up in such earthy, temporal matters as social and economic improvement; they are to 'preach the gospel.' " He did not find it easy himself making the leap in his professional preoccupation from personal salvation to public weal.* In later years, he would acknowledge a resentment toward "preachers riding around in big cars, living in fine homes, but not willing to take part in the fight." Yet, over the years, there had been an ambiguity in the black church that made it far more than a passive partner in the status quo.

The black church, from the beginning, took from Christianity a dual, and contradictory, message: submission to slavery and the equality before God of the human soul. The whites, in offering blacks their faith, emphasized the virtues of the former. The blacks, in accepting it, dwelled upon the implications of the latter.

During the decades of slavery the black church, shunned by whites, acquired increasing autonomy, and drew further and further from the influence of the masters. The Negro church in American history served as the incubator and transmitter of an indigenous black culture, and the mainstay of the concept of black dignity. By the nineteenth century, black Christianity possessed a clear political character, which whites hardly noticed. The Negro spiritual was a signpost on the road that black culture traveled. Whites countenanced it as a lament, and a statement of resignation. Blacks upheld it as a hymn of faith in the ultimate triumph of justice for all men. To many blacks, the mission of the church lay not so much in the gospel as in pursuing that triumph.

But whatever its role, the church created leaders. "The

---

* King's ideas had matured enough by 1963 for him, in his celebrated "Letter from a Birmingham Jail," to write: "I have watched white churchmen stand on the sidelines and mouth pious irrelevancies and sanctimonious trivialities. In the midst of a mighty struggle to rid our nation of racial and economic injustice, I have heard many ministers say: 'Those are social issues, with which the gospel has no real concern.' And I have watched many churches commit themselves to a completely otherworldly religion which makes a strange un-Biblical distinction between body and soul, between the sacred and the secular."

35

Preacher," wrote W. E. B. Du Bois in *The Souls of Black Folk*, "is the most unique personality developed by the Negro on American soil. A leader, a politician, an orator, a 'boss,' an intriguer, an idealist—all these he is, and ever, too, the centre of a group of men, now twenty, now a thousand in number." The church was the only training ground that blacks had.

Of the slave revolts in American history, most were led by preachers, but more often preachers kept the flame of freedom alive more discreetly, within the church's walls. After the Civil War, preachers became the political chiefs of the emancipated slaves but, like black political power generally, they went into eclipse near the end of the century. Martin Luther King, Jr., and the many black preachers who followed along with him, represented not a new phenomenon in leading black resistance to white oppression, but the reemergence of an old one.

King followed long-standing church practice, too, in eliciting, and controlling, the emotions of his congregation from the pulpit. His practice had deep roots in the black ministry, perhaps in Africa itself. One Sunday morning, in the Ebenezer Baptist Church in Atlanta, I saw that side of King, and I understood that the political inspiration he gave his followers came, first, from his powers as a preacher of the gospel. King excelled in the pulpit, and enjoyed it, both its high theatrics and warm spontaneity.

Dressed in his black robe, King performed like an orchestra conductor, rolling out pronouncements in his deep baritone voice, to which the crowded pews responded on cue. Almost mystically, the congregation answered with handclaps and shouts of approval, periodic laughter, with the rhythmic counterpoint of "yessir, yessir," by an occasional shriek of pain or a rapturous moan of deep involvement. Du Bois called it the "frenzy," and considered it a means of achieving a collective spiritual union. King's contribution was that he put this worship openly to political ends, in direct challenge to the system of segregation.

It was only through the medium of the church, in fact, that King could imagine a movement to assert the rights of blacks. When the question was asked, "Why Montgomery, in December of 1955?" King had little doubt about the answer. He addressed it in *Stride Toward Freedom,* and concluded that "every rational explanation breaks down at some point . . . it cannot be explained without a divine dimension." A divine dimension may indeed have been present in Montgomery, but it was Martin Luther King who moved it out of the churches and into the streets to create real political power.

In the first few months of the boycott, King deepened his grasp of the concept of nonviolence, gradually transforming it from a personal commitment to a strategy for provoking political change. He was helped by at least two others, whose experience with nonviolence dated back to the Fellowship of Reconciliation, a pacifist organization which in the 1940s set out to apply to the United States the new ideas that Mohandas Gandhi was practicing in India within an altogether different context. Though never more than a tiny organization, the FOR had a profound influence on the development of the civil rights movement.

One of King's teachers was Glenn E. Smiley, a white Methodist minister from Texas, who was then field secretary for the Fellowship of Reconciliation. The other was Bayard Rustin, a black pacifist, former FOR activist, a protégé of A. Philip Randolph and an organizer of great renown. Rustin fed King on the thinking of Gandhi, worked to organize support services for the boycott outside Montgomery and finally signed on as King's secretary and factotum.

Yet what distinguished Montgomery from the experiences of these two men in FOR was that, for the first time in America, nonviolence had acquired a mass following. The work of Smiley and Rustin had always been with small groups, selflessly practicing nonviolence to desegregate a restaurant here or a theater there; but in Montgomery blacks were marching by the thousands. These two men, and others familiar with Gandhian principles who passed through Montgomery, shared their understanding, both theoretical and practical, with King. But it was King himself who had to make the leap, to apply nonviolent direct action on a massive scale, on the inhospitable terrain of the American South.

In *Stride Toward Freedom,* King wrote that, until he read Gandhi as a divinity student, he was convinced that the ethics of Jesus had application only to individual relationships. He said he accepted the view that "turn the other cheek," while a valid personal philosophy, was irrelevant to the conflict between races. Gandhi, he

37

wrote, was "probably the first person in history to lift the love ethic of Jesus above mere interaction between individuals to be a power and effective social force on a large scale." Gandhi convinced him, he said, that nonviolent resistance, lovingly conducted, was a strategy in the freedom struggle that was not only moral but practical.

But only after the bus boycott began, King wrote, did he come to understand the real power of nonviolence. "Many of the things that I had not cleared up intellectually," he noted, "were now solved in the sphere of practical action."

In Montgomery, the campaign was limited to a boycott, a quiescent, even stoic, form of nonviolent direct action. In future years, King's nonviolent strategy would become more aggressive, evolving into mass marches and other forms of physical confrontation with authority. Near the end of his life, he was seeking tactics which would be still more dynamic, and he spoke of massive "dislocation" of transportation systems, of local bureaucracies, perhaps of the government itself. But Montgomery was the start.

King acknowledged that, even for him, it was not easy to reach an appreciation of how love could serve as an instrument of social change. Nonetheless, he made a commitment in Montgomery to pursue no other political course. His example persuaded thousands of others, black and white, that this was the right road to the achievement of racial equality.

King made a basic distinction: nonviolent direct action was not to be confused with passive nonresistance to evil. It was an active nonviolent *attack* upon evil. Its aim was not to defeat or humiliate an opponent but to win his friendship, and persuade him of his error. Its target was not the evildoer but the evil, and its practitioner had to be willing to turn the other cheek to violence, and even to accept jail when necessary. King believed that the suffering of a nonviolent activist would educate his opponent, and transform him.

Nonviolence, furthermore, contained a pledge to shun "internal violence of the spirit," King believed, no less than physical violence. The nonviolent activist had to refuse to hate. He was to seek to create a community of *agape*, a Greek word which King defined as an overflowing love, or a redeeming goodwill for all men, even toward those who do one evil. King also said that the nonviolent activist had to understand that suffering without retaliation was an act of faith in the future, and had to believe that the universe was ultimately on the side of justice.

These were the principles that King worked to impart to the blacks of Montgomery, chiefly during the biweekly mass meetings that became an intrinsic part of the MIA movement. The meetings rotated from church to church and in many ways, were indistinguishable from religious services. They regularly drew thousands of people, cutting sharply across class lines in the black community. The agenda of the meetings was unvarying in its sequence of songs, prayer, Scripture reading, remarks by the leader, donations, reports from various MIA committees and an inspirational talk.

King presided over a large proportion of the meetings, but whether it was he or another minister who spoke, their purpose was, more often than not, indoctrination in the theories and practices of nonviolence. The meetings made Gandhi a household word, King noted, and "people who had never heard of the little brown saint were now saying his name with an air of familiarity."

By insisting upon the principles of nonviolence, King asked a great deal of those who gave him their allegiance. The doctrine was foreign to the experience, the history and the vision of life of most blacks. Only a few in Montgomery ever really grasped it, and most accepted it only out of confidence in King, and in his assurance that it represented "Christianity in action." But the doctrine's prospects for survival as a commanding force depended on the results it yielded.

E. D. Nixon, for one, had no use for it. He had been raised in the atmosphere of savagery that was intrinsic to race relations in the South. His life had many times been threatened, sometimes because he was a black leader, sometimes simply because he was black. He envisaged the boycott not as King did, as a witness against evil, but as a means for applying pressure, inflicting pain, demonstrating a power of revenge over the whites who had brutalized him. Nixon's experience told him that brute force was the method to which whites would turn to maintain the structure of their supremacy. And it told him that force was the only way for blacks to deal with them in return. To E. D. Nixon, nonviolence was an incomprehensible folly.

"I had all kinds of guns here in the house," he told me, "and a whole lot of times I carried one in my pocket. I told Reverend King that I didn't go along with non-violence, and I told him I wouldn't. 'Cause I knew if anybody hit me in the face, I was goin' to hit them back.

39

"Now Reverend King wouldn't do that. But I told him point blank that I couldn't agree with him. And he said don't go around and preach it, and I said I won't. But I told him I'll stay out of your parades where I might get hit, 'cause I know I'm going to fight back."

The personal test of King's commitment, and the black community's, came when the boycott was two months old. Though blacks complained of long walks, sore feet and lost time, the sight of the empty buses buoyed their satisfaction and sense of solidarity. Hundreds of volunteers had been enlisted for the car pools. Despite the wintry weather, seventeen thousand people got to work each day, while whites looked on in angry impotence. Then, on January 30, when King was at the pulpit leading a mass meeting, his house was bombed, and only by chance did his wife and ten-week-old baby escape unharmed. Later that night, a thousand angry black men and women assembled on his lawn, many of them carrying guns, knives, clubs or broken bottles. They were ready to spill blood, even their own, and waited only for a command from King when he appeared on his devastated front porch. It was a climactic moment for the movement, and for nonviolent protest, and King did not hesitate.

"If you have weapons, take them home," he told the wrathful crowd. "If you do not have them, please do not seek to get them. We cannot solve this problem through retaliatory violence . . . We must love our white brothers, no matter what they do to us. We must make them know that we love them. Jesus still cries out in words that echo across the centuries: 'Love your enemies; bless them that curse you; pray for them that despitefully use you.' This is what we must live by. We must meet hate with love."

The crowd responded grudgingly with cries of "Amen," and fitfully drifted away.

The demands formulated by the Montgomery Improvement Association at the start of the boycott were extremely modest. That the MIA did not call for an immediate end to segregation was an index of what appeared realistic, even proper, in the American South at that time. It is true that when Rosa Parks was found guilty of violating the Jim Crow ordinance and fined $14, the MIA looked

to the Supreme Court to vindicate its efforts by sweeping bus segregation away. But that was for the federal government, in its majesty, to do. The program submitted by the MIA to the city fell far
short of such a demand.

The MIA's three conditions for ending the boycott were (1) courteous treatment of blacks by bus drivers, (2) seating on a first-
come-first-served basis, blacks back to front, whites front to back,
(3) employment of black operators on routes through predominantly black neighborhoods. This proposed modification of Montgomery's Jim Crow system was hardly audacious. It was, in fact,
the procedure followed in Atlanta, Mobile and other Southern
cities. But a committee composed of Montgomery's mayor, several
city commissioners and representatives of the bus company insisted the demands would violate the local segregation laws, and
turned them down cold.

Within a few days after the start of the boycott, all negotiations
collapsed, and were never resumed. The feeling among whites toward the MIA was not quite unanimous. A businessman's group
called Men of Montgomery promoted compromise as preferable to
economic disruption and bad publicity for the city. A few white
ministers, and a handful of private citizens, spoke out courageously
for a new attitude toward blacks. But an overwhelming majority
opposed any concessions, and seemed to sense—as did Montgomery's blacks—that a victory for the MIA would be the beginning of the end of the structure of white supremacy. So, after the
initial flurry of meetings, the city's white leadership turned its attention to destroying the blacks' organization.

On January 22, 1956, the *Montgomery Advertiser* ran an article
containing an announcement by the city commission that it had
reached a "settlement" with three prominent black ministers. King
was tipped off to the story the night before and found the three
ministers, none of them prominent, who admitted having been ca-
joled into a meeting by white leaders, but denied making any
agreement with them at all. That night, King and other MIA members made the rounds of the black community to denounce the hoax
and the next morning, Sunday, all of the city's black ministers reaffirmed from their pulpits that the boycott was still on. The city
commission was confounded, and the buses continued to ride
empty.

41

The police then embarked on a series of harassments to disrupt the MIA's car pools. Drivers were stopped for questioning about their licenses and insurance, ticketed on dubious charges and sometimes jailed. People waiting for rides were threatened with arrest for hitchhiking or vagrancy. King himself was arrested on a traffic charge, intimidated during a long ride in a police car and locked in a cell for several hours. The tactic brought the city some success, frightening away a number of volunteer drivers, but the car pools survived and the boycott went on.

Then came a profusion of threatening letters and phone calls, followed by the bombings. King's home was the first target, E. D. Nixon's the second. "I was coming down from Chicago and I got to Birmingham that morning," Nixon recalled. "A redcap came out when he saw me and gave me a paper and said, 'Hey, Nick, they blowed up your house.' They tried to throw the bomb in the up-stairs window but it hit the side of the building and slided off the porch and hit the driveway."

King wrote in *Stride Toward Freedom* that, after this savagery, he felt intimations of impending death, and urged his followers to face up to carrying on without him. It was a feeling that was to stay with him for the rest of his life. King understood by now that the violence in Montgomery was not random. If the bombings were not actually ordered by the white hierarchy, the lackadaisical investigation by the Montgomery police was persuasive evidence that violence had its sanction. Some reports indicated, in fact, that the dynamite had passed through the hands of the police.

Then late in February, 1956, a Montgomery County grand jury indicted King and more than a hundred other activists in the MIA, at least a fourth of them preachers, on an obscure state antiboycott law. King was out-of-town that day and, according to a diarist,* Nixon was the first to appear at the police station to surrender. "You are looking for me? Here I am," he declared.

Soon hundreds of blacks assembled outside the police station to applaud as, one by one, the other indicted leaders appeared. "A once fear-ridden people had been transformed," King wrote. "Those who had previously trembled before the law were now

* Bayard Rustin kept a diary on some of his Montgomery experiences. It was published in the April 1956 issue of *Liberation*, and reprinted in Rustin's book, *Down the Line*.

proud to be arrested for the cause of freedom." Many who were not arrested on the indictment were disappointed, King reported, and checked at the police station in the hope that they had been inadvertently overlooked.

King was tried in a test of the law on March 19. His team of NAACP attorneys brought twenty-eight defense witnesses to the stand to show, as the statute required, that the boycott had just cause, and they testified at length on the indignities they had suffered on the buses. After four days of trial, the two sides rested and the judge immediately found King guilty. The sentence was a fine of $500 or 386 days at hard labor. The indictments against the other defendants, now reduced to eighty-nine, were stayed pending King's appeal.

Meanwhile, the city's white leadership continued the campaign against the car pools, reasoning now that they were the MIA's weakest link. The city succeeded in having the MIA's liability insurers cancel the policies on its station wagons, several of which it had acquired through donations. King, in bewilderment, turned to a black insurance broker in Atlanta, who then went to Lloyd's of London, which solved the problem by issuing new policies.

Then the mayor instructed the city's legal department to file a suit to stop the operation of the car pools outright. It alleged that the car pools were an illegal private enterprise, operating without license or franchise, depriving the city of legitimate tax revenues. An MIA petition in Federal court to have the suit dismissed was rejected. As summer turned to fall, and blacks looked forward to a second winter without buses, it appeared quite possible that the city's suit would succeed, thereby bringing MIA and the entire boycott effort to collapse.

But the city was up against more than a local association of blacks, for, within a few months after it was founded, the MIA had become a cause that captured imaginations, and contributions, everywhere. The heaviest response came from black church groups throughout the country and local chapters of the NAACP. Whites were also enthusiastic, however, and important gifts were made by labor and civic organizations. Individual contributions came from as far away as Europe and Asia. Every mail brought in checks, King

43

reported, a few as large as $5000. More often, the letters contained one or two dollar bills.

E. D. Nixon, who was treasurer of the MIA, recalled that he was always out trying to raise money. "I'd come in here at nine o'clock in the morning on my run, take a bath and catch a flight out of here, and at nine o'clock at night I'd be in Detroit, Chicago, New York and so forth," Nixon said. "I raised ninety-seven thousand dollars and brought back five automobiles. The United Automobile Workers one night gave me thirty-five thousand dollars."

For Nixon, the most exhilarating event of the year was a fund-raiser for the MIA in New York's Madison Square Garden at the end of May, 1956. Eleanor Roosevelt and A. Philip Randolph were there. So were Roy Wilkins, executive secretary of the NAACP, and Congressman Adam Clayton Powell of Harlem. Tallulah Bankhead, Sammy Davis, Jr., and Pearl Bailey were the entertainers, and eighteen thousand enthusiastic supporters were in the audience. Nixon and Rosa Parks were guests of honor.

"When it got to me to talk it was five minutes of twelve," Nixon reminisced, "and I'd been sitting there so long I could hardly stand up. I got up and thanked the people, and I said that, according to this program, I'm supposed to speak thirty minutes, but if that's true it means I'll start talking today and end tomorrow. They didn't catch that at first, and then someone started laughing in the corner and they all started applauding.

"I don't think I talked for over ten or fifteen minutes. I started out by saying, 'I'm E. D. Nixon from Montgomery, Alabama, a city that is known as the Cradle of the Confederacy and the city that has stood still for more than ninety-three years until Rosa Parks was arrested and thrown in jail like a common criminal, and fifty thousand Negroes—"We weren't using the word 'black' then," he whispered to me—rose up and caught hold to the cradle and began to rock it till the Jim Crow rocker began to reel and the segregated slats began to fall. I'm from that city.' The people screamed. I never shall forget it."

As MIA treasurer, Nixon had more unusual financial responsibilities, too. One of the MIA's fears was that the city would somehow manage to seize its bank accounts, or at least freeze its balances, leaving it financially impotent. So the executive board decided to deposit MIA's money outside Alabama. "You know what," Nixon told me, "I left here once with eighty-five thousand dollars in a briefcase. I went to Atlanta, Raleigh, Richmond, Washington, Philadelphia and New York, and I scattered that money out and put it in the bank."

King has written that the MIA collected $250,000 during the boycott. But Nixon, who was often unhappy about the organization's loose bookkeeping procedures, said the figure was too low. "I cut checks myself for four hundred and fifteen thousand," he said, and there may have been more.

More than money came to Montgomery. The boycott was the object of incessant attention from the press and television, which kept it constantly before the eyes of the nation and the world. Without television to maintain a level of popular concern, the boycott would not have been able to endure. Without television, in fact, it is probable there would not have been a civil rights movement. Television and the press kept up heavy coverage because the country was interested in Montgomery, but it is also true that the country remained interested in Montgomery because television and the press kept up heavy coverage.

King proved to be a luminous media personality, receptive to questioning, invariably articulate, always composed. He quickly became nationally, then internationally, known, and he was deluged with invitations to appear before audiences to tell the Montgomery story. He made regular visits to black colleges, where he carried the doctrine of nonviolence to a generation of black students. He preached in the nation's most celebrated churches, where he helped turn the religious impulses of whites toward civil rights.

In August of 1956, King appeared before the Democratic National Convention in Chicago. He urged the Democrats to commit themselves to strong federal action in behalf of civil rights, but they were scarcely more supportive of the Supreme Court's *Brown* decision in 1956 than Eisenhower was. Adlai Stevenson, the Democratic nominee, failed to sense that civil rights was a rapidly maturing political issue. He preferred being vague, in the hope of retaining the electoral votes of what had once been the Solid South. In spite of Montgomery, civil rights was hardly discussed in the 1956 campaign. But four years later, and for the rest of the decade, civil rights would be central to American politics.

45

From the start of the boycott, an underlying assumption of Martin
Luther King and the MIA was that, ultimately, the Supreme Court
would come along to declare bus segregation unconstitutional. The
boycott gave urgency to the cause. It tested the political strength of
blacks. It gave a moral component to the court deliberations. But,
by itself, it would not end Jim Crow. The MIA's strategy was an
acknowledgment that, even with the weapon of nonviolent direct
action, Southern blacks were still dependent on the federal government to change the law.

The city of Montgomery had made a serious mistake in charging
Rosa Parks with violating the local desegregation ordinance. Had it
brought her to court on a conventional disorderly conduct charge,
the MIA's lawyers would have had no real case to appeal. But by
convicting her on the basis of a law whose constitutionality could
be challenged, Montgomery defined the MIA's case. MIA's lawyers
felt confident that they had only to hold out while the appeals
ascended, slowly but surely, through the judicial system. They
underestimated, however, the canny ability of Southern officials to
rectify their blunders by manipulating justice.

"One day it came to me, I just thought about it off the top of my
head," E. D. Nixon told me, "about this woman named Viola White,
and her case had never been heard after ten years. It was a bus case
just like Mrs. Parks'. The only thing was she didn't get up and the
bus driver attacked her, and she beat him almost to death on the
bus. They arrested her and put her in jail, and I hired a lawyer to
represent her. They found her guilty, and we appealed her case to
the Circuit Court of Alabama. The case never got docketed on appeal and she died. That was ten years before."

Nixon said he shared his fears with J. Clifford Durr, a white
lawyer in Montgomery. One of the few whites to support civil
rights, Durr confirmed that the state was likely never to put the
Parks case on the appeals court calendar. It was Durr's opinion that
the MIA was wasting its time trying to get the Parks case to the
Supreme Court via the Alabama court system. He said it would be
better to get four or five plaintiffs to swear they had been mistreated
on the bus, and then file a civil suit directly in federal court.

"I came in from my run on the second Sunday in January 1956,"

Nixon recalled, "and I called Reverend King and Reverend Abernathy, and I told them, I got news for you boys. I said I can call you 'boys' because I got a son that's older than either of you. I said, you all think we goin' to the Supreme Court in Mrs. Parks's case. The city fathers knows we feels that the only outlet we got is that case, and they goin' to freeze us out. I told them what we would have to do."

The MIA found some women who were willing to join a complaint in federal court, and Fred Gray, the NAACP lawyer who represented Mrs. Parks, put the case together. Four women filed at first. Later one dropped out, and the city used the pretext to seek disbarment of Gray, on grounds that he had sought to represent her without permission. The woman, who worked for the city, subsequently told Bayard Rustin, "I had to do what I did or I wouldn't be alive today," and the disbarment was averted only after Nixon, who had been forewarned of the trap, produced a tape recording of the MIA's negotiations with the women. Later, the MIA paid off Mrs. Parks's sentence with a check to the Alabama courts, and a hearing on the women's civil suit was set in Federal Court on May 11, 1956.

"No one can understand the feeling that comes to a Southern Negro on entering a Federal court," King wrote, "unless he sees with his own eyes and feels with his own soul the tragic sabotage of justice in the city and state courts of the South. The Negro goes into these courts knowing that the cards are stacked against him . . . But the Southern Negro goes into the Federal court with the feeling that he has an honest chance of justice before the law."

The case was argued before a panel of three federal judges. Robert Carter of the NAACP's national office, representing the MIA, contended that the judges should apply the *Brown* precedent to overthrow the separate-but-equal doctrine which guided Montgomery's bus operations. The city's attorneys responded that, if segregation were abolished, Montgomery would become a bloody battleground.

King wrote that he knew the MIA would win when one of the judges asked, "Is it fair to command one man to surrender his constitutional rights, if they are his constitutional rights, in order to prevent another man from committing a crime?" The judges deliberated for about three weeks, and on June 4 ruled in the MIA's

47

favor by a two-to-one margin, declaring the municipal bus segregation ordinance unconstitutional.

King and his followers then waited with anxiety while the Supreme Court considered the city's appeal. Throughout the summer and into the fall, meanwhile, city officials raced the court by applying their heaviest pressure against the car pools in a last-ditch effort to break the MIA.

The Supreme Court did not speak until November 13, 1956. That very day, King was sitting in municipal court with E. D. Nixon and Ralph Abernathy, listening to the city present its case for the injunction to break the MIA transportation system. As King had foreseen, the Supreme Court vindicated the MIA position, and affirmed the lower court judgment without argument. It was irrelevant that the municipal court judge later granted the city's bid for the injunction. Segregation on the city buses was declared illegal, and the fight in Montgomery was over.

Yet the city did not concede gracefully. The city commission refused to make any move until it received official notification from the Court, which was to be more than a month away. In the interval, King's people put great stress at the continuing mass meetings on the need for nonviolence in the integration of the buses, and they made special visits to black schools to impress on students their responsibility for averting conflict. Neither the city nor private white organizations, however, would take the initiative in preparing the white community for the change.

On December 18, 1956, the city commission promised that it "will not yield one inch, but will do all in its power to oppose the integration of the Negro race with the white race." The White Citizens Council, to which several members of the city commission publicly belonged, threatened that enforcement of the decision would lead to riot and bloodshed. The Ku Klux Klan had already initiated a campaign of terror, and rumors of new bombings circulated throughout the city. But having stood fast through a year of struggle, Montgomery's blacks were not tempted to surrender at the moment of triumph. The MIA would not let Montgomery ignore the law.

On December 20, 1956, the Court's order finally reached Montgomery. At the MIA's mass meeting that night, King said, "As we go back to the buses, let us be loving enough to turn an enemy into a friend. We must now move from protest to reconciliation." Later

King asked the ministers from the MIA to ride the buses during rush hour for a few days, to give blacks the courage to integrate and to handle provocations nonviolently.

Before television cameras and newsmen, King and E. D. Nixon boarded an early bus together the next morning. They were joined by Abernathy and Glenn Smiley, the white minister from the Fellowship of Reconciliation. The boycott officially over, the bus driver greeted them politely. The relative quiet of the next few days provided hope that Montgomery would accept the blacks' offer of reconciliation cordially.

Montgomery, however, did not. King noted that the public officials who had predicted violence needed violence to save face. Within a week, bus riders were being subjected to a reign of terror. Shots were fired at buses as they rode through poorly lighted neighborhoods, and at least one black was struck by a bullet. A teenage girl was beaten by a band of white thugs as she left a bus. The city commission, rather than protect the buses, chose to suspend runs after 5:00 P.M., leaving black workers once again without transportation. The white leadership's prophecy that integrated transportation would not work was now self-fulfilled.

By the start of the new year, tension had grown even worse. King was in Atlanta with Abernathy when, early in the morning of January 10, 1957, he received a phone call that bombs had again exploded throughout Montgomery. Abernathy's home was struck. So, for the second time, was that of Reverend Robert Graetz, a white Lutheran minister of a black church. Three black Baptist churches had also been hit. Though a few responsible white voices were finally raised in protest, King said he had never felt so depressed, not even during the grimmest days of the boycott.

Then, on January 28, twelve sticks of smoldering dynamite were found unexploded on the front porch of King's home. Blacks at two other sites were less fortunate; a home and service station were leveled by bombs. King wrote that, in touring the wreckage, he witnessed the arrest of two blacks who had done nothing more than berate policemen aloud for acquiescing in the bombings. Montgomery's blacks had never been angrier than they were that day, but there was no riot, and nonviolence prevailed.

Whatever King had hoped, the Christian nonviolence practiced by the blacks had not transformed the hearts of white Southerners. If the brutal character of Southern resistance had not been apparent before, it became unmistakable during and after the Montgomery confrontation. Since the beginning of King's campaign, relations between the races in the South had become more fragile than ever. It seemed possible that any kind of incident could snap the self-restraint of blacks, and provoke a catastrophe.

In fact, King wondered after it was over what, apart from the desegregation of the buses in Montgomery, the boycott had accomplished. By the peculiarities of the American judicial system, the decision the courts rendered for Montgomery applied nowhere else. The Supreme Court had set a precedent in the Montgomery case to which civil rights lawyers could refer, but blacks in every city in the South needed to file lawsuits to get all the buses desegregated. Meanwhile, bus segregation remained, along with job discrimination, a devious judicial system, disenfranchisement, brutal police forces and segregated restaurants, theaters, sports, housing and—the *Brown* decision notwithstanding—schools. Even in victory King could not underestimate the magnitude of the task of desegregation that lay ahead.

Nonetheless, King had proven something fundamental in Montgomery. It was that nonviolence was not a strategy of weakness, passivity and cowardice, as many had once believed. Nonviolence was not valuable merely in demonstrating the moral superiority of the oppressed over the oppressors. The experience had shown that it was a positive strategy, to which blacks could adapt, which the South could not ignore, and which the world would applaud. The challenge would now be to apply it to other situations, for more grandiose ends.

King was not at all sure after his victory in Montgomery how to proceed. Three weeks after the integration of the buses, he called a meeting in Atlanta of some sixty black activists, most of them ministers who had been part of a network of MIA supporters in the South. They founded an organization which, shortly afterward, they named the Southern Christian Leadership Conference. King was elected its president. None of its members knew how next to apply the strategy of nonviolence, either, but ideas were fermenting among them, and their banding together in itself represented a commitment to continue the struggle.

What was clear was that the white South intended to defy the school desegregation order, and every other desegregation order the courts issued, as long as it could. When blacks realized they faced this defiance, as E. D. Nixon put it, "That's when our feets hits the ground." Recognizing they would have to fight, they knew they could not win alone. They needed the Supreme Court. They needed the moral sanction of a white majority to pressure the government. They needed money. But, until Montgomery, the white South never thought it had an adversary. At Montgomery, blacks showed not only that they could come together for the struggle, but knew how to win.

The Montgomery bus boycott did not instantly ignite the blacks of the South. Few Southern black communities had a man like Martin Luther King, Jr., to inspire and lead them. Fewer still had such a man in combination with a strong force like E. D. Nixon to transform an angry sense of grievance into active resistance. Many Americans in the late 1950s dismissed Montgomery as an isolated episode, praiseworthy perhaps but without important consequences. King himself was unsure of the influence it would have on others. But within the mass of Southern blacks the lesson of Montgomery was incubating, and a new decade had barely begun before it blossomed forth spectacularly.

II
ALLEN GINSBERG:
The New Values

"Burroughs and Kerouac saw my family as being like a rich advantage. . . . Meeting them was connecting with people who were already spiritually open. They turned me on, so instead of developing into a Columbia College prick with a prep school tie running around trying to get a job in advertising, and unconsciously making that my image, I found myself honored and valued for my personal eccentricities, and the subjectiveness of my activities, like that of a mortal weeping over my mother, and a heartfelt farewell to existence."

M

ORE WAS INCUBATING in the 1950s in America than the black revolt. Most Americans behaved according to the strictures of Eisenhower's morality and McCarthy's politics, challenging little, daring less. They lived beneath a blanket of conformity, scarcely aware that it was suffocating. Only a few brave spirits were gasping for air, and they seemed like anomalies, perhaps even lunatics, agitators who scarcely threatened the society's placid temperament. It is only in retrospect that these few have been granted credit for tugging at the edges of the blanket, to admit a breeze that would ultimately permit Americans to breathe more freely.

They were an odd assortment, as the avant-garde often is. Some were intellectuals, some were not, but they reacted in common against an America they found surfeited with authority, which denied intuition and stifled emotion. They exacted physical sensations that most Americans had been frightened to feel, moral perceptions that most had been unwilling to contemplate. Like those who spoke for the black movement, they asserted the right of people to be themselves, take risks with their own fate, defy the limitations the society imposed on them. If they eluded designation as radicals, because they were nonpolitical, the message they proclaimed was nonetheless radical for the social standards of the time.

Allen Ginsberg was surely the most influential of this avant-garde. Ginsberg was a Jewish, homosexual poet, son of a minor poet of the 1930s. He broke out of the middle-class confines of Paterson, New Jersey, to play a role, in a phrase he used without extravagance, as a "wizard of the heart."

With a handful of others, most notably Jack Kerouac and William Burroughs, Ginsberg made up the school of writers known as the Beat Generation. They wrote, Ginsberg told me, to encourage a "liberating insolence of recognizing one's own feelings and acting one's own feelings rather than acting Madison Avenue feelings of careerism." The Beat writers were at the core of those who, by what they did as well as by what they said, merchandized the idea of spiritual emancipation from what they regarded as social tyranny. Hardly anyone supposed they were also pioneers on the frontier of the impending decade.

These few, as it turned out, were expressing what many Americans, especially the young, seemed to sense but could not articulate. In retrospect it appears that the generation at the edge of adulthood, or at least a noteworthy part of it, was getting ready to rebel against the mood of the 1950s. The avant-garde performed its traditional function of contributing to it a set of justifying ideas.

By the later 1950s, colonies had been established, mostly in California, populated by several thousand people, most of them young and children of the white middle class, that challenged the values of the adult generation. They were called "beats" or, more pejoratively, "beatniks," after the Beat Generation writers. In the 1960s, the colonies multiplied, the numbers grew and the general term of reference became "hippies." In due course, the phenomenon became sufficiently widespread to earn the more generic name "counterculture."

Many of the tenets of the counterculture were absorbed into a pervasive new consciousness of the 1960s, which became identified as the "youth movement." The nonconformist notions of a tiny minority in the 1950s had emerged as common social currency a decade later. Conventions on dress, sex and drugs, personal identity, even politics had retreated before the doctrine of personal liberation. The daring of an avant-garde had been transformed into a set of habits and mores that went beyond the young to exercise an impact on Americans of all ages.

The spreading civil rights rebellion undoubtedly stimulated, occasionally collided with, often shared experiences with the rising counterculture. Young blacks provided the dynamic element for the one, young whites for the other. For a time they provided mutual reinforcement and moral support. But they remained distinct forces, developing parallel to each other, suffusing the society with their separate values. Their coupled challenge to the status quo served early to define the 1960s, and endow it with its unique and tremulous character.

Norman Mailer was one of those who understood in the 1950s that something important was going on. In 1948 Mailer had published *The Naked and the Dead,* remembered as the best, if not the most original, novel to come out of World War II. His subsequent work, like his personal life, revealed an increasing restlessness, a need to throw off political and social restraints, a tendency to swashbuckle. Mailer conducted himself in the image of the American existentialist, which is how he perceived himself, and he never wrote the great works of fiction that had been anticipated by his early success. Though he missed becoming a writer of the first rank, Mailer's sensitivity never abandoned him, and in an essay called "The White Negro," published in 1957, he noted the appearance of a new phenomenon among American whites. He called it the "hipster," and he recognized it as a widely emulated model.

Mailer said the hipster was a "philosophical psychopath" who, like the American black, lived immoderately and for the moment. He smoked marijuana and spoke a special language in which the words most often heard were "man, go, put down, make, beat, cool, swing, with it, flip, creep, hip, square." He sought not love, Mailer said, but a good orgasm, and espoused a nihilism which at best could be creative and at worst murderous.

The hipster was not necessarily a political radical, Mailer wrote, but he would inevitably be embittered by the attempts of society's conservative forces to deny him his freedom and be driven thereby to a "radical comprehension" of society's horrors. Mailer estimated the number of hipsters at not more than a hundred thousand, but he noted that they were armed with the ruthlessness of an elite and a language attractive to adolescents. Their potential power, he said, lay in the identity between their view of existence and the adolescent propensity to rebel.

Mailer's analysis is stunning prophecy, not only of what the counterculture would become very shortly but of the various directions it would take later on. Adolescents did emulate what they thought blacks were doing, as Mailer foresaw, and they adopted in huge numbers the special language, the sexual freedom and the drugs that he saw in hipster life. What Mailer called the "nihilism" of the hipsters stimulated brilliant creativity in the Beatles at the start and, perhaps, savage murder in the Manson gang at the end. As he said it would, society's conservatism drove the counterculture to a radical evaluation of America's ills, but even he did not anticipate the repercussions on the stability of the society that this rejection of conventional values would set off.

Characteristically, Mailer sought to go beyond describing the hipster phenomenon, and its future, to deal with the more elusive question of its cause. It was his contention that the black behavior which became the hipster model was the product of the physical jeopardy in which all Negroes passed their lives. "The cameo of security for the average white: mother and the home, job and the family, are not even a mockery to millions of Negroes," he wrote, "they are impossible." Mailer declared that the American black lived in constant fear and humiliation, apprehensive of violence in even the most casual encounter, deliberately cultivating a paranoia as a mechanism of survival.

". . . and so," Mailer wrote, the black "kept for his survival the art of the primitive, he lived in the enormous present, he subsisted for his Saturday night kicks, relinquishing the pleasures of the mind for the more obligatory pleasures of the body, and in his music he gave voice to the character and quality of his existence, to his rage, and the infinite variations of joy, lust, languor, growl, cramp, pinch, scream and despair of his orgasm."

Such exquisite feelings, however, had spread beyond the private domain of the black man, Mailer wrote. Since the atom bomb, whites had come to share the black's perception of the fragility of life. The gas chambers and crematoria of World War II had revealed how handily masses of people could be finished off. Mailer argued that the bomb, and the knowledge that men without qualms about mass extermination have possessed the power to use it, and so might again, had introduced a permanent state of terror into the human condition.

58

The hipster is a man, Mailer wrote, "who knows that if our collective condition is to live with instant death by atomic war, relatively quick death by the State as *l'univers concentrationnaire,* or with a slow death by conformity with every creative and rebellious instinct stifled (at what damage to the mind and the heart and the liver and the nerves no research foundation for cancer will ever discover in a hurry), if the fate of twentieth century man is to live with death from adolescence to premature senescence, why then the only life-giving answer is to accept the terms of death, to live with death as an immediate danger, to divorce oneself from society, to exist without roots, to set out on the uncharted journey into the rebellious imperatives of the self."

And, indeed, a generation did set out on this journey, but not with the grim feelings of resignation that Mailer attributed to it. Mailer had logic to his argument that the collective psyche of the first generation born under the cloud of nuclear annihilation—the generation which reached maturity in the 1960s—had been permanently darkened. But the evidence to support this logic was absent and, in fact, those who undertook this rebellious journey seemed to do so joyously, and with a sense of wonder. This generation, after all, had adapted its psyche to many innovations, besides learning to live with the bomb.

The generation of the 1960s was also the first to grow up in persistent affluence, with divorce commonplace in the family, experiencing incredible geographic mobility. It was the first to be given an inoculation against virtually every disease and, perhaps more important, a pill against the contingency of pregnancy. It was the first to be raised on television. It was the first to be influenced by Dr. Spock's liberal notions of child-raising, and to consider itself entitled in adolescence to an extended retreat in college. It was a generation diapered in throwaways, nursed with plastic bottles, strengthened on a diet of protein and weakened by endless snacks of sugar-coated cereals. It was the first dressed in synthetic fibers and freed of household chores by laborsaving devices. The inventory is long, and one can add to it or subtract from it at will.

In fact, it is quite possible that, to explain the passion of the 1960s, one need go no further than the ghostly reserve of the 1950s. History has been rather faithful to sequences of action and reaction.

59

The theme of the decade of the 1950s was security: internal security (McCarthy), international security (massive retaliation), personal security (careerism). And yet no one felt secure. It is hardly surprising that Mailer's hipsters should have decided "to explore that domain of experience where security is boredom and therefore sickness," and that a larger audience was excited by their explorations. If America in the Eisenhower era was the paragon of a sane society, it is quite reasonable that some of the multitude would have preferred to be crazy.

"I wasn't embarrassed by craziness," Allen Ginsberg told me. "The way was prepared because my mother had gone through bughouses and I had to take care of her when I was young. In a way, hell was dedicated to her. She died in a mental hospital in the mid-1950s. I had to deal early with the realities of irrationality."

Ginsberg, whose hair and beard were unkempt and long, and whose clothes were shabby, was a familiar figure to me. Though he was a few years older, we had been raised in the same Jewish middle-class milieu in Paterson, New Jersey, and we had gone to the same high school. I remembered him as one of the serious students, neatly dressed and wearing horn-rimmed glasses, with a reputation for brilliance. Now he was almost fifty and, as we sat talking on the grass in a park in Washington, D.C., he sucked insouciantly on an ice-cream cone, while I questioned him in the hope of finding out why, in Mailer's language, he had become hip while I remained drearily square.

"So I already had my mind caved in when I was about ten," Ginsberg said, "in terms of ability to reexamine things for what was what and what was not. It took me years to accept my mother with her madness as being a human being sent to hell-in-your-mind. Finally I knew craziness was a family matter, a human matter, rather than something you swept under the carpet. It was impossible to ignore it."

Madness is a theme that runs consistently through the writings of the Beat Generation. Not only Ginsberg but Kerouac and Burroughs were personally touched by it. Another of the beats' consistent themes was homosexuality.

"Whatever my mother's condition," Ginsberg continued, "because I was a homosexual, my person was already different from the norm. I knew that at nine, fooling around with little boys. I didn't tell my family what was going on in my heart until much later.

"Finally I said to my father, 'I have some sex problems and should go to a psychiatrist,' and he wanted to know what. Very diffidently I said, 'Well, I have a problem with homosexuality.' My father really freaked out. He said, 'Do you mean you like to take men's penises in your mouth?' So that was my father's reaction. Of course, I said, 'Oh, no, no, no.' And that was the end of it for another five years.

"The only reason I went to Columbia College was because of a young student I knew there that I was in love with. Out of this hopeless homosexual virginal longing, I took the entrance exam. When I told that to Kerouac he laughed. He appreciated it for its humor, and the sweetness of the situation."

Jack Kerouac was driven, spontaneous, intense. He could have been the prototype for Mailer's hipster. The Kerouac that Ginsberg met hung around Harlem bars and, faithful to Mailer's portrayal, imbibed black culture through the channels of jazz. "Kerouac took his whole consciousness from the private Harlem attitude of the black musicians," Ginsberg recalled, "which is the attitude of complete tolerance, complete openness, 'Yeah man, anything you say, of course. Whatever your drug is that's your pleasure, whatever your love is that's your love. We just want to play a little horn.' " To a young man fresh from New Jersey, Kerouac's was an attitude that dazzled the mind.

William Burroughs, in contrast, was withdrawn to the point of inscrutability, but an intellectual adventurer with a quiet, almost suicidal daring. Burroughs was a teacher, who introduced Ginsberg to the experimental work of Blake and Rimbaud, Kafka and Céline, to Wilhelm Reich's psychoanalysis and Cocteau's musings on opium. He also helped Ginsberg, who was still consumed by ambivalence about his family and his homosexuality, to acquire a sense of personal worth and dignity. Burroughs was, in Ginsberg's eye, the most brilliant man he had ever met, and a confirmation of the validity of antibourgeois values.

"Burroughs and Kerouac saw my family as being like a rich advantage," Ginsberg said to me, "because I could talk about it and deal with it, rather than make-believe I was interested in accounting and market research statistics.

"Meeting them was connecting with people who were already spiritually open. They turned me on, so instead of developing into a Columbia College prick with a prep school tie running around trying to get a job in advertising, and unconsciously making that my image, I found myself honored and valued for my personal eccentricities, and the subjectiveness of my activities, like that of a mortal weeping over my mother, and a heartfelt farewell to existence. They were fully conscious when I fell into their midst, and they provided a social context and permission and encouragement to think my own thoughts and accept my own thoughts."

Bored by the rigid routine of Columbia College, Ginsberg at eighteen became the disciple of Kerouac and Burroughs. Together they experimented with sex and drugs, dabbled at the fringes of the underworld and explored options for self-expression in writing. Describing the evolution of his poetic style, Ginsberg reminisced about how he and his beat friends broke down the barriers between writing and talk:

"We all talk among ourselves and we have common understandings, and we say anything we want to say, and we talk about our assholes, and we talk about our cocks, and we talk about who we fucked last night, or who we're gonna fuck tomorrow, or what kind of love affair we have, or when we got drunk, or when we stuck a broom in our ass in the Hotel Ambassador in Prague—anybody tells one's friends about that.

"So I began finding in conversations with Burroughs and Kerouac and Gregory Corso,* in conversations with people whom I knew well, whose souls I respected, that the things we were telling each other for real were totally different from what was already in literature . . . So then—what happens if you make a distinction between what you tell your friends and what you tell your Muse? The problem is to break down that distinction: when you approach the Muse to talk as frankly as you would talk with yourself or with your friends." †

---

* Corso, another of the Beat Generation poets, served a term in prison in his teens and, on his release, met Ginsberg, who recognized and encouraged his talents.

† This and several other quotes in this chapter are from Thomas Clark's interview of Ginsberg that appeared in the *Paris Review*, May 1966. It was reprinted in *Writers at Work: The Paris Review Interviews*.

And when I talked with Ginsberg two decades later, he was no less indignant.

"I knew about *Time* as a social phenomenon in the early 1950s," he said. "It delivered a funny, phony, CIA vision of cleanliness, the kind of cleanliness you get with airline stewardesses and, you know, 'Throw away a plastic cup after you use it,' 'How dare there be a spot on my seat!' 'What am I paying the airlines for with the smell of vomit, the human smell, the family smell?' which is part of a large-scale image of America which meant ultimately covering up mass bombing in Indochina because it's inconvenient, plasticizing it and packaging it to make it sound like enemy losses . . .

"This was a vast propaganda effort to fake a personal consciousness in America and to present a fake personal consciousness as the real, internal, sensitive self . . ."

Gradually, Ginsberg drifted from New Jersey back to New York, for a few more years of meaningless jobs and personal depression. Kerouac and Burroughs were in and out of town often, carrying manuscripts, which Ginsberg tried to market for them. Both of them were at last published, Kerouac with *The Town and the City* in 1950 and Burroughs with *Junkie* in 1953. Neither attracted much notice, but for Ginsberg the period was even more frustrating. Publishers consistently rejected his poems on the grounds that they were too rambling or too vulgar or too despondent.

In his journal in mid-1952 Ginsberg penned the following notation, which he entitled "A Novel":

> At 14 I was an introvert, an atheist, a Communist and a Jew, and I still wanted to be president of the United States.
>
> At 19, being no longer a virgin, I was a cocksucker, and believed in a supreme reality, an anarchist, a hipster totally apolitical Reichian; I wanted to be a great poet instead.
>
> At 22 I was a hallucinating mystic believing in the City of God and I wanted to be a saint.
>
> At 23, a year later, I was already a criminal, a despairing sinner, a dope fiend; I wanted to get to reality.

It was as a consequence of a caper with Kerouac that Ginsberg was suspended from Columbia in the spring of 1945. Contrary to the rules, Kerouac was living in Ginsberg's dormitory room and, the story goes, when a chambermaid reported the violation, Ginsberg reacted by mischievously inscribing on the dusty film of his window, "Fuck the Jews" and "Nicholas Murray Butler has no balls."* The deans were mortified, and Ginsberg was saved from outright expulsion only by the promise that he would see a psychiatrist.

The ensuing interlude away from the campus was important to him. It allowed him to take to the road, a practice that Kerouac a few years later would immortalize in his fiction, and which became a hallmark of the Beat Generation.

Ginsberg worked as a welder, a night porter and a dishwasher in a seedy cafeteria, an obscure figure, as he put it, "on the landscape of the common world." He enrolled in a training course at the Merchant Marine Academy, and shipped out on a voyage that took him to Atlantic and Gulf ports. He hitchhiked to Denver for an aborted love affair with Neal Cassady, one of the shadowy figures in the beat circle, then went on to Texas, where Burroughs had gone to live. From there he shipped out again, aboard a freighter bound for Marseilles and Africa. When he returned to New York to reenroll in school, his psychological problems had not left him but he was a more self-possessed man.

In the summer of 1948, Ginsberg was living in a squalid apartment in East Harlem, working part-time as a file clerk while he labored on for his degree. With Burroughs and Kerouac both gone, he felt lonely, and was chronically depressed. Life seemed hopeless, he said, at a dead end. That was the summer he had a series of visions of William Blake, an episode celebrated in Ginsberg lore, which gave him a new sense of his mission. Some of the later visions, he recalled, were induced by drugs. The genesis of the first was more mundane.

"There I was in my bed in Harlem, jacking off," Ginsberg said, "with my pants open, lying around on a bed by the windowsill, looking out into the cornices of Harlem and the sky above. And I had just come. And had perhaps hardly even wiped the come off my thighs, my trousers, or whatever it was. . . . a Blake book on my

* Nicholas Murray Butler (1862–1947) was president of Columbia from 1902 to 1945.

lap—I wasn't even reading, my eye was idling over the page of 'Ah, Sun-flower,' and it suddenly appeared—the poem I'd read a lot of times before . . . and suddenly I realized that the poem was talking about *me*.

"And simultaneous with understanding it, heard a very deep grave voice in the room, which I immediately assumed, I didn't think twice, was Blake's voice . . . the voice was so completely tender and beautifully ancient. Like the voice of the Ancient of Days. But the peculiar quality of the voice was something unforgettable because it was like God and had a human voice, with all the infinite tenderness and anciency and moral gravity of a living Creator speaking to his son.

"I suddenly realized . . . that this was the moment I was born for, this initiation . . . My second thought, never forget—never forget, never renege, never deny. Never deny the voice—no, never forget it, don't get lost mentally wandering in other spirit worlds or American or job worlds or advertising worlds or war worlds or earth worlds. But the spirit of the universe was what I was born to realize . . ."

Save to himself and literary historians, Ginsberg's visions might be of little interest, but for their appearing, in retrospect, to be a milestone on the road to the counterculture. In some measure, at least, they seem to be responsible for transforming Ginsberg from a would-be professional poet, with debilitating feelings of insecurity, to a missionary, a zealot, a would-be Messiah.

It is no coincidence, furthermore, that Ginsberg's apparition was of William Blake, the eighteenth-century English mystic, poet and artist, antirationalist and social rebel. Blake was a figure who had deeply influenced Ginsberg, and the 1960s resurrected much that was suggestive of him. The counterculture challenged not only the political authority but those values in modern industrial society that Blake himself would have considered inhumane: intellectuality, technology, discipline.

Private as were Ginsberg's visions of Blake, they seemed to foreshadow the popular swing in America to a counterculture which valued Blake's kind of mysticism. The fascination with drugs, as a vehicle to a higher vision, was intrinsic to this counterculture. So was its exaltation not only of the sexual and emotional but the intuitive, the spiritual, even the supernatural in human affairs. If

Blake was Ginsberg's inspiration, Ginsberg was the herald of change.

Visions or not, however, Ginsberg still had great difficulty es[cap]ing from the circle of desperation in which he seemed capture[d in] New York. In late 1948, he was arrested for hiding the stolen g[oods] of a band of petty thieves with whom he became involved thr[ough] Herbert Huncke, another of the shadowy figures who stalke[d the] beats.

By now Ginsberg was notorious at Columbia, but he wa[s also] recognized as a bizarre genius, and the college deans took [great] pains to save him from jail. By prearrangement with the d[istrict] attorney's office, Ginsberg pleaded psychological disability [and,] like his mother before him, went off for confinement in a [mental] institution. He spent eight months there, talking with a Fre[nch] psychoanalyst, reading French surrealists and writing poem[s.]

After his release, he returned briefly to live in Paterson, [where] he spent many hours with William Carlos Williams, an old[er poet] made controversial by his dissent from the reigning forma[lism of] T. S. Eliot and Wallace Stevens, yet highly esteemed in so[me cir]cles. Williams was author of a long poem called *Paterson*[, which] explored the commonplace characteristics of the grimy old [mill] city where Ginsberg and I were raised.

Ginsberg told me he considered Williams "a great m[aster of] American speech, of how to say it in American rather tha[n En]glish, or highfalutin." Williams helped Ginsberg looser[his] work, and reshape it along nontraditional lines in both s[tyle and] content.

Ginsberg emerged from these bitter years with little re[spect] for American orthodoxy. He even found a scapegoat to em[body] diverse objects of his contempt. It was *Time* magazine. A [decade] later, in a poem called "America," he would write:

> *I'm obsessed by Time Magazine.*
> *I read it every week.*
> *. . . It's always telling me about responsibi[lity. Busi]*
> *nessmen are serious. Movie producers a[re serious.]*
> *Everybody's serious but me.*

*At 24, after being a jailbird, a schizoid screwball in
the bughouse, I got layed, girls, I was being psychoan-
alyzed.*

*At 26, I am shy, go out with girls, I write poetry, I am
a freelance literary agent and a registered democrat;
I want to find a job.*

Who cares?

At the end of 1953 Ginsberg decided to abandon New York in
search of an enhanced personal consciousness. He hitchhiked first
to Key West, and took a plane to Havana. Then went on to Yucatán
in Mexico, where he spent four months in the jungle exploring
Mayan ruins.

Having then crossed Mexico to the California frontier, he made a
journal entry in the early summer of 1954 which said, "Enter U.S.
alone naked with knapsack, watch, camera, poem, beard." A few
weeks later he wrote from Los Angeles, "As now I am 28 for the
first time older than I've dreamed of being. The beard a joke, my
character with its childish core a tiring taste . . . Must find energy
& image & act on it." From there Ginsberg went directly to San
Francisco, a city quickening with intellectual excitement.

San Francisco in the mid-1950s was in ferment, the first of the
cities to be touched by what would later be known as the counterculture. It was the logical place. San Francisco was the only city in
the West to be settled from the sea, thereby escaping the fetters of
the Puritans who trekked overland. It had traditions of dissent with
roots in the labor movement, populism, the New Deal and European radicalism. It was accustomed to heterogeneity in its population, and brought a bemused tolerance to bohemians. Its climate
was mild, which encouraged street life, and its wine, locally produced, was cheap. Even in the 1950s, young rebels were gravitating to San Francisco, where they could turn on comfortably with
marijuana and experiment with sex forms in communal pads.

San Francisco's bohemian life when Ginsberg arrived was concentrated in the neighborhood known as North Beach, the cultural
hub of which was the City Lights Pocket Bookshop. Run by the
poet Lawrence Ferlinghetti, City Lights stayed open long into the
night for browsing and gossip. Its bulletin board displayed notices

of art exhibits and odd jobs. In 1956, it extended its cultural influence further with the founding of City Lights Books, the imprint under which Ginsberg's *Howl* was finally published. Ginsberg relished the moments at City Lights, along with those at the Old Spaghetti Factory, the Coexistence Bagel Shop, the Purple Onion and the many cellars now forgotten where aspiring poets read their verses, often accompanied by jazz.

In North Beach, and across San Francisco Bay in Berkeley, Ginsberg also encountered a kaleidoscope of poets, dedicated feverishly to their work. Kenneth Rexroth, the dean among them, admitted Ginsberg into his salon, where he met Robert Duncan, Philip Lamantia, Michael McClure and Ferlinghetti. Duncan, teacher and gadfly of the group, then introduced Ginsberg to Philip Whalen and Gary Snyder, a student of Zen. "Out here," Ginsberg wrote to a friend in New York, "there are a few hidden and excellent poets —a kind of buddhist influenced post Pound post Williams classicism full of independence and humor AND gift of gab, native wordslinging." These people were not intimate pals like Kerouac and Burroughs, but Ginsberg experienced with them a level of artistic fellowship he had never known before.

Between these poets and Ginsberg there was a fruitful exchange. They exposed him to various "schools" of writing, bearing such names as the Anarchist Circle, the Black Mountain experiment, the Berkeley Renaissance and the San Francisco Renaissance. Within the circle, he found an audience for his own poems, and circulated the manuscripts of his beat friends. Among them was Kerouac's kinetic novel, *On the Road*, which would become one of the seminal works of the counterculture. Though the exchange went both ways, Ginsberg's contribution was clearly the more powerful, and influenced the work of the entire group. Within a few years, each of their reputations, in some measure, would become associated with the name of the Beat Generation.

What was most appealing for Ginsberg among the available offerings in San Francisco, however, was Zen Buddhism, which gave him a new way to look at the mind. Its reigning expert was Gary Snyder, an attractive young intellectual from the backwoods of Oregon with a special taste for Eastern religions. Ginsberg said that under Snyder's tutelage he became a serious reader of the *Tibetan Book of the Dead* and *Tibetan Buddhist Documents*, the ideas of which were a major revelation to him. In contrast to the Freudian influence that pervaded New York intellectual circles, he said, Zen Buddhism was in the soul of San Francisco, and he embarked resolutely on its study.

Zen did not replace but complemented the ideas Ginsberg brought with him from New York. It forced him to examine more deeply the virtues of meditation over achievement, intuition over reason, insubstantiality over materialism. Zen postulated a harmony between the inner self and the outer world, but it insisted on no rigid orthodoxy to attain the goal. It was an excellent ethic for those seeking an antidote to what they perceived as the excesses of industrial civilization, and Ginsberg absorbed many of its tenets into his poems. Through him, and others of the beats, the influence of Zen passed into the counterculture, doctrine from the Orient that vindicated for those who accepted it a distaste and disillusion for the reigning values of the West.

Yet congenial as San Francisco was, life for Ginsberg remained a struggle there. He still had enough ambivalence about a career to get a job as a market researcher, which he kept for a whole year. He survived on unemployment compensation for six months, then enrolled in Berkeley to take a master's degree but, he wrote to a friend, "threw up my hands inside of a month and was back on wine and poetry with the zen lunatics." Later he shipped out on a government cargo ship carrying radar equipment to military installations in Alaska.

Not the least of Ginsberg's struggle was his search for love. It was consolation that Kerouac came out to visit during this period, as did Gregory Corso, but these were not loves. Then, about a year after he arrived in San Francisco, Ginsberg found Peter Orlovsky, a lithe blond, seven years younger than himself. The two made a lifetime commitment to each other, sexually and intellectually. They became, as Ginsberg put it, "two merged souls." *

Shortly after the meeting, on a weekend in the late summer of 1955, Ginsberg sat down to write *Howl*. Orlovsky, Zen and his

---

* It was an enduring relationship. Orlovsky was at Ginsberg's side when I interviewed him for this book in 1974.

circle of literary friends provided him with unaccustomed support, and generated within him a new self-esteem. On the wall of his room in North Beach was tacked a set of literary instructions from his mentor Kerouac. It was entitled "Essentials of Modern Prose." According to Ginsberg, its principal tenet was: Don't revise. Ginsberg admitted that he did not at first grasp the meaning of Kerouac's admonition, but he decided to accept it.

"What Kerouac said," Ginsberg remembered, "was that it was sort of like lying if you revised, in the same sense that you make believe you didn't say that. Like you revealed what was on your mind, but he felt that most revision would be motivated by embarrassment—in other words you'd be embarrassed by the truth of what you were saying, therefore revise."

It was characteristic of the beats to be absorbed by the question of truth, not Keats's "beauty is truth, truth beauty," but something almost directly contrary, a truth that is unbeautified, unmodified, uncompromised by the false standards of a corrupting civilization. It was no coincidence that the truth of the beats was normally ugly, undisciplined, cruel. The beats' concept was truth as protest—and so the concept passed into the consciousness of a generation which seemed convinced that the defining characteristic of America was hypocrisy. The generation took delight in being personally unkempt, using vulgar language, living in filthy pads. This was truthful. This was authentic, like the unrevised line of a poem.

There were other elements of beat thinking in the process of creating *Howl*, among them a conviction that more important than the response of the audience was the experience of the writer. Making poems, like other forms of action, was valuable as a vehicle for personal exploration and sensation.

"What Kerouac's kind of writing proposes," Ginsberg said, "is an absolute, almost Zenlike, complete absorption, *attention* to your own consciousness, to the act of writing, to a focus of the mind, so that attention does not waver while writing, and doesn't feed back on itself and become self-conscious . . ." *

Howl was also written, at least in part, while Ginsberg was under the influence of drugs. The second section of the poem, he said,

* These lines were delivered in a dialogue with Robert Duncan at Kent State University on April 7, 1971. The colloquy is reprinted as "Early Poetic Community" in *Allen Verbatim*.

was "composed during a peyote vision." Ginsberg explained that "drugs were useful for exploring perception, sense perception, and exploring different possibilities and modes of consciousness . . ."

When Ginsberg finished his poem, he sent a copy to Kerouac with a note which said, "The pages I sent you of 'Howl' (right title) are the first pages put down, as is. I recopied them and sent you the 100% original draft. There is no preexistent version. I typed it up as I went along, that's why it's so messy . . . What you have *is* what you want. I realize how right you are . . ."

Ginsberg was probably sincere in saying that he never expected *Howl* to be published. In those days publishers were unenthusiastic about controversial works, even works that promised commercial success. One of New York's most prominent houses had refused to honor its contract to publish Mailer's *The Deer Park* on the grounds that it would be liable to an obscenity prosecution and, before it finally appeared, six other houses rejected it for the same reason. *Howl* seemed an even less likely candidate for publication.

"At the time," said Ginsberg, explaining further, "writing *Howl* —for instance, like I assumed when writing it that it was something that *could* not be published because I wouldn't want my daddy to see what was in there. About my sex life, being fucked in the ass, imagine your father reading a thing like that, was what I thought . . . I assumed that it wouldn't be published, therefore I could say anything that I wanted.

"So literally, just for myself or anybody that I knew personally well, writers who would be willing to appreciate it with a breadth of tolerance—in a piece of work like *Howl*—who wouldn't be judging from a moralistic viewpoint but looking for evidence of humanity or secret thought or just actual truthfulness."

What Ginsberg had in mind in *Howl* was a public reading, scheduled for the fall of 1955 in San Francisco's Six Gallery. Ginsberg himself planned the reading, and personally handled the publicity. Some have attributed to him a prescient understanding that the time had arrived for a cultural breakthrough, but it is more likely that the date of the event was set to coincide with one of Kerouac's visits. In addition to Ginsberg, Rexroth was to read and to introduce Lamantia, McClure, Snyder and Whalen, who would also recite

71

from their works. In the publicity, Ginsberg announced that there would be a small collection for wine and postcards.

Kerouac, with characteristic frenzy, recorded the evening in *The Dharma Bums,* a novel about his beat friends, which was published in 1958. With Alvah Goldbrook as Ginsberg and Rheinhold Cacoethes as Rexroth, he wrote:

> Everyone was there. It was a mad night. And I was the one who got things jumping by going around collecting dimes and quarters from the rather stiff audience standing around in the gallery and coming back with three huge gallon jugs of California Burgundy and getting them all piffed so that by eleven o'clock when Alvah Goldbrook was reading his poem "Wail" drunk with arms outspread everybody was yelling "Go! Go! Go!" (like a jam session) and old Rheinhold Cacoethes the father of the Frisco poetry scene was wiping his tears in gladness . . . It was a great night.

It may even have been a night in which the course of American society shifted, if only a little, not because Ginsberg spoke new ideas but because he crystallized sensations and perceptions that he shared with others into a document of great dramatic power. The reading of *Howl* was electrifying. As Ginsberg has said, the poetry was itself "like a rhythmic articulation of feeling . . . like an impulse that rises within—just like sexual impulses."

Some of it, being spontaneous, did not even make sense, but the best of it, Ginsberg has said, touched absolute truth. Certainly, by all testimony, the audience that night, high on emotion, drugs, alcohol, responded as if it understood exactly what Ginsberg was saying.

> *I saw the best minds of my generation destroyed by
> madness, starving hysterical naked,
> dragging themselves through the negro streets at
> dawn looking for an angry fix
> angelheaded hipsters burning for the ancient heavenly connection to the starry dynamo in the machinery of night*

These words, with which *Howl* opens, are harsh and evocative, pounding with an outrage that seemed inconsistent with the gentleness of the young man who spoke them. They were a sad lament for his friends and a vow of hostility against the forces which he believed had destroyed them. Indeed, transformed but recognizable, here is Ginsberg's life, which he mourns in the name of victims . . .

> *who were expelled from the academies for crazy &
> publishing obscene odes on the windows of the
> skull,*
> *who cowered in unshaven rooms in underwear, burn-
> ing their money in wastebaskets and listening to
> the Terror through the wall,*
> *who got busted in their pubic beards returning
> through Laredo with a belt of marijuana for New
> York,*
> *who ate fire in paint hotels or drank turpentine in
> Paradise Alley, death, or purgatoried their torsos
> night after night*
> *with dreams, with drugs, with waking nightmares,
> alcohol and cocks and endless balls . . .*

and, one can indeed imagine Ginsberg's father cringing at the line about those . . .

> *who howled on their knees in the subway and were
> dragged off the roof waving genitals and manu-
> scripts,*
> *who let themselves be fucked in the ass by saintly
> motorcyclists,* and screamed with joy.*

The language is, indeed, inelegant, the argot of another set of values, a tongue meant to strip away the pretense of life, a fist—or, perhaps, only a finger—to dismay the middle class. Relentlessly, through seventy-five long lines, Ginsberg related the bizarre, often

---

* These "saintly motorcyclists"—brutal thugs in black leather jackets to most of the world—were somehow a fascination that persisted among those who lived within the counterculture.

ugly, experiences of his generation destroyed, until he shifted to the question of what destroyed them. "What sphinx of cement and aluminum bashed open their skulls and ate up their brains and their imaginations?" With heavy rhythm, he answers.

> Moloch! Moloch! Nightmare of Moloch! Moloch the loveless! Mental Moloch! Moloch the heavy judger of men!
> Moloch the incomprehensible prison! Moloch the crossbone soulless jailhouse and Congress of sorrows! Moloch whose buildings are judgment! Moloch the vast stone of war! Moloch the stunned governments!
> Moloch whose mind is pure machinery! Moloch whose blood is running money! Moloch whose fingers are ten armies! Moloch whose breast is a cannibal dynamo! Moloch whose ear is a smoking tomb!
> Moloch whose eyes are a thousand blind windows! Moloch whose skyscrapers stand in the long streets like endless Jehovahs! Moloch whose factories dream and croak in the fog! Moloch whose smokestacks and antennae crown the cities!

It is not until the last section of the poem, which he calls "Footnote to Howl," that Ginsberg permits his tender, meditative side to appear. Here he draws from Buddhism to offer an answer to the pitiless power of Moloch. To deprive Moloch of the capacity to corrupt, Ginsberg seemed to advocate recognition of the sacredness of every object that man is likely to encounter. The holiness of which he spoke seemed to be a kind of universal love.

> The world is holy! The soul is holy! The skin is holy! The nose is holy! The tongue and cock and hand and ass-hole holy!
> Everything is holy! everybody's holy! everywhere is holy! everyday is in eternity! Everyman's an angel!

Given the magnitude of the ills Ginsberg identified, his plea for universal love, for the recognition of an all-pervasive holiness,

74

seems in last analysis to make *Howl* a weak manifesto. If the essence of revolution is uprising against injustice, *Howl* is not a revolutionary document. Full as it is of Old Testament indignation, it retreats from the conventional summons to smite the enemy. Ginsberg invited his audience not to revolution but to apocalypse, to a new and more humane vision of society. He sought redress not in social reform, not even in politics, but in regeneration and rebirth, perhaps in epiphany.

Ginsberg disagreed vigorously when I suggested in our interview that his interests, at least as represented in *Howl*, were not political. To me, politics was defined in terms of power to affect the organization of society. I said to Ginsberg that his concerns were individual perfectibility, which was quite different and not political at all. Ginsberg expressed irritation with that interpretation, and nearly walked away from our talk.

"I say there's no problem," he argued. "It's the same thing. If literature is public revelation of private thought, politics is only the same thing, public manifestation of what people know already. Once you open up your personal feelings and liberate your personal feelings and find out how you are, then you do it in public. Once you begin meditating and find your identity, then you can play a public role.

"Political activity without first discovering your own identity or nonidentity is in vain because it's just mechanical . . . The experiences through which you've gone, in conjunction with many others, is an indispensable state for reorganizing the system."

To illustrate what he meant, Ginsberg recounted an anecdote of an early meeting with Bob Dylan, the sandpaper-throat rock singer who served as troubadour to the generation of the 1960s. Ginsberg told me of an article about the beats which appeared in *Time*, his favorite magazine, "with my saying 'I'm Allen Ginsberg and I'm crazy as a flower,' and Peter said, 'I'm Peter Orlovsky and I'm crazy as a daisy,' and Gregory said, 'I'm Gregory Corso and I'm not crazy at all.'*

"Dylan saw that in *Time* and, many years later, said he read between the lines. It was the reliance on humor that Dylan picked up on. It was to transform consciousness, and I don't think you can create new structures until you have transformed consciousness.

* *Time*, February 9, 1959.

75

The statement we were making was a spontaneous mind statement rather than a calculated political statement." But to those who saw how it cut through the hypocrisy and cant, Ginsberg made clear to me, its political meaning was unmistakable.

Ginsberg also understood the civil rights movement in terms of personal transformation. At one point in our talk, he spoke of its essence being, for blacks, "a rediscovery of their own private self," much as the beat movement was for members of his circle and for those who were brushed by it.

"That culminates in LeRoi Jones in 1958," Ginsberg told me, "when we all got into contact and he was writing poems making fun of his sister who likes Tschaikovsky. 'My sister likes Tschaikovsky and Rudy Vallee—She straightens her hair—She goes to the university and studies literature—She doesn't like bad talking niggers—She doesn't like the blues, she loves Tschaikovsky.'* So there was a realization that blacks had been brainwashed, just like white kids around Columbia who had been brainwashed to think that their actual humanity lay in getting a fifty-dollar-a-week job on Madison Avenue advertising cigarettes or something."

Politics for Ginsberg was different from what it was for me. I remembered seeing him making the rounds in Washington in the early 1960s to lobby for the legalization of marijuana. That, at least, was politics as I understood it, whatever the legislative objective. More characteristically, his political involvement took the form of poetic expressions of indignation. He walked no picket lines for

---

* The lines come from the seventh stanza of *Hymn for Lanie Poo*, a poem by LeRoi Jones, a black poet who changed his name during the nationalist phase of the civil rights movement to Imamu Amiri Baraka. The actual lines read:

> my sister drives a green jaguar
> my sister has her hair done twice a month
> my sister is a school teacher
> my sister took ballet lessons
> my sister has a fine figure: never diets
> my sister doesn't like to teach in Newark because there are too
>   many colored in her classes
> my sister hates loud shades
> my sister's boy friend is a faggot music teacher who digs Tschai-
>   kovsky
> my sister digs Tschaikovsky also
> it is because of this similarity of interests
> that they will probably get married.

The poem is published in *New Negro Poets*, edited by Langston Hughes.

civil rights. In 1962, after a year and a half in India studying Buddhism with Gary Snyder, he and Orlovsky stopped over in Vietnam, and were appalled by what they saw of the war there. Back in the United States, they became politically active, "formulating scenarios for flower power," Ginsberg said, "chanting mantras to keep things cool" at antiwar demonstrations. The other demonstrators regarded him with affection, and considerable bewilderment.

Yet, for Ginsberg, chanting mantras was a kind of politics. In *Howl*, he created the image of an America that was so vicious and corrupt that only spiritual revelation—not political revolution—could save it. Vietnam aroused passion in him because it was an example of merciless Moloch seeking to devastate a culture that was more primitive, and thus purer. As Ginsberg understood politics, society could be redeemed only by the cumulative transformation of individuals to a higher sense of self. It was a millenarian rather than a practical vision. It pervaded *Howl*, as it did the counterculture, and much of the radical politics of the 1960s.

It is true that by the time he was interviewed by the *Paris Review* in 1966, Ginsberg seemed to recognize that the spiritual rebirth he hoped for had little prospect of application to most people.

"Everybody too intransigent. Everybody too mean," he said. "I don't suppose it'll take place but . . . somebody has got to sit in the British Museum again like Marx and figure out a new system; a new blueprint. Another century has gone, technology has changed everything completely, so it's time for a new utopian system."

Many of the radicals in the movement were having similar thoughts about that time. But, in case one be tempted to take Ginsberg's remark as serious political commentary, he continued, "Burroughs is almost working on it."

The real lesson of *Howl* was that conditions were beyond repair. *Howl* condemned not just American society, not just modern society; its criticism seemed to go on to encompass all that was worldly. No campaign of personal salvation seemed to promise enough conversions to make a difference. The problem was social, but it was so severe that the only logical response to it was antisocial. "Tune in, turn on, drop out," became the slogan of those who found their relief from a contemptible world in withdrawal from the normal vocation of life. Whatever Ginsberg intended, this was the message, above all others, that he conveyed.

Meanwhile, Elvis Presley and James Dean had appeared on the scene, emitting many of the same signals as Allen Ginsberg. If Ginsberg was an index of restlessness among those of the young who felt at home on the campus, Presley and Dean made clear that the restlessness extended to a range well beyond. The popularity of Presley the singer and Dean the actor was so instantaneous, so sweeping, so intense that, in retrospect, it seemed as if the country had been waiting for them.

Until Presley and Dean came along, the world of mass entertainment, as one might expect of it, affirmed the mores of refinement and circumspection which Eisenhower's society professed. A black guitarist named Chuck Berry, who strummed rhythm and blues, and a white actor named Marlon Brando, who played in a film called *The Wild One*, conveyed an exciting new sensuality in the early 1950s but their following was limited. More popular were the musicians whose standard fare was insipid sentimentality and the movies which were tailored to a censorship code that treated sex as an oddity.

Then, within a few weeks of Ginsberg's reading of *Howl* in the Six Gallery, Presley appeared for the first time on nationwide television and Dean's *Rebel Without a Cause* was released. What Presley and Dean brought to the public was a kind of undisciplined, primitive energy. Without articulating it, they repeated Ginsberg's exhortations to personal liberation, and with their appearance, the mores of the 1950s started giving way.

Presley had just turned twenty-one when he was presented on the Tommy and Jimmy Dorsey show in January of 1956, and shortly afterward on the even more prestigious Ed Sullivan show. Born in Mississippi and raised on a farm, Presley had never gone beyond high school, and was working as a truck driver in Memphis while he tried to establish a career as a singer of country music. He made some records at the local radio station and appeared from time to time in hillbilly concerts, but nobody noticed him until he put a heavy beat into his music and began to shake and rock onstage with a frenzy that was considered not quite respectable.

Only then did Presley start to sell his records and get out-of-town bookings, to which he traveled in his secondhand Lincoln sedan. Shortly afterward RCA discovered him, and offered him a big contract. Within a few years, he was a multimillion-dollar performer.

78

Musically, what Presley did was to incorporate into his country style a black influence that whites had stubbornly ignored during the long years of segregation. Country was the native music of Southern whites, which drew heavily from the gospel as it was sung in the church. Southern blacks, meanwhile, had developed a style which they called "rhythm and blues," that had much of the spontaneous, emotional quality of early jazz. Chuck Berry had brought rhythm and blues to white audiences in the early 1950s and, by the time Bill Haley's white group made "Rock Around the Clock" the top hit of 1955, the style was being called "rock 'n' roll." Presley fused these various strains of music with the thundering volume of his electric guitar and the unconcealed sexuality of his body to become the hottest thing in show business.

It is important to note that, by now, the entertainment business had been transformed by economics and technology. Presley was accessible to multitudes on television the way no earlier performer had ever been. He was also accessible at home, at all hours, on records, and prosperity had put all these possessions within teenagers' reach. Record players in the 1950s were as common a possession as radios a generation before. By 1958, according to one authority, 70 percent of all records were bought by teenagers. The recording companies, having found their audience, were happy to earn their profits catering to it.

What teenagers by the mid-1950s were demanding—at their record stores, on the jukeboxes, from the disc jockeys—was rock 'n' roll. What they got was Presley and, after him, a stream of spectacular young performers who, like him, answered to their hunger. Searching incessantly for new forms and new messages, the restless guitars of rock 'n' roll proceeded to become the full-time accompaniment to the social ferment of the 1960s.

Certainly there was nothing consciously rebellious in Presley. Those who knew him agreed that, offstage, he was polite, even bashful, and never quite comfortable with his fame. He said his prayers at night and was genuinely devoted to his mother and father. He had nothing of the counterculture's aversion to material goods, and he possessed a well-publicized fleet of Cadillacs. The lyrics of many of his songs were unabashedly romantic, and even those that were a trifle angry, like "You Ain't Nothin' but a Hound Dog," scarcely qualified as social protest.

79

But, onstage, Presley conveyed a sullenness and defiance, a contempt for civility and for the intellect. His greasy hair, slickly cut with long sideburns, bespoke vulgarity. The costumes he affected —"an elegant hybrid of nigger and neck," one writer said of them —were a challenge to refinement. His guitar, booming electronically to the farthest row of the auditorium, made a mockery of subtlety and nuance.

As for the voice, it corresponded astonishingly with a description Allen Ginsberg once gave of his own reading of poetry, a voice "that begins somewhere in the pit of the stomach and rises forward in the breast and then comes out through the mouth and ears, and comes forth a croon or a groan or a sigh." Its singular purpose was to imitate the sounds of the sex act. All this added up, among Presley's huge following, to a praiseworthy blow struck against hypocrisy, against repression, against stuffiness, against pomposity. Like Ginsberg, Elvis Presley was an affront to the bourgeois world, and millions of young people loved him for it.

By the time Presley appeared on the Dorsey show, and *Rebel Without a Cause* had started circulating in the movie houses, James Dean was already dead. He had made three films, all idealizing the rebellious young, with whom he had himself become identified. Taciturn and surly, blond and with handsome features which, like Presley's, were a touch effeminate, he had a wantonness about him expressed in a passion for fast sports cars and high-powered motorcycles. He died on a California highway on September 30, 1955, in a smashup of his silver Porsche, which he had affectionately named "Little Bastard."

It was a frivolous death, almost devil-may-care, an existential act that seemed to shout defiance at the kinds of people that Ginsberg said in *America* were "always telling me about responsibility." In death, James Dean was canonized as the rebellious adolescent he epitomized in life.

Born on February 8, 1931, Dean spent most of his boyhood in Indiana. His mother died when he was nine. After that he saw little of his father, who turned him over to an aunt and uncle living on a farm in Fairmont, forty miles north of Indianapolis. Dean's roots went back to the *Mayflower*, his church was Quaker, his adolescent years were typically Midwestern: varsity sports, debating and theater, dates and parties. Dean's biographers agree he led a good life on the farm, well cared for and well loved.

At eighteen Dean left Indiana to become an actor. He lived awhile with his father in Los Angeles, attending Santa Monica Junior College and then UCLA, hanging around studio lots in Hollywood seeking bit parts in movies. In 1951 he moved to New York and was accepted at the Actors' Studio, where Marlon Brando had preceded him, to learn "Method" acting. Those were the days of the live television drama, and the following year he obtained the first of his many television parts. His mumbling, intense style seemed to fit him particularly well for young delinquent roles, often quite violent, and he soon acquired a reputation as a serious and talented professional.

After two appearances in Broadway plays, both well received, Dean was selected for the starring role in the movie *East of Eden*, a modern Cain-and-Abel story in which he played the neurotic and sensuous central character, an antihero named Cal Trask. Elia Kazan, the director, constructed the story as a confrontation between the son, angry and disobedient, and the father, who represented oppressive patriarchy. Dean fitted the role so perfectly that many, Kazan included, believed he *was* the role. He slouched and prowled, pouted and sputtered, and succeeded in romanticizing a mixed-up kid who triumphed over his better-natured brother by perversity. Many critics objected to the moral turnabout from conventional movie morality, but *East of Eden* became a big hit among teenagers, who clearly identified with its star.

In the spring of 1955, Dean made *Rebel Without a Cause*, the film which identified him indelibly with a set of ideals that seemed genuinely his own. Its theme was the search of confused and angry adolescents for an honest role in a hypocritical adult world.

Dean's character, Jim Stark, was portrayed in the publicity as a teenager with "a chip on both shoulders . . . caught in the undertow of today's juvenile violence." With great conviction, Dean conveyed brutality and tenderness, outraged innocence, a sense of persecution and basic decency, a youth who remained faithful to his dreams. It was the ultimate youth movie, a calculated response to the discerned demands of the teenage market. It became the core of the James Dean cult.

Giant, Dean's third movie, added relatively little to the myth, though it helped codify what was to become the young people's uniform of the 1960s, the faded blue jeans and tattered shirt. It was a costume of protest, rough enough to mock a culture that overval-

81

ued the mind, sloppy enough to shock those who preached the bourgeois value of neatness. For young people, it became a statement of authenticity that contrasted with the falsity of the uncomfortable business suit and tie.

In *Giant*, Dean once again played the outsider, furiously challenging the established order, endowed with a narcissism that was seen not as self-indulgent but as pride in being heretical, individualistic, nonconformist. *Giant* was not crucial to Dean's popular deification but, given the scarcity of icons produced in such a short life, it helped the cult to flourish.

Dean's death four days before attached a special mystique to the opening on October 3, 1955, of *Rebel Without a Cause*. Dean and the film became inextricably entwined, speaking the same message to its largely adolescent audiences. Fueled by death, the cult flourished almost immediately, in James Dean fan clubs, a profusion of fan letters to a dead star, memorial editions of magazines, a scramble for memorabilia, even a pervasive reaching out to the occult. Dean became an object of emulation around the world, and the obsession did not diminish as the decade wore on.

"There is nothing much deader than a dead motion picture actor," wrote John Dos Passos, the novelist and poet,

> *and yet,*
> *even after James Dean had been some years dead,*
> *when they filed out of the close darkness and the*
> *breathed out air of the second and third and fourth*
> *run motion picture theaters*
> *where they'd been seeing James Dean's old films, they*
> *still lined up:*
> *the boys in the jackboots and the leather jackets,*
> *the boys in*
> *the skintight jeans, the boys in broad motorbike belts*
> *before the mirrors in the restroom*
> *to look at themselves*
> *and see*
> *James Dean;*
> *the resentful hair*
> *the deep eyes floating in lonesomeness,*
> *the bitter beat look*
> *the scorn on the lip.*

> *Their pocket combs were out; they tousled up
> their hair
> and patted it down just so* *

It was apparent as the 1950s faded that there was something about James Dean that a generation wanted to be and perhaps would try to become.

While the fame of Presley and Dean was spreading, Allen Ginsberg remained a figure barely known outside San Francisco's bohemian circles. Getting *Howl* published was not easy. No American publisher would touch it. An English house finally agreed to do it, and ship copies to the United States, on the condition that the editors could replace with asterisks whatever words might be considered offensive. But when copies arrived in San Francisco in early 1957, the collector of customs promptly confiscated them. The copies were released a few months later, only after the customs office in Washington decided to avoid a court fight over arbitrary confiscation procedures.

By that time Lawrence Ferlinghetti had established City Lights Books, to produce inexpensive editions called "Pocket Poets" of the work of controversial artists. Ferlinghetti had already published three books of poetry, including one of his own. Though willing to publish his friend Ginsberg, he had no particular interest in challenging the government. But when the Customs Service dropped its action against the censored English version, Ferlinghetti reasoned that an uncensored edition of *Howl* would encounter no problems. *Howl and Other Poems*, a forty-four page soft-cover volume without asterisks, became the fourth work in the "Pocket Poets" series. William Carlos Williams wrote the introduction.

Ferlinghetti was genuinely surprised, then, when two officers from the Juvenile Bureau of the San Francisco police department entered his bookstore, paid 75 cents for a copy of *Howl and Other Poems*, arrested his clerk and left a warrant for him. The warrant charged that Ferlinghetti did "wilfully and lewdly print, publish and sell obscene and indecent writings, papers and books, to wit: 'Howl and Other Poems.'"

* From Dos Passos' profile of Dean in *Mid-Century*.

The *Howl* prosecution seemed to confirm everything Ginsberg had said about the repressive, uptight nature of American society. Belying San Francisco's reputation for tolerance, Captain William Hanrahan of the Juvenile Bureau said that, if the prosecution was successful, he would seek to banish a long list of other "filthy" books. When a reporter asked him waggishly whether he planned to confiscate the Bible he said no, but he added, apparently with some solemnity, that "what King Solomon was doing with all those women wouldn't be tolerated in San Francisco."

Fortunately for Ferlinghetti, who could not have afforded an ambitious defense, the Northern California chapter of the American Civil Liberties Union volunteered to take the case. The ACLU, a traditional bulwark of constitutional rights, had been in a condition of languor for some years. In the eyes of many, it had been flaccid in dealing with McCarthyism. But in 1958 McCarthyism was in decline, liberals were emerging from trepidation, and free speech issues were again attracting supporters. The ACLU in general was becoming more resolute and its Northern California chapter, an unusually freewheeling branch, decided to go after a constitutional precedent by getting Ferlinghetti acquitted.

The ACLU assured attention to the trial by enlisting as its chief counsel, without fee, Jake Ehrlich, the most flamboyant and esteemed of San Francisco's criminal lawyers. Ehrlich had defended Sally Rand, the fan dancer. He had also defended Caryl Chessman, an articulate kidnapper who captured the sympathy of young Californians and who, to widespread dismay, would be executed in 1960. Ginsberg was himself absent in Europe during the *Howl* trial, but dozens of his long-haired neighbors from North Beach enlivened the proceedings from their seats in the courtroom.

Ehrlich's principal witness was Mark Schorer, professor of English at Berkeley, a novelist and a critic. Schorer testified that the theme and structure of *Howl* "create the impression of a nightmare world in which 'the best minds of our generation' are wandering like damned souls in hell." Asked whether the obscenity was relevant, he said, "The poem uses necessarily the language of vulgarity." When challenged by the prosecution to explain "angelheaded hipsters," Schorer answered, "You can't translate poetry into prose. You don't understand the individual words taken out of context.

84

You can no more translate it back into logical English prose than you can say what a surrealistic painting means . . ."

In contrast to the defense's presentation of nine expert witnesses, the prosecution made a weak case. It offered two unknown academicians, who made a poor impression. The judge, a teacher of Bible classes at a Sunday school, had not been thought to be favorable, but he listened carefully and read the precedents conscientiously. In his ruling he said, "Would there be any freedom of press or speech if one must reduce his vocabulary to vapid innocuous euphemism? An author should be real in treating his subject and be allowed to express his thoughts and ideas in his own words." He found *Howl* not obscene and Ferlinghetti not guilty.

The two San Francisco papers covered the trial heavily, and their stories encouraged press attention around the country. *Life* and *Time* seized the occasion to do the first of their recurring accounts of Ginsberg and the beats, whom *Life* called the "James Dean school of poetry." Most of the other national magazines also took note. Their attention made *Howl* a best seller, and gave Ginsberg his first big boost to fame.

The Eisenhower Administration's reaction to the *Howl* decision, a setback in its ongoing struggle against obscenity, was like a caricature of a Ginsberg poem. Postmaster General Arthur Summerfield, calling smut "one of the most serious moral and social problems of the United States," initiated one of the most rigorous censorship campaigns in American history. He established a national speakers' bureau against obscenity, persuaded Congress to tighten penalties against offensive mailings and stepped up confiscations. Then he put the material he had seized into a private exhibit known in Washington as the "Chamber of Horrors." Admission to this celebrated display was strictly limited, and invitations to it were among the most highly solicited in town. To the young, Eisenhower and his people had come to look like a bevy of old fools.

"Here it was," Ginsberg said to me, "G-men and post office agents and the very president of the United States who was supposed to be a big, intelligent military leader, diddling around on the desk saying, 'Terrible, we can't have that.' That was the point that Burroughs and others were making at the time, that censorship of sexual imagery was censorship of the single largest area of private consciousness that existed, except maybe for death and hunger.

"Repression of such a vast chunk of the senses is something out of *1984*. But, as Orwell said, a functioning police state doesn't need police to enforce it. They get people to internalize. In *1984*, the people don't realize there's a war at the other end of the planet. Then, suddenly, they wake up to the fact that there has been some vast conditioning. Brainwashing may be too strong a word, but it's accurate. It was a conditioning so that the public was able to amnesiaize vast areas of its own consciousness.

"So once there was a breakthrough in that central area, and a breakthrough in the gray room, then everything was called into question. After sex was made conscious, what about money? What about capital exploitation? What about plastic? What about tearing up the earth and replacing it with asphalt? What about the murder of one hundred million buffalo?

"So, step by step, the whole pattern of reality appeared to be like a phony hallucination, the whole pattern of publicly accepted reality values was revealed to be a hallucination."

In spite of Eisenhower's wounded morality, the judiciary's attack on censorship continued. Local courts struck down the bans against one book after another in the late 1950s and publishers, feeling more audacious, rushed new titles into print. In 1959, Summerfield barred from the mails D. H. Lawrence's *Lady Chatterley's Lover*, recently published by Grove Press. A federal judge in New York overturned the action, with the comment that it would be "inimical to a free society." When the judge was affirmed by the Supreme Court, arbitrary literary censorship was all but dead.

A year after Ferlinghetti's edition of *Howl*, Jack Kerouac's *On the Road* was published. In 1959, after another struggle, William Burroughs's *Naked Lunch* appeared. The three, the basic texts of the Beat Movement, had attained notoriety during the extended publication battles. When they finally became available, the public snapped them up.

"All of a sudden, people could read everything," Ginsberg said. "They could recognize themselves in it, recognize their own longings and their own private understanding. Suddenly all of this private literature was public, and everyone could wonder who had been banning it all the time."

86

Kerouac's *On the Road* was probably the most influential of the Beat Movement texts. Its raw spontaneity and dynamic imagery made it thrilling to read. Its characters, forever on the move, transmitted their own restless dissatisfaction about their lives, and their sense of exhilaration in escaping from middle-class strictures. Burroughs's *Naked Lunch*, written from the perspective of a deranged drug addict, dwelled more angrily on the control mechanisms of the bureaucracy. It was far more morbid and pessimistic than *On the Road*. It was also more brutal and more sensuous, and certainly more subtle in its blurring of distinctions between reality and fantasy. Artistically, both *On the Road* and *Naked Lunch* may have been more important pieces of work than *Howl*.

But neither Kerouac nor Burroughs possessed Allen Ginsberg's messianic spirit, or his personal charisma. Ginsberg was more than beat poet; he was the prophet of the Beat Movement, committed to spreading its word. He was furthermore a luminous teacher, emanating a personal warmth and quality of love that many, especially the young, found nearly irresistible. In his shabby clothes, with unkempt beard and thinning hair, he seemed to personify the values he proclaimed: material abnegation, spiritual liberation, inner peace, total truth.

"Ginsberg is the lion of the poetry-reading circuit," declared *Life* in a long article on the beats in 1959. "He declaims his own startling verse with wild fervor, and hecklers attack him at their peril. At a recitation in Los Angeles last year a man stood up and demanded to know what Ginsberg was 'trying to prove.' 'Nakedness,' said Ginsberg. 'What d'ya mean, nakedness?' bawled the unwary customer. Ginsberg gracefully took off all his clothes."

Ginsberg was astonishingly testy, I found, about the bemusement, often mixed with hostility, which crept into articles in the press about the beat writers. "The distortion of them into Frankenstein imagery," he said to me, "and making up the idea of a bunch of creeps who had dirty beards, dirty hair, did not take baths, had lice in their hair, had bugs, who drank too much, had bad breath, smelled bad, who were violent and knife slashers, held back the cultural growth of America by at least a decade."

Actually, the contrary was probably true. The shocking appearance the beats deliberately cultivated was meant as protest against conformity. Calculated to advertise a philosophical position, it was a form of showmanship, and Ginsberg was himself champion of the showmen. This showmanship helped to get not only him but his ideas into the public press. It also won him invitations, and in the decade after *Howl* was published, Ginsberg brought his beliefs before, literally, thousands of audiences, composed of hundreds of thousands of young people. Whatever Ginsberg's quarrels with the media, he was among the first of the personalities of the 1960s to learn how to enlist them into trumpeting his cause.

Though *Howl* kept selling by the tens of thousands each year, it was more by force of personality than poetry that Ginsberg's influence grew. In the mid-1960s, *Life* wrote that Ginsberg "speaks today to the young of the world at large as the most famous and admired American poet." *The New York Times* went a step further and said, "To university students all over the world today, Allen Ginsberg is a kind of culture hero and sometimes a true prophet." His fame did not make Ginsberg rich, vain or bourgeois; it was rather an index of the spread of his ideas through an entire generation.

THE
CREATION

III
JOHN LEWIS:
Sitting In

1960

"It was the first time in my life I had ever been arrested. This cop came up and said, 'You're under arrest,' and hundreds, maybe thousands, of angry whites who were standing on the streets applauded when they took us away. I had a certain amount of fear, because growing up in rural Alabama I had instilled in me that you don't get in trouble with the law. . . . Yet, in a strange way, I found it was also a good feeling. I felt at the time it was like a crusade. All of us then believed that we were in a holy war."

FOR MOST AMERICANS, the decade of the 1960s began the day that four freshmen from North Carolina Agricultural and Technical College—an all-black school in Greensboro—walked into the local Woolworth's, sat down at the lunch counter and asked for a cup of coffee.

The date was February 1, 1960, the place a conventionally segregated, middle-sized Southern city. The four students politely presented their order to an astonished waitress. She, faithful to the practices enshrined in the tradition and law of the South, refused them service. When they declined to leave, a new word—"sit-in" —was added to the nation's vocabulary. Politics, normally practiced in the legislature and the courtroom, moved dramatically to the streets, and the "movement" entered American life.

February 1, 1960, is not the date that the movement began, however. It is, rather, the day most Americans took notice of it. For some years, a new mood had been incubating within the black community, especially among the young and the middle class, more notably in the South than in the North. Evidence of it had appeared from time to time. Many Americans had cheered on Martin Luther King, Jr., during the bus boycott in Montgomery, and admired the demeanor of such blacks as Daisy Bates and Autherine Lucy during the desegregation crises at Little Rock, Arkansas, and the University of Alabama. But, to most Americans, these seemed like almost random incidents, far removed from daily life, interest-

93

ing to watch but hardly cataclysmic in meaning. In contrast, in the years after Greensboro, no one who lived in America would miss the impact of the movement.

The four young men—whose names were David Richmond, Franklin McCain, Ezell Blair, Jr., and Joseph McNeil—have said they had made no particular preparations for their fateful undertaking. But the tactic of nonviolence which King had introduced in Montgomery was by now widely known in the black South, and the idea of the sit-in had for some time been growing in the minds of black students.

Almost as a whim, though scarcely as a frolic, the four entered the store. They were neatly dressed, directed their request to the waitress matter-of-factly and, when informed that Woolworth's policy was not to serve "colored," engaged articulately but futilely in a dialogue with the manager. They remained on their stools at the lunch counter until the store closed at the end of the day.

Planned or not, however, the Greensboro sit-in continued the next day, when some twenty students joined the original four at the Woolworth's counter. In the succeeding days, hundreds more arrived as reinforcements, including students from the white colleges in and around the city. By then, local white ruffians and Ku Klux Klansmen were appearing regularly to challenge the demonstrators inside and outside the store. Though some of the students were attacked, and others were arrested on charges of disturbing the peace, none breached the wall of nonviolence. By the end of the week, in an atmosphere of rising hostility, Woolworth's decided on a moratorium, however, and closed its doors.

Meanwhile, the movement spread, as if black students had been poised. Within little more than a week, sit-ins were started by students from small Southern colleges which most whites, at least Northern whites, never knew existed. These were the colleges which, year after year, quietly graduated the doctors and lawyers, the pharmacists and businessmen, ministers and teachers who served the nation's blacks. After Greensboro, sit-ins were staged by students from Shaw in Raleigh, North Carolina College in Durham, Johnson C. Smith in Charlotte, Fayetteville State Teachers College in Fayetteville, Hampton Institute in Hampton, Virginia. Scarcely any of the hundred or so black campuses in the South were untouched, as the wave spread from the Upper South into the Deep South, then back up to the Border States.

Though black, these colleges did not seem a likely place to spark a movement. They were supported, for the most part, either by public funds voted by white legislatures or by private donations provided by white philanthropists. They were thus conservative institutions, administered by men with the prudence to dampen racial passions and unattainable dreams. Students on these campuses were encouraged to pursue status, income and consumption, not culture or learning, and certainly not the well-being of the race. For generations, the graduates of these colleges were notorious for their social indifference, and their white benefactors liked it that way.

But by the start of 1960 civil rights had become a national preoccupation. Blacks had not forgotten the promise of the *Brown* decision, or allowed the lesson of Montgomery to fade. The crises at Little Rock and the University of Alabama had polarized the races in the South more than ever. White liberal allies had taken the offensive and, in 1957, had won the enactment of the first civil rights bill since Reconstruction. In 1960, a second bill was being debated, not just in Congress but in the media, and it was apparent that civil rights would be a central issue in the impending presidential election campaign.

In Nashville, Tennessee, Martin Luther King's most disciplined band of followers had assembled, and they sensed as 1960 began that they were about to embark on a great venture. Students throughout the black South had been familiarizing themselves since 1958 with the practices of nonviolent direct action. But in Nashville a band of young men and women worked intensively toward the day when they would lead the movement to a new stage of development. At the start of 1960 their preparations were nearing a climax.

John Lewis, who would emerge as one of the significant civil rights leaders of the 1960s, was part of the Nashville group. A small man, stockily built, with a plain brown face, Lewis was born in 1940, and was raised on a farm fifty miles south of Montgomery. Speaking in the slurred accents of the rural South, with a lisp he worked constantly to control, he seemed like an average Alabama farm boy. But beneath his unassertive manner lay a fierce inner zeal, which gave him incredible courage and inflexible will. Of the ten children in his family, he was the only one who aspired to college, and the only one who partook in the movement.

Lewis and I spoke for the first time in the mid-1970s in his office in Atlanta, where he directed the Voter Education Project, an outgrowth of the bitter registration campaigns of the 1960s. Later, he ran unsuccessfully for the congressional seat vacated by Reverend Andrew Young, who had once been executive director of King's Southern Christian Leadership Conference. I last spoke to Lewis in Washington, where he was serving the federal government as an associate director of Action, with responsibility for antipoverty and other social welfare programs.

"There was a black world and a white world in rural Alabama when I grew up," Lewis reminisced, "and our world was strictly black, strictly segregated.

"My father had been a tenant farmer, until he saved three hundred dollars and bought a hundred ten acres of land. We raised cotton and peanuts. We would work many, many days literally from sunup to sundown, not just in our fields but in the white man's fields. We received very little pay, and my father was always in debt. Our house was on a hill, a red-clay hill. We didn't have electric lights, we didn't have indoor plumbing, anything like that."

To get away from this life, many of Lewis's relatives had migrated to the North. In those days, blacks in the rural South were on the move. Mechanization had made much of the farm labor superfluous, and from 1940 to 1960 at least a third of the black people in Alabama left to seek work elsewhere. Most went to the North. Nearly as many moved to towns and cities in the South. But the elder Lewis was one who stayed.

"I used to argue with my father that there must be a better way," Lewis recalled. "But, with ten children, he didn't think he had much of a choice. I don't remember we ever had a single discussion about moving, certainly not about moving to the North."

Still, the migration shaped the outlook of John Lewis, as it shaped all those who stayed behind. Lewis said his own relatives favored Buffalo, where, at the age of eleven, he spent several weeks visiting an uncle. That was his first trip outside the South, and it was a revelation. But so were the trips that his uncles and cousins from the North made back home, wearing city clothes, driving shiny cars, telling stories about a good life where there was no

96

formal segregation. Lewis said that he, and the kids he went to school with, came to realize from these visits that they could aspire to something better than the world of blacks in the rural South.

The memories of segregation that remained most vividly with Lewis were the black children traveling to school in broken-down buses, while white students rode in gleaming new ones, the schools he attended with holes in the walls, which meant going out for wood in winter to keep a fire alive, the textbooks that were hand-me-downs from the white school. He remembered peering into the clean washroom marked White in the municipal bus station in town, and having to use the dirty washroom marked Colored. He remembered the local five-and-ten, where the white kids had a water cooler with a chrome spout and the black kids had a rusty spigot in the corner. He remembered he was not allowed to use the local public library, and in his family the system was never questioned, never even discussed.

"When I was fourteen years old, the Supreme Court issued its decision on school desegregation," Lewis said. "I remember it very well. I thought that the next year I would go to a real high school, and not the kind of training school that blacks were sent to. I thought I wouldn't have to be bused forty miles each day, past white schools, to maintain a system of segregation. I thought we would have new buses.

"But integration didn't happen when we returned in September. Nothing happened, really. I went all the way through high school and graduated in 1957, without attending a single desegregated school."

Lewis said his mother and father were much more interested in his staying out of trouble than in indulging his desire for a higher education. They had no objection to his going to college to become a minister, or to prepare for a job that would provide financial security. But they never contemplated education as a vehicle for opening the mind, much less for challenging the social system.

They even objected to his walking around Troy, the county seat, for fear he might somehow provoke the police, Lewis said. In their world, blacks who were arrested were "riffraff," he said, and no matter how oppressive the police were, his mother and father believed that decent black folks stayed out of trouble. In rural Alabama, blacks lived in a state of "psychological slavery," scarcely

97

distinguishable from the real thing of a century earlier, Lewis said. The shadow of insecurity was forever present, and people were always afraid.

The conventional response of American blacks to this life of torment had been, under slavery and since, to turn to the church, and John Lewis was no exception. "Between the ages of six and twelve," he said, "I would get together with my brothers and sisters, my first cousins and my friends, and we would literally play church." The Christian doctrine which Southern white society had bestowed upon blacks, in emphasizing the generous rewards available in the next world, made the suffering in this one seem a little more tolerable. The church, moreover, produced the only black authority figures that a young man like John Lewis was likely to know. When Lewis played church, he was the minister, and he knew that when he grew up he wanted a ministry of his own.

The crucial event in his growing up, Lewis said, was the Montgomery bus boycott, the unfolding of which he followed with passionate intensity. "There was a black radio station in Montgomery," Lewis explained, "a sort of rock 'n' roll, religious and gospel type. I guess you'd call it a soul station today. We listened to it every day, and we talked a lot about everything we heard. My grandfather also had a subscription to the *Montgomery Advertiser*, and I would go to his house and bring it home two or three times a week, after he read it. At school, we got *Ebony* and *Jet*, and the *Pittsburgh Courier*, the black newspaper. From all of them, I knew what was happening in Montgomery, and in civil rights."

As a partisan of the boycott, Lewis acquired a hero in Martin Luther King, who was not otherworldly like the preachers he knew but instead was leading black people in resistance to injustices in the here and now. King made him understand, Lewis said, that blacks could challenge the system of racial segregation, not in some distant domain of the spirit but in the familiar world he lived in.

The boycott loosed a surge of insight, Lewis said, unlike anything he had ever experienced before. "I saw fifty thousand black people," he said, recalling a fifteen-year-old's sense of wonder, "refusing to ride segregated buses any longer." Furthermore, behind their rejection of complicity with Jim Crow was the force of the black church, which he loved, and the stubborn leadership of black clergymen.

As early as 1957, the Montgomery boycott had inspired emulation throughout the South. In Tallahassee, a black preacher named C. K. Steele founded an organization modeled after the MIA, and it started its own bus boycott. In Orangeburg, South Carolina, blacks initiated an economic boycott. In Tuskegee, the faculty of the Tuskegee Institute, founded in 1881 by Booker T. Washington, undertook a voter registration drive which so upset the Alabama legislature that it gerrymandered the college outside the city limits. Tuskegee's blacks then retaliated with a boycott against the downtown stores. The practical results of these and other initiatives were mixed but they were proof that black forces, aroused by Montgomery, were marshaling throughout the South.

In the summer of 1957, King and the alliance of black ministers that had coalesced around the Montgomery bus boycott finally chartered the Southern Christian Leadership Conference. To avoid any hint of rivalry with the NAACP, its founders agreed that the SCLC would desist from court litigation and the mass recruitment of members. It had no long-range civil rights strategy, and its improvisations meant that it had to reestablish its leadership constantly. Instead, the SCLC conceived for itself the role of channeling the force of the black church into the civil rights struggle through nonviolent direct action, and as long as King was at its head it was generally successful.

To capitalize on its churchly character, the ministers decided after some debate to incorporate the word "Christian" into the organization's name. But their reasons went beyond credibility in the black community. The 1950s were still fearful times, when Americans were suspicious of change. The country drew away reflexively from organizations said to have Communist sympathies, which the white South attributed to the entire civil rights movement. It was only logical, as a semantical shield against demagogy, for the SCLC to advertise its Christianity. But it sought to convey in its name that it was moderate, and respectful of the basic values of American society, as well. In fact, militant as it sometimes became, SCLC's objectives never strayed from a conventional American context. It was respectable, even bourgeois, and the end it pursued was racial integration within a constitutional framework.

99

In institutionalizing the victory of Montgomery, the founding of SCLC had further significance. Until the *Brown* decision, the civil rights movement was symbolized by Thurgood Marshall and the NAACP. It was basically Northern and intellectual, with a legal and political orientation, and had a heavy component of white leadership. After Montgomery, the movement would be symbolized by Martin Luther King and the SCLC. It would be basically Southern and religious, oriented toward mass-supported direct action. With the founding of SCLC, control of the movement also shifted dramatically to the hands of the blacks.

At about this time, John Lewis was preparing to go away to college. His first choice was Morehouse in Atlanta, the school that his idol Martin Luther King had attended. But Lewis had no way to raise the money to go to Atlanta, and he was unable to obtain a scholarship. His family could not even afford Alabama State Teachers College, a substandard public college for blacks in Montgomery, where most of Lewis's schoolteachers had been trained.

"One day I was reading a newspaper put out by the Alabama Southern Baptist Convention," Lewis said, "and there was a little ad in it about a black school in Nashville called the American Baptist Theological Seminary. It is a school that is owned jointly by the Southern Baptist Convention, which was predominantly white, and the National Baptist Convention, which was almost all black. The school was founded in the early 1920s to keep black men and women who were interested in a religious education out of the white seminary in Louisville and get them into a black seminary. You didn't have to pay any tuition and you could work. I applied to go there."

Lewis mailed his application in May of 1957 and was accepted. With $100 as a gift from a generous uncle, he set off in the fall, traveling by bus from Troy to Montgomery to Birmingham to Nashville. Room and board at the college, he remembers, was $42.50 a month. To pay his expenses, he worked through the first two years in the kitchen, washing pots and pans. In his last two, he did janitorial work at the school.

Shortly after he arrived at the American Baptist Seminary, Lewis proposed to organize a campus chapter of the NAACP. Though

100

enjoined by state law in Alabama and elsewhere in the Deep South, the NAACP thrived in Tennessee, and Lewis said he wanted nothing more than to carry a membership card. The college administration refused its permission, however, out of fear that existence of an NAACP chapter would jeopardize the support of the college's white donors.

Lewis, instead, joined the existing Nashville chapter of the NAACP, and shortly afterward he attended his first "freedom rally," addressed by Reverend Martin Luther King, Sr., Martin's father. Sponsored principally by local NAACP units, such rallies were held frequently in the 1950s, and were an index of an increasing boldness among blacks in their campaign for civil rights. The effort by the American Baptist Theological Seminary to isolate itself from the civil rights struggle was, at the same time, the index of a timidity within the black community that would not vanish.

In his freshman year, Lewis had a personal experience which reflected this ambivalence. Lewis decided to apply for admission to Troy State, an all-white college near his home. Troy State was well regarded and he sincerely wanted to attend, Lewis said, though he was aware that if he set the precedent he would also make it possible for other blacks to go there after him. Troy State was inexpensive, and he could commute by bus while living at home. He submitted his high-school transcripts and the other necessary forms, he said, but never received a reply from the registrar.

Lewis then sent a letter to the Montgomery office of Fred Gray, the NAACP lawyer who had represented the MIA during the bus boycott. When he arrived home for vacation in the summer of 1958, he phoned Gray, who sent him bus fare to travel to Montgomery for a meeting. At the meeting, he was thrilled to find Martin Luther King, along with Ralph Abernathy, who were larger-than-life figures to him. They told Lewis that if he really wanted to study at Troy State, Gray would file a lawsuit and they would help him pay the fees.

"It was left entirely up to my parents to decide," Lewis remembered. "At the last minute, my mother and father literally refused to sign the suit and I had to drop the whole thing. Though my family owned the land we lived on, my father was still paying for the tractor and the machine tools he used. He had loans at the bank. He was literally afraid to get involved, so I went back to Nashville."

101

In Nashville in the fall of 1958, black students were beginning to be touched by the civil rights fever. Lewis recalled looking forward to a mass rally sponsored by the Nashville branch of the SCLC—called the Nashville Christian Leadership Council (NCLC)—which King was scheduled to address. During a visit to Harlem in September, however, King had been stabbed in the chest by a deranged black woman. During the weeks that he hovered near death, the future of the movement seemed to be in suspense, and it was months before King resumed his normal schedule. Lewis recalled that King's wife Coretta came to replace him at the rally, which even in his absence was a huge success. Similar rallies followed one another in rapid order throughout the school year, and Lewis attended them all.

Young blacks were also excited by a message that they received from abroad, Lewis recalled, from the sweeping liberation movements in black Africa. Ghana, initiating the postcolonial era, had won its independence in 1957, and the African empires of Britain, France, Belgium and Portugal were giving way rapidly to a series of free states. The black peoples of Africa were emerging from centuries of colonial ignominy into an era of self-government, endowing them with a positive new image, in their own eyes and those of others.

American blacks, cut off abruptly from their past, had always had more confused feelings about their heritage, and about the lands of their origins, than did most American whites. Now, however, was a time for blacks to take pride in their native continent. Exultantly, American blacks for the first time found reason to measure themselves and their achievements against those Africans who for so long had been so distant.

"Sure we identified with the blacks in Africa," Lewis said, "and we were thrilled by what was going on. Here were black people, talking of freedom and liberation and independence, thousands of miles away. We could hardly miss the lesson for ourselves. They were getting their freedom, and we still didn't have ours in what we believed was a free country. We couldn't even get a hamburger and a Coke at the soda fountain. Maybe we were slow in realizing what this meant to us, but then things started moving together.

102

What was happening in Africa, finally, had tremendous influence on us."

In 1958, Lewis met James M. Lawson, Jr., a soft-spoken, almost retiring clergyman working for his Ph.D. in theology. Tall, medium brown in complexion, Lawson was thirty years old at the time. Born and educated in Ohio, son of socially prominent blacks in a small Ohio town, he had made a commitment as a young man to what he called "New Testament pacifism." During the next few years, Lawson would shape a student movement in the South and become more influential than King in imparting to it a nonviolent character.

True to his pacifist beliefs, Lawson in the 1950s chose to go to prison rather than be drafted for the Korean War. Paroled to Methodist officials, he spent three years as a missionary in India, where he became familiar with Gandhi's ideas. When he returned home he enrolled in theology school at Oberlin in Ohio, but became excited by Martin Luther King's work—a "prophetic thrust on black people," he called it—in Montgomery. What impressed Lawson about King, he told me, was his placing the burden for attaining freedom on blacks themselves.

Lawson met with King in Montgomery in 1957, and conveyed to King his interpretations of Gandhi's methods. After the meeting, he quit Oberlin to disseminate the concepts of nonviolent direct action as Southern field secretary for the Fellowship of Reconciliation. His office was in Nashville, where John Lewis encountered him.

In the final years of the decade, Lawson traveled constantly throughout the South, conducting workshops on nonviolence for groups of blacks. Sometimes he traveled with Glenn Smiley, the white minister from the Fellowship of Reconciliation who had worked beside King during the boycott. Sometimes he conducted the workshops with King himself, or with Ralph Abernathy, or with some other minister familiar with Gandhian principles and the Montgomery experience.

Usually the workshops took place during a three-day weekend, and training sessions went on morning, afternoon and evening. Over these years, Lawson kept a low profile to the outside world, and few whites knew of his mission. But he recruited adults to

103

nonviolence in hundreds of churches, and became known to students on virtually every black campus in the South.

Lawson's special target was Nashville. Considered reasonably tolerant for a Southern city, Nashville had long had an active chapter of the Fellowship of Reconciliation. In the ministers of the Nashville Christian Leadership Council, it also had excellent black leadership. Nashville had a large population of black students, all potentially militant, at Fisk, Tennessee State and the American Baptist Theological Seminary. It also had whites sympathetic to civil rights in Vanderbilt, where Lawson planned to resume his own theological studies, and in other nearby colleges. Lawson reasoned that Nashville, still rigidly segregated, was the Southern city best fitted for the next nonviolent offensive.

Glenn Smiley actually organized the first workshops in nonviolence in Nashville, and Lawson joined him in the fall of 1958. John Lewis was recruited by Reverend Kelly Miller Smith, head of the Nashville Christian Leadership Council, who was one of the professors at his seminary. At first the workshops were held sporadically, Lewis said, but before long they were fixed for every Tuesday night. Participants came from all the black colleges around Nashville, and from some of the white ones, although the core of regulars never exceeded a dozen. By the fall of 1959 Lawson had resumed his studies in theology at Vanderbilt and had cut back on his traveling. He took personal charge of the Nashville workshops then, and imposed upon them a rigorous discipline.

"Jim was really the thinker in this group," said Lewis, who remembered Lawson as a gentle man, willing to inspire but reluctant to lead. "In his own right, he was a great moral force. We regarded him as our real teacher in nonviolence. I think he could have been the most important man in the civil rights movement, if he wanted. There was tremendous support and respect for him, especially among the young people."

John Lewis recalled that the workshop program began with lectures on the philosophy and discipline of nonviolence. They traced the ideas of nonviolence from the early Christians, emphasizing New Testament concepts of love, and they carried the process up to Martin Luther King and the bus boycott. He said the workshops dwelled at length on Gandhi and the goals to which massive nonviolent action had been put in India. He remembered discus-

104

sion of American theories of civil disobedience, and of the lessons
of the American black experience.

"We started mostly with talk, but later we turned to what we
called sociodrama," he said. "We actually acted out roles, trying to
foresee the varieties of possible alternatives, and how we could
apply nonviolence to different situations. But we also talked of how
do we bring about an open society, through SCLC.

"The phrases that kept coming up were, 'How do you use soul
force?' and 'How do you redeem this city and this community and
this nation?' The workshops became almost like an elective to students like me. It was the most important thing we were doing. We
became a real group of believers."

By the end of 1959, the Nashville Student Movement had been
established by the workshop participants, and a Central Committee, composed of about twenty-five students from the city's black
colleges, had been formed. It was to be the decision-making body,
and have a rotating chairmanship. But its natural leader, and first
chairman, was Diane Nash, a slight, pretty, light-skinned black Chi-
cagoan, with a soft voice and iron determination. Nash was to remain a dominant force among black students in the movement for
some years. Lewis, who was also a member, said the nucleus of the
Central Committee formed a "beloved community," friends and
crusaders who leaned on one another like a family.

The challenge Lawson put to the Central Committee was to
translate a commitment to the theory of nonviolence into a blueprint for action. Gandhi had taught that nonviolence required a
calculated program to have meaning. Lawson charged the committee with devising a set of plans that would get results.

Lawson told the Central Committee that, in some of his church
workshops, he had learned from the black women of Nashville that
the segregation they most detested was practiced at the downtown
department stores. These stores charged black women no higher
prices than the white women but allowed them nowhere to rest
their feet or give their children a moment's respite. Sometimes they
could not even try on the dresses they were invited to buy.

Lawson proposed the department stores as the target. He asked
the Central Committee to study it, to explore the ramifications of
choosing it and, if the target was found suitable, to reach a consensus among themselves. The decision-making process he proposed

was not efficient, but he strongly favored it over willful or manipulative leadership. Finally, in late 1959, the committee came to a decision to conduct a campaign in downtown Nashville, though not limited to the department stores. The campaign was to begin in February of 1960, after final exams.

The principal weapon of the campaign was to be the sit-in, derived from the sit-down strikes of American labor in the 1930s, and adapted to Gandhi's tenets of nonviolence. Gandhi had instructed his followers to be better prepared in confrontations than their adversaries, Lawson said, and he proposed a series of tests as the last stage in their preparations. In November and December of 1959, the Nashville students conducted their first "test sit-ins."

The test sit-ins, Lewis recalled, were designed to elicit a maximum of information about the enforcement of segregation. It was not that blacks were unsure whether Jim Crow would be applied, but that no one remembered any challenges. The test sit-ins were to establish how whites would react, and how the students would react themselves. The Jim Crow system needed a test, they reasoned, just to reaffirm that it was still in working order.

Sitting in at department store restaurants and lunch counters, the students carefully scrutinized the astonished responses of the management and the patrons. As the clusters of students came and went, Nashville's whites had no idea that anything momentous was impending, and even the black press paid these practice sessions only slight attention. Once the students were refused service, they engaged in a minimum of polite dialogue, Lewis recalled, and then departed.

Lewis said that, after the test sit-ins, the Central Committee proposed desegregation talks with the head of the chamber of commerce, the managers of the department stores and a variety of downtown businessmen. The overtures were uniformly rebuffed, he said. In late January, the Central Committee called a meeting at Fisk, which five hundred students attended, far more than had ever participated in the nonviolent workshops. The student leaders described the events of the previous weeks, and laid out a plan of direct action to put the system under siege.

But, before the Nashville campaign got started, four unknown young men in Greensboro, North Carolina, seized the initiative

106

themselves. Franklin McCain, one of the four, has denied any out-side influence. "Four guys met, planned and went into action," he has said. "It's just that simple." Ezell Blair, Jr., another of the four, recalled reading a "comic book" on the nonviolent movement, pub-lished by FOR and widely circulated, entitled *Martin Luther King and the Montgomery Story*. Whatever they remembered, however, these young men were functioning not in a vacuum but in an at-mosphere created by King, Lawson and the times. On February 1 they started the sit-ins, and the 1960s were under way.

Within a few days, the campus network that Lawson had been instrumental in creating was activated. Lawson received a phone call from a young minister at a college in Durham, fifty miles away from Greensboro, to ask for a display of support from the Nashville students. Nashville was ready, Lawson said, though the Central Committee decided not to rush in impulsively.

About seventy-five of the workshop students met with Lawson at Fisk on February 11 to put final touches on the Nashville plans. The next night, the First Baptist Church in the heart of downtown Nashville overflowed with the first of many mass student meetings, and the program for the direct action campaign was outlined pub-licly. The following day, Saturday February 13, the Nashville sit-ins started. Of all the sit-ins in the South in early 1960, they were to be the largest, the best-disciplined and the most influential.

"About ninety or ninety-five percent of the people who showed up at the church the week before had no training in nonviolence," said John Lewis, "but they were ready to go. We tried to catch them up on the essentials. They were instructed not to engage in any form of aggression or retaliation, to sit right up at the lunch counters and be quiet, literally to study, to do their homework. We in-structed people to prepare to go to jail, if necessary. Later, we appointed leaders and captains. It was almost like military disci-pline.

"The day the sit-ins began was a very nice day. The men all wore coats and ties. The ladies had on stockings and heels. It was like going to church. We sent people to the department store restau-rants, and to other restaurants and lunch counters. The city of Nash-ville didn't know how to deal with it. Most of the places just closed down."

The city's leadership responded, at first, more in bewilderment than in anger. Like the businessmen, the politicians had never had

107

much contact with blacks, and almost none at all with black students. Not knowing the source of the sit-ins, they had no idea what to do about them. The local branches of national chains felt some early pressure for a solution, since many of their stores in the North were being picketed in sympathy. But Nashville's whites, whether bigots or not, were accustomed to segregation, having lived with it all their lives, and could scarcely conceive of changing it.

In the absence of any city policy, the sit-ins continued intermittently throughout February, mostly on Tuesdays and Thursdays, when class schedules were light. The police did not arrest any students, and allowed no attacks by the white thugs who often clustered menacingly around them.

Late in February, the Nashville *Tennessean* wrote of the sit-ins by 350 students downtown. It treated the subject almost routinely, in a tone which suggested more resignation than indignation on the part of the city's whites. The article said:

> As in the previous demonstrations, when the Negro students took seats and asked to be served, the store manager ordered the lunch counters closed and stopped all service.
>
> The students sat there until 3:45 p.m., when they adjourned to a mass meeting at the First Baptist Church, Eighth avenue North.
>
> Although crowds of white youths gathered in several of the stores, there was no violence. Plainclothesmen and uniformed police kept a watchful eye on all five stores but made no arrests.
>
> Many of the Negro students did their homework as they sat at the counters. Others read books or magazines. One, John Lewis, a ministerial student at American Baptist Seminary, worked on a sermon.

But then the city changed its policy and arrests began. It was February 27, a cold and snowy day, when the sit-ins in Nashville were exactly two weeks old. Eighty-two students—seventy-seven blacks and five white supporters—were taken in and charged with disorderly conduct.

"A young white minister who had good contacts in the city had told us there would be trouble if we went downtown that day,"

Lewis recalled. "Some of the black community leaders had been tipped off, too, and they warned us that if we got arrested they would not have the money in their churches to get us out of jail. So we had a meeting of the Central Committee, and decided to go down anyway."

As if to emphasize that the period of tolerance was over, the police set loose the white rowdies who had hovered around the fringes of the demonstrations from the start. "A group of white boys," the *Tennessean* reported, "attacked two Negro demonstrators at Woolworth's after receiving no response from comments such as, 'Go home, nigger,' and 'What's the matter, you chicken?' " Much of the attack that day was verbal, but some of the whites abused the sit-ins with fists, lighted cigarettes and stones. As the demonstrators were hauled off to jail, the ruffians cavorted with impunity.

"It was the first time in my life I had ever been arrested," said John Lewis. "This cop came up and said, 'You're under arrest,' and hundreds, maybe thousands, of angry whites who were standing on the streets applauded when they took us away. I had a certain amount of fear, because growing up in rural Alabama I had instilled in me that you don't get in trouble with the law. But I guess all of us had a great deal of fear.

"Yet, in a strange way, I found it was also a good feeling. I felt at the time it was like a crusade. All of us then believed that we were in a holy war. Back on the campuses, the students heard we had been arrested and, after an hour or so, there were about five hundred more students occupying our places."

Most of the black community of Nashville supported the sit-ins. Dr. Stephen J. Wright, president of Fisk, said that, arrests notwithstanding, he had no intention of trying to stop the demonstrations. The Nashville Christian Leadership Council raised money to get the students out of jail, and the Nashville branch of the NAACP said it would back the students in every way. City councilman Z. Alexander Looby, a black lawyer long active with the NAACP, agreed to represent the students in court. The day after the arrests, a thousand supporters rallied on the Fisk campus, and in the ensuing days the black community showed its feelings at mass meetings in the local churches.

Some blacks expressed reservations about the students' actions,

109

of course, most conspicuously those who were subject to political or economic pressure. At the end of February, for example, Governor Buford Ellington issued a thinly veiled warning against student participation in the sit-ins to the administration of Tennessee A & I, a state institution. The dean of students responded quite differently from the officials of Nashville's private black colleges. "The school is not involved in any way," he said, "and the school has no intention of becoming involved."

John Lewis recalled that his parents were shocked at his arrest, which reinforced their disapproval of his involvement in the movement generally. "My mother, especially, felt ashamed," he said. "I don't think she could make a distinction between getting arrested for being drunk and getting arrested for demonstrating in civil rights." Everyone in the county, Lewis said, knew of his arrest—"the son of Eddie and Willie Mae Lewis up there in Nashville gettin' in trouble"—and because it was for civil rights, his family was naturally apprehensive of retaliation by local whites.

"We had decided in advance on staying in jail," Lewis said. "That's very much in keeping with the Gandhi philosophy. We felt we did not commit a crime, that we did not do anything wrong, that we were not going to cooperate with the system. The press was giving us a lot of attention then, and the television, and we wanted to use the jail to involve our parents, the university, the people of Nashville and the entire country."

Lewis was among those convicted of disorderly conduct for the February 27 protest, and he chose the city workhouse rather than pay the $50 fine. Diane Nash and fourteen others made the same decision.

In behalf of them all, Diane Nash issued a Gandhian statement in explanation. After thanking those who made the fine money available, she said, "We feel that if we pay these fines we would be contributing to and supporting the injustice and immoral practices that have been performed in the arrest and conviction of the defendants." Sixty-two others who had been released earlier rejoined them in jail as an assertion of solidarity.

On March 3, after meeting with a delegation of black clergymen, Nashville's Mayor Ben West announced the appointment of a bi-

110

racial citizens' committee to deal with the intensifying dispute. Even to blacks, the step appeared to advance the prospect of a settlement, and a truce seemed justified. Diane Nash, Lewis and the other students in the city workhouse agreed to have appeals bonds posted and accepted release. Then they announced that, as long as there was progress toward a settlement, further sit-ins would be suspended.

Shortly afterward, a city prosecutor jeopardized the truce when, in the mayor's absence from Nashville, he filed conspiracy charges under state law against seventy-nine of the demonstrators. He then added to the list of defendants Reverend James Lawson, whom he ordered arrested. It seemed for a moment as if the students had been betrayed, until a higher official announced that the city would not prosecute, and a semblance of calm was restored.

Lawson's name had not previously appeared in discussions of the sit-ins. He had been an observer at some of the demonstrations, but had stayed in the background. He was virtually unknown to the white community when, on March 1, he joined the group of black ministers who met with Nashville's mayor. He emerged from anonymity at that time by telling the mayor, to his face, that the local segregation ordinance was a "gimmick to manipulate the Negro." That afternoon, when people began asking who Lawson was, he held a press conference in which he revealed to the startled white community that he was, in effect, the principal adviser to the demonstrating students, who had been planning the protests for eighteen months or more.

Two days later, Lawson was expelled from Vanderbilt for involvement in unlawful acts. The expulsion seriously divided the campus. The divinity school's white faculty had paid Lawson's bail when he was arrested a few days earlier. Only his gratitude for this gesture, Lawson had said, persuaded him to leave the jail. For a time, the attention his expulsion received threatened to overshadow the sit-ins themselves, and in the end Lawson had to go elsewhere to finish his doctorate. But sympathy for the sit-ins seemed to crystallize among whites over the Lawson incident, first at Vanderbilt, then in Nashville itself.

By the time the mayor's biracial committee convened during the second week of March, white resistance was crumbling at the edges. Diane Nash, whom Lewis called "the most daring of our

111

leaders," had led a handful of black students into the lunch counter at the Greyhound bus terminal. To widespread public surprise the management agreed to serve them.

The bus terminal was different from the downtown restaurants, however. Judicial decisions had established that bus terminals, like public schools, were subject to the federal Constitution. In suits brought in recent years before the Interstate Commerce Commission, the Supreme Court had raised serious questions about the validity of segregation in terminal facilities. Most Southern cities found the Court's equivocation good reason for keeping segregation intact. But in 1960, the management of the Nashville terminal decided not to fight, and turned to assorted ICC rulings as the excuse for abandoning its segregation practices. None of the city's white leadership seemed to mind.

Department stores and their restaurants, in contrast, were in the unregulated world of private enterprise and, until the Civil Rights Act of 1964, there was no requirement that an owner serve anyone he chose to refuse. Nor did Nashville's political leadership have the power to issue such a desegregation order. At most, the city could repeal its segregation ordinance but repeal would affect only the city's enforcement powers and still not require merchants to serve blacks.

By mid-March, a few of Nashville's merchants indicated they would integrate if the city rolled back the ordinance, but none would accept the onus of integrating without the others. Most downtown merchants explained that they could not retreat because integration would give their suburban competitors an economic advantage. The mayor's biracial committee could recommend a solution to the deadlock, but there was no way it could compel the merchants, any more than the rebellious blacks, to comply.

Meanwhile, rumors circulated that the committee would propose a compromise based on "token" segregation. Diane Nash addressed the prospect at the committee's hearing in mid-March by declaring that segregation was an evil which could not be compromised. "I told them," she said to reporters after the meeting, "that no form of token segregation would be acceptable as a solution . . . By token, I meant part of a lunch counter segregated and part desegregated." The business spokesmen, for their part, told the committee that they could not imagine accepting any desegregation at all.

During the weeks that the biracial committee deliberated, the truce was broken by a major demonstration only once. On the last Friday in March 1960, 120 blacks held sit-ins at nine downtown eating places, allegedly to protest the committee's slow pace. Governor Buford Ellington charged, however, that the sit-ins had been staged for the benefit of a CBS television crew which had come to town to film a documentary.

It was not to be the only time in the 1960s that a television network would be charged with staging a "media event" disguised as news. Both the makers and recorders of the news were still refining their techniques, and throughout the decade the two would engage in mutual exploitation in the effort to capture TV audiences. There is no doubt that the presence of cameras aroused a behavior which became news, and that on occasion events were actually staged as news.

The chairman of the biracial committee complained that, whether or not the demonstration had been arranged for TV, it had wiped out three weeks of hard work. The governor called for an investigation into the abuse. But the truce resumed the next day, and no discernible damage had been done.

Blacks, meanwhile, applied more pressure indirectly. In a local election at the end of March, the churches mobilized black voters who reversed earlier patterns to vote against the mayor's candidates by a four-to-one ratio. In early April, black leaders admitted that they had quietly organized a boycott of the downtown stores, which the merchants had recognized for some time. At a mass meeting, the leaders said the boycott was 60 percent effective, and in a few weeks had cost the storekeepers several million dollars.

To underscore the pressure, black students periodically conducted "prayer vigils" at City Hall, and appeared at white churches on Sunday mornings. "We sent integrated groups down to the churches," Lewis said, "and they were almost never turned away." The students asked the white ministers for support of the movement, and many of them responded favorably.

The mayor's biracial committee finally announced its recommendation on April 5, 1960. The key proposal was precisely the "token" solution that Diane Nash had earlier rejected. The committee recommended that downtown eating facilities be divided into two parts, one reserved for whites, the other desegregated. The proposal meant that exclusion would end for blacks, but that a segre-

113

gated section of each restaurant would, in effect, be assigned to them. The committee suggested a ninety-day trial period for its plan and, as bait to the blacks, proposed that, if it worked, the city should drop all the sit-in prosecutions.

Neither side liked the proposals. Diane Nash and James Lawson, joined by Reverend Kelly Miller Smith, president of the Nashville Christian Leadership Council, met with the merchants to discuss their differences. But two hours of discussion only confirmed that they were as far apart as they had been when the sit-ins began two months before.

In a statement released after the meeting, the downtown merchants turned down the committee proposals with a touch of self-pity. They said they had an "unenviable" relationship with their competitors. "The very nature of our business," the statement said, "is such that it was most impractical for a small group of stores to assume the role of leading such a social change." They did not accept the reasoning that if Nashville's downtown were desegregated, desegregation would inevitably follow in the suburbs.

The same day Kelly Miller Smith, speaking for the blacks, declared that the biracial committee's "token" proposals were actually a plan for resegregation, which ignored "the moral issue involved in the struggle for human rights." Smith said the restricted areas in the restaurants would convey "the same stigma of which we are earnestly trying to rid the community." He emphasized that blacks would accept no such solution.

Smith said also that the ninety-day trial period placed "the principle of desegregation on trial and we submit that it is not." The trial period would encourage segregationists to wreck the experiment, he declared, and then claim proof that integration would not work.

The students resumed large-scale sit-ins in April, after the collapse of the committee's efforts, adding to their protests the picketing of Nashville's central square and the courthouse. The tension became considerably more severe than before, and the police sought to abate it by arresting both demonstrators and the white rowdies who repeatedly attacked them. The few whites who picketed in support of the black students were special targets for arrest.

One afternoon, the *Tennessean* noted, there were competing pickets. Blacks carried signs saying "Let's Break Bread Together,"

114

and "Make Nashville Great, Desegregate," and hostile whites carried signs saying "We Don't Like Jiggs," and "We Don't Like Jungle Bunnies." On several occasions that day, the newspaper noted, violence was averted only by the appearance of news photographers on the scene.

The situation in Nashville appeared to be at a stalemate in mid-April. There were no more negotiations. The two sides stared silently at each other. Observers sensed that Mayor West, despairing of a solution, had abdicated leadership. He made no response to the blacks who regularly demonstrated beneath his office window, he made few public statements, he contrived to be out of the city often. The students suspected that his strategy, and that of the storekeepers, was to wait for the school vacation, in the hope that the demonstrators would leave Nashville and lose their ardor at home.

Then, in the early hours of April 19, a bomb wrecked the home of City Councilman Looby, the NAACP leader and lawyer for the sit-ins. Looby and his wife were somehow saved from serious injury, but the blast was so severe that the house was almost totally wrecked. Two neighboring houses were damaged by the concussion and 147 windows were shattered in the Meharry Medical College across the street. The chief of police told reporters that, "These were killers. You don't throw that much dynamite to scare somebody." The bombing startled the entire city into a recognition of the imminence of racial warfare, unless steps were quickly taken to resolve the crisis.

"The Looby bombing brought everything to a head," John Lewis recalled. "We convened a meeting the next day of the Central Committee, and we also met with the Nashville Christian Leadership Council. The only idea we came up with was that we should have a mass march. We sent a telegram to Mayor West telling him to meet us on the City Hall steps, that we were going to have a nonviolent march to protest the bombing.

"We started the march at Tennessee State, which must be ten or twelve miles from the heart of downtown, and by the time we got to the City Hall, I really think we had over six thousand people walking with us.

"That was the turning point. Looby was highly respected. It was no longer the students and a few civil rights activists and the NCLC

115

people. Blacks and whites from all over came and participated. It was the total community, white people and black people. And the mayor finally told us he favored opening up the restaurants. That's what the headline in the Nashville *Tennessean* said the next morning."

On April 20, 1960, the *Tennessean* wrote not of the six thousand blacks and whites whom John Lewis remembered but of "3000 demonstrating Negroes" whom the mayor, telegram still in hand, received at 1:30 P.M. on the steps of City Hall. But the paper confirmed that the mayor indeed stated for the first time that the restaurants should end racial segregation. The encounter at City Hall was, indeed, the turning point in the struggle.

According to the newspaper account, the meeting between the mayor and the demonstrators started badly. A black minister, speaking for the Central Committee and the Nashville Christian Leadership Council, read a statement sharply criticizing West for failing to lead. The crowd applauded lustily. When the mayor attempted to respond, the minister interrupted him, and the two men argued for some minutes.

Then the mayor took the floor to defend himself, declaring that he would enforce the law without prejudice to blacks or whites but that he had no power to tell restaurant owners how to run their affairs. The audience stood in cold silence. Finally the mayor intoned solemnly, "We are all Christians together. Let us pray together." To that, a black student in the audience shouted, "How about eating together?"

Diane Nash, determined to clear up the ambiguity in the mayor's statements, then took the microphone for a series of questions. She asked whether West, as mayor, would use "the prestige of your office to appeal to the citizens to stop racial discrimination?" West answered directly: "I appeal to all citizens to end discrimination, to have no bigotry, no bias, no hatred."

Pursuing the attack, she asked: "Do you mean that to include lunch counters?" West, somewhat evasively, answered: "Little lady, I stopped segregation seven years ago at the airport when I first took office and there has been no trouble there since." *

---

* Though there was some vague federal law in the 1950s banning airport segregation, not until the 1960s was it explicitly outlawed.

116

Persevering resolutely, Nash asked: "Then, Mayor, do you recommend that the lunch counters be desegregated?"

To the crucial question, finally posed, the mayor said, "Yes."
Then, hesitating an instant, he added, "That's up to the store managers, of course." But the disclaimer proved unequal to the affirmation. What the newspaper readers of Nashville saw the next day
was that the mayor had endorsed an end to segregation. That was
what the store managers read, too.

On the day after the march, Martin Luther King, Jr., came to
Nashville to help the black community to celebrate. Four thousand
people, a substantial proportion of them white, crowded into the
Fisk gymnasium, then evacuated it for an hour when police received a bomb threat. By the time the search was over, thousands
more had arrived, to sit outside and hear King's talk over a loud-
speaker.

King called the Nashville movement, with accuracy, "the best
organized and the most disciplined in the Southland." He said, "I
came to Nashville not to bring inspiration but to gain inspiration
from the great movement that has taken place in this community."

Indeed, the students in Nashville had carried the strategy of nonviolence to a new level of effectiveness, beyond the Montgomery
bus boycott, beyond what had been achieved in any of the cities in
the South where sit-ins were taking place. King surely felt he was
not overstating matters when he told the throng at Fisk that "segregation is on its deathbed now, and the only uncertain thing about
it is the day it will be buried."

The negotiations to desegregate the downtown stores went
smoothly enough after the Looby bombing and the confrontation
with the mayor at City Hall. The students agreed to accept a decent
interval before testing desegregation, and to begin the process in
small numbers, during slack hours.

On May 10, 1960, black customers were served for the first time
at the lunch counters of three five-and-tens, a drugstore and two
department stores, all of them major targets of the sit-ins. Store
officials reported that their white customers accepted the change
with no serious complaints.

Throughout the spring, an atmosphere of change pervaded the

South. According to the Southern Regional Council, a research group based in Atlanta, sit-ins took place in more than a hundred cities. At least seventy thousand persons, most of them black, participated actively. An estimated thirty-six hundred of them were arrested at some point, but the demonstrations, nonetheless, were overwhelmingly peaceful. Victories over segregation followed one another, though not all of the sit-ins, by any means, were successful. According to a calculation made in August, segregation of lunch counters ended that year in twenty-seven Southern cities and of five-and-tens in sixty-nine cities. The wave appeared irresistible.

These victories, however, had required a monumental expenditure of courage, of time and money, of energy, of personal stamina. Notwithstanding Martin Luther King's claim that nonviolence would fill its opponents with "moral shame," the resistance of the segregationists remained bitter, resourceful and potent. In the Deep South states of South Carolina, Georgia, Alabama, Mississippi and Louisiana, no desegregation whatever occurred. That the triumph in Nashville should have consisted of six lunch counters, grudgingly conceded, and nothing more, seemed ludicrously disproportionate to the effort it demanded.

Yet King had been right in foreseeing that the sit-ins, as an expression of Christian nonviolence, would win the approval of whites outside the South. The evidence lay in letters to the editor, in political statements, in church sermons and, more meaningfully, in the thousands of dollars in financial contributions sent in for the sit-ins' support. A national consensus seemed to have been established, from which only the white South was excluded. It acknowledged the justice of the sit-ins, as it had earlier endorsed the Montgomery bus boycott. Without this consensus, the South's repressive power would surely have prevailed, and blacks, as they had in the past, would have paid heavily for rebellion.

That is not to say that Americans were completely at ease with the sit-ins. White Americans knew very little of Gandhi, and civil disobedience was still an unfamiliar concept in the American context. Liberals remained committed to the belief that blacks could attain their rights through the political process, despite a century of experience which refuted it. Yet most liberals squirmed uncomfortably when former President Harry Truman, political patriarch of civil rights, said of the sit-ins, "If anyone came into my store and

118

tried to stop business, I'd throw him out. The Negro should behave himself and show he's a good citizen." The sit-ins had clearly made Truman's kind of liberalism obsolete.

What persuaded so many Americans to approve of the sit-ins was, precisely, that the young black sitting quietly at the lunch counter *was* a good citizen. He was asking for his rights, peacefully and with dignity. The surlier the white South showed itself to the blacks' Christian pacifism, the more deeply the blacks' tactics touched the rest of the country. Like the stoic marchers in Montgomery during the bus boycott, the young men and women of the sit-ins possessed a majesty to which most Americans responded.

The gap would never close between those who favored the political process and those who turned to direct action. Thurgood Marshall, when asked about the sit-ins, sighed, "The young people are impatient . . . and, if you mean are the young people impatient with me, the answer is yes." Ultimately, the tension of their differences would split liberals and activists apart. But, in the euphoria of the early 1960s, it was a warmhearted alliance. Truman was an exception. Few on either side carped at the other.

The problem was, after Nashville as after Montgomery, something new was needed to maintain the momentum. Among the lessons of Nashville was that the sit-in, used on a wide front, was a good weapon with which to start the campaign to desegregate American society. But young blacks could hardly be blamed for concluding that, for all their labors, most of Nashville remained as segregated as ever. If blacks had to rely everywhere on the pressure of sit-in campaigns, segregation would outlast them. Like Montgomery, Nashville proved that the system was not impregnable, and that blacks could attack it successfully. But it showed also that, like the bus boycott, sit-ins alone could not finish the job.

To establish a strategy for finishing the job, the sit-in veterans met in the spring of 1960. The organizer of the meeting was Ella Baker, a black woman who had spent most of her sixty years in civil rights, many of them organizing in the field for the NAACP. Since 1958, Ella Baker had been executive director of Martin Luther King's SCLC. Her relentless prodding of SCLC to be more aggressive made King uncomfortable, however, and their differences

119

were soon to cost Ella Baker her job. But in the weeks after the sit-ins, she persuaded the SCLC board to sponsor the conference of sit-in leaders. What she foresaw was that the students would surpass the ministers as a dynamic force in the civil rights movement.

The meeting was held during spring vacation on the campus of Shaw University in Raleigh. It was conceived as a gathering of a hundred or so, but there was no containing the momentum of the movement, and more than three hundred students attended. They came from fifty-six colleges in the South and nineteen in the North. The meeting began on April 15, Good Friday, and lasted until Easter Sunday.

The Nashville Movement, recognized for its high degree of organization and discipline, was preeminent among the delegates. Reverend Lawson received particular deference for his initiatives. Diane Nash and John Lewis were greeted as heroes. The only delegation that could compete for acclaim came from Atlanta, whose campuses had higher academic standing but whose demonstrations had been less effective. North Carolina A & T sent Ezell Blair, one of the four original sit-ins. Within the gathering were many of the young men and women who, in the ensuing years, would become famous in the civil rights struggle.

Martin Luther King, Jr., delivered the keynote address, and Raleigh's black middle class turned out in greater numbers than the students to hear him. At the conference, King was indisputably the most revered figure, but James Lawson was much more special to the young. Though the same age, King's role seemed to identify him with an older generation, Lawson's with the movement of campus protest. What emerged from the euphoria of the sit-ins was that the students believed they had a contribution of their own to make, free of the leadership of Martin Luther King.

Ella Baker encouraged this belief. She made no secret of her conviction that King and the SCLC had not kept pace with the demands of the times. "She kept daring us to go further," John Lewis remembered. "She was much more radical than King, more like Philip Randolph in his youth, well to the movement's left. She was very creative. She did not want the students used by the SCLC or the NAACP. She left a deep imprint on us."

Ella Baker insisted that the students not rush into establishing an organizational structure, which would inevitably have required af-

filiation with SCLC. At her suggestion, the delegates voted to create a Temporary Student Non-Violent Coordinating Committee. Its
instructions were to recommend by fall the shape of a permanent
organization.

Had James Lawson wanted, he could surely have assumed the
leading role in the organization. But he had a profound wariness of
leadership, including his own. He had promoted "group-centered"
decision-making in Nashville, and he did not retreat from it in
Raleigh. The students were guided by his thinking, and in fact
went further.

The students at Raleigh conveyed a deep skepticism of age, of
experience, of reputation and office, of authority in general. They
promoted the powers of the rank and file over the leaders, and
enshrined the decision-making process over the decision. Much as
they admired King, they were apprehensive of his magnetic qualities. They set out consciously at Raleigh to build an organization in
which leaders were weak, in which decisions were reached by
consensus. Ultimately, their ideas evolved into the doctrine called
"participatory democracy," a major ideological innovation of the
1960s. It was an exciting notion, though the aversion to leadership
that was intrinsic to it proved finally to be a fatal flaw.

Other germs, later to flourish, also appeared in Raleigh, though it
is surely easier to see them in retrospect. No public debate took
place over the commitment to nonviolence. Nonviolence was even
incorporated into the name of the students' organization. All the
delegates deferred to Lawson, whose commitment to nonviolence
was unequivocal, and who wrote the organization's statement of
principles. In language much like King's, Lawson said the "philosophical and religious idea of non-violence [is] the foundation of
our purpose, the presupposition of our faith and the manner of our
action." John Lewis agreed with that statement. So did Diane Nash
and the others of the "beloved community" of the Central Committee in Nashville. But many in Raleigh did not.

Lawson could not quell the skepticism which, if rarely spoken in
floor discussion, was whispered frequently in the corridors. Students were willing to accept nonviolence as a tactic, but were unwilling to commit themselves to it as a way of life. It was that
distinction, whose importance would later loom larger, that separated the students philosophically from King. It was hard to quarrel

121

with success, and King's ways had brought great victories in the boycott and the sit-ins. But unlike King and Lawson and Lewis, most of the students at Raleigh would not pledge themselves to nonviolence permanently.

More immediately, a major difference arose over the role of students from the North. The sit-ins had sparked excitement on Northern campuses, among whites as well as blacks, and Northern students were in search of an outlet for their enthusiasm. The presence of these Northerners was flattering to the Southerners, and little attention was paid to their color. Since the undisputed objective of the civil rights movement was still racial integration, the rejection of racial distinctions was natural enough. Yet the battle-hardened veterans at Raleigh were ambivalent, even tense, about the newcomers' arrival.

As Ella Baker remembered it: "There was a high degree of protectiveness on the part of the Southern students. I think it became evident to some of the youngsters for the first time that the Northern students—who came from Yale, Harvard, Brown, City College of New York, Chicago and so forth—were much more articulate in terms of social philosophies. The Southern students had come with a rather simple philosophical orientation, namely the Christian nonviolent approach. They had demonstrated, however, their capacity for suffering and confrontation to a degree that the Northern students had not."

Among the blacks, the largest Northern delegation came from Howard University in Washington. James Lawson remembered the Howard students as bombastic, skeptical, indifferent to nonviolence. Lawson conducted the business sessions at Raleigh much like a prayer meeting at a Southern black church. During particularly heated discussions, he would propose that the students stop for interludes of singing or prayer. The Southern majority was comfortable with such procedures but the Northern blacks were intolerant, and made fun of them.

Clearly, the Southerners had no intention of losing their leadership to the more adroit Northerners, as they felt blacks had lost out to whites within the top ranks of the NAACP. After considerable acrimony, a decision was reached that a Northern Student Movement would be established, as an auxiliary, and that by individual efforts Northerners could earn full participation in the activities of the main organization.

The decision left the field open for the development of Southern black leaders, better fitted on the whole than Northerners to serve the black South. But the debate did not end at Raleigh. Rather, it foreshadowed a breach that would ultimately debilitate the emerging organization beyond recovery.

Finally, the Raleigh meeting debated strategy. Ella Baker understood that economic issues lay beyond segregation. She had little use for King's contention that the movement had to inspire American whites to a higher level of morality. It is she who is usually credited with coining the endlessly repeated question, "What's the use of integrating lunch counters when Negroes can't afford to sit down to buy a hamburger?" There was a touch, or more, of Marxism to Ella Baker's thinking, and it would be years before King would incorporate economics into his social analysis. Even when he did, however, he was unwilling to surrender his conviction that Christian doctrine, not economic doctrine, was the key to ending racial inequality.

The strategy the students argued at Raleigh was within a narrower range, but its implications were momentous enough. One group proposed to teach the techniques of nonviolent mass action throughout the South, reasoning that whites would respond to the demonstrations and force the various institutions of government to act. The basis of this strategy was the enlistment of white allies to the goals of the movement.

The contending strategy called for a program of grass-roots organizing throughout the South to register black voters and make them aware of their own political power. At the basis of this strategy was a philosophy of independent black strength, which would later emerge into the doctrine of Black Power. It was in this direction that the organization was turning but, in the warm atmosphere of Christian love at Raleigh, few were able to see very far ahead.

A month after the Raleigh meeting, an organizing committee convened in Atlanta in SCLC facilities. Under Ella Baker's watchful eye, the student representatives later consulted with King, as well as with leaders of the Congress of Racial Equality, the National Student Association, the NAACP and other friendly organizations.

In the fall of 1960, after it became clear that the students would strike out on their own, SCLC fired Ella Baker and withdrew the use of its office space. In October, with a grant from the AFL-CIO, many of the students who had been at Raleigh met again and officially established the Student Non-Violent Coordinating Committee. SNCC—known by all as "Snick"—would soon become a household word.

Like the SCLC, the parent it had disowned, the Student Non-Violent Coordinating Committee was not structured as a membership organization. In 1960, virtually every black campus in the South had a direct action group eligible to become a SNCC affiliate. As its name indicated, SNCC at that time envisaged its role to be nothing more than a "coordinating committee" for these groups, each of which would function autonomously. SNCC would create a small staff to provide information and guidance to those who sought it.

But the premise on which SNCC was established proved false. In short order, the powerful ardor of the campuses would wither and the direct action groups would vanish. SNCC, then, would evolve into a significant organization on its own, made up of the staff that had once been recruited to serve others. Its first budget was $14,000, scarcely enough to run an office. But within a few years the budget would grow to nearly $1 million annually.

In a compromise between the two power bases, it was agreed that Nashville would provide the SNCC chairman, while Atlanta would be the site of the headquarters. Marion Barry of Fisk was named the first chairman.* John Lewis later succeeded to the office, and served for the three most productive years of SNCC's history.

In SNCC, the civil rights movement acquired a detachment of professional shock troops, small in numbers but extraordinarily dedicated, gifted and brave. Ella Baker had been correct in foreseeing that the students would become the chief combative force in the blacks' campaign for equality. It would not be long before SNCC would demonstrate the power to transform the civil rights movement, and contribute mightily to the tempestuous character of the 1960s. Embodiment of the spirit of the sit-ins, SNCC would become an aggressive, impatient, angry force, driving the society to change.

* In 1978, Barry was elected mayor of Washington, D.C.

124

IV
JAMES FARMER:
Freedom Riding

1961

vinced. As nearly as one could tell in midcampaign, blacks
e going to cancel themselves out as a political force by voting
it equally for each candidate.

hen, near the end of October, an incident occurred which
iged the course of the election. Like so many other crucial
lents of the period, it concerned Martin Luther King, Jr. In
mon with most of the black leadership, King had seemed to
er Kennedy over Nixon, but he remained scrupulously neutral
ie campaign unfolded.

ng lived in Atlanta now. In 1959, the year before the election,
ad resigned his post in Montgomery to join his father as copas-
f the Ebenezer Baptist Church. Atlanta meant returning not
to home and the family pulpit, but being at the seat of the
hern Christian Leadership Conference, institutional base of
owers within the civil rights movement.

lanta was also the most dynamic city in the South, a pacesetter
isiness and industry, and a model of Southern racial relations.
ough its buses had been desegregated by the spring of 1960,
est of the city was still rigidly Jim Crow. Then the sit-ins came
the students of Atlanta University, King's own alma mater,
/ the city into turmoil. By fall, after dozens of arrests, the stu-
had acquired enough confidence to take on the citadel of the
e elite, Rich's Department Store. They insisted that King be
leader.

n Allen, Jr., president of the Atlanta Chamber of Commerce,
Mills Lane, a prominent banker, agreed to meet with a dele-
i of students prior to the sit-in at Rich's. Allen, who was to
ne Atlanta's mayor in 1962, described the encounter in his
oirs.* With remarkable candor, he captured much of the char-
of the relations that existed in 1960 between Southern whites
lacks.

> The students told us about how they could go into
> Rich's and buy all they wanted, but could neither take
> a seat at the lunch counters or even try on clothes. It
> was, frankly, the first time Mills and I had given any
> thought to most of these difficulties faced by the
> Negro. We listened to them and said we would take

Allen, Jr., *Mayor: Notes on the Sixties.*

130

"On the bus I noticed some of the students writing notes,
boys writing notes and putting them in their pockets, and
girls putting them in their brassieres. I went across the aisle
to find out what it was. They were writing names and addresses of next of kin. They really had not expected to live
beyond that trip. But it was something they had to do, and
they were determined to go."

THE SPRING OF 1961 was a period of testing for
John F. Kennedy and his new Administration. He had won the
presidency on a promise of ending the drift of the Eisenhower
years, of getting the country moving again. In his inaugural address,
he had announced exultantly that "the torch has been passed to a
new generation of Americans," which he characterized as courageous, disciplined and proud. He had surrounded himself with
men and women who were young and attractive like himself, and
who helped him generate an excitement, and a sense of expectancy,
unknown in Washington since the early days of the New Deal. In
his first months, Kennedy transformed the torpid atmosphere of the
country by the freshness and energy of his leadership.

In quick succession, Kennedy sent to Congress a range of important proposals, covering both foreign and domestic policy. He was
more at ease with executive action, however, operating outside the
constraints of Congress. Even when he blundered at the Bay of
Pigs, he appeared to vindicate himself by his daring, and by a self-
mocking candor which seemed to say that what he did not know he
would apply himself to learning. Rather little of his attention in
these months was given to the problems of blacks, though he remained faithful in his public statements to the ideals of equality on
which he had campaigned.

By spring the world was indisputably charmed by this engaging
man, though the quality of his leadership had yet to be confirmed.
Khrushchev in the Kremlin watched him warily, but so did America's farmers, businessmen, educators and workers. As for American

127

blacks, having voted overwhelmingly for him, they thought they had earned the right to expect more than the others. But, having too often been disappointed by government, they tempered their hopes in Kennedy with an intrinsic skepticism.

James Farmer, a barrel-chested man of forty, was among the more skeptical. Farmer served as director of the Congress Of Racial Equality (CORE), a civil rights organization with roots that dated back to the pacifist movement of the 1940s. He had studied Gandhi's teachings for twenty years, believed deeply in racial integration, had spent most of his adult life working to dismantle the barriers that separated the races. Farmer felt himself titillated by the vision that the time to sweep away the barriers had actually come, but the experience of a lifetime of crushed hopes had left him cynical. He insisted that Kennedy's commitment to civil rights could not be taken for granted and remain subject to Kennedy's convenience. He wanted this commitment to be tested in combat. That spring, Farmer and the CORE staff hit upon the idea of the Freedom Ride.

"Sure I responded positively to Kennedy in 1960," Farmer told me many years later, "but I was not looking for well-intentioned rhetoric. My attitude was, whoever was president we had to put pressure on him to move. Eisenhower moved in Little Rock only when he had to. And we figured the government would move only when it became politically more dangerous not to move.

"We planned the Freedom Ride with the specific intention of creating a crisis. We were counting on the bigots in the South to do our work for us. We figured that the government would have to respond if we created a situation that was headline news all over the world, and affected the nation's image abroad. An international crisis, that was our strategy."

And in May of 1961, Farmer's Freedom Ride did become an international crisis. Southern bigots behaved precisely as Farmer and the CORE staff had foreseen, focusing the attention not only of the nation but of the world on the savagery endemic to racial segregation. The brutality that the Freedom Riders suffered in the effort to exercise their rights forced the Kennedy Administration, hesitant at first, to take a forthright stand on the constitutional rights of black Americans. After Farmer's Freedom Ride, there was no longer any doubt about the side to which the federal government was committed in the struggle.

the matter up with the other members of the Chamber, but then we made no serious moves toward eliminating segregation.

I think what we were doing was closing our eyes and hoping the problem would go away. It was in the nature of our upbringing that we had seldom come into contact with the problems of the Negro in America. A part of the Southern Way of Life was that you didn't really *see* Negroes when they were in a store or walking the streets downtown. You didn't happen to think that maybe they had no restroom to use while shopping, or that they had to buy dresses or slacks without first being able to try them on for size, or that when they became hungry they had the choice of either waiting until they got back to their neighborhood grill or else sidling up, hat in hand, to the back door of the white man's restaurant and ordering something to go. I was on the board of directors at Rich's then, and we began discussing the students' demands, going so far as to determine the exact volume of Negro business, which wasn't much in dollar value, and giving consideration to making Rich's an all-white store. That is how naive we were on the race issue at that point, on the verge of the greatest civil-rights struggle in the history of the United States.

King did not want to lead the students in their sit-in, but he understood that, unless he did, he risked forfeiting the preeminence of SCLC, and of nonviolent direct action. The students' success in the sit-ins during the spring had made them exultant over their power. They found SCLC too cautious, and they resented the wealth brought to it by the contributions that King attracted. They talked of a "generation gap," though they recognized that King remained the strongest spokesman the movement had. For his part, King understood that he could not be less daring than his followers, and on October 19 he led a band of seventy-five students out of Atlanta's black ghetto into the center of the city. Entering Rich's, he and his followers sat down at the lunch counter, singing "We Shall Overcome." The management, unwilling to negotiate, promptly had everybody arrested.

The arrests would have had little lasting importance, except for a

131

decision by Judge Oscar Mitchell in neighboring De Kalb County. Mitchell remembered that King had been arrested some months earlier for failing to obtain a Georgia driver's license when he moved to Atlanta from Montgomery. In chains, King was taken from the Atlanta jail to the De Kalb County court, where the judge ruled that King, in getting arrested at Rich's, had violated his probation. King was then sentenced to four months at hard labor in the state penitentiary at Reidsville, where blacks were commonly beaten, and sometimes shot. With barely a week to go before the presidential election, King was transferred the three hundred miles to the prison, and locked in solitary confinement.

Nixon missed the opportunity to protest the imprisonment. In his memoir, *Six Crises,* he wrote that he considered it improper for a lawyer to pressure a judge.* He also wrote that he asked the attorney general to look into a possible infringement of King's rights, whereupon the Justice Department drafted a statement critical of the judge's action for Eisenhower's use. Characteristically, however, Eisenhower chose to remain silent, and Nixon's press secretary, when questioned about the case, answered "no comment." Political observers at the time conjectured that Nixon was less concerned about legal propriety than about maintaining the narrow lead in three Southern states credited to him by the polls.

Kennedy's camp reacted differently. The initiative came from Harris Wofford, a thirty-four-year-old staff aide responsible for civil rights. Wofford had studied under Gandhi in India, worked as a lawyer with the Civil Rights Commission, was a friend of James Lawson and lectured on nonviolence on black campuses in the South. Nixon's staff had no counterpart to him. Wofford proposed that the candidate phone Mrs. King with a promise of help, and the idea was conveyed to Kennedy, then barnstorming in Chicago.

Coretta King was attractive, intelligent and poised. Soon to give birth to a child, she was potentially a major asset to any presidential campaign. As she remembered it, Kennedy phoned her and said, "I want to express to you my concern about your husband. I know this must be very hard for you. I understand you are expecting a baby, and I just wanted you to know that I was thinking about you

---

* As the country learned during Watergate, Nixon later became less scrupulous in his dealings with judges.

132

and Dr. King. If there is anything I can do to help, please feel free to call on me." Kennedy did not touch on the substance of King's legal difficulties, or state any support for the Rich's sit-ins.

The next day Robert Kennedy, the candidate's younger brother and campaign manager, went a step further. The future attorney general, undeterred by Nixon's reservations, telephoned Judge Mitchell in De Kalb County with a plea for King's release on bail. When the news of the action was leaked to the press, it received nationwide attention. Judge Mitchell reversed himself, and Martin Luther King was released from Reidsville. On his return to Atlanta his elated father, Reverend Martin Luther King, Sr., declared to a cheering crowd, "I've got a suitcase full of votes, and I'm going to take them to Mr. Kennedy and dump them in his lap." *

"Daddy" King, with some help from John Kennedy's publicity machine, delivered on his word. On the Sunday before election day, he and hundreds of other black ministers around the country promoted Kennedy's cause from their pulpits. A precipitous economic decline just before the election, which refreshed a nostalgia for Democratic activism, accelerated the momentum among blacks. On election day, seven out of ten black voters cast their ballots for Kennedy. Black voters provided Kennedy's margin of victory in Illinois, New Jersey, Michigan, South Carolina and Delaware, and perhaps in six other states as well.

Ironically, despite his avid courtship of the South, Nixon won only Florida, Tennessee and Virginia among the Southern states. The misjudgment was costly. Had a few thousand black votes in two or three crucial Northern states switched to the Republican column, he would have become president. Black politicians exulted, with some justice, that it was the black vote which sent John F. Kennedy to the White House.

James Farmer became national director of CORE on February 1, 1961, a few days after Kennedy's inauguration. His selection represented a decision by CORE to embark on a militant direct action campaign. CORE had pioneered in the strategy of nonviolence in

* The quote is from Theodore White's *The Making of the President: 1960*, p. 323. Mrs. King's version was, "He roared out to the crowd, 'If I had a suitcase full of votes, I'd take them all and place them at Senator Kennedy's feet.' "

133

the 1940s, but throughout the decade of the 1950s little had been heard of the organization. During the Montgomery bus boycott King drew on CORE's experience, and during the sit-ins CORE came alive again with field counseling throughout the South. Now CORE, aroused by the times and challenged by SCLC, wanted to reassert its eminence. In choosing Farmer, CORE found a dynamic and eloquent leader with a long history in civil rights demonstrations. Farmer was impatient to get back into the battle.

Born in Texas in 1920, James Farmer was, like Martin Luther King, Jr., the son of a minister of the gospel. James Leonard Farmer, Sr., a Methodist, was no ordinary preacher, however. Long before blacks thought much about scholarship, the elder Farmer had acquired a doctorate of divinity at Boston University, where King acquired a doctorate many years later. An Old Testament scholar and a master of languages, Farmer's father would undoubtedly have held an esteemed pulpit, or a chair at a fine university, were he not black. Instead, he moved from one small black college to another, culminating his career at Howard University in Washington, D.C. In a quiet college atmosphere, sheltered by books from a racist society that loomed beyond the walls, Jim Farmer grew up.

Farmer received his bachelor's degree from Wiley College in Marshall, Texas, and from there entered the divinity school at Howard to follow in his father's footsteps. But at Howard he found himself growing wary of the black church and was strongly influenced by critical interpretations by Max Weber and R. H. Tawney of Protestant orthodoxy. He wrote a thesis which held that the black clergy's function, intentional or not, was to preserve the dominant racial values of the society. Far from seeing black ministers as instruments of social change, Farmer ridiculed them for their dependence on segregation for their livelihood and status. As for the Methodist Church, in which he had been raised, it had recently been reorganized, only to reaffirm its segregated structure, and Farmer felt deceived by it. In 1941, he received his degree in divinity from Howard but, to his father's dismay, he declined to be ordained.

I interviewed Farmer several times as he moved from job to job during the 1970s. Since the golden days of the civil rights movement, his career had had ups and downs, but he continued to work tirelessly for racial equality, in government and labor unions and

134

foundations. Whenever I saw him, he was brimming with energy, and seemed still a bit disorganized, but he transmitted the restlessness of a young racehorse.

"Martin King and I saw the Church quite differently," Farmer said to me. "I must admit I was surprised at the extent to which the black church became involved in the civil rights battle, in Montgomery and after. I didn't realize how much the ministers had changed in the 1940s and 1950s, when I was out of contact with the South. During the Freedom Ride, CORE relied heavily on the black churches. But I can't take back the fact that I lost interest in the church very early. Faced with problems on this earth, I looked for answers in the secular world."

While he was still at Howard, Farmer's thinking had led him to the circle of Howard Thurman, a black professor of theology who was national vice-chairman of the Fellowship of Reconciliation. Since World War I, FOR had been a tiny flame that kept alive the radical ideals of Christian pacifism and racial equality. In 1940, A. J. Muste became FOR's chief executive, and brought with him Gandhian concepts of nonviolent direct action to apply to these ideals. Farmer became a part-time field organizer for FOR, and began to study Gandhi's lessons.

Meanwhile, World War II approached, and FOR's hope of finding "nonviolent alternatives" to the conflict faded. Most of FOR's members were conscientious objectors, despite their loathing for the racism of the Nazis, and many were to go to jail for their convictions. Farmer said he would have gone to prison himself, but for a black draft board in Washington which refused to prosecute him. Instead, at Muste's invitation, he went to Chicago to serve at FOR's headquarters as secretary for race relations. Serving with him on the staff was Bayard Rustin, FOR's secretary for youth.

Farmer said that, shortly after taking the job in Chicago, he sent Muste a memorandum proposing that FOR undertake a campaign against racial barriers, using Gandhi's techniques. Only the NAACP, working through the courts, had a civil rights program at that time. Not only was the NAACP's pace glacial, however, Farmer said, but its objectives, such as equal pay for black teachers in segregated systems in the South, conveyed a reluctance to make a final break with the "separate but equal" doctrine. The NAACP did not take warmly to rivals in the field. But Farmer said he thought

135

the NAACP's methods were not working, and that it was time to experiment in nonviolent direct action.

In reply to Farmer's memo, Muste in 1940 authorized establishment of the Committee of Racial Equality, which was renamed the Congress of Racial Equality on becoming autonomous the following year. The name was chosen with the acronym CORE in mind, Farmer said, to present notice that the aim of its work was nothing less than the heart of racism. Administratively and financially, FOR was for many years the chief supporter of CORE. But because CORE rejected a permanent commitment to nonviolence, which Muste maintained and King would adopt many years later, Farmer said, it had to sever its official ties and establish an identity of its own.

"We dreamed of a mass movement," Farmer said, "and we did not think then that a revolution could be conducted by pacifists. For CORE, nonviolence was never more than a tactic. When a person participated in a CORE project, he was required to be nonviolent. But I agreed with Gandhi, and I quoted him as saying, 'I would rather have a man resist injustice with violence than fail to resist out of cowardice.' Nonviolence did not have to be the personal philosophy of a CORE member, and he could be quite violent in other circumstances if he chose."

CORE's first target in Chicago was a roller-skating rink which excluded blacks, several blocks from the Southside ghetto. He and an FOR band tried conscientiously to follow Gandhi's sequence of investigation, negotiation, publicity and, finally, demonstration. But after the investigation, he said, the negotiation got nowhere, and the newspapers provided no publicity. For several months, however, CORE maintained picket lines at the rink, which brought business virtually to a halt, Farmer said, and at last management gave in.

It was an exhilarating moment for the members of the young organization, and America's first victory for Gandhian nonviolence. The second victory came in May 1943, when Chicago CORE conducted the first successful sit-in—still generally called, after labor movement tactics, a "sit-down"—against segregation at the Jack Spratt restaurant. By then, CORE chapters had been formed in at least seven Northern cities, and Farmer remembered that he was feeling extremely hopeful.

Farmer had nostalgia in his voice when he said, "We were young

136

then, and we'd stay up all night planning and scheming. We really felt we were at the edge of a great wave."

Farmer was by now the national chairman of CORE but the members, as well as most of the leadership, were largely white. "The reaction of blacks when you said nonviolence in the 1940s and '50s," Farmer recalled, "was, you must be some kind of nut. Somebody's going to hit you and you're not going to hit back?" It was easier to find a few idealistic, well-educated whites and train them in nonviolence, he said, than to find blacks willing to go through the pain and humiliation of trying to integrate a restaurant. Farmer remembered that CORE by then had become not only three or four to one white, but increasingly elitist. It was also overwhelmingly Northern, having hardly penetrated the South at all.

Gradually, the early euphoria ebbed, Farmer said. The members tried Gandhi's techniques at swimming pools and theaters, as well as restaurants. They even made efforts to apply the method against segregated jobs and housing. But more often than not, encounters ended in defeat. The prospect of desegregating America restaurant by restaurant, theater by theater seemed hopeless. Momentum was absent, and what few victories CORE won gave no hint of the massive, nonviolent uprising of which its founders had dreamed.

"At one point, we wondered whether we had to give up the ghost," he said. "We weren't growing. We weren't getting any publicity. There seemed to be no interest in the black community. It was hard to keep the chapters alive." Finally, Farmer said, he and the others in CORE's tiny revolutionary band had to take nonrevolutionary jobs to earn a living.

CORE's most spectacular achievement during its early period was the Journey of Reconciliation in April 1947. Initiated by Bayard Rustin, it was conceived in response to the Supreme Court's *Irene Morgan* ruling that segregation on buses traveling interstate routes was unconstitutional. Rustin organized a contingent of eight blacks and eight whites to ride Greyhound and Trailways buses through Virginia, Kentucky and North Carolina to test the decision. They were, for the most part, highly disciplined, confirmed pacifists like himself. Before embarking on the trip, the volunteers received intensive training in responding nonviolently to the abuses they expected to receive from drivers, policemen and hostile crowds.

The NAACP opposed the Journey of Reconciliation, and Thurgood Marshall warned Southern blacks to keep their distance from the "well-meaning radical groups" that were headed their way. Nonetheless, the riders were warmly taken in by church and college groups, and even by NAACP chapters, along their route. The talks they gave to their hosts, and the considerable publicity received in the press, helped spread the name of CORE and the message of nonviolence.

In fact, the riders on the Journey of Reconciliation encountered relatively little abuse and virtually no violence. But their goals were modest. Since the Supreme Court, in the *Irene Morgan* decision, had not addressed itself to the issue of segregation within terminals, the volunteers tested desegregation only in the buses themselves. Furthermore, they limited their trip to the Upper South, knowing the greater dangers of the Deep South. Still, twelve arrests were made and, after all the appeals were exhausted, Rustin and two of his white companions served twenty-two days on a North Carolina road gang.

In his report on the Journey of Reconciliation to CORE and FOR, Rustin reaffirmed his belief that the NAACP's litigation strategy would leave segregation in the South untouched. "Without direct action on the part of groups and individuals," he wrote, "the Jim Crow pattern in the South cannot be broken." Rustin and his comrades were jailed for exercising a constitutional right, as defined by the *Irene Morgan* decision, and yet the federal government did nothing. It would take fourteen years and a major change in the social climate before blacks and whites were again willing to test their right to ride interstate buses through the South together—and some of them would be brutally beaten even then before the federal government came to their aid.

"In the 1940s, at every one of the annual CORE conventions," Jim Farmer said, "a motion would be made that we begin activities in the Deep South, try to start the nonviolent movement, with noncooperation and civil disobedience throughout the South. The motion was regularly defeated. As a matter of fact, I spoke against these motions on several occasions.

"My feeling in the 1940s was that there would have been lynchings, that we would have been killed right there on the spot. Even in the 1960s, Southern sheriffs were able to respond to nonviolent protest with police dogs and cattle prods, and in the 1940s, there

138

was no supportive federal government to protect us, and no television to put it all on display before the country. We could very well have had a massacre."

Organizationally, CORE survived the 1940s and 1950s, but it had lost its earlier audacity. At the start of the 1960s, it was little known and without resources. Secular at its start, it had never expanded its Northern, predominantly white base, and it was ignored by Southern blacks. CORE was hardly in step in 1960 when the civil rights movement suddenly emerged from obscurity—church oriented, overwhelmingly Southern, popularly based, almost wholly black.

Yet what CORE had done through all these years was critical: it had kept alive the flame of an idea. The idea was of nonviolent direct action, which it had inherited from FOR, which in turn had acquired it from Gandhi. CORE had helped pass the idea on to King at Montgomery. Bayard Rustin was the most important figure in the transmission to King, but he was assisted by others who had continued to live with the heritage, including Farmer himself.

Now, after a decade in the wilderness, Jim Farmer was ready to lead CORE back to what he regarded as its rightful place of preeminence in the civil rights movement. He never quite succeeded; the burdens that CORE carried with it were too great. But for a few weeks in the spring of 1961, the Freedom Ride dominated the nation's attention, and everyone spoke of CORE with awe.

President Kennedy's failing in the spring of 1961 was in looking upon civil rights as a political problem like any other, rather than as an irresistible moral issue. Kennedy was a practical man, not given to meaningless gestures. As a senator he had experienced the difficulties of passing two civil rights bills with a Republican in the White House. His political arithmetic told him he could not pass another over the opposition of Republicans and the Southern wing of his own party. Rather than lose on civil rights, he preferred to win on the other measures in his legislative package. Kennedy insisted he wanted a civil rights law as much as anyone, but would propose one to Congress only when it had some reasonable prospect of approval.

Meanwhile, he left no doubt about his position in the exercise of his executive powers. He appointed blacks to posts of unprece-

139

dented visibility in his Administration, and he called for aggressive recruitment of blacks for the civil service. He tightened enforcement of antidiscrimination rules in government contracting and, though he tarried on his promise to eliminate housing bias with "a stroke of the pen," he named a black as head of the Housing and Home Finance Agency. He cleaned up the last pockets of segregation within the armed forces, and had his brother Robert, the attorney general, step up the pace of lawsuits to compel the registration of black voters in the South. No one could mistake the civil rights stand of Kennedy's Administration for that of Eisenhower's.

If Kennedy hoped that blacks and their allies would be quieted by his efforts, however, he was mistaken. It is in the nature of politics that the energy of political forces quickens as their goal approaches, and the civil rights movement was no exception. Kennedy's executive actions and public demeanor only sharpened its appetite. Martin Luther King, Jr., pressed for more Federal initiative to enfranchise blacks in the South. The NAACP's Roy Wilkins argued for faster school integration. Joseph L. Rauh, Jr., speaking for the liberal Americans for Democratic Action in a tense meeting with Kennedy, called for confronting Congress head on with civil rights proposals, including establishment of a fair employment practices commission. Jim Farmer, meanwhile, laid plans for the Freedom Ride.

Farmer said it came to him that CORE would have to re-create the Journey of Reconciliation when the Supreme Court, a few weeks before Kennedy took office, completed the work of the *Irene Morgan* decision of 1946. In *Boynton* v. *Virginia,* the court extended the ban on segregation in interstate travel to the restaurants, rest rooms and other facilities in interstate terminals. The federal government, however, made no greater effort to enforce *Boynton* that it had to enforce Morgan when Bayard Rustin and his friends were arrested in North Carolina in 1947. CORE's original impulse, Farmer recalled, was to call their project Journey of Reconciliation II but, after some discussion, it was agreed that few people would remember the first journey well enough to understand the allusion. Moreover, CORE felt the time had passed for talk of "reconciliation." The movement now defined its goal as "freedom," and with little further debate CORE adopted the name Freedom Ride.

In early March, Farmer sent out invitations to a carefully

140

screened list of CORE members and others who had a record of participation in nonviolent protest. He recalled receiving twenty-five or thirty applications, from which eleven men and two women were selected, of both races. One was Farmer himself. Another was John Lewis, who by now was a veteran of five civil rights arrests. A third was James Peck, a lifelong pacifist and early stalwart of CORE, the only Freedom Rider who had also been on the Journey of Reconciliation. All six whites, in fact, had roots in the pacifist movement, and a long history of involvement with civil disobedience. Apart from Farmer, who was now forty-one, the blacks were all of student age, and had only recently begun the practice of nonviolent direct action.

While proceeding with plans to bring the Freedom Riders together, Farmer sent out a scout along the proposed routes. The scouting report said that segregation was not enforced as rigorously in Virginia and North Carolina as it had been in 1947, but that in the Deep South states of Alabama and Mississippi it was as severe as ever. The report singled out Anniston, Alabama, as a particularly "explosive trouble spot without a doubt." It also indicated that, while some local blacks would welcome the Freedom Riders, others would be much too frightened to be hospitable. Farmer concluded from the report that, unlike the Journey of Reconciliation, the Freedom Ride would probably have bloody consequences.

The thirteen Freedom Riders assembled in Washington for a workshop in nonviolence a few days before the scheduled departure date. As veterans of nonviolent demonstrations, all had attended such workshops before. But Farmer calculated that the Freedom Ride would be different from anything they had ever encountered on picket lines in the North, different even from sitting in at lunch counters in the South.

The workshop agenda began with the conventional readings of Gandhi, Thoreau and other theoreticians. It then went on to an exploration of the Jim Crow structure of the South, with particular attention to bus terminals. Farmer also brought in lawyers to lecture on the rights of Freedom Riders under the *Boynton* decision, and the legal responses available to them when these rights were denied.

"Finally, we engaged in role-playing," Farmer said. "Three of the Freedom Riders would sit in at a simulated lunch counter and

141

ask for a cup of coffee, and would remain seated when they were refused service. Then a half-dozen other Freedom Riders, playing the role of white hoodlums, would come in and assault and attack them, clubbing them over the head, knocking them to the floor, kicking them and hitting them. Those playing the role of the victims were coached on how to protect vital parts of their bodies, head, groin, ribs and so on, so that if they could absorb punches, they might be able to escape serious injury. Then we'd reverse roles."

Farmer recalled with a sardonic laugh that the role-players "bent over backwards to be realistic, I must say. When we finished I was aching all over." But no one argued that the training was irrelevant, or that the Freedom Ride was unlikely to encounter violence.

"If, at any stage of this training," Farmer explained to me solemnly, "a Freedom Rider felt he was getting to the end of his tolerance or patience, and that he could not control himself nonviolently, then he was obliged to withdraw from the project. But nobody did."

Among the duties Farmer performed before leaving Washington was to write letters to the president, the attorney general, the FBI, the Interstate Commerce Commission and the two bus companies. He did it, Farmer said, in observance of the Gandhian admonition to keep the authorities informed of plans when engaging in civil disobedience.

The letters stated that on May 4, blacks and whites together were going to leave Washington aboard commercial buses, deliberately violating segregated seating requirements in Southern states and the segregated use of terminal facilities. The letters stated further that the Freedom Riders intended to continue their journey until they reached the Gulf of Mexico at New Orleans on May 17, the anniversary of the Supreme Court's *Brown* decision desegregating the public schools.

Farmer acknowledged that the persons to whom the letters were addressed had probably never heard of CORE, and knew nothing of him. The letters were sent through the public mails, without any effort to notify officials via other channels to be on the alert. Kennedy's people have insisted that the letters were never received or, if received, were diverted at some subordinate level, unrecognized for the warning they contained. No replies came back from any of

142

them. When the Freedom Ride began, the Kennedy Administration was taken completely by surprise.

On the night of May 3, the thirteen Freedom Riders went out to dinner together at a Chinese restaurant in Washington. John Lewis said he remembered the evening well. It was the first time in his twenty-one years that he had eaten Chinese food. "We were joking, and saying that this was like the Last Supper," he recalled, "because we were headed for the Deep South."

Farmer's reflection was even more grave. "I felt by the time the group left Washington," he said, "that they were prepared for anything, even death. This was a possibility, and we knew it, after we got to the Deep South." The next morning, May 4, 1961, the Freedom Riders, dividing up between a Greyhound bus and a Trailways bus, set out on their mission.

The first few days of the Freedom Ride were uneventful. The group made its way at a leisurely pace through Virginia and North Carolina, successfully challenging the segregation of waiting rooms, restaurants and toilets. Farmer said he was told by local blacks that, with news of the Freedom Ride preceding it, the "white only" and "colored only" signs came down.

The first incident occurred only on May 8, when Joseph B. Perkins, Jr., a black Freedom Rider, was refused a shine at a terminal barbershop and arrested for trespassing. He remained behind in jail while the Freedom Ride moved on, and rejoined the group after he was tried and acquitted two days later.

The day after Perkins's arrest, the Freedom Riders in Rock Hill, South Carolina, encountered the first violence of the trip. "John Lewis started into a white waiting room and there were several young white hoodlums, leather jackets, ducktail haircuts, standing there smoking," Farmer recalled. "They blocked the door and said, 'Nigger, you can't come in here.' Lewis answered, 'I have every right to enter this waiting room according to the Supreme Court of the United States in the *Boynton* case.' They said, 'Shit on that,' and as Lewis tried to walk past they clubbed him and knocked him down. One of the white Freedom Riders, Albert Bigelow, who had been a Navy captain during World War Two, big, tall, strapping fellow, very impressive, from Connecticut, stepped between the

143

hoodlums and Lewis. They then clubbed Bigelow and finally knocked him down, and he didn't hit back at all."

Eventually the police arrived and put an end to the beating. The police made no arrests, Farmer said, although they did ask if the Freedom Riders wanted to press charges. The Freedom Riders declined, however, and went on their way.

On Saturday, May 13, the Freedom Ride reached Atlanta, staging area for the incursion into Alabama and Mississippi. Martin Luther King, Jr., and a crowd of black activists welcomed the group when they arrived, and King had dinner with them.

It was at Atlanta that Jim Farmer left the Freedom Ride to bury his father in Washington. "My mother said he willed his death," Farmer recalled, "because he had my schedule before him and believed I would be killed." But Farmer vowed to return to his comrades as soon as the funeral was over.

In Atlanta the Freedom Riders stayed only overnight. On Sunday, May 14, which happened to be Mother's Day, they resumed their journey. News reports told them that angry mobs had assembled ahead to meet them.

Serious violence first took place about a hundred miles down the road in Anniston, where Farmer's scout had predicted it would happen. Anniston was a town of some thirty thousand inhabitants in eastern Alabama. The Greyhound bus carrying the first contingent, scheduled for a half-hour rest stop there, was attacked as it pulled into the depot by thirty or forty whites carrying chains, sticks and iron bars. They broke windows in the bus, dented the body and slashed the tires. While policemen stood by watching, they pulled Freedom Riders from the bus and badly beat them. Policemen finally waved off the attackers and escorted the bus from the depot to the street. As it drove away toward Birmingham, the assailants jumped into their cars and gave chase.

One of the cars kept ahead of the bus to keep it from gathering speed. Then, about six miles out of Anniston, the bus was forced to stop when a damaged tire gave way. The mob attacked again, shattered several windows, and threw a fire bomb, which exploded inside. At first the attackers kept the door closed, trapping the passengers amid the smoke and flames. After the doors were opened, they administered more beatings as the passengers fled.

Finally the Anniston police arrived to disperse the mob, just be-

144

fore a convoy of cars driven by armed blacks rolled up to make the rescue. The convoy, organized by Reverend Fred Shuttlesworth, King's friend and supporter in SCLC, took the Freedom Riders to Birmingham, some fifty miles away. The charred hulk was left on the road, while the Freedom Riders were treated in Birmingham for smoke inhalation and other assorted injuries.

Meanwhile, Trailways's bus, which arrived in Anniston an hour behind Greyhound's, was forcibly boarded at the depot by eight white men. They ordered the Freedom Riders off the bus, and then began their beating. Walter Bergman, a sixty-one-year-old sociology professor who was participating in the Freedom Ride with his wife, was knocked to the floor and struck repeatedly. He suffered permanent brain injuries. The entire contingent was then forced back into the bus, pushed to the rear and, with the driver subject to the orders of the attackers, driven on to Birmingham.

In Birmingham, a crowd of young whites carrying iron bars and baseball bats waited for the bus on the platform. As the Freedom Riders disembarked, five or six whites rushed furiously at each one. Jim Peck was knocked unconscious, and required fifty stitches. Several others were injured badly enough to require hospitalization. It was fifteen minutes before the first police arrived to put a stop to the mayhem.

Testimony given Congress many years later indicated that the Birmingham police had actually promised the Ku Klux Klan enough time to inflict the beatings. In due course, the savagery of Birmingham's Chief of Police Eugene ("Bull") Connor would make him a legend within the civil rights movement. But the ways of the police in Birmingham, and the rest of the South, were still largely unknown to the world. Asked by reporters why the cops were not at the bus depot to stop the violence against the Freedom Riders, Connor answered innocently that most were off visiting their mothers for Mother's Day.

Back in Washington, Jim Farmer learned from the newscasts of the attacks in Anniston and Birmingham. He recognized at once that the contingent of Freedom Riders which had left Washington under CORE's sponsorship had been decimated. "Our group couldn't go on," he said. "I was the only one, because I had missed the bitterest part." It was no longer a question of whether the Freedom Riders would keep to their scheduled arrival in New Orleans on May 17. It was a question of whether the Freedom Ride could be sustained at all.

Had the Freedom Ride been called off, it would have meant the triumph of segregation over the Constitution, of violence over non-violence, of hatred over justice. Farmer sensed that the federal government was now alert, and champing nervously, but it was nonetheless dead-still at the gate. He was not optimistic. Unless he could find new recruits to prolong the journey, the Freedom Ride would have to be counted a catastrophe, not just for CORE and civil rights but for the country.

What Farmer did not understand was that CORE's few zealots were no longer alone, as they had been in the postwar years, in the fight against racism. A new day had dawned. When he looked around, Farmer found a whole army of young blacks ready to take over, willing to seize the torch, as John Kennedy had put it in his inaugural address, from the hands of the old generation.

The country had become increasingly aware of the Freedom Ride through the crescendo of news reports. White faces contorted with hate, the charred wreckage of a bus, the heads swathed in bandages, all had become familiar pictures in newspapers and on television. After Atlanta, the country followed the progress of the buses through the South with regular bulletins. After Anniston, Americans understood that the Freedom Ride had become a national crisis, which required federal intervention.

Attorney General Robert Kennedy was, like his brother, a practical man. The adjectives generally applied to him since he began serving as his brother's campaign manager were "tough" and "ruthless." Robert Kennedy readily acknowledged that he had had little contact with blacks in his life, and had little feeling for their grievances. Nor did he make a claim to having a civil rights program when he took command at the Justice Department. But, like his brother, he disapproved of the South's abuse of blacks, he understood that racism undermined America's standing in the world, and he acknowledged a debt to black voters. Perhaps most important of all, he took seriously his responsibilities as attorney general to uphold federal law.

Burke Marshall was Kennedy's assistant attorney general for civil rights. His post was a relatively new one, established under the

146

Civil Rights Act of 1957. As the framers of the law had intended, it gave the Justice Department a strong, in-house advocate of civil rights. But Marshall had been a corporation lawyer, whose only brush with blacks before he joined the Justice Department was a brief professorship at Howard. He was intelligent, incisive and fair. He had been recommended by Harris Wofford, the campaign adviser who had initiated the celebrated phone call to Mrs. Martin Luther King. Marshall had been appointed, it was said, because Robert Kennedy, sensitive to the criticism that he had never practiced law himself, wanted respected lawyers as his assistants. But, in early 1961, Marshall knew almost nothing about civil rights.

"I think I would have to say I was ill-suited for the job when I started out," Burke Marshall said, in a characteristically self-effacing way. I interviewed Marshall in the 1970s, after he had returned to the practice of corporate law. "But I'm not sure that somebody who did know about it would have been able to do any more, except in the very, very first stage of the Kennedy Administration.

"I guess that was the stage of the Freedom Ride. I had just been confirmed a few weeks before, and when the Freedom Ride started I was actually home sick. I knew nothing about it in advance. The Freedom Ride was an education to me, to the attorney general and to the White House. When it started, we were still too ignorant of our jobs to recognize its implications and its dangers."

Until Mother's Day, the Justice Department had done nothing about the Freedom Ride except keep track of the buses as they penetrated more deeply each day into hostile territory. The attorney general's office, with Kennedy himself prowling from one corner to another in the labyrinth of offices, was the command post. Marshall was the chief operational officer. The sources of information were the news reports, and the observations sent in sporadically by the FBI agents on the scene.

But the FBI was not reliable. Over the years it had grown increasingly autonomous under its irascible director, J. Edgar Hoover. Though officially under the Justice Department's jurisdiction, it operated outside the attorney general's control. Because Hoover had an animosity toward blacks, furthermore, Kennedy could not count on it to see to equal enforcement of the law. Kennedy knew he would have to turn elsewhere for the execution of any plan the Department of Justice might devise to save the Freedom Ride.

"Once the Freedom Ride got interrupted in the Mother's Day

attack in Birmingham," Marshall said, "the attorney general and I didn't even discuss the possibility of not taking charge. The attitude that the federal government might have taken at some point in history, at the University of Alabama in 1956 and at Little Rock in 1957, that they could ignore the situation and let the violence control it, was unacceptable.

"The decision was intuitive with me, and I think with Bob. It was impossible, unsatisfactory, unconscionable for the federal government not to do something so that these buses could go through. There was no debate on that."

While Jim Farmer was despairing about the fate of the Freedom Ride, the Justice Department under Robert Kennedy was gearing up to move. President Kennedy was to meet with Chairman Khrushchev of the Soviet Union two weeks later in Vienna, and the foreign papers were headlining mob violence in Anniston and Birmingham. Kennedy did not want to convey personal weakness or national division either to Khrushchev or to Europe. Farmer had predicted that an international crisis would be needed to elicit federal intervention. It now seemed to be shaping up.

Burke Marshall acknowledged that, in the week after the Mother's Day attack, he proceeded without a tactical plan, unsure from one moment to the next what he had to do. He worked twenty hours a day, he said, commanding, exhorting, bluffing, arguing, always extemporizing as the circumstances seemed to require. Only the goal was clear. Under the Constitution, the federal government possessed jurisdiction over interstate travel. Once it was decided that the Freedom Ride would continue, he said, the Justice Department took the responsibility for getting the buses safely to their destination.

John Lewis, like Farmer, had skipped the Atlanta-to-Birmingham leg of the Freedom Ride. Having applied to serve for two years in East Africa with the International Volunteer Service, he had been called to Philadelphia for an interview. On his way to rejoin the Freedom Ride, he stopped in Nashville, where he learned from news reports of the attacks in Anniston and Birmingham. The reports said that CORE was abandoning the Freedom Ride. Lewis made contact with Diane Nash of the Nashville Student Movement, and the two set to work immediately to recruit a relief force to continue it.

Farmer remembered getting a phone call while he was still in Washington from Diane Nash. She asked, he said, whether CORE would resent Nashville's bringing in a platoon of SNCC students to keep the Freedom Ride going. He said he told her he would welcome them, but that he had to warn her they could be massacred. "She told me that if the Freedom Ride could be stopped by massive violence, the movement would be dead," Farmer recalled. "She said they would take their chances on getting massacred." Farmer told me that Diane Nash phoned reports to him at each succeeding stage of the preparations, until the two finally met for the first time in the bus depot in Montgomery.

John Lewis said he stayed up most of the night following Mother's Day arguing with leaders of the Nashville Christian Leadership Council to provide funds for the students' reinforcement of the Freedom Ride. By early morning, he said, it was agreed that $900 would be made available for student expenses. Throughout Monday and Tuesday, volunteers were recruited and drilled on what they were likely to encounter. At 6:30 A.M. on Wednesday, seven men and three women—eight blacks and two whites—left Nashville aboard a bus bound for Birmingham.

Though no announcement had been made of the departure, Lewis said, the Alabama police were alert. Just outside Birmingham, a policeman stopped the bus, boarded and approached a young white and a young black who were sharing a seat. When both refused to move, he placed them under arrest, and took them off and drove them away in a police car. A second policeman then came aboard and escorted the bus into the city.

At the Birmingham bus terminal, the policeman inspected the tickets of all the passengers, and those who had started in Nashville and were booked through to New Orleans were assumed to be Freedom Riders. They were ordered to remain in their seats, Lewis said, while policemen ominously pasted newspapers on the windows. Unable to see out, the students were kept seated for three hours, while anxiety rose. Then Chief Bull Connor came aboard and announced that the passengers were being placed in protective custody for their own safety. They were all herded into paddy wagons, Lewis said, and taken to the city jail.

149

"We spent Wednesday night in jail on a hunger strike," Lewis remembered. "On Thursday, a city lawyer came and told us they would let us out if we agreed to go back to Nashville. We refused.

"About two o'clock on Friday morning, without any warning whatever, Bull Connor and several of his men, along with a reporter from the *Birmingham News*, came to our cells and said, 'We're taking you back to Nashville.' We answered, 'We're not going back to Nashville. We're on a trip. We have a right to travel and we're not going.' Then we all went limp."

Lewis said the Birmingham police picked up the students and carried them into two limousines, their baggage tied on top. The original group of ten was now down to seven, all blacks. It had lost the two men arrested on the bus and its one remaining white, a young woman whose father had arrived from Buffalo to take her home. But the group grew to eight when Connor climbed into the limousine with them, Lewis said, and the hours on the road passed with friendly, sometimes funny, shop talk. The students really believed they were going back to Nashville, Lewis said, but Connor dropped them off instead at the state line in a little town called Ardmore.

"We didn't know a soul," Lewis remembered. "We just stood there in the dark, thinking maybe we had been set up. Then we located the railroad tracks. In the South, black people usually live near the railroad tracks. We found two broken-down shacks and knocked on the door of one of them. There was an elderly black man and woman, in their late sixties or early seventies. They had heard about the Freedom Ride and recognized us. They were very frightened, but they put us all in the back room of their house. They had a telephone, and I called Diane Nash in Nashville and told her to send a car for us.

"By this time we were very, very hungry, because we didn't eat anything during the hunger strike, and the elderly man went to three different stores to buy food for our breakfast, so that no one would get suspicious. When the car came the seven of us, plus the driver, got in with all the baggage. This was Klan territory, and we were all scared. We heard on the car radio that the students, meaning us, were apparently back in Nashville now, on their college campuses. But none of us gave any serious thought to turning back. It was something we felt we had to do. We told the driver to take us back to Birmingham."

150

Lewis and his companions went first to the home of Reverend Shuttlesworth, the SCLC head in Birmingham, then joined forces with ten other students who had arrived from Nashville by train. Meanwhile, news of the attack at the bus depot was attracting still more students to Birmingham. Lewis's plan was to board the Greyhound bus to Montgomery that very afternoon, and to have as many Freedom Riders as possible along with him.

The problem was, Lewis recalled, that Greyhound canceled the three o'clock bus, then canceled the bus scheduled for five thirty when the driver refused to go. "I'll never, never forget," he said, "what the driver told us when we tried to get on the bus. 'I have one life to give, and I'm not going to give it to CORE or the NAACP.' " The students then went into the waiting room, but the next bus, scheduled for eight in the evening, was canceled, too.

There were about twenty students assembled by then, most of whom identified with SNCC, and they decided to spend the night in the waiting room. Lewis remembered that the local officials locked up the toilets and disconnected the telephones. Late that night a mob surrounded the bus station and, though Bull Connor's policemen kept the mob at a safe distance, rocks were thrown through the windows and threatening noises persisted for hours. After a fitful night on the benches, the new Freedom Riders awoke, to be informed by a news reporter that Attorney General Kennedy had been in contact with Greyhound, which would take them to Montgomery at 8:30 A.M.

In Washington, the first problem of Attorney General Robert Kennedy and his staff was to get drivers into the buses. Alabama's Governor John Patterson had declared that none of Alabama's resources would be spent to protect "outside agitators." His words were taken as an invitation to the mobs, which was how they were intended. Prudently the bus drivers, backed by their unions, refused to get back behind the wheel without some certainty of being safe.

"Our first job was to get the state of Alabama to make a commitment," Burke Marshall said. "The governor tried to duck us, but our position was that this was a situation that could not be ducked.

"We tried to get him to listen to reason. We put as much pressure as possible on conscience, politics, money, any kind of thing that

151

would make him act like a responsible governor. But we didn't get a commitment until Friday of that week—and, of course, it didn't hold once we got it. Meanwhile, there were endless conversations with the bus companies before they turned around."

The man who finally obtained the commitment was John Seigenthaler, Robert Kennedy's personal aide, who had flown to Montgomery on Friday at Governor Patterson's invitation. That night, Seigenthaler met with the governor, from whom he extracted an assurance that Alabama had the ability and the will to keep the peace. In Patterson's presence, Seigenthaler phoned Kennedy to communicate the understanding. Based on this assurance, which Seigenthaler confirmed with the chief of the Alabama Highway Patrol, the Justice Department passed the word that the Freedom Ride could resume, and the buses should roll.

John Lewis and his companions, twenty-one students in all, pulled out of the Birmingham terminal aboard a Greyhound bus at the scheduled hour on Saturday morning. Governor Patterson had a small plane flying over the bus and sixteen patrol cars escorting it at intervals along the highway. Lewis remembered it as a "nice ride" for most of the way. But, as the bus approached the Montgomery city limits, the plane and the patrol cars ominously vanished.

Lewis recalled an eerie feeling that came over the bus as it pulled into the terminal. When the Freedom Riders stepped onto the platform, they stood for a few minutes in silence. The bus driver walked quickly away, and there was no one else nearby. Then, from around a corner, a mob of several hundred whites led by a phalanx of shrieking women rushed toward them. The police were nowhere in sight.

While the women screamed, "Kill the nigger-lovin' son of a bitch," a wave of young men with ax handles attacked Jim Zwerg, a young white student from Wisconsin. They knocked him to the ground and left him there, unconscious. Then they turned on William Barbee, a black student, and beat him viciously. In the ensuing confusion, many students outran their attackers and found shelter in a nearby post office and in neighboring churches. But most of the Freedom Riders, as well as some out-of-town reporters and photographers, took blows from fists or clubs. "The last thing I remember," Lewis said, "someone took a crate and hit me in the head." As he lay on the ground in a daze, an Alabama official came up and presented him with a court injunction. It said that blacks and whites were prohibited from sitting together aboard public transportation.

John Seigenthaler, Kennedy's representative, was another victim. As he tried to stand between the mob and two young women who were trying to flee in a taxi, he was struck from behind and left lying on the sidewalk. Twenty-five minutes elapsed before police took him to a hospital. Later, an official explained that Seigenthaler would have been rescued earlier, except that every white ambulance in town had broken down.

That afternoon President Kennedy issued a statement pledging "all necessary steps" by the federal government to meet its responsibilities in Alabama. John Doar, Burke Marshall's chief deputy, went into federal court in Montgomery to obtain an injunction prohibiting interference with interstate travel. Additional teams of FBI agents were sent to Alabama, although those already on the scene had not made the slightest effort to keep the peace. Finally, late in the day, Attorney General Kennedy ordered federal marshals to Montgomery, and by the next morning four hundred men were standing by for duty at an air base just outside the city.

"One of the things we'd done that week," Burke Marshall said, "was assemble a small army of federal marshals. Marshals are not policemen, but it was simply not feasible to try to get the Bureau [FBI] to perform the kind of police work that was necessary. So we had to improvise."

President Kennedy ordered the mobilization of the marshals in order to avert the need for sending in the army. As a senator, Kennedy had criticized Eisenhower for failing during the Little Rock crisis to be ready with enforcement procedures short of military occupation. Eisenhower had, in fact, initiated a program of riot training for federal marshals but it never advanced very far. The two presidents successively agreed that it was better to send civilians in mufti than uniformed soldiers shouldering rifles into American cities, but readying a force for such a mission was not easy.

"Some of the marshals were really marshals. That is, they were reliable employees of the federal courts," Marshall explained. "Then we also deputized some prison guards, some alcohol and tax people, and some border patrol. The border patrol were the only ones that could shoot.

"This made a force of sufficient number but, as a practical matter,

most of them were the product of senatorial patronage, middle-
aged, fat, lethargic people with no law enforcement experience.
Many of them came from the South, and really thought they were
being asked to protect black people whom they considered Communists, or worse. We weren't sure which side they would be
on.

"But we recruited, deputized and brought them together in a
week. We got them there by air or by private car. Many didn't like
what they were doing, but a large number performed heroically.
They probably salvaged the day for us."

On Sunday night, May 21, Martin Luther King, Jr., joined his
friend Ralph Abernathy to lead a mass rally in Montgomery in support of the Freedom Ride. More than fifteen hundred blacks, along
with a handful of friendly whites, assembled in Abernathy's First
Baptist Church, where King had so often aroused audiences for the
Montgomery Improvement Association during the turmoil in 1956.
And yet the tension the night the Freedom Ride came to town was
worse than it had ever been during the long months of struggle
over the boycott.

The U.S. marshals stood in a rigid circle around the First Baptist
Church. Beyond them an unruly crowd of a thousand whites milled
restlessly, as if waiting for some signal to rush for the doors. Periodically a rock would soar from the crowd's midst and crash through
a stained-glass window. Stink bombs followed the rocks, the gases
penetrating the tightly packed auditorium.

King and Abernathy, inside the church, sought in turn to maintain the morale of the frightened audience. They appealed to courage, to love and to nonviolence. The gathering in the pews sang
"We Shall Overcome," anthem of the movement, and repeated
choruses of hymns and spirituals, which fell coldly on the ears of
the angry men and women in the street. Occasionally the marshals
fired a tear gas bomb to keep the rabble in check, but their force
would have been nowhere near adequate had the crowd turned
and attacked. The whites were primed for bloodshed, and for hours
the scene hovered on the edge of catastrophe.

Jim Farmer arrived in Montgomery that night, his week of
mourning in Washington over at last. He was picked up at the
airport by Reverend Fred Shuttlesworth, and the two set out for the
church. As they neared their destination, Farmer recalled, they

were unable to get through the densely packed streets, and several times they had to change course. Eventually, Farmer said, a black taxi driver told them how to reach within a few blocks of the church by driving through a cemetery. To cover the remaining distance, the two men had to maneuver through the gauntlet on foot.

"That Shuttlesworth, who's just a little fellow, was either insane or the most courageous man I have ever met," Farmer said with awe. "I tried to hide behind him but I didn't fit. Fortunately, those people didn't know who I was. Shuttlesworth just walked through them, cool as a cucumber. I think they were intimidated by his boldness. I'm sure they thought, No nigger could do that, and they parted so we could get through."

Farmer's arrival raised the spirits of those seated in the church. Between turns at the pulpit, he and King explored the prospects for lifting the siege. At one point, a band of whites actually kicked in a door and entered the church, but a squad of marshals was on hand. Using clubs, without drawing their guns, the marshals drove the intruders out. They then dispersed clusters of whites who stood near the entrances, forcing them to back away to less menacing points. Somehow, no signal for general attack was ever given and, after midnight, the crowd began to tire. Burke Marshall has said he was convinced that, but for the marshals, King and the others would surely have been slaughtered that night.

King had by now phoned Robert Kennedy to report personally on the tense situation. Kennedy in turn phoned Governor Patterson to warn that he was ready to reenact a scene from Reconstruction, if necessary, and more recently from Little Rock, by sending federal troops to the city. Shortly afterward, Patterson declared martial law, and ordered eight hundred National Guardsmen to immediate duty.

As the Guardsmen arrived at their posts, the federal marshals withdrew. King once again phoned Kennedy, this time to inquire whether the blacks in the church were being betrayed. Kennedy impatiently assured him that they were not, but he took the precaution of calling Patterson again to warn against any change of mind. By dawn, weary and defeated, the remnants of the mob at last drifted away, and shortly thereafter the Freedom Ride's supporters filed into the street. Many of them were driven home by the Guardsmen in their jeeps.

155

The next night, May 22, Farmer met with Martin Luther King, Jr., Ralph Abernathy and John Lewis to discuss the advance of the Freedom Ride into Jackson, Mississippi, the next scheduled stop. Farmer no longer made the decisions alone but shared them, not just with SCLC but, as the presence of the twenty-one-year-old Lewis indicated, with SNCC. It was with SNCC, after all, that the dozens of young people who came to Montgomery, ready to ride into Jackson, chiefly identified. Without SNCC, there would have been no recovery of the Freedom Ride.

On Tuesday, May 23, Farmer, King, Abernathy and Lewis announced jointly at a press conference in Abernathy's backyard that the Freedom Ride would indeed go on. SNCC's substitution for CORE as the dominant force, however, meant that the Freedom Ride had been transformed from a carefully controlled demonstration by trained professionals, patterned after the Journey of Reconciliation, to a spontaneous expression by the young on a major, if not massive, scale. Farmer, true to the teachings of Gandhi, announced that the Freedom Riders were now ready to fill Mississippi's jails to show the depths of their dedication.

"We were all scared about going into Mississippi," Farmer said. "The SNCC kids expected Martin to go with them, but he refused. As he put it, he had to choose the 'when and where of his Golgotha.' He also said he was on probation, and the ride would be a violation. The SNCC people wouldn't accept that. They said, 'Look, I'm on probation, too,' and 'So am I,' and 'Me, too.' They were furious with him, and accused him of being yellow.

"In fact, I wasn't sure I was going myself. They attacked Martin but they didn't even ask me. I was waving good-bye at the bus, and they looked sort of puzzled. I felt sheepish, so I tried to make excuses. I did have a lot of CORE paper work that was being neglected, but the real reason was that I was scared shitless. Then a young girl looked out the window and said to me, patronizingly, 'Jim, please.' That's when I got my baggage out of the car and got in.

"I had seen fear in the eyes of some of the kids as they climbed the steps of the bus. But there was also something there that transcended fear. On the bus I noticed some of the students writing

156

notes, boys writing notes and putting them in their pockets, and girls putting them in their brassieres. I went across the aisle to find out what it was. They were writing names and addresses of next of kin. They really had not expected to live beyond that trip. But it was something they had to do, and they were determined to go."

The Freedom Riders' bus left on Wednesday morning, May 24, 1961. The Alabama National Guard, fully armed, had escorted the passengers to the station. Guardsmen kept vigil as Farmer and twenty-six students ate breakfast at the "white" lunch counter, then made the final preparations for departure. After the Freedom Riders climbed on the bus, the Guardsmen went aboard after them.

On the road to Jackson, National Guard cars rode in front and behind the buses. Three National Guard reconnaissance planes and two helicopters roared overhead. A thousand Guardsmen patrolled shoulders of the highway. Watching the spectacle were seventeen newsmen who were seated among the Freedom Riders, and twenty carloads more that followed in the convoy.

At the state line, the Mississippi state police took over from the Alabama Guard. Farmer admitted to some apprehension over rumors of an impending ambush, but he was reassured when he saw Mississippi Guardsmen standing at the roadside scanning the adjacent woods.

The Mississippi state police escorted the Freedom Riders into Jackson with scrupulous care. The crowd waiting at the terminal consisted of plainclothesmen and reporters. The terminal itself had been cordoned off, and police held dogs on the leash. With civility, the players in the drama played out their respective roles. As they left the buses, the passengers began testing the terminal's facilities. In each instance, they were promptly but courteously arrested. Farmer was apprehended at the "white" lunch counter, John Lewis while urinating in the "white" men's room.

On the afternoon that the bus reached Jackson, Robert Kennedy made what some considered his only blunder of the Freedom Ride crisis. In the manner of a trained lawyer, Kennedy had apparently concluded that enough fact had been established for the courts to resolve the issue of segregation in interstate transportation once and for all. "What is needed now," he announced, "is a cooling-off period."

But the Freedom Ride was now going exactly as Jim Farmer, in

157

his wildest moments, had dreamed it might, and he had no intention of taking the pressure off. "We'd been cooling off for a hundred years," he snorted at Kennedy. "If we got any cooler, we'd be in a deep freeze."

Led by Farmer the Freedom Riders, convicted of violating the Jim Crow laws in Jackson, refused to pay the $200 fine levied on each and chose instead to go to jail. As Gandhi had recommended, they overwhelmed the city's jail facilities, and drew increasing attention to their cause. Locked up in Jackson, the Freedom Riders failed to reach their destination in New Orleans, but they had become great heroes. The Freedom Ride was over—to be succeeded by dozens of impromptu Freedom Rides, organized spontaneously all over the South.

CORE sought to accommodate to the quickening zeal by establishing organization and training centers in New Orleans, Atlanta and Chicago. In a few hours of briefings before they boarded their buses, volunteers were introduced to the theories and techniques of nonviolence. They left with a heedlessness of danger and an unflinching willingness to go to jail.

Though the massive beatings did not recur, some three hundred sixty Freedom Riders were arrested that summer, three hundred in Jackson alone. Many of them were inhumanly treated in jail, particularly in Mississippi's notorious penitentiary at Parchman. Those with rigorous training in nonviolence were said to have endured the ordeal the best. But most stood up well to the punishment, even those with little or no training.

Meanwhile, Attorney General Kennedy had petitioned the Interstate Commerce Commission to issue rules banning segregation within interstate bus terminals. Like most Supreme Court decisions, the ruling in *Boynton* was not self-enforcing. Normal procedure to obtain compliance would have required a lawsuit for every depot in the South, a process which would have taken years. To shorten it, Kennedy asked the ICC to issue a rule, based on the *Boynton* principle, under its regulatory authority. Such use of this authority was unprecedented, but Kennedy and the force of public opinion constituted strong pressure and, with some misgivings, the ICC concurred.

158

The ICC ruling was announced on September 22, after the summer wave of Freedom Rides, and it took effect on November 1, 1961. It not only ended segregation in interstate travel but required buses and terminals to announce that service was offered "without regard to race, color, creed or national origin." It also stipulated that by 1963 a similar notice be printed on all interstate bus tickets.

A few smaller Southern cities, like McComb in Mississippi and Albany in Georgia, exhausted virtually every legal and extralegal remedy before complying. Neither city would be free of violence for some time. But after the Freedom Ride, Jim Crow was doomed in every facet of interstate transportation, and it was a rare facility where segregation survived the year 1962.

The Freedom Ride accelerated the pace of the civil rights movement, and few now doubted that the momentum could be stopped short of full desegregation. The Freedom Ride was a step forward in the evolution of nonviolent direct action. It put nonviolence on wheels, gave it motion, took it into the enemy camp. It dramatized, to any who remained doubters, that segregation was a national concern, rather than a series of local problems. It challenged Martin Luther King and the other leaders of the movement to find new applications for nonviolence, to push their strategy still closer to its potential as an instrument of social change.

Though the Freedom Ride restored Jim Farmer to the front ranks of the civil rights leadership, it left CORE depleted, and without a clear role to play. Daring as CORE's action had been, the young people of SNCC had to finish the Freedom Ride, and in the end CORE's veterans had to share their glory with SNCC's upstarts. SNCC was a new generation, on the rise, and CORE was yesterday's radicalism, not quite able to fit into the framework of the 1960s. For the remaining years of the movement, SNCC would be at the leading edge of the combat while CORE, though surviving, slipped again into eclipse.

Yet, in the Freedom Ride, CORE had made a contribution that was vital to the movement. It was Farmer's triumph to bring the federal government unequivocally to the side of civil rights. He had forced Kennedy to quit straddling, and he thereby increased the isolation of the white South. He had conceived his mission clearly, had calculated the strategy with skill, and he had succeeded in shifting the balance of forces in the civil rights struggle. The Freedom Ride, politically, was a turning point of the 1960s. With the federal government as its ally, the civil rights movement had acquired the power to kill Jim Crow off.

V
TOM HAYDEN:
Manifesto Writing

"I mean, we inevitably began saying, 'If the problems were there all these years, why did *we* have to discover them?' Where was liberalism at? What you got was this dynamic where young people were putting their bodies on the line, and maybe their parents or older people would give them some money, but that was as far as it went. It had to lead to the idea that liberalism was an armchair ideology."

From the moment black students came off the campus to sit in at the five-and-ten, they acquired stature in the eyes of their white counterparts in colleges across the nation. They were engaged in a noble cause. They were brave. They were selfless. They created excitement at a dreary moment. It should hardly have been a surprise that, at least in the North, young whites admired them and yearned to emulate them.

Challenging the rules of society almost always appeals to the young, preoccupied as they are with establishing their own station in life. The 1950s had provided them with little stimulation. The generation in college in 1960, replacing a generation that was neatly combed and showed respect for its elders, had been nurtured on McCarthyism and social orthodoxy. Now, however, McCarthyism was fading into an embarrassing memory and, without advance notice, black contemporaries had presented white students with a model for attacking the ancestral structure. The rebellious instincts of the young, surging by some natural process toward the surface, found in the civil rights movement a glittering vehicle for personal expression.

Students, in fact, seemed to be acquiring a special sense of themselves, and of their political potential, around the world. In Korea and Venezuela, in Japan and Turkey, college students taking to the streets had very recently shaken governments with their political power. Throughout the American South young blacks, organized not as soldiers or as workers but as students, had jolted the status quo. This was new to the American experience, and young whites were stirred by the lesson.

163

Furthermore, the American university itself was changing, under the impact of the country's growing affluence. In 1960 the number of college students had reached more than three and a half million, a third more than in 1955, and by 1965 the enrollment would increase by another two million. By then, nearly half the whites in late adolescence would be studying in college, and so would about a fourth of young adults between twenty-one and twenty-four. Such a ratio of students in society was without precedent in history. If nothing else, just the number of students was enough to change the character of the universities, and influence the attitude of American students toward themselves and the world.

Most of these students lived in campus communities segregated from the working society. They had little need to earn money, few mundane responsibilities and plenty of leisure time. Unburdened by commonplace worries, they were free to cultivate their individuality and inflate their grievances. Life, experienced within a commonwealth of students, was conducive to the contemplation of the special nature of students, the membership of students in a distinct social class, the potential of students to wield political power.

Within this special world the student movement was born, the progeny of the civil rights movement but groping for its own way to challenge the past. It never consisted of more than a minority at any university, but its members were consistently the brightest and most energetic on campus. Jews were disproportionately represented, and so were the "red diaper" children of old-time radicals. But if there was a typical activist, among the huge diversity within the movement, it was the offspring of a family of professionals, usually well-to-do, with liberal political convictions. Unlike the young black in civil rights, the white student had no identifiable self-interest in promoting his cause. For better and worse, his concerns were less practical than moral, his goals not just reformist but often millenarian.

From the start, the student movement claimed that its objective was a radical transformation of society. But by linking itself to the cause of racial equality, it was assured of the sanction of a major segment, perhaps even a majority, of the very society it vowed to dismantle and remake. Later, when students shifted their concern from civil rights to Vietnam, they made common cause with opponents of the war and retained this popular sanction. Indeed, the

164

reformist temperament of the 1960s, fostered by a liberal tradition, kept the student movement, sometimes in spite of itself, close to the center of political activity. The sympathy enjoyed by the students created an illusion, which was long in dying, that young people could rebel against the inherited structure of society—with widespread parental approval.

Of the student radicals of the 1960s, none had more influence than Tom Hayden, who seemed to be everywhere, making his presence felt. He was an early organizer of Students for a Democratic Society, and the chief drafter of the "Port Huron Statement." He was in Mississippi with SNCC, in Newark for the ghetto riots, at the Pentagon for the famous march. He went to Hanoi for the antiwar movement and led the demonstrations at the Democratic National Convention in Chicago. He was arrested again and again, and was tried as one of the Chicago Seven. Brilliant, dedicated, courageous and cunning, Hayden probably understood the radical movement of the 1960s better than anyone else. Yet there was nothing in his background that predestined him to it.

Hayden was born in 1940 of working-class Irish-Catholic parents who had no interest whatever in politics. He remembered his father as cold, his mother as generous, himself as insecure about his small size, his homely face and his physical immaturity. In his boyhood his parents separated and his Catholicism lapsed. At the local high school in Royal Oak, Michigan, an all-white suburb of Detroit, he was one of the brightest students, but his principal interest was in sports and the school newspaper. He remembered identifying with James Dean of *Rebel Without a Cause,* with the nonconformist hero Holden Caulfield of J. D. Salinger's *The Catcher in the Rye,* and with the antics of *Mad* magazine, a monthly that poked fun at social hypocrisy, but tens of thousands of other teenagers in the mid-1950s identified with them, too.

In the fall of 1957, Hayden enrolled in the University of Michigan at Ann Arbor, the only college that had ever interested him. He found there a world of personal freedom and intellectual excitement he had never known before. He plunged deeply into his studies, and was particularly fascinated by philosophy. Yet he remained largely indifferent to politics. His principal enthusiasm was the

165

campus newspaper, the *Michigan Daily*, and throughout most of his undergraduate years he planned on a career as a writer or foreign correspondent, commenting upon rather than participating in great events.

I interviewed Hayden in the mid-1970s in a run-down little house near the beach in Los Angeles that he shared with his wife, the movie actress, Jane Fonda. With ancient furniture and Ché Guevara posters, the interior conveyed the feeling of a 1960s crash pad. Hayden still talked of himself as a radical, with little esteem for the electoral process, though he would soon thereafter conduct an energetic campaign for the Democratic senatorial nomination in California. I found Hayden's conversation thoughtful and astute, critical but not cynical. After a few hours he became impatient to finish, having promised to relieve his wife at baby-sitting with their son, Troy.

"I was disheveled in those days at Michigan," Hayden remembered. "I carried my green bag around, with a lot of books on philosophy in it. I was interested in the bohemians, the beatniks, the coffeehouse set, the interracial crowd, but I wasn't really part of them. I didn't get interested in politics at all until after the sit-ins."

It was about the time of the sit-ins that Hayden, working as a reporter for the *Michigan Daily*, met Al Haber, a stocky and already balding young man. Born in 1936 and a Michigan freshman in 1954, Haber was a periodic dropout who had still not graduated in the spring of 1960. "He was the campus radical," Hayden said of him. "He had a beard and lots of books and he just knew a lot. He was much older than anyone else, and he came over to talk to me." Hayden said that Haber gave him a lecture on sit-ins, from the trade-union movement to the civil rights movement, trying to persuade him that the *Michigan Daily* should support the cause.

Haber, son of an economics professor at Michigan, was brought up in Ann Arbor, where a resurgent left-wing community had developed in the waning years of McCarthyism. Haber was recruited into the New York–based Student League for Industrial Democracy, child of the venerable League for Industrial Democracy, whose Socialist origins dated back to such radical luminaries as Jack London and Upton Sinclair early in the century. Jim Farmer had been an organizer for LID in the early 1950s. Though its doc-

166

trine had turned social democratic and its posture anti-Communist, it was nonetheless considered radical during the McCarthy years. Despite its radicalism, Haber found it tame, quipping that "SLID too much represented its experience in its name," and he vowed to infuse it with a dynamic new spirit.

Haber's ardor appealed to the SLID leadership, which sensed a quickening of political interest on campuses as the old decade ended. Haber rose rapidly in the SLID hierarchy, and in the spring of 1960, when SLID received a $10,000 grant from the United Automobile Workers, he was hired to serve full time in the capacity as field secretary. SLID also sponsored a civil rights conference that spring at the University of Michigan, where Jim Farmer, Bayard Rustin and others talked about the sit-ins. Determined to make a new start, SLID had by then changed its name to Students for a Democratic Society, and elected Haber its president.

Hayden, of course, had attended SLID's civil rights conference on the Michigan campus, and for the first time encountered real political activists. By now he had also marched on picket lines at Woolworth's in Ann Arbor in support of the sit-ins, though he continued to think of himself chiefly as a journalist. His appointment as editor of the *Michigan Daily* at the end of the school year seemed to confirm him in the role, but he acknowledged to himself that the sit-ins had evoked political stirrings. Then, after he read a recently published book by Jack Kerouac called *On the Road*, the "beat" life called out to him. The book persuaded him, he said, to spend the summer of 1960 hitchhiking to the West Coast.

"I got to Berkeley," Hayden said, "and immediately went to the first person I saw who was giving out leaflets. I'd never seen anything like this before. I told her who I was and what I was interested in and, being political, they took me home and gave me a room to stay in for a few weeks, and tried to educate me politically."

With its fifteen thousand undergraduates and eight thousand graduate students, Berkeley seemed in a kind of frenzy when Hayden arrived in June of 1960. Like campuses elsewhere, the University of California had suffered through the long winter of McCarthyism, but the demands for political conformity there had been particularly severe, and the battles particularly bitter. Now

Berkeley was awakening, a little earlier than other campuses, and with more verve. The counterculture, crossing the Bay from San Francisco, had established colonies in the Berkeley community, and the street scene was already highly animated. Student politics, so long tedious and bland, was beginning to touch serious social issues.

The year before Hayden reached Berkeley, a loosely structured organization of leftist students called SLATE had won a student government election. The university administration was upset not so much by SLATE's fiery resolutions in favor of civil rights and academic freedom as by its refusal to subscribe to an anti-Communist disclaimer. To the administration, SLATE's argument that anti-Communism constituted a sterile premise for politics was incomprehensible, but the argument itself was a signal that a new generation no longer hysterical about Soviet power had come of age. Berkeley was leading the nation's colleges into a new decade.

The first school year of the 1960s began contentiously, when the Berkeley administration expelled a seventeen-year-old freshman, son of an Air Force colonel, for conducting a seven-day fast to protest compulsory ROTC. The restlessness grew when Caryl Chessman, a convicted rapist whose eloquent pleas for clemency had won him a wide following, was executed at San Quentin prison, while a large body of students stood vigil outside. Then, the Board of Regents stirred up a furor on the campus by apologizing to right-wing organizations for allowing a mild criticism of the FBI to appear in a university document. When Director J. Edgar Hoover rushed to the defense of the Regents, the *Daily Californian*, the student newspaper, told him in an editorial that the FBI resembled the Gestapo, and the furor intensified.

By now, the sit-ins in the South had begun, and CORE's student chapter was picketing the local Woolworth's. Students for Racial Equality staged a jazz concert to collect money to send to the South. These activities conflicted with the controversial "Kerr directives" —named for Clark Kerr, president of the university —which barred student organizations from taking positions on off-campus issues. For the moment, a collision was averted by the university's restraint, though four years later civil rights would ignite the Free Speech Movement, and the university administration would shun such restraint. But, in the meantime, the sit-ins gave Berkeley an

168

electrifying new vision of the possibilities of direct action, which students were impatient to test.

In May 1960 the House Un-American Activities Committee came to San Francisco to hold two weeks of hearings at City Hall on disloyalty and subversion. For years HUAC, tireless in its efforts to impose an ideological orthodoxy upon the nation, had symbolized to liberals everything that was wrong with anti-Communist politics. Berkeley responded to the news of HUAC's intentions with the formation of a group called Students for Civil Liberties, which circulated anti-HUAC petitions that a thousand students and three hundred faculty members signed. When the HUAC members arrived on May 12, waiting to greet them at San Francisco City Hall was a picket line of several hundred students.

The proceedings the first morning were conducted without incident, and at noon the students held a rally in Union Square. Tension did not begin to rise until the afternoon session, when only a handful of students were allowed into the hearing room. Indignant at being excluded, students in the City Hall rotunda began to chant, "Let us in, let us in!" When their comrades inside the chamber heard them, they joined the chorus. On committee orders, police dragged the chanting students from the hearing room, which created the kind of publicity that assured a much larger crowd of demonstrators for the following day's session.

The next morning several hundred students lined up in the second-floor rotunda, but only about twenty were admitted. When the hearings reconvened at two o'clock, an additional few were permitted to enter, and about a dozen more forced their way past a police guard to occupy vacant seats. Some two hundred stayed in the hall, seated on the stone floor, showing no disposition to violence but singing loudly enough to distract the proceedings within.

Then, without warning, police officers with fire hoses appeared in the rotunda and began bowling the students over with powerful jets of water. The hosing stopped only after all the students were drenched, and several inches of water covered the floor. Few of the students had been driven off, however. Sodden and bedraggled, they resumed their places on the wet stone and began to sing a civil rights song, "We shall not be moved . . ." That was when the police attacked again.

Swinging their clubs wildly, the cops sent bodies sprawling and

169

skidding across the slippery marble. Within a few minutes, most of the rotunda had been cleared, with dozens of students limping away to nurse bruises. Then the police picked up the hoses a second time and directed the nozzles at the fifty or sixty students who remained. When the hosing stopped, motorcycle troopers arrived as reinforcements and began to fling the demonstrators down the stairs, one by one. Bodies cascaded over the stone, and blood mixed with the water. As they bounced to the bottom of the staircase, sixty-three students were arrested for disorderly conduct.

"Black Friday"—as May 13, 1960, came to be known in Berkeley lore—was the decade's first violent encounter between militant white students and the society's peace-keeping forces. It would probably never have taken place had not the sit-ins preceded it, but it was more than a civil rights protest. The anti-HUAC demonstration was the first salvo of the student movement, directed at elements that students found "repressive" within the society.

The pattern was to become familiar. It began with defiant students feeling morally superior confronting angry policemen accustomed to using physical duress. It was followed by mutual provocation and ended in brutal contact, from which the students emerged battered and bloody. What began with clubs on Black Friday in San Francisco ended almost precisely ten years later with M-1 rifles at a college in Ohio called Kent State. Black Friday's bruises were still sore when, a few weeks later, Tom Hayden arrived in Berkeley.

"I met this guy I had heard was a leftist,"[*] Hayden recalled. "I didn't know what that was, but he drove me out to Livermore and showed me the nuclear reactor, where all the hydrogen bombs were made, with the fence around it, and he described the nuclear weapons and the arms race. And then another day he drove me out into the fields and valleys, and he told me about the Chicanos and the farm workers, and the conditions under which they labored. He took me to the camps where the organizing committee would go out on week-ends, and he told me of his dreams of some day organizing the farm workers.

"Before Berkeley, politics was unimaginable to me. I'd never

---

[*] This quote, and several others in this chapter, are from the Tom Hayden interview in *Rolling Stone*, October 20, 1972.

seen or heard a demonstration, and I had no sense that it was a form of political protest.

"Maybe I already was a radical but then it didn't have a name. It was like trying to mimic the life of James Dean or something like that. But the other half of me was in the establishment, the ambitious young reporter who wanted to be a famous correspondent. What Berkeley did was define my politics, and turn me on to the idea of student power. I got very exhilarated by that, and within a year I had plunged deeply into SDS."

From Berkeley, Hayden hitchhiked to Los Angeles for the 1960 Democratic National Convention, which he had agreed to cover for the *Michigan Daily*. The candidate who interested him the most, he said, was John F. Kennedy, whose youthfulness and energy he found appealing. At the convention, however, he found himself more attracted to Reverend Martin Luther King, Jr., who led a picket line of several thousand people, white liberals and blacks, in an appeal for a Democratic commitment to civil rights legislation. Hayden interviewed King for the paper, then switched from reporting to marching with him on the picket line.

Meanwhile, he sent articles on his California experiences back to his college paper for publication. In one of them, he proclaimed the birth of an American student movement, which seriously upset university officials. He liked what he had seen in Berkeley, he said, but he was confused by it. "I didn't know where I was at," Hayden said, "and by the end of the convention the divisions in me had grown further." It was at Los Angeles that he converted to King's cause, and to Kennedy's, Hayden remembered, and probably crossed the psychological barrier from journalist to activist.

Hayden acknowledged that Kennedy, first as candidate and then as president, had much to do with creating the atmosphere in which the student movement subsequently thrived. Kennedy brought a renewed sense of dynamism to the country, and an unembarrassed idealism, both of which were exciting to the young. Hayden himself was particularly fascinated by the Peace Corps, with its notion of service to humanity. "I was, in part, tied to the Kennedy image," he said, with apparent reluctance. Hayden conceded that Kennedy conveyed a measure of hope to young people, gave them a sense

171

that great visions could be realized, bestowed a certain legitimacy upon their effort to redirect the course of events.

Yet, like most of the young radicals of the 1960s, Hayden was quick to see another side of Kennedy. When I asked him whether young people were inspired by Kennedy, he said, "No, just politicized by him. It was indirect. You couldn't be politicized by Eisenhower, or Nixon." Kennedy's contribution, Hayden said, was to make young people feel that politics was something that involved them. When I asked whether this was because Kennedy was more interesting than other political figures, he answered grudgingly, "Not interesting, just relevant. It was a younger set of politicians, more in tune with people on the campus."

As Hayden saw it in retrospect, this characteristic of relevance by giving Kennedy a cushion of student support may have made him more dangerous. It protected him when he attacked the Cubans at the Bay of Pigs in 1961 and when he threatened the world with nuclear war in the missile crisis a year later. It allowed him to inflate the military budget and send the first troops to Vietnam. "In reality he, or the forces around him, were taking advantage of the discontent of youth, and channeling it into certain directions that could be beneficial to their image of the United States." With some bitterness, Hayden concluded: "We didn't know that."

From Los Angeles Hayden headed back to Michigan, stopping in Minneapolis for the *Daily* to cover the annual congress of the National Student Association. On the agenda was the issue of how strongly NSA should support the Southern sit-ins. John Lewis was there, along with other prominent figures in the movement, and they were treated as heroes. Though opposition was strong among delegates from the white colleges of the South, it was overwhelmed on the part of the majority by commitment to social activism and civil rights. "You could feel a sense of power and excitement," Hayden remembered, "at the prospect of young people being able to change things drastically." When he returned in the fall to begin his senior year, Hayden found the same sense of exultation at Michigan.

Though he worked conscientiously on the newspaper, Hayden also found time now for politics, and when *Operation Abolition*

172

was released in fall of 1960 he organized a showing on the campus. *Operation Abolition* was a movie produced by the House Un-American Activities Committee from newsreels of San Francisco's Black Friday. Narrated by J. Edgar Hoover, it purported to show that the anti-HUAC protest was the responsibility of the Communist party, which was engaged in a vast conspiracy to subvert American youth.

Operation Abolition was a huge success with right-wing groups, but it was an even bigger success on college campuses, where it played a trick on its makers. College audiences identified not with the authorities but with the demonstrators. They took the film as evidence of anti-Communist mindlessness, and of the hypocrisy of the political system that sustained HUAC.

"The room was packed," Hayden said of the Michigan showing. "There were three hundred people, which at that time was unprecedented. I don't think most of them understood the formal issues, like contempt of a congressional committee. To them, Red-baiting was a new word. Witch-hunting was a new word. Nobody was tied into the tradition of the 1930s or 1950s, that would make those words have an emotional meaning.

"But what the movie made clear was that there were really outdated and irrational people on congressional committees who were behaving in, you know, insane ways, and the San Francisco police were their allies. Young people like ourselves were being washed down the stairs of City Hall, getting their heads broken. Those people were like us."

Hayden had, in a sense, taken over as chief political activist at Michigan for Al Haber, who had moved to New York to head the SDS national office. The two were in constant contact, searching for ways to exploit the interest in politics that Kennedy's presidential campaign had generated in the fall of 1960. Taking another page from his Berkeley lesson book, Hayden founded a left-wing political coalition fashioned after SLATE. He called it VOICE, which in due course became the Michigan chapter of SDS. Thanks largely to the imprint of Hayden's personality, it remained one of SDS's key chapters, even after Hayden was long gone.

That fall similar groups, vaguely leftist and wary of the American government but with no fixed orthodoxy, were being established by enterprising young men and women on campuses elsewhere.

173

There was POLIT at Chicago, the Political Action Club at Swarthmore, the Liberal Study Group at Wisconsin, ACTION at Columbia. At Harvard, a former math prodigy named Todd Gitlin was working to build TOCSIN. At Oberlin, a former 4-H club champion in chicken judging named Rennie Davis was organizing the Progressive Student League.

All took their nourishment from the atmosphere created by the Kennedy campaign and the sit-ins. All were conceived out of a sense of quitting the 1950s, leaving the McCarthy-Eisenhower era behind, starting something politically new, especially in civil rights. Ultimately these groups were absorbed by SDS, but each began autonomously, possessed of an individual spirit, led by students of considerable diversity.

Todd Gitlin was a New York Jewish intellectual. His parents, both graduates of City College, had master's degrees and worked as teachers. As a child he had read widely and, drawing from the East European origins of his family, thought of himself as some kind of Socialist. He attended the Bronx High School of Science, an elite school within the New York public education system, where he specialized in mathematics, and he worried about the social responsibilities of scientists. Graduating as valedictorian of his class, Gitlin entered Harvard in 1959.

"I went through my whole freshman year oblivious to politics," Gitlin told me. "That summer, I got a job as a computer programmer. It was a good job, programming a machine to multiply and divide, and I was obviously making my way into the technocracy.

"But all that summer I was reading *The Rebel* by Camus and Kafka's *Diaries*, so you can see what was going on in my mind. I guess I was saying to myself, This is not a human existence, these people are boring, the work I'm doing is absolutely meaningless, this is no way to spend a life, sitting in a cubicle getting paid more and more money. I knew I felt like an alienated laborer, and two weeks before the end of the summer I quit the job. Though I didn't realize it, I had severed my connection with the technocracy forever."

Gitlin said that, like Hayden and so many others, he got involved in politics in the fall of 1960, though not because of the sit-ins, to

174

which he had paid little attention. He had not even been attracted to Kennedy, whose campaign speeches he considered "Cold War rhetoric." What crystallized in 1960, Gitlin told me, was the fear of the atomic bomb that had always hung over his head, and his uncertainty about Kennedy's commitment to peace. He was drawn to TOCSIN at Harvard because of its serious concern for peace. The task he assigned himself, he said, was to become an expert in the problems of disarmament, and before long he had read three or four shelves of books on nuclear arms control.

Gitlin acknowledged that, being a Harvard student with excellent academic credentials, he had easy access to a wide range of government officials, some quite close to Kennedy, many of them with Harvard connections themselves. He was often in Washington, making use of his contacts to lobby for disarmament.

"I knew that whole world inside out. By then I could meet those people at their own level of expertise," he said matter-of-factly, without conceit. "I started out believing they were all gentlemen, that we all spoke the same language, that we were all committed to liberal values, of which peace was preeminent. Imagine my chagrin at discovering that, after all, they were very different, that in some fundamental way they weren't reasonable at all."

Gitlin said he started out in politics identifying himself with the liberal wing of the Democratic party. After the Bay of Pigs in April 1961, and the rebuffs to his disarmament notions, he began drifting left, toward student radicalism. He became active in SDS and, in 1963, at the expiration of Tom Hayden's term, he became its president.

Rennie Davis, in contrast to Hayden and Gitlin, was an Anglo-Saxon Protestant who had spent his childhood in Washington and his adolescence in rural Virginia. His father, John C. Davis, had been an economics professor, then became a member of President Truman's Council of Economic Advisors. When Davis was in the seventh grade, Truman left office and his father moved the family to a five-hundred-acre farm in the Blue Ridge Mountains.

Davis remembered it as an "idyllic environment, a beautiful place" to grow up. At high school, he made straight A's, was student body president and editor of the paper, and played varsity basketball. He scarcely noticed, he said, that the school was racially segregated. For him, winning the 4-H clubs' Eastern U.S. chicken

175

judging championship, he said, was the finest moment of his high-school years.

"I loved the farm and didn't see any reason ever to leave," Davis recalled, "until my senior class made a trip to New York City. Going through Harlem, spending some time in the Bowery, just experiencing New York, was very traumatic. When I came home I spent the summer in a kind of teenage reflection, walking through hills and pastures, struggling with myself. It was a moral dilemma, wondering whether to stay where I had everything I could ever want, or to try to deal with the evils and crime and vices of the world that I saw in New York. At the end of the summer I decided to go to college."

Having turned down a scholarship to study animal husbandry at Virginia Polytech, Davis in 1958 entered Oberlin, a small liberal arts college in northern Ohio. He spent his first year trying to catch up with academic deficiencies, he said, and in his second he became involved in student politics, helping to found the Progressive Student League, a campus party that served chiefly as a forum for the dissemination of left-wing ideas. At a small college in Ohio, McCarthyism was slower to fade than in California, or on the East Coast or even at a big Midwestern campus like Michigan, and students resented the disruptiveness of the Progressive Student League, Davis remembered. Then the sit-ins came.

"Here were four students from Greensboro who were suddenly all over *Life* magazine," Davis said. "There was a feeling that they were us and we were them, and a recognition that they were expressing something we were feeling as well, and they'd won the attention of the country.

"Communications made a tremendous difference. I can't remember a conversation that ever went, 'Man, do you realize what we've got at our fingertips? This generation can actually command the media. We can shape public opinion.' That all came much later. What I did experience on the campus was a subtle reinforcing of the belief that, if we took action, we could get results."

What the sit-ins did, according to Davis, was to reinforce a generation that already possessed huge confidence in itself. At the disposal of students in 1960 was important new technology, particularly in communications. Having never worried about a meal, these young people were free as no generation before to involve

176

themselves in social issues. By the start of the 1960s, after a decade of campus passivity, the young had reached the shocking conclusion that society's practices were far removed from its principles. This generation, Davis said, was unique in the conviction that it could do something about those practices, about war, racism and economic injustice.

"We never asked, 'Jesus, what are we talking about?' The assumption was, 'Of course.' We were never in doubt. We realized that we had to work not only around civil rights but around the other big issues, and we began immediately to get down to particulars." In the annals of SDS, Rennie Davis ranked second only to Tom Hayden in intensity of involvement in radical action throughout most of the 1960s. "From 1960 onward," Davis noted, "I considered myself a full-time activist in what was then called the 'student movement,' and later just the 'movement.' "

Meanwhile, Haber was having serious troubles in New York running the tiny SDS organization. In a dingy office downstairs from the LID headquarters on the Lower East Side, he wrote and circulated a civil rights newsletter. By the end of the year, he had distributed ten thousand copies, two thousand of them to the South. He also promoted SDS at student conferences, and succeeded in establishing SDS chapters on a half-dozen campuses. But the pace of organization was too slow to satisfy Haber, who saw the moment as unique, and in his impatience he ran into head-on conflict with his LID patrons.

Haber wanted to link up SDS with existing campus groups of various shades of the left, like Tom Hayden's VOICE at Michigan, Todd Gitlin's TOCSIN at Harvard and Rennie Davis's Progressive Student League at Oberlin. In the jargon of the day, he proposed creation of a "multi-issue movement," which would diversify not only SDS's character but its range of concerns. LID objected to this strategy, on the grounds that the lack of control would loosen its hold over its student affiliate. LID's directors were even more alarmed at the prospect of opening a door to Communist infiltration. In March of 1961, LID went so far as to fire Haber. Then, when he threatened to put the issue to the SDS national convention, it agreed to hire him back.

177

Haber often returned that year to Ann Arbor, his base of political support. There he found Hayden, who had built VOICE into the strongest left-wing campus organization in the country. Sometimes the two of them would go off together on recruitment missions to other colleges. Rennie Davis remembered their visit to Oberlin in the spring.

"We sat in our room together," he said, speaking of himself and his roommate, "and they were saying we had to form a national communications network they called SDS. Paul and I were feeling intruded upon, that it was kind of heavy coming in here, and that we had a nice scene going at Oberlin.

"But we recognized, especially in Tom's analysis of the defense establishment, that this was a brother who was really opening our horizons, really showing us a greater perspective than just this campus. He was saying, 'Let's help shape what's taking place.' By the summer we had let go of our provincialism, and really wanted to serve with Tom and people like him on a national scale."

Davis joined Haber and Hayden in the summer of 1961 at the annual congress of the National Student Association at the University of Wisconsin. It was the first of a series of NSA conferences at which SDS people provided guidance to a blossoming student left. For SDS, NSA proceedings were a platform and a recruiting ground. SDS became an important force in the National Student Association in the early 1960s, and yet it failed consistently to win any but the lesser offices of the organization.

Not until *Ramparts* magazine in 1968 revealed that the CIA had controlled the organizational structure of NSA throughout the decade did anyone know why, but Tom Hayden said he had been aware for some time of something unusual. In the spring of 1961, he had applied for admission to NSA's international relations seminar, a six-week course given to outstanding student body leaders. Those who took it became NSA delegates to international student conferences, which normally turned into arenas for the East-West struggle. The veterans of these conferences, in turn, came to dominate the elected offices in the organization. The objective of the CIA, which secretly paid for NSA's foreign operations, and subsidized some general expenses as well, was to assure the orthodoxy of the international delegates. To achieve its ends it wanted no dissidents in NSA's positions of power.

178

"By now I was consciously with the left wing of NSA," Hayden told me, "and identified with wanting to overthrow the Establishment. I was interviewed for the seminar by two guys who I'm sure now were CIA. They wrote me a letter saying that I was already so well informed, and really so brilliant, that I could not benefit. So I was kept out of it."

Hayden said that, having failed in the international field, he decided to run for national affairs vice-president. This was an office, as it turned out, on which the CIA placed a much lower priority. Occasionally, even militants were elected to it. In fact, the CIA made no effort to control NSA policies on domestic matters, which were usually determined spontaneously, in tumultuous floor debate. In the course of the 1960s, NSA strongly supported the activities of SNCC, and of the civil rights movement generally, and often took positions in sharp conflict with the government on the Vietnam War and the draft. Nonetheless, Tom Hayden did not win his election.

"One day, just before the congress, I was in the office of the NSA president," Hayden said, "and lying on his desk, on a yellow pad drawn in his hand, was a chart of the power bases at the meeting. Me, Haber and other SDS people were listed on the left. Then there was a center and a right, and at the top was a Control Group, capital C, capital G. This guy was in it, along with all the people from abroad, and a couple of people from the national office. You know, people came to that Control Group every night while the congress was on to report how things were going.

"I didn't steal that piece of paper. It was before those days. You didn't steal things and expose it, but I think it would have blown the NSA apart if I did.

"Well, virtually every one of those people in the Control Group turned out to be CIA. We ran against them, attacking them as an older elite that wasn't really from the campuses, and into the Cold War too much, and so forth. But, through all their string-pulling, we narrowly lost."

Hayden's defeat deprived him of access to hundreds of thousands of students through the National Student Association, but it provided him with another constituency. When he graduated from Michigan, Haber offered him a job as field secretary for SDS in the South. He took the offer. Thus Hayden's prodigious energy

179

was diverted from the mainstream of student politics to the full-time service of the radicalism that was growing on American campuses.

In the fall of 1961, Hayden set up a small SDS office in Atlanta, not far from the headquarters of SNCC. Perceived as the embodiment of the sit-ins, SNCC to many white students possessed heroic stature. For SDS, SNCC was also a model. As a "coordinating committee," SNCC was founded to serve autonomous campus units. In a general way, this corresponded to Haber's idea of building SDS upon a base of diverse campus organizations. That SNCC's campus groups were lapsing into inactivity, while SNCC itself was becoming an independent force, was hardly a distraction. Mostly, it was SNCC's radical spirit that persuaded militants like Hayden to look to it for guidance. As much as anything, Hayden's task as Southern field secretary was to serve as SDS's liaison to SNCC.

Hayden assigned himself to touring SNCC's projects in the South, and to sending reports back in the form of newsletters to the campuses of the North. For this work, he resumed his identity as journalist. He wore a coat and tie so he could talk to Southern officials, and he tried to understand all sides of the story. Though hardly dispassionate, Hayden wrote with careful attention to accuracy and detail, and he has left some of the best accounts of the period of SNCC's field activities.

Hayden recorded SNCC's efforts at voter registration in McComb, an isolated town of twelve thousand in the Mississippi Delta, where whites showed they would stop at virtually nothing to maintain their supremacy. He also joined black students riding a bus into McComb in one of the last of the Freedom Rides, a mopping-up action to test the enforcement of the ICC's integration order. He wrote of the beatings of civil rights workers and, associating with them, was himself beaten up by some of McComb's white toughs.

"Perhaps this situation cannot be adequately conveyed . . . ," Hayden wrote in one of his reports. "Does it become real in recognizing that those Negroes are down there, digging in, and in more danger than nearly any student in this American generation has faced? What does it take? When do we begin to see it not as remote

180

but as breathing urgency into our beings and meaning into our ideals?"

Hayden recalled to me with unabated anger that, even as a journalist, he had to function like a guerrilla behind enemy lines, hiding on the floor of cars to go to meetings held in dark cellars. Once the McComb police took him to the station and told him he had the choice of going to jail or leaving town. Yet, what he was seeking to write about was a campaign to register voters, which seemed to him like a most reasonable, even conservative goal. "What we were up against was a whole organized system that was out to kill us," Hayden said, "and that was a very devastating thing to discover." Whatever the impact of his reports on their readers, the experience in Mississippi did much to advance Hayden's own radicalization.

In a memo he sent back to Haber on SNCC in the fall of 1961, Hayden wrote of a "crazy new sentiment that this is not a movement but a revolution." He said the activists were identifying not with black figures from their own past but with the revolutionary leaders of the new nations. SNCC people, he said, recognized that "beyond lunch counter desegregation there are more serious evils which must be ripped out by any means: exploitation, socially destructive capital, evil political and legal structure, and myopic liberalism which is anti-revolutionary."

With more than a touch of prophecy, he told Haber that, in dealing with SNCC, SDS "should be aware that they have changed down there, and we should speak their revolutionary language without mocking it, for it is not lip service . . . It is good pure struggle, the kind that can bring hope to Africans and Asians and the rest of the hungry people, and it's a struggle that we have every reason to begin in a revolutionary way across the country . . . The Southern movement has turned itself into that revolution we hoped for, and we didn't have much to do with its turning at all . . . Now they are miles ahead of us, looking back, chuckling knowingly about the sterility of liberals . . . In the rural South, in the 'token integration' areas, in the cities, they will be shouting from the bottom of their guts for justice or else. We had better be there."

Representing the cause of the SNCC workers, Hayden went to Washington, where he told John Doar of the dangers they faced in Mississippi in their voter registration campaign. Doar was deputy to Burke Marshall, head of the Justice Department's Civil Rights

181

Division. He would become known during the 1960s for his strong dedication to civil rights, and for his considerable physical courage in seeking to avert bloodshed during racial confrontations.* Hayden said Doar told him the Justice Department could do nothing to protect SNCC workers because of jurisdictional limitations upon the federal government.

"In other words," Hayden said, "this Justice Department official, this top law enforcement officer of the United States, was encouraging us not to register people to vote because we would be getting into trouble of the kind he could do nothing about. From that time on it was clear."

In my interview with Burke Marshall, he said he thought Hayden's anger, however understandable, was unfair. He cited the Freedom Ride, for which "the use of specially deputized marshals was . . . unprecedented. . . . The legal issues to be decided involved the most difficult of the relationships between the states and the Federal government . . . and were the object of disagreement and debate among the most experienced lawyers." † Marshall argued that what Hayden and SNCC wanted, furthermore, would have required not just a few marshals, like the Freedom Ride, but military occupation of Mississippi. That, he said, was manifestly out of the question.

To Hayden, Marshall's argument was hairsplitting. The attitude of Marshall and Doar, he said, proved that liberals, however sincere their commitment to the Constitution, were impotent in the face of the South's organized racism. He said liberals were less dedicated to civil rights than to legalisms, which they were unwilling to violate and unable to change.

Hayden's Southern experience left him with the conclusion that liberals were an integral part of the ugliness of American society. Whether their responsibility was active or passive was of small consequence. That it might be accompanied by noble motives was irrelevant. That the liberal vision of American society had much in common with his own did not make it any less the object of his scorn. Liberalism was an enemy.

---

* He later became known as chief special counsel to the House Judiciary Committee during the inquiry into the impeachment of Richard Nixon.

† Quote is from Victor Navasky, *Kennedy Justice.*

What Hayden expressed was a position intrinsic to the student movement of the 1960s. Liberals—many of whom had dedicated their lives to the causes young radicals seemed only recently to have discovered—had a great deal of trouble understanding these sentiments. Why had an older generation of liberals—having created the welfare state, having defeated Fascism, having worn down McCarthyism, having made the most progress in a century against racial discrimination—to apologize to fresh kids? For Hayden and the young militants, however, those liberal achievements were ancient history and not enough. Tom Hayden's perceptions of liberalism, more than any other grievance against American society, translated themselves into his program of radicalism for SDS.

"Here was brutality authorized by the state, or at least tolerated by the state," he said. "It was a test of the implications of liberalism. Liberalism on the one hand was espousing all these noble ideals and on the other was unable to do anything about them.

"I mean, we inevitably began saying, 'If the problems were there all these years, why did *we* have to discover them?' Where was liberalism at? What you got was this dynamic where young people were putting their bodies on the line, and maybe their parents or older people would give them some money, but that was as far as it went. It had to lead to the idea that liberalism was an armchair ideology.

"It reinforced our disposition that activism was necessary, even where there wasn't a blueprint for where it was leading. We wanted SDS to become a direct action organization, not a Fabian organization. By that I mean that SDS was not to become simply a forum for ideas. We would try to get those ideas adopted, by mass organizations for instance. But SDS was a Bolshevik group, or a Jesuit group. That's what the civil rights movement was. It was small groups of people taking action to achieve things."

During the Christmas vacation of 1961, Haber invited Hayden, along with about a dozen other campus activists, to a meeting at Ann Arbor to prepare a program for SDS. He already sensed that SDS lacked a goal for its radicalism, and a strategy for its energies. With accuracy he called SDS nonpolitical and, in an SDS bulletin, he wrote: "It is non-political largely because of a lack of faith in the

183

political process or in the established instrumentalities of change, but to these it offers no alternative beyond direct action. It operates on the assumption that ... if we speak loud enough and in sufficient numbers, 'something will happen.' There is no recognition ... of institutional forces with which the movement must ultimately deal." Haber called the Ann Arbor meeting in order to create for SDS a sense of where it was going.

Haber had asked each of the participants at Ann Arbor to prepare a paper containing recommendations and, as might be expected of a "multi-issue" organization, the proposals that arrived were diverse. The Penn delegate argued for organizing against poverty, the Cornell delegate for pressing university reform, the North Carolina delegate for educating Southern whites about civil rights, the Michigan delegate for establishing peace centers to disseminate antiwar information. Others proposed that SDS give its support to SNCC's voter registration campaign, to disarmament negotiations or to left-wing candidates running for elective office.

In addition to his concerns about doctrine, Haber had organizational problems to solve. On the one hand, he wanted to retain SDS's "multi-issue" approach, to appeal to the widest possible range of radically disposed students and campus organizations. On the other, he wanted to identify SDS with specific principles that would be helpful in promoting campus organization and recruitment. The Ann Arbor meeting concluded without resolution. Haber turned the working papers over to Hayden, with instructions to draft a manifesto to be submitted for endorsement to the SDS national convention in the spring.

Throughout early 1962, Hayden worked on preparing various drafts. He rejected the contention of some members that the approach should be narrowly political, and decided instead to put principal emphasis on social and moral values. He also decided against a short, pithy statement in favor of a more ambitious, perhaps even grandiose, document. Marx had prepared the model, appealing to the proletariat in the Communist Manifesto of 1848. Hayden, confident that Marx was out-of-date, aspired to writing the manifesto of the New Left, as an appeal to the student movement.

Hayden read widely for his work, consulted with other SDS members and circulated a number of drafts for criticism and comment. What emerged from his effort was the celebrated "Port Huron Statement."

184

The philosophical presence behind Tom Hayden was a maverick sociologist from Columbia named C. Wright Mills, who died the year the "Port Huron Statement" was adopted, at the age of forty-six. A rural Texan by origin and temperament, Mills wrote from the Populist tradition of outrage at the established bases of power. An angry intellectual, he violated academic orthodoxy by harnessing scholarship to moral commitment, and he created a fresh body of radical thought.

As a student at Michigan, Hayden had written a research thesis on Mills. Haber, Rennie Davis and Todd Gitlin all knew Mills's work well. It was Mills who invented the term New Left, and whose thinking, more than anyone else's, gave the student movement its early intellectual content.

Mills's *The Power Elite* was published in 1956, the same year as Allen Ginsberg's *Howl*. Though one spoke to the mind and the other to the senses, they bristled equally at a repressive and unjust society. Both, furthermore, deplored the powerlessness they said the average American felt to influence his own destiny. Ginsberg, the poet, blamed greed for the society's miseries, and saw no better response than turning-on and dropping-out. Mills, the sociologist, blamed increasingly powerful political institutions, run by a handful of decision-makers accountable to no one. Mills's analysis, in contrast to Ginsberg's, led logically to political action. No doubt the influence of the two men overlapped during the 1960s, but if Ginsberg was the guru of the counterculture, C. Wright Mills was surely the mentor of the New Left.

"The powers of ordinary men are circumscribed by the everyday worlds in which they live," was the way Mills opened *The Power Elite*, "yet even in these rounds of jobs, family and neighborhood they often seem driven by forces they can neither understand nor govern. 'Great changes' are beyond their control, but affect their conduct and outlook none the less. The very framework of modern society confines them to projects not their own, but from every side, such changes now press upon the men and women of the mass society, who accordingly feel that they are without purpose in an epoch in which they are without power."

Mills identified the "power elite" which made society's great decisions as a closely knit clique that directed the giant corporations, the government and the armed forces. He did not accuse it of fascism. In fact, he condemned it for the lack of a coherent conservative philosophy. The danger of the power elite, he wrote, was not that its members sought to do evil but that the only good it understood was determined by the codes of their own circle. Cut off from the mass of Americans, they acted arbitrarily and insensitively, with no awareness that their conduct was detrimental to the majority.

Mills had no illusions about the Soviet Union. Whatever his objections to American democracy, he rejected any notion that the Communist left offered a viable alternative. The Soviet Union, he wrote, was governed by its own power elite, which had shamelessly distorted the structure of Marxist ideas into a system of permanent repression. The only advantage that Russians had, he wrote, was that they knew they lived under a tyranny, while Americans were unmindful of their own persecution.

The liberals were the object of Mills's heaviest scorn. Crediting them with important contributions to American life under the New Deal, he castigated them for their loss of courage and vigor in the postwar era. "The New Deal used up the heritage of liberal ideas," he wrote, "made them banal as it put them into law; turned liberalism into a set of administrative routines to defend rather than a program to fight for."

Nor did Mills entertain the slightest hope that liberalism could recover its vitality. "As a rhetoric," he wrote, "liberalism has become the mask of all political positions, as a theory of society it has become irrelevant. . . ." Mills fixed the New Left's attitude toward liberalism by conceding the liberals' decent intentions, while treating their effectiveness with contempt.

For all its analysis, Mills gave little attention in *The Power Elite* to how, or with what alternative, to replace the system he loathed. But he was a prodigious worker. In the years after 1956, he wrote books on the arms race, on sociological methodology and on the revolution in Cuba. At his death, he was working on a book about Marxism, to which he had become increasingly attached, and the growing number of his admirers looked forward to a valuable reformulation of socialist theory.

From his study of Marx, Mills concluded that a "historic agency of change" would arise to sweep away the rotten old system. Marx

186

had taught that the proletariat would serve that function, but Mills considered that facet of Marx's analysis to be outdated. Mills reflected much on what might replace the proletariat, and in the spring of 1960 he published his answer. It could hardly have been more thrilling or come at a better time, for the nascent student movement.

In an article he called "Letter to the New Left," Mills scolded radicals for their continued dedication to "Victorian Marxism," which enshrined the working class. He had himself suspected for some time, he wrote, that the motor for revolution might be the intellectual classes, and he argued that recent history had confirmed his hypothesis. Repressive regimes had been shaken or overthrown by students in Turkey, South Korea, Cuba and Japan, he wrote. There were massive protests in universities in England, and even Hungary and Russia felt under attack by intellectuals. The conclusive proof for his contention seemed to be in the American South. "Who is it that is thinking and acting in radical ways?" Mills asked. "All over the world—in the bloc, outside the bloc and in between—the answer's the same: it is the young intelligentsia."

Mills's declaration was good news for American students of militant disposition, especially the whites who, feeling envious of the certainties enjoyed by their black counterparts, were unsure whether they themselves had a role to play. Hayden, however, understood that Mills had not yet answered the crucial question. Assuming Mills was right in seeing young intellectuals as the agency of change, what should they seek to change the society to?

Hayden replied to Mills not long before the Port Huron conference in an essay he entitled "Letter to the New (Young) Left." Despite his admiration for Mills, he deplored a pessimism which "yields us no formulas, no path out of the dark." He cautioned young militants that, if they were serious, they would have to prepare for a long, painful and often frustrating struggle. Meanwhile, he warned, "the student movement which has rejected so many institutions and instruments of social change—the Southern courtrooms, by and large the Democratic party, the military, often the Congress—has invented no substitute save a noble morality and in some cases a commitment to nonviolence that will dissipate soon if not secured in a new social structure." Hayden did not suggest the

187

suspension of action pending the resolution of uncertainty, but he admitted: "I am beset by doubt."

At the time of the Port Huron meeting, SDS was still far from a thriving organization. It claimed only eight hundred members, whose single commitment was the payment of a dollar a year in dues. It ran on an annual budget of $10,000, which was carefully doled out by LID. It had a dozen chapters, but even Haber conceded that they were not uniformly active.

Until two weeks before the national convention, the New York office had still not found a suitable site, and gratefully accepted the invitation of the United Auto Workers to use the camp that gave the meeting its name. Port Huron is forty miles north of Detroit. SDS records show that fifty-nine people attended, forty-three of them with the power to vote. Among those enfranchised were not only delegates of SDS chapters but, in keeping with Haber's theory of the "multi-issue" organization, representatives from SNCC, the Young Democrats, Campus ADA, the Student Peace Union, the NAACP, the Young People's Socialist League and CORE. The conference opened on June 11, 1962, and lasted for four days.

The document that emerged at Port Huron, some twenty-five thousand words in length, was grand in its conception, and in execution alternately thoughtful and banal, daring and timid, provocative and dull. Much of what it contained was already well within the spectrum of ongoing debate, and rather little was said to which liberals themselves would take serious exception. In its time, whether or not it was a radical document was much debated. Many of its proposals were conventionally liberal. But its concerns were millennial, and its sweep conveyed ideals that few considered attainable. In that sense, it was radical, indeed.

Hayden compared the experience at Port Huron—the endless argument, the writing and rewriting, the all-night sessions—to giving birth. Though the final statement was not basically different from his original draft, SDS modestly characterized it as "a beginning in our own debate and education, in our dialogue with society." But, as witness to the anguish and discontent within a generation of the young, the "Port Huron Statement" was one of the important pronouncements of the 1960s.

The tone of the "Port Huron Statement" was set in its opening line: "We are the people of this generation, bred in at least modest comfort, housed now in universities, looking uncomfortably to the world we inherit." The line was, at once, an assertion of uniqueness, an acknowledgment of chagrin, a claim of virtue. It contained the feelings of guilt and superiority which, in the 1960s, seemed to set apart so many middle-class whites emerging from adolescence from the rest of the culture. Feelings of uniqueness, chagrin and virtue, guilt and superiority were all intrinsic to the student movement, and pervaded the work done at Port Huron.

The young, in search of adult models that shared their ideals, had been routinely betrayed, the statement said. The culprits were the liberals, who established a "perverse unity" with racists, and the older left, "perverted by Stalinism." As for the Kennedy Administration, it had been opportunistic at best, and in the name of "tough-mindedness" had failed to abate either racism or the Cold War. The consequence had been the crushing of the idealism of the young, since "to be idealistic is to be considered apocalyptic, deluded. To have no serious aspiration, on the contrary, is to be 'tough-minded.' "

The statement lamented the disillusion that had set in among young people when they discovered the "hypocrisy of American ideals." It cited the "paradoxes" of racism and militarism in a society that boasted of being egalitarian and peace-loving. It contrasted the "sense of urgency" of the young to solve pressing social problems with the paralysis of the institutions responsible for solving them. The nation's success in accumulating wealth, said the paper, did not, as many believed, signal a golden age but, on the contrary, the decline of an era.

Pervading the "Port Huron Statement" was the countercultural contention that radicalism's role was not just social change but metamorphosis. Intrinsic to it was the peculiarly American commitment to personal freedom, and the preeminence of the individual over society. "We oppose the depersonalization that reduces human beings to the status of things," the document proclaimed. Society, it argued, had a responsibility to man's "self-cultivation, self-direction, self-understanding and creativity." Hayden's own commitment remained essentially political, but this millennial imperative—Ginsberg's gift to Jeffersonianism—was never fully absent from the radicalism of the 1960s.

189

The ideas of C. Wright Mills dominated the political analysis. "The American political system is not the democratic model of which its glorifiers speak," the paper declared. "Business elites" run foreign policy, while "labor elites," once an important force for reform, had become bureaucratic, materialistic and corrupt. "Military strategy, including the monstrous decision to go to war," is determined by uniformed and industrial elites, who exploit patriotism for "boondoggling, belligerence and privilege," while elected politicians passively stand by. "And who," the paper asked rhetorically, "controls the elites anyway, and are they solving mankind's problems?"

The specific proposals made in the paper were, by and large, already on the liberal agenda: universal controlled disarmament and supervised military disengagement; an enlarged foreign aid program to assure the economic and social development of the Third World; realignment of the political parties to give voters clearer choices, and restructuring of corporations to provide for more social responsibility; expansion of the economy's public sector to create more jobs; and establishment of an antipoverty program to enable the poor to make their own way in life.

The principal structural change that the paper proposed was a shift to "participatory democracy," which stemmed from an observation that "the people" were too easily manipulated by the procedures of representative democracy. The paper recommended, instead, that decisions be made at a more popular level, where disagreements could be resolved through discussion and, ultimately, consensus. Participatory democracy, according to the "Port Huron Statement," would let "the individual share in those social decisions determining the quality and direction of his life." The idea was summed up in the slogan, "Let the people decide," a favorite among radicals through much of the decade.

The origin of the idea of participatory democracy is obscure but surely came, at least in part, from the suspicion of elites, and ultimately of leadership itself, with which C. Wright Mills imbued the age. The concept appeared first as "group-centered" decision-making in James Lawson's nonviolence workshops in the late 1950s and it passed from there directly into SNCC. One of its conse-

190

quences was to make decisions in SNCC impossible without endless deliberation. SDS would adopt these same practices of decentralized authority to the point that often no decisions were possible at all. Though SNCC and SDS both had extraordinary personalities associated with them, both were characterized by a pervasive hostility to leadership, which left them as organizations throughout their history with weak and ineffective direction.

Nonetheless, the concept of participatory democracy had a huge impact on the 1960s. The theory justifying it held that the quality of a decision was less important than the manner in which the decision was reached. Participatory democracy would overcome a sense of powerlessness by having people partake directly in making the decisions that affected their destiny. The concept was meant as the answer to the feelings of impotence among that majority that Mills had identified. Its proponents maintained that participatory democracy would promote the growth of "indigenous" political and economic institutions among the poor, and thereby enable them to compete on more favorable terms in a highly demanding society.

SNCC sought to apply the concept from the start in organizing disfranchised blacks in the rural South. It was the premise behind SDS's most ambitious organizational experiment, the Economic Research and Action Project (ERAP), which Rennie Davis directed. ERAP's aim was to organize the poor in Northern urban ghettos. To the dismay of SDS, the Johnson Administration injected the idea into the federal antipoverty program, where it was applied to community action projects in dozens of cities. In many of these cities, the poor created such effective institutions that.the existing elites felt threatened. After a series of furious battles, these elites succeeded in having the antipoverty program dismantled.

Of the concepts that were actually tried, participatory democracy was surely the most radical of the 1960s. It embraced both the process and the goal of Hayden's ideal of a "new social structure." It was surely too radical for the federal government, which abandoned it, and though it could have served as the basis of SDS's organization for revolutionary ends, its success demanded more hard work and patience than most young radicals were willing to give. Hayden, organizing in Newark, and Rennie Davis, organizing in Chicago, were willing to make a long-term commitment to its

191

development. For most of the others, however, the Vietnam War became a more exciting target, and the ERAP experiment collapsed.

Participatory democracy alone probably justified Tom Hayden's defense of the "Port Huron Statement" as a radical document. Hayden, however, saw it as radical through and through.

"They were not new ideas but they were not liberal ideas either," he said. "I think one thing that has to be erased is this notion that the early SDS was liberal reform and then became Marxist. The early SDS was *New* Left. Certain ideas may look reformist in time but you have to look at the context that they were anchored in and know what the motivation of the people was. The motivation was toward revolution.

"When I wrote the economic section, everybody had a good laugh when it was said that the draft was by Brother Hayden as amended by Brother Karl Marx. Now, our notions of Marxism were in many ways fucked up. We had no experience, no intellectual background. But everybody there knew what we were doing. We had certain deviations from what we considered to be Marxism because we preferred ourselves to be *New* Left. But we were conscious of what we were driving at, which was a revolutionary change in the American structure.

"We were never reformers who became disillusioned and, therefore, more radical. That might have been true of the generation as a whole. It might have been true of the mass phenomenon. It was not true of the SDS people.

"We were opposed to foreign ideology, to doctrines imposed from the past. In that sense, we were not Marxist. It was much easier to identify with Mills. Everything for us had to be new. We named *ourselves* New Left. If we were liberals, why did we name ourselves New Left? Because we thought our vision lay in the traditions of the left, but that they had to be reconstructed all over again, in our time and place. That reconstruction was our mission."

The "Port Huron Statement" also called for university reform, though it hardly made a powerful argument that reform was neces-

192

sary. The document complained of the cumbersome nature of academic bureaucracy and of the demeaning supervision over student behavior. It lamented the triviality of university education, from which students graduated "somewhat more 'tolerant' than when they arrived, but basically unchallenged in their values and political orientations." On the whole, the section on the inadequacy of the universities had the ring of traditional campus gripes.

Hayden had little patience, however, for the argument that grievances against the university system were the product of student self-indulgence rather than genuine abuse. "I'd say the university was a more powerful issue in forming SDS than any other," he said. "SDS could not have been founded without the civil rights issue and, perhaps, without the New Frontier. But the thing that was the most immediate source of alienation in the environment of my generation, what we were concerned with, was the campus."

The "Port Huron Statement" touched upon something real, which two years later would manifest itself in the outburst at Berkeley. The Berkeley protest was succeeded by a wave of disorders on campuses across the nation, which served as proof that students were indeed aggrieved. Some of these disorders were provoked over campus complaints, but far more were started over other issues, notably the Vietnam War. Whatever Hayden's contention, students were reacting to a malaise that went much beyond dissatisfaction with the university, though its identity was never easy to determine.

A more interesting discussion on the universities accompanied the endorsement in the "Port Huron Statement" of the Mills thesis that students had become the world's principal agency of social change. The very term "New Left" could scarcely be understood outside a university setting, the paper said. The university's "social relevance, accessibility of knowledge and internal openness" made it the ideal "seat of influence" for the assault upon the status quo. The university's task, the "Port Huron Statement" proclaimed, was to train young people to fulfill their responsibilities as this "agency of change." It seemed to be saying, critical as it was of other elites, that a student elite had now to be forged on the campuses to realize the New Left's vision of the future. This elitism remained with the New Left throughout its history.

193

However radical the rest of their work, the drafters at Port Huron knew that their most provocative assertion would be their statement on anti-Communism. It was the subject that most dramatically separated the New Left from the Old, the radicals from the liberals, the young with little sense of history from the not so young who had lived through the Berlin crisis, the Hungarian uprising and a hundred other inflammatory episodes in East-West relations. It was also the issue that divided SDS from its financial patron, the League for Industrial Democracy.

Anti-Communism in American politics, said the "Port Huron Statement," is a mindless paranoia. The document did not defend the Soviet Union, which it conceded was militaristic, or the Communist system, which it acknowledged to be antidemocratic. But American anti-Communism, it argued, "leads not only to the perversion of democracy and to the political stagnation of a warfare society, but it also has the unintended consequence of preventing an honest and effective approach to the issues." By perpetuating a dubious assumption that the Soviet Union is inherently expansionist, the paper said, "the monstrous American structure of military 'preparedness' has come to rule the society." The students at Port Huron urged the replacement of irrational anti-Communism by a reasoned analysis of national needs.

Before it adjourned, the Port Huron convention elected Tom Hayden president of SDS. It also adopted a new constitution, in which, for the first time, it declared itself an association of the left. It formalized Haber's "multi-issue organizational conception by opening affiliation to practically any campus group. Finally, it relaxed the strictures against the membership of Communists and asserted SDS's functional independence of LID.

When the directors of LID learned what had happened at Port Huron, they were predictably outraged. Michael Harrington had been there as an observer, and his advice had consistently been ignored. Harrington, a veteran Socialist, had recently written *The Other America*, a powerful condemnation of poverty that helped spark the federal antipoverty program. Like Hayden, he was a Midwestern Irish-Catholic radical, and the two were warm friends. But Harrington was also an uncompromising anti-Communist, and it was he who led LID's fight against SDS.

194

Hayden and Haber were ordered to appear before an LID committee on July 6, 1962, to answer for their heresy. In the strange jargon in which the Old Left still talked, Harrington accused SDS of "united frontism" for its willingness to make peace with the Communists. According to minutes of the meeting, Harrington said, "You knew this would send LID through the roof. This issue was settled on the left ten or twenty years ago—and that you could countenance any united frontism now is inconceivable." That an issue of political dogma is ever "settled" hardly corresponds to man's experience, much less to the special experience of SDS, for whom ten or twenty years ago was prehistory.

After several tumultuous hours of debate, LID agreed to have Haber present a defense of SDS in writing. But before a word was put on paper, LID cut Haber and Hayden from the payroll and suspended all of SDS's subsidies. Even more humiliating, members of SDS's small staff of volunteers found when they came to work in New York on Monday morning that LID had locked them out of their office. The lockout became a celebrated episode in SDS history, proof that the Old Left could be neither trusted nor persuaded.

After some weeks of negotiation, SDS and LID reached an unfriendly truce, and LID's dingy office space and tiny budgetary allocation were once again put at SDS's disposal. The price SDS paid was Haber's departure and this time he was not allowed to return. With ill-concealed resentment, Haber gradually drifted away from the organization. In the months that followed, Hayden as president did very little to put SDS on a firm administrative footing, and mismanagement would in fact remain chronic until SDS's end. The office did, however, function with relatively little interference from its patron. SDS and LID were a mutually acknowledged mismatch, with two political conceptions more in conflict than in harmony. And, as might have been expected, in due course they broke apart for good.

But SDS was in far greater measure a religion than a bureaucracy, and the "Port Huron Statement" became its scripture. Hayden surely exaggerated when he told me that "the effect of those ideas on other people was electric." Whether it changed many minds is doubtful. The chief importance of the "Port Huron Statement" was that it articulated what many students, at some level of consciousness, already believed, and it thereby legitimized their beliefs.

195

The "Port Huron Statement" circulated widely on the nation's campuses, conveying a sense of solidarity among the persuaded. It created excitement, not because what it revealed was new but because its familiarity was reassuring. And so SDS, however incompetent its management, became an inspiration for campus militancy. In those years its presence was still hardly noticed. But the radical consciousness it embodied was gestating, as the disposition to direct action had gestated among young blacks throughout the late 1950s. When the student movement dramatically surfaced, the world would again be dumbstruck, and SDS would be its avant-garde.

VI
BAYARD RUSTIN:
Marching to Washington
1963

"I came out of prison realizing that talking to individuals about being good is a pile of crap. You've got to have a social organization which helps people to bring out the goodness in them, not one that brutalizes them. That's basically what Randolph always said."

To MANY AMERICANS, the March on Washington in August of 1963 *was* the civil rights movement. A quarter of a million people were there. By rough calculation, one of every hundred black Americans was at the Lincoln Memorial that day. But the character of the March on Washington was no less established by thousands of whites, by the institutional strength of Protestants, Catholics and Jews, by organized liberals and by labor. It was the biggest, and surely the most diverse, demonstration in history for human rights.

Here was a coalescence of citizens whose consciences had at last been roused to the conviction that blacks could no longer be denied the rights that other Americans enjoyed. It was a day of reverence, and of exaltation, and of rejoicing. It was also a day of unprecedented harmony for the races in America and one could hope, if not believe, that its spirit would endure. The March on Washington was a unique moment in the American experience, and no one who was there would ever forget it.

Even today it is hard to say what its significance was. It may have changed no votes in Congress on a civil rights bill; it may have changed no minds in the South on racial segregation. It was the apogee of the struggle against racism in American history, and yet the struggle went on, bitterly, as if the March had not occurred. It provided a fleeting glimpse, perhaps, of what the 1960s might have been, before the assassination of Kennedy, the burning of Watts, the Vietnam War, filled those years with despair. It offered a vision of the melting pot realized, of the injustice of three centuries remedied by nonviolence and decency, of the two societies fused into one. And then it ended, leaving a warm memory.

199

A. Philip Randolph had conceived of the March on Washington as far back as 1941, and even then had Bayard Rustin working on it. Randolph, the eloquent president of the Brotherhood of Sleeping Car Porters, had already done more than any other man of his time in the cause of Negro rights, and half a lifetime of service still lay ahead of him. Randolph believed that unless blacks organized they would remain forever powerless and, with war raging in Europe, he threatened President Roosevelt with a massive descent on Washington unless the government recognized blacks' rights as citizens, no less than their wartime duties. Bayard Rustin was one of the young men who volunteered to help him organize the march and, off and on for two decades, Randolph and Rustin worked together. When the March on Washington was actually realized after twenty-two years of longing, A. Philip Randolph was presiding, and Bayard Rustin was in charge.

Rustin was born in 1910 in the small Pennsylvania town of West Chester, near Philadelphia, where the Quakers had established a colony of black freedmen before the Civil War. He traced his high cheekbones and narrow features to the Indian in his background. His chocolate skin and bushy hair came from his mother, a sixteen-year-old black woman to whom he was born illegitimately.

Thinking of his mother as his aunt, Rustin said, he was raised by his grandmother, a strong woman in the home and a leader in the local black community. She was a nurse, and a board member of the new organization called the NAACP. She was also a committed member of the Quakers, the only Christian denomination with an uninterrupted tradition of opposition to slavery and a belief in the inherent equality of the races. Through the Quakers, Rustin was introduced early to the idea of pacifism, of service and of racial equality.

Rustin remembered a boyhood that was essentially segregated, but West Chester's black population was small and whites felt no threat from the Negro presence. Fewer than 2 percent of American Negroes lived in the North in this era, and growing up in West Chester was far different from the persistent tension of growing up in the South. Rustin said he mixed comfortably with Jews and Irishmen and Chinese, no less than with the Quakers whose parents ran

200

the town. He won esteem, furthermore, as a football player and as an accomplished tenor. In his generation, Rustin said, West Chester represented an unusual opportunity for a young black to experience a wide range of contacts in a nonblack world.

After high school, Rustin's tenor voice won him a scholarship to Wilberforce, a black college in Ohio, but a year later he transferred to Cheyney State in Pennsylvania, a black teachers' college not far from his home. He stayed two years before accepting the invitation of his "sister" Bessie—who was actually his mother's sister—to move to New York, where he enrolled in City College. To earn money he sang folk songs in white nightclubs, sometimes with such celebrities as Josh White and Leadbelly.

I talked to Rustin in his apartment in a high-rise in midtown Manhattan. Randolph, who died in 1979, lived in the same development. It was within walking distance of the A. Philip Randolph Institute, an organization responsible for promoting job training among young blacks. Randolph founded it, and Rustin was its director. Rustin's apartment was crowded with art objects, many of them from Africa. He smoked constantly, and spoke with an elegant British accent, cultivated during long visits to England and India. I found Rustin hard to interview. His memory, a treasure of experiences in the struggle for equality, jumped almost at random between episodes that were decades apart.

"I discovered at City College during the Depression," said Rustin, explaining an association that stigmatized him during the McCarthy years, "that when Tom Mooney was in trouble, it was the Communists who came to his assistance. When it was the Scottsboro boys, it was the Communists. When it came to speaking out against Jim Crow, it was the Communists. Every black who got into trouble, the Communists made a great deal of fuss about. So I got involved in the Young Communist League."

Rustin never made apologies for his years of association with the Communists. Nor has he sought to conceal them. As late as the March on Washington, the enemies of civil rights sought to use them to discredit the movement. Rustin never even claimed, as did so many others, that he had been duped by the Communists. He has said simply that when he learned the real nature of their objectives, he quit.

"Why did I leave the Communists?" he said. "Well, in 1939 they

201

called me in and asked me to set up a statewide committee against discrimination in the armed forces. They said discrimination was wrong, and that blacks should not be fighting in any war of Franklin Delano Roosevelt's. They said that, as Communists, they were deeply dedicated to eliminating discrimination of *all* types, against *all* people, social, economic and political discrimination. This appealed to me greatly, so I set up the committee.

"Then, in June 1941, Hitler turned against Russia. The day after the invasion took place, they called me in and told me to disband the committee. They said this was now a people's war, that we must all come together and demand the opening of a second front by Allied forces.

"I raised a series of questions with them, to have it revealed to me that at that moment the Communists were interested only in what was good for the Soviet Union. They were not really interested in justice, as I had thought. I therefore resigned."

Rustin said that in the weeks after he left the Communists he felt a deep sense of loss. "I had faith in the Communists," he said, "and I had no underpinnings. Bessie was not at all political, and she was not able to help me." He turned to the Fellowship of Reconciliation, whose ideas were close to his own Quaker pacifism. He also went to see A. Philip Randolph, who was reaching the climax of his preparations for the March on Washington.

Rustin told me that, even while he was in the Young Communist League, he had worked as a volunteer in the youth division of the March on Washington. He had never met Randolph, he said, but he had no doubt about Randolph's militancy in the racial struggle. In the Stalinist lexicon, Randolph was a reactionary for resisting Communist efforts to exploit his trade union leadership. Rustin said he had not quite swallowed the Communist line on Randolph, but going to see Randolph was nonetheless a big psychological leap. When he did, he became so impressed with Randolph that he became a disciple, and the two men established a working relationship that lasted until Randolph died.

Even when he was a boy, Rustin knew of A. Philip Randolph, who had long before acquired a reputation as the most outspoken militant in Harlem. A Socialist and a pacifist, he had defied both

202

Booker T. Washington and W. E. B. Du Bois, the black community's most esteemed thinkers, by arguing that black people, if organized around economic issues, could stamp out America's color caste. As editor of the *Messenger* during World War I, he was called the country's most dangerous Negro for exhorting blacks to resist army duty until they were granted equal rights.

Rustin remembered that Randolph also rejected the black nationalism of Marcus Garvey in the years between the wars. "It was a very despairing period," Rustin said. "The ghettos were being formed. Blacks were being run off the land in the South. Lynching was at its height. So out of the despair they attempted to turn someplace else, and it is always to Africa, or into your own bosom." * But the exclusionism of black nationalism, Rustin said, was an escape, not a solution. Forty years later, he and Randolph together were denounced as "Uncle Toms" for arguing that a new nationalism, called Black Power, was self-segregation, not salvation, and a hopeless cause to follow.

Rustin remembered Randolph best, however, as president of the Brotherhood of Sleeping Car Porters, serving as the chief spokesman for the black working classes. Unlike Rustin, Randolph understood by the 1930s that the Communist party was, above all, an instrument of Soviet foreign policy. Randolph was particularly outraged when American Communists defended Stalin's pact in 1939 with Hitler, whom he recognized as more racist than the worst American. When he excoriated the Russians for joining Hitler in the invasion of Poland, Rustin waded in with his fellow communists and denounced Randolph as a reactionary.

In the fall of 1940, while Roosevelt flirted with intervention, Randolph resumed the campaign he had started in World War I to have the government abolish racial discrimination in the armed forces. Roosevelt responded by inviting him, along with Walter White of the NAACP and T. Arnold Hill of the Urban League, to the White House. When their meeting was over, the White House issued a statement saying that segregation had been reaffirmed "after Roosevelt conferred" with the three black leaders. The implication that Randolph and his two companions had somehow en-

---

* This and several other Rustin quotes are from the interview by Peter Joseph in *Good Times.*

dorsed segregation was both false and dishonest, and the three men were justly indignant.

It was then that Randolph proposed the mass march on Washington, to demand racial integration of the armed services and equal access to jobs in defense industries. At first he talked of a march of ten thousand blacks. Gradually the number of which he spoke grew to a hundred thousand. Randolph promised nonviolence as it was practiced by Gandhi, whose strategy for freeing India from colonial rule had recently begun to attract attention. But, nonviolent though his intentions were, Washington was a city that was totally segregated—restaurants, hotels, rest rooms, drinking fountains, buses—and the prospect of tens of thousands of Negroes coming in from out-of-town looked like an invitation to massive disorder.

Nonetheless, on January 14, 1941, Randolph issued a call for support of the march. "Only power can effect the enforcement and adoption of a given policy," he declared, in an unusually candid formulation of his strategic thinking. ". . . Power and pressure do not reside in a few, an intelligentsia. They lie in and flow from the masses. Power does not even rest with the masses, as such. Power is the active principle of only the *organized* masses, the masses united for a definite purpose."

Randolph fixed the day for the March on Washington at July 1, 1941. The response from the nation's blacks exceeded his hopes by far. The NAACP and the Urban League, both much more conservative than he, agreed to join in the sponsorship. So did many black church groups. Committees sprang up all over the country, frequently under the inspiration of Randolph's army of traveling emissaries, the sleeping car porters. Only the Communists were not welcome, Randolph made clear, as active participants in the event.

"We organized around bread-and-butter issues," Bayard Rustin recalled. "All whites had to do was be able to breathe, and they were making fantastic salaries in airplane factories. To put it simply, the blacks wanted a piece of the action. They had sons, uncles, cousins going to war, and they figured that whites shouldn't be the only ones to get some economic benefits from it. We organized Chicago, New York, Los Angeles, San Francisco, Washington. I didn't see such fantastic meetings, such enthusiasm, again until I went into Montgomery with King in 1956."

204

Toward the end of spring, 1941, the enthusiasm among blacks was too great for the government to ignore. On June 18, with less than two weeks to go, Roosevelt invited Randolph to the White House for an encounter which, according to firsthand accounts, was not pleasant. Before a roomful of officials, Randolph told the president he would not abandon his plans without explicit concessions in return. He offered to drop his demand for immediate integration of the armed forces only on condition that Roosevelt promulgate an executive order barring job discrimination both in industry and in government.

Incredulous at Randolph's obstinacy, Roosevelt finally agreed to appoint a committee to draft an executive order. But Randolph still refused to call off the march. The actual drafting of the order was assigned to a young government lawyer from Cincinnati named Joseph L. Rauh, Jr., then embarking on a lifetime of activism in civil rights. Before Randolph approved it, Rauh had written and revised a half-dozen versions. Finally on June 25, six days before the scheduled event, Roosevelt signed the paper.

Executive Order 8802, as it was known to history, declared that "there shall be no discrimination in the employment of workers in defense industries or government because of race, creed, color or national origin." Shortly afterward, Roosevelt kept a pledge to Randolph by appointing a Fair Employment Practices Commission (FEPC), endowed with powers to enforce the order. Unimportant as it appears from the perspective of a later era, Executive Order 8802 was the government's most significant action in behalf of black citizens since Reconstruction, and it would have no rival in the field of civil rights for another quarter of a century.

When Randolph canceled the March on Washington, the federal government relaxed, but some of his supporters were furious. Rustin was then cochairman of the young division, arranging for buses to take young people to Washington. He was among those in the division who protested Randolph's decision. The protesters reasoned that a demonstration of the power that blacks could mobilize would, in the long run, have been more valuable even than the jobs that the FEPC could deliver.

Randolph was indignant at the dissidents, though they were only reciting back to him the organizational philosophy that he had taught them. He called them romantics, "who apparently were

205

more interested in the drama and pyrotechnics of the march than in the basic and main issue of putting Negroes to work."

One of Randolph's considerations was surely his fear that far fewer than the hundred thousand blacks that he claimed would come to Washington, conveying an impression of very little power at all. In fact, there was a widespread belief that the talk of a march was altogether nothing but a bluff. Nonetheless, Randolph's cancellation was a huge disappointment to the many blacks who had, in a few months, come to identify with the March on Washington as an expression of their rising discontent.

Randolph prolonged the March on Washington Committee, to serve both as a watchdog over the FEPC and as the machinery for future action. The FEPC did deliver a large number of jobs and, after it was dismantled in a surrender to Southern power at the end of the war, remained as a discarded symbol of the federal government's compassion. No further use was ever made, however, of the March on Washington Committee's organizing machinery. Periodically, in the years after 1941, Randolph announced consideration of other marches, to protest other grievances, but none of them ever took place.

"During the riots in Harlem in 1943," Rustin remembered, "one of the things destroyed was the March on Washington headquarters on a hundred and twenty-fifth street. The destruction was intentional. Scrawled on the wall was, 'Randolph, why don't you march?' I think the writers were trying to say to him, 'Get on with it. We're in a bad state. Do something!' "

Rustin went his own way after the cancellation of the March on Washington. The Fellowship of Reconciliation had actually paid his salary to work on the march, and, when Randolph no longer needed him, he decided to go back to it, to carry FOR's principles of nonviolence into the struggle against racial segregation.

Fighting racism through civil disobedience in those days was lonely work, and required incredible courage. In 1942, Rustin wrote of a trip from Louisville in which he was pulled from the bus by four policemen for refusing to sit with blacks in the back. After an initial round of kicks and blows, he wrote, he stood up, spread his arms parallel to the ground and said, "There is no need to beat

206

me. I am not resisting you." Nonetheless, the assault continued. Even in his pain, however, Rustin saw a victory in the plea made in his behalf by three white passengers, and in the reaction of a young policeman who averted his eyes during the drive to the station in a police car.

Later in the day, having won the respect of the assistant district attorney for his pacifism, he was addressed as "Mister Rustin," and was told that he could leave without charges. "I left the court-house," he wrote, "believing all the more strongly in the non-violent approach." Rustin said that from these small signs he took hope that ultimately nonviolence would liberate the white hearts and black bodies held in bondage by segregation.

His solitary experiences emulating Thoreau in civil disobedi-ence, Rustin said, led him to the study of Gandhi's methods for practicing nonviolence on a massive scale. "Randolph taught me that while Thoreau was great," Rustin said, "Gandhi was greater, because he organized masses." Still, Randolph was skeptical about whether a language familiar to Indians could be made comprehen-sible to oppressed Negroes in America. For himself, Rustin said, he felt compelled to make the try. He had reached a conclusion that without massive nonviolence there would be a massive racial con-flict that would not be nonviolent at all. Such a conflict, he said, would be a catastrophe.

"Having lived in a society in which church, school and home problems have been handled in a violent way," Rustin wrote dur-ing World War II, "the majority of blacks at this point are unable to conceive of a solution by reconciliation and non-violence. I have seen schoolboys in Arkansas laying away rusty guns for the 'time when'. I have heard many young men in the armed forces hope for a machine gun assignment 'so I can turn it on the white folks'. I have seen a white sailor beaten in Harlem because three Negroes had been 'wantin' to get just one white' before they died. I have heard hundreds of Negroes hope for a Japanese military victory, since 'it doesn't matter who you're a slave for'."

Rustin argued within FOR to have it step up the effort to per-suade the Negro that his best hope for progress lay in nonviolent direct action. He acknowledged that a commitment to nonviolence would demand terrible sacrifice and long suffering, and even a willingness to die. But, quoting Gandhi, he said, "freedom does not

207

drop from the sky." Rustin insisted that American Negroes could create a dynamic force, based on a Christian technique, that would free not only themselves but others who were oppressed throughout the world.

"Certainly the Negro possesses qualities essential for non-violent direct action," Rustin wrote prophetically in 1942. "He has long since learned to endure suffering. He can admit his own share of guilt and has to be pushed hard to become bitter. He has produced, and still sings, such songs as 'It's Me, Oh Lord, Standin' in the Need of Prayer' and 'Nobody Knows the Trouble I've Seen'. He follows this last tragic phrase by a salute to God—'Oh! Glory, Hallelujah'. He is creative and has learned to adjust himself to conditions easily. But above all he possesses a rich religious heritage and today finds the church the center of his life."

In 1943, Rustin went to prison for refusing to be drafted. He had registered early in the war as a conscientious objector, which made him eligible for non-combatant service. Later he withdrew his claim, on the grounds that any kind of military service was inconsistent with his beliefs. He also told his draft board he had to refuse to do duty in a segregated army because "I must use my whole being to combat by non-violent means the ever-growing racial tension in the United States." Rustin remained in Lewisburg Penitentiary in Pennsylvania until the war was over in August, 1945.

"I came out of prison," Rustin said, "realizing that talking to individuals about being good is a pile of crap. You've got to have a social organization which helps people bring out the goodness in them, not one that brutalizes them. That's basically what Randolph always said."

In the decade after World War II, Rustin was something of an eclectic in humanist movements, promoting pacifism and equality, confident like his friend Jim Farmer that an uprising for civil rights one day would come. He moved back and forth between CORE and FOR, sending speakers here and there for conferences on racism, conducting workshops on nonviolent disobedience, lecturing in black churches and colleges.

His most dramatic action was the Journey of Reconciliation, which he undertook in the belief that young blacks returning from

208

the war were ready to strike back at Jim Crow. He turned out to be mistaken, and young blacks did not respond to it at all. His experience did impart to him a certain renown among the movement's faithful, but it was not until fifteen years later in the Freedom Ride that the Journey yielded a major harvest.

At Randolph's instigation, in 1948 Rustin organized and ran the League for Nonviolent Civil Disobedience Against Military Segregation. The league's program was directed at President Truman's universal military training bill, which Randolph insisted was "pregnant with indecency" for perpetuating military segregation. In a meeting that duplicated the encounter with Roosevelt in 1941, Randolph told an angry president that Negroes would no longer take up arms for the United States if they were denied democracy at home. When Truman refused to change his mind on desegregation, Randolph promised a massive civil disobedience campaign.

The league's program corresponded to Rustin's beliefs in two ways. Rustin was hostile not only to a segregated army; he was hostile to any army whatever. "The organizers and perpetuators of segregation are as much the enemy of America as any foreign invader," he declared. "The time has come when they are not merely to be protested. They must be resisted." These were strong words, and made even stronger in 1948 in the context of an accelerating Cold War. Rustin announced plans to establish "disciplined cells" across the country, to offer advice on draft resistance and provide spiritual, financial and legal aid to draft resisters.

At the Democratic National Convention in 1948, Randolph led a picket line carrying a sign that read, "Prison Is Better Than Army Jim Crow." Inside, Hubert H. Humphrey, the young mayor of Minneapolis, was leading a drive to commit the party to a strong civil rights program. His chief strategist was Joe Rauh, the civil rights lawyer who had worked with Randolph in 1941 to draft the FEPC order. Truman, fearful of dividing the party, resisted Humphrey's effort. But when Humphrey won on the convention floor, and the Southern delegates stalked out, Truman was forced to turn to black votes in the Northern cities for reelection. Within weeks, he had ordered an end to segregation in the armed forces, and Randolph called off the civil disobedience campaign.

Rustin was annoyed, as he had been over Randolph's abandonment of the March on Washington in 1941. But Randolph, unlike

209

Rustin, had left his pacifism behind him. Much to Randolph's irritation, Rustin kept the league alive, and engaged in pacifist agitation for almost six months after Truman's order. Finally, Randolph squeezed off its funds and the league collapsed. Once again rebuked, Rustin gravitated back to the FOR.

In 1950, FOR sent Rustin to India for a year and a half to study nonviolent direct action with Gandhi's disciples. When he returned, he and some friends from the FOR established a committee against apartheid in South Africa. From 1953 to 1955, Rustin served as executive secretary of the War Resisters League. He also traveled several times, at FOR's behest, to West Africa to serve as an adviser to black political leaders during the wave of peaceful decolonization there. Between his other assignments, Rustin appeared on platforms and in print to argue that racial discrimination was not only immoral, but ought to be fought vigorously.

When the bus boycott began in Montgomery at the end of 1955, Rustin saw the budding of the nonviolent revolution he was waiting for. He considered the Supreme Court's *Brown* decision the year before a radical break with history, but it was overshadowed, in his mind and in Randolph's, by the huge popular response to Martin Luther King's call in Montgomery for nonviolent action. His first instinct was to go to Montgomery to offer his help to King, and Randolph agreed to send him.

But a troublesome problem intruded, which in the conformist atmosphere of the mid-1950s threatened to neutralize Rustin's potential to the movement entirely. Rustin admitted having been a Communist, and had gone to jail for refusing the draft. As if that were not enough, however, he took no serious pains to conceal that he was a homosexual, and on at least one occasion he had been arrested in a homosexual episode. His past thus made Rustin a natural target in the age of McCarthy for whoever wanted to smear the civil rights cause.

As a consequence, some of Randolph's comrades objected when he proposed to send Rustin to Montgomery. According to Rustin, Norman Thomas, leader of the Socialist party and a member of the Fellowship of Reconciliation, said, "This young King is doing very well. Bayard is considered a homosexual, a Communist and a draft

210

dodger. Why do you put such a burden on King?" Rustin said the consensus seemed to be to keep him at home, until Randolph phoned King himself. King answered that he knew of Rustin's reputation within the movement, and that his need for help superseded his concerns. So Rustin went to Montgomery and became a member of King's inner circle, where he remained off and on through the rest of King's life.

Rustin performed a variety of tasks while he was in Montgomery, and was actually designated King's secretary. But he was careful not to become, as Norman Thomas had feared he might, a burden upon King. He had been warned by King's people, Rustin noted in his diary, that "they are trying to make out that Communists and New Yorkers are running our protest." So he remained inconspicuous, and his presence around King was rarely noted.

Rustin was an organizer, who shared with the Montgomery Improvement Association his experiences in such mundane areas as money-raising, car pools and press relations. He was the principal drafter of the plan that established the structure of the Southern Christian Leadership Conference. He told me he also tried to complement King's orientation toward Christian morality with some hard economic thinking, to turn the Montgomery protest to consideration of jobs, but King's mind was still far from economics. Rustin said he had much more success helping King to apply Gandhi's strategy to Montgomery's conditions. Probably more than anyone else, Rustin helped King give nonviolent direct action the new dimension it acquired in Montgomery.

Randolph, meanwhile, began laying plans to maintain the momentum that King had started. Though Randolph's own prestige remained high, the strength of the Brotherhood of Sleeping Car Porters, never great, continued to wither with the decline of passenger traffic on the railroads. Randolph's vision was to merge the NAACP's wealth and membership with King's moral preeminence to create a powerful political force. The task required reconciling the secular and the religious, New York and the Deep South, litigationists and evangelists in the American black community. Only a project of compelling magnitude could unite black leaders, Randolph knew, and mobilize the energy of the black masses. Naturally, his mind turned back to his vision of a March on Washington.

In March of 1957, Randolph, along with King and Roy Wilkins of

211

the NAACP, reached an agreement to sponsor the first of annual civil rights demonstrations at the Lincoln Memorial in Washington. In deference to King's Christian orientation, it was not to be called a March on Washington, a name that hinted of coercion, but a Prayer Pilgrimage. Out of respect for Wilkins's organizational needs, it was scheduled for May 17, third anniversary of the *Brown* decision, the NAACP's great judicial triumph. Bayard Rustin was put in charge of organization, though he was considered too controversial to be listed publicly as director.

The crowd at the rally, estimated at twenty-five thousand people, covered the steps of the Lincoln Memorial and spilled over as far as the Reflecting Pool. Washington's *Evening Star* noted that it was composed of "predominantly colored persons," among them celebrities from sports, entertainment and politics. The mayors of New York and Los Angeles, and the governors of four states, endorsed the demonstration. Randolph presided, and King delivered one of his famous speeches, in which he called out to the nation to "Give us the ballot, give us the ballot." Wilkins's NAACP paid most of the bills, and King's SCLC joined with Randolph's Brotherhood to pay the rest.

Though the event made no impact on Eisenhower, and the public response appeared to be negligible, Randolph refused to be discouraged. In the succeeding two years, he had Rustin organize similar demonstrations. They were both called the Youth March for Integrated Schools; the first drew eight thousand, the second, twenty-five thousand. To Randolph, they were important in keeping the King-Wilkins coalition together and, in retrospect, it is even fair to say that they were test runs for the great March on Washington of 1963. But more important, these rallies proclaimed, at least to the nation's blacks, that, in spite of Eisenhower and McCarthyism and massive resistance, there was an active civil rights movement gestating in America. The next spring, in Greensboro and on college campuses throughout the South, it was born.

The generation of Greensboro, however, was not particularly generous to A. Philip Randolph. The young men and women whose sit-ins transformed the 1960s in an instant were contemptuous of the 1950s, and indifferent to the men who had preceded them.

212

What did it matter that Randolph had crusaded against segregation for nearly fifty years, when they believed it was their own implacability at the lunch counters that broke down the first barriers? If they knew of Randolph at all, it was as a remote and largely irrelevant historical figure.

The others fared hardly better. King himself was regularly accused of timidity. Farmer, audacious as he had been at the start of the Freedom Ride, had been eclipsed when the going got tough. Wilkins seemed like the stodgiest of all, even if the NAACP remained the bulwark of the movement and its principal bankroller. As for Rustin, his commitment to an austere pacifism and to the details of organization seemed to offer nothing at all to the buoyant, aggressive, self-confident generation that had cracked open the decade.

For Rustin, the late 1950s and early 1960s were especially painful years, when he was not always able to keep ahead of the controversy that doggedly pursued him. In 1958, King chose not to offer him the directorship of SCLC because of the homosexuality issue. In 1960, King, under attack from conservative Baptist churchmen, decided he did not need Rustin among his advisers at all. Even SNCC snubbed Rustin, presumably for the Communist stigma, in order to obtain a grant from the AFL-CIO. Rustin continued his practice of free-lance consultations, but he busied himself mostly with the pacifist concerns of the War Resisters League, and remained in the twilight on civil rights.

Then, after the flurry of the sit-ins in 1960 and the Freedom Rides in 1961, the civil rights movement settled down, as if in preparation for a difficult siege. The Kennedy Administration continued to identify itself with the Negro cause, but in 1962 introduced only two minor voting rights bills. The president stepped up administrative sanctions to achieve school integration, but eight years after the *Brown* decision it was calculated that only 7.6 percent of black children in the South were enrolled with whites. Though more slowly, the campaign of nonviolent activism went on, allowing neither Southern white society nor the Federal government nor the public at large any respite from the irritating awareness of racial injustice. But the mere involvement of blacks in action, persistent and heroic though they were, resulted in no consistent pattern of victories.

213

The focus of civil rights activities in 1962 was Albany, Georgia, a middle-sized market city, where the whites who made up 60 percent of the population refused even minor concessions to local blacks. The campaign began with a series of Freedom Rides to challenge the city's defiance of the Interstate Commerce Commission's desegregation orders. Gradually, the various segments of the movement reached a consensus to make Albany its target for the year. Their theory held that a single major confrontation was more valuable in enlisting nationwide support for the movement than a scattering of skirmishes. The execution of the theory, however, required unified leadership, clear objectives and wholehearted support. In Albany, none of these components was present.

SNCC started the campaign, first establishing an office for voter registration, then sponsoring a series of Freedom Rides to open the city's segregated transportation facilities. King came in next, and generated SNCC's resentment by capturing the bulk of the publicity. The NAACP, as usual, grumbled at receiving no appreciation, but wound up paying the bills. CORE, seeing the terrain already overcrowded, made scarcely any pretense whatever of helping. The nominal direction of the campaign was conferred upon local blacks, through an umbrella organization called the Albany Movement. But it failed to mobilize more than a fraction of the city's black population, much less agree upon a set of objectives or keep the various participating groups from squabbling.

Though the campaign received nationwide attention, events were dominated not by the protesters but by Chief of Police Laurie Pritchett. To neutralize the impact of nonviolence, his police conducted themselves with great restraint. Before arresting demonstrators, Pritchett sometimes even prayed with them. King, vowing to stay in jail after one arrest, was mysteriously bailed out. In spite of mass jailings, the support of Protestant, Catholic and Jewish clergymen who came down from the North to march, and the city's stubbornness, the campaign petered out. The white violence which had inspired solidarity among civil rights forces in other battles remained absent, and in the fall of 1962 King went home defeated, feeling angry with himself.

The Justice Department was clearly grateful and Attorney General Kennedy even wired congratulations to Chief Pritchett for keeping the peace. The Justice Department was no doubt aware of repeated instances of brutality inflicted behind the jailhouse doors, but chose to ignore them. Washington's signal seemed to be that the South could do as it liked if it maintained a facade of order. The civil rights movement recognized dangerous implications in this message, and feared that the Kennedy Administration was beating a serious retreat.

President Kennedy did intervene once in 1962, under circumstances that left as little choice as Eisenhower had faced in 1957 in Little Rock. Governor Ross Barnett of Mississippi had defied the explicit order of a federal court to enroll James H. Meredith, a black Mississippian and an Air Force veteran, in the state university. The president had negotiated personally with the governor, who, having been found in contempt, announced that he would rather go to jail than enroll a black in Ole Miss.

As registration day neared, the president federalized the Mississippi National Guard, dispatched units of the army to nearby positions and ordered 320 federal marshals to the campus. On the night of September 30, a mob of twenty-five hundred—of which only a small fraction were students—defied a televised plea by the president and attacked the marshals. By dawn, more than half of the marshals had been injured or wounded, and two men, one of them a foreign journalist, were dead.

Federal troops finally drove the rioters off, and at 8:30 A.M. the marshals escorted Meredith to his enrollment. Federal forces remained on the Mississippi campus to keep order, and the principle of law enforcement had been upheld. But it seemed unlikely that Washington could withstand many such crises without acknowledging an outright state of rebellion.

By the end of 1962 a few harsh truths, obscured earlier by the euphoria of the sit-ins and the Freedom Rides, had been demonstrated to the civil rights leadership. There was no question now that the movement was unlikely to win significant victories, even with the help of the courts, without enlisting the enforcement powers of the federal government. It was also apparent that the white South could survive an endless series of local battles, and only sweeping federal legislation could transform the terms of the struggle. It was equally clear that the movement had its best chance of succeeding if it devised a unified strategy and concentrated its forces on big, dramatic ventures. It was with such considerations in

215

mind that the idea for the March on Washington of 1963 began to crystallize.

A. Philip Randolph, from whose thoughts a March on Washington was never very distant, first raised the prospect with Bayard Rustin during a chat at the Brotherhood's headquarters in Harlem in December 1962. The two men—the one now seventy-three, the other fifty-one—were both conscious of the movement's recent failures, and of their own estrangement from it. Both were impatient to get back into the struggle.

Randolph's preoccupation was, as usual, with economic power for blacks, to which he knew neither King nor Wilkins nor Farmer gave high priority. Randolph proposed to Rustin that an Emancipation March for Jobs be held in Washington, to commemorate the centenary of the Emancipation Proclamation in 1963. Rustin agreed at the Brotherhood office that day to draw up some plans along the lines that Randolph contemplated.

Rustin turned over the actual drafting of a memo to Norman Hill, an assistant program director at CORE, and Tom Kahn, a white graduate student at Howard University. Both had met Rustin years before while working in the Young People's Socialist League. Hill had been a volunteer in the two Youth Marches to Washington. Kahn had been active in the League for Industrial Democracy, and was one of Tom Hayden's antagonists at the Port Huron convention the previous spring. Like Randolph and Rustin, both identified themselves as Socialists, closer to the Old Left than the New. They saw civil rights as part of the class struggle, and visualized the march as an instrument for rectifying economic injustice.

The two proposed in the memo that the March be conducted under the sponsorship of the Negro American Labor Council, an association of black trade unionists which Randolph had formed within the AFL-CIO. They suggested a two-day program, for a Friday and Saturday in May, with the first day dedicated to visits to the White House and Congress by labor, church and civil rights leaders, the second to a mass rally to project a specific "emancipation program" of federal economic intervention. They proposed that Randolph seek support from Walter Reuther of the Automobile Workers and other "progressive" union officials. Almost as an after-

216

thought, they suggested that Randolph also be in touch with King, Wilkins and Farmer.

Randolph quickly accepted the conception contained in the Kahn-Hill memorandum. On March 7, 1963, he issued to the Negro American Labor Council a call for a "vast, massive, nationwide Emancipation March on the Nation's Capital for Jobs." In a voice that recalled the labor movement of the 1930s, he continued: "Let the black laboring masses speak! Negro workers, ARISE and MARCH." When the response to this call was barely discernible, Randolph talked further with Rustin, and decided to include among the goals the breakdown of racial barriers over a wide range of American life. Randolph and Rustin also agreed to change the name of the demonstration to the March on Washington for Jobs and Freedom.

Meanwhile Martin Luther King, Jr., still smarting over the setback in Albany, had seized the initiative in Birmingham, Alabama. Just as the March on Washington of 1941 remained Randolph's strategic model, so the mass action in Montgomery of 1956 was King's. Just as Randolph's organizing principle was creation of the widest possible coalition, so King's was to work through the churches, and keep control in the hands of ministers. In the spring of 1963, while Randolph's plans languished, King enjoyed a spectacular triumph. Ultimately the Birmingham campaign set the stage for a more dazzling March on Washington than anyone ever dreamed of, but it was months before King was ready to turn the attention of the movement back to Randolph's idea.

Birmingham had the reputation of being the most inflexibly segregated city in the South. Under Bull Connor, the police force was known as the South's most brutal. In the spring of 1963, furthermore, Bull Connor was running for mayor.

For a year Reverend Fred Shuttlesworth, the fearless bantam who headed Birmingham's SCLC affiliate, had tried to persuade King to lead a confrontation with the city. Shuttlesworth argued that Connor was psychologically incapable of adopting Albany's tactics of restraint, and that official savagery would demonstrate the evils of segregation to the world. Shuttlesworth insisted that, by taking on and conquering the toughest city in the South, the movement could prove that segregation's day was indeed finished. King was finally won over, and pledged that, to expiate the failure at Albany, he would stay on in Birmingham until the job was done.

To avoid fueling Connor's mayoral campaign, King delayed the start of demonstrations until after election day. Connor lost, but when he contested the count, King rejected further postponement. On April 2, 1963, twenty blacks were arrested trying to integrate a Birmingham department store. Three days later, forty-two more were jailed during a protest march to City Hall. The next day, Palm Sunday, snarling police dogs followed at the heels of twenty-five marchers on a "prayer pilgrimage," in which all were arrested. On Good Friday, King himself, leading a column of fifty hymn-singing blacks, was seized and thrown roughly into a police van.

For the first time, King shed his usual coat and tie for the march, in favor of the denim workclothes that had become the trademark of SNCC. The new costume was King's signal that he had embarked on a more militant phase of his career. His arrest added a new dimension to the campaign. President Kennedy phoned Mrs. King, as he had in 1960, to tell her that FBI agents had been instructed to see that her husband was not mistreated. Meanwhile, the growing harshness of the police, particularly the snapping police dogs, had become good copy for newspapers and television. Connor was falling into King's trap.

By the time King was bailed out of jail eight days later, public indignation was widespread, and Birmingham had become the focus of international attention. The campaign had so far failed to provoke the federal intervention that its planners sought, however. Kennedy made no public statement on the Birmingham situation, and the Justice Department insisted that no legal violation within its jurisdiction had occurred.

On May 2, 1963, King unveiled the controversial weapon of children's marches and nearly a thousand kids from six to sixteen were arrested. The next day, when the children marched again, Connor brought out water hoses, and used the dogs to attack them. On Sunday, May 5, blacks conducted "kneel-ins" at fourteen white churches, ten of which coldly turned them away. By Tuesday another thousand demonstrators had been arrested and, with the jails too crowded to take more inmates, Connor took to breaking up the marches with powerful blasts of water. When Shuttlesworth was

218

injured and hospitalized, the discipline of nonviolence began breaking down. Connor responded to rock and bottle attacks by calling in reinforcements from the state troopers, who were reputedly even more ruthless than his own men.

Robert Kennedy, fearful now of massive disorder, issued a statement supporting the demonstrators' goals, while deploring their "timing," and sent Burke Marshall to Birmingham to seek a settlement. Having learned from the blacks of their terms, Marshall turned to the white business leaders, and found they were disposed to reach an agreement. At Kennedy's request, but over Shuttlesworth's objections, King on Wednesday agreed to a twenty-four-hour truce.

President Kennedy conceded at a press conference that the Birmingham conflict had become a "spectacle which was seriously damaging the reputation" of the country. But he continued to resist federal intervention by denying that federal statutes had been violated. King did not agree. He responded publicly to the president that among the laws which Birmingham had broken was the arrest of blacks going to the courthouse to register to vote.

King continued to meet with the city's businessmen, however, and on Thursday, May 9, he announced that agreement had been reached on most of the Negroes' demands. But a sticking point had developed over the city's plans to prosecute 960 demonstrators who were still in jail. That afternoon, the Kennedy Administration began a feverish effort to establish a bonding fund for the jailed demonstrators. Meanwhile, in the absence of an accord, King and the black leadership prepared for resumption of the marches the next morning.

Before the demonstrations started on Friday, King announced that the agreement had been concluded. It provided for the desegregation of most public facilities in downtown Birmingham, the hiring and promotion of blacks in local business and industry, and the establishment of a permanent biracial committee to deal with ongoing problems between the races. The hard work of the Kennedy Administration resolved the remaining issue: the AFL-CIO, along with its constituent unions, raised $160,000, and the 960 demonstrators were released on bond.

King called the settlement "the most significant victory for justice we've ever seen in the Deep South" and characteristically, he

219

added that, "We must now move from protest to reconciliation." The white diehards were not disposed to reconciliation, however. Bull Connor promptly called for a white boycott of desegregated businesses. Outgoing Mayor Arthur G. Hanes called the negotiators "quisling, gutless traitors." Alabama's Governor George Wallace declared that any "compromise on the issues of segregation" was unacceptable.

The next night, after the Ku Klux Klan held a rally on the edge of town, dynamite blasts demolished the home of King's younger brother, Reverend A. D. King, and blew a hole in the side of the Gaston Motel, a black establishment which served as King's head-quarters. About midnight a large crowd of irate blacks gathered at the Gaston Motel. Shouting its contempt for nonviolence, the crowd set off on a rampage. Several whites were dragged from their cars and beaten, several white-owned stores were looted and set ablaze. State troopers used rifle butts to disperse the rioters, and it was not until dawn that peace was restored.

The disorders persuaded President Kennedy to alert military units trained in riot control for deployment in Birmingham. Gover-nor Wallace protested armed enforcement of "a worthless agree-ment made by a so-called biracial committee," but there was no rioting the next day and the troops were not needed. Birmingham businessmen endorsed the desegregation agreement and promised to implement it. The *Birmingham News*, long an ally of Jim Crow, also lined up behind it. Then, before the month was out, the Su-preme Court ruled on Birmingham's contested mayoralty election, and confirmed Bull Connor's defeat. The new city administration, though far from integrationist, promised to uphold the law, against white violence no less than black. For the Deep South the promise was, indeed, a major change.

Still, the Jim Crow system had not been broken. Businessmen had agreed to let Negroes use the same facilities as whites in Bir-mingham. In separate action, the Supreme Court rendered a deci-sion on May 20 that declared Birmingham's municipal segregation ordinances unconstitutional. But no positive right had been estab-lished that blacks could use the same public facilities available to whites. If Jim Crow was dying, there was still no law which said that Southern society could not, by private regulation, keep segre-gation alive a little longer. The conquest of Birmingham was a monumental achievement, but its chief meaning seemed to be that blacks had the power to beat Jim Crow by conducting comparable campaigns in every city in the South. This would have meant years of chaos. The only prospect for avoiding such chaos was federal enactment of sweeping antidiscrimination laws.

President Kennedy finally addressed himself to this need on June 11, 1963, proposing the most comprehensive civil rights bill in American history. It was the commitment on the part of the federal government that blacks, and their white liberal allies, had been urging Kennedy to make for two and a half years. The Birmingham struggle had made up his mind.

"The heart of the question," Kennedy declared, "is whether all Americans are to be afforded equal rights and equal opportunities, whether we are going to treat our fellow Americans as we want to be treated. If an American, because his skin is dark, cannot eat lunch in a restaurant open to the public, if he cannot send his children to the best public school available, if he cannot vote for the public officials who represent him, if, in short, he cannot enjoy the full and free life which all of us want, then who among us would be content to have the color of his skin changed and stand in his place? Who among us would then be content with the counsels of patience and delay? . . . The events in Birmingham and elsewhere have so increased the cries for equality that no city or State or legislative body can prudently choose to ignore them."

Kennedy's bill proposed to give all Americans the right to be served in facilities open to the public, authorize federal intercession in lawsuits to end school segregation, and provide greater protection of the right to vote. When it was sent to Capitol Hill a week later, the bill contained, in addition, a proposal to establish a Community Relations Service to act as an intermediary in racial crises. It also promised the enforcement of equal employment practices, though the section was weaker, ironically, than the executive order Roosevelt had delivered to Randolph a quarter-century before.

Meanwhile, the Birmingham demonstrations sent reverberations through black communities across the nation. Within two days of Kennedy's civil rights speech, there were demonstrations as far afield as New York, Columbus and Tallahassee. According to Jus-

221

tice Department calculations, blacks engaged in 758 demonstrations in 186 cities of the South in the succeeding ten weeks. The Southern Regional Council estimated that nearly fifteen thousand persons were arrested in the wake of Birmingham in 1963, far more than during the wave of sit-ins in 1960.

The race struggle in the spring of 1963 also took a more violent turn. On April 23, William L. Moore, a white postman from Baltimore, was shot dead on an Alabama highway while carrying a sign saying "Equal Rights for All." On June 12, Medgar Evers, field secretary of the Mississippi NAACP, was murdered by a sniper's bullet outside his home in Jackson. Black violence was less deadly, but Birmingham was not the only city in which orderly demonstrations had led to mob rioting. The discipline of nonviolence seemed to be slipping away.

"No longer can white liberals merely be proud of those well-dressed students, who are specialists in non-violent action," Bayard Rustin wrote prophetically in the days after Birmingham. "Now they are confronted with a Negro working class that is demanding equal opportunity and full employment."

Rustin predicted that the battle would soon move North, where despairing blacks would turn against racist political and economic institutions. "The Negro masses," he noted somberly, ". . . are going to move. Nothing can stop them from moving. And if Negro leadership does not move rapidly and effectively enough, they will take it into their own hands and move anyhow."

This is the argument that Randolph made when he described the plans for the March on Washington to President Kennedy on June 22, 1963. The president had invited the top civil rights leaders to the White House to urge them to give their highest priority to his civil rights bill. Though Kennedy did not express opposition to the March, he contended that his bill had a better chance of passing if blacks stayed off the streets and appeared unthreatening.

"The Negroes are already in the streets . . . ," Randolph answered. "Is it not better that they be led by organizations dedicated to civil rights and disciplined by struggle rather than to leave them to other leaders* who care neither about civil rights nor nonviolence?" Having been conceived in the winter as an instrument for

* Randolph was no doubt thinking specifically of the Communists.

222

grumbled about a White House tactic to use them. The March was to bring thousands of demonstrators to Washington to make a declaration against injustice—and President Kennedy had adroitly established the position that his government was innocent of any blame.

The shift deprived the March of its anger. It also turned attention away from Randolph's early themes of economic power and employment. The change became irrevocable when three prominent clergymen—Mathew Ahmann of the National Catholic Conference for Interracial Justice, Dr. Eugene Carson Blake of the National Council of Churches and Rabbi Joachim Prinz of the American Jewish Congress—joined the black leadership as sponsors. In all, some one hundred civic, labor and religious organizations announced their support. The most prominent dissenter was George Meany, the stubborn president of the AFL-CIO, who was the backbone of the civil rights lobby on Capitol Hill but who disliked demonstrations. He started no trend. In fact, as the days passed, the March increasingly adopted the posture of a moral witness against evil; participation became not a matter of politics but of conscience, and support swelled.

One of the few ugly notes during the weeks of organization came when Senator Strom Thurmond of South Carolina, who had been the Dixiecrat candidate for president in 1948, took to the floor to denounce Rustin as a Communist, a draft dodger and a homosexual. That the attack had been anticipated did not make it any less upsetting. Rustin issued an answer refuting the first two charges, and said he would not condescend to reply to the third.

In Rustin's files I found a briefing paper with the answer Randolph would have given had he been questioned by the press on the subject. "Twenty-two arrests in the fight for civil rights attest, in my mind, to Mr. Rustin's dedication to high human ideals . . . ," it said. "That Mr. Rustin was on one occasion arrested in another connection has long been a matter of public record, and not an object of concealment. There are those who contend that this incident, which took place many years ago, voids or overwhelms Mr. Rustin's ongoing struggle for human rights. I hold otherwise." Nothing more was heard of the matter, and Thurmond's effort to make Rustin an issue failed completely.

A week before the March, *Life* provided its readers with a fore-

stirring up the black masses, the March had been transformed by spring, at least in the mind of Randolph, into a channel for containing them.

Arthur Schlesinger, Jr., who was present at the meeting with the blacks, remembered that Martin Luther King acknowledged to the president that the March might seem ill-timed, but had then added: "Frankly, I have never engaged in any direct action movement which did not seem ill-timed. Some people thought Birmingham ill-timed." According to Schlesinger, the president replied to King wryly, "Including the attorney general."

King, whose preeminence in the movement had been affirmed once more at Birmingham, was the key to Randolph's plan for a coalition to sponsor the March. To John Lewis at SNCC and James Farmer at CORE, the idea of a March seemed unduly tame, and they were skeptical of what it would achieve. Roy Wilkins at the NAACP and Whitney Young at the Urban League, though both increasingly militant, feared that a March on Washington might get out of hand. Once Randolph recruited King, however, the others would not risk being left out, and they promptly fell into line.

With King in the coalition, it seemed assured that the March on Washington would be unthreatening. SNCC's militants had to give up the thought they once entertained, which the old radical in Randolph had at least for a moment considered, of turning the event into a massive exercise of civil disobedience. By introducing the civil rights bill, Kennedy himself had acquired a stake in the civil rights movement, and his interests could not be ignored. Though the slogan for the March on Washington remained "for Jobs and Freedom," the goal shifted almost spontaneously to "Pass the Bill."

Bayard Rustin, whom Randolph had nominated as director of the March, was the only source of disagreement among the leaders. As Rustin remembered a leadership meeting in late June 1963, Wilkins complained that he, Rustin, "had too many scars—all the talk about his sex life, his political life, and his being a draft dodger. I just think he would be too much of a liability."

Wilkins's objections could not be ignored. Though the initial funds for the March had been put up by a New York trade union, the NAACP's treasury and manpower were indispensable to its success. The others in the room argued that no one could organize the March like Rustin, and Wilkins finally agreed to a compromise. Randolph would be named director, and Rustin would hold the title of deputy. The date of the March was fixed for August 28.

During the first week in July, Rustin set up headquarters in a four-story walk-up at 170 West 130 Street in Harlem. The original staff was composed of delegates from the sponsoring organizations, but volunteers rapidly swelled the ranks. Open virtually round-the-clock, the headquarters was a hive in which the crescendo of activity rose as the day drew closer.

"We had about two hundred people working in the national office and we had people working in almost every city in the country," Rustin remembered. "If you want to organize anything, assume that everybody is absolutely stupid. And assume yourself that you're stupid. What would I do under the circumstance? Or if this happened? There is just something about people moving in numbers which reduces their ability to function carefully.

"We wanted to get everybody, from the whole country, into Washington by nine o'clock in the morning and out of Washington by sundown. This required all kinds of things that you had to think through. You had to think how many toilets you needed. Where they should be? Where is your line of march? We had to consult doctors on exactly what people should bring to eat so that they wouldn't get sick. We even told people what to bring in their lunches. We had to arrange for drinking water. We had to arrange what we would do if there was a terrible thunderstorm that day. We had to think of the sound system. There were just a million things. We had to set up a bank. We had to notify everybody where the bank was in the event that anybody got lost or lost their pocketbook and didn't have money to get home.

"The interesting thing is that there were over a quarter of a million people and we only had to spend something like four hundred dollars for welfare. Absolutely fantastic!"

Rustin's planning was based on the estimate of a hundred thousand demonstrators, which had been Randolph's magic number for the March when the dream was born in 1941. Based on that figure, a budget of $65,000 was fixed and, to avoid any hint of corruption, Rustin set up rigorous accounting procedures. In the end, both the

attendance and the expenditures exceeded the estimate[s] than twice, but there was no scandal to comfort the enem[y] March, and Rustin's organizational structure survived int[act].

In his press conference of July 17, President Kenne[dy] known that he had become a convert. He called the [...] "peaceful assembly for the redress of grievances," and [...] "They are going to express their strong views. I think [...] great tradition. I look forward to being there." His state[ment] a lift to the civil rights cause, and signaled the federal b[ureau] to cooperate on arrangements with Rustin's staff.

Rustin himself did most of the crucial negotiating with [Washing]ton police officials. The capital was no longer the tens[e segre]gated city it had been in 1941, and blacks would have [...] finding places to eat. Rustin, moreover, had recruited tra[ined New] York policemen, from a black association called the Gu[ardians to] serve as volunteers in crowd control. But, without polic[e coopera]tion, the March could have been a disaster, and the W[ashington] police were not known for a fondness for blacks. With [orders] from Kennedy, however, they conducted themselves v[ery profes]sionally and, like the other federal agencies, cheerfull[y gave] support.

Still, no one could predict how several hundred thous[and pro]ters might behave on a torrid August day, especially if p[rovoked by] black militants or white antagonists. Much was beyond [the reach] of the organizers and the police. Rustin himself raised a [chilling] prospect when he said to officials, "If Negroes comin[g up] from Mississippi were attacked and the buses burned, [as hap]pened in our recent history, let us say the night before, t[hen we are] faced with a totally new psychological situation." A[s the day] neared, in spite of a rising euphoria, a dread of the [unknown] surrounded the March.

Yet Kennedy's blessing imbued the March on W[ashington,] which had begun as a massive protest, with a positi[ve public] purpose. Unlike the march that Randolph had promise[d in 1941,] the March of 1963 was not directed against the g[overnment.] Though it began that way, President Kennedy had turne[d it around] and made it an instrument of his domestic policy. N[ot everyone] approved of the transformation. While members of Co[ngress com]plained of a White House effort to intimidate them, ma[ny] cast of the scope of the event: two trains and three planes had already been chartered from Chicago, and four planes from California; six hundred buses had been reserved in New York alone. *Life* reported that "freedom trains" were scheduled to head north from Miami, Jacksonville and Birmingham, stopping throughout the South to pick up demonstrators. "Altogether, according to Rustin's headquarters," *Life* said, "as many as 30 special trains, a score of planes and 2,000 chartered buses may reach Washington on the 28th." The estimates, in fact, proved modest.

The March began at dawn on August 28, 1963, with one thousand people already gathered at the foot of the Washington Monument. By 10:30 the crowd had grown to fifty thousand, and police reported that highways leading to the city were packed bumper to bumper with cars and buses. As the hours passed the temperature rose to 84 degrees, but clear skies and a cool breeze kept the day comfortable.

The signs the marchers carried, faithful to Rustin's instructions, were uniformly friendly. As a precaution, bars and liquor stores had been closed, and government workers urged to take the day off. But the few disruptive incidents that occurred were handled expeditiously by the marshals or the police. In all the atmosphere was amiable, fraternal, even affectionate, no less so as blacks and whites pressed closer and closer together to accommodate the arriving waves.

At 11:20, having had its fill of entertainment by such celebrities as Josh White and Joan Baez, the crowd became impatient to get on with the main program of the day. Gradually the marchers converged and began a majestic walk down Constitution Avenue. Hand in hand in the first rank were Randolph, King, Wilkins, Young and other stalwarts of the movement. For Rustin it was a working day, and he remained back at the local headquarters, monitoring every facet of the event. By early afternoon, a quarter of a million people covered the acres in front of the Lincoln Memorial, standing, sitting on the grass, dangling their bare feet in the waters of the Reflecting Pool.

A. Philip Randolph presided over the official rites from the Lincoln Memorial steps. At seventy-four, he was unknown to much of

227

the crowd. Only a few were aware of his lifetime of service to the cause of racial equality, and fewer still recognized this day as the realization of a twenty-two-year-old dream. Randolph had suffered long years of disappointment and frustration. But, without him, there would have been no March on Washington, nor a civil rights movement of such diversity and strength.

"Fellow Americans," he declared in opening the program, "we are gathered here in the largest demonstration in the history of this nation. Let the nation and the world know the meaning of our numbers. We are not a pressure group, we are not an organization or a group of organizations, we are not a mob. We are the advance guard of a massive moral revolution for jobs and freedom." Then, in acknowledgment of the years of struggle that remained, he said, "We here today are only the first wave . . . We shall return again and again to Washington in ever-growing numbers, until total freedom is ours."

Perhaps better than any of the speakers, Reverend Eugene Carson Blake of the National Council of Churches struck a theme that pervaded the March, a theme of moral identification by whites with the cause of racial justice, of white guilt for past neglect. "Late, late we come," declared Blake, ". . . to march behind and with those amazingly able leaders of the Negro Americans who, to the shame of almost every white American, have alone and without us mirrored the suffering of the cross . . ." Blake's words vindicated, for a glimmering moment, King's contention that the power of love, as expressed through Christian nonviolence, could transform men's hearts. They acknowledged no likelihood that, after the sun set, squalid days would follow.

Martin Luther King, as one might have expected, delivered the speech which evoked the highest emotion. It was a revivalist sermon, like all of King's great speeches, relying not on any freshness of content but on the repetition of a theme, and eloquent phrases to which the audience could make its own cadenced response. "I have a dream," King declared again and again, as he elaborated on his vision of American society, North and South, where no man had to pay a price for the color of his skin. The audience picked up his rhythm and joined in his delivery, and for a moment the crowd was a huge congregation, united in Godly purpose.

SNCC, which had never been happy at the prospect of the

228

March, provided the day's discord. John Lewis, the chairman, had prepared a speech reflecting SNCC's growing militancy, castigating the Kennedy Administration for refusing to protect the workers in their voter registration efforts in Mississippi. Lewis had planned to denounce Kennedy's civil rights bill as inadequate, and declare that SNCC could not support it. He saw an opportunity for SNCC to shatter an illusion that the palliatives of liberal America could achieve the goals of racial justice. SNCC's rhetoric was now of revolution.

Holding to Rustin's rules, Lewis had handed in his text the night before, and when Archbishop Patrick O'Boyle of Washington, who was to deliver the invocation, learned what it contained he threatened to withdraw from the ceremonies. In a tiny room inside the Lincoln Memorial, Randolph and Rustin argued with Lewis that O'Boyle was not alone in his objections, and they pleaded with him to make revisions to preserve a facade of unity. After consultations with his SNCC colleagues, Lewis made the key compromise by agreeing to support the Kennedy bill "with reservations." Then he and his SNCC friends sat down to rewrite a final draft, which was finished only minutes before he stepped up to speak.

Lewis's speech was still, by far, the toughest of the day. "By the force of our demands, our determination and our numbers," he declared, "we shall splinter the segregated South into a thousand pieces, and put them back together in the image of God and democracy." His words were free of the love, the conciliation, the sweetness that characterized the other addresses.

What the crowd did not know, though a text had been leaked to the press, was what Lewis had intended to say, "We will march through the South, through the Heart of Dixie, the way Sherman did." "We shall pursue our own 'scorched earth' policy and burn Jim Crow to the ground—non-violently . . . We will take matters into our own hands and create a source of power, outside of any national structure, that could and would assure us a victory." These words foreshadowed SNCC's course, as it embarked toward the repudiation of black-white harmony, of nonviolence, of democratic change, of the spirit of the March on Washington. Before long, SNCC would leave even John Lewis behind.

But SNCC did not chill the day, and the March on Washington ended with an unprecedented throng of Americans, black and

229

white, basking in the contentment of a rare and special experience, which the millions more who watched on television in some measure shared. Though he declined to appear at the March itself, President Kennedy received the sponsors in his office late in the afternoon, then released a statement to the press. "One cannot help but be impressed," he said, "with the deep fervor and the quiet dignity that characterizes the thousands who have gathered in the Nation's Capital from across the country to demonstrate their faith and confidence in our democratic form of government . . . This nation can properly be proud of the demonstration that has occurred here today."

The fears of violence had proven groundless, and the predictions of administrative chaos vanished as the last buses left for home. Bayard Rustin had even provided for a contingent of volunteers to clean up the debris on the grounds around the Lincoln Memorial after the March was over.

"The March on Washington," Rustin said, "took place because the Negro needed allies . . . [It] broadened the base of the civil rights movement. The March was not a Negro action. It was an action by Negroes and whites together. Not just the leaders of the Negro organizations, but leading Catholic, Protestant and Jewish spokesmen called the people into the street. And Catholics, Protestants and Jews, white and black, responded."

In itself, the March probably made few converts. But it crystallized an evolution of national conscience that had been under way since World War II and had quickened irresistibly since 1960. It consecrated, for a fleeting but crucial moment, an alliance between American blacks and a wide community of liberal whites. When the March was over, there was no disputing any longer the breadth of the consensus on civil rights. The March did not work magic on the political system. The trauma of President Kennedy's death, and the skillful invocation of Kennedy's spirit by President Johnson, were required to pass the civil rights bill. But the March on Washington was the alchemy that prepared America for the change.

What the March on Washington did not do was respond in any significant way to black poverty. An on-the-scene survey by the Bureau of Social Science Research established that three-fourths of the marchers held white-collar jobs, and that virtually no poor or unemployed people were among them. Of the sponsors, neither blacks nor whites fully understood the insistence of Randolph and Rustin upon jobs, which seemed so banal an objective. Rustin's early proposal to bring jobless workers to the March was never financed. The sponsors were preoccupied, in Rustin's words, with "the problem of dignity." Only Rustin and Randolph seemed to understand that, even after the civil rights bill was enacted, there would be no dignity for those who did not have work.

Rustin acknowledged that, as he put it, "the problem of how to get jobs for Negroes is really the problem of how to get jobs for people." This problem was largely outside the special competence of the civil rights movement. Nonetheless, the civil rights movement could not ignore it, because jobs were crucial to the stability of black society. After the civil rights bill was passed, Rustin said, "economic issues were bound to emerge, with far-reaching implications." The problem lay in urban ghettos, where an ever larger number of blacks were concentrated. The March on Washington was largely irrelevant to them, and its goodwill was unequal to ameliorating the conditions of life. Yet it was with these problems that the civil rights movement would be increasingly preoccupied in the years that followed.

VII
JOSEPH L. RAUH, JR.:
Organizing Mississippi
1964

Automobile Workers, which carried with it a seat on the Leadership Conference for Civil Rights. The Leadership Conference was the direct descendant of the National Council for a Permanent FEPC, a lobbying coalition that Randolph had established after the March on Washington campaign of 1941. Its founding members were civil rights, religious and fraternal organizations, both Negro and white, and a handful of liberal labor unions, most notably Walter Reuther's United Automobile Workers. During the McCarthy years, the Leadership Conference encountered only indifference to civil rights, but Randolph's stature and Rauh's energy kept alive a hope that the federal government would someday be persuaded to act.

Lyndon B. Johnson, the Senate majority leader, was Rauh's chief antagonist in those days. Johnson, a New Deal liberal in his congressional years, had turned conservative under the influence of his Texas constituency after he entered the Senate in 1948. Throughout the 1950s, as Senate majority leader, Johnson frustrated all efforts to modify the Senate's filibuster rule, which was then regarded as the principal obstacle to the enactment of civil rights laws. Even in 1957, when Johnson cooperated with President Eisenhower to win passage of a modest civil rights bill, Rauh was unforgiving. "To give the devil his due," Rauh reminisced, "he got us the first civil rights bill since Reconstruction, but he also took out its teeth." In a speech as ADA chairman, Rauh complained that the Democrats under Johnson were practically indistinguishable from right-wing Republicans.

I met Joe Rauh when I first moved to Washington as a reporter for the *Washington Post* in the 1950s. I had known him by his reputation, which in those days was rooted in his resistance to McCarthyism more than in civil rights. I remember marveling, in the context of the times, at his courage. Later I covered Rauh in his capacity as leader of the Democratic party in the District of Columbia, his small political power base. As a news source, I found him open, accessible and generous.

In 1960, Rauh's first choice for the Democratic presidential nomination was his friend, Hubert Humphrey, then senator from Minnesota. When John Kennedy emerged far stronger in the primaries, Rauh worked to get Humphrey the vice-presidential nomination. Then, at the Democratic convention, Kennedy's people announced that the nomination would go instead to his nemesis, Lyndon John-

238

"Walter was cooler than I would have expected. I think he saw it immediately as a possible confrontation with (President) Johnson. At that point, the possibility hadn't even occurred to me."

A YEAR AFTER the March on Washington, the battlefield for racial equality had shifted from the cool shade of the Lincoln Memorial's gardens, where whites and blacks had united in common purpose, to the hot sun of Atlantic City's boardwalk, where the delegates of the Democratic party were convening for their national convention. The country had not yet emerged from the shock of John Kennedy's assassination. It had carried on intrepidly, trying to hide a sense of uncertainty. But the shabbiness of the old New Jersey beach resort to which the Democrats repaired seemed to bespeak the condition of America's morale.

Lyndon Johnson, Kennedy's successor, had served the country well. He had assumed the presidency somberly, and with dignity, promising to advance Kennedy's ambitious legislative program. He had applied himself diligently to the task, had even expanded on it, and by the time the Democrats reached Atlantic City he had made the elusive civil rights bill into law. Blacks and liberal whites had never worked more productively, or more harmoniously, than in the first months of the Johnson presidency. On the surface, the spirit of the March on Washington flourished, but the experience in Atlantic City would shatter the illusion.

No man embodied the March's spirit more than Joseph L. Rauh, Jr. One of the more familiar mementos of the day was a photograph of thousands of demonstrators, most of them casually dressed, flooding down Constitution Avenue between the elms. At their head was a rank of serious-looking men, bareheaded in the midday sun, wearing somber blue suits and dark neckties. They walked hand in hand, as brothers. A. Philip Randolph was among them. So were Martin Luther King, Jr., Whitney Young of the Urban League and Roy Wilkins of the NAACP. At their center was Joe Rauh.

235

The man in the photograph was in his fifties, tall and barrel-chested, and white. His facial features were coarse, his hair gray. He wore glasses and, as usual, a bow tie. Those who knew him were made comfortable by his absence of pretension, and many knew him, for Joe Rauh had for two decades been at the leading edge in battles across the nation for liberal causes. He marched that day as leader of the biracial lobby that worked the halls of Congress promoting enactment of the civil rights bill.

A profile of Joe Rauh would have shown him fairly typical of the white liberals who supported the civil rights movement. He was a white-collar professional, quite wealthy, a Democrat, a nonpracticing Jew. He had walked picket lines for desegregation but he was, basically, a lawyer and political tactician rather than an activist. He would have called himself a reformer, with a healthy suspicion of revolutionaries, and he worked zealously to achieve the movement's goals within the framework of the democratic process.

Joe Rauh was not involved in the March on Washington for its symbolism, its ultimate historical message, its spiritual values. He was not there to atone for sin or confess guilt. He had an uncomplicated, high-spirited, eminently practical instinct for social justice, and he saw the march as an instrument for applying pressure in Congress on representatives and senators.

Joe Rauh represented the long and noble tradition of service that white liberals rendered to the cause of racial equality. Over the years, white liberals gave most of the money, performed many of the chores and provided much of the expertise that the movement needed to survive. Most blacks had long considered whites like Joe Rauh an important asset in an otherwise unfriendly society. Among whites, few made more valuable contributions to civil rights than he had.

But within a year of the March on Washington, at Atlantic City, Joe Rauh was being bitterly denounced by blacks within the movement. It was not easy to understand why. President Johnson had been the most effective champion of civil rights in a century. As his running mate he would choose Hubert Humphrey, a politician who had again and again put his career on the line for civil rights. The party had promised more civil rights legislation, until genuine equality was achieved. Atlantic City was a triumphant moment for white liberals like Joe Rauh, but something had gone wrong.

At Atlantic City, the civil rights coalition shattered into frag-

ments. The aims and intentions of the Democratic party had be called into question. White liberal had become a term of reproa The movement's most dynamic segment was denouncing its form ally, Joe Rauh, as a turncoat. Militant blacks had acquired a ne orthodoxy, and declared that you could never trust a "dirty whi liberal."

Joseph L. Rauh, Jr., was born in Cincinnati in 1911, son of German immigrant who had prospered in business and industry He attended Harvard College and Harvard Law School. In 1935 he went to Washington to take a job as an assistant in the White House, then served as law clerk successively to Justices Benjamin Cardozo and Felix Frankfurter. He first became known in the area of civil rights in 1941, when he worked with A. Philip Randolph to draft the celebrated Executive Order 8802, signed by Roosevelt to establish the FEPC. When he came back from the war, Rauh started a law practice which permanently identified him with civil liberties and civil rights.

In 1947, Rauh joined with a handful of like-minded young men, Hubert H. Humphrey among them, to found a political organization they called Americans for Democratic Action. ADA was to be a gathering place for liberals interested in promoting a non-Communist left, and it quickly became a major influence on the Democratic party. In 1948, Rauh and Humphrey engineered the floor fight at the Democratic National Convention which led to the adoption of an aggressive civil rights plank. When the South walked out, Harry Truman was forced to turn to urban blacks for votes, and the part was embarked on a pro-civil rights course from which it neve turned back.

Rauh told me of an evening in 1950, after he won a case again union discrimination for A. Philip Randolph's Brotherhood. wanted to go out for a drink with Phil to celebrate," he recalle "but there was no place in Washington we could go. Washingt was the most legally segregated bastard of a town in the wh United States. So Phil, with his great dignity, simply said, 'Go night, Mr. Rauh. We'll make it another time.'" After that, Rauh his ADA friends began picketing in Washington, and helped Jim Crow there before the barriers crumbled elsewhere.

In the 1950s, Rauh became counsel for Walter Reuther's Un

son. Grabbing a microphone on the convention floor, Rauh declared angrily before a nationwide television audience, "Wherever you are, John F. Kennedy, I beseech you to reconsider." Kennedy did not reconsider, and Johnson left the Senate for the vice-presidency, leaving Rauh's hostility publicly exposed.

Liberals were bewildered then, when Lyndon Johnson emerged as the Kennedy Administration's most persistent advocate of civil rights. From the start, word filtering out of the White House held that Johnson was arguing for strong legislation. On June 21, 1963, two days after introduction of the civil rights bill, President Kennedy summoned Rauh and the other members of the Leadership Conference to a meeting. Johnson was there and, in Kennedy's presence, he endorsed a strategy of trying to expand the Administration's own proposals through amendments in committee and on the floor.

Throughout the summer of 1963, Rauh and the Leadership Conference lobbied to toughen the Administration bill, over the objections of a presidential contingent led by Robert Kennedy. "What I want is a bill, not an issue," said the attorney general in arguing for practicality. But public opinion shifted discernibly toward a strong bill after the March on Washington on August 28, and it took an even more decisive shift on September 15, when four teen-age black girls were murdered by a dynamite explosion during a Bible class in a Birmingham church. In October, the legislation approved by the House Judiciary Committee was much closer to Rauh's version of the civil rights bill than President Kennedy's.

Nonetheless, the bill was still bogged in a legislative morass of Southern making when, on November 22, the president was shot in Dallas. The country initially took the assassination to be a climactic act of violence in the wave of racial hatred that was sweeping the South. Out of the confusion that has since enveloped the episode, it is unlikely that a final judgment on culpability for the murder will ever be rendered. But in 1963 the contest between nonviolent blacks and violent whites had become increasingly brutal, and Kennedy's assassination seemed to many to be the ultimate proof that restoration of public order depended on eliminating racial injustice.

In his first message to Congress, five days after Kennedy's death, Johnson not only endorsed the civil rights bill but insisted it was

239

his first legislative priority. "No memorial oration or eulogy could more eloquently honor President Kennedy's memory," he told a joint session and a nationwide television audience, "than the earliest possible passage of the civil rights bill for which he fought so long. We have talked long enough in this country about equal rights. We have talked for a hundred years or more. It is time now to write the next chapter—and to write it in the books of law."

Rauh and the rest of the civil rights leadership had, understandably, been apprehensive about a Johnson presidency. But, on the day of his address to Congress, Johnson invited Rauh to fly with him aboard Air Force One to attend the funeral of an old New Dealer, former Senator Herbert Lehman of New York. It was Johnson's way of saying that he would let no old grudges stand in the way of the bill's enactment.

Johnson never wavered in his support of the bill. But equally vital to its passage was the nation's state of mind. Rauh, who had long worked the corridors of the Capitol in behalf of civil rights, said his old feeling of solitude had given way. "Instead of our being alone in the hall," he said, "there were a couple of dozen of the most beautiful ministers, most of them young and handsome, some wearing their full collars. It was one thing for those guys [Congressmen] to brush past me and vote against the Leadership Conference, but it was another to brush past the church and vote against them. You can't underestimate that factor." Rauh said he believed Kennedy would have surrendered one or two key sections of the civil rights bill in the bargaining for enactment. Johnson was emphatic in his unwillingness to surrender anything at all.

After a favorable vote by the House on February 10, 1964, the bill went to the Senate, where Majority Whip Hubert Humphrey had taken responsibility for beating the Southern filibuster. Throughout the late winter and the entire spring, Rauh and the civil rights leadership performed the grueling work of changing senators' votes, one by one. Rauh made the trip to Capitol Hill every day to meet with Humphrey, to explore the latest intelligence and examine prospects for swinging over one marginal senator or another. At any time during the exhausting weeks of filibustering, the Southerners probably had it within their capacity to bring the struggle to a close, as they had during the civil rights debate of 1957, by seducing a majority with a reasonable compromise. The debate dragged into the summer, however, as the Southerners vowed to fight to the bitter end.

Meanwhile, SNCC's young militants were moving in a different direction, as if the civil rights bill did not matter. Integration had ceased to look as attractive to them as it had at the time of the sit-ins. The SNCC people, though hardly indifferent to the end of Jim Crow, had come to recognize through their work in the field that the right to check into a motel or order dinner in a restaurant had no bearing on the life that poor blacks led in the rural South. SNCC acquired a growing concern with power. Its workers reasoned that rural blacks could upgrade their lot not by possessing a right to mingle with whites, which would be of scant use to them. Rather, they had to wrest from the white power structure control over the conditions in which they lived.

This thinking evolved only gradually within SNCC, and after much reflection and debate. The strategy King had brought to the civil rights movement and which SNCC had supported at the start, was to conduct demonstrations to draw public attention to injustice. Directed at segregation, the strategy had been repeatedly vindicated. But SNCC saw a deeper evil in the economic powerlessness of the rural poor, much as Randolph and Rustin did for urban blacks. SNCC people reasoned that they must fix their objective not on attitudes but on institutions. They came to worry less about touching the conscience of the white majority and more about mobilizing the political potential of the black masses.

SNCC's strategy required organization—and, even as SNCC workers became increasingly skeptical of the value of the democratic process, they identified the most logical issue on which to organize as the exercise of the right to vote. The strategy meant that SNCC had to go where the voters were. Time had reversed the reasoning of the civil rights workers of the 1940s, who held that bringing their message to blacks in the Deep South was hopeless, even foolhardy, because whites there were too intransigent, and too dangerous. SNCC saw the Deep South as its natural target because, whatever the character of whites, blacks had the numerical potential there to exercise real political power.

The Kennedy Administration actually sponsored SNCC's early

241

voter registration efforts. Attorney General Robert Kennedy believed in the ballot as the blacks' best weapon for attaining their rights, and he was not indifferent to the prospect that it would be cast in most instances for Democrats. He could not believe the South would seriously obstruct a voter registration campaign, though history belied this conviction. Southern resistance had frustrated many registration drives, most recently a major effort by the NAACP to test the voting protection written into the civil rights act of 1957.

Robert Kennedy also preferred an unobtrusive voter registration campaign to a disruptive protest like the Freedom Ride. Unfortunately, he failed to understand that Southern resistance to such a campaign, though less conspicuous, would not necessarily be less brutal. Nor did he foresee that the encouragement he gave blacks to participate in the political process would in due course lead SNCC into angry conflict with the Democratic party, culminating in Atlantic City in 1964.

Indeed, with great good will in the summer of 1961, before the clouds of dust from the Freedom Rides had settled, Assistant Attorney General Burke Marshall began talking up the notion of a voter registration campaign. Marshall met several times in New York with the heads of philanthropic foundations, notably Field and Taconic, that supported liberal causes. Later, the leaders of the NAACP, CORE, SCLC, the Urban League and SNCC were invited to join in the deliberations. A program called the Voter Education Project grew out of these meetings, and to it the foundations agreed to allocate nearly a million dollars.

SNCC did not leap at the money. The offer was made while SNCC was still debating its program. A substantial segment of the organization, led by Diane Nash and the Nashville contingent, favored pursuing the more familiar strategy of nonviolent direct action. In the interval between the sit-ins and the Freedom Rides, Nash had led a SNCC group in a "jail, no bail" protest over segregation in Rock Hill, which ended for several of them in a stretch on the South Carolina road gang. Though they had failed to enlist widespread black support, they moved from Rock Hill to the success of the Freedom Rides. Diane Nash was convinced that highly publicized nonviolent demonstrations were the key to defeating segregation.

242

Nash opposed the voter registration proposal when it came from Washington. One of her arguments was that SNCC ought not to identify itself too closely with the government's goals. SNCC, however, was on the point of insolvency, and the financing was an incentive which those who favored organizing the rural poor used to tip the decision. In taking the money, SNCC virtually abandoned mass action, and set off on the back roads of Mississippi to spawn black political power.

Out of the negotiations also came a major misunderstanding. SNCC, and its allies on the front lines, interpreted the participation of the Kennedys as an implicit promise of government protection. Robert Kennedy, however, never anticipated a need for protection, and his people had made no provision for it. They had promoted voter registration over mass action precisely because it seemed innocuous, and thus unlikely to lead to physical confrontation. Both benefactors and clients were to pay dearly for their miscalculation.

A team of its field workers was already installed in Mississippi when SNCC submitted its formal application to the Voter Education Project in February 1962. "We have people strategically located in each of the five Congressional districts within the state," said the SNCC letter. "The field workers . . . are going to live with the people, develop their own leaders and teach them the process of registration and effective use of the franchise." Over the objections of the NAACP, which regarded the program as impractical, the VEP gave SNCC $5000, a sum that was disappointingly small but which conveyed with it the apparent blessings of the white liberal establishment.

With the decision to move into political organizing, power within SNCC gravitated toward James Forman, who had become executive director in the fall of 1961. Forman, by then, was already in his thirties, a decade older than most of the SNCC people. Though born in the South, he had been raised in the bristling ghetto of Southside Chicago, where he remembered attending rallies in 1941 for Randolph's March on Washington. He spent three years in the Air Force, obtained a degree from Roosevelt University in Chicago and earned an M.A. in African studies at Boston.

After the Montgomery bus boycott, Forman worked sporadically

243

in civil rights. In 1961 he was demonstrating in Monroe, North Carolina, with Robert Williams, one of the first civil rights figures to renounce nonviolence, when he met Ella Baker. She was impressed with his intelligence and dynamism, and recommended him to SNCC. Forman in the succeeding years became SNCC's stern and able taskmaster. A large man, he was high-strung but with enormous physical stamina. He was brave and cynical and angry, and he was an important influence in moving SNCC steadily to the left.

While Forman ran SNCC's central office in Atlanta, a dark-skinned young man named Robert Moses who spoke softly and wore horn-rimmed glasses gradually came to dominate SNCC's operations in the field. Moses, in a way, was characteristic of a new generation that enlisted in the organization after the ardor of the sit-ins ebbed. SNCC's campus chapters had mostly withered and died, and the Southern black colleges ceased to furnish the bulk of the recruits. The cadre which then took over SNCC's operations was more Northern than Southern, more sophisticated, its character formed more by the hard knocks of the urban ghetto than by the love of the Christian church.

Moses, a Harlemite, was then twenty-six years old. He had a B.A. from Hamilton College and an M.A. in philosophy from Harvard, and he had taught math in a high school in New York. His outlook was not doctrinaire, either Christian or Marxist, but was shaped, rather, by Camus's existentialism, which left to individuals the responsibility for distinguishing good from evil.

Bayard Rustin first remembered Moses as a volunteer during the organization of the Youth March on Washington in 1958. After the sit-ins in 1960, Rustin recommended Moses to SCLC, where he worked first as a volunteer in the New York office. That summer he went to Atlanta to join the SCLC staff, but Ella Baker, still SCLC's executive director, diverted him to SNCC. A few weeks later he left SCLC's payroll and, as SNCC converted from its original mission of service to campus chapters, Bob Moses more than anyone became the model of the dedicated professional organizer.

Moses seemed to possess a magnetic power over people, which at times frightened even himself. "I admire Bob, you know," said Mary Lane, who was a field secretary under Moses. "He was very —he was one you could sit down and talk with. After talking to

244

him, you would really understand, you'd be a little broader than you were at first . . . He also had this thing about him, like if it was Bob who said it, you knew it had to be done. I think a lot of other people felt the same way about him. He was just one of those persons."

Moses was genuinely uncomfortable with leadership. Rustin said that during the organization of the Prayer Pilgrimage, Moses wanted only to lick envelopes. When he proposed a bigger job, Rustin said, Moses replied contemptuously that he disliked the centralized way the office was managed, and he stayed with his envelopes. Already fermenting in him, no doubt, was the concept of "group-centered" leadership, which on a wider scale became "participatory democracy," the concept SDS enshrined in the "Port Huron Statement" and SNCC adopted as its organizing principle in Mississippi. As SNCC's man in the hazardous precincts of Mississippi, however, Moses found that, like it or not, he could not keep his subordinates from deferring to him. Ultimately, the burden became so overwhelming to Moses that he fled.

Moses went down to Mississippi for the first time in the fall of 1960, and met Amzie Moore, a courageous black man who was a local NAACP chairman, and who argued that SNCC should bring a voter registration campaign into the Delta. Tom Hayden, in one of his reports for SDS, wrote that "Moses and Moore saw the possibility of getting out on those dirt roads and into those old broken homes, talking the language and living the life of the oppressed people there, and persuading them to face the trial of registration. The trial past, a Negro community with an actual voice in local, if not regional, politics might be built . . . Most of all, a spirit that is vital . . . might replace the spiritual apathy which now characterizes the Negro community." After meeting Moore, Moses designed a campaign of rural organization, and the following summer he went back.

In August of 1961, Moses set up the headquarters of SNCC's voter registration campaign in the Mississippi Delta in the town of McComb in Pike County, where two hundred blacks out of eighty thousand eligibles were registered. With a team of about fifteen SNCC workers, he established a citizenship school to teach blacks how to answer the questions on the registration forms. But its primary task, Hayden wrote, was "morale building, encouragement

245

and consequent group identification which might inspire the exploited . . ." Over the course of a few weeks, the SNCC workers set up additional citizenship schools in two neighboring counties.

Within a few days of Moses's arrival, the McComb newspaper had taken note of the project, and a black who attempted to register was shot. Several days later, Moses escorted three elderly blacks into the registrar's office in nearby Liberty, seat of Amite County, and was asked to leave while the three filled out the forms. All three applicants were rejected, and told not to return for six months. When the four left the building, a highway patrolman followed them in his car, pulled them to the side and ordered them to drive to McComb, where Moses was arrested and charged with obstructing an officer. He was fined $50, which the NAACP paid, and given a suspended sentence. Then he phoned the Justice Department, collect, but he received no promise of assistance when he recounted what had occurred.

On August 29, 1961, Moses was beaten in front of the registrar's office in Liberty while escorting two more blacks to register. By now the black community in the Delta was aroused and, in the following days, two hundred people testified to their support of the campaign by attending a rally, and several hundred high-school students conducted a sit-in at the lunch counter in the bus station. SNCC workers, meanwhile, persisted in bringing eligible voters to register, and the registrars just as persistently turned them away.

Meanwhile, angry whites stepped up the level of violence, with more shootings, and with the beating and jailing of SNCC workers. The violence reached a climax on September 25, when Herbert Lee, a fifty-two-year-old father of ten who had been active in voter registration and NAACP work, was killed by a prominent white citizen before numerous eyewitnesses. No arrest was made.

One hundred high-school students, led by two SNCC workers, marched to the McComb City Hall on October 4 to protest the killing. Robert Zellner, a white SNCC worker, was attacked as he watched. "There were about fifteen or twenty beating me," Zellner remembered, "and they tried to carry me out into the street where hundreds of people carrying sticks and chains and pipe wrenches were waiting, and I realized that if they got me in the street they would kill me. The mob was screaming, 'Bring him to us. Bring him to us.' It was obvious the cops were not going to do anything."

246

Zellner said he was saved by Moses and Charles McDew, then the SNCC national chairman, who shielded him from the mob with their bodies, allowing him to work his way up the steps and into City Hall. Moses, McDew and Zellner were later sentenced to four months in jail for contributing to the delinquency of minors. The local SNCC workers who led the protest each got six months.

When Bob Moses was released from jail at the end of 1961, the voter registration project in McComb was standing dead still. Most blacks were paralyzed by fear, and whites were congratulating themselves on victory. SNCC had to decide on another tack and, early in 1962, nominated black candidates for Congress in the Democratic primary in two Mississippi districts. Both lost decisively, but the attention drawn to them kept SNCC's flag aloft and maintained at least a trace of black pressure on the all-white political system.

The money from the Voter Education Project, turned over to SNCC in the summer of 1962, gave Moses a new opportunity and provided a surge to his staff's morale. By fall, SNCC had opened regional offices throughout Mississippi. Moses was everywhere, supplying inspiration and courage, as well as administrative direction. Most of the workers who manned the offices were local blacks, in their late teens or early twenties. They understood the physical risks to which they subjected themselves, and the economic reprisals to which they subjected their families. Wherever they canvassed, death stalked them. Beatings were almost commonplace.

The Justice Department knew of this savagery, of course, but it followed the line that Washington had no authority to interfere with the police functions of the state. As Assistant Attorney General Burke Marshall acknowledged to me, the department could have devised legal arguments for sending in federal marshals. But it determined—notwithstanding their value as a deterrent, or as a symbol of federal concern—that marshals would have been unequal to the task, which only a military occupation could have accomplished.

In February 1963, a car in which Moses was riding was splattered with fourteen bullets, three of which seriously wounded James Travis, who was driving. The next month, the Justice department

247

filed for a court injunction against official toleration of violence. It promptly dropped the suit, however, after receiving a vague, and unkept, promise from Mississippi authorities.

The FBI in Mississippi was of no help whatever. Director Hoover saw the civil rights movement as challenge to public order, and he regarded all civil rights workers as troublemakers. Hoover adopted the position, on civil rights abuses, that the Bureau was an "investigative" rather than a "law enforcement" body, a distinction which would have astonished Dillinger. The neatly dressed FBI agent, who characteristically spoke with a Southern accent himself, was a familiar enough figure outside the registrar's office, or along the line of a protest march. But he became a cynical joke in SNCC lore, as he calmly took notes while civil rights workers were being beaten.

SNCC workers still recall wryly the desperate phone calls to Washington in which Robert Kennedy himself, or else Burke Marshall or John Doar, would reply to their pleas for help with genuine compassion, and then reassert their impotence to act. Believing they had undertaken their work with the Kennedys' sanction, the SNCC people were convinced they had been grossly betrayed.

Out of necessity, SNCC people developed their own pattern of life. Unable to travel safely in daylight, they learned to roam the dirt roads of rural Mississippi by night. They became intrepid drivers, accustomed to dodging roadblocks and outracing pursuers, often without headlights. They followed strict rules to keep one another constantly informed of their whereabouts through elaborate communication systems. Sometimes, in spite of their pledges of nonviolence, they carried guns, though rarely were they so foolhardy as to use them.

The SNCC workers lived together, communally, to economize resources but, more important, for mutual protection. Though relations were not always harmonious among them, the life they shared created a deep intimacy and sense of mutual concern. They invariably wore faded denim overalls and T-shirts, at first because such dress was inconspicuous on the landscape, later because it became a badge of self-esteem and honor. The SNCC workers developed a strong *esprit de corps*.

Still, it was a lonely life, with the workers reaching out to the black community and yet isolated from it. "Women told their daughters, don't have anything to do with me," one aggrieved worker wrote to the Atlanta office. "I was there to stir up trouble, that's all. So if I walked down the street, people would say, 'Ain't that the Freedom Rider?' Anything that you do there, their eyes are dead on you." Now and then SNCC workers were granted a weekend of paid leave in Atlanta, to unwind, to have a time. But the rate of psychosomatic ailments within the group was high, an index of the tension under which they lived.

Inevitably, this way of life created an elitist sense among the SNCC workers, at once self-righteous and parochial. It manifested itself in SNCC's contempt for the March on Washington, which Moses would not attend on the grounds that he had more important work in Mississippi. When Mississippi blacks, nonetheless, asked for chartered buses to take them to Washington, Forman denounced the trip as a waste of money. SNCC's way of life bred an attitude of brash absolutism, and an implicit condescension which irritated people in other civil rights organizations. SNCC kids were known throughout the movement as arrogant and haughty. And yet there was no denying that SNCC was waging a gallant attack in the South, on terrain which everyone had always considered impregnable to civil rights.

In the fall of 1963, SNCC stepped up the campaign by conducting a mock election it called the Freedom Vote. Nominally, the Freedom Vote was run by COFO—the Council of Federated Organizations—which was a coalition of SNCC, CORE, the NAACP and SCLC. It had been established to widen the base of action in Mississippi, and received funds directly from the Voter Education Project. COFO's chairman was Aaron Henry, state president of the NAACP, but SNCC remained the principal power, and Moses ran both COFO and the Freedom Vote.

Moses's brainchild, the Freedom Vote was conducted on the same day as the regular election. On the white man's ballot were the duly nominated party candidates. On the Freedom Ballot were Aaron Henry for governor and Reverend Edwin King, a white chaplain at Tougaloo, a Negro college in Jackson, for lieutenant governor. The purpose of the Freedom Vote was to show that, contrary to the assertions of Mississippi whites, Negroes would register and vote, if they could. It was also designed as a forum for blacks to speak out on politics.

For the Freedom Vote campaign, one hundred white students were recruited from Yale and Stanford by a white activist named Allard Lowenstein to join the SNCC workers. Together, whites and blacks fanned out into almost every community in the state. It was the first massive infusion of white volunteers into Mississippi, and the state harassed them as if they were black. At least one of the white students was beaten, and several were jailed. Local Negroes volunteered in unprecedented measure to participate in the campaign, however, and in unprecedented numbers attended rallies at which the "freedom candidates" spoke. On election day, eighty thousand freedom votes were cast, and the Aaron Henry slate "won" an overwhelming victory.

The following week Bob Moses called a meeting of SNCC's Mississippi staff to contemplate the next step in the offensive. From this meeting emerged the daring notion that SNCC organize an insurgent Democratic party to challenge, and try to supplant the Mississippi regulars at the Democratic National Convention the following summer at Atlantic City. In 1960 the Mississippi regulars had bolted the party after John Kennedy's nomination to support a slate of unpledged electors. Given the party's commitment to Kennedy's civil rights bill, they were surely not going to support the Democratic candidate in 1964. The Freedom Vote had shown that Mississippi blacks could be relied upon, in spite of intimidation, to come forth in large numbers. SNCC reasoned that if it could offer the Democrats a loyal delegation, fairly chosen by a substantial electorate, the party would be unable to disregard it.

Having determined their strategy, the SNCC workers then had to consider whether they again wanted white students to help them. Though the Yale and Stanford volunteers had labored conscientiously during the Freedom Vote, SNCC people had not been uniformly happy with them.

The young blacks resented these outsiders, self-confident and inevitably bossy, who moved in, expected cavalierly to take over, and then departed. They were particularly irritated by Allard Lowenstein, the thirty-four-year-old political activist who had recruited the whites and then, they said, conducted himself as if the Freedom Vote were his personal domain, to run as he saw fit. Not least im-

250

portant, the SNCC workers came to feel that their program was blacks' work, which they had earned the right to perform, without selling out for reasons of expediency to liberal whites.

And yet there were sound reasons for welcoming volunteers, of which manpower was only one. SNCC workers understood that the presence of young whites from good families would attract more attention from government and the press than they could alone. It was argued that whites would keep SNCC's program on the front pages and on the evening news and, in a whisper, it was added that a good white murder was likely, at last, to bring in the federal forces that had remained aloof to racist violence. Some of the SNCC workers said candidly that enough Negro blood had been shed for justice, and now it was the turn of whites.

Ultimately, Moses swung the decision, arguing that SNCC had to look to its roots and resist the exclusionary racism of its enemies. But only by staking his full prestige did he win. A narrow majority agreed that, when SNCC announced the Mississippi Summer Project, whites should be invited to join. One of Moses's five district directors, however, declared that he would not go along. His name was Stokely Carmichael, and he said he would work the Summer Project with blacks only. Within a year, Moses would drift into the camp with Carmichael and announce that he would not work with whites any longer either.

Throughout the first half of 1964, while SNCC prepared for the Mississippi Summer, signs of the integrationist spirit of the March on Washington were still plentiful. The National Council of Churches made a major financial contribution, and several liberal foundations declared a willingness to follow suit. Throughout the North, recruiting centers were set up on campuses, staffed by SNCC workers and the "Friends of SNCC," most of them white. The response from students was enthusiastic. White liberals showed their affection for the movement by holding fund-raising parties, and numerous white doctors and lawyers volunteered for service in the field.

There were disquieting signs, too. The elders of the movement, always suspicious of SNCC, grew more distant as reports drifted in of its growing radicalism. COFO remained intact, ostensibly the

251

sponsor of the Summer Project, but the NAACP and SCLC had for all purposes withdrawn from it. Except for one district left to CORE to organize, SNCC had Mississippi to itself. Then the Voter Education Project declined to renew its grant to COFO, and the SNCC leadership blamed white liberals for playing politics. Far from seeking to accommodate the liberals, however, SNCC outraged them by engaging the National Lawyers Guild, an association well to the left of the organized bar, to do much of the Summer Project's legal defense work.

A more ominous development for the Summer Project was the swell of what had come to be called backlash. During the years that the civil rights movement was capturing the conscience of more and more whites, a rarely spoken truth was that working-class and poor whites in the North resisted any change in their attitudes. The AFL-CIO, and the leaders of several powerful unions, gallantly promoted the civil rights cause, but rank-and-file union members continued to regard blacks as a threat to their security, and union locals continued to exclude blacks from membership. The more victories the movement won, furthermore, the more demanding working whites found that blacks became, and backlash was their response.

In the spring of 1964, Governor George Wallace of Alabama brought his quixotic campaign for the Democratic presidential nomination into the North. Running on a platform of bigotry, he won a third of the primary vote in Wisconsin, 30 percent in Indiana and 43 percent in Maryland. Precinct analysis revealed that his chief supporters were white ethnic industrial workers, the backbone of Democratic majorities since the New Deal.

Though Wallace was himself never a real contender, Senator Barry Goldwater of Arizona, the favorite for the Republican nomination, was fueling his own presidential campaign by opposition to civil rights. By the end of the spring, many liberals had acquired reservations, not so much about the civil rights movement but about those of its activities which seemed likely to provoke a politically harmful backlash.

Meanwhile, Mississippi's whites mobilized for the Summer Project. The state government recruited two hundred additional highway patrolmen, and the city of Jackson doubled the size of its police force. Jackson even bought a tank, with thick steel walls and bul-

252

letproof windows. The newspapers treated SNCC's program as a foreign invasion, and whipped up the white population into a state of anxiety and frenzy. Mississippi's leaders left no doubt that they would receive their visitors without pity.

The plan that Bob Moses and Jim Forman formulated during the winter and spring of 1964 was based upon the establishment of the Mississippi Freedom Democratic party. MFDP was to be the mirror image of the regular party, except that blacks would be equal participants with whites. It would be Democratic in its affiliation and hierarchical in its structure. Unlike Mississippi's regular organization, however, MFDP would follow the party rules so scrupulously in the election of a delegation to the national convention that its claims to legitimacy would be beyond dispute. MFDP, according to the plan devised by Moses and Forman, would go to Atlantic City in August and make the case before the Democratic delegates that it had a more valid claim than the regulars to Mississippi's convention seats.

Joseph L. Rauh, Jr., first heard of the Mississippi Freedom Democratic party during a chance encounter with Moses and Forman on March 20, 1964. He had been invited by an organization called the National Civil Liberties Clearing House to preside at a symposium on direct action. Forman had been invited as a speaker, and he brought Moses along. The minutes say the following:

> Robert Moses, SNCC worker in Mississippi: "Should the Democratic Party tolerate the Democratic delegates from Mississippi at its national convention?" He outlined current plans to send a rival delegation from that State to the convention. Mr. Rauh responded, "I can assure you that if you send a civil rights delegation, we will do our best to see that it is seated," and Mr. Moses said, "We'll be there, Mr. Chairman."

The man Moses and Forman saw in Rauh was an insider in the Democratic party, its foremost champion of civil rights and a pipeline to the important liberals whose support was vital to MFDP's success. Rauh, having directed the floor fight at the 1948 conven-

253

tion when Hubert Humphrey won adoption of the first civil rights plank, also had more experience than any other Democrat in conducting party challenges. Rauh told me that the moment he heard Moses's proposal he was excited. He said his on-the-spot assessment, based on his knowledge of Democratic delegates, was that, if the issue could be brought into open battle on the convention floor, MFDP would win.

Two days after their Washington encounter, Moses and Forman joined Rauh at the annual convention of the United Automobile Workers, of which Rauh was general counsel. The three of them asked for support from the UAW president, Walter Reuther, the labor movement's most avid partisan of civil rights. "Walter was cooler than I would have expected," Rauh remembered. "I think he saw it immediately as a possible confrontation with Johnson. At that point, the possibility hadn't even occurred to me. Walter was a much more sensitive political animal than I." Reuther had by now committed himself totally to Johnson's reelection. Though he raised no objection to Rauh's serving as MFDP's legal counsel, Reuther's refusal to help was an inauspicious beginning.

Throughout the spring of 1964, Rauh was preoccupied with breaking the Senate filibuster of the civil rights bill, and when he had time he campaigned for his own election as a District of Columbia delegate to the Democratic National Convention. But on several occasions he met with Moses, and they worked on the strategy for MFDP.

Moses and Rauh agreed that Mississippi's blacks would demonstrate their good faith by seeking to participate in the precinct, county and state conventions of the regular Democratic party. When their exclusion was established beyond doubt, they would create a parallel organizational structure, within which they would select their own convention delegates. Rauh would then prepare a detailed legal brief, which would present the evidence and the arguments for supplanting the Mississippi regulars to other delegates at Atlantic City.

Under Mississippi's pyramid system, the process for selecting delegates began at the precinct level, where any Democratic voter was eligible to participate in the election of representatives to a county convention. At the county level, delegates were elected to a district convention. The districts would then elect representatives

254

e volunteers, and he conveyed the sympathy of the John-
nistration for the cause of civil rights. But when he was
at the federal government would do to provide protection
ippi, he answered simply, "Nothing. There is no federal
ce. The responsibility for protection is that of the local
e can only investigate."

conspired quickly to affirm the irony of the "protection"
the Mississippi police. On Saturday, June 20, at the close
t week of training, a group left Oxford on a sixteen-hour
eridian, in CORE's sector of Mississippi. In the car were
chwerner, a twenty-four-year-old social worker from New
James Chaney, a twenty-one-year-old Mississippi black,
E staff members who had worked to set up the Meridian
y center. Also with them was Andrew Goodman, a
e-year-old volunteer from New York.

up reached Meridian safely on the twenty-first, and
apsacks and suitcases into the CORE office. After a few
eep, Schwerner, Chaney and Goodman set out to inspect
of the Mount Zion Methodist Church, fifty-five miles
eshoba County. The church, which had been serving as
school, had been burned to the ground a few days before.
rough Philadelphia, county seat of Neshoba, their car
ed for speeding by Deputy Sheriff Cecil Price. The three
sted, taken to jail, fined $20 and released. They were
alive again.

s of the three missing civil rights workers spread quickly
country. At the training center in Ohio, Summer Project
waited apprehensively for word. With the media follow-
nt carefully, millions of others waited, too.

I, breaking precedent, acted promptly in sending four
hiladelphia. On instructions from the White House, one
ailors from a nearby naval station were ordered to under-
ch and, a few days later, their number was increased to
ed. Among the volunteers at the Ohio training center,
SNCC workers in the field, it did not go unnoticed that,
vhites among the missing, the government had promptly
SNCC's hypothesis that nothing would draw attention
ppi like the blood of young whites appeared confirmed.
st 4, as the result of an informer's tip, the bodies of the

to a state convention, which was empowered to choose the delegates to the national convention in Atlantic City.

On June 16, blacks showed up for most of the 1884 precinct
meetings scheduled by the party regulars as the base of the pyramid. In fact, three-fourths of those meetings were never held.

The MFDP brief which Rauh later prepared recounted that in
Ruleville, for example, Negro voters found no one present and so
"convened the precinct meeting on the lawn of the Community
House. A resolution was passed pledging support of the National
Democratic Party. Delegates were elected for the county conven-
tion. After a short prayer and singing 'We Shall Overcome,' the
precinct meeting adjourned." The Ruleville blacks were fore-
sighted enough, however, not to let their effort go unrecorded.
"The entire operation," the brief noted, "was filmed by CBS News,
TV."

A week later, blacks claiming to represent the precincts where
the meetings were never convened presented themselves to
eighty-two county conventions, to which they were refused admit-
tance. The MFDP record, which Rauh prepared and was uncon-
tested by the party regulars, showed that blacks, having been
squeezed out of the system at the county level, were never allowed
back in. The two final tiers, the district and state conventions, were
all white, as was the delegation sent by the regulars to Atlantic
City.

By now Barry Goldwater was virtually assured of the Republican
nomination, and successful exploitation of his backlash strategy
seemed to provide the only prospect for his election. Johnson took
the prospect with some seriousness. Whether or not backlash could
beat him, it appeared to have the potential to cut deeply into
his margin of victory, and Johnson yearned for a huge mandate to
reaffirm his right to the office he had acquired indirectly through
Kennedy's murder. Johnson also wanted a mandate from the voters
for his ambitious legislative program. To get it, while still pressing
for enactment of the civil rights bill, he reasoned that he had to
dampen the fires of civil rights controversy.

To Johnson, the Mississippi Summer Project meant only trouble.
He was a politician, a man not given to symbolic struggle. His mind
was oriented toward the machinery of government in Washington,
and he did not understand the point of what SNCC was trying to

achieve in Mississippi. He considered his own legislative program —not just the civil rights bill but the antipoverty program and a half-dozen other social welfare proposals—far more important to blacks than the Mississippi Project.

Roy Wilkins of the NAACP, among other elders of the movement, agreed with Johnson. Wilkins called a meeting that summer, from which emerged the promise of "a moratorium of all marches, picketing and demonstrations" until after election day. Even after the word "moratorium" was amended to read "broad curtailment," John Lewis of SNCC and Jim Farmer of CORE would not go along. But King, Whitney Young of the Urban League, Bayard Rustin and A. Philip Randolph concurred in the proposal.

In June, Johnson sent Louis Martin, a black who handled minority affairs at the Democratic National Committee, to ask Joe Rauh to proceed cautiously with the MFDP challenge. At the same time, Reuther discreetly pressured Rauh to quit as MFDP counsel. Ironically Ella Baker, who turned up working in MFDP's Washington office, came to Rauh one day from the opposite side of the political spectrum to suggest that he surrender his representation to the National Lawyers Guild. Rauh did not like Ella Baker, and found her too radical for his taste. He accepted neither her invitation nor Reuther's to withdraw, and kept preparing his case on the assumption that MFDP had an excellent chance to win.

The first group of volunteers for Mississippi gathered at the Western College for Women in Oxford, Ohio, on Monday, June 15, 1964. They numbered three hundred, both men and women, of a total of eight hundred who would join the project. They were almost all middle class and from the best universities. All had been screened for psychological stability.

Only one of six was black. The meagre ratio was blamed on the requirement that volunteers pay their own transportation and living expenses, any hospital bills they might incur and even their own bail bonds if they were arrested. Few blacks could afford such luxury, and the Summer Project could not subsidize them. Unfortunately, much of the money that had been expected from the liberal foundations had never arrived.

The week of training was intense, and in some ways traumatic.

White volunteers did not like to hear them But the objective of the instruction was to ings of blacks who knew whites only as a misery, and of physical danger. The volu attitudes, ranging from politics to sex, both organize and those working with them.

They listened to the swaggering SNCC ently as the "jungle fighters"—describe th centers and freedom schools, SNCC's g ening black consciousness and political of the onerous labor of voting registrati were introduced to the strategy of the M ocratic party, and led to hope that the effort would be triumph in Atlantic City

They took practical instruction in non Bayard Rustin, elaborating on the theo love Eastland,* it sounds preposterous— ple. But . . . you *love* Eastland in your which will redeem his children." They in mind when they practiced the techni ings of clubs and fists.

Many of the volunteers shuddered a like these:

Jim Forman—"I may be killed and y

R. Jess Brown, a Jackson lawyer—" where and a cop stops you and starts though you haven't committed any cri not the place to start conducting cons licemen, many of whom don't have a f

Bob Moses—"If we can go and c something. If you can go into Negro that will be a huge job . . . [Negroes white half of the integrated bus term against having their houses bombed think the key is in the vote."

John Doar, representing the Depar

* James O. Eastland, senator from Mississip the Judiciary Committee, which had jurisdicti

three young men were found. Goodman and Schwerner had been shot in the head. Chaney had been brutally beaten to death. In December, the FBI arrested Deputy Sheriff Price and twenty other white Mississippians in connection with the murders, but the charges were subsequently dropped.*

It was during the week of the murders that the filibuster against the civil rights bill was finally broken in the Senate. The key shift was that of Senator Everett Dirksen of Illinois, conservative leader of the Republican minority, who finally gave way before the heavy lobbying of the White House, the churches, the Leadership Conference, the labor unions and much of industry. Quoting Victor Hugo, Dirksen declared, "Stronger than all the armies is an idea whose time has come," and, with the approval of the civil rights coalition, Humphrey modified the bill slightly to make Dirksen's reversal of position a bit easier. Dirksen brought twenty-seven Republicans with him to the cloture vote, which carried the total to well above the necessary two-thirds.

Among the senators who voted against cloture, and then against the bill itself, was Barry Goldwater of Arizona. He justified his opposition on the standard conservative grounds that enforcement would require "creation of a police state." A few weeks later, Goldwater became the Republican nominee for the presidency. His position on the bill guaranteed that the issue of civil rights would be at the center of the election campaign.

In Mississippi, SNCC received the news of the bill's passage with little interest. Moses's headquarters in Greenwood announced that it would not test the law, since it saw no use in a black's risking his life to eat a hamburger in the company of a white man. Some SNCC workers were excited by the implications of the law, however, and so were some of the local blacks. They insisted on challenging segregated facilities, and their forays into restaurants and theaters made life in the Summer Project more dangerous than ever.

Despite the dangers, however, only a few volunteers had quit the

* On the basis of new testimony, and a changed atmosphere, Price was convicted on a federal conspiracy charge in connection with the murders in 1967. He served forty-four months in prison.

259

Summer Project and by early July, the network of volunteers had spread throughout the state. Under the supervision of the SNCC professionals, the newcomers accustomed themselves to the routine of telephone check-ins and two-way radios, quit the streets by nightfall and learned to dodge the fists and shotguns of white vigilantes. They grasped the lesson that a cop was someone they ran from in fear rather than turn to for help. They lived the life of the SNCC field worker, in short, except that it was an adventure, and they knew that after two months they would go home.

Part of the adventure was the communal living. Having arrived open-minded and egalitarian, the white students willingly adapted to the ways of the Southern blacks they worked with. In return, they brought in their baggage something of the counterculture— shaggy hair, disdain for bras, bare feet, marijuana, and a zest for sex that was often interracial. If much of their work irritated the local whites, the challenge that mixed mating presented to Southern phobias was explosive. SNCC veterans shuddered when they saw a white girl promenading hand in hand with a black boy, and usually tried to shove them indoors before everybody was slaughtered.

There was also discord. Black women complained of their men being taken away by girls with fair skin. And women of both races, in what were the budding signs of a new and powerful liberation movement, complained of being relegated by overbearing men to the most routine and uninspiring kind of tasks, usually referred to as the "shit work." Inevitably, too, the Northern whites complained that the Southern blacks were disorganized, while the Southern blacks complained that the Northern whites were domineering.

Yet, whatever the internal problems, the Summer Project flourished. However contemptuous Southern whites may have been of these bizarre and troublesome outsiders, the volunteers were characterized far more by self-discipline than self-indulgence, far less by bohemianism than by bravery.

The political work was backbreaking. The conditions of life among blacks hardly encouraged political involvement. One volunteer described her experience at organizing in a letter home:

> You climbed on the porch by stepping on a bucket— there were huge holes on the porch for the unwary. The woman was sitting dejectedly on the bed as she

260

couldn't talk very well. She was surrounded by shy children, some of them naked . . . We tried to explain what Freedom Registration meant—it seemed like a rather abstract approach to her problems . . .

The volunteers appealed to potential voters in churches and marketplaces, as well as in their homes. They held meetings in the community centers, classes in the freedom schools. Martin Luther King, James Farmer and Bayard Rustin all came to Mississippi to help them. But, for some reason, the number of blacks who agreed to enroll in MFDP was not as great as had participated in the Freedom Vote the year before.

Still, fifty thousand blacks were on the rolls when MFDP began holding precinct meetings on July 19, 1964, to elect delegates to its county conventions. Another volunteer, writing home, described a concurrent meeting of several Leflore County precincts held in Greenwood on July 21:

> We got some of the community leaders together and had a workshop with them on how to run the meetings. The meetings were run by the local people, with the snicks [SNCC's] as "parliamentarians" . . . The meeting hall was done up like a convention hall. There were placards for the different precincts, and banners proclaiming LBJ FOR PRESIDENT and ONE MAN—ONE VOTE, and so on. The place was jammed.

Still another volunteer wrote of the same event:

> What a meeting it was—a totally unorganized group of people had come together for the first of many steps in organizing a local political party. And it was truly democratic. Hundreds of people came from each precinct, compared to the five or ten Mississippi whites who show up for their precinct meetings . . .

The following week, MFDP held conventions in thirty-five of Mississippi's eighty-two counties. Several more conventions were convened in Jackson because it was deemed too dangerous—in

Neshoba, for example, where the three young men had been murdered—to hold them locally.

A few days later, the delegates who were elected at the county level met in the district conventions. Meanwhile, on July 28, the regulars held their state convention, which was all-white and Goldwaterite, and abstained conspicuously from any pledge of support for the national ticket. The Freedom Democrats met for *their* state convention in Jackson on August 6, and chose a slate of delegates —sixty-four blacks and four whites—pledged to Lyndon B. Johnson.

Joe Rauh was at the MFDP convention in Jackson, and he was a center of attention. "We're not a paper party," he declared boldly from the platform. "When you have two parties that claim to represent the regular party, you take the loyal one. There's not a Goldwater fan in the house."

Rauh, in explaining procedure, said that MFDP was unlikely to win its battle in the Democratic party's 108-member credentials committee, which Johnson dominated and which would consider the contest first. He said his strategy was to invoke party rules which provided that a seating dispute could be brought from the credentials committee to the convention floor with the votes of as few as eleven committee members, and that a roll call on the floor could be required at the request of eight states. If the "elevenand-eight" barrier could be overcome, Rauh said, he was confident MFDP could win a roll call on the convention floor.

One of the volunteers at the Jackson convention noted that, "Mr. Rauh presented quite an optimistic picture concerning the chances of getting the [MFDP] seated in Atlantic City . . . Bob Moses didn't seem so confident." Rauh was less confident than he acknowledged, however. He knew that Lyndon Johnson did not share the logic of his argument that, of the two Mississippi parties, the Democrats at Atlantic City should pick the loyal one. Unlike Kennedy in 1960, Johnson was certain of winning the black vote in 1964, but he also wanted to win as many Southern states as possible. Party structures, like the voters, in these states were white. Johnson saw MFDP not as an issue of right versus wrong but as a needless provocation to the white South. "LBJ is the single most important factor," Rauh told the MFDP delegates with some foreboding. "I would be very happy with his benevolent neutrality."

262

The proceedings at Atlantic City opened with a silent vigil conducted by whites and blacks in support of MFDP on the boardwalk outside Convention Hall. On Saturday, August 22, prior to the opening of the convention itself, the credentials committee began its deliberations. Television had turned to the committee as the only newsworthy event of the day, and stayed with it in preference to the tedious stage management which Johnson had imposed on the rest of the proceedings.

Joe Rauh was a delegate from the District of Columbia and himself a member of the credentials committee. He called on Mrs. Fannie Lou Hamer of Ruleville, vice-chairman of the delegation, to explain MFDP's case.

A large, dark-skinned woman in her middle years, Mrs. Hamer perspired profusely under the television lights. She told of being fired by her boss and beaten unconscious by the police for her MFDP work. In a deep and mellow voice, between intermittent sobs, she testified:

> They beat me and they beat me with the long flat
> blackjack. I screamed to God in pain. My dress worked
> itself up. I tried to pull it down. They beat my arms
> until I had no feeling in them. After a while the first
> man beating my arm grew numb from tiredness. The
> other man, who was holding me, was given the black-
> jack. Then he began beating me. . . . All of this on ac-
> count we want to register, to become first-class citi-
> zens, and if the Freedom Democratic party is not
> seated now, I question America . . .

Far from getting Johnson's "benevolent neutrality," as Rauh had hoped, MFDP became the object of the President's wrath. Watching Mrs. Hamer's testimony in his White House office, Johnson became so alarmed that, on a transparent pretext, he called a televised press conference to divert the country's attention. The ploy, however, came too late. Mrs. Hamer was already a star, and her testimony was rerun on the evening news. Rauh had awakened the nation to the nature of politics in Mississippi, and won the sympathy of most liberal Democrats to MFDP's cause.

263

"As an avant-garde campus, Berkeley was going to be in trouble at some point. It didn't have to be at that time over this issue. But given the nature of San Francisco and the tradition of the Berkeley campus and what was going on around the world, in Japan in 1960 and the movement of the blacks, Berkeley was going to be in trouble at some time."

A MERICANS WERE no better prepared for the student movement when Berkeley made the headlines in the fall of 1964 than they had been when those four freshmen from North Carolina A & T walked into Woolworth's in Greensboro to herald the start of the civil rights movement.

There had been instances of white student protest during the early 1960s, but they appeared random, and noninfectious: an anti-HUAC demonstration in San Francisco, an antiwar march organized by Todd Gitlin in Washington, an unsuccessful sit-in against the administration's racial policies at the University of Chicago. Large numbers of white students had worked for civil rights but that was in support of someone else's movement, not their own. The "Port Huron Statement" might have been taken as a signal that serious discontent lay beneath the surface of the society, but few people outside the academic community had given it much notice. Not until Berkeley did student protests take on a significance of their own.

And, even after the uprising began, the issues at Berkeley seemed obscure. Few Americans were blind to the racial discrimination which aggrieved the country's blacks But the students at Berkeley were white, far from poor, psychologically secure, unoppressed. Americans had learned to tolerate the occasional hijinks —like goldfish swallowing and panty raids—which periodically swept over campuses, and even welcomed them as harmless diversions of energy. But American students had no grand traditions of political activism, as did students elsewhere, and only a tiny minority in most colleges ever seemed interested in politics at all.

275

What, Americans asked, were the Berkeley students complaining about, anyway? There were the stated issues, revolving around free speech, but they scarcely seemed large enough to excite such a massive reaction. A prescient young teaching assistant at Berkeley had published a small book in 1962 in which he wrote that the students looked upon the university as a factory, where the quest for knowledge was conducted on an assembly line. "A man is not a product," he wrote, anticipating the declamations of 1964, "nor is he an IBM record card." * Was he expressing just an everyday student gripe, or grounds for student rebellion?

If there was going to be a student rebellion, then certainly Berkeley, California, was a logical place for it to start. The name Berkeley stood, at the same time, for a city, the principal campus of California's higher education system, and a scholastic style. By conventional standards of academic measurement, Berkeley in 1964 was the undisputed leader among public universities in the nation, and it conceded little to even the best private ones. It was also esteemed, as a community, for sophisticated and gracious living, and for its tolerance of the wide diversity of people clustered within.

Blessed by a pervasive sun and a spectacular view across San Francisco Bay, Berkeley routinely attracted not only excellent academic minds but committed bohemians and other free spirits. As a community, it had shaken itself free before others of the stodginess of the 1950s. By the early 1960s, the long hair and beads of the counterculture were established along its avenues, the old-fashioned boy-girl strictures had withered among the students and a noisy radicalism had invaded the political dialogue. Quick to the point of faddishness in responding to the times, Berkeley in those years trembled with excitement over Kennedy and Castro, civil rights and nuclear disarmament, rock music and marijuana. As events were to show, Berkeley was not so different from other academic communities; rather, it was at the leading edge.

Clark Kerr understood in the early 1960s that something special was happening at Berkeley. Kerr was president of the University of California, a sprawling establishment of nine campuses and nearly

* David Horowitz, *Student*, a prophetic piece of writing.

100,000 students, plus another 200,000 students enrolled in extension courses. At his disposal was an operating budget of $500 million, plus another $100 million for construction. His university had 40,000 employees, 10,000 courses in its catalog and projects in 50 countries. Berkeley, the most highly esteemed of his campuses, boasted the most rigorous academic standards and the largest graduate school in the system. Because his office was located in Berkeley, Kerr was able to exercise closer personal supervision there than over any of the other campuses.

In April 1963, Kerr delivered the prestigious Godkin Lectures at Harvard, which he entitled "The Uses of the University." With sensitivity he observed that, "The undergraduate students are coming to look upon themselves more as a 'class.' Some may even feel like a 'lumpen proletariat.'" Kerr said that, in giant universities like California, the student "has problems of establishing his identity and a sense of security." He warned that students had revolt on their minds, some directing it against the university, others against society itself. Tom Hayden could hardly have conveyed these points any better.

One expected Clark Kerr to be perceptive. He was not a popular figure, but by his shrewd manipulations he managed simultaneously to hold the esteem of the Board of Regents and the alumni, the state government and most Californians, the faculty and the students. What had been remarkable about his career was a capacity for accomplishing contentious ends without creating strife.

Kerr even looked inoffensive, with a bullet-bald head and a nondescript face, on which steel-rimmed glasses were perched. His voice was disarmingly soft, his manner strangely mousy. I spoke with Kerr in Berkeley some years later, after he had been fired as president of the university, in the office of a prominent educational foundation which he headed. We talked again in Washington, during one of his many trips to the East. I found his style ingratiating but not warm, smooth but not open, plain but not direct.

Kerr still showed indignation at having been abandoned by California. He had been supremely loyal, he explained to me, but had been done in by subordinates insensitive to the shifts in the times, and unadaptable to changing relationships between competing constituencies. As president, Kerr had taken pride in being the master bureaucrat: selfless, nonideological, effective. But a master

277

bureaucrat's first requirement is to keep his institution intact, and in the autumn of 1964 Berkeley turned into a debacle.

Born to Quaker parents in 1911, Clark Kerr was raised on a farm in eastern Pennsylvania. While a student at Swarthmore College, he spent summers and weekends as a "peace caravaner" seeking converts to the League of Nations and to international disarmament. During the Depression, he distributed food through the Society of Friends among poor blacks in the Philadelphia area. Kerr said the hardship he witnessed persuaded him to specialize in economics, and attracted him first to socialism, then to the New Deal. He did graduate work in economics at Stanford and the London School of Economics, and received his Ph.D. in 1939 from Berkeley.

While at graduate school, Kerr drifted into labor relations, a new academic specialty. In 1933, he got his first taste of labor-management violence when he worked as an investigator during a strike of cotton pickers. Three years later, when the sanction given collective bargaining by the Wagner Act made the study of trade unionism popular, Kerr was one of the few specialists in the field. Following a series of professorships, he was appointed vice-chairman of the War Labor Board and spent the World War II years working in Washington.

After the war ended, Governor Earl Warren of California decided to establish an Institute of Industrial Relations at Berkeley, and appointed Kerr to head it. While directing the institute, Kerr also worked independently as a labor arbitrator. His skills as a negotiator, and his impartiality, made him known as the best arbitrator on the West Coast. These abilities were essential to him as his career advanced within the university structure.

In the postwar years McCarthyism seriously infected California, and in 1948 the Board of Regents* enacted a requirement that all employees of the university sign an oath disclaiming membership in the Communist party. Most of them did, but some of the more

* The California state university system is governed by a Board of Regents appointed by the governor. The Regents appoint the chief executive officer, who is the president. Each campus is under the direction of a chancellor, although Berkeley's chancellor tends to be overshadowed by the president's geographical proximity.

distinguished professors, staunch conservatives among them, stood firm on the grounds that the oath was a violation of academic freedom.

The dispute dragged on for two years, during which none of the nonsigners was ever accused of being a Communist. The Regents, however, were unwilling to concede the right of a few men standing on principle to challenge their authority. Ultimately the nonsigners were fired. Though they were later reinstated by the courts, enduring bitterness between Regents and faculty led to a wave of resignations that sent Berkeley into serious academic decline.

Among the few faculty members who distinguished themselves in the angry dispute was Clark Kerr. Still a junior professor, Kerr had been appointed to the Committee on Privilege and Tenure, which normally had only perfunctory responsibilities. But the committee played a pivotal role during the oath battle, trying to find a compromise that would satisfy both sides. Kerr, by demonstrating his bargaining skills, was made committee chairman, and argued strenuously against the firings. Though his efforts failed, Clark Kerr established himself as a unique figure who, in a tough situation, was able to retain his credibility with all contending factions.

"It was out of that that the Berkeley faculty nominated me to be the chancellor of the Berkeley campus," Kerr told me. "I'd never been a department chairman, never been a dean, never been on any committee of real importance. But I think that the Regents at that time were appalled at what they had done and wanted to make a gesture toward the faculty.

"I had never had any plan to go into academic administration at all. In fact, I had my research planned out for ten years and had my work as an arbitrator. But my friends were all saying that anybody whom the faculty wants and the Regents will accept has an absolute duty."

The Board of Regents, thanks to some changes in membership, had by the time of Kerr's appointment in 1952 shifted to a policy of reconciliation. Kerr proved excellent at the work, deliberately and without flamboyance turning to one after another of the grievances that had alienated the teachers. Though the state's irrepressible rightists baited Kerr as the "red chancellor," the Regents regarded him with increasing esteem. Kerr was adroit in dealing not just with the faculty but with California's business and industrial elite, a

279

power in university affairs. He also showed an unforeseen talent at budget-making, long-range planning, campus management and the other bureaucratic chores of university administrators.

In recognition of his success as chancellor, the Regents—to his surprise, Kerr said—selected him in 1958 to be president of the University. His mandate was to get on with the healing. A major building program was undertaken, with the establishment of new campuses and the upgrading of old ones. Kerr granted considerable administrative autonomy to the campuses and made certain the new administrators he selected, particularly for the still volatile campus at Berkeley, had strong support from both faculty and students.

Under Kerr, the university again began to attract outstanding scholars and, by the early 1960s, Berkeley had actually pulled ahead of Harvard as the country's leading center for graduate education. In early 1964 Kerr, jointly with the Regents themselves, won the Alexander Meiklejohn Award from the American Association of University Professors for their contributions to academic freedom. To say that the scars of the McCarthy era had vanished would be an exaggeration, but Kerr was universally credited with having restored the liberal atmosphere that education requires, and the university was considered to be in remarkably good health.

Yet Kerr found that, as Regents and professors became more calm and less belligerent, the students, particularly those at Berkeley, were moving in precisely the opposite direction. Since the Chessman vigil and the anti-HUAC riot in 1960, campus issues had come and gone: racial discrimination, compulsory ROTC, controversial campus speakers, atmospheric nuclear testing, the Cuban missile crisis. Some were in the university's domain, some were public questions. Yet all seemed to be accompanied by harsh attacks by the students, directed chiefly at campus regulations.

Harassed as usual by the powerful right wing in California's politics, Kerr was in a dilemma when responding to the student attacks. He maintained that the campus rules were not, as the conservatives insisted, too liberal. On the contrary Berkeley, compared with other universities, was strictly supervised, he said, with restrictions that hung on stubbornly from past decades. Kerr, to avoid provoking his right-wing antagonists, tended to give ground only slowly before student pressure. But he was conscious of a rising tempo of demand from the students that the university recognize their right to speak out as they chose, act according to their consciences, manage their personal lives as they saw fit.

Kerr perceived that there was a malaise among the students, which went beyond their articulated complaints. Words like "meaningless" and "powerless" had crept into their discussions of their lives, and they talked of being "manipulated" by the adult world. "We oppose the depersonalization that reduces human beings to the status of things," SDS had declared in the "Port Huron Statement." Were it more poetic, this was a statement Allen Ginsberg might have made. People outside the university, scarcely aware of the counterculture, had no idea of the influence of such thinking on the campus. But Kerr had a vague feeling that the restlessness he perceived might cause him a problem.

In his lectures at Harvard in the spring of 1963, Kerr dissected the changes which seemed to have left "depersonalization" as their debris. The postwar university, he said, had become a "multiversity," serving the national purpose, contributing to military, scientific, economic and social objectives. The federal government fed the multiversity on money, but exacted a submission to federal priorities in return. The new university had risen to educate an ever-rising proportion of the young, but in the process had become an industry of its own. As the "knowledge industry," Kerr said, it had inherited the role played earlier by the railroads and the automobile as the dynamo of national growth.

As for the undergraduates, Kerr said, the "multiversity" was a confusing and unsatisfying place. "Recent changes," he noted, "have done them little good—lower teaching loads for the faculty, larger classes, the use of substitute teachers for the regular faculty, the choice of faculty members based on research accomplishments rather than instructional capacity, the fragmentation of knowledge into endless subdivisions . . . The students find themselves under a blanket of impersonal rules for admissions, for scholarships, for examinations, for degrees." The worst offenders, he acknowledged candidly, were the large state universities, which left their students with feelings of insecurity, impersonality and neglect.

Yet Kerr conspicuously declined to accept any burden for reform.

281

On the contrary, when describing his duties as president of the multiversity, he fell back on his professional training and attributed the greatest importance to his function as mediator. Though he conceded that on occasion "the mediator needs to become the gladiator," he conveyed a peculiarly passive vision of himself. It was the vision of a leader who denied responsibility for the condition of the groups within his domain, except as a condition might disrupt their fragile relations with other groups. His concern was with the equilibrium of the institution as a whole.

The mediator's first task, Kerr proclaimed, is peace: "Peace within the student body, the faculty, the trustees; and peace between and among them . . . Peace between the internal environment of the academic community and the external society that surrounds and sometimes engulfs it."

Kerr added that peace depended on the moderation of the leadership within each of these constituent groups. "When the extremists get in control . . . ," he said, "then the 'delicate balance of interests' becomes an actual war." He failed to make the obvious point that if the president neglected the problems that troubled students, extremists might then fill the void, and the war he so dreaded might inevitably ensue.

In the fall of 1963, President Kennedy was assassinated. If students were already restless and confused, as Kerr had noted at Harvard in the spring, it is probable that the assassination shattered further their sense of security, their belief in a relatively predictable future, their faith in existing institutions and processes. Kennedy had been a popular figure among Berkeley students. He had been welcomed tumultuously when he spoke on the campus in 1962. The Peace Corps had obtained more recruits from Berkeley than anywhere else. To many students, the lesson of the murder was that liberal democracy was doomed to defeat by forces that held the rules of society in contempt. The assassination gave the procedures of law a pathetic appearance, and exalted coercion as an effective instrument of social change. Kennedy's death, shocking and depressing, was also disorienting to those who had accepted a premise of order in the social structure.

Late that fall, Berkeley students turned with renewed zest to

282

bune's information, the Berkeley administration decided that Knowland could not be ignored. Furthermore, the administrators themselves regarded political activity on campus as getting out of hand, and saw the *Tribune*'s overture as a choice opportunity for restoring their own control.

The Bancroft Strip was a patch of sidewalk just outside the campus gates. The Strip had long been tolerated by Berkeley administrations as a bazaar of free speech. Student organizations set up folding tables there, and year around they displayed literature, collected donations and signed up volunteers. It was here that recruits were obtained for the civil rights demonstrations in the spring, for the anti-Goldwater picketing at the Republican convention in the summer, and for the protests at the *Tribune* in the previous weeks. For the university administration, the Strip was a safety valve, diverting student energies into relatively harmless enterprises. Noisy, colorful, forever animated, the Strip, more than anything else, gave Berkeley its reputation as America's most uninhibited campus.

Then, under the prodding of the *Tribune*, the Berkeley administration decided that the activities on the Strip were no longer so harmless. On September 14, the dean of students announced that tables would be permitted on the Bancroft Strip no more, and that speechmaking and leafleting would also be prohibited. It was the administration's effort to suppress the established traditions of the Bancroft Strip that sired the Free Speech Movement and became the *casus belli* of the Berkeley uprising.

Kerr himself was absent when the trouble started, having left California in July, even before the Republican National Convention. After participating in a series of seminars in Eastern Europe, he flew to Hong Kong and then to Tokyo, for the ceremonial opening of University of California extension centers there. It was typical work for the president of the nation's largest university system, and Kerr was normally on hand to preside over the growth of his empire.

But he was familiar with the ample evidence that trouble was likely to accompany the students' return for the fall semester. He also knew of the sensitive referendum questions on the November ballot, and even of the *Tribune*'s search for a pretext to put the university in its place. "I told the chancellors," Kerr said to me,

285

"that I thought the student situation was becoming more volatile. I said to them, let's be awfully careful that we don't do anything which excites the situation." But he left no clear directives and, if he actually conveyed the admonitions he described to me, those who remained in charge simply paid no attention to him.

The administrators of the Berkeley campus were a team of Kerr's choosing. They were known, much like Kerr himself, as energetic, sympathetic and liberal, and disposed to place a high priority on being effective. The chancellor of the Berkeley campus was Edward Strong, a sociologist, who at the time of his appointment in 1961 was considered a Kerr protégé. When Kerr was on hand, the division of authority between the two men was unclear, but in Kerr's absence Strong was in charge. Until the new directives on the Bancroft Strip were announced, Strong had been regarded as friendly to the students. But he was uncomfortable with the atmosphere of political license which he saw, and he was anxious to reestablish what he considered reasonable standards of discipline.

The differences between the administration and the students at the time of the announcement on September 14 seemed hardly monumental. Any number of compromises—of scheduling or location or procedure—appeared possible, even likely. But the administrators, feeling political pressures, were determined to stand firm, while the students, stimulated by fresh winds of freedom, had no intention of submitting. Combinations of blundering and daring, of stubbornness and cheek, of stuffiness and insouciance, produced the uprising at Berkeley. But it had been waiting for the right moment. The high drama of the events set off the differences between generations in 1964, and persuaded each side to seek refuge behind its own barricades.

Clark Kerr returned from Tokyo the day after the directive was issued. He sensed trouble at once but, by nature conciliatory rather than abrupt, he was loath to rush to a decision. He told me he advised Strong to take the order back, but Strong refused. Only because he himself had decentralized power in the university, Kerr said, was Strong able to defy him.

"If I had it to do over again," Kerr said to me, "I would make that an order. Strong might still have refused. If he had appealed it to the Regents, some of them would have liked what he had done, but they would have taken my advice. I've often wondered why I didn't do it."

The reason he did not do it, no doubt, was that the two sides of Kerr, the administrator and the liberal, were at war with each other. Since the uprising, Kerr has often said publicly that he argued with Strong in favor of patching up the differences with the students. Memoranda in the university's files, however, indicate that, at least in the early stages of the disorder, Kerr not only supported but promoted a hard line.* Kerr was in fact uncertain, as were the other Berkeley administrators, about the wisest tactics for restoring peace. This uncertainty led them to zigzag through the crisis, and commit one grave error after another.

Only the students, at the beginning, had a clear sense of what they wanted. To them, the directive of September 14 represented one more effort by the administration to enclose their lives in rules. Chancellor Strong feared that retreat on the directive would cost him control of the campus, but a wide range of student leaders perceived almost immediately that he had reversed cause and effect. If Strong did not retreat, the students would surely unite in a campaign against the Berkeley administration.

On September 17, 1964, all of the principal campus political organizations—civil rights, Democratic and Republican, radical and Socialist, religious and pacifist, conservative and even Youth for Goldwater—formed a coalition called the United Front to protest the new rules. In response to their appeal, the administration issued a "clarification," which was intended to mollify the students by promising a reasonable interpretation of the directive. But the "clarification" left intact the pivotal ban on fund-raising, recruitment and advocacy of partisan positions. The United Front, after meeting for hours, rejected the administration's concession.

At noon on September 21, the opening day of the fall semester, the first protest demonstrations took place, with a picket line of two hundred students in front of Sproul Hall, the main administration building. In the ensuing week, hundreds of students participated in picketing, rallies and all-night vigils. A large proportion of them had never before been involved in campus politics. On September

* See Max Heirich, *The Beginning: Berkeley 1964.*

regulations. Shortly before noon, two deans approached a man at CORE's table, the largest in the plaza, and informed him that he was under arrest. Campus policemen then stepped forward to place him in custody.

The man was Jack Weinberg, the twenty-four-year-old mathematics dropout who had brought Savio into the movement. Refusing to be led away, Weinberg made a series of speeches to the crowd as the police waited for reinforcements to arrive. When a squad car drove into the middle of the plaza, Weinberg, in classic nonviolent fashion, went limp, and several policemen bundled him inside. Spontaneously, student bystanders sat down around the squad car, tentatively at first, then in great numbers. When the policeman at the wheel signaled them out of the way, they refused to move.

As the students poured out of their classes for the lunch hour, the plaza filled up, until the crowd numbered in the thousands. To be heard, Mario Savio climbed barefoot on the roof of the stranded police car, in the back of which Weinberg was still uneasily seated. "We were going to hold a rally here at twelve o'clock," he declared, "and we were going to have to shout our lungs out to get people. I'm so grateful to the administration of this wonderful university. They've done it for us! Let's give them a hand."

Savio then turned to the policemen ringing the plaza, and mockingly praised them for enforcing the university's rules so well. "Just like Eichmann," said a voice from the crowd, referring to the Nazi chief who had recently been tried and executed in Israel for running the bureaucratic apparatus of the death camps. "Yeah, very good," Savio answered. "It's very, you know, like Adolf Eichmann. He had a job to do. He fit into the machinery." The crowd cheered in knowing response.

Savio then departed for Sproul Hall, to meet for negotiations with the administration. While he talked, one speaker after another succeeded him on the rooftop rostrum. Savio told the administrators that the students would disperse in return for Weinberg's release, reinstatement of the eight expelled students and a start toward discussions on the disputed campus rules. Kerr refused to make himself available to hear him, and Strong rejected Savio's terms categorically.

In midafternoon about five hundred students left the plaza for the Regents, some of them would have liked what he had done, but they would have taken my advice. I've often wondered why I didn't do it."

The reason he did not do it, no doubt, was that the two sides of Kerr, the administrator and the liberal, were at war with each other. Since the uprising, Kerr has often said publicly that he argued with Strong in favor of patching up the differences with the students. Memoranda in the university's files, however, indicate that, at least in the early stages of the disorder, Kerr not only supported but promoted a hard line.* Kerr was in fact uncertain, as were the other Berkeley administrators, about the wisest tactics for restoring peace. This uncertainty led them to zigzag through the crisis, and commit one grave error after another.

Only the students, at the beginning, had a clear sense of what they wanted. To them, the directive of September 14 represented one more effort by the administration to enclose their lives in rules. Chancellor Strong feared that retreat on the directive would cost him control of the campus, but a wide range of student leaders perceived almost immediately that he had reversed cause and effect. If Strong did not retreat, the students would surely unite in a campaign against the Berkeley administration.

On September 17, 1964, all of the principal campus political organizations—civil rights, Democratic and Republican, radical and Socialist, religious and pacifist, conservative and even Youth for Goldwater—formed a coalition called the United Front to protest the new rules. In response to their appeal, the administration issued a "clarification," which was intended to mollify the students by promising a reasonable interpretation of the directive. But the "clarification" left intact the pivotal ban on fund-raising, recruitment and advocacy of partisan positions. The United Front, after meeting for hours, rejected the administration's concession.

At noon on September 21, the opening day of the fall semester, the first protest demonstrations took place, with a picket line of two hundred students in front of Sproul Hall, the main administration building. In the ensuing week, hundreds of students participated in picketing, rallies and all-night vigils. A large proportion of them had never before been involved in campus politics. On September

* See Max Heirich, *The Beginning: Berkeley 1964.*

28, the administration announced another modest liberalization of the directive but did not retract the controversial bans. The United Front the next day set up "advocative" tables on the Bancroft Strip in direct challenge to the administrators.

Two days later members of the dean's office, accompanied by campus police, approached some of the tables, gave students seated at them an opportunity to leave, then requested identification of those who remained. Mario Savio, back from his summer in Mississippi, was raising funds for Friends of SNCC at one of the tables. It is recorded that a student at an adjoining table asked him whether he thought there would be student support if disciplinary action were taken. Savio replied that he did not know but was willing to explore the prospects of a mass protest. That day, five students were cited for violation of the university's rules.

When the five appeared at the dean's office in Sproul Hall, they were accompanied by five hundred others, who insisted upon receiving comparable disciplinary treatment. Savio, not among the original five, was promptly added to the list, along with two more students, for organizing the protest. After a meeting in which the dean declined to drop any of the charges, the five hundred students commenced a sit-in in the corridors of Sproul Hall.

As the hours passed, Savio maintained the solidarity of the sit-in, speaking at length of the denial of democracy in the operation of the university. At midnight, the administration announced the indefinite suspension of all eight students who had been cited. At that point, the sit-ins converged in the corridors and decided to transform their United Front into a permanent organization called the Free Speech Movement. As FSM, it gave its name to the Berkeley rebellion. At 2:40 in the morning, the students disbanded and went home.

Mario Savio, to whom leadership now gravitated, was a tall and slender Italian-American, with dark brooding eyes and frizzy hair. Born in New York in 1942 of working-class parents, he was indoctrinated in Catholicism, attended Manhattan College, which is Catholic, and then Queens College, where he was president of the Confraternity of Christian Doctrine. Though a brilliant physics student, he shifted his interest at Queens to philosophy, and embarked on reading the great philosophers. In 1963, after a summer of community work in a Mexican village, he moved with his parents to Glendora, a Los Angeles suburb, and enrolled in Berkeley. He had

288

excellent grades and, in the autumn of the Berkeley uprising, he needed three semesters to complete his degree.

Savio had become active in politics only after he encountered the civil rights movement in 1963. He participated in the various demonstrations for minority hiring, and he was among those arrested in March during the mass picketing at the Palace Hotel. While in jail, his cellmate was Jack Weinberg, who had dropped out of graduate work in mathematics to organize for CORE, and who urged Savio to volunteer for the Mississippi Summer Project. Savio did, and spent much of his tour in McComb, the brutal Delta town where Bob Moses had labored for four years. One time in Mississippi he was attacked by white men with clubs. Back in Berkeley in the fall, Savio was designated chairman of University Friends of SNCC, and started organizing a program for the co-workers in Mississippi whom he had left behind.

Savio thought of his involvement in the Berkeley rebellion as an extension of his commitment to civil rights. "I witnessed tyranny," he said later. "I saw groups of men in the minority working their wills over the majority. Then I came back here and found the university preventing us from collecting money for use there, and even stopping us from getting people to go to Mississippi to help." But for the civil rights movement, Savio would have been a bystander to FSM, and there were many others like him. It is virtually certain, in fact, that, but for the civil rights movement, there would not have been a Berkeley uprising, or a white student movement at all.

Timid in private meetings, even given to stammering, Savio became electrifying on the public platform. His eloquence stemmed not so much from a commanding style but from a remarkable capacity to see beyond immediate issues and articulate deeper concerns. On the night of the Sproul Hall sit-in, he argued that the protesting students had caused a breakdown in Clark Kerr's "multiversity machine," and that the university wanted to expel the parts that were "gumming up the works." It was through Savio's inspiration that FSM transformed a petty dispute over university regulations into a confrontation of philosophical dimensions.

On the morning following the sit-in, Berkeley administrators looked out the windows of Sproul Hall and saw students, this time in the heart of the campus, sitting at tables industriously violating regulations. Shortly before noon, two deans approached a man at CORE's table, the largest in the plaza, and informed him that he was under arrest. Campus policemen then stepped forward to place him in custody.

The man was Jack Weinberg, the twenty-four-year-old mathematics dropout who had brought Savio into the movement. Refusing to be led away, Weinberg made a series of speeches to the crowd as the police waited for reinforcements to arrive. When a squad car drove into the middle of the plaza, Weinberg, in classic nonviolent fashion, went limp, and several policemen bundled him inside. Spontaneously, student bystanders sat down around the squad car, tentatively at first, then in great numbers. When the policeman at the wheel signaled them out of the way, they refused to move.

As the students poured out of their classes for the lunch hour, the plaza filled up, until the crowd numbered in the thousands. To be heard, Mario Savio climbed barefoot on the roof of the stranded police car, in the back of which Weinberg was still uneasily seated. "We were going to hold a rally here at twelve o'clock," he declared, "and we were going to have to shout our lungs out to get people. I'm so grateful to the administration of this wonderful university. They've done it for us! Let's give them a hand."

Savio then turned to the policemen ringing the plaza, and mockingly praised them for enforcing the university's rules so well. "Just like Eichmann," said a voice from the crowd, referring to the Nazi chief who had recently been tried and executed in Israel for running the bureaucratic apparatus of the death camps. "Yeah, very good," Savio answered. "It's very, you know, like Adolf Eichmann. He had a job to do. He fit into the machinery." The crowd cheered in knowing response.

Savio then departed for Sproul Hall, to meet for negotiations with the administration. While he talked, one speaker after another succeeded him on the rooftop rostrum. Savio told the administrators that the students would disperse in return for Weinberg's release, reinstatement of the eight expelled students and a start toward discussions on the disputed campus rules. Kerr refused to make himself available to hear him, and Strong rejected Savio's terms categorically.

In midafternoon about five hundred students left the plaza for another sit-in at Sproul Hall, but they withdrew after several hours. Throughout the late afternoon and early evening, the crowd remained packed around the police car, listening quietly to whomever chose to speak. Near midnight some fraternity men came by, hollered some epithets and threw some eggs, but there was no serious violence. After midnight the bulk of the demonstrators drifted away, leaving several hundred students bedded down in the plaza, many of them in sleeping bags, to pass the night.

In the morning, the crowd around the stranded police car swelled once again, reaching four thousand by noon. By now, the protest had become a Bay Area tourist attraction, and no one could tell the demonstrators from the spectators. But student solidarity remained intact. The coalition of campus political groups that made up FSM —from the W. E. B. Du Bois Club on the left to the Youth for Goldwater on the right—had weathered a series of internal stresses in a tumultuous meeting, and their solidarity emerged unbroken.

Kerr that morning spent several hours meeting with his administrators, as well as with representatives of the governor and law enforcement agencies. In a luncheon speech in San Francisco, he said he would make no concessions "in the face of mob action." Late in the afternoon, policemen from Berkeley, Alameda County, Oakland and the California Highway Patrol positioned themselves strategically on the campus. Then Kerr reversed himself on discussions, and agreed to meet with the demonstration leaders after all.

News of the police arrival brought a new rush of students to the plaza, raising their number beyond seven thousand. Though Kerr pledged not to use the police until after he had met with protest leaders, the scene was tense. Veterans of civil disobedience in the crowd passed out instructions on arrest techniques—remove valuable rings and watches, take sharp objects from pockets, loosen clothing, pack closely together, do not link arms, go limp, give no information beyond name and address, ask to see your lawyer.

About 7:30 in the evening, arriving exhausted from the meeting with Kerr, Mario Savio climbed to the now flattened roof of the marooned police car. He then read a document that would be known as the October 2nd Agreement. In return for student abstention from further illegal protests, Savio said, the university would submit the rules dispute to a joint committee of students, faculty

291

and administrators for recommendations. It would also place the eight student suspensions before a faculty committee for reconsideration and would take no disciplinary action against Jack Weinberg after his booking by police. Kerr also promised to support the deeding of the Bancroft Strip to the city, so that it would fall outside campus jurisdiction.

When he finished the reading, Savio said, "Let us agree by acclamation to accept this document. I ask you to rise quietly and with dignity, and go home." The huge crowd responded as Savio asked. A few minutes later, the police began to withdraw. At eight o'clock Joan Baez, the folk singer, held an open-air concert on the campus to celebrate the students' victory.

The police car episode summed up much of the character of the Free Speech Movement, and of the student rebellion that swept campuses in the succeeding years. There was indignation, sacrifice, comedy, surrealism, self-absorption. There was also—in keeping with the spirit of the times—a calculated disorganization, a leadership based on consensus rather than authority, a do-your-own-thing absence of structure which functioned only because a sense of solidarity went with it. FSM had set up an executive committee to make policy, and a steering committee for tactical decisions. But both represented a kaleidoscope of viewpoints, and neither offered a process to replace the high-spirited spontaneity which often determined the course of events.

Savio did not regard himself as an FSM chief. Having spent the summer with SNCC in Mississippi, he came to share SNCC's suspicion of leadership, including his own. When he returned to Sproul Plaza after his meeting with Kerr, he apologized to the crowd for not having submitted the agreement he had negotiated for real democratic consideration.

Once, when a reporter asked him about FSM's intentions, he answered reproachfully, "This is not a cult of one personality or of two personalities. It is a broadly based movement, and I will not say anything unless it is made clear." Another time, in discussing whether majority decisions were binding, he said, "You cannot bind individual consciences. Those who want to go are not, therefore, finks." In pondering his own power to sway crowds, he mused, "I've been criticized because they say mass democracy is dishonest. I've watched Fidel Castro, and I agree. But I have tried

292

to feel what those who commit themselves on the line are feeling. I have really tried."

Like the civil rights movement, the student movement would not always possess this openness, this innocence, this love. It, too, would take an ugly turn. But in the heady autumn of FSM, the movement seemed genuinely to be a confrontation between beauty and blemish, ideals and compromise, purity and hypocrisy. Mario Savio appeared incorruptible, Clark Kerr seemed tired. In time, it would be understood that the issues were more complicated than they seemed then, but in 1964 the student movement was still very young and very virtuous.

In the weeks after the October 2nd Agreement, various bodies and delegations met, separately and together: faculty and students, Regents and administration. It was clear that the administration felt itself under considerable pressure from the Regents to reassert disciplinary control over the campus. The faculty, on the other hand, was generally sympathetic to FSM's demands. FSM was seriously divided over whether to return to demonstrations as counterpressure, but protest activity remained at a nondisruptive level. Nonetheless, an uneasiness ruled the campus during the simmering debate over the agreement's implementation. Kerr, as usual, tried to mollify all sides, and Savio, on the few occasions that he spoke at rallies, urged his followers to be patient and calm.

On November 24, Chancellor Strong finally announced the revised rules, applicable not only to the Bancroft Strip but to other areas of the campus. They authorized student political organizations "to accept donations and membership sign-ups, and to distribute political and social action material from tables." Though there was a shade of equivocation in the text which upset some of the more radical members of FSM, the changes made it appear that the administration had carried out its part of the bargain. FSM, as Savio put it, could now "fold up shop."

Then, the next day, the administration shattered the illusion, addressing to Savio and three other students letters which arrived during Thanksgiving recess. The letters accused the four of having "led and encouraged numerous demonstrations in keeping a university police car and an arrested person therein entrapped on the

293

Berkeley campus for a period of approximately 32 hours . . ." The four students were ordered to appear before a faculty committee, whose recommendations would be advisory to the administration.

To the FSM leadership, the four "Thanksgiving letters" were a betrayal. Though technically within the terms of the October 2nd Agreement, they were no doubt a violation of its spirit. The Bancroft Strip regulations, which had provoked the Sproul Plaza demonstration, had by now been canceled. The four letters were contrary to faculty recommendations, and the administration had not even hinted in the previous weeks of deliberations at the action they initiated. The letters were a piece in a compromise between the hard-liners and the soft-liners around Kerr, but they were sure to destroy the prospect of stability on campus. It could have come as no surprise that they forged a new solidarity within the student body around the Free Speech Movement.

When classes resumed on the Monday after Thanksgiving, and Strong reaffirmed the charges, FSM announced a mass sit-in at Sproul Hall, to be held on Wednesday. The teaching assistants, all graduate students, met next and voted to strike. Meanwhile, FSM sympathizers on other campuses planned action, and there was talk of closing down the entire university. At noon on Wednesday, six thousand people appeared for a noon rally on Sproul Plaza, and Joan Baez sang "Blowin' in the Wind," the new anthem of the generation's protest.

That was the rally at which Savio delivered the most celebrated statement of the Berkeley uprising. Inspired by the civil rights movement's exhortation to personal freedom, Savio fused the political analysis of C. Wright Mills with the counterculture's rejection of industrial society to articulate a painful insight into a generation's malaise. Grappling to explain the discontent, he said:

> "We have an autocracy which runs this university. . . .
> This is a firm, and if the Board of Regents are the board
> of directors, and if President Kerr in fact is the man-
> ager, then . . . the faculty are a bunch of employees
> and we're the raw material. But we're a bunch of raw
> material that don't mean . . . to be made into any prod-
> uct, don't mean to end up being bought by some
> clients of the university. . . . We're human beings.

"And that brings me to civil disobedience. There's a time when the operation of the machine becomes so odious, makes you so sick at heart, that you can't take part, you can't even tacitly take part. And you've got to put your bodies upon the gears and upon the wheels, upon the levers, upon all the apparatus, and you've got to make it stop. And you've got to indicate to the people who run it, to the people who own it, that unless you're free the machine will be prevented from working at all."

Even from the perspective of a decade later, it is not easy to evaluate Savio's statement. Was it simply the traditional complaint of sons against fathers, a declaration of evanescent ideals of those who had not yet inherited the earth, a cliché dignified within the context of civil rights? Or was it the herald of a new set of values for what was modishly called by many who had no material cares the "postscarcity age"? Certainly those who had been thrilled by the "Port Huron Statement" believed that Savio's words contained some transcendental wisdom, appropriate to the era. When Savio finished, more than a thousand of those people marched defiantly into Sproul Hall, with Joan Baez strumming the cadence on her guitar.

The students took seats along the corridors and, arranging themselves one or two deep from the first floor to the fourth, sang songs, played cards or read. A few classes of a "freedom school" were held. A study hall was reserved on the top floor, and quiet was enforced. FSM monitors, wearing armbands, made certain no offices were invaded, but the administration gave most employees of the building the day off anyway. As the dinner hour approached, FSM volunteers brought in food from the outside.

When the administration met to consider tactics, Kerr favored doing nothing about the sit-in, on the grounds that boredom and fatigue would ultimately take over, and the students would leave voluntarily. But Governor Pat Brown, with other considerations, intruded into the debate. Brown felt his political career had already been endangered by his appearing too soft on the students. Kerr said it was the governor himself who gave the order to clear Sproul Hall, and Strong endorsed the decision.

At 7:00 P.M., the campus police took possession of the doors, allowing anyone to leave but no one to enter. Inside, movies were shown to pass the time. By one o'clock the hall lights were out, and the demonstrators had settled in for the night. At 3:00 A.M., Strong entered the building with a clatter and proceeded to read the students a final order to disperse. After a few minutes of scurrying and confusion, some six hundred policemen went to work.

With great solemnity, they started clearing on the fourth floor, and moved downward. Many of the students went limp and were dragged down the stairs, but most obeyed the arrest orders, and only one scuffle was reported. At first the police were courteous, but they grew harsh as they tired. The paper work, conducted in the basement, took twelve hours, and by morning a large crowd of FSM supporters had congregated around Sproul Hall. The arrested students, driven away in buses and vans, were taken first to local jails, but almost all wound up at the Santa Rita Rehabilitation Center, known as an internment camp for Japanese-Americans during World War II. It was promptly dubbed the "Santa Rita campus."

In all, some eight hundred demonstrators were locked up, which made the arrest the biggest in California history. All were released during the day, having posted bail ranging from $56 to $110, most of it raised on campus. Driven back by fellow students, the demonstrators arrived on the campus in triumph.

Who the eight hundred were soon became a matter of intense interest, particularly since appalled conservatives were quick to characterize them as rowdies and beatniks, or as professional agitators. In fact, a survey conducted by sociologists within Sproul Hall, later checked for accuracy against the arrest list, indicated that the eight hundred bore a remarkable resemblance to the campus population as a whole.

The sex predominance was roughly six to four male, and the level of academic performance was well within the normal range. The ratio of participants was disproportionately high for the social sciences, arts and humanities, and disproportionately low for engineering, but every subject major except business was represented. Where the eight hundred departed significantly from the norm was in the unusually high educational level of the parents, in the underrepresentation of Catholics and overrepresentation of Jews, and in the proportion of Protestants who denied any religious affiliation. Refuting the notion of outside agitation, the survey showed that of the total arrested less than 10 percent were nonstudents, and half of the nonstudents were recent dropouts.*

On Thursday morning, while the police were still clearing Sproul Hall, the teaching assistants' strike in support of FSM, which had been scheduled to begin the next day, started spontaneously. Picket lines formed at dawn at the campus entrances and around the main buildings. They thickened as students arrived for classes, and made the decision to identify themselves with FSM. By eleven o'clock, five thousand or more students had crowded into Sproul Plaza for a rally that FSM had scheduled for noon. An antistrike protest, held nearby, drew only a few hundred. After the speeches on the plaza began, a squad of policemen attempted to seize FSM's sound equipment, but the crowd was so dense that it could not get through.

The next day, the strike was estimated to be 60 to 70 percent effective. Most of the teaching assistants—nine hundred out of twelve hundred, according to an estimate—canceled their classes. At a heavily attended meeting, the regular faculty passed by acclamation a resolution endorsing the FSM position, and a substantial number of professors also canceled classes for the day. Campus service employees refused to cross the picket lines, and Bay Area trade unions spoke up for the strike. Around the country, as well as at other University of California campuses, student groups declared their solidarity with FSM.

By Friday, a sense that the strike concerned issues larger than the rules also permeated the campus. Posters appeared with such statements as "My Mind Is Not the Property of the University of California" and "Shut This Factory Down." The IBM card became a symbol of the protest. A student who worked at the university's computer center had punched hundreds of cards with the words "strike," "FSM," and "Free Speech," and students wore them around their necks. One protester coined what became the most celebrated slogan of the uprising, when he displayed a sign saying, "I am a UC Student: Do Not Fold, Bend or Mutilate."

* These findings concur basically with the profiles drawn of student activists of the 1960s around the country. For example, Richard Flacks, a sociologist with a long interest in the student movement, reported in *Protest: Student Activism in America* that campus protesters as a whole tended to have intellectual tastes, good grades and secular attitudes, as well as parents with superior educations, high incomes and liberal political preferences.

Faced with an impending set of recommendations from the faculty, Kerr chose the moment to try to recapture the initiative. Canceling classes, only a few of which were being conducted anyway, he announced with some fanfare that he had a series of new proposals to make. On Monday, December 7, he convoked the entire student body, with the faculty and the administrative staff. On the stage of the campus's open-air theater, Kerr spoke solemnly before a semicircle of sixteen thousand tightly coiled people. In the front row, directly before him, sat Mario Savio, audibly muttering "hypocrite."

Kerr's recommendations, made after consultation with Governor Brown, were unequal to the drama of the setting. He agreed to revoke the charges contained in the "Thanksgiving letters," and to restrict discipline of the Sproul Hall eight hundred to the charges brought by police. But he put no limitation upon the discipline of those involved in the massive student strike, which was the product of the Sproul Hall arrests. Since each event of the escalating rebellion was related to the previous one, Kerr seemed to ignore logic by placing liability on the students for only the last of them. To the students, the proposals were another inexplicable shift in policy, and no compromise at all.

Kerr's procedure, furthermore, was a severe irritant. In his bland style, he presented his points, refusing then to entertain either questions or discussion. Yet, the essence of the Free Speech Movement was the insistence of students on being heard, and fundamental to its character was a commitment to dialogue. Standing at the podium, Kerr seemed to personify the deafness of the bureaucracy against which the students were rebelling.

After Kerr finished speaking, a strange incident occurred. Mario Savio, having been refused permission earlier to reply, mounted the stage and sauntered toward the microphone. Before the entire audience, two policemen grabbed him roughly and, when he went limp, dragged him backstage. Several students, attempting to come to his aid, were pushed off. The amphitheater was degenerating into pandemonium over the seizure when Kerr, reacting quickly, ordered that Savio be released and allowed to speak.

Savio's intentions in approaching the microphone were never

298

made clear. He said later he wanted simply to make an announcement. Kerr explained that the police, having been alerted to the
possibility of disruption, had grabbed Savio on their own. But, to
the audience, this was allegory: here was the contest that was central to the FSM struggle, between free speech and authority. By
only the narrowest of margins was bedlam averted.

When Savio reappeared from behind the curtain, he was disheveled and obviously unnerved. He spoke briefly, announcing what
had become a regular campus event, FSM's noon rally. "Clear this
disastrous scene," he said, "and get down to discussing the issues."
When he returned to the plaza, a crowd of ten thousand was there
to listen. Then democracy prevailed: Kerr's proposals were rejected by an overwhelming roar.

In the ensuing December days, as the strike dragged on, the
Berkeley administration's isolation from its campus constituencies
was unmistakably established. In an undergraduate election, in
which the turnout was unprecedented, a slate that supported FSM
gained control of the student government. At a general meeting of
the faculty, after a long and tumultuous debate, a resolution supporting FSM was passed by 824 to 115. The consensus of the faculty seemed to be that the students had shown admirable discretion
in applying nonviolent civil disobedience to the laudable objective
of free speech. But there was a discernible anxiety, at least among
a minority, that a successful rebellion at Berkeley could open the
way to a period of campus disarray such as America had never
known.

After hints from the Regents that they would recognize the mandate for reform expressed by the students and the faculty, the campus strike dissolved, and the weeks before the Christmas recess,
though edgy, were calm. The Regents met on December 18 and
passed an ambiguous set of resolutions which, on the whole,
seemed to endorse FSM's position on free speech. Though Savio
called it "horrendous," their action indicated that positions had
shifted significantly. If the administration had once adopted a hard
line to mollify the Regents, the Regents had now moved to a softer
line than the administration to mollify faculty and students.

Then, on January 2, 1965, the Regents met again and, quite un-
expectedly, fired Ed Strong, the Berkeley chancellor, who had long
since become the hard-liners' champion. Strong's departure ap-

peared to announce the end of the administration's disputes with FSM over discipline, as well as over the original issue of campus rules.

Kerr, delighted to be rid of his truculent subordinate, took the resolution as a personal endorsement. "We didn't give away the university, you know," he said to me. "We made virtually no concessions. We really gave back the students what they'd had before the unfortunate order in September 1964." Though Kerr may have gloated, the Regents' move looked to the students like a huge victory. With final exams approaching, the taste for struggle waned, and FSM voted to disband.

January and February of 1965 in Berkeley provided an interlude of geniality. Under the tolerant eye of the new chancellor, Martin Meyerson, students put up their tables, not only on the Bancroft Strip but at other sites on the campus. The campaigns for civil rights and other causes, interrupted since the fall, were resumed with their old vigor and zeal.

Campus CORE returned to picketing, prudently shifting from the *Oakland Tribune* to some downtown restaurants, but the times were also beckoning energies in new directions. A group of graduate students who had tutored FSM activists to help them through exams established a Free University to offer "socially relevant" subjects not included in the campus curriculum. Another group, most of them FSM veterans, founded a controversial magazine called *Spider* to satisfy the current attraction to radical politics, drugs, liberated sex and rock music.

Meanwhile, the street scene intensified, and increasingly bizarre forms of dress appeared, both on campus and off. Strolling folk singers provided free entertainment and poets read their verses. Some Californians looked upon the atmosphere as license. Others saw it, after the tensions of the autumn, as a restoration of Berkeley's easygoing charm.

The idyll ended abruptly on March 3, when a young man from New York, unaffiliated with the university, wandered onto the Berkeley campus wearing a sign lettered FUCK. Campus police arrested him on the steps of the Student Union.

The next morning, several students associated with FSM appeared at the office of Chancellor Meyerson, to demand that the

charges be dropped. When Meyerson refused, they proceeded to call an "obscenity" rally on the Student Union steps. About 150 students showed up, obviously amused rather than troubled by the latest crisis. Treating the matter playfully, several students spoke, including the chairman of the Conservative Club, who announced that a thousand "Fuck Communism" signs had been ordered for distribution. Later, a table was set up in behalf of the "Fuck Defense Fund," and a graduate student read aloud passages containing the disputed word from *Lady Chatterley's Lover*.

Hastily reconvened, the FSM executive committee debated how to get out of a controversy in which it had no interest and which reflected unfavorably on its cause. The newspapers treated the "obscenity" rallies as another round in the free speech struggle, and before long the FSM initials were being said to signify "Filthy Speech Movement." Once arrests took place, the FSM people felt compelled to acknowledge some responsibility for the students involved. Yet FSM saw itself being trapped, and it tried to limit its involvement in the controversy to a discreet plea for "due process" for the accused.

Kerr, always aiming to keep his constituencies in equilibrium, felt squeezed by the unremitting tension between California's right-wingers and the student body. From his perspective, excessive power had tipped to the students in recent months but now, with FSM vulnerable, he saw the opportunity to recoup. A week after the forbidden word appeared on the campus, he described the situation as "a new confrontation potentially filled with great passion." FSM pretended to see it as no confrontation at all, called Kerr a liar and said his statement was "an insult to students, faculty and local administrators." But, this time, Kerr moved nimbly.

His wedge was a question left unresolved by the Regents: whether the administration could limit expression on the campus which would be constitutionally safeguarded elsewhere. "The university must have the right," Kerr declared, "to augment civil law with rules that will protect and enhance educational purpose." A few months earlier the faculty would have challenged such a contention, and the Regents at that time seemed resigned to backing the professors. But the speech at issue was no longer exhortation in behalf of the noble cause of civil rights but public proclamation of the word "fuck," and old allies were scurrying away.

On March 9, 1965, the chairman of the Board of Regents, Edward

301

Carter, phoned Kerr with an ultimatum to expel any offending students at once. Kerr, in spite of his designs on student power, declared he was shocked to encounter such an intrusion upon his professional domain. "It occurred to me for the first time," Kerr said to me later, "how much more scared they were of Freud than of Marx. The chairman was just violent about the whole thing." For the master bureaucrat, FUCK became the pretext for putting not only the students but the Regents in their place.

Very adroitly, Kerr called a press conference a few hours after he received Carter's order and announced that he and Meyerson would resign. "If the board had stepped in without having gone through any judicial process and gotten rid of these kids," he said to me very solemnly, "it would have been a terrible thing. Martin and I really laid our lives on the line to stop it." Meyerson actually submitted a letter of resignation. Kerr said he would, but never did.

The reaction from the campus was immediate, with sympathetic messages to the administration from the faculty and from the student government. At a mass meeting three days later, the professors condemned the students' "willful flaunting of obscenity," and overwhelmingly voted their support of Kerr and the Berkeley bureaucrats in their conflict with the Regents.

The following day, Kerr and Meyerson met with the Board of Regents in closed session and, afterward, announced that they would remain. In an accompanying statement, Kerr said, "The Regents and both of us completely disapprove of the obscene behavior which took place recently on the Berkeley campus . . . Proceedings are now under way to discipline the students involved in an orderly and prompt way." Kerr's feint had worked superbly, leaving him in the lee of the rising winds of the right, and once again the recognized mediator among the university's various constituencies. Only the militants of the Free Speech Movement were now excluded from his consensus.

Late in April, Meyerson dismissed one student from the university and suspended three others for their role in the obscenity incident. When Savio, before a noon rally of fifteen hundred people, declared "the end of our honeymoon with Marty," the university cut off the power for his loudspeakers. A few days later, the faculty endorsed Meyerson's disciplinary action and, in a campus election the following week, only a small minority of the pro-FSM candidates won seats to the student government.

302

Tired after so many months of unremitting tension, Savio knew that he had also been defeated. Like Bob Moses after the MFDP delegation limped back to Mississippi, he withdrew from FSM after the obscenity episode, and from virtually all further involvement in the student struggle. He condemned the faculty for abandoning the cause of students' rights, but he made clear that his decision to go was personal rather than political.

"If the student movement at Berkeley must inevitably fail without my leadership," he said, "then it were best that it fail." At his last student rally, Savio told his startled audience, "Lest I feel deserving of the charge of 'Bonapartism,' which even I sometimes have made against myself, I'd like to wish you good luck and good-bye." With that, Mario Savio ebbed back into obscurity.

The FSM era continued to claim its victims, however, as the political pendulum in California swung relentlessly rightward. In the summer of 1965, Martin Meyerson was refused permanent appointment as chancellor of the Berkeley campus because he insisted that the Regents desist from further intervention in administrative affairs. A year later, the conservative Ronald Reagan supplanted the liberal Pat Brown as governor, largely on a campaign against "the sit-ins, the teach-ins, the walkouts" at Berkeley, and on the promise to "organize a throw-out" within the University of California, with the first target being Clark Kerr.

"See, I'd spent my life really fighting off the right as chancellor and as president," Clark Kerr said to me, explaining why he had been fired. "The left in California had no power of its own. It could draw headlines, but that just set off the right. One of the things that so disturbed me during the FSM thing was to see the left feeding into the hands of the right. When the final decisions were going to be made, it would be the right that would make them."

Kerr, no doubt, considered himself a man of the left. He thought of himself as a liberal, as devoted to free speech as Joe Rauh to civil rights. In his own terms, he played the role in Berkeley that Rauh had played in Atlantic City—a practical and responsible man, a lightning rod for the assaults of the right, a defender of a set of liberal values he shared with a group farther to his left. A bureaucrat, Kerr admittedly played an artful game, and made compromises. But, he argued, under difficult circumstances he had served free speech well. He did not enjoy it that, like Rauh, he was turned by the young into a symbol of the shabbiness of American liberalism.

To Kerr, the fact that he had rendered service to liberalism was proven by his selection as target, and finally victim, of California's right-wingers. In the campaign for governor in 1966, Reagan had called Kerr too soft on students and, at the first Regents' meeting after the election, he kept his campaign promise. The new governor fired the man FSM had denounced as a tool of the conservatives, for being an instrument of liberal ideas.

In the end, no one was quite sure what the Berkeley uprising had been all about. The immediate issues were easy enough to define and, by normal democratic standards, the administration's position was substantially weaker than the students', who had a right to their indignation. But the magnitude of the students' response suggested that there were surely underlying issues, and these remained much more elusive. They would provoke the best thinking of sociologists, philosophers, psychiatrists and others, on the campus and off, as the student movement grew throughout the decade.

"As an avant-garde campus, Berkeley was going to be in trouble at some point," Kerr said to me, when I questioned him about causation. "It didn't have to be at that time over this issue. But given the nature of San Francisco and the tradition of the Berkeley campus and what was going on around the world, in Japan in 1960 and the movement of the blacks, Berkeley was going to be in trouble at some time.

"I think the campus itself had nothing to do with it, that it came out of the external atmosphere. Student movements are terribly volatile as to when they rise and fall, as to what issues they're going to take, and what their tactics are going to be. The students came in with a style picked up from the black movement. I don't think the multiversity or the IBM card had really much of anything to do with it."

Mario Savio agreed, in statements made during the turmoil, that the Free Speech Movement came out of the black movement. In fact, he said, "there appears to be little else in American life today which can claim the allegiance of men." He called middle-class life "flat and stale" and a "wasteland," and he tried hard in his own mind to reconcile his commitment to civil rights with his role in

304

the Berkeley rebellion, which was conducted overwhelmingly by the white and the privileged, and directed to their concerns.

"Last summer I went to Mississippi," he told his fellow students during the Sproul Hall sit-in, "to join the struggle there for civil rights. This fall I am engaged in another phase of the same struggle, this time in Berkeley. The two battlefields may seem quite different to some observers, but this is not the case. The same rights are at stake in both places—the right to participate as citizens in a democratic society and to struggle against the same enemy. In Mississippi an autocratic and powerful minority rules, through organized violence, to suppress the vast, virtually powerless, majority. In California, the privileged minority manipulates the university bureaucracy to suppress the students' political expression."

Yet, when Savio got down to some of his specific grievances, the case he made was weak. Having encountered the "organized status quo in Mississippi," he said, he found "it is the same in Berkeley." The example he cited was that in Berkeley "we find it impossible usually to meet with anyone but secretaries. Beyond that, we find functionaries who cannot make policy but can only hide behind the rules." Such treatment was no doubt frustrating, but it was hardly like being beaten with clubs, as Fannie Lou Hamer was, or shot dead, like Herbert Lee, or even denied the right to vote, which was the grievance of the Mississippi Summer Project.

Still, even conceding that FSM was a derivation of the black movement, and that some of Savio's gripes were trifles, more than a little of his refrain rang painfully true. His words had their echo in the "Port Huron Statement." His tune was hummed through the counterculture, and would reverberate throughout the student movement. "Society provides no challenge," Savio declared. "It is a bleak scene, but it is all a lot of us have to look forward to . . . American society is simply no longer exciting . . . America is becoming ever more the utopia of sterilized, automated contentment . . . This chrome-plated consumers' paradise would have us grow up to be well-behaved children."

These were not petty complaints. They went to the heart of contemporary American culture, and the analysis was widely shared among youth. The conditions that Savio lamented were scarcely susceptible to liberal reform. As social criticism, his message was profoundly radical.

305

Savio offered a foreshadowing of the remainder of the decade when he said, "The most exciting things going on in America today are movements to change America." Though the young had been raised in intellectual and moral sterility, he went on, "an important minority of men and women coming to the front have shown that they will die rather than be standardized, replaceable, and irrelevant." Savio, as it turned out, overstated in predicting that they would die, but they surely proved they were willing to raise a lot of hell.

After the Free Speech Movement was subdued in the spring of 1965, a sullen rage invaded the Berkeley campus. The good-natured atmosphere of the police car episode would, in the annals of student rebellion, be remembered with nostalgia. FSM was suppressed and Savio was gone, but the Berkeley students' achievement in making a great university quake became lore on every campus in the country. The genie out of the bottle, before the spring of 1965 was past there were demonstrations over a wide diversity of issues at a dozen colleges, among them Yale, Penn, the University of Colorado and Notre Dame.

Strangely, the war in Vietnam was barely mentioned during the Berkeley rebellion, nor was Goldwater's challenge to President Johnson. While Berkeley students discussed hypocrisy and the nature of man, and conducted rallies and sit-ins, the rest of the country argued about the first American bombing of North Vietnam and civil rights and world peace, and went to the polls to vote. FSM waged the struggle, at least in part, as if its concern was not human politics but human perfection, as if the boundary of its jurisdiction was the psyche, or at most San Francisco Bay.

In February, 1965, during the lull just prior to the "filthy speech" outburst, the American government initiated a war policy of sustained bombardment of North Vietnam. Even then, the campuses were in no hurry to notice the nature of the war. But, if there was among students in the mid-1960s a vague malaise in search of an issue, President Johnson now provided the issue. Before long he, not Clark Kerr, would be the object of campus fury. Riding a wave of opposition to the Vietnam conflict, the student movement would soon thrive.

306

IX
PAUL WILLIAMS:
Exploding Watts

1965

"I finally got to the supermarket. It hadn't burned down yet and I went in. I took some groceries home and then my mother wanted me to get some eggs. I had to go back in a giant burning building. It could have caved in on me to get some eggs. The eggs could have been hard-boiled by the time I got home. But it was the principle of the thing. Going into a store was uplifting yourself."

"WHY WATTS?" everyone asked in August of 1965, while the buildings were still smoldering and the bodies lay uncounted. Compared to the slums of America's older and more crowded cities, Los Angeles's black ghetto looked almost splendid. Its streets were wide and uncongested, its homes detached and set on decent-sized lots, its location central to the city's concentrations of industry and commerce. No authority with a white face stopped Watts's blacks from casting a vote, or from using the rest rooms at the train station. In a survey conducted nationally by the Urban League in 1964, Los Angeles ranked first among sixty-eight American cities in the conditions of Negro life.

Even as the National Guard patrolled among the rubble along Watts's boulevards, Governor Pat Brown, a man genuinely concerned about the poor and the powerless, could say with bewilderment, "Here in California, we have a wonderful working relationship between whites and Negroes. We got along fine until this happened."

It was not that signs of trouble in the nation's ghettos had been lacking when Watts exploded. The summer before, there had been a riot in Harlem in which 144 were injured, and in rioting in Rochester, in addition to hundreds of injured, four were killed. In Birmingham the year before that, discipline had snapped among the ghetto poor and, despite the presence of Martin Luther King, a non-violent campaign degenerated into an orgy of rock-throwing and looting. In Watts itself, several tense encounters over the previous two or three years between police and small crowds would, in

309

retrospect, have to be classified as near-misses. Black leaders everywhere were issuing regular warnings that the strains and despair of ghetto life might soon lead to catastrophe.

The men and women who rioted in Watts were newcomers to Los Angeles, even for a city of newcomers. In the quarter-century since the start of World War II, the overall population of Los Angeles County had tripled, but the black population rose nearly three times as fast, from 75,000 to 650,000. Two-thirds of the blacks had gravitated into south-central Los Angeles, of which Watts was the core. In a city formed of an amalgam of separate communities, Watts was long known as Negro and, as blacks spilled over into neighboring communities, Watts loosely gave its name to what became about fifty square miles of ghetto area.

Most of the blacks in Watts had come from the rural South, where the misery of their existence was at least mitigated by a certain stability in their environment. Negro life in the South, unlike Los Angeles, contained few illusions about equality but, instead, it offered the comforts of warm, human contacts. In Los Angeles, conditions may have improved materially over the South—though probably not by much—but at the cost of familiar ways, loving relationships, reliable anchors in uncertain seas.

Watts, compared to back home, had no strong institutions of social control. Church and family had not traveled well. Watts was a community without leaders. Its disappointment tended to turn in upon itself, and its internal disarray, its crime, drugs, idleness and squalor demonstrated that the first index of a slum was not its buildings but its minds. Though much of Watts's wretchedness was the product of the callously applied power of whites, much also came out of insecurity and confusion, and the pain that blacks, awash in a world they could not master, inflicted upon one another.

Yet Los Angeles, with its sunshine and sprawl, seemed to its white leadership somehow immune to social tempest. Who worried that the L.A. freeways had become the symbol of the aristocrat who sped through the neighborhood without noticing? Who savored the irony that nearby Hollywood produced the reminders for nightly television of a better world out of reach? If there was poverty, President Johnson had a war against it; if there was unemployment, Governor Brown had a liberal agenda to take care of it. Unlike the poor crowded into Cleveland's Hough or New York's Harlem, the

310

blacks in Watts had room to let off steam without colliding into hostile whites next door.

Hardly anyone noticed that the civil rights movement had given Watts's blacks a different sense of themselves. It occurred to very few that the rising expectations prevalent in the mid-1960s had transformed everyday discontent into an angry rejection of the status quo.

The best answer to "Why Watts?" may be "Why not?" Rioting could have started in any of a dozen cities in 1965, and by chance circumstances conspired to select Watts. Nobody wanted the riot, nobody plotted to start it, nobody led the marauding bands into battle. But, as if they had been coiled for a signal, ten thousand blacks took to the streets that week to loot and to burn, a few of them to maim and to kill.

When the rioting was over, 34 persons were dead, almost all of them black. Whole blocks of buildings were burned to the ground, and 3500 adults and 500 juveniles had been arrested. An army of 14,000 National Guardsmen, in addition to 1600 police officers, had been required to restore order. From Watts, the "long, hot summer" spread, to become an established phenomenon of the 1960s.

Paul Williams was the product of Watts, born there in 1948. He hardly knew his father, who was away during most of his boyhood in a federal penitentiary. His mother was a shampoo girl in a Beverly Hills beauty shop, conscientious enough to move the family out of public housing and into a small bungalow which she had bought with her savings. Though as angry as any young man in Watts at the conditions of his life, Williams somehow acquired a determination not to let them destroy him.

"My grandmother fed me while my mother worked," he said. "My sister raised me in the streets." He said the women in his early years were strong, but they left him room to "develop some techniques of becoming a man for myself." Williams said he never had illusions about the family's social ranking, but that his home life conveyed to him at least some of the values that America looked upon as middle class.

In the world of Watts, the whites that Williams encountered were, if not oppressors, then strangers. He recalled a time in the

311

early 1960s when some well-meaning white liberals from a West Los Angeles church made friendly overtures. "Their kids would come into our community," he said, "and we would go into theirs. We'd shake hands and sit down, eat cookies and talk. I remember a little white girl who came up to me and asked, 'Are you a ghetto kid?' My attitude was, 'Wow, she must really be out of it.' You couldn't blame the problems on the kids, or even the old people who were trying to be sincere. But any type of move for integration in Watts at that time was a dead issue." The Watts in which Paul Williams grew up was not a world of cookies and genteel conversation.

"I hate to say it, but when I was twelve or thirteen I didn't think I'd live to be thirty," Williams recalled. "Many of my friends did not. I got into my first knife fight at the age of seven, with a guy who was fourteen years old.

"Then, another time, I was about sixteen, and a guy about twenty asked me for a quarter and I said no. He had just migrated from Mississippi. He wanted to jump on me. He wasn't physically big enough to jump on me, but he was, as we say, 'country' enough. I ended up tussling with this guy, and before I knew it he was on the ground and I was pounding his head on the pavement.

"Then three of his brothers, I mean blood kin, proceeded to pull out chains and just do me a number. I'm getting there whipped to death by chains, my mother's at work, friends standing by afraid to get involved, and a lady on the corner comes out with a shotgun and says, 'I'm going to blow you suckers away if you don't leave that boy alone.' Now, believe it or not, I might have to fight these people even to this day if I go back to my mother's house, and the guy's loaded or something. I might have to do a number right there."

When I talked to Paul Williams, it was in a small house he lived in not far from the beach in West Los Angeles, a half-hour drive from Watts. A sturdy young man, he spoke with detachment, but he conveyed the feeling nonetheless that, despite college and a tranquil neighborhood, he could not quite shake the ghetto from his mind. Working to develop a specialty in African studies, he became a teacher at a local community college but, even as he neared thirty, Paul Williams did not find it easy making his way in a white man's world.

312

Williams said it was as much by chance as anything that his future was not fixed by involvement with a gang in Watts. For a time he tried to get accepted by the Little Egyptians, before he changed his mind. His sister, he said, was not as fortunate in keeping clear of the gang world. "Most girls, they wouldn't associate with but one gang," he said. "My sister was kind of hard core. She ran with a lot of Gladiators, but she would associate with any number of dudes." Sometimes gang members from different parts of Watts, he said, had fights over his sister right out in the front yard.

Gangs were an intrinsic part of life when he was growing up in Watts, Williams said, and on the street where he lived there was no way you could avoid dealing with them. Though the Watts gangs were not as large or as elaborately organized as some in the nearby neighborhoods, Williams said, they all had criminal attributes of one form or another.

"The Little Egyptians were more of a self-defense gang, against the bigger gangs," he said, "but they would still rip off a nickel or a quarter from some kid whenever they could." He said a young man's reputation turned upon his behavior with the gang. "Watts gangs were known for having not one leader but maybe five," he said. "One guy was probably known for fistfighting, another guy for the knife, another guy for brass knuckles, another guy for carrying a chain. I have a couple of friends who were known for having single-handed duels with the police and the sheriff's department. That's how the guys got respect."

To get admitted as a full gang member, Williams said, "you might have to commit a crime, or you might have to beat up someone, or you might have to shoot heroin." Once initiated, furthermore, gang members, particularly the leaders, were regularly called upon to commit fresh acts of bravado to renew their mandate. Personal loyalty was a negligible value. Williams said his mother's house was once broken into by one of his best friends as a way of asserting his manhood.

"I guess his thing of gaining respect was to jump on his own people," Williams said. "It's the survival of the fittest. You never look at anybody as your enemy in Watts. I never found an instance when one brother would shoot another in the back. But what you learn is that you never look at anybody as a friend, either."

313

Yet much as Watts suffered from the tyranny of the gangs, it resented the oppression of the police even more. The patrolling of Watts was shared by the County Sheriff's Department and the Los Angeles Police Department. Neither was beloved, but the LAPD was regarded as by far the crueler. If the community in part forgave the gang members their sins because they were black, and because all blacks in Watts experienced a torment in common, it had no sympathy for the police at all. Had the behavior of the cops been exemplary, Watts would still have looked on them as the occupying army of white America, a hostile power. But they often behaved as savages, as captors without mercy, and they were loathed.

That "police brutality" was not departmental policy was hardly credible to the residents of Watts. Yet it probably was not. Los Angeles Police Chief William H. Parker, anathema though he was to blacks, prided himself on the professionalism of his force. He scorned the fire hoses and dogs that had become a trademark of Southern police work, and he enforced strict rules on the use of firearms and tear gas. He had implemented racial integration among police officers and promulgated admirable guidelines for eliminating racial prejudice in day-to-day relations with citizens.

But Parker took satisfaction in being a "tough" cop and, whatever the guidelines, his only real concern was with public order. He proclaimed that he had no responsibility to sociology, and flatly rejected programs to improve police-community relations. Moreover, he considered it his duty to stick by his men when they were criticized, and he showed no interest in complaints about the special form of justice reserved for Watts.

No one would have said, of course, that policing Watts was easy work. It was a high crime area, tortured by violence, prostitution, drugs, petty gambling. Parker understood, on some level, that excessive crime among blacks was, as he put it, "something that has grown out of the dislocation he [the Negro] has suffered in our society." Nonetheless, he demanded no civility of his police, and he tolerated no back talk among blacks, in the process of upholding the law in Watts.

The Los Angeles cops read Parker's message to mean that, within the wide limits of professionalism, they were free to conduct them-

314

selves as they chose. To Watts, this meant that a policeman could, with impunity, vent whatever racist animosities suited his fancy, and Watts replied with an equal degree of hate. The result was warfare, normally low-level but unrelenting, between citizens and police on the ghetto streets.

"There was no place in Watts you could go," said Paul Williams. "The police were the Gestapo. There was a cop we used to call 'Cigar,' white guy, big guy, riding around with a cigar. He intimidated you, slapped you around the side of the head, kicked you down to the ground. Sometimes he'd arrest you, sometimes he wouldn't. Everyone's dream was to kill this man."

There was no question that the police engaged in an almost random program of intimidation, as if keeping the black men of Watts off-balance would somehow reduce the crime rate. Among police, Watts was known as a "duck pond," where they could stop whomever they chose, whatever the pretext, for interrogation. They seldom felt any constraint about using terms like "nigger" and "boy," and rare was the black male who reached adulthood without acquiring some kind of arrest record. But arrests were an instrument of social control, not a step in the law-enforcement process. One study showed that, after arrest, 90 percent of the juveniles never had charges filed against them.

"On a hundred and third street in Watts, which was crowded with kids day and night," Williams said, "you could always see red lights blinking every quarter of a mile or half a mile, where the cops were lining them up, searching them against the wall, for nothing. I don't know how many times the police have jacked me up, with a billy club stuck in my ribs.

"Do you know what it's like to live like that? You go home and want to argue with your family. You want to take out your frustrations on any authority. Really, that's the thing I hated most about Watts, the treatment by police. It really burns me up when I think about it. The sheriff, he wouldn't beat you up but he'd pull his gun out. Maybe they were afraid. But the LAPD beat you with the sticks and the guns."

If nothing else, the blacks who migrated from the South to Watts, and the other Northern ghettos, thought they had established a right to freedom, and a smattering of dignity. Even at its worst, no doubt, Watts was freer in a hundred ways than the cramped, sti-

315

fling, segregated life imposed upon blacks in the South. But the cops seemed determined to snatch away the chief advantage that Los Angeles life had over the South, and Watts was ready to grab it back. In the summer of 1965, rightly or not, Watts perceived the police as growing more oppressive than ever. The Watts riot, like the other ghetto riots of the 1960s, was more than anything a protest against indignity, largely imposed upon the black community by the cops.

Then, as if fairness required that he put his experience in perspective, Williams said: "I remember we would have to run to school to get away from the gangs in the morning, and walk down the side streets and the back streets to keep from getting stopped by the police at night. If either one got you, you could come away with your head bandaged and a knot on the side of your eye."

What saved Paul Williams from running with the gangs was that, beginning in junior high school, he turned his attention to athletics. "I remember a lot of kids who were in junior high with me, instead of going to school they'd go buy a bottle of Silver Satin or something, or a joint or two, or some heroin, or go gamble on the street. That could have happened to me but I was lucky. I played football and ran track."

Williams acknowledged that he was never a very good student. He could scarcely read, in fact, until.he finished high school and entered junior college. But sports, he said, gave him the opportunity to turn his mind to something constructive. At the same time, sports put him in contact with a group of black students who were determined to make something of themselves, and maybe even something of Watts.

Richard Townsend, who was Williams's classmate at David Starr Jordan High School, was one of these young men. Born in Lowndes County, Alabama, in 1948, Townsend was brought to Los Angeles as an infant and, like so many of the children of Watts, was raised without benefit of father, chiefly in public housing, by a strong and enterprising mother.

Though small in size, Townsend was husky and muscular, and he became an all-league running back in football and a star in track. He was also a conscientious student, with a good academic record. The yearbook of Jordan High's Class of 1966—which pictures fewer than a half-dozen nonblacks in a class of four hundred—conveys Townsend as a poised and self-confident young man, winner of numerous offices and awards. To Williams, Townsend was a clean-cut hero, a sharp contrast to the dope dealers, street-corner sharps and incipient alcoholics of the gangs.

As early as 1963, when he was still in junior high, Williams was invited by his English teacher—a young white woman named Sue Welsh—to join a self-improvement club which she had persuaded some of her students to form. Richard Townsend was among its leaders. Williams remembered bringing some of his girlfriends to the early meetings, at which twenty or thirty teenagers sat around deploring "the older kids beating up on them, their parents getting drunk and stuff. We was just fed up."

Before long, the kids had established the Student Committee for the Improvement of Watts (SCFIW—pronounced skee-foo) and had embarked on a community uplift program. On weekends, with materials donated by local merchants and church societies, they painted houses, or cleared alleys of trash. They even sponsored a few civil rights demonstrations, in support of black activists in the South. They won the praise of local politicians, and occasional notice in the press. But they did not attract much support, or even approval, among the young dudes who roamed Watts's streets and were no more concerned about Birmingham than about their own neighborhood.

"We were laughed at all the time," said Paul Williams. " 'Look at the NEE-groes.' That's what they called us. 'The NEE-groes with the white girl.' They figured we were following the white woman, Sue Welsh, around. They accused us of kissing ass with the white folks.

"The Student Committee was a good branch of kids. There was a bad branch in Watts, too, and they knew each other. And then there were kids like myself who were in the middle. Some of them would say, 'Yeah, I'll come to a meeting for community improvement.' And the next day I'd go down and see them on the corner with the fellows drinking wine. I really went to the meetings a lot of the times."

Like Williams, Richard Townsend did not find the course he took to be easy, even though his self-assurance equipped him better for the ridicule.

"No, it wasn't very comfortable," he said. Richard Townsend,

317

now a lawyer, spoke softly, with better grammar and diction than Williams's. "I was always uneasy. I had a lot of public acclaim, on the campus and around the community, because of track and other things, so I think my acceptance was due in large measure to that. I did not feel a part of what I call the gangster element and, though there was some intermeshing, I wasn't involved in their activities. I was ostracized from them.

"Instead, I was accepted by a group of peers who were also pursuing acceptable types of activity in school, running for student offices, being good students, successful in sports. Looking back on it, I was a goody-goody. But what I did led me to want to achieve certain things, do something worthwhile, be involved in the community."

In the fall of 1964, nearly a year before the Watts riot, Townsend and another of SCFIW's leaders, William Armstead, prepared a paper called "Watts: Its Problems and Possible Solutions." It was a remarkable document, not simply because it was written by two sixteen-year-olds without training in sociology, statistics and the other tools of urban analysis. What was more important was its unusual insight into the reasons for the sense of doom that surrounded Watts.

The paper talked of absentee landlords and wretched housing, broken families and indifferent parents, high-school dropouts and teenage pregnancies, alcoholism and drug addiction. It lamented the inadequacy of educational, cultural and health facilities in the neighborhood. It dealt with chronic unemployment among the young and resultant juvenile crime.

The statistics of the era readily confirmed the impressions of Townsend and Armstead. They show that, while the Negro's income relative to the white grew substantially during and immediately after World War II, the increase since the late 1950s had slowed considerably. In fact, between 1959 and 1965, median income in the Watts area had dropped by 8 percent.

Furthermore, while the rest of the country prospered between 1960 and 1964, unemployment in Watts rose to almost 20 percent. It was as high as 30 percent for males and nearly 50 percent for teenagers. More than 50 percent of Watts's adults were functionally illiterate, and three times as many youths as in the rest of the city were classified as delinquent.

318

Meanwhile, some two thousand Negroes a month continued to pour into Los Angeles from the South, and most of them settled in Watts. By 1964, 60 percent of the Watts residents were on relief.

The Townsend-Armstead paper dwelt in some length upon the black churches in Watts, deploring their failure to give the community some institutional stability. "Churches are built," the paper said, "because of a so-called preacher who decides to make it a business venture. These churches are usually used by these so-called preachers as a stepping-stone to wealth."

No doubt, preachers abused their office, but in fairness it should be noted that the principal secular duty of the church—to provide for the poor—had been usurped. With a majority in Watts on welfare, the churches confronted in a benevolent government an institutional rival with which they could not compete. Deprived of their traditional role, the churches were, if not corrupt, then incurably weak.

"I don't think the church had any impact on the kids," said Paul Williams, corroborating Townsend's observation. "The reason they gave up on the church is that Sunday was just like Saturday night, a continual party, get high to get rid of your troubles. We had one big preacher riding around in a Cadillac. Most people that ride around in a Cadillac in the black community are looked at as hustlers, pimps. There was no way we could respect that man riding around in a Cadillac. What I'm saying is, most times when you looked at a preacher, you were looking down the throat of a guy who was beating you out of your nickel. People just gave up on the church."

The church that Williams knew in Watts had fallen a long way from its station in rural Alabama, where religious belief had inspired John Lewis to enter the struggle for black rights, where Martin Luther King served the young as the model of Christian mission.

Perhaps the most important observations of the Townsend-Armstead paper were directed at the "overwhelming feelings of inferiority" present in Watts. In part the young authors blamed white community leaders, some for failing to grasp the magnitude of Watts's social and economic problems, others for outright racism. They left no doubt of their anger at the white world.

But they noted candidly the internal factors responsible for the

319

failure of the people of Watts to build a strong community. "A person cannot very easily have respect for others if he hasn't any self-respect to begin with," they wrote. "The low degree of pride in Watts," they said, "causes a low degree of action and thinking."

Without denying discrimination, Townsend and Armstead expressed their impatience with blacks who made no serious effort to surmount it. They delivered the observation that the blacks of Watts were sullen and angry at their conditions of life, which they were unable to overcome because they were so sullen and angry. What Richard Townsend and his friend were expressing was the inherent, perhaps insoluble, dilemma of America's black ghettos.

The paper by the two young SCFIW leaders, Townsend and Armstead, was considered so valuable that, in August of 1965, it was published as an addendum to a long study prepared by the U.S. Department of Commerce on "Hard-core Unemployment and Poverty in Los Angeles." On August 7, SCFIW sent a delegation to testify at a hearing on the operation of the federal antipoverty program held in Los Angeles by the House Committee on Education and Labor. The following week was to be SCFIW's second annual Community Improvement Week, featuring a parade down the main avenue of Watts and a neighborhood-wide clean-up day. Paul Williams was chairman of the Community Improvement Week.

Concerned young men like Paul Williams, Richard Townsend and William Armstead were still very few, but they were making a start in the summer of 1965 at filling the leadership void in Watts. That they were considered such oddities is an indication of the shallowness of community involvement. Indeed, the void was so wide that, at best, SCFIW could have filled only a small corner. But even this modest hope proved vain. The Community Improvement Week never took place. The rioting in Watts began on the night of August 11, and lasted for six agonizing days.

But, history shows, the dispirited, the demoralized, the defeated, do not normally rise up. Nor does economic want alone spark rebellion. People take to the streets when some privilege to which they are accustomed is abruptly taken away, or when some hope on which they had relied appears suddenly unattainable. Only the aggrieved rise up, but not under conditions that are otherwise stable. Rebellion is not a first step, but a step along the way in a dynamic process. It takes place not when there is stagnation but when there is change.

Certainly life in Watts was dreadful. But it was not so dreadful that it slowed migration from the South, or sent migrants fleeing back to Alabama or Mississippi. Most blacks knew, before arriving in Watts, that they were unlikely to find financial security and social stability. Though economic opportunities were declining in the summer of 1965, Watts probably did not riot over despair about a future it never believed in. Watts that summer was about as bad as, or only marginally worse than, it ever was.

In many ways, however, the summer of 1965 was dynamic, and one of the changes was that submission among blacks had gone out of style. Every Negro who had a television set—and, in Watts, nine out of ten homes did—had found on the screen a model of protest, the choice ranging from the sit-in in Greensboro to the marcher in Birmingham. These models evoked the image of the hero which lives in every man. It was not central that these protests were Southern or nonviolent or against a segregation that did not exist in the North. These protests were black, and the enemy was white, and there was not a man or woman in Watts who failed to perceive that as a personal message.

"All I know about what was coming out of the South," said Paul Williams, "was that there was a bunch of mad niggers down there who thought their situation was worse than ours. King, and all his talk about nonviolence, didn't mean much. Watts had respect for King, but the talk about nonviolence made us laugh.

"Watts wasn't suffering from segregation, or the lack of civil rights. You didn't have two drinking fountains. You had the police, but no German shepherds. When Johnson signed the civil rights bill in sixty-four, nobody even thought about it in Watts. You were too worried about getting your head beat in by your buddy next door to worry about civil rights. It had nothing to do with us."

In the early 1960s Watts had chapters of both the NAACP and CORE, but both actually lost strength during the flourishing years of the movement. The NAACP was concerned with police brutality in Los Angeles, but was too legalistic to attract a wide following. CORE was as much white as black, and was accused of overlooking the ghetto black in the interest of integrating middle-class blacks

321

into the country clubs. Both were more preoccupied with injustices in the South than in Watts, and were without influence at the time the riots began.

"You understand what I'm saying," Williams continued. "You go into a local market in Watts. Besides the rats and the roaches, the food was rotten. There would be some Jewish guy* or a white guy standing there saying, 'The hell with you, you're going to have to buy this anyway.' Those are the first places the people went, to burn down the store. What we didn't have in Watts wasn't civil rights. It was jobs, housing and education. It was a positive image of ourselves. We didn't know what they were complaining about in the South."

The man who spoke to the young people of Watts, far more than Martin Luther King, was the charismatic Black Muslim leader who called himself Malcolm X. Product himself of a black ghetto in the Middle West, orphaned in childhood by a Ku Klux Klan murder, a dope peddler and pimp in his teenage years, Malcolm converted to Islam during a long term in prison. Living in Harlem from the late 1950s until his assassination† in 1965, Malcolm X increasingly captured the country's attention—rabble-rouser to some, prophet to others—as the most brilliant and eloquent proselytizer of the black separatist movement called the Nation of Islam.

"The white Southerner, you can say one thing—he is honest," Malcolm declared. "He bares his teeth to the black man; he tells the black man, to his face, that Southern whites will never accept phony 'integration' . . . But the Northern white man, he grins with his teeth, and his mouth has always been full of tricks and lies of 'equality' and 'integration.'

* Many Jews, especially those who had given much of themselves to the civil rights cause, were disturbed by a recurring strain of anti-Semitism which appeared in the movement in the mid-1960s. In *Where Do We Go From Here?* Martin Luther King wrote: "The limited degree of Negro anti-Semitism is substantially a Northern ghetto phenomenon; it virtually does not exist in the South. The urban Negro has a special and unique relationship to Jews. He meets them in two dissimilar roles. On the one hand, he is associated with Jews as some of his most committed partners in the civil rights struggle. On the other hand, he meets them daily as some of his most direct exploiters in the ghetto as slum landlords or gouging shopkeepers . . . [They] are remnants of older communities. A great number of Negro ghettos were formerly Jewish neighborhoods; some storekeepers and landlords remained as population changes occurred. They operate with the ethics of marginal business entrepreneurs, not Jewish ethics, but the distinction is lost on some Negroes who are maltreated by them. Such Negroes, caught in frustration and irrational anger, parrot racial epithets. They foolishly add to the social poison . . .".

† Presumably the product of internal conflict within the Muslims.

"When one day all over America, a black hand touched the white man's shoulder, and the white man turned, and there stood the Negro saying, 'Me, too . . .,' why, that Northern liberal shrank from that black man with as much guilt and dread as any Southern white man.

"Actually, America's most dangerous and threatening black man is the one who has been kept sealed up by the Northerner in the black ghettos—the Northern white power structure's system to keep talking democracy while keeping the black man out of sight somewhere, around the corner."

Malcolm's "tell-it-like-it-is" style made him much in demand as a speaker, and gave him frequent access to the media. He wrote a regular column in black Los Angeles's newspaper, the *Herald Dispatch*, and his statements were disseminated nationwide in the Muslim weekly, *Muhammad Speaks*. Paul Williams remembered that when Malcolm spoke in Los Angeles, a year before the riot, young blacks left the hall declaring, "We have a leader now." Though he made few actual converts, Malcolm X crystallized feelings among the ghetto youth whom King had left indifferent. If any set of ideas provided the powder for the Watts explosion, it was Malcolm's.

To a young black in California, with its liberal governor and state legislature, where Jim Crow never lived and the exercise of the right to vote was encouraged, Malcolm's words provided an explanation for the squalor of Watts. Malcolm's ideas drew no attention for their originality. They were popular because, in the context of the 1960s, when Southern blacks and liberal whites exulted in the pace of racial change, they told ghetto blacks why they were being left out.

Malcolm dared to articulate thoughts, appalling to whites in their overt hostility, that ghetto blacks carried in the recesses of their minds but left discreetly unsaid. "He voiced for the people of Watts," said Paul Williams, "what the people could not voice for themselves." Once spoken, such ideas became a summons, rattling in the public brain.

The doctrine of change that Malcolm preached was a separation of the races. It found a receptive following as militants of the mid-1960s grew tired of the goal of integration, and it accelerated the transformation of SNCC, already gravitating toward the ideology which would be called Black Power. It was accompanied by Malcolm's plea for black pride, addressed to the kind of self-hatred which upset Richard Townsend. Bayard Rustin found the notion— "how you wear your hair, what you eat, black poetry, the cultural revolution"—a diversion from the real work of changing the black condition. But if Malcolm's doctrine was not strong enough to transform black psyches, it was too strong for most young blacks to ignore, and it served to rationalize a deep loathing for whites.

"The worst crime of the white man has been to teach us to hate ourselves," Malcolm declared. "We hated our head, we hated the shape of our nose—we wanted one of those doglike noses, you know. Yeah, we hated the color of our skin.* We hated the blood of Africa that was in our veins . . . It made us feel inferior. It made us feel inadequate. It made us feel helpless. And when we fell victims to this feeling of inadequacy or inferiority or helplessness, we turned to somebody else to show us the way."

Malcolm said that, though the white man was to blame for them, the black man had to correct his own deficiencies. "The black man needs to start his own program to get rid of drunkenness, drug addiction and prostitution," he said. "The black man in America has to lift up his own sense of values." And the Muslims were rigorous in demanding traditional, even puritanical, moral conduct from whomever accepted the strictures of the faith.

Malcolm's lessons on violence were less clear. When he was accused of advocating violence, which was often, he pretended to great innocence. But he left little doubt of his contempt for the pacifist message of Christianity, or for the Christian ministers who promoted a nonviolent discipline.

"It is a miracle," Malcolm once said, "that twenty-two million black people have not risen up against their oppressors—in which they would have been justified by all moral criteria, and even by democratic tradition. It is a miracle that a nation of black people has so fervently continued to believe in a turn-the-other-cheek and heaven-after-you-die philosophy . . .

"The miracle is that the white man's puppet Negro 'leaders,' his preachers and the educated Negroes laden with degrees, and others who have been allowed to wax fat off their black poor brothers, have been able to hold the black masses quiet until now."

* He did not mention here black surnames. His own was Little. He traded it in for X on the grounds that Little was his "slave name."

In his autobiography, which was finished shortly after the Harlem riot of 1964, Malcolm wrote of the "human combustion" that was packed into the ghettos, waiting to be ignited. He spoke of "social dynamite" in New York, Washington, Chicago, Detroit, Cleveland, Philadelphia, San Francisco—and Los Angeles.

Insofar as his warnings were prophecy, they possessed a self-fulfilling quality. Malcolm had gone beyond justifying outrage, as other civil rights leaders had done, to sanctioning conflict. "I remember people out there during the Watts riot," Paul Williams said, "crying 'Long live Malcolm X.' " Even if Malcolm did not explicitly advocate violence, he unleashed emotions by his doctrines which were difficult to contain, and which seem in retrospect to have brought collision in the ghettos one step closer.

As the Watts riot approached, there was recurring evidence that the traditional restraints which kept the rage of the American black community from bursting into physical convulsion were eroding. Two black psychiatrists in San Francisco noted that the times offered a growing sanction for lashing out. In a book written during the riot era,* they presented a series of case studies, among them that of a black professional who

> had been a "nice guy" all his life. He was a hard-working non-militant who avoided discussions of race with his white colleagues. He smiled if their comments were harsh and remained unresponsive to racist statements. Lately he has experienced almost uncontrollable anger toward his white co-workers, and although he still manages to keep his feelings to himself, he confides that blacks and whites have been lying to each other. There is hatred and violence between them and he feels trapped. He too fears for himself if his controls should slip.

These two psychiatrists then asked rhetorically: "If these educated recipients of the white man's bounty find it hard to control their rage, what of their less fortunate kinsman who has less to

* William H. Grier and Price M. Cobbs, *Black Rage.*

325

protect, less to lose, and more scars to show for his journey in this land?"

By the eve of the Watts riot, such anger had become almost palpable. A Los Angeles fire inspector, after a four-year absence from Watts, told a writer* he was shocked by the change in attitude he found on his return. No longer, he said, could he move around without fear or harassment in making his inspections. Firemen, he noted, were met with constant verbal abuse, and regular communication with the people of Watts no longer existed.

The year prior to Watts was fraught with incidents that might have served in the suggestible as stimuli to riot. One of them was in the north of California, in Berkeley, where university students were expressing mass defiance of campus authorities. Richard Townsend said that blacks were accustomed to the different measure that applied to whites who provoked authority. "We knew there were things other people could get away with that blacks could never do," he said. But Townsend said that the brazenness of the Berkeley students became something of a dare to the dudes in Watts.

"I don't think I ever heard anyone in Watts say, 'Well, if they can do it I can do it,'" Townsend said. "But I heard people say, 'Look at those kids up there. What are they doing?' And in their voices was an amazement at what these kids thought they had a right to do, and the guts to do.

"I heard a lot of admiration. I'm not sure there was any conscious change. You can't figure out all the elements that went into the Watts riot. But something moved."

At the same time as the affair in Berkeley, California's voters were being called, in effect, to pass upon Malcolm X's contention that the ghetto walls would never be dismantled peacefully. The year before, the California legislature had passed the Rumford Act, which prohibited racial discrimination in the sale and rental of housing. The state's real-estate interests immediately undertook a campaign to repeal it, and succeeded in getting the question on the ballot as Proposition 14. All during the fall of 1964, Californians

* Robert Conot, *Rivers of Blood, Years of Darkness*.

debated, as blacks perceived it, whether bigotry was lawful. The contest over Proposition 14 overshadowed even the presidential campaign.

"I was very agitated by Proposition Fourteen," said Richard Townsend, "and I was involved in the campaign. It was a big thing in the churches, the first time I ever heard of anything political going on in the churches. I think very few got out and knocked on doors, but it was really important to people."

At stake in the battle was not the state's residential pattern, since relatively few blacks could actually afford to move into white neighborhoods. The issue was the liberal ideal of an open society, which Malcolm had acidly mocked but which many aspiring blacks believed in.

"It was a class thing," Townsend said, "and it depended on what kind of future you were interested in. It was probably more of a worry to middle-class blacks than police brutality, which was a situation they usually managed to keep themselves out of. But don't exaggerate the differences, because the middle class, like other blacks, still has the feeling of being black in a white society, and I think everybody in Watts was aware that something was going on about fair housing. Even the blacks who couldn't move anywhere discussed it."

For months the debate over the vote on Proposition 14 raged, while the polls showed backlash in California getting worse. On election day, the outcome was not even close. By a margin of two-to-one, the voters approved repeal of the law that barred racial discrimination in housing.

"Everyone was angry that it had even come up," Townsend said, "and, of course, everyone was angry at the way it turned out. Everybody in Watts was aware that they were being rejected by somebody, by somebody white."

Then, in early 1965, came King's Selma demonstrations, accompanied by the white South's last and most furious counterattack against the demands of blacks for equality under the law. King, in late 1964, had won the Nobel Peace Prize, and was at the summit of his prestige. He planned at Selma to maintain the dynamism of the civil rights movement by forcing enactment of new federal leg-

327

islation to guarantee the right of blacks to vote. Selma was a city of twenty-eight thousand in Alabama's Black Belt, where only three hundred of the county's fifteen thousand voting-age blacks were registered. Sheriff Jim Clark promised to be an antagonist there in the tradition of the celebrated Bull Connor.

In demonstrations from January to March of 1965, more than a thousand protesters were arrested. King himself served five days in jail. A young black was beaten to death by Alabama state police, a Boston minister was killed by a band of white hoodlums and a Detroit housewife was murdered by Klan gunmen in her car. On March 7, known as Bloody Sunday, state troopers attacked a peaceful column of six hundred blacks, fracturing the skull of John Lewis,* sending some fifty demonstrators to the hospital. For weeks, the television networks covered Selma, recording the unembarrassed barbarity of the white police, and the remarkable courage of the blacks.

"Selma was the culmination of all the demonstrations. It seemed like the one where blacks were treated the worst," Richard Townsend recalled. Like other blacks, Townsend watched the reports from Selma every night on television, and tended to forget that hundreds of whites marched there, too. Joe Rauh was at Selma, along with clergymen of all three faiths. Many whites were injured, and several were killed. "I was incensed, with a feeling like I had no reason at all to be particularly kind or gracious to anyone, particularly to white society or white persons in the Establishment, with all this going on."

Once more, at Selma, King's strategy of massive demonstrations paid off. Supportive marches were staged in Detroit, New York, Chicago and Los Angeles. Sympathizers in Washington conducted sit-ins at the White House and the Capitol and, during rush-hour traffic, on Pennsylvania Avenue. Several thousand clergymen presented a petition to the president, and picketers maintained a round-the-clock vigil at his gates. Then, on March 15, President Johnson went before a joint session of Congress to ask for the passage of a bill, stronger than any ever written before, to assure the voting rights of all Americans.

"What happened in Selma," Johnson declared, "is part of a far

* Because SNCC had refused to endorse the Selma demonstrations, Lewis marched on his own.

larger movement which reaches into every section and state of America. It is the effort of American Negroes to secure for themselves the full blessings of American life. Their cause must be our cause, too. Because it is not just Negroes, but really it is all of us, who must overcome the crippling legacy of bigotry and injustice."

Then Johnson spoke a line which to many Americans was unforgettable. "We shall overcome," he declared, referring to the nation's heritage of racial injustice. "We Shall Overcome" had been the motto of the civil rights movement, chanted in a thousand street demonstrations. "The real hero of this struggle is the American Negro," Johnson went on. "His actions and protests, his courage to risk safety and even to risk his life, have awakened the conscience of the nation." As many Americans saw it, the president of the United States had sanctioned the actions of blacks in taking to the streets, and had almost become a demonstrator himself.

Townsend acknowledged that while the police of Selma showed how white authority brutalized blacks, Johnson affirmed the corollary, which was that "blacks might actually win because the law was not completely stacked against them." Townsend said Selma encouraged blacks, even in Watts, to indulge the notion that protest could succeed.

The federal antipoverty program seemed to show again in the summer of 1965 that, without Washington's help, nothing would happen. The program had been passed with much fanfare. For months afterward, Watts had heard promises of an infusion of federal funds, and even cynical teenagers talked hopefully of getting jobs at $1.25 an hour, which was better than hanging around on the street corner. But the money became clogged in a dispute, classic to the politics of the poverty program, between Los Angeles's mayor, who wanted its patronage benefits, and community representatives, seeking power of their own over the local projects.

What funds became available before the riot, according to the street wisdom, went into the pockets not of the needy but of the "poverty pimps," the brokers who formed a new privileged class within the community. "There was no poverty program in Watts before the riot," said Paul Williams irascibly, "there wasn't nothin'." In the end, the highly touted war on poverty became the latest deceit, another white man's tease, one more hope shattered.

If Selma was a victory for black activism, which even the presi-

329

dent endorsed, the failure of the antipoverty program to deliver on its promises proved once more that submissive blacks got nothing. From the Selma experience, Townsend said, the "average black on the street" concluded that when whites felt the stability of their system threatened they would act.

Still, Watts was different from Selma. It had no Martin Luther King, nor did it have the teachers and the pupils, the discipline and the issues, to conduct King's style of nonviolent protest. Unlike Selma's blacks, the community lacked a strong faith, a sense of solidarity, a vision of the future. In the summer of 1965, blacks in Watts had the will to win a victory like Selma, but rioting was the only form of collective protest that they knew.

Congress worked on Lyndon Johnson's voting rights proposal for seven months, and finally passed a bill. Tens of thousands of blacks would register under its provisions, and in the ensuing years the law would have huge political ramifications throughout the South. It was the last of the great civil rights bills of the 1960s and, though only a few then recognized it, brought the revolution to an end. In a ceremony televised from the Capitol rotunda, Johnson said the measure would "strike away the last major shackles" of the Negro's "ancient bonds." The bill became law on August 6, 1965, five days before the Watts riot began.

August 11, 1965, the night the controls snapped in Watts, was hot and humid. The precipitating incident was commonplace. Officer Lee W. Minikus of the California Highway Patrol stopped a ten-year-old gray Buick at the corner of 116th and Avalon, in the heart of the ghetto area. At the wheel was Marquette Frye, twenty-one, a black. Next to him was his brother Ronald, twenty-two. Both had been drinking. Minikus, according to undisputed testimony, was courteous, and the encounter was untroubled until he announced that Frye had flunked a sobriety test he administered and would have to go off to jail.

Conventionally enough for a summer night, a crowd from the neighborhood, all black, had gathered to watch the spectacle. Equally normal was the arrival of several cars of police reinforcements, mostly white. Rena Frye, the young men's mother, promptly reached the scene, and pleaded with her son Marquette to go

child of the ghetto, he was less certain of himself than Townsend, and the line between right and wrong was for him more blurred. Williams was drawn on the one hand by a sense of community responsibility. On the other, he was propelled by the excitement, the defiance, the comradeship of the streets.

"The day after the riot broke out," Williams remembered, "I'm on my way to an emergency meeting of SCFIW to see what we could do as kids to slow down some of the violence. There was no way I could cross a hundred and third to get to this meeting, man. You could look a mile down the street and it's packed with people looting. It was like this wall of people. Everybody I knew was there. I just got sucked into the vacuum.

"It was a day I'll never forget in my whole life. People were really happy. It was like, 'Get 'em. Do it.' They were breaking in stores, grabbing what they could. Watts was known as a little Jewish enclave of stores. All those people were run off that day, the Jews, the whites.

"I remember one guy who barricaded himself inside his store with a gun. They beat that guy and dragged him out the front end, then came around the back through the store again. It was where I used to buy my shoes at. They just emptied the whole store out. They went through it like locusts, like an army of ants. They left devastation behind. I always wanted to be part of the in-crowd. Here was the big opportunity. Everybody was doing it. And before I knew it, I was in a band of roaming looters.

"My dedication to SCFIW suddenly vanished. It was like I always believed in serving the community and the people in it, the masses. But I saw the masses of the people in the street.

"I felt sorry as hell that I couldn't get to the emergency meeting, but that was a joke. Do you understand? It was a big joke. People didn't look at themselves as committing a crime. They had lived through all that deprivation, and now they were uplifted. I nearly wanted to cry right there on the street when I saw all those people."

The worst day was Friday the thirteenth. At 9:00 A.M. Chief Parker decided to call for the National Guard and at 10:00 A.M. he officially requested a thousand men but, due to a sequence of administrative errors, not until twelve hours later were the first troops deployed. Throughout the entire day, the police had no control of the streets.

333

Mobs roamed at will, systematically burning. Filling stations, selling gasoline for Molotov cocktails, did a land-office business and a hundred fire companies, harassed by rock throwers and occasional snipers, tried vainly to keep up with the blazes. Looters swarmed through supermarkets, furniture stores, liquor stores and pawnshops, and twice they invaded the post office. By nightfall the first fatality was recorded, a black bystander caught in a cross fire between police and rioters, and the chaos was still spreading.

Yet, for all its apparent spontaneity, the mob seemed to be guided by a certain design. No residences were deliberately burned, and little damage was done to schools, libraries, churches and public buildings. Bayard Rustin, who remembered the terrible destruction inflicted by blacks on blacks in Harlem the summer before, wrote after an inspection of the ruins that Watts "marked the first major rebellion of Negroes against their own masochism." No doubt he exaggerated. But the mob knew where it was putting the torch: to white businesses, particularly to the white businesses that exploited their customers. Black businessmen, inscribing "soul brother" on their store windows, were generally spared.

"I remember breaking into a camera shop and taking cameras out, cleaning it out," said Paul Williams. "I remember guys telling me about breaking not only into pawnshops but into gun shops, and taking all the guns. A liquor store wasn't nothin'. I remember having trash cans full of liquor. And when I came out, the most natural thing I would say to myself was that I had paid for it. It was like revenge.

"There was a supermarket on a hundred and twentieth, and my mother told me to get some groceries, because there was going to be a problem getting food eventually. She gave me the car and I went out on a hundred and twentieth and Central, and all you can hear is the ambulance screaming and people yelling and gunshots. You could see a stream of smoke from five or six miles away.

"I finally got to the supermarket. It hadn't burned down yet and I went in. I took some groceries home and then my mother wanted me to get some eggs. I had to go back in a giant burning building. It could have caved in on me to get some eggs. The eggs could have been hard-boiled by the time I got home. But it was the principle of the thing. Going into a store was uplifting yourself."

Williams said his mother, with middle-class aspirations for her

334

son, was more troubled than he by the lawlessness all around. Marooned by the breakdown of transportation, she was unable to get to her job in Beverly Hills. She watched him go out into the tempest each day, he said, and was tortured by ambivalence.

"I had a young mother who tried to give me some proper direction," he said. "She didn't tell me to go out there. She said, when you're out there, if you're doing anything, be careful. She told me, don't be a fool for no one else's game. But even to this day, my mother cries when she thinks about my involvement in the Watts riot."

On Saturday, National Guardsmen in battle dress finally arrived, and were deployed in succeeding waves. Many of them were assigned to conduct "sweep and clear" operations in jeeps with mounted machine guns. Others rode "shotgun" on fire engines to stop the sniping and rock throwing. Braced by the reinforcements, the police roamed the streets with bullhorns, prepared for the first time to enforce orders to the rioters to disperse.

On Saturday morning, the arrest of looters began, although the police were often too outnumbered by the still-roaming hordes to be effective. A curfew was imposed on the riot area, making it unlawful to be on the streets from 8:00 P.M. to dawn. Roadblocks were established at key intersections, to monitor the movement not only of potential troublemakers but of foolhardy sightseers who came to witness the drama.

Before the momentum was turned back, satellite riots had broken out in nearby Pasadena, Monrovia, San Diego and Long Beach. But on Saturday night the worst was over. As the riot waned, however, the police seemed to loosen their trigger fingers, and before the sun rose on Sunday the number of fatalities had surpassed twenty.

"It was like you were always in fear of death," Paul Williams remembered. "Everybody was scared. My mother cried two or three days in a row. My grandmother cried the whole time. People were worried they were going to have their relatives killed. But it never really crossed your mind when you were right there in a critical situation. At one time, when we were in a camera shop, I kept saying, 'This is going to be the last one,' but it wasn't. I made two more attempts.

"A friend of mine socked in a plate-glass window, hit it with his fist and the window went down. He kicked his way through the show stand there, and we were inside. Before we know it, we were all out, and there was one old drunk standing there on the sidewalk, saying, 'I'm going to fight the police.'

"Before we could get away from the block, six cars with sheriffs just unloaded at the corner. Everybody in our car got out but me, and the doors were standing open, the car sitting there with all this merchandise. I said to myself, I know I'm going to jail today, and I was even asking what I was going to get when I got there. But, believe it or not, all the guys got away, hopping fences. It was my car, and even I got away, by slowly driving down the street.

"The only guy who got busted was the old guy standing there loaded, talking about how he was going to fight the police."

On Sunday, Watts showed some signs of resuming a normal life. People emerged from their homes to go to church, to inspect the ruins, to perform the errands left undone since Wednesday night. To fill the gap left by the burned-out food stores, provisions were distributed through official and charitable channels.

Chief Parker reported on Sunday that the police and the military had jointly reestablished law enforcement authority over the area, but he did not dismiss the difficulty of the mopping-up. In fact, Governor Brown's visit to Watts on Sunday afternoon had to be cut short for fear of sniper fire and, in some respects, the forty-eight hours until Brown terminated the curfew on Tuesday were the most vicious of the week. Parker was sure that Watts swarmed with snipers, although no policeman or Guardsman was killed by sniper fire and it is not clear that any were even struck. For two days and nights, however, uniformed men patrolled the streets with their weapons poised, their fire sometimes rash, as they sought to flush these snipers from their lairs.

"I remember the last day, when a hundred and third was still in flames," Paul Williams said, "and we were sitting on the corner watching the National Guard protect the street. I think the only thing that stayed there was the bank, the police station and the fire station. They wanted to accuse us of sniping.

"It was like sitting there watching a movie. There were about two hundred or three hundred people in the street, and we were all laughing at the National Guard protecting this street that had been burned down. To me it was just funny.

"I also remember some Chicano cat who was loaded on heroin or

336

stuff, and he tried to drive his car through a barricade where the National Guard was. His car was riddled with bullets and he was killed.* That's what I think about in dreams of the Watts riot, the National Guard and the police riddling that car with bullets.

"I almost got killed the last day myself. I was standing on the corner of Manchester and Broadway, and a guy had thrown a rock from behind a house and it hit a policeman on the head. He fell down, and on his way to the ground he hit a fire hydrant and busted his head wide open. He's sitting there bleeding from the head, and the police start to shoot up the house. Then they turn the guns on people like myself standing on the street corner. They unloaded everywhere. They sprayed the tree I was leaning on.

"I just took them seriously, and went home."

And so, with the vanishing of the sniper threat, the Watts riot officially ended. Despite some fiery rhetoric about going downtown to get Whitey, it never spilled out of the ghetto. Whatever retribution blacks exacted upon the hated police, and on the white man who abused them, the rioting was conducted on their own terrain. On August 18, 1965, the National Guard packed up its gear and departed. Just a week had passed since the fateful encounter at 116th and Avalon between Officer Minikus and Marquette Frye.

Two years after the explosion in Watts, President Johnson established the Kerner Commission † to explore the causes and character of urban unrest. By then ghetto riots had become commonplace— Chicago, San Francisco, Atlanta in 1966, Newark, Detroit and New Brunswick in 1967, to cite just a few. The commission pursued its task conscientiously, and drew from its mass of data patterns that were remarkably consistent with what had occurred in Watts.

Among the findings were:

> Virtually every major episode of urban violence in the summer of 1967 was foreshadowed by an accumulation of unresolved grievances by ghetto residents

---

* According to the records of the Watts riot, the victim was apparently Ramon L. Hermosillo, nineteen.

† Officially known as the National Advisory Commission on Civil Disorders, it was commonly called the Riot Commission or the Kerner Commission, after its chairman, former Governor Otto Kerner of Illinois.

against local authorities (often, but not always, the police). So high was the resultant underlying tension that
routine and random events, tolerated or ignored under
most circumstances . . . , became the triggers of sudden violence.

Having fixed a pattern of detonation of the great urban riots, the
Kerner Commission went on to draw up a profile of the "typical
rioter," who bore an uncanny resemblance to Paul Williams. It
found him to be between fifteen and twenty-four, locally born, the
economic peer of his black neighbors, somewhat above average in
education, reasonably informed about politics but distrustful of politicians, racially proud, sensitive to discrimination.

It is quite likely that Williams's feelings about his involvement
in the tumultuous days of Watts were also typical. To Williams, the
riot was a transcendental experience, permanently vivid, and to it
he attached qualities that were almost mystical.

"We used to talk a lot building Watts," Williams said. "We talked
about improving the community, burn the trash, baby, don't throw
it on the street, don't litter. And in 1965 we literally burned it down
to clean it up. That was the attitude people had, 'You want to burn
some trash, baby? Here we go.' You didn't worry about sweeping
up no alley when they were burning down the street.

"Everybody felt high. You didn't have to be high to feel high
during those times. Why did a lot of people have to riot and burn,
or die in a revolution? I didn't like to look at it as a revolution. But
if you ever felt you had some human rights, that's when you had
some. They couldn't call me a Negro anymore. They couldn't call
me a boy anymore. I was respected as a man.

"In those five days I knew that I was right there at the center
between freedom and liberation. It was like an out-of-memory period, where you go into a time capsule, where before you were
hoping for freedom within the civil rights movement and when you
came out the other end you hoped for liberation. In those five days,
I experienced things I wouldn't normally have experienced, like
drinking liquor in my mother's house. It was a free feeling.

"After, people liked to project that it had to be some belief, like
it was nationalism or Pan-Africanism or whatever ism that was responsible. I like to look at it as a movement that was generated
thousands of years ago in Africa, where people who saw cruelty

338

would rise up against it. I think Watts was just a perpetuation of the linear movement that began thousands of years ago.

"The people had no control over the Watts riot. It was natural. If someone would say was it organized? I would say no. If they would say was it unorganized? I would still say no. Because people had enough in themselves to say that they were going to have no more of this shit. 'Hell, no,' that was the attitude. There was no leadership. Watts as a community was the leadership.

"A lot of people like to say the Watts riot was a negative thing, but it was a positive thing. I look at it as a symbol of hope. It's hard to remember the true feeling. Even today, the political implications are not clear. But those days were like I was sucked into a void that was beyond my comprehension."

After the fires died and the rioters went home, the debate began over who was to blame for Watts. The ruling establishment in California tried mightily to demonstrate that it was a passing social aberration, the work of an evil few.

Mayor Sam Yorty of Los Angeles blamed the riots on "criminal elements," Governor Brown on "hoodlum gang elements." Chief Parker estimated that just 1 percent of the blacks in Los Angeles participated. These assessments served conveniently to mitigate official responsibility, or the responsibility of society as a whole, which would have been implied by an acknowledgment of massive black identification with the uprising.

It was the estimate of the McCone Commission that ten thousand blacks took to the streets. The commission, appointed by Brown to determine the causes of the riot, served largely as an arm of California's political and economic elite, and its report emerged as a pallid apology for government and the police. Even accepting the commission's figure, ten thousand blacks were a significant proportion of the adults of the ghetto area. By commending "the admirable effort of hundreds, if not thousands" to restore order, however, the commission affirmed its belief that most blacks strongly supported the existing social system.

In fact, independent surveys* conducted shortly afterward indicated that at least thirty thousand blacks were involved in the riot,

---

* See Robert M. Fogelson, ed., *The Los Angeles Riots*.

and that the number may have been as great as eighty thousand. If the higher figure was correct, the ratio of adult participation approached a majority. Based even on the lower figure, participation far exceeded any "criminal" or "hoodlum gang" element.

Far from being a narrow slice of the population, furthermore, the surveys showed that in age and economic status the participants represented a broad cross section of the ghetto area. They also revealed that most blacks in the nation sympathized with the riot, and believed it had a positive impact on the black community. The chief remorse seemed to be that blacks, rather than whites, suffered most of the casualties.

"Initially, it was a spontaneous thing," said Richard Townsend, the young man who stood for responsibility and restraint in Watts, "but as it grew it was joined by a lack of moral feeling about taking, the breaking of things that weren't yours and that belonged to people who didn't care about you. There was this feeling that the community owed no special obligation to abide by certain rules that society had set forth, and that certain types of things were perfectly okay.

"I don't think there was any feeling that what was taking place was morally wrong. Perhaps not politically right or tactically wise. Or just risky and dangerous if you were a thinking person. But, morally, the taking of things during the riot was not condemned. The feeling was, yes, you can rise up and do those things. And I sensed that type of thinking coming on more and more afterwards, after Watts."

Somewhat the same view emerged in a controversial dissent within the McCone Commission report. It was written by Reverend James Edward Jones, the commission's "token" black, whom the governor had considered a safe appointment. Jones refused to call Watts a "riot," and by referring to it as "protest" he gave it his implicit sanction.

The ghetto black, Jones wrote, "has a right to protest when circumstances do not allow him to participate in the mainstream of American society. Protest against forces which reduce individuals to second-class citizens, political, cultural and psychological nonentities, are part of the celebrated American tradition. As long as an individual 'stands outside looking in,' he is not part of that society; that society cannot say that he does not have the right to protest . . ."

The Kerner Commission, a much more serious examination than the McCone Commission, made a different point. Addressed chiefly to whites, it directed its attention candidly to the question of white responsibility. "What white Americans," the report said, "have never fully understood—but what the Negro can never forget—is that white society is deeply implicated in the ghetto. White institutions created it, white institutions maintain it, and white society condones it." What the Kerner Commission was weaker on was what white society had to do about it.

But why, when what white America saw was a community lying in ruins, were blacks so thrilled by the turbulence that had leveled Watts? The practical consequences certainly brought no comfort. Watts would long be digging out of the debris, and even longer rebuilding. A few new social programs came in, both public and private, but very little that promised to reach to the heart of problems. The riot had not evoked much remorse or guilt in white society. King's strategy of nonviolence evoked much more. So what was it that made so many blacks exult?

Bayard Rustin told of an encounter, during the tour he and King made through the embers of Watts, with an unemployed young man of about twenty. The young man shouted joyously to him, Rustin remembered, "We won!" And Rustin recalled answering, "How have you won? Homes have been destroyed, Negroes are lying dead in the streets, the stores from which you buy food and clothes are destroyed, and people are bringing you in relief."

Rustin marveled at how well the young man dealt with his paradox. The mayor for the first time had come to Watts. The chief of police had visited personally. Thousands of newsmen had descended, with their cameras and their pads. Watts was on the radio all day long and on the TV news every evening. Americans everywhere suddenly learned where Watts was, and what its people were doing.

"We won because we made the whole world pay attention to us," the young man told Rustin. "We made them come."

The boost that the events in Watts gave to the sense of community, to black stature in an era of black assertion, to black self-esteem was surely enormous. The world had noticed Watts and, in ghettos throughout the land, other blacks stood up and demanded to be noticed, too.

341

X

STOKELY CARMICHAEL:
Blackening Power

1966

"Wilkins came to the meeting and he already had a statement. He was going to make the march to support some legislation, some nonsense that Johnson had. And when he came up with that, everyone else was mad, because they didn't like him much anyway. So I started acting crazy, cursing real bad. I said, 'You sellin' out the people, and don't think we don't know it. We gonna' getcha' . . . Wilkins couldn't believe it. He went to Dr. King, and Dr. King might have been shocked, too, but he didn't say a word."

B̲Y 1966, the great reformist phase of the civil rights movement was over. The work that Martin Luther King, Jr., began so tentatively at Montgomery ten years before had been completed. The Civil Rights Act ended the formal practices of segregation once and for all. The Voting Rights Act guaranteed that Southern states would be able to bar the ballot to blacks no longer. On the federal statute books was even written the fair employment practices principles that A. Philip Randolph had won in 1941, had watched slip through his fingers and had then labored for decades to regain. The legal pillars of black subservience were gone, and it all happened far more quickly than anyone, when the movement dawned, had believed possible.

And yet the millennium remained at a distant horizon. In Mississippi, the blacks who had at last acquired the right to eat a hamburger at a lunch counter did not have the quarter to pay for it; in Watts, the blacks who had crossed a continent in search of jobs and a little dignity had looted and burned to show that they had never found them. Once before, after the Civil War, the North gave blacks freedom and the vote, but defaulted on the promise to accompany them with "forty acres and a mule." With no way out of economic dependency, the Negro in the Reconstruction era lost both his freedom and his vote. Some blacks wondered in 1966 whether it would happen again.

After Selma, King wrote, a new phase of the civil rights move-

345

ment had opened. "For the vast majority of white Americans," he wrote, "the past decade—the first phase—had been a struggle to treat the Negro with a degree of decency, not of equality. White America was ready to demand that the Negro should be spared the lash of brutality and coarse degradation, but it had never been truly committed to helping him out of poverty, exploitation or all forms of discrimination." King wrote that few Americans realized the implication of the shift from one phase of the movement to the next. During his many years of preoccupation with Jim Crow, and redeeming America's racist soul, he had scarcely contemplated a second phase himself.

Some blacks, of course, had long understood how racial discrimination fed on economic and political impotence. A. Philip Randolph had looked for racial equality first in socialism, then in trade unionism. Bayard Rustin, his apostle, had tried to focus the March on Washington less on lofty spiritual principles than on the reality of jobs. Ella Baker had sounded the warning to the young men and women who were founding SNCC in 1960 that, ultimately, the struggle would be not over the right to sit at a lunch counter but over the money to pay the check. Throughout its meteoric history, SNCC had always grasped better than the rest of the movement that power was essential for dealing with the economic and political components of racism.

This understanding of power explained why, almost from the start, SNCC had turned to organization, to create within the black community of the rural South the capacity to stand on its own. It was very nice, SNCC reasoned, that after a great deal of commotion whites had bestowed upon blacks the laws to end segregation and disfranchisement. But Northern whites had lost interest in blacks before and, when they did, the white South promptly reestablished a system of racial oppression. Much of SNCC spoke with contempt of the civil rights laws. SNCC's interest was in making blacks independent of the sufferance of others, by guaranteeing racial equality through the power that blacks themselves could exercise.

Early in its life, SNCC began to define its mission as the creation of autonomous political and economic institutions. It took its theoretical framework from the concept of participatory democracy, with which the organization was imbued from the start. From SNCC, the doctrine had gone on to invade virtually all the thinking

346

on social change in the 1960s, political and professional, liberal and radical. The federal government itself experimented with it in the antipoverty program. SNCC already had wide experience with participatory democracy in the field—in building the Mississippi Freedom Democratic Party, for instance—and it had even had some noteworthy success.

But what SNCC added to the idea in the mid-1960s was an unmistakable antiwhite animus, and a retreat from nonviolence. Never fully integrationist in its ideology, like King's SCLC or the venerable NAACP, SNCC turned abrasively in the second half of the decade to black nationalism. The years of federal failure to protect its field workers, the bitter resentment over Atlantic City, the intensifying white backlash and finally Johnson's shift in priorities from social justice to the Vietnam War—all were taken as proof of the faithlessness of whites, and led to the crystallizing of a set of separatist notions that, in diverse forms, had periodically surfaced during the long struggle of American blacks for equality.

In 1966, a charismatic SNCC militant named Stokely Carmichael attached to these notions the slogan "Black Power." The slogan carried with it a promise not just to build institutions but to build them alone, in beleaguerment, in defiance of even the friendliest whites. Black Power was a flat rejection of Martin Luther King's appeal for integration, nonviolence and love. Carmichael's ideas were to dominate the last phase of the civil rights movement, and bring it to an end.

Stokely Carmichael brought black nationalism to the United States with him. He was born in 1941 in Trinidad, a West Indian island ruled by the British and populated by blacks. His father, a carpenter by trade, was deeply committed to the independence movement which, in the early 1950s, was sweeping the Caribbean, but his father gave up his political involvement to emigrate to the United States in search of a more secure future for his family. At the age of eleven, Carmichael arrived in New York, to become an American.

"All my father's friends, all the people who came to the house," Carmichael said, "were from the West Indies. They all talked about the independence movement. Within the family network, I didn't

347

see myself so much as an American as a West Indian. And the nationalism of the West Indies was a black nationalism. It had a much more precise form—getting independence—than it ever had here in the United States. But the idea lay deep inside me, ready to take an American form later on."

I interviewed Carmichael in the house in the Bronx in which his parents still lived. It had been hard catching up with him. Carmichael spent most of his time in the 1970s in Guinea, where he lived with his African wife, the singer, Miriam Makeba. But he still promoted the cause of revolution from the lecture platform. Through an intermediary, I intercepted him between lectures, during one of his visits to the United States.

I could readily see why Carmichael had captivated so many young people, white as well as black. He was tall, and had a deep bronze color and flashing eyes. He had gained some weight since, as a skinny youth, he roamed the back roads of the rural South, but he possessed the same easy smile, infectious enthusiasm and outgoing charm. Carmichael answered questions freely, and we talked for many hours. He started speaking with a crisp West Indian accent but, as he warmed to the reminiscences of the years with SNCC, he shifted into the drawl of the black South.

Though neither of his parents had finished high school, Carmichael said, they stocked the shelves of the house with books, and transmitted to him a hunger for knowledge. After grammar school, he passed the competitive exam for admission to the Bronx High School of Science, an elite school within the New York public education system. There, he said, all his friends were the children of college graduates, if not of Ph.D.s and M.D.s. Todd Gitlin, the math prodigy who helped found SDS, attended the school. To keep up with classmates like these, he had to devour huge numbers of books, Carmichael said, which gave him a strong sense of himself and of his potential.

Carmichael said he gravitated naturally at school to students involved in left-wing politics, bearers of a rich tradition in New York. They were Young Socialists or Young Communists, supporters of SANE or the Fair Play for Cuba Committee or the League for Industrial Democracy, out of which grew SDS. These students welcomed him to their diverse picket lines, he said, and introduced him to Lenin and Trotsky. By his middle years in high school, he said, he had already made up his mind to be a Socialist.

348

But he found missing among his left-wing friends, Carmichael recalled, a concern for the condition of blacks. Stimulated though he was by their company, he preferred to spend his free time in Harlem, drinking in the racial politics of the street-corner orators. In the decorous debates of his Marxist friends, all talked of socialist revolution, Carmichael said, but they failed to understand that the likeliest place for it to start was among blacks.

These mentors taught him to apply scientific analysis to social problems. They also taught him that strong organization was essential for dealing with social problems, he said. "The trouble was," he said, "that they couldn't identify with the problems that I saw," and their analysis left him no room to act on racial discrimination, the problem which troubled him the most.

"When they talked about workers, you understand, they didn't talk about black workers," Carmichael said. "Their line was that blacks had to move into the unions, but the white workers wouldn't let the blacks into the unions. The few black workers who attended the meetings with me, they'd taken on the complete line, so they became like nonracial people.

"But I knew what was going on, because my father was a black worker, and he couldn't move for the racism. The Italians—the Mafia actually—ran the unions here in the Bronx. In the wintertime, when the work was slow, all of the black people were fired. They used to come here to my house and talk about how bad it was. My father even used to ship out in the merchant marine during the winter months. He hated it, because he was away from the family, but he couldn't work here because of the union.

"I'd go to the left-wing meetings when I was in high school and come back with these theories about the unions. My father would laugh, and say it doesn't work that way. So it seemed to me—or, at least, it seemed to my father and his friends, who used to discuss it all the time—that blacks needed their own unions to deal with these problems. Even though it wasn't the line, that was reality."

Bayard Rustin was the man Carmichael credited with reconciling his social philosophy and his racial ideals. Rustin excited him, Carmichael said, because he was black and a socialist, eloquent, energetic and courageous, and oriented to action rather than theory. In those days, the period between Montgomery and Greensboro, Rustin did a lot of speaking around New York. Carmichael said he followed Rustin from one speech to the next, licked envelopes in

Rustin's office for the Youth Marches of 1958 and 1959, and finally became a part-time union organizer for Rustin among black workers in a paint factory.

"Bayard played a crucial role in my life," Carmichael recalled. "He was one of the first people I had direct contact with that I could really say, 'That's what I want to be.' He was so at ease with all the problems. I mean, he was like Superman, hooking socialism up with the black movement, organizing blacks. You could see the beginnings of something happening. Even today, it's a problem for the white left to match theory with activity. But for me, with civil rights, Rustin did it.

"Now, today, to see this man in the struggle, you know things change all the time. The man who made me see through Bayard Rustin best of all was Malcolm X. I can't say that Bayard had ever been revolutionary. But, at that point in my life, he appeared to be the revolution itself, the most revolutionary of men."

In the spring of 1960, his last semester in high school, Carmichael attended rallies protesting the excesses of the House Un-American Activities Committee, and he helped raise money to defend the Berkeley students who had been arrested in the anti-HUAC demonstration in San Francisco. Once he joined a caravan to Washington to picket HUAC hearings. What excited him most about the trip was not picketing HUAC, however, but meeting a group of students from Howard University who told him of their activities as sit-ins in the neighboring Jim Crow states of Maryland and Virginia.

Carmichael said he found the student sit-ins throughout the South that spring much more important to him than the various causes in which he had been enlisted by his left-wing friends in New York. At first, he said, he was bewildered by the sit-ins, because nothing in his socialist education had prepared him for them. But then, like other blacks, he became intoxicated. In April, he followed with some envy the deliberations of the sit-in leaders in Raleigh, who proceeded to organize SNCC. The whites among his left-wing friends, he said, were indifferent to the mobilization of black students under SNCC, as they had been unmoved by the sit-ins themselves.

"One of the things the hard-liners inside the radical white left pushed was, 'Don't look for spontaneity, look for hard organization,'" Carmichael explained. "We had read Engels's *Scientific Socialism* over and over again. So when the sit-ins started, they were taking the line, 'Oh, it's all right, but it's only crude and spontaneous.'

"The people in the white left had this theory that the revolution needed a vanguard. And they thought they were the vanguard, so the blacks couldn't be. Anything that happened outside the theoretical framework they could not look on as serious. But the sit-ins were all that black people were talking about, everywhere you went. I couldn't be against them.

"Then, seeing they couldn't stop the sit-ins, the white left began to organize activities to raise funds for SNCC. What they hoped was to tame the movement, and finally come to lead it. They kept saying, 'These people need leadership.' To them, of course, within a scientific framework, providing leadership was not an elitist concept. It was just scientific analysis. But the leadership the students needed was leadership the white left was incapable of giving."

Carmichael's exposure to the Howard sit-ins, and the persistent nonchalance of his white friends to the burgeoning black movement, led him to a decision. Howard University had a dynamic group of civil rights activists on campus, and Washington was a center of civil rights activity. Carmichael decided not to go on with his studies within the integrated framework of a white college, but to go to college among blacks. That fall, Carmichael enrolled in Howard, planning to use it as his springboard to the movement.

At the time, the Student Non-Violent Coordinating Committee was still a loose federation of student organizations. Its Washington affiliate was a citywide body called the Non-violent Action Group (NAG), integrated in its membership but dominated by whites. Carmichael had barely arrived at Howard before he joined with some fellow students to take NAG over. With cool dispatch, he recruited enough new members from the campus to tip the balance in the organization to blacks, and vote the whites out of power. It was Carmichael's coup within NAG that introduced the movement to him, and it was NAG that served as his original channel to SNCC.

351

Beginning in the fall of 1960, his freshman year at Howard, Carmichael spent most of his weekends on picket lines, with dozens of demonstrations in the Washington area to choose from. During the Christmas vacation, he worked on a project set up by Jim Forman in Fayette County, Tennessee, to help evicted sharecroppers. In the spring of 1961, he answered SNCC's call to join the Freedom Ride, suffered his first beating, got arrested in Jackson with the rest of the SNCC contingent, and spent forty-nine days in Mississippi's Parchman Penitentiary. When he was released, he went to McComb to help Bob Moses get the voter registration project started in Mississippi.

Even then, Carmichael said, he already had serious questions about his commitment to nonviolence. Though the doctrine of nonviolence was still intrinsic to SNCC, he began to wonder about it as he sat in the cell of the Mississippi prison. Carmichael said he was not alone, and he could sense doubt about the value of nonviolence working its way through many of the young militants.

"Whew! They used to whip us every day," Carmichael said. "There were brothers and sisters in the jail who wanted to fight. They were afraid to put forth their position, and I was putting it forth for them. I didn't know at first that it was my position, too. We couldn't see each other through the jail cells, but we could talk, and we talked about what we really believed in."

Between Parchman and McComb in the summer of 1961, Carmichael attended a workshop for black student leaders sponsored by SNCC at Fisk University in Nashville. At the time, students were picketing again in downtown Nashville, to maintain the pressure on segregation barriers, and each evening the pickets were attacked by white hoodlums. Carmichael said that after a few evenings on the picket line he and another Howard student made contact with a gang of black teenagers, and the two of them promised to create a pretext the next night for going after the attacking whites. Though he personally remained nonviolent, Carmichael said, there was a ferocious fistfight, after which he joined several of the gang members for a night in jail.

"James Lawson and John Lewis and the other preachers saw what we had done," Carmichael recounted with a mischievous laugh, "so at the meeting the next day I was scared. I thought I was going to be kicked out of SNCC. They told me I would have to

352

leave SNCC if I could not adhere to nonviolence, and I felt pushed and finally said 'bullshit' to that nonsense. 'I'm not going to let somebody hit up the side of my head for the rest of my life and die. No! You got to fight back. We don't demonstrate to get beat up. We demonstrate to show people what has to be done.'

"Then Lawson made the whole theological argument about how Jesus Christ advanced the world beyond the eye-for-an-eye, tooth-for-a-tooth principle. 'Yeah,' I said, 'but Jesus said I come to bring the sword, not the shield, and no remission of sin without the shedding of blood.'* After that, an argument really blossomed, and people inside of SNCC began to raise questions about this non-violent stuff. Lawson and Lewis were really on the defensive. That was the last time they ever raised the question with me."

Carmichael also recalled that one of the heroes among his segment of SNCC militants in those early days was Robert Williams, a black ex-marine who had been head of the NAACP chapter in Monroe, North Carolina. For years, Monroe's black community had been subjected to beatings and harassment by local whites, with the complicity of the police. In 1959, Williams stood on the courthouse steps and declared, "We cannot rely on the law . . . We must meet violence with violence." For this, he was suspended from his NAACP office by Roy Wilkins, whose decision was affirmed by the NAACP convention.

Undeterred by the banishment, Williams and his followers began carrying arms for self-defense. In August of 1961 Jim Forman accepted Williams's invitation to bring a band of Freedom Riders, on their release from Parchman, to demonstrate in Monroe. All of them were beaten, and Forman was nearly killed. Williams, at the climax of the tension, seized a white couple as hostages and, though they were released unharmed, he fled with his wife to avoid kidnapping charges. Williams spent much of the 1960s in Cuba, a fugitive from the law and anathema to the main body of the movement, but something of a cult figure among the SNCC militants, who moved further and further from nonviolence.

As long as nonviolence served as an effective tactic, however, Carmichael and his friends were not prepared to abandon it.

* The verses to which Carmichael referred were presumably: "I came not to send peace but a sword" (Matt. 10:34), and "Without shedding of blood is no remission" (Heb. 9:22). The former statement is generally attributed to Jesus, but not the latter.

Throughout his undergraduate years, Carmichael was involved in demonstrations almost every weekend, frequently winding up arrested, often getting back to class only after his release from jail on Monday or Tuesday. In the spring of 1963, he was in the center of a prolonged confrontation between blacks and the police in Cambridge, Maryland, and, though he himself remained faithful to nonviolent discipline, the National Guard had to come in to quell rioting. When he was not demonstrating, Carmichael worked with NAG at recruiting others for demonstrations, at getting food and clothing to send South, at soliciting money for bail.

These were the verdant days of SNCC, when spirits were high and optimism pervasive. Everybody worked hard and cheerfully and, though there were factions, no one felt that factionalism threatened the organization. Carmichael and the people around him were recognized as being more radical than the rest of SNCC. They came from the North, they knew about Marx, they sneered at the church. Within SNCC, they were dubbed the "black masses contingent," and they were a trifle intimidating to the gospel-singing SNCC kids from the South. But there was a selflessness within SNCC in those early days that overcame suspicion. SNCC knew the enemy was white racism, and it had no time left over for organizational squabbles.

Carmichael said he would have dropped out of college to work on voter registration in Mississippi during those years, but he was afraid of being drafted. On a few occasions, SNCC suspected that white politicians in the South were putting pressure on local boards to get civil rights workers out of the field and into the Army. During the year or so that SNCC thought its voter registration project had Robert Kennedy's endorsement, it often notified the Justice Department of its suspicions. But Kennedy refused to intercede in any way in the draft process. So Carmichael decided, to avoid risking his student deferment, to limit his work in Mississippi to school vacations.

Much as Carmichael liked demonstrating, he regarded the voter registration work in Mississippi as far more important. Demonstrations were all right for raising black consciousness, he said, and useful for keeping up the momentum of the struggle while he was

in college. But the impact of demonstrations was inevitably tran-
sient, while organizing could produce lasting change. Demonstrations were mobilizing without organizing, he said, and the lesson
he learned from his Marxist friends in New York was that organization alone meant power.

Being committed to registration did not mean, however, that Carmichael believed in elections. "I came from the North," he said.
"Black people *did* have the vote in Harlem, but it didn't make any
difference. To me, the only good the vote could do was to wreck
the Democratic party and spring off a revolution in America." Carmichael said that in the South the act of registering was itself important, because it gave the black man the opportunity to stand up
and defy the white-run system. It was not the ballot itself, he said,
but infusing blacks with this kind of courage that was the road to
transferring power.

During the summer of the March on Washington, Carmichael
had a serious falling-out with Bayard Rustin over the principle of
demonstrations. Until then, the two had maintained a warm relationship. Rustin once spoke at Howard at Carmichael's suggestion,
and had spent a long evening with campus militants in Carmichael's apartment discussing the movement. When the decision on
the march was reached in 1963, Rustin asked Carmichael and his
friends to help. Some did. But Carmichael told Rustin that the
march, especially after plans for civil disobedience were abandoned, was of no interest to him.

In June, Carmichael went off to Mississippi. Throughout the
summer, he flatly opposed SNCC's cooperation with the march. In
August, he refused to return to Washington to participate in it.

During the discussions in early 1964, Carmichael led the opposition within SNCC to the proposal to invite white students to join
the Mississippi Summer Project. He said his concern was not simply that the white volunteers, with their superior education and
management skills, would dominate the black field workers. "They
said to me," he recalled, " 'Now, don't tell us that you can't control
some white kids, you big bad black nationalists.' But it wasn't controlling them. It was the spin-off." Carmichael said he worried
about what would happen after the white volunteers left.

His worry, he said, was that the Summer Project would again be
mobilization without organization. He was concerned that the army

355

of volunteers would generate the same popular expectations as mass demonstrations, and then there would be no one around to follow up with the detail work. "The question was," he said, "could we control this monster, the Summer Project, that we were creating? I felt we could not." He said Moses shared his apprehensions, but decided there was ample reason for going ahead anyway with the recruitment of whites.

Carmichael's opposition did not stop him from serving the Summer Project with prodigious energy. Moses put him in charge of the Second Congressional District, one of the five administrative subdivisions in the state. Carmichael promptly announced he wanted only blacks working in it, and he and his supporters independently canvassed the campuses of the North in search of black volunteers. He did not get enough, and in the end he had to accept some whites. But he enforced a policy of having the whites train blacks, rather than replace them at essential tasks.

Carmichael's district quickly became known as the best run in Mississippi. From his headquarters in Greenwood Carmichael organized excellent communications and security networks. As a consequence, Jim Forman, to involve all of SNCC more fully in the action, moved national headquarters from Atlanta to Greenwood for the summer. Moses regularly sent inquiring newsmen to interview Carmichael, who was charming and extremely articulate. The ensuing publicity led other workers to dub him "Stokely Starmichael," and with the admiration in which he was held there was mixed a touch of resentment. Carmichael's special status created some of the first tensions discernible within SNCC.

Carmichael had never had good relations with John Lewis, whose piety offended him, and whose churchy style was so different from his own. In age, the two were only a year apart but, in SNCC's terms, Lewis was from another generation. Lewis, by now twenty-four, was a founding father of the civil rights movement, a creator of the sit-ins, a charter member of SNCC. He was Southern and Christian, and believed in redemption through moral transformation. Though his kind of thinking was on the way out in SNCC, his contributions to the organization were undeniable, and in June of 1963 he was elected SNCC's national chairman.

Lewis spent very little time in Mississippi, however. The SNCC chairman's job was not to lead, since SNCC did not really believe

356

in leadership. It was to raise money and generate popular support for SNCC, particularly in the North. Lewis performed the job well, but at the price of losing touch with the rank and file in the field. He had an especially bitter clash shortly after he was elected, when Carmichael tried to keep him from speaking for SNCC at the March on Washington. Though Lewis won the battle, the support Carmichael received from his fellow field workers was a sign of the direction in which SNCC was moving.

During the Summer Project in 1964, Carmichael clashed repeatedly with Lewis over nonviolence. Carmichael insisted on the right of field workers to carry guns for self-defense. He argued that guns had a deterrent effect on trigger-happy whites. When a SNCC staff member was arrested with a gun, Carmichael and Lewis argued bitterly over the use of SNCC funds for bail. "We understood why he was carrying a gun," Carmichael said disdainfully. "John didn't." Finally, Carmichael said, a policy was adopted: if a worker was arrested with a gun, SNCC would pay to keep him out of jail, but would cut him from the payroll. The compromise stilled the dispute only temporarily, as Carmichael kept up his attacks on nonviolence, and on John Lewis.

Carmichael also quarreled with SNCC's leaders over the MFDP strategy. He did not favor establishment of the Mississippi Freedom Democratic party, which he said was a relic of the day when blacks went hat in hand to the white man requesting approval. He argued for the creation of a black political party, totally independent of the Democrats. Carmichael charged Moses with deluding the people by telling them MFDP had a chance to be seated at the Democratic National Convention. Even if MFDP was a useful issue around which to organize the community, Carmichael said, SNCC had no right to raise the false hope that it might succeed.

"We knew that the Democratic party wasn't going to seat no niggers," Carmichael told me. "No question in our mind about it. For those in the Second [Congressional District], we told people we're going over to our own independent party if they don't seat us."

Whatever his reservations about MFDP, Carmichael worked hard for it all summer, without ever conveying his misgivings to the contingent that worked under his leadership. During the Democratic convention in Atlantic City, he was assigned to keep the

357

picket line on the boardwalk constantly manned, and he labored with his customary diligence. But when the Democrats rebuffed MFDP's petition, he considered himself freed of further obligation. Carmichael returned to Mississippi at the end of the summer, determined to build a black political base in the South, independent of liberals, Democrats, whites, what-have-you.

The MFDP's rejection at Atlantic City was a more severe defeat for SNCC than was at first suspected, not because SNCC had performed poorly but because it had set the standard of victory so high, and had invested so much of itself to win. On the strength of the summer's publicity, contributions in the fall of 1964 ran higher than ever. With the extra money, SNCC added eighty-five volunteers to the permanent field staff, which more than doubled its forces in Mississippi. Many young men and women who had gone down for the summer stayed on their jobs, teaching in the Freedom Schools or canvassing for MFDP. But the signs of health concealed a loss of direction, since SNCC was no longer quite sure of the end to which it would put its furious organizing.

Though SNCC lost interest in its Summer Project after the Atlantic City convention, the Mississippi Freedom Democratic party, ironically, took on a life of its own. To retain its claim on the national Democratic party, MFDP supported the Johnson-Humphrey ticket during the fall campaign, while the Democratic party regulars in Mississippi backed Goldwater. MFDP also tried to get congressional candidates on the ballot in three of the state's five congressional districts, and, when that failed, conducted a mock Freedom Election, much as it had done before.

In January of 1965, MFDP persuaded Congressman William Fitts Ryan, a liberal Democrat from Manhattan, to challenge the seating of the five congressmen elected in Mississippi the previous November. Ryan's argument was that the election was illegal, because blacks had been systematically excluded from the balloting. President Johnson was not enthusiastic about the challenge and both Martin Luther King and Roy Wilkins, still ruffled over the fracas with MFDP in Atlantic City, remained aloof. So did most white liberals, including Joe Rauh, who was displeased to see MFDP represented by two attorneys from the National Lawyers Guild. Nonetheless, Ryan's motion received 149 votes in the House, and, after a sequence of hearings that kept Mississippi's racism in the public eye for months, received 143 in a rematch. MFDP had lost but once again its body of support was large enough to constitute a serious warning that Mississippi's lily-white political structure was doomed.

SNCC's decision to abandon MFDP was a serious mistake. MFDP had turned out to be precisely the kind of indigenous institution that participatory democracy had been designed to create. Autonomous and self-sustaining, MFDP was to play an important role in the years to come in giving Mississippi's blacks a real share of political power. A few SNCC people helped MFDP in the fall campaign in 1964, and over the next few months SNCC gave MFDP some money from its brimming treasury. But most of SNCC's people regarded MFDP's support of the Johnson-Humphrey ticket a betrayal of the fight that had been waged in Atlantic City, and the two organizations drifted irreversibly apart.

Early in the fall of 1964, a delegation from SNCC led by Jim Forman accepted an invitation to visit the Republic of Guinea, the most radical of the newly decolonized African states. For some time, Malcolm X had been promoting the doctrine that American and African blacks should identify with one another's cause. Carmichael, among many in SNCC, was strongly attracted to the idea. All of the SNCC delegation was moved by the experience of the African visit, but no one more than Forman. When he returned home, he began speaking of "Mother Africa, our homeland," referring to the American black community as a colony, and talking of SNCC's goals as "national liberation."

This fascination for Africa, which had been steadily growing in SNCC, led many of its members to an exploration of the thinking of Cuba's Ché Guevara, North Vietnam's Ho Chi Minh and Algeria's Frantz Fanon, all of them theorists of Third World liberation. Gradually Fanon, a Martinican who had fought the French in Algeria and died of cancer in 1961, became the favorite. Carmichael read his books, and so did Forman. Fanon's message was that national liberation required violent revolution, not simply for the colonized to drive out the colonizers but to establish their own cultural identity.

Full as they were of exciting ideas about the Third World, however, Forman and the others who returned from Africa had little to offer to help SNCC find a strategy. Forman suggested extending the voter registration campaign from Mississippi to the entire South, but the field staff showed no interest in the proposal. Still, no one came up with a better idea.

The touch of anarchy that had always been in SNCC's soul was now exacting its price. As long as the organization agreed on a goal, the field workers were able to marshal themselves to pursue it. In his quiet way Moses had provided dynamic leadership when it was needed, but after Atlantic City he became hostile to leadership and abdicated his role completely. Though SNCC's drift was apparent, the talk at staff meetings continued to dwell more on the process for reaching decisions than on what the decisions should be. When Forman proposed greater centralization and tighter control, the field workers turned him down cold.

The money that came rolling in after Atlantic City contributed to the anarchy. It reduced the sense of austerity, of beleaguerment, of personal sacrifice that had pervaded the field operations. It brought in the new field workers, mostly from Northern campuses, and the bulk of them promoted countercultural values. As revolutionaries, these newcomers resisted discipline in favor of "doing your own thing" for the cause. They could be hardworking and brave, but, more than the older hands, they smoked pot, made love and talked philosophy. The older hands accused them of being on a "freedom high," and it was true that they could not be aroused to treat organizational matters as seriously as SNCC's battle-scarred veterans.

Stokely Carmichael may have been a dissident within SNCC, but he was not on a "freedom high." Though sometimes mistaken for a blithe spirit, he understood the difference between dissent and self-indulgence. Far from a martinet, he recognized that it was necessary in the conditions of Mississippi occasionally to blow off steam. But there was enough of the New York Socialist left in him to realize that, without leadership, there would be no organization and, without organization, there would be no revolution.

When Carmichael was director of the Second District during the Summer Project, he once fired a volunteer who each day performed some noble act of protest that would get him arrested. Carmichael appreciated the volunteer's courage, but to get him out of jail every day cost the organization time, money and lawyers. Carmichael believed that, whatever the character of individual acts, they had to correspond with an ultimate organizational goal. In the fall of 1964, having received his B.A. in philosophy from Howard, Carmichael was ready to work full-time for the movement. Unlike so many others in SNCC, Carmichael had an objective, and he had the personal discipline to set out on his own to attain it.

What Carmichael wanted was to make SNCC into an all-black organization, working to create a black society free not only of dependence on but of contact with whites. The concept, known as black nationalism, had appeared repeatedly throughout American history, most spectacularly under the banner of Marcus Garvey in the 1920s.

SNCC's white field workers recognized that they would have no place in the organization that Carmichael envisaged. Bob Zellner, whose many battle scars testified to his devotion to SNCC, was furious at what he considered Carmichael's betrayal. SNCC's black veterans, many of whom shared Carmichael's views, acknowledged the injustice to Zellner and other brave whites who had served SNCC. Many had misgivings, furthermore, about the practicality of trying to realize as radical a notion as Carmichael advocated.

By the end of 1964, Carmichael had calculated that he could not possibly attain his goals within SNCC's Mississippi framework. He resigned his directorship of the Second Congressional District and announced that he was going to rural Alabama, a still unchartered hinterland for political work. He would set up his own SNCC project in Lowndes County, he said, where four-fifths of the population was black, and he would organize it as he saw fit.

Lowndes, Carmichael told me, was "the epitome of the tight, insulated police state." According to a study by the U.S. Civil Rights Commission in 1961, not a single black in the county was registered to vote, and the distribution of wealth was scarcely more equitable. The principal road between Montgomery and Selma ran straight through Lowndes, which would have an impact on Carmichael's mission, and Martin Luther King's people had sometimes sought allies in the county for their work. But the Lowndes police were notorious for their brutality, and the civil rights movement seemed to have passed Lowndes County by.

Carmichael arrived in Lowndes County in March of 1965, while

361

King's campaign to register voters was raging in nearby Selma. Carmichael had been among those in SNCC who, thinking the Selma campaign would fail, wanted nothing to do with it. He opposed the participation of John Lewis, now a board member of SCLC in addition to being chairman of SNCC, but he acceded to Lewis's participation in the Selma demonstrations in a private capacity. On March 7, Lewis had his skull fractured by police in Selma while he marched at the head of a column headed for Montgomery. Two weeks later, after Johnson's voting rights speech, King led a second Montgomery march which actually reached its destination. By that time, Carmichael had changed his mind and joined in.

He changed his mind, Carmichael said, because the march passed straight through Lowndes County, where King was a hero. Despite Forman's objections, he said, he had no intention of missing the chance to identify himself with King. "I told Forman," Carmichael explained to me, " 'I'll be at the front of that line and I'll be looking for everybody from Lowndes County, get their names, see who the strong people are and make my move.' I took my momentum from the personality of King. Later Lowndes County people used to call me King's boy, and I said, 'Ye-ah.' " After the Selma demonstration, Forman agreed to dispatch a half-dozen field workers to Carmichael's support, and the SNCC campaign for registering black voters in Lowndes County was on.

The SNCC people, with Carmichael at their head, worked hard to get blacks on the voting rolls throughout the spring and summer of 1965. They explained very carefully to potential voters, Carmichael said, how election of a black sheriff might end police brutality, and how election of a black tax assessor could channel funds into better roads and schools for blacks. They conducted meetings every Sunday night, and actually managed to enlist a substantial contingent of local people willing to support them. As they had done in Mississippi, they roamed the back roads often at night, sometimes in disguise, to persuade blacks to act.

Even though SNCC people admitted they carried guns for self-defense, Martin Luther King was impressed enough with Carmichael's work to send in some of his pastoral volunteers to help them. In August, a white sheriff in Hayneville gunned down two of them, both white, killing Jonathan Daniels, an Episcopal seminary

362

student from New Hampshire, and wounding Father Richard Mor-
risroe, a Chicago priest. "We're going to tear this county down,"
Carmichael declared in a protest rally after the shootings. "Then
we're going to build it back, brick by brick, until it's a fit place for
human beings." Despite the effort and the sacrifice, however, by
the end of August the names of only fifty or sixty black voters had
been inscribed on the Lowndes County rolls. By then the Voting
Rights Act, the recompense for the suffering of Selma, had become
law, however, and federal registrars were heading South.

In the summer of 1965, SNCC was beginning to feel the financial
pinch of the decline of the civil rights movement. The contributions it had come to expect from churches, labor unions and foundations, as well as from individual donors, had fallen substantially.
For the first time in several years, SNCC was running a deficit.
Convinced that the decline was temporary, SNCC borrowed, but
by early 1966 contributions had dried up further and SNCC was
unable even to service its debts.

Martin Luther King and the American liberal community
watched with dismay as SNCC edged increasingly leftward, and
assumed an increasingly antiwhite posture. The Vietnam War had
become a central issue in SNCC's debates, and neither King nor
the liberals had yet made a commitment to oppose it. Though both
disliked the war, they were reluctant to break with Lyndon Johnson, their patron on domestic political issues. Equally important,
neither King nor the liberals wanted to precipitate a schism in the
civil rights movement by openly attacking SNCC.

In deference to their friends, the SNCC people also hesitated.
But SNCC's Third World orientation drew it inevitably to the conclusion that Vietnam was a colonial war, conducted by whites
against people of color, like themselves. Restraint within the organization finally snapped when a Tuskegee student named Samuel
Younge, who had worked on SNCC campaigns, was shot dead after
using a whites only rest room in an Alabama filling station. The
murder made the Civil Rights Act, with its "public accommoda-
tions" guarantees, look to SNCC like a mockery. After the Younge
killing, SNCC seemed indifferent to the risk of rupture with King,
Johnson, the white liberals, even with America itself.

363

In January 1966, after the acquittal of Younge's murderer by an all-white jury, SNCC released a statement that said:

"The murder of Samuel Younge in Tuskegee, Ala., is no different from the murder of peasants in Vietnam, for both Younge and the Vietnamese sought, and are seeking, to secure the rights guaranteed them by law. In each case, the United States government bears a great part of the responsibility for these deaths.

"Samuel Younge was murdered because United States law is not being enforced. Vietnamese are murdered because the United States is pursuing an aggressive policy in violation of international law . . . We maintain that our country's cry of 'preserve freedom in the world' is a hypocritical mask behind which it squashes the liberation movements which are not bound, and refuse to be bound, by the expediencies of United States cold war policies. . . ."

It was the kind of statement that would be echoed again and again in the following years by civil rights militants and by the New Left. But what troubled the public in 1966 more than criticism of the war was SNCC's encouragement to draft resistance. "We are in sympathy with, and support," SNCC's statement said, "the men in this country who are unwilling to respond to a military draft which would compel them to contribute their lives to United States aggression in Vietnam . . ." Not yet an accepted anti-war tactic, draft resistance upset even critics of the war. SNCC, however, had always been the avant-garde. Bolstered now by the thinking of Frantz Fanon, it was moving quickly away from the mainstream of the civil rights movement, and the whites of the New Left were just a step or two behind.

In the short term, the heaviest price for the statement was paid by Julian Bond, SNCC's director of public information, who had been elected to the Georgia legislature in the fall of 1965. A Supreme Court ruling which required legislative reapportionment to provide representation for urban blacks had made his candidacy possible. Many in SNCC had not wanted Bond to run, especially as a Democrat, reasoning that the Democrats were now the party of the war, as well as of Atlantic City. But Bond dismissed them and, backed by an energetic contingent of SNCC veterans who swapped in blue jeans for coats and ties, he conducted an excellent campaign and won.

But Bond, one of seven blacks elected to the legislature that fall, endorsed SNCC's antiwar statement a few days before he was to be sworn in, and the next day the *Atlanta Constitution* ran a headline which said, "SNCC and Legislator Back Draft Card Burnings." It was something of an exaggeration, but Bond did not say he had been misrepresented either on the war or the draft. Alone of the elected blacks, Bond was denied his seat by the Georgia legislature in January.

A month later, Bond ran to fill his own vacancy and won, and in November of 1966 he ran for the full term and won again. But it took nearly a year of litigation before the Supreme Court ordered him admitted to his seat. Meanwhile, Bond's case intensified public awareness of SNCC's contention that racism was at the heart of the war, and it pushed SNCC further into the black nationalist position that was to mark it for the remaining years of its life.

Ever since his triumph in Selma early in 1965, Martin Luther King had found it frustrating trying to hold on to his leadership of the civil rights movement. SNCC threatened to abandon his carefully cultivated tenets of nonviolence. CORE, the granddaddy of American nonviolent direct action, had shrunk to a bickering vestige of itself. Malcolm X, offering Islam and race hatred, had become more attractive to the young than was he, offering Christianity and universal love. Then in the summer came Watts, the kind of cataclysm he had warned about but for which he was nonetheless unprepared.

The civil rights movement, in the belief that its proper target was the South, had never established inner-city projects. SDS still had a small ghetto program, but it was dying from lack of enthusiasm and funds. Only the federal government, in the antipoverty program, was doing promising work within the inner city.

By late 1965 the Office of Economic Opportunity, under the audacious direction of R. Sargent Shriver, was establishing community action programs in cities everywhere. Openly based on citizen participation, the federal antipoverty program, like SNCC and SDS, aimed at building black political and economic institutions, and its projects were siphoning off the energies of young blacks who might once have been attracted to the movement. In city after city, antipoverty projects were running head-on into established political and economic power, and were maintaining a high level of urban instability. Still, there was evidence that they were effective in laying the groundwork for ghetto blacks to break the cycle of poverty and despair.

In mid-1966, King, still in search of a way to adapt nonviolence to the next phase of the civil rights movement, announced an "end-the-slums" campaign of his own in Chicago. The local civil rights organizations supported him but, because their concerns were not with the problems of poor blacks, he had little popular base with which to work in the ghetto. For weeks King marched the streets of Chicago, demanding major reforms, but it was never clear to whom his campaign was addressed.

Chicago's powerful mayor, Richard J. Daley, no great friend of blacks, was a different kind of target from Bull Connor. Chicago, a volatile mix of black and white ethnic communities, was one of the nation's most heavily segregated cities, and Daley's policy of concentrating public housing in already black neighborhoods produced much of the segregation. But public housing developments were not going to be torn down, and even a change in city policy would not have affected the subtle segregationist processes in which banks, real-estate brokers, builders, state and federal agencies and residents themselves privately conspired. The segregation of neighborhoods, unlike schools, was not vulnerable to a court order. Unlike lunch counters, neighborhoods were not susceptible to a deal that could be put into effect overnight. Neighborhood segregation was a condition that would not be easy to uproot from American culture, nor was it likely to yield victories to nonviolent direct action.

Because he depended heavily on black votes to keep his machine in power, Daley treated King with courtesy. He parried King's demonstrations with promises of swimming pools and playgrounds, employment and training programs, health and welfare benefits, all presumably to be paid for by Washington. By his deference he kept King off balance, and by his maneuvering he thwarted King's efforts to undermine the black community's allegiance to his political machine. The bleak experience confirmed for King that the targets of the second half of the 1960s would not fall to the techniques of the first. In Carmichael's terminology, King mobilized the Chicago ghetto but he did not organize it, and the campaign inevitably failed. King did not give up his search to regain the initiative in civil rights but, like SNCC, he turned increasingly to the Vietnam War, which he regarded with growing horror.

Since the enactment of the Voting Rights Act, a team of federal voting registrars had arrived in Lowndes County, and in contrast to the frustration encountered by SNCC, the federal authorities enjoyed remarkable success. The whites in Lowndes did not give in easily. Sharecroppers were evicted from their land for registering, workers were fired from their jobs. Nonetheless, the disfranchised came to sign up and, within two months, nearly two thousand blacks became eligible to vote.

Carmichael did not want the blacks in Lowndes County competing for power in the Democratic primary. With a heavy black majority in the county, his dream was to establish an all-black party, which would take power away from the local whites. Yet Alabama's blacks, much as they identified the Democratic party with George Wallace and the brutes who served as sheriffs, were reluctant to go off on their own. Only with much persuasion did Carmichael get enough of them to follow his advice and found their own political party. It was called the Lowndes County Freedom Organization and its symbol, which gave the party its popular name, was the black panther.

The Black Panther party needed only 20 percent of the votes in the May 1966 primary in Alabama to get its candidates on the ballot for the general election, but it received little encouragement as it prepared its campaign. Democratic liberals at the national level made no secret of their preference for having the newly enfranchised blacks take the state's Democratic party away from the local Dixiecrats. The labor unions and other major political donors saw nothing hopeful in third-party precedents, and dismissed third-party politics as useless. As for the old-line civil rights leadership, it would have nothing to do with a party that espoused black nationalism—now criticized as "reverse racism"—and which abdicated all prospect for influence at the presidential and congressional level of the Democratic party.

Among the leaders hostile to the Black Panther party was the SNCC chairman, John Lewis. An Alabaman himself, Lewis knew that, to rural blacks in the state, voting was synonymous with voting in the Democratic primary. In the South's one-party system, it was in the Democratic primary that candidates had always been elected. In the MFDP campaign SNCC had fought to have blacks recognized as Democrats. Furthermore, Lewis agreed with the liberals that unless blacks took the Southern Democratic party away from the racists, they would remain powerless in national politics.

"John came into Alabama during the height of the primary campaign," Carmichael told me, "and he gave a speech that was heard all over the state. He was on the radio every five minutes, telling people to vote in the Democratic primary.

"I didn't go to him. Others did. He said that we didn't understand, that we were Northern people. He said he remembered all his life that people wanted to vote, and he couldn't tell them not to vote. Of course, that wasn't the issue at all. Here was the chairman going against his own organization. Even if he disagreed, this independent organizing thing was SNCC policy. After that, I wanted his blood."

A year after Carmichael arrived in Lowndes County, the Black Panther party obtained about nine hundred votes for a slate of seven candidates for county offices, and succeeded in qualifying for the general elections. In the ensuing months federal authorities continued to register new voters, and by election day in November 1966 blacks actually constituted the county's voting majority.

During the ensuing election campaign, Carmichael made no pretense of nonviolence, and Black Panther party workers all carried guns. When a county sheriff announced that he could not protect a Black Panther campaign meeting near the courthouse, Carmichael was quoted as saying, "That's okay, baby, we're going to bring our own guns," and the meeting went on. Carmichael flaunted the slogan "Power for Black People," so there would be no mistaking, for either race, what the party's purpose was. Yet some blacks were doubtful and some were intimidated, and not all rallied to the Black Panther banner during the election drive.

On election day, Black Panther candidates each received an average of sixteen hundred votes, but that was not enough, and all of them were defeated by the regular Democrats. Nonetheless, it was a remarkable showing, considering the atmosphere of tyranny in Lowndes County, in the first elections in which blacks had participated since Reconstruction. The mathematics established beyond doubt that the day of white political monopoly in Lowndes County was ended and, indeed, within a few years a black was sheriff and blacks held several other county offices.

Stokely Carmichael was fresh from the triumph of organizing the Black Panther party and getting its candidates on the ballot when SNCC, in the spring of 1966, held its annual staff meeting at Kingston Springs, near Nashville. He felt he had a personal grudge to settle there with John Lewis. But he phrased it in the ideological terms of revolution versus reformism, black nationalism versus integration, armed self-defense versus philosophical nonviolence. In the nearly two years that had passed since Atlantic City, SNCC had moved a long way toward Carmichael's positions. Now Carmichael talked of spreading the organization of the Black Panther party from Lowndes County into all of Alabama, of going on then to the entire South.

Many in SNCC saw the Lewis-Carmichael contest differently. Though he had been chairman for three years, Lewis did not have many friends in the field. He conveyed an impression that his mandate emanated independently from SNCC, and he had become increasingly pontifical. Having insisted on an exemption from SNCC policy to march in Selma, he demanded the right to participate with the other elders of the movement in a White House Conference on Civil Rights, which Johnson was sponsoring and which SNCC proposed to boycott. If the chairman was to be SNCC's symbol to the outside world, Lewis no longer qualified, because SNCC's policies had moved so dramatically away from his beliefs.

About 130 staff members attended the meeting, substantially fewer than were on the roster in the fall of 1964. After a few days of desultory debate on administrative matters, the meeting turned to whether the twenty or so whites still on the staff should remain. The indomitable Bob Zellner argued strongly for their retention. Finally, out of deference to Zellner, a proposal was made to readopt an old policy requiring white members to organize only in the white community. The compromise was adopted but the vote left little doubt that only time kept whites from being swept out of SNCC completely.

369

On the night of May 14, 1966, debate began on the election of officers. Jim Forman, whose strong hand had given SNCC five years of administrative stability, had decided that ill health required him to withdraw as executive secretary. He would remain close to SNCC, and his black nationalism would be a major influence, but SNCC would from then on miss his solid good sense. Ruby Doris Robinson, a woman who had given long service to SNCC, was elected to replace him. Cleveland Sellers, a close friend of Carmichael, was elected program secretary. The climax of the agenda was Carmichael's challenge to Lewis. Culminating hours of discussion, embittered by the attacks and counterattacks of what had become savage factionalism, the vote did not come until midmorning, after many members had gone off to sleep. Lewis won by a wide margin.

But the results were challenged on the grounds that Forman, as acting chairman, had violated a promise to notify the members who had gone to bed. Lewis stood adamant on the result, and a nasty argument followed. Forman ruled finally in favor of a revote and, in support of the ruling, Robinson and Sellers resigned from the offices they had just won. In a moment of panic Lewis, seeing his strength erode, overplayed his hand, and threatened to resign from SNCC if not reelected. In an organization riddled with suspicion of overbearing leaders, the statement was catastrophic. The revote was not a match-up between two philosophies but a response to Lewis, and Carmichael won overwhelmingly.

Yet, however haphazard the circumstances, there was logic to Carmichael's election. Lewis had become an anachronism in SNCC, increasingly isolated, painfully irrelevant. He represented an era of the civil rights movement that was no more, and which could not be recaptured by him or Martin Luther King or James Lawson. In the end he tried sincerely to reconcile SNCC's burgeoning black nationalism with his own spiritual values, and he failed. True to his vow on the night of his defeat, he soon withdrew from the organization.

In his victory statement to the press after the election, Stokely Carmichael reaffirmed his Lowndes County strategy, his Third World identification and his revolutionary commitment. He ended with a gibe at the government of the United States for the "deception" in its claims of concern for democracy. At the end of the meeting, Carmichael went back to organizing in Alabama.

But Carmichael moved quickly to identify SNCC publicly with the philosophy he espoused. On June 6, 1966, three weeks after his election as chairman, he was waiting for a flight in the Memphis airport when he was paged to take a phone call. He was informed by SNCC headquarters in Atlanta that James Meredith, while on a lone protest march from Memphis to Jackson, had been ambushed by a white gunman ten miles inside the Mississippi state line. Meredith had been taken to a hospital back in Memphis, where he was to be visited the following day by King, Roy Wilkins and other civil rights leaders.

James Meredith was one of the lonely activists of the 1960s. An Air Force veteran, in 1962 he became the first black admitted to the University of Mississippi, after a night of mob carnage on the campus. Meredith never identified himself with any of the civil rights organizations but occasionally performed some solitary act of bravery. The march through Mississippi was his own idea, conceived as a symbol of encouragement to blacks to banish the fear of registering to vote.

When Carmichael learned of the shooting, he perceived its potential at once. Meredith's route from Memphis to Jackson passed straight through Mississippi's Second Congressional District—just as the Selma-to-Montgomery road had bisected Lowndes County —and the Second was where he had organized voters throughout the Mississippi Summer of 1964. When Carmichael arrived at the hospital he found King, who had already persuaded Meredith to authorize the continuation of the march as a statement by the entire civil rights movement. Carmichael told King that, despite SNCC's aversion to marches, he would go along.

Joined by several of his companions from SNCC, Carmichael attended a meeting the next day in James Lawson's church in Memphis. King was to be there, along with Wilkins, Whitney Young of the Urban League and Floyd McKissick, who had recently succeeded Jim Farmer as CORE's national director. Carmichael told me he and the SNCC people wanted the march to be a dramatic affirmation of black nationalism, but the presence of Wilkins of the NAACP and Young of the Urban League threatened to restrain any swing in that direction.

"King's role was dangerous to us," Carmichael recounted, ob-

371

viously enjoying the mischievousness of his story. "Not only did he occupy the center stage in terms of public popularity. He had the strongest personality. King could take a middle position among the organizations and appear to be the real arbitrator. We wanted to pull him to the left. We knew if we got rid of Young and Wilkins, the march is ours."

Carmichael said he and the SNCC contingent discussed the strategy they would follow at the meeting, then laid out what they calculated might be the scenario. He acknowledged that he was "a little ashamed" of the ruse they planned, but it worked spectacularly.

"Wilkins didn't know me," he said, "and neither did Young. All they knew about me was the image they'd seen on television of this crazy black man. But King knew me before I was chairman, not like an equal but like a young man in SNCC. He knew me as a worker and there was some respect there.

"Wilkins came to the meeting and he already had a statement. He was going to make the march to support some legislation, some nonsense that Johnson had. And when he came up with that, everyone else was mad, because they didn't like him much anyway. So I started acting crazy, cursing real bad. I said, 'You sellin' out the people, and don't think we don't know it. We gonna' getcha'.' And all the SNCC people in the meeting were yelling, 'Right on! We ought to shoot him on the spot.' We wanted to let them know that it would be impossible to work with us.

"Wilkins couldn't believe it. He went to Dr. King, and Dr. King might have been shocked, too, but he didn't say a word. King was just beautiful. Young and Wilkins fell completely into the trap and stormed out of there."

In his own account of the Meredith march, King never mentioned the deliberations with Wilkins and Young, and said simply that he, Carmichael and McKissick made the arrangements. He wrote also that he rejected Carmichael's efforts to limit participation to blacks, and he refused to authorize the presence along the line of march of the Deacons for Defense, a group of blacks armed to deter white violence. King recalled that, at a press conference prior to departure, he affirmed the nonviolent and interracial character of the march.

Carmichael and his followers, as they had anticipated, nonetheless dominated the march. They knew where to go to line up the churches for the evening meetings, to get the tents for sleeping outdoors, to reserve the land to pitch the tents. They arranged the meals and the sanitary facilities wherever the marchers stopped. They encountered friendly veterans of the SNCC campaigns in virtually every community, and they profited from the enthusiasm generated by the march to conduct a simultaneous voter registration drive. Whatever King's objection, furthermore, they saw to it that the Deacons for Defense were on hand, scanning the road as the marchers passed, checking on suspicious bystanders.

As Carmichael remembered it, King became increasingly smitten by black nationalism as the days went on. "At the mass meetings each night," he said, "the SNCC workers would speak before King did, and that set the nationalist tone. The people had been hearing it from us for a long time. They knew this talk, and they would go wild." Carmichael said King started out on the march using the word "Negro," which SNCC had long before abandoned in favor of "black," and turned gradually to more militant rhetoric. Before long he was saying "black is beautiful," Carmichael recalled, and the crowds loved it.

In his account in *Where Do We Go From Here?* King wrote that he argued the implications of black nationalism with Carmichael and his SNCC friends throughout the march. He acknowledged that his own presence generated large crowds, and huge enthusiasm, during the many days en route, and he insisted that, whatever the SNCC people said, his own message was one of continued commitment to integration and nonviolence. At one point, King wrote, Carmichael revealed to him candidly that it had been SNCC's deliberate strategy to make the most of his prestige. With good humor King wrote: " 'I have been used before,' I said to Stokely. 'One more time won't hurt.' "

When Carmichael saw the enthusiasm of the crowds, he began to contemplate an act of further daring. He sent out an advance man named Willie Ricks to test the slogan "Black Power." Ricks was in the tradition of the fearless SNCC organizer, willing to risk anything for the cause. "Ricks came back with fantastic reports," Carmichael said. "It's electrifying. The people are going wild." Afraid Ricks was exaggerating, Carmichael said he sent out others, who confirmed the reports. The only question was where to drop the

373

slogan so that the media would pick it up, he said. After a short deliberation, they decided the logical place had to be Greenwood.

Everyone remembered Stokely in Greenwood, the blacks for his gallantry, the whites for his outrageousness. Greenwood, a city of twenty-two thousand, had been Carmichael's headquarters in the Second Congressional District, and the site of SNCC's national office during the Mississippi Project. On July 17, 1966, Carmichael returned to Greenwood with several hundred marchers. He was promptly arrested for illegally pitching a tent on the grounds of a black high school.

The mass meeting in Greenwood that night was all SNCC's. King had gone to Memphis to tape a television show, and everyone's mind was on Carmichael, sitting in the jail. For hours Willie Ricks, a dynamic speaker, held the platform, haranguing the crowd of three thousand with condemnations of the arrest. At the high point of the crowd's ardor, a group of SNCC workers left the rally, arrived at the lockup, bailed Carmichael out and speeded him back. The crowd cheered as he sprang athletically to the platform.

"The only way we gonna stop them white men from whuppin' us is to take over," he cried. "We been sayin' 'freedom' for six years and we ain't got nothin'. What we gonna start sayin' now is—" and then he shouted, "Black Power!"

At that, Willie Ricks leaped to the podium and yelled, "What do you want?" And the crowd, instead of responding with the usual "Freedom!" shouted back, "Black Power! Black Power!" And so that night a powerful new slogan was born, which would dominate the civil rights movement for the rest of its days.

Black Power was on everyone's mind throughout the remaining nine days of the march. Carmichael continued to use the slogan, and monopolize the publicity. King dissociated himself from it on June 20, saying "black supremacy would be equally as evil as white supremacy," but he decided to stick with the march itself.

Before it had ended, King and 250 followers were stoned by whites in the Mississippi town of Philadelphia, where they had detoured to commemorate Andrew Goodman, James Chaney and Michael Schwerner, the three murder victims of the Mississippi Project. In Canton, on the last leg of their journey, the marchers were attacked by Mississippi highway patrolmen using tear gas, clubs and rifle butts. Finally, on June 26, fifteen thousand people

374

marched triumphantly into Jackson. At their head were King, Carmichael, McKissick and James Meredith, who had been released
from the hospital a few days before. As they paraded through the
city, the cry heard most frequently from the ranks was "Black
Power!"

The Black Power slogan evoked extraordinary interest throughout the country. Even before the march reached Jackson, Carmichael was invited to appear before reporters on *Face the Nation*, a
network television panel. In the following months, he spoke on
platforms almost daily, drawing large audiences and major attention from the press. So captivating was his personality that the
nation seemed almost to expect that, at some point, he would announce with his easy laugh that it had been a practical joke. But
while he equivocated about the meaning of Black Power, Carmichael never retreated from his allegiance to it.

In a book bearing his name,* written not long after the Meredith
march, Carmichael described Black Power rather innocuously as:

> . . . a call for black people in this country to unite, to
> recognize their heritage, to build a sense of commu-
> nity. It is a call for black people to define their own
> goals, to lead their own organizations and to support
> those organizations. It is a call to reject the racist insti-
> tutions and values of this society.

He sought to attribute to Black Power an almost cherry-pie American quality, arguing that:

> . . . group solidarity is necessary before a group can
> operate effectively from a bargaining position of
> strength in a pluralistic society. Traditionally, each
> new ethnic group in this society has found the route
> to social and political viability through the organiza-
> tion of its own institutions . . . Studies in voting behav-
> ior specifically, and political behavior generally, have
> made it clear that politically the American pot has not

* Stokely Carmichael and Charles V. Hamilton, *Black Power*.

375

melted. Italians vote for Rubino over O'Brien; Irish for Murphy over Goldberg, etc. This phenomenon may seem distasteful to some, but it has been and remains today a central fact of the American political system.

Yet most Americans took Black Power to mean something more than an organizational strategy, as Carmichael suggested, and more even than the armed self-defense of which he occasionally spoke. In less guarded moments, he talked of revolution and strife, and of bringing down the American power structure. No doubt his ambivalence was calculated. It served his purposes to be misunderstood. But, whatever his real intentions, both blacks and whites perceived in the Black Power slogan—probably correctly—a hidden agenda that was a menace to the society.

Of the old-line civil rights leadership, only CORE, which was without influence, supported Black Power. Roy Wilkins rejected it as "anti-white power . . . the ranging of race against race." Bayard Rustin, Carmichael's former idol, said it "not only . . . lacks any real value for the civil rights movement but its propagation is positively harmful." A. Philip Randolph, an ex-radical but an inveterate foe of separatism, joined with Whitney Young and other prominent blacks to reaffirm their commitment "to the common responsibility of all Americans, both white and black, for bringing integration to pass."

Exciting as Black Power was, it only accelerated SNCC's decline. After Greenwood, financial contributors fled faster than ever. Nonetheless, seemingly hypnotized by its slogan, SNCC plunged forward and, in December 1966, eliminated the inconsistencies in its position by firing the five remaining whites on its payroll. Meanwhile, more and more of the dedicated old hands went off to other work, too tired or too alienated to keep going. Thanks to Black Power, Carmichael had become a celebrity but his organization had eroded away beneath him. Black Power had not given SNCC new life, but had sealed its doom.

"Yeah, SNCC worked for Black Power, and Black Power killed SNCC," Carmichael said to me. I thought that he spoke wryly, almost whimsically, rather than bitterly. "But we couldn't control what was happening in America.

376

"I had seen spontaneous rebellions, been involved in spontaneous rebellions, since the early sixties. Cambridge, Maryland, was where I first saw it, where black people not only threw bricks and bottles but shot at the National Guard. I saw it in Birmingham, in Jackson, in Greenwood. I saw the feeling, I saw the energy, and I myself was nervous about it. But it was building and there was no way to stop it.

"SNCC could try to stop it or play a neutral role, which was not possible. Or SNCC could push it. Black Power was the only constructive way to go.

"By the time Black Power came, it was clear to a lot of us what revolution actually calls for. Watts had already rebelled. As you moved around, you saw what the black masses felt about Watts. They were happy. But we had a problem: while most of us were from the North, most of our work was in the South. We never looked at the North for organizational bases. We saw them only as support groups, Friends of SNCC. But it was in the urban areas that the real repercussions of the Black Power movement could be felt. These areas needed sure, heavy organizing, and that's where we were weakest. We couldn't keep up with the momentum.

"After the Black Power march, we looked around and we didn't have but a handful of people. And most of them were burned up, exhausted. And then, when the white man heard about Black Power, he said SNCC definitely had to be crushed. He let some of the SNCC people go easy by giving them jobs in the poverty program, or scholarships and fellowships, but even these tactics were eating away at SNCC. There was no question about it: SNCC had to be crushed.

"As the chairman of SNCC, I tried to educate the masses, to add fuel for the urban rebellion, to encourage a new way of thinking. But there was no organization capable of meeting the challenge. In the year after the Black Power march, it became clear that SNCC had run its course."

Carmichael did not even stay around for SNCC's final days. Promoting Black Power on the lecture circuit was more exciting than administration, and organizational responsibilities at the Atlanta headquarters languished. The SNCC workers in the field saw that they were being forgotten, and resented Carmichael for it. Jim Forman, who remained SNCC's gray eminence to the end, fought hard to keep the organization intact. But Carmichael admitted candidly that he was willing to write SNCC off.

"I never saw organization as supreme to the revolution," he told me. "I've been in and out of too many organizations—been fired from some, resigned from others—to worry about organization. If a Ford can take me on this leg tomorrow, fine. If a Cadillac can take me the next leg, fine. All I need is the vehicle."

In 1967, after a year in office, Carmichael declined to run for reelection as SNCC's chairman. He decided, instead, that the next step in his revolutionary career was to promote Black Power in the ghetto, and he moved to Washington, D.C., where he had begun his career as a militant seven years before. There he started over, organizing on the streets.

But as a celebrity in the tradition of Ché, Ho and Frantz Fanon, he was also invited to give lectures extolling Third World revolutions in Cuba and North Vietnam, Africa and the Middle East. As one of his last acts within SNCC, he was influential in elaborating a strongly pro-Arab position against Israel, a country which he decided was a tool of Western colonialism. This stand exposed the remnant of SNCC to the charge of anti-Semitism, which was the final nail in its coffin. At the end, SNCC had strength only to conduct internal squabbles, and in the course of one of them Carmichael was actually expelled from the organization, but by then it hardly mattered.

In the few years of its life, SNCC had scattered sparks across a wide landscape. It had never been a mass movement. At its most it was composed of only a few hundred young men and women. Yet it was what the Marxists called a vanguard. It transformed the politics of the Deep South, and more. It planted seeds that germinated as important influences in the student movement, the poverty program, the women's movement, the peace movement. SNCC was the most dynamic, the most creative, the most daring band of social activists of the 1960s. Its work had an impact on the entire culture. But, by 1967, SNCC had nowhere to go.

The civil rights movement was over. Public opinion polls showed that the sympathy of the white majority for the movement's goals had fallen precipitously. A decline in membership and contributions had put all the major civil rights organizations in financial jeopardy. Even Congress, after years of support, reversed its course, and rejected President Johnson's final, modest civil rights program. Martin Luther King said the defeat "surely heralds darker days for the social era of discontent," but no one paid much attention. The country was tired of civil rights.

King, persuaded now that poverty and powerlessness were the proper target of his endeavors, continued his search for a new strategy to revive the movement. While rejecting Black Power, he talked often of civil disobedience, even of massive social disruption. After his disastrous end-the-slums campaign in Chicago, he tried his hand at organizing a Poor People's March to descend on Washington and at supporting a strike of sanitation workers in Memphis. Convinced that blacks were paying disproportionately for the American adventure in Vietnam, he committed himself fully in the last year of his life to the campaign against the war.

But, persistent as King was, nothing could revive the days of glory. The civil rights movement had served its purpose brilliantly. It had transformed the relationship between the races, not only in the South but in the nation. It had changed attitudes, mores, laws, values. But when it could find no further role for itself, it died. Black Power was its epitaph.

XI
ALLARD LOWENSTEIN:
Dumping Johnson

1967

"I was always sure that the great bulk of the antiwar movement was conventional, moderate, liberal, whatever you call
it, reformist, mainstream. The SDS view was that, if they
could command the support of people against the war, they
had an opportunity to radicalize the whole of society. . . .
There was a very profound philosophical difference between those two positions. . . . You can make a case for
either one, but you have to see that they were not always
compatible."

BY 1967 the Vietnam War had displaced all other
political issues in the mind of Lyndon Johnson, and in the concern
of the public. Liberals still talked longingly of stepping up programs in civil rights and poverty. Conservatives called for increasing the efforts against urban rioting and crime. For both consumers
and businessmen, inflation was becoming a heavier burden. But
attention to all these problems languished, as the fighting in Vietnam intensified and the federal government kept pace by enlarging
the American military commitment.

By the start of 1967, the number of American troops in Vietnam
had climbed to nearly four hundred thousand. Americans on the
battlefield were being killed at the rate of almost five hundred a
month, and total casualties in the war had surpassed forty-four thousand. During the year just ending, the government's expenditures
in Vietnam had been $22 billion or more, compared to $1.2 billion
for the president's highly touted war on poverty.

Despite these sacrifices, the prospects for a successful end to
American involvement in Vietnam continued to fade. Frustrated by
failure, the Pentagon asked for more men and more money, which
seemed to assure only that losses would grow. The process of
enlargement of the American commitment came to be known as
"escalation," and to all the Pentagon's requests, Lyndon Johnson
concurred.

In retrospect, the least that can be said of the American presence

383

in Vietnam is that it was the wrong war at the wrong time. It was fought against a resourceful and tenacious opponent, who neutralized America's advantages in manpower and technology. This opponent appeared to pose so little threat to the United States that, whatever the Cold War rationale, the government succeeded in mobilizing little of the nation's ardor. The war contained a smell of racism and colonialism, when racism was a universal embarrassment, and colonialism was dying. It had a David-and-Goliath quality, with most of the world cheering for David, and most Americans uncomfortable playing Goliath.

Notwithstanding these drawbacks, the American people might conceivably have rallied to it, as they had to in past wars, if the president had not been Lyndon Johnson. With only slight exaggeration, Johnson himself lamented that what Americans readily forgave in the engaging John Kennedy they would not tolerate from him. Johnson had never been personally popular, though he brought the country together with dignity and purpose after Kennedy's assassination, though he broke a legislative logjam on major social reforms which had existed for decades, though he won a huge mandate in the election of 1964. Even in these moments of triumph, there was no concealing the qualities of character which disturbed many Americans, and caused them to distrust him.

Johnson had assumed the presidency with many assets. He was smarter than Truman, more conscientious than Eisenhower, more experienced than Kennedy. His Southern origins and his liberal convictions permitted him to forge a genuinely national coalition. He was visionary and daring, even courageous, and he was a brilliant legislative tactician. No doubt, his objective was to create a nation of social justice, with prosperity, living in peace. Yet, as the years in office passed, his attributes seemed to slip away from him, and his reputation came to be dominated by a penchant for mendacity. It was for Johnson that the term "credibility gap" was invented.

Lyndon Johnson may have been the hapless victim of the television revolution. He did not convey the directness of Truman, the simplicity of Eisenhower, the gallantry of Kennedy. Johnson was meant to persuade nose to nose in a back room of the Senate, not to address a hundred million people on a television screen. He did not have the face or the manner for that. No matter how he dressed, combed his hair or set his glasses, he looked like a riverboat gambler. No matter how deeply he felt his words, or practiced his phrases, he came across like a charlatan. Lyndon Johnson may not have been the most unattractive man who ever served in the presidency, but he was surely the most unattractive of the electronic age.

At first, the country tended to dismiss the credibility gap as a relatively harmless human foible, of no greater consequence than Johnson's penchant for fast driving, pretty women, hard drinking and frontier language. Even Kennedy had sometimes strained belief, and evoked complaints of "managed news." But, as the months stretched into years, especially after the tensions of Vietnam worsened, it became increasingly clear that Johnson did not understand the acceptable boundaries of public manipulation. It seemed that he abjured candor gratuitously, without reason, as if he had an addiction. Gradually, the public came to believe nothing, and he became a president whose every word carried an assumption of untruth.

As 1967 started, Johnson's personality seemed to poison whatever support the war had. His speeches dwelled on peace, while he intensified the bombing of North Vietnam. He boasted of military success, while the enemy's capacity to inflict damage remained unabated. He heaped praise upon the regime in Saigon, while its tyranny and corruption were common knowledge. As for his countrymen who had doubts about the war, he dismissed them haughtily, calling them "nervous Nellies," and he impugned the loyalty of the antiwar movement by contending that its protests encouraged the enemy and prolonged the fighting.

The antiwar movement, by the start of 1967, was a highly diverse, extremely uneasy coalition ranging from the mildly liberal to the actively radical. The Vietnam War, for the liberals, was a horrendous diversion of national energy from the pursuit of reforms that were vital to the society. But to the radicals, the war served as proof that American society was beyond salvation, and it became the opportunity to rally the uncommitted to the cause of revolution. As the war took on the character of an endless nightmare, radicals increasingly exploited antiwar protest as a revolutionary vehicle. By 1967, liberals understood that, if the war went on, the antiwar movement, no matter what they did, was likely to leap the bounds of the democratic system.

Allard Lowenstein was one of those liberals. Lowenstein recognized that, as long as Johnson was president, there was no prospect of getting out of the war and, the longer the war lasted, the more radical the protest would become. What distinguished Lowenstein from other liberals, however, was his conviction that Johnson's presidency could be brought to an end by hard work within the democratic process.

In 1967, Lowenstein undertook a lonely campaign, with little but his own zeal to sustain him. In due course designated the "Dump Johnson" movement, the campaign was hardly a secret, and far from a conspiracy, but at first it was barely noticed. When Lowenstein began, it was still an article of political faith that a sitting president could not be denied the nomination of his party. Only a man given to lost causes, and imbued with an almost naive trust in democracy, would have chosen to challenge that notion.

Personally ascetic, energetic to the point of frenzy, indignantly self-righteous, Lowenstein set out on his mission. The task he set for himself was to find the foes of Johnson scattered throughout the Democratic party and prove to them that they were not alone. He resolved to bring them together, then to select a candidate who would end the war.

One at a time, Lowenstein helped peel away the layers of skepticism, beneath which lay hidden a huge wave of sentiment against Johnson, and against the war. Finally, the movement acquired a dynamism which outran Lowenstein himself. One of the stunning episodes of the 1960s, the Dump Johnson campaign achieved its goal of deposing the president—only to find, in its triumph, that it had failed dismally in its larger objective of ending the war.

Al Lowenstein did not look the part of leader of a nationwide political movement. His hair was thin, his face undistinguished, and his body belied almost an obsession with physical fitness. He wore thick eyeglasses and ill-fitting clothes. His table manners were frightful and, being a teetotaler, he made a poor drinking partner. He appeared to be the prototype of the New York Jewish intellectual, which, among the various species of Americans, was not one of the more popular in the hinterlands.

Furthermore, Lowenstein had no political base. This was less of a disadvantage than if he had been seeking office for himself. Still,

Democratic politics in the 1960s was not organized for loners, and Lowenstein was not only a loner but a free-lancer, a liberal jack-of-all-trades who rarely lived in the same place, or served the same cause, for two years in a row. It is true that, on the platform, Lowenstein was a spellbinding speaker, capable of arousing even the most apathetic audience. But the public platform was no substitute for a power base, and the only credibility Lowenstein possessed was what, face-to-face, he could convey.

Allard Lowenstein was born in 1929 in Newark, New Jersey, and raised in New York. His father had been brought from Lithuania as a child, attended an Ivy League college and achieved a certain distinction as a scientist but, during the Depression, had given up science to go into the restaurant business with a brother. Lowenstein remembered that his father and mother lost interest early in politics, voted only sporadically and made no effort to imbue their four children with political values. Neither could understand the interest their son Allard showed in liberal causes, like the Spanish Loyalists, from a very early age.

"When I was a kid I skipped in grade school," Lowenstein said, "so I was smaller than the other kids. I wore glasses and I was funny-looking. I was picked on and left out a lot. Maybe because of that I always identified with ugly girls at dancing school, with blacks in the back of the bus, with anybody that was in some way hurt or excluded. My political involvement, I think, came from some emotional identification with people like that, rather than from some ideology."

It seemed to me that I interviewed Al Lowenstein a dozen times for this book. The first was in his chaotic campaign office in Brooklyn, when he was trying to get the Democratic nomination for the Senate in 1974. Then we adjourned to his house, and talked while he ate supper with his young kids. Another time we had lunch in a seedy luncheonette, where he consumed an overcooked hamburger and drank two Cokes. One time, I turned on the tape recorder in my car as I drove him to an airport. Once we met at the State Department, once at the UN, and several times he phoned me late in the evening and showed up at my house at midnight.

After a while I learned that this had always been Al's way of doing business, disorderly and frenetic and yet, in its own bizarre way, shrewdly organized. People all over America, it seemed, had

387

memories of Lowenstein only on his way to or from an airport. His style left him little time for introspection, which I concluded was the way he wanted it.

The only social commitment in his household when he was growing up, Lowenstein recalled, was to Jewishness and to Zionism. "I remember my father pushed the value of being Jewish," he said, "especially during World War Two and Hitler's destruction of the Jews." For himself, Lowenstein, like most second-generation Jews, preferred assimilation to Jewishness, and yet the fate of the Jews was a subject that recurred repeatedly in his speeches and writing. I suspected that Lowenstein's Jewishness intensified his outsider feelings, and that his awareness of the Hitler era sensitized him to the barbarity that often accompanies the disintegration of the orderly processes of government.

When Lowenstein graduated from high school in 1945, he and his parents found much to disagree on. He wanted to go into the Army, Lowenstein said, but, being only sixteen, needed their consent. They agreed, but only on the condition that he complete a summer session in college.

"Besides that," Lowenstein said, "I wanted to be an athlete. They wanted me to be a scholar. I wanted to go to a big state university. They wanted me to go to the Ivy League, where my father and brothers had gone. I wanted to go to a small town, and to a co-ed institution. They didn't like any of that. It was the Sam Levenson sense of what Jewish parents expected of their children. I just had a different vision of what I wanted my life to be."

Lowenstein enrolled in the University of North Carolina at Chapel Hill, an unlikely place for a New York Jew at that time. Two months after he entered, Japan surrendered, and he abandoned his plans to enlist in order to give his full attention to college.

Lowenstein told me he went to North Carolina without having given any thought to segregation. Save for the maids in his neighborhood, he had never known a black. But, from the start, he said, he found himself offended by segregation, and campaigned against it in Chapel Hill. Rather promptly, the board of trustees, the state legislature, the student body and the North Carolina press all came to know him, and resent him as an intruder, a New York Jew who flouted the local folkways, perhaps even a deliberate agitator.

388

In his sophomore year, Lowenstein attended his first convention of the National Student Association. As the only delegate from a Southern university who would speak out against racial discrimination, he attracted attention from a wide range of liberal students. Lowenstein was excited meeting with these students, felt comfortable in the milieu and, from the start, entertained notions of a liberal student movement.

After graduating from college, Lowenstein was elected president of NSA and, in the succeeding years, would speak frequently at NSA congresses. Even during the era when NSA's agenda was—secretly, and unbeknownst to him—tightly controlled by the CIA, the liberal sentiments of students on issues of domestic politics resonated throughout the organization. Lowenstein's ongoing relationship with the liberal multitude within NSA would be of huge importance to the Dump Johnson campaign, nearly two decades after he himself finished college.

"The value of NSA," Lowenstein said to me, "was that it reached a broad stream of American students. It was a mass movement, and at the conventions every year were fraternity jocks and Midwestern pom-pom girls, kids from little Catholic colleges and student body presidents who were not particularly interested in partisan politics. It was not narrowly based, like the SDS conventions, where the students were mostly intellectuals, and some of them fanatic.

"I think if you took a vote in the NSA congresses on the Eisenhower-Stevenson races in 1952 and 1956, Eisenhower would have won. Yet I think NSA contributed to liberalizing a wide range of student opinion."

While at North Carolina, Lowenstein had frequent occasion to meet with the university's president, Frank P. Graham, a gentle liberal who took pains to protect dissenters from the anger of conservatives in the state. When Graham served briefly in the Senate in 1949 and 1950, Lowenstein worked for him, as an assistant with responsibilities for racial and poverty matters.

Later Lowenstein worked for Eleanor Roosevelt, having first served as national chairman of Students for Stevenson in the 1952 presidential campaign, graduated from Yale Law School and fulfilled a boyhood ambition by enlisting for two years in the Army. Mrs. Roosevelt hired him as an assistant in an international education project sponsored by the American Association for the United

389

Nations. Later, she would write of Lowenstein, "He will always fight crusades because injustice fills him with a sense of rebellion." Mrs. Roosevelt and Frank Graham, Lowenstein has often said, were political parents to him.

In 1958, while he was employed on the Senate staff of Hubert Humphrey, Lowenstein was sent on a fact-finding trip to the south of Africa. He returned to South Africa the following year in a private capacity, and smuggled himself into the mandated territory of South-West Africa to collect tape recordings, photographs and other documents as evidence of colonial oppression. In the fall of 1959, he testified on his findings before a United Nations committee and, later, he recorded them in a book he called *Brutal Mandate*. The trip was a typical Lowenstein undertaking—unofficial, presumptuous, financially improvised, almost innocent in heedlessness of danger, and effective.

After the African experience, Lowenstein dabbled in Democratic reform politics in Manhattan, managing the successful congressional campaign of William Fitts Ryan, exploring unsuccessfully the prospect for himself of a race for the state senate. In 1961, he went off to California to teach political science at Stanford, and the following year he returned East to teach in Raleigh at the North Carolina State College of Agriculture and Engineering. On both campuses he was a center of controversy, at Stanford on a civil liberties issue, at North Carolina State by leading demonstrations to integrate local public facilities.

On the Fourth of July weekend, 1963, Lowenstein made his first trip to Mississippi, in response to a plea from SNCC for lawyers to represent civil rights demonstrators. He told me he was unprepared by his experiences with segregation in North Carolina for what he found there. He was struck, Lowenstein said, by the brutality in race relations that was visible right on the surface. Mississippi was more like South Africa than the rest of America, he said.

His first contact was in Clarksdale with Aaron Henry, state president of the NAACP. Henry had been a delegate to NSA from Xavier College in Louisiana, and had known Lowenstein. He referred Lowenstein to Bob Moses, who was working in McComb on voter registration. Lowenstein said he and Moses put their heads together in a search for ways to make the voter registration campaign more productive.

"I remembered that I had been in South Africa on election day," Lowenstein told me. "The African National Congress had called a day of mourning so that blacks would demonstrate their discontent. So I thought, in South Africa, where blacks can't vote, they have a day of mourning but, in Mississippi, they are supposed to be able to vote. So why not have a day of voting?

"But then the problem arose of how to vote, because if any black in Mississippi tried to vote he'd be arrested, and the bail would be so great that no one would be able to put it up. That's what led to the idea of the Freedom Vote, which was that you could vote where you would be safe—in black churches, barbershops, community centers, funeral parlors, whatever you could find, as a way of massive protest."

SNCC people have not shared Lowenstein's version of the genesis of the Freedom Vote, but there is no doubt that Lowenstein established a close working relationship with Moses. In the fall of 1963, Lowenstein traveled to Stanford and Yale, the two Northern campuses where he had the strongest ties, and recruited white volunteers to work with the SNCC field staff. The students' work was essential to the success of the Freedom Election, and provided the model for the Mississippi Summer Project the following year. But a barrier quickly developed between Lowenstein and the bulk of the SNCC workers, who resented what they considered his efforts to take their program over.

"Of course, there were the usual problems of ego and power," Lowenstein said to me, "but what was being born in Mississippi at that moment was what was to come to full flower in the antiwar movement later. You could say our purposes—that is, the civil rights traditionalists who followed Martin Luther King—were to get the white community to accept blacks, to open the society, to create the opportunity for poor people and black people to be included in the American way of life.

"The radicals in Mississippi—Stokely and Jim Forman, like the SDS leadership later—insisted that the white middle-class way of life was itself sick, and they did not want to get poor black people into it. They thought that would only add to the problem, which was to change the whole society."

391

In his memoirs, Forman attributed far more sinister motives to Lowenstein. "Seven years had passed since I had seen him in action at the NSA conference," Forman wrote, "slickly manipulating a conservative victory . . . I was disturbed to see him in Mississippi now and very briefly mentioned to Bob Moses that I had reservations . . . It would take us still longer to understand the full implications of Lowenstein's presence in Mississippi in 1963. We would discover that he represented a whole body of influential forces seeking to prevent SNCC from becoming too radical and to bring it under the control of what I have called the liberal-labor syndrome."

Forman defined the liberal-labor syndrome as powerful elements of the liberal establishment with close ties to the Johnson Administration. Its principal members, he said, were Walter Reuther of the UAW, Michael Harrington, who had been Tom Hayden's nemesis at LID, Bayard Rustin and Joe Rauh, all of whom he credited with being skilled Red-baiters. Forman said he was sure, on the basis of the NSA experience, that Lowenstein was close to the CIA, if not actually on its payroll. Lowenstein, he wrote, was assigned by the liberal-labor syndrome to "infiltrate" SNCC, to check the power of the Stalinists and keep SNCC out of the hands of Communists.

Lowenstein, while dismissing the conspiratorial aspects of Forman's analysis, did not deny that from the start he perceived a struggle between liberals and radicals in Mississippi over the direction the movement would take. He acknowledged that he was upset by the antiwhite tenor discernible in SNCC by 1964, and by SNCC's decision to turn to the National Lawyers Guild for legal representation. He had, in fact, decided not to participate in the Summer Project, he said, until he received the report of the murder of Chaney, Goodman and Schwerner. Then he returned, and spent the rest of the summer traveling around Mississippi to encourage the volunteers, and to tell blacks at freedom rallies that there was concern for them in the outside world.

At the Democratic National Convention in Atlantic City in August, 1964, Lowenstein said, he helped Hubert Humphrey try to get agreement on the seating of the two delegates from MFDP. At the famous church meeting on Wednesday morning, he spoke in favor of SNCC's accepting Lyndon Johnson's offer of two at-large seats, while insisting on MFDP's right to send the delegates of its choice. He acknowledged that the nuances of his plan were lost in SNCC's sweeping rejection of Johnson's offer. As a result of what happened, he said, he became one of the white liberals accused of complicity with Johnson's racism.

In the fall of 1964, Lowenstein signed on as a speechwriter for Humphrey's vice-presidential campaign. After the election, he held such temporary jobs as consultant for the Ford Foundation and director of a youth camp for political education. One night in March of 1965, while he was speaking at a rally of the Free Speech Movement in Berkeley, he received word that his father had died. He returned to New York, and for the next year or so gave most of his time to the legal affairs of the family's restaurant business. He also married, and made an unsuccessful attempt to win nomination as a Reform candidate from Manhattan for Congress. Mostly, he chafed at his relative inactivity, while the war in Vietnam intensified.

The Students for a Democratic Society, strangely, was slow in seizing upon the war as an organizing issue. SDS had grown to a couple of dozen functioning chapters on scattered campuses by the spring of 1964 and, after the Berkeley uprising that fall, the number roughly doubled. But student radicalism was still far from a popular wave, and SDS remained tentative about how to transform it into one. SDS opposed the war, of course, but regarded Vietnam as too narrow an issue on which to build a radical movement. It was also apprehensive that if Johnson abruptly ended American involvement, SDS would be left embracing a dead cause.

Community organizing in the Northern slums was by far SDS's most ambitious project during these middle years of the 1960s. The Economic Research and Action Project—known as ERAP—started in the summer of 1964 with several thousand dollars in foundation grants. Consciously modeled on SNCC's experience in Mississippi, it was based on the principle of participatory democracy. SDS's strategy was to organize the urban poor, both white and black, to stimulate a sense of solidarity, social consciousness and self-reliance. From the organizations of the poor, SDS postulated, there would emerge a radical political base, the prerequisite of social revolution.

393

Tom Hayden was central to organizing the project in Newark, Rennie Davis to the project in Chicago. Other projects were founded in Baltimore, Philadelphia, Cleveland and smaller cities. SDS people worked at organizing their constituencies over grievances ranging from unemployment to poor schools to inadequate trash collections.

At different intervals, about four hundred students worked in these projects, living communally as did the SNCC kids in the South, in conditions of extreme austerity. But they rarely established the warm relationship with their clients that SNCC did in rural Mississippi. Having romanticized the urban poor, SDS organizers were disappointed to find that in reality they were suspicious, insensitive and quite often unlikable. Furthermore, the premise that radicalism would thrive as the capitalist foundered was invalidated by the prosperity of the middle 1960s, from which even the poor benefited.

About half of the original ERAP projects failed the first summer, and only a few survived more than a year or two. Much of the reason was that the students were heedless of Tom Hayden's admonition that radicalism was a longtime political commitment; most wanted instant revolution. Hayden was also disturbed that many saw their objective not within a political framework, but as a personal and countercultural experience, to fuse a revolutionary character in themselves, to purge bourgeois failings, to "get in touch" with feelings and redeem the soul. Hayden stayed in Newark until Black Power persuaded him to withdraw, and Rennie Davis remained tenaciously in Chicago until he decided, with some misgivings, that Vietnam had a higher priority. But most of the SDS militants had left their projects long before.

Almost inadvertently, SDS decided at its national council meeting at the end of December 1964 to sponsor a protest march against the Vietnam War in the spring in Washington. No one showed much enthusiasm for the proposal, and the issue was finally decided on the argument of campus organizers who said that anything which gave SDS some publicity would be useful to them. Then, five weeks later, Johnson ordered the bombing of North Vietnam, escalation was under way and liberals were taking the war seriously. Suddenly, endorsements of the march started arriving, from liberals as well as radicals, individuals as well as groups. An antiwar movement had begun, and SDS was fortuitously at the center of it.

Americans for Democratic Action tried to discourage liberals from participating in the SDS protest, and Bayard Rustin conveyed his disapproval within the civil rights movement. The Selma demonstrations were taking place in the early spring of 1965. Johnson had made his celebrated "We Shall Overcome" speech and the momentum was growing for enactment of the Voting Rights Act. ADA and Rustin, though both opponents of the war, feared jeopardizing the Voting Rights Act by alienating Johnson. They were also loath to participate in any protest that might put them on the same platform with diverse radicals, Communists included, whose interests went far beyond the war. SDS's protest rally created a dilemma for liberals and the civil rights leadership which they would not resolve as long as the antiwar movement endured.

SDS's demonstration took place on Saturday, April 17, 1965, and the twenty thousand who attended were far more than its planners had anticipated. At least fifty colleges sent delegations, and students were clearly the majority on the Washington Monument grounds. Most of them were middle class and white, neatly dressed and clean, and they exhibited little of the anti-Americanism, or the spleen, which was to characterize later antiwar rallies. A range of liberal speakers took the podium to denounce the follies of the war but, as ADA and Rustin had foreseen, SDS took the occasion to convey a much broader message.

"In many ways this is an unusual march, because the large majority of people here are not involved in a peace movement as their primary basis of concern," said Paul Potter, the president of SDS. Potter, who had grown up on a farm in Illinois, had been Rennie Davis's roommate at Oberlin. He had been an officer of NSA, was once beaten with Tom Hayden by Mississippi whites, and had worked in the ERAP project in Cleveland. He was currently enrolled in graduate studies at Michigan. "What is exciting about the participants in this march," he said, "is that so many of us view ourselves consciously as participants in a movement to build a more decent society."

According to Potter's analysis that afternoon, it was not malicious officials but the system itself that brought power to bear to crush the Vietnamese, deny blacks a meaningful existence, control lives through bureaucracy, favor material values over human values. Potter said the United States had chosen Vietnam as a "testing ground" for a counterrevolutionary attempt to suppress "the social revolution that is sweeping through the impoverished downtrodden areas of the world." Then he spoke words which took a place among classic statements of the radicalism of the 1960s.

"We must name that system," Potter declared. "We must name it, describe it, analyze it, understand it and change it. For it is only when that system is changed and brought under control that there can be any hope for stopping the forces that create a war in Vietnam or a murder in the South tomorrow or all the incalculable, innumerable, more subtle atrocities that are worked on people all over—all the time."

Potter's statement was criticized by a subsequent generation of radicals, four or five years later, for lacking the courage to say that the name of the system was "capitalism" or "imperialism" or even "liberal democracy." But, in 1964, student radicalism was still exploratory, open, nondogmatic. The statement was radical enough for most, and certainly clear enough in laying out a strategy for bringing down "the system" through a campaign against the Vietnam War. Ending the war gave SDS a purpose and, within another year, its rolls had surged to more than 150 chapters.

Yet SDS, for reasons endemic to the radicalism of the 1960s, failed to capitalize on its momentum. SDS had always followed the intellectual lead of SNCC. In the summer of 1965, SNCC was experiencing a crisis that focused on decision-making. Members of the same generation whose ideas on leadership had already rocked SNCC—influenced by the counterculture, and by the ideals of participatory democracy—now turned to SDS.

At SDS's national convention in June, this new generation denounced the principle of strong leadership, exalted "do-your-own-thing" radicalism, argued that life-style was as important as politics in making revolution. Those members were the counterpart to SNCC's "freedom high" people. They tended to be less intellectual, less disciplined and less austere than the founding generation of SDS. At the convention they persuaded a majority to abolish the post of national secretary, the only officer with ongoing responsibilities for administration, and they nearly succeeded in doing away with the national office itself.

396

Emulating SNCC's flight from leadership, the SDS convention also declined, incredibly, to take a formal stand on the Vietnam War. Its aloofness did not dampen antiwar enthusiasm on the campuses, or discourage SDS chapters from assuming a central role in antiwar protests in their local communities. But the national leadership's unwillingness to lead prevented the organization from devising a strategy of growth based on opposition to the war, from elaborating a conception that might somehow link the war to its revolutionary vision, even from providing tactical guidance to its scattered followers on how to profit from antiwar sentiment. By 1969, SDS would be ready to make up for the lost time, but by then the opportunity had passed.

It is possible that the Vietnam War never really possessed the revolutionary potential which, in the most tumultuous days of the 1960s, was so encouraging to some, so threatening to others. But it was, in any event, the most promising instrument the radicals possessed, once civil rights withered as an issue. The war was Lyndon Johnson's gift to the radical movement, and SDS did not know what to do with it.

In its "freedom high" mood, what SDS did at its 1965 convention was modify its membership policies, to follow SNCC in rejecting Red-baiting, to loosen further the exclusionary clauses against Communists. When asked whether there was the chance that Communists might take SDS over, the cavalier quip of the time was, "They'll have to find us first." In fact, before many years had passed, they did find SDS, despite its organizational disarray, and they nearly did take over. What SDS did not understand in 1965, however, was how different it was from SNCC. SDS had found a purpose, just as SNCC was losing one. SDS seemed indifferent to the opportunity the war presented, in the interest of a higher truth, and a gossamer future.

Both on and off the campus, in the meantime, there was no dearth of volunteers to promote the antiwar movement. Some of the activity was quite spontaneous, like the "teach-ins," which began at the University of Michigan in March of 1965, shortly after the first bombings of North Vietnam.

In mid-March, forty-nine Michigan faculty members proposed to

397

the administration that classes be suspended for a day to permit a campus-wide exploration of the implications of the American intervention. For a time, the university community agonized, while campus radicals sought to transform the proposal into an issue for a Berkeley-type confrontation. As a compromise, the various parties agreed that public discussions of the war would begin at the end of classes one afternoon and go on, if necessary, throughout the night. News of the Michigan plan spread quickly through the academic world, and faculty-student groups elsewhere hurried to make similar arrangements.

On March 24, thirty-five hundred students and professors crowded into four lecture halls on the Michigan campus and, as the hours went by, teachers spoke about the war, students questioned them or argued, seminar groupings formed and re-formed, and the sessions went on until dawn. Columbia held a teach-in the next night, and in the following days the University of Wisconsin, New York University, Rutgers and the University of Oregon adopted the model. Much less celebrated institutions—from Western Reserve to Flint Junior College—also joined spiritedly in the movement. On May 15, a "national teach-in" was held in Washington, connected by telephone to 122 campuses across the country.

For the most part, the teach-ins were an honest effort to present conflicting viewpoints on the war, to enable an audience to reach an understanding of American policy. Even the White House seemed to acknowledge as much by authorizing McGeorge Bundy, a former Harvard dean who was serving as the president's national security adviser, to speak at the national teach-in, though he withdrew on a vague pretext at the last minute. Nonetheless, at the Washington meeting, as at others, the Administration received its fair share of the time. It was not until Berkeley, where twelve thousand assembled at the end of May, that the teach-in was transformed into an antiwar rally. After that the school year ended and the teach-ins faded. They had not influenced the government, but they left behind the unmistakable message that, on the nation's campuses, opposition to the war was overwhelming.

In August of 1965, the sequence of antiwar demonstrations that would mark the rest of the decade received a fresh spark from a coalition of peace groups which called itself the Assembly of Unrepresented People. A weekend of protest began on August 6 with a prayer vigil outside the White House. Names which would recur repeatedly throughout the antiwar years—David Dellinger, Staughton Lynd and the indefatigable octogenarian A. J. Muste, founder of the Fellowship of Reconciliation—were among its leaders. Before the weekend of protests was over, more than 350 demonstrators had been arrested, and Dellinger, Gandhi-style, had gone to jail. From that weekend emerged the National Coordinating Committee to End the War in Vietnam, a broader coalition of some thirty-three groups to plan further protests.

On the weekend of October 15, the National Coordinating Committee sponsored protests of various degrees of militancy in sixty cities, in which an estimated hundred thousand persons participated. In California the Vietnam Day Committee, whose leadership came largely out of Berkeley's Free Speech Movement, led a march of fifteen thousand on the Oakland Army Terminal, threatening a free-for-all before retreating in the face of heavily armed police. In New York, at the Whitehall Army Induction Center, David Miller of the Catholic Worker movement burned his draft card, an act for which he ultimately served two years in jail.

Officially, SDS had nothing to do with the protests, but it was SDS campus chapters that were the most active organizers on the local level. The University of North Carolina chapter marched on a chemical-biological warfare center at Fort Bragg, the University of Texas chapter conducted a "death march" on the state capital, and the Michigan chapter conducted a sit-in at the office of the Ann Arbor draft board.

A few weeks later the protests took on a more solemn tone. On November 6, 1965, Norman Morrison, a Quaker and a father of three, immolated himself outside the Pentagon. A week later Roger La Porte, another Catholic Worker, did the same at the United Nations. Though the public was horrified, the personal sacrifices —like the teach-ins and the demonstrations—had no impact on the government's Vietnam program.

On the Saturday after Thanksgiving, 1965, the Committee for a Sane Nuclear Policy, an organization of liberals whose campaign to abate the Cold War extended back to McCarthy days, brought twenty-five thousand people to Washington to march. Because of SANE's liberal credentials, the ADA abandoned its resistance to antiwar protest and joined in the sponsorship, as did the Union of

Hebrew Congregations, the Methodist Board of Christian Social Concern and the National Student Association. The radicals were there, too, but SANE did its best to keep their anti-American banners hidden from the television cameras.

Nonetheless, SDS largely captured the day. Carl Oglesby, the SDS president, delivered the rally's most quoted speech, in which he said: "The original commitment in Vietnam was made by President Truman, a mainstream liberal. It was seconded by President Eisenhower, a moderate liberal. It was intensified by the late President Kennedy, a flaming liberal. Think of the men who now engineer the war—those who study the maps, give the commands, push the buttons and tally the dead: Bundy, McNamara, Lodge, Goldberg,* the president himself. They are not moral monsters. They are all honorable men. They are all liberals." The statement was not quite fair, since it was liberals who had provided Oglesby with his audience, and with whom he walked arm in arm in antiwar protest. But it represented what Oglesby believed of liberals, and growing numbers of young people thought as he did.

In 1966, when the democratic process seemed unable to curb Johnson, these young people, more than any other age group, kept the antiwar spirit alive. Congress argued increasingly about Vietnam, and the debate had become acrimonious, but results were negligible. In the spring primary elections, the closest any peace candidate came to winning was in Berkeley, where Robert Scheer, a radical with close ties to the Free Speech Movement, won 45 percent of the vote against a liberal, pro-Johnson congressman. In the general election in November, two "doves" were added to the Senate, but thirty "hawks" were added to the House. The tireless A. J. Muste lamented at the end of the year that he discerned a "feeling of letdown, of hopelessness, which overcomes at times because the Johnson war-machine grinds on." But on the campus, protests were becoming more frequent, and more daring.

Part of the reason was that the Selective Service System, in January of 1966, had abolished the long-standing policy of granting automatic draft deferments to college students. Until then, students could look upon the war as a distant evil, fought by someone else. The change in policy was designed to equalize the military burden,

* McGeorge Bundy, special assistant to the president for national security affairs; Robert McNamara, secretary of defense; Henry Cabot Lodge, U.S. ambassador to South Vietnam; Arthur J. Goldberg, U.S. ambassador to the United Nations.

which had fallen unduly on the poor and the black. What Selective Service instituted was a looser structure, which authorized local draft boards to take into account class standing, and the results of federally administered exams, when making its choices. Students tended to see the shift not as a needed reform, however, but as a vicious attack. With the monthly draft calls steadily rising, the war was transformed for many into personal peril.

The change in the rules shifted much of the focus of campus protest from the war in general to the draft in particular, and SDS acquired a new following. Talk turned to draft resistance, closing induction centers, burning draft cards. At Chicago, the SDS chapter organized a Berkeley-style sit-in to protest the university's transmission of scholastic information to draft boards. SDS chapters at Antioch, Buffalo, Cornell and Oberlin followed with their own antidraft demonstrations.

There were other forms of campus protest, too. At Brown, Kentucky, Maryland and Queens, SDS led protests against recruiters from the CIA and the arms industry. Berkeley was the scene of another major campus strike, triggered by a Navy recruitment program. SDS provoked a particularly nasty confrontation at Harvard, when Secretary of Defense McNamara came to talk. And on some campuses, like Davidson and Penn State, SDS organized demonstrations that had nothing to do with the war at all, but with tuition increases, proprietary rules and bad food.

So, despite official indifference to the war at the national level, SDS became increasingly known in the public mind as the spearhead of campus disruption. By the fall of 1966, SDS listed nearly two hundred chapters, and almost every one of them had some sort of demonstration on its agenda. When supporters of the war, in Congress for example, wanted something to denounce, SDS provided an easy target. Even the attorney general singled out SDS in a statement on groups under investigation. Campus protest, thanks largely to SDS, had for the first time in American history become a factor in the nation's politics, and campus turmoil a feature of college life.

Meanwhile, Allard Lowenstein was working to arouse the non-radical students, or to convince students that they need not be radical to be against the war. In August of 1966, he spoke at the annual NSA convention, and came away persuaded that many students were relieved to be assured they could be antiwar without being anti-American.

During the following months Lowenstein rounded up several hundred signatories, among student body presidents and student newspaper editors, to a letter to the president. The letter warned solemnly that, "Unless this conflict can be eased, the United States will find some of her most loyal and courageous young people choosing to go to jail rather than to bear their country's arms." It was published as a news article with the first hundred signatures on December 30, 1966, on page one of *The New York Times*.

Then Lowenstein went to England and came back with another letter to the president, this one signed by fifty American Rhodes Scholars. In January 1967, he recruited some help from students at the Union Theological Seminary in New York, and began to widen the net. In due course further letters to Johnson, from Peace Corps returnees as well as more student leaders, were published as advertisements in *The Times*. Few knew whose mysterious hand was behind all these missives, and many wondered, but they created an undercurrent of excitement on campuses and within the antiwar movement and left no doubt that student radicals were not alone in standing on the side of peace.

"I was always sure that the great bulk of the antiwar movement," Lowenstein said to me, "was conventional, moderate, liberal, whatever you call it, reformist, mainstream. The SDS view was that, if they could command the support of people against the war, they had an opportunity to radicalize the whole of society. I was for social change, too, but first of all I wanted to see the war end.

"There was a very profound philosophical difference between those two positions. If you wanted to end the war you did it one way. If you wanted to radicalize America you did it another. You can make a case for either one, but you have to see that they were not always compatible."

Lowenstein told me that at the start he did not regard himself as anti-Johnson. He said his campaign was designed to enlighten the president, by bringing to his attention all the decent people who objected to his policies. At most, he said, it was heavy lobbying.

In January of 1967, however, he had a meeting in the White House with Walt Rostow, who was regarded as Johnson's chief theoretician of the war, and a few weeks later he joined some of his student followers for a talk with Secretary of State Dean Rusk in the State Department. Lowenstein said of the first meeting, "I found Rostow's position so arrogant, and so completely askew from my point of view, that there wasn't much we had to say to each other." The students, he said, felt equally disturbed about their encounter with Rusk. By early spring, he recalled, he admitted that he had to think in terms of a complete break with the Johnson Administration.

Lowenstein, at that point, turned for help to Curtis Gans, whom he had met a decade before at the University of North Carolina, and who shared his taste for political struggle. Over the years, the two had often worked together, and become close friends. Dark and intense, Gans had the organizational skills and persistence to complement Lowenstein's powerful but untidy charisma.

Lowenstein had helped Gans become editor of the North Carolina *Daily Tar Heel;* Gans, after becoming a vice-president of NSA, helped Lowenstein with some of his antiapartheid work in South Africa. Lowenstein helped Gans's efforts in behalf of the sit-ins in the South; Gans helped Lowenstein in his abortive efforts to win a seat in Congress from New York. Gans was actually among the founders of SDS but, being a practical man, left before Port Huron, in the conviction that SDS was destined to remain without influence in American politics.

When Lowenstein made his proposal, Gans was working for Americans for Democratic Action, as newspaper editor, foreign policy lobbyist and field organizer. He had earlier helped Lowenstein get elected to the ADA national board, and Lowenstein subsequently became ADA chairman. In November 1965, Gans was coordinator of the SANE peace march, of which ADA had been a sponsor. A year later he helped Lowenstein draft some of the antiwar letters for the signature of student leaders. Now thirty years old, he agreed in the spring of 1967 to join Lowenstein in what many would have considered one more frivolous effort to end the war.

The initial battleground was ADA itself, and specifically the mind of Joe Rauh, its most respected figure and still the principal channel to the Democratic party's liberal wing. Rauh was already in open opposition to the war, and most ADA members shared his sentiments. But, like liberals generally, ADA remained faithful to Johnson's domestic programs, and agonized over the prospect of a break with the White House. At the urging of Lowenstein and Gans, Rauh crossed the barrier in April 1967 by persuading ADA to go on record against Johnson's war policy. ADA's trade union wing bitterly opposed him, and their differences heralded a widening gap between liberals and the labor movement, but Rauh's antiwar resolution signaled a liberal commitment from which there was no retreat.

Rauh also agreed to sound out potential Democratic challengers to Johnson, the most likely of whom was the late president's brother Robert, now the senator from New York. In the previous year or so, Robert Kennedy had spoken out increasingly against the war. But in their meeting he affirmed to Rauh what he had said in public, that he would not challenge Johnson for the nomination. Rauh reported he also called on Senators Frank Church of Idaho, George McGovern of South Dakota and Eugene McCarthy of Minnesota. All refused, Rauh said, and McCarthy, furthermore, seemed so lackadaisical that Rauh felt it would be particularly hopeless to encourage him.

In fact, Rauh was fearful that, if he found a candidate, Johnson would claim that a poor performance conveyed public endorsement of the war. He worried also that an internal struggle would so divide the Democrats that a right-wing Republican, committed to expanding the war, would wind up in the White House. In the end, Rauh tentatively settled on the strategy he had successfully pursued against Truman in 1948. Until a viable candidate for the presidency came along, he would push for approval of a strong peace plank at the Democratic National Convention.

Meanwhile, in February of 1967 *Ramparts*, an aggressive New Left magazine published in San Francisco, broke the story that the National Student Association had been receiving subsidies from the CIA since the early 1950s. The story acknowledged that, during the 1960s, "NSA responded to the militant mood on the campuses. It supported students against the draft, opposed the war in Vietnam, and participated in civil rights struggles." But the article provided clear evidence that the CIA exercised virtually total control over NSA's international programs, a control which the student generation of the 1960s, long since alienated from the Cold War, found outrageous.

Sam Brown, a Harvard divinity student who was chairman of the NSA supervisory board, was not among those who had known the secret. An activist who opposed the war, he had rejected SDS as "too bitter and too flamboyant" and had helped Lowenstein round up signatures of student body presidents for one of the antiwar ads. As soon as the *Ramparts* story broke, Brown called the affair "morally disgusting," and used his NSA office to sever CIA's last remaining ties to the organization.

Brown then took leave from Harvard and embarked on a nationwide tour of campuses to denounce the CIA and the Vietnam War. If the *Ramparts* revelations weakened the student organization, they also evoked in many of the thousands of young people who identified with NSA a determination to reaffirm their independence of the government. Lowenstein, still an important figure within NSA, had emerged untainted from the scandal. Brown's tour served to establish contacts with students on dozens of campuses. They would later prove indispensable to Lowenstein's Dump Johnson campaign.

The president's commitment to the war was still escalating, and his credibility still declining, when the Spring Mobilization brought radicals and liberals together in New York and San Francisco on April 15, 1967, for the biggest demonstrations to date against the war. The legendary A. J. Muste had died in February but new faces appeared. Dr. Benjamin Spock, the celebrated pediatrician, Reverend William Sloane Coffin, chaplain of Yale, and, most important, Martin Luther King, Jr., had stepped forward from liberal ranks to assume leading roles in the antiwar movement.

Reverend James Bevel of King's SCLC, who directed the Mobilization, announced that any antiwar group would be welcome to participate in the spring protests. With considerable success, he worked to widen the net to bring in not only political groups but church associations, women's clubs and professional organizations, which together moved the equilibrium point of the coalition significantly toward the center. When asked about the politics of the Mobilization, Bevel replied, "We're going to get to the left of Karl Marx and left of Lenin. We're going to get way out there, up on that cross with Jesus."

For the radicals, the high point of the Spring Mobilization came

405

in the dawn light at the Sheep Meadow in New York's Central Park, where a crowd of several hundred, including newsmen and investigators, had assembled to watch 150 young men burn their draft cards. The Cornell SDS chapter had initiated the event, and had promised that it would be held only if five hundred card holders were willing to join the ceremony. A fraction of that number appeared, but the ceremony took place anyway. Later in the day, the Cornell contingent marched under a flag which read, "We Won't Go," suggesting that the war might end by the simple measure of young men refusing to fight.

For liberals the high point was Martin Luther King's address at United Nations Plaza. King had in the past months spoken out increasingly against the war, which he saw not only as a diversion from the issues of poverty and civil rights but, in the ever-growing violence of the battlefield, a moral stain upon the nation. Roy Wilkins of the NAACP now vigorously opposed King, on the grounds that the cause of civil rights had to remain divorced from foreign policy. But King, after painful self-examination, had concluded that his personal commitment to nonviolence included the Vietnam War, even if he had to burn his bridges to Johnson and to some within the civil rights coalition.

The Spring Mobilization was a triumph for the antiwar movement. In New York, it drew a crowd estimated by police at 150,000, by its leaders at 300,000 to 500,000. In San Francisco, where the "numbers game" was also played, police estimated the crowd at half the 65,000 seats in a stadium that supporters said was filled with demonstrators. Whatever the real figures, the demonstrations this time seemed too great for even Johnson to ignore. But Secretary of State Dean Rusk said the president spoke for the two hundred million Americans who did not march, and Johnson publicly scoffed at the importance of the throngs.

In April 1967, shortly after the Spring Mobilization, Lowenstein called a meeting at his family's restaurant in Manhattan. Gans was there, and Gans's wife Genie, who was doing many of the administrative chores for the Dump Johnson campaign while holding a job with the government. Reverend Andrew Young, executive director of the SCLC, was also there, representing Martin Luther

King. So were James Wechsler, the liberal columnist for the *New York Post*, and Norman Thomas, the veteran Socialist and pacifist.

The group explored the various strategies available in 1968, among which was formation of a third party, with King its presidential candidate. Although Young made clear that King was unlikely to run, Thomas, inveterate candidate on third-party tickets, favored such a course. Gans, however, argued that the antiwar movement was too strong to settle for a symbol, which a third party would be. He also said the nomination of a black, whatever King's virtues, would be a mistake, because it would only obscure the antiwar issue.

Gans argued that the best course was to try to deny Johnson the nomination through the Democratic primaries and the state party caucuses. He outlined some exploratory work he and Lowenstein had already done, relying on ADA and NSA contacts. After considerable debate, the skepticism of the group began to soften. Its conclusion was not that the strategy would succeed, but that it was worth the attempt.

After that meeting, Lowenstein set out on his odyssey, with Gans working closely beside him. Conventionally, Gans went first to the various states, and held as many meetings as he could with two sets of people, political leaders and peace activists. When he had stimulated enough interest, Lowenstein would arrive to address them, usually in separate groups, attempting to galvanize the first group into a political campaign, the second into a citizens lobby called Dissenting Democrats.

The two concentrated particularly on Minnesota, New Hampshire and Wisconsin, where the delegates were chosen early, and on New York and California, where they were elected in great numbers. Gans calculated, however, that he visited thirty-two states in all in the first three months of the campaign, and Lowenstein probably as many.

David Hoeh, a Dartmouth professor who would head the McCarthy campaign in New Hampshire, recalled that Gans, with his dark eyes and intense manner, generated mystery in his early visits, and Lowenstein seemed at least as alien. Hoeh remembered that Lowenstein once arrived for a speech, disheveled and without a tie, surprised that his appearance might, in proper New Hampshire, create some unease. The two rushed to a gift shop, Hoeh said, where Lowenstein chose a tie "that almost matched his shirt and suit." Both Gans and Lowenstein, however, quickly won the confidence of New Hampshire's antiwar Democrats, the first with his quiet self-assurance, the second with his openness and obvious sincerity.

Hoeh gave me his files, a position paper that Lowenstein had helped to write, and that Gans also used, to buttress their arguments in the New Hampshire campaign. One of its paragraphs read:

> ... if a president is wrong but popular, political realities may make opposing him difficult, however right; if a president is right but unpopular, supporting him may be a duty, however difficult. But when a president is both wrong and unpopular, to refuse to oppose him is a moral abdication and a political stupidity.

Hoeh said New Hampshire's antiwar Democrats found such arguments persuasive. Lowenstein remembered he had no trouble convincing Democrats that Johnson was wrong, but that he had difficulty persuading them that they were part of a mass of opposition that was struggling to reach the surface.

Late one night in August 1967, Lowenstein phoned Gans from California to announce that he had received some key commitments to an anti-Johnson campaign. One, he said, came from Gerald N. Hill, a San Francisco lawyer and chairman of the California Democratic Council, which represented thirty thousand liberals within the state party. The other was from Donald O. Peterson, a dairy products salesman from Eau Claire, Wisconsin, who was on the board of ADA and Democratic chairman of the Tenth Congressional District. Neither was, in national terms, a prominent Democrat, but they were a start.

On the basis of this start, Lowenstein and Gans agreed to set up an organization they called the Conference of Concerned Democrats. Lowenstein, along with Hill and Peterson, became cochairmen. Gans took the title of national director. Its office was the living room of Gans's house on Capitol Hill in Washington.

Lowenstein told the National Student Association about the Conference of Concerned Democrats, and the Dump Johnson campaign, on August 16, at its national convention. Gans recalled that he had to drag Lowenstein to the meeting, because his wife was in labor.* It was a particularly tumultuous convention, the first since the CIA revelations which had sent NSA students reeling to the left. SDS took advantage of the moment to hold a "counter-conference" nearby. Lowenstein remembered that students were incredulous at his argument that they could stop the war by beating Johnson at the polls.

Sam Brown was defeated for NSA president at that convention, and promptly went to work with Lowenstein and Gans. Brown had spent most of the summer ringing doorbells on an antiwar project called Vietnam Summer. At the NSA convention he put together a group called Alternative Candidate Task Force '68—to be known as ACT-68—and he became its chairman. The relationship with Lowenstein assured that its membership would be liberal, not radical. ACT-68 became the student arm of the Dump Johnson campaign, and Brown became the Conference of Concerned Democrats' student coordinator.

Throughout the fall of 1967, the Conference of Concerned Democrats' only assets were the energy of Lowenstein and Gans, and the office in the Gans town house on Capitol Hill, where Genie Gans kept a reference file of names collected. Lowenstein traveled more than ever, Gans remained more often at home, working the phones and the files to build precinct, district and state support. A trickle of small contributions was enough to pay for plane tickets and phone bills, and almost nothing more. The enterprise appeared to be making little headway, and the press virtually ignored it.

Crucial to the organization's credibility was a presidential candidate. At every meeting Lowenstein was asked about it, and at each one he answered that he would have one by the end of the year. But until he did, Johnson would be unthreatened.

In September, Lowenstein resumed the courtship of Robert Kennedy. Since Kennedy's solicitation of Lowenstein's advice for a trip he took to South Africa in 1965, the two had been on friendly terms. Kennedy was opposed to the war, and it was no secret that he

* The baby was named Frank Graham Lowenstein. The Lowensteins' two subsequent children were named Thomas Kennedy and Katherine Eleanor Lowenstein.

detested Johnson. Endowed with the family's magnetism, he had a nationwide following, particularly among the young. He had ambitious aides who urged him to run. But Kennedy felt certain of getting the nomination in 1972, after Johnson's second term, and he was loath to make enemies in an intraparty fight, which he was unsure of winning. Lowenstein finally reconciled himself to Kennedy's caution, and to seeking a candidate elsewhere.

In October, Lowenstein met with Senator McGovern, whom Rauh had failed to persuade several months before. McGovern told Lowenstein that he could not be distracted from his own reelection campaign in South Dakota. Lowenstein also saw James Gavin, a retired general who had gone repeatedly on record against the war. Gavin, too, declined to take Johnson on.

Lowenstein's next prospect was Senator Eugene McCarthy of Minnesota, who had actually ruminated on running since the spring, when the war began to upset him seriously. Tall, with a strong face, McCarthy was not a politician of conventional ambition. A Catholic ex-seminarian with an extremely subtle intellect, he seemed less interested in power than in warning of its excesses. He was outraged by Johnson's manipulations, deceptions and encroachments, and thought of his own running as a moral service. He proposed first the multiple candidacy of favorite sons, each standing against Johnson in the region of his strength. In late October, he finally agreed to make the race himself. Ebullient, Lowenstein concluded that with McCarthy's acquiescence the campaign's major problem had been resolved, though in fact it had just begun.

Lowenstein and Gans quietly began to spread the word and, on November 2, McCarthy confirmed surmises by announcing a tour of the country to explore his prospects. Gans made sure that, at each stop, McCarthy encountered Democrats who would encourage him with their support. The behavior of crowds, however, was beyond Gans's control, and yet wherever McCarthy went large numbers gathered, and they greeted him with cheers. McCarthy was persuaded and, on November 30 in the Senate Caucus Room, he officially announced his candidacy.

Yet, even the announcement was unusual. McCarthy emphasized the heavy costs of the war, which he promised to end. Then he made his declaration, which consisted of the diffident assertion

410

that, "I intend to enter the Democratic primaries in Wisconsin, Oregon, California and Nebraska. The decision with reference to Massachusetts and New Hampshire will be made within two weeks." At no point did he actually say he was running for president. In fact, as the months passed, it became increasingly unclear whether he was.

When they were certain that McCarthy would run, Lowenstein and Gans arranged for a grand welcome in Chicago by the Conference of Concerned Democrats. On December 2, some 350 delegates from forty states appeared at the meeting, which was organized to look conspicuously like a party convention. On the night of McCarthy's speech, four thousand well-wishers, in addition to the delegates, were in the audience. What had been foreseen as a climactic moment, however, turned into a fiasco.

McCarthy, who was to follow Lowenstein on the program, arrived late. Told to use up some time, Lowenstein proceeded to deliver an old-fashioned, tree-stump oration, to which the crowd responded deliriously. Lowenstein said that when he saw the signal that McCarthy was backstage, he stopped as quickly as he could. Others said he apparently forgot which of the two was the candidate, and went on for twenty agonizing minutes, mentioning McCarthy's name only once. Genie Gans, who was with McCarthy, remembered that it felt like eternity. While Lowenstein wound up his speech, McCarthy stood in the kitchen, kicking furiously at bits of glass lying on the floor.

When the candidate finally reached the platform, he was sulky, and did nothing to acknowledge the rounds of cheers. He delivered a lifeless, pointless lecture, and said virtually nothing about the Conference of Concerned Democrats, out of which his candidacy had been created. McCarthy conveyed no feeling that he was part of a collective effort, which was an omen of the months ahead. When the speech was finished, he passed up the chance to mingle with the delegations that were laying plans to get him the nomination, as well as with the thousands who had turned out to cheer him.

While Lowenstein and Gans worked at pushing the antiwar movement back into political channels, the orderly processes of

411

society in America seemed to be unraveling irresistibly. The ghetto riots in the summer of 1967 were the worst ever, ranging over twenty-three cities, large and small. In Newark, 26 people were killed and 1200 were injured. In Detroit, 43 lay dead and 7200 were arrested. The National Guard had to put an end to violence in both cities. Confronted by anger and the brutality, by the abandonment of rules that maintained society in a state of reasonable cohesion, by a growing contempt for simple decency and civility, many Americans wondered whether the country was coming apart.

While the embers still burned, the National Conference on Black Power convened in Newark. More than a thousand black delegates, many dressed modishly in dashikis to convey their identification with the Third World, voted to resist the draft as a fraud upon black youth, reject birth control programs as black genocide and establish black universities to train black revolutionaries. They also voted to start "a national dialogue on the desirability of partitioning the United States into two separate nations, one white and one black."

Over the Labor Day weekend of 1967, two thousand radicals met in Chicago for the National Conference of New Politics, ostensibly to resolve on a strategy for the forthcoming presidential election. A four-hundred-member black caucus immediately announced a boycott unless a majority accepted, without revision, a thirteen-point program which required an equal division of powers between whites and blacks at all sessions. The caucus's program also required endorsement of reparations to all blacks, and a blanket condemnation of Israel. The conference acquiesced to the thirteen-point program by a three to one majority.

Acquiescence, however, did not connote approval. Many of the delegates recognized that the black caucus's program constituted blackmail. Even then, blacks from the caucus could not be restrained from endless antiwhite diatribes, as if Black Power somehow conveyed the privilege, if not the obligation, to be scurrilous. "Honky" had become for radical blacks what "nigger" once was for racist whites. Israel, as a "colonial" power, became the target of outrageous accusations. Jews among the militants, always a disproportionate number, were especially troubled by this turn.

Mindlessly laden with slogans, the conference marked the distance that radicalism had traveled since the Port Huron meeting only five years before. At that time, radicals engaged in genuine intellectual discourse, with respect for one another. The Chicago meeting, in contrast, was tumultuous, abusive, philistine. In the end, a majority could agree on nothing, except to abstain completely from participation in the 1968 presidential campaign.

On October 16, 1967, four thousand people gathered at the Arlington Street Church in Boston to watch fifty young men burn their draft cards. Two hundred fifty others handed their cards to Reverend William Sloane Coffin, who carried them to Washington, where they were dropped into a briefcase on the steps of the Justice Department with draft cards collected from several hundred other young men in ceremonies around the country. Before television cameras, Coffin took the overflowing briefcase inside, where an attorney general's representative refused to accept it. The government's action was interpreted by many as timidity in the face of growing draft resistance and, in fact, prosecutions for draft resistance had been sporadic for some time. But in a sharp reversal of policy, Coffin and four others were indicted three months later on charges of conspiring to violate the Selective Service Act.*

On the day the draft cards were burned in Boston, antiwar groups in the San Francisco Bay Area, led by Berkeley radicals, started their Stop the Draft Week. Local SDS activists had been arguing for months that the antiwar movement had to establish a "second front" at home to put pressure on the government. Protest in the Bay Area that week snowballed from a peaceful sit-in at the Federal Building in San Francisco on Monday to a series of angry brawls between police and marauding students on the street of Oakland on Friday. Once again Berkeley was in the vanguard, and students exulted in the new "mobile tactics." Some thought they had at last found a way to strike back at a society that would not respond to their demands.

On the day after the Oakland street battles, the antiwar movement staged the March on the Pentagon, celebrated by Norman Mailer in the best-selling *The Armies of the Night*. The National Mobilization, its sponsor, was unable to compromise differences within the coalition over whether to make the demonstration peaceful or militant. The Mobe finally resolved the dilemma in the "do-your-own-thing" style of the 1960s. In the sunshine of the

* Besides Coffin, they were Dr. Spock, Michael Ferber, Mitchell Goodman and Marcus Raskin. All were ultimately acquitted on appeal.

413

morning, fifty thousand people assembled at the Lincoln Memorial for what had become a standard peace rally. Some went home from there, others crossed the Arlington Memorial Bridge into Virginia. From there the militants took over, and a thousand, most of them identified with SDS, raced for the Pentagon for what had been advertised as an effort to shut down the American military machine.

About twenty-five demonstrators actually slipped through the line of MPs that guarded the building, and were arrested inside. The remainder stationed themselves at various points on the Pentagon grounds. A few hundred spent the night there, and on Sunday the number swelled to two thousand. Some taunted the soldiers who guarded the entrances, others offered them food and flowers, seeking to cajole them to "Join Us." A few demonstrators were beaten by federal marshals. At midnight on Sunday, those who hung on were ordered to leave, and most did. But several hundred protesters were arrested, Norman Mailer being the most eminent among them.

The concern over America in disarray extended beyond antiwar politics into the counterculture, which by 1967 showed symptoms of serious illness. The "hippie" communities of many large cities, which had once seemed innocent and gentle and in many ways quite attractive, had in fact long lived at the edge of violence. Traffic in drugs and sex attracted the psychopathic, the venal and the criminal in society. The number of deaths from overdoses had risen alarmingly among hippies and their friends, and a few well-publicized sex murders spread more dismay. The street scene of the "flower children" appeared less charming now, and an older generation that was mystified by the curious political and social behavior of its young wondered how badly damaged were the tenuous bonds that kept America intact.

Such was the atmosphere in the country when McCarthy's campaign for the presidency began in December 1967. Some of his supporters hoped the turmoil would persuade law-abiding voters to turn to him for the reestablishment of tranquillity. Lowenstein said he did not think it would. He said he feared too many Americans failed to distinguish among opponents of the war, and could not tell an antiwar liberal carrying the Stars and Stripes from a

414

student radical waving a Viet Cong flag. Too many Americans in 1967, Lowenstein said, thought the choice facing the country was between chaos and repression. McCarthy had to prove, amid this turbulence, that he could end the war by pursuing a democratic course between the two extremes, but the beginning of his campaign was not promising.

McCarthy himself was uninterested in the campaign organization, and it was slow in taking shape. Obviously, his personality was so different from Lowenstein's that the two could not work harmoniously together. Cut off, Lowenstein drifted toward the periphery of operations. McCarthy named as his campaign manager Blair Clark, a decent low-keyed man of culture like himself, with little political experience. Clark moved Gans, whom McCarthy also shunned, into a top executive position, and Gans brought with him the organizational structure of the Conference of Concerned Democrats. Clark also hired Sam Brown as his youth director. Thus the Lowenstein machine, but without Lowenstein, was kept intact, and moved directly into the McCarthy campaign.

McCarthy, apprehensive about New Hampshire's reputation for hawkishness, hesitated over entering the primary there. But New Hampshire had an excellent antiwar organization, cultivated for months by Lowenstein and Gans, and it was anxious to take Johnson on. David Hoeh, the Dartmouth professor who had worked with the Lowenstein-Gans team from the start, collared McCarthy when he came in for a look and argued that no serious candidate could afford to duck the first of the presidential primaries. Hoeh finally persuaded McCarthy that, in size and resources, New Hampshire was an excellent place for a long shot to test his chances. On January 3 McCarthy announced his candidacy, and a few days later Hoeh set up a storefront headquarters for student volunteers in Concord, the state capital.

During the next few weeks, McCarthy campaigned desultorily throughout the state, maintaining his dry speaking style, seeing few local politicians, keeping largely to himself after dark. Through these early weeks, student groups from the New England colleges made occasional forays into New Hampshire in his behalf, but McCarthy seemed unable to broaden his appeal. The polls conceded to him not more than a few percent of the vote, and Johnson continued to appear invulnerable.

415

But events, as McCarthy himself had predicted, marched in favor of insurgency. At the end of January, the Communists in South Vietnam embarked on their Tet offensive. With several hundred thousand men in the field, they attacked all of South Vietnam's major cities and quickly took much of Saigon, where they penetrated the walls of the American embassy itself. Within a few days, the American army of a half-million men had, with help from the South Vietnamese, repulsed the offensive. Yet the losses were heavy and, for most Americans, the lesson of Tet was not the Communists' defeat but their ability, in the face of Johnson's ongoing claims of military success, to undertake an attack of such magnitude.

It was an index of the president's credibility that when he boasted on February 2 of Tet's having been an American victory, no one took him seriously. Furthermore, another victory hardly seemed to matter. Tet showed that, whatever the president said, the war was not coming to an end, and that current policy was likely only to keep it going indefinitely.

Even before the New Hampshire balloting, in fact, the president was faltering. In Massachusetts, Johnson seemed unable to decide whether to put his own or some stand-in's name on the ballot. Inexplicably, he chose neither, and the filing deadline passed, giving McCarthy seventy-two convention delegates by default. In McCarthy's home state of Minnesota, where Lowenstein and Gans had organized early, the challengers had to take on the power of Vice President Humphrey, the state's favorite politician, in the party caucuses. McCarthy supporters appeared in unanticipated numbers, however, and by the end of the caucuses they had about thirty delegates.

In New Hampshire, after Tet, McCarthy's dry, reasonable style —setting him off starkly from Johnson—began to yield returns, and he rose steadily in the polls. Gans traveled up from Washington to take charge of the campaign, and student volunteers appeared in droves. Virtually none were radicals. Almost all came "Clean for Gene," well washed and neatly dressed. The Lowenstein-Gans-Brown connection, which had started with NSA in the summer, now paid off in the New England snows. With an ardent young army at his disposal, Gans arranged to have every house in New Hampshire canvassed three times in person and twice or more by

phone. And at least six pieces of literature were sent to every registered voter in the state.

When the New Hampshire returns came in on March 12, Mc-
Carthy had 42.2 percent of the votes in the Democratic column,
and enough crossovers from the Republicans to give him a shade
under 50 percent of the total. McCarthy, furthermore, captured
twenty of the twenty-four convention delegates. To call the results
an anti-Vietnam mandate would have been an overstatement.
Clearly, many who favored or were indifferent to the war were
aroused to vote against Lyndon Johnson. That McCarthy had not
won a majority of the votes went almost unnoticed. New Hampshire had been perceived as a contest between the incumbent with
all the power of the party behind him, and an unknown whose
brigades of youthful volunteers sang his praises. To the country,
Eugene McCarthy had won.

The day after McCarthy's victory Robert Kennedy, who as late as
January 30 had promised not to challenge Johnson "under any fore-
seeable circumstances," declared that he was reassessing his decision. Three days later he announced that he would run.

McCarthy and his supporters were understandably outraged.
Kennedy had not even left them a moment to savor the New Hampshire victory before stepping in to steal the nation's attention.
When asked why he had waited until after New Hampshire to enter
the race, Kennedy replied that McCarthy had proven Johnson vulnerable. But he added that he alone could win.

The entry of Kennedy, to whose candidacy McCarthy had been
willing to defer a few months earlier, added a new dimension to
the anti-Johnson campaign. If McCarthy was aloof, Kennedy was
personal, committed, passionate, magnetic. If McCarthy ran with
pious detachment, Kennedy ran with zesty combativeness. If
McCarthy had won the hearts of legions of the young who endorsed
the system, Kennedy had shown he could reach out to radicals, too,
and somehow win their confidence.

After New Hampshire, however, McCarthy felt he had earned
the right to represent the antiwar movement all the way to the
convention, and many who had once preferred Kennedy agreed
with him. Independently, the two men now set out to defeat Lyn-

417

don Johnson, and each other. Never again in the 1968 campaign would the antiwar forces within the Democratic party be united, not even after Robert Kennedy's death.

For Al Lowenstein, Kennedy's decision did not make a difficult period any easier. He admired Kennedy and felt a personal attachment to him. He tended to agree that Kennedy was a more likely winner and, when called for advice during Kennedy's deliberations, he did not discourage Kennedy from running. Yet, he said, he was angry when Kennedy announced. Uncomfortable as he was with McCarthy, he remained grateful to him for alone being willing to challenge Johnson. Though he was hurt at being ostracized from the campaign, he would stump for McCarthy in Wisconsin, as he had in New Hampshire. But he never denounced Kennedy, and wherever he spoke he reminded his audiences that their foe was Lyndon Johnson and the Vietnam War.

Kennedy was sympathetic to Lowenstein's dilemma. A week after his announcement, Kennedy asked Lowenstein to abandon McCarthy. When Lowenstein declined, Kennedy scribbled out a note and handed it to him. It said, "For Al, who knew the lesson of Emerson and taught it to the rest of us: 'They did not yet see, and thousands of young men as hopeful, now crowding to the barriers of their careers, did not yet see if a single man plant himself on his convictions and then abide, the huge world will come round to him.' From his friend, Bob Kennedy."

After the Tet offensive, Johnson faced a more critical military situation than ever before. General William Westmoreland, the commander in Vietnam, had asked for reinforcements of 206,000 men, which would have brought the American troop level to some 750,000. In the year just ending, the American presence in Vietnam had cost 9000 dead, 62,000 wounded and $32 billion, without the slightest success to show for it. Though Johnson had claimed Tet as a victory, the Pentagon acknowledged the need for more and more men to "stabilize the battlefield," and there was no prospect of an end. Support of the war was vanishing, and the atmosphere in the country verged on desperation.

On March 1, 1968, Johnson appointed Clark Clifford, a well-established hawk, as Secretary of Defense. Clifford immediately

418

announced a complete reevaluation of the Vietnam effort and, from the ensuing flurry of activity in the White House, it was clear that serious deliberations were under way. Still, Johnson alone was responsible for final decisions, and his reputation led to the assumption that all the meetings were a sham, a cover for a mind already made up. Few Americans doubted that the latest request for escalation, like the previous ones, would be approved.

Meanwhile, Johnson and McCarthy forces confronted each other in Wisconsin, where the second presidential primary was scheduled for April 2. There the polls showed Johnson's earlier strength eroding rapidly, and the same was true in the other primary states. To compound the problem, old-line party leaders faithful to the president were having trouble containing rebellions, most notably in such crucial states as New York and California. A few days before the voting, Postmaster General Lawrence O'Brien went out to Wisconsin as Johnson's special observer. On March 29, O'Brien notified the president that his campaign effort there was virtually moribund, and that he would be badly defeated.

Two days later, on March 31, 1968, Lyndon Johnson astonished a nationwide television audience by announcing that the Pentagon's plan for a further escalation of the war had been rejected. In the interests of peace, he said, the bombing of North Vietnam would be halted and the United States would unilaterally reduce the level of ground hostilities. Furthermore, he said, an effort would be made at once to enter into negotiations for a peace settlement.

Then Johnson went on to some paragraphs that were not in his previously distributed text. He said that, in view of the strains created by the war, he felt he should not involve the presidency in the partisan divisions of an election year. With war and peace in the balance, he said, he had also concluded that he should devote his full efforts to the duties of his office and divert no time to politics. "Accordingly," he said, "I shall not seek, and I will not accept, the nomination of my party for another term as your President . . ." And so, before a stunned nation, Lyndon Johnson bowed out.

Al Lowenstein's long and improbable Dump Johnson campaign had won. The trickle of anti-Johnson sentiment present in the spring of 1967 had turned into an avalanche in the spring of 1968. Johnson would have been beaten in Wisconsin, and his campaign for renomination would never have recovered but, had Lowenstein not believed Johnson's defeat possible, there would never have been an anti-Johnson candidate, an anti-Johnson campaign, an anti-Johnson victory. In doing what radicals and conservatives alike had said could not be done, he had vindicated the electoral system and the democratic process.

When it was over, Lowenstein slipped away. He had wanted the Democratic senatorial nomination from New York, but the Kennedy and McCarthy factions had not been able to agree on his candidacy. He had then been offered the support of antiwar Democrats in Long Island to run against a regular Democrat in a congressional primary. But he had put off a decision and gone campaigning to Wisconsin. He was sitting in an airport, where he always spent an inordinate amount of his life, when he learned of Johnson's withdrawal. He knew at once that the remainder of the contest would be between Kennedy and McCarthy, and he did not want to be involved. For the rest of the campaign he remained loyal to McCarthy, but his heart was with Kennedy. He gave his last speech for McCarthy in Wisconsin, then turned to his own congressional campaign.

Yet the success of the Dump Johnson movement proved, in a larger sense, to be an illusion. Lowenstein and his followers had perceived Johnson as the personification of the Vietnam War. Their mistake lay in failing to recognize that if they deposed him without capturing his party they left alive the policies he represented. They had struck down a president, not a party leader. So, in the end, Johnson proved to be not the embodiment but only one in a line of Democratic stewards of the Vietnam War.

As Johnson prepared to pass on the powers of office to a successor, what the radicals had said about the meaninglessness of the electoral process seemed to be vindicated. Millions of Americans who had risen up with McCarthy and Kennedy found that the system, as they thought they understood it, had played a terrible trick on them. They had defeated a man, but had only discredited his ideas, and another man seeking to succeed him would come along to resume them. For a euphoric moment after Johnson's downfall, it seemed likely that the fire in America's streets would subside and then go out. Instead it flared up, and the flames would soar higher than ever before.

XII
JERRY RUBIN:
Assaulting Chicago

1968

"We wanted exactly what happened. We wanted the tear gas to get so heavy that the reality was tear gas. We wanted to create a situation in which the Chicago police and the Daley administration and the federal government and the United States would self-destruct. We wanted to show that America wasn't a democracy, that the convention wasn't politics. The message of the week was of an America ruled by force. That was a big victory."

NOT SINCE THE CIVIL WAR ERA had American life seemed so whimsical, arbitrary, confusing, and so murderously violent, as it did in 1968. Al Lowenstein's struggle for rational political process was uphill, and the ascent was becoming steeper. Jerry Rubin's championing of unreason, and the dissolution of political process, was downhill, and the slide was getting faster, and more out of control. 1968 was the year in which a society that had traditional values, deep roots and serious concerns seemed genuinely in danger of being washed away.

Two of the nation's most gifted leaders, Martin Luther King, Jr., and Robert Kennedy, were assassinated. The wafting of tear gas became a normal occurrence not just in ghettos but on campuses and in the major business districts of the cities. Demagogy seemed to crush calculation in the black community, and brute force seemed to be driving intellect from the university. The Kerner Commission, after examining the urban riots, concluded glumly that "Our nation is moving toward two societies, one black, one white—separate and unequal."

Then, on the streets of Chicago that August, while the Democrats were meeting to choose their presidential candidate, the madness of the decade seemed to crystallize before a disbelieving, and mortified, television audience. Long-haired youths, and many young men and women with tidy hair and neat clothing, stood their ground before the flailing billy clubs of frenzied policemen. The script played by the Democrats deliberating in the amphitheater seemed inconsequential compared to the spontaneous violence, anger and bloodshed that dominated the city streets. "The whole world is watching, the whole world is watching," the crowds chanted as the cameras turned, and hundreds of millions of spectators wondered what had happened to America.

Al Lowenstein, the improbable hero of the Dump Johnson campaign, had become a bit player in the Chicago drama, as the effort to end the war through electoral politics collapsed ignominiously. On center stage now was Jerry Rubin, chieftain of the Yippies, bare to the waist and in grease paint, declaiming against "Amerika" and tripping on drugs. He was part hippie, part revolutionary, part clown.

Rubin's upbringing was conventional enough—like Tom Hayden's, and like that of so many of the young white rebels of the 1960s. His father drove a bread truck, his mother kept house. Despite a limited income, the family's style of life was comfortably middle class, thanks to the grandparents with whom they lived. In his autobiography,* Rubin entitled a chapter "The Making of a Dissident," in which he discussed at some length his rebellion against parents and grandparents. Nothing he wrote, however, explained how his private revolt, hardly distinguishable from that of most adolescents, grew into a general attack upon the society.

Born in 1938, Rubin was Jewish but not religious, smart but not very good in school, small but not notably belligerent about it. He played softball and joined the Cub Scouts. He campaigned for Stevenson in 1952. He was committed to the short hair and dapper dress of the 1950s, and the only black person he knew was the maid. He attended Oberlin for a year and finished at the University of Cincinnati, while working full-time as a sports reporter for the local paper.

In the late 1950s, his father became a Teamsters' organizer, without conveying to his son any special zealotry for trade unionism, or the oppressed classes. Though his parents were Democrats, politics played a very minor role in the household. His parents' chief contribution to Rubin's later calling, it seemed, was to leave him a

* Growing (Up) at 37.

small inheritance at age twenty-two, which freed him to pursue his newly acquired revolutionary objectives.

Yet beneath the banal exterior, something was obviously in ferment. At college in the late 1950s, Rubin, like Hayden and so many others, read and was thrilled by C. Wright Mills.

"I used to carry his paperback book, *The Marxists,* around with me, and I came to a Marxist understanding of the world," he told me. "I remember, having lunch with the other reporters when I was working on the newspaper, I would say, 'Look, it's so obvious that big business owns everything,' and then they would say, 'Don't you know you're advocating Communism?' I got very upset."

After his Mills period, Rubin said, he moved into a Walter Lippmann phase, and in his senior year he wrote a paper on Lippmann's thought. "If you go back to read his books of the 1930s, before he became a stodgy newspaper columnist," Rubin said, "you'll find the best writing on socialism that has ever been done." For a while Lippmann was his idol, and reading Lippmann made him want to go to graduate school to study.

I first interviewed Rubin in the early 1970s in a park in San Francisco's North Beach section. It was a warm spring day and, as we lay on the grass, it seemed to me that he was waiting for the high-spirited days of the 1960s to be reborn. I met Rubin again some years later, after he moved to an apartment in New York, and he seemed more resigned to charting a new course in life. He still talked buoyantly, however, of his revolutionary career, mixing nostalgia with pride.

Having been primed by Mills and Lippmann, Rubin said he felt ecstatic when, in May of 1960, he learned of the tumultuous anti-HUAC demonstration in San Francisco, then saw *Operation Abolition,* HUAC's film about the demonstrations. It was about that time, he said, that he became fed up with the newspaper business, felt that he was being used and exploited and shuddered at the dead end reached by veteran reporters. "I kept looking at *Operation Abolition* and saying 'fantastic!' and 'great!' " he told me. That was when he decided he wanted to go to Berkeley, to be near the action.

It took awhile, however, because his parents died in quick succession, leaving him as legal guardian of his brother Gil, nine years younger than he. Restless, he thought of going to India to

425

study Gandhi, but had to stay in Cincinnati while his brother finished school. Then, in 1962, he took off with Gil for Israel, but in place of the socialist community he had envisioned, he said, he felt himself in a bourgeois world not very different from Cincinnati. After a year and a half of sporadic study, he left Israel for California, arriving in Berkeley in January 1964, as the fever of student radicalism was rising.

It took much persuasion to get the Sociology Department to accept him as a Ph.D. candidate, Rubin said, and then six weeks later he dropped out. By then, he had met every radical in town, and had inscribed the answers to a million political questions in a notebook. "I went to every meeting. I went to every rally. I was obsessive-compulsive," he told me. He helped create chaos at the celebrated "shop-in" in the supermarket on Telegraph Avenue, joined CORE and became, as he called it, a "full-time picket-line walker."

Rubin described himself as being, at the time, "pretty straight but Marxist inclined, ambitious, looking for something, and very angry, very angry, really angry. I had a chip on my shoulder." He still wore his hair short and had not yet smoked marijuana. But that summer, while others were leaving to work in the Mississippi Project, he joined a Progressive Labor party tour, in defiance of U.S. law, to visit Castro's Cuba.

"Fidel Castro goes right up there with C. Wright Mills and Walter Lippmann," Rubin told me. "As a matter of fact, in the fifty-yard dash, Lippmann falls out very quickly, and C. Wright Mills falls out, too. Castro takes off.

"Remember, Mills had the intellectuals changing the society, the intellectuals leading the workers. He created a whole new thing about the intellectuals, and I thought I was an intellectual, too. Well, I got to Berkeley and found out that the intellectuals were just justifying the system. The real people were in the streets. I saw the real people were the Cubans. The real people were the Vietnamese and the blacks. So I took my C. Wright Mills with me into the street."

When Rubin returned from Cuba in the fall of 1964, the Free Speech Movement was getting under way. He said Mario Savio reminded him of Fidel. Though not a leader during the protests, he became a familiar figure as an FSM follower. He was smoking dope now, and moving away from books. "I was a genuine Berkeley

426

street person," he said. "You could always find me in the coffee shop, on Telegraph Avenue, at the rallies. I always knew the first sign of anything happening, the gossip, the stories." Later, when FSM broke up over the "filthy speech" issue, Rubin was among those who stood up defiantly for the students' right to say 'fuck.'

"FSM was precounterculture, you understand, when we were free to protest racism but not to say fuck," he told me. "Near the end, the idea of the students as community was beginning to come in. 'Filthy speech' was the beginning of irrationality in the student movement, of the cultural revolution. It had a strong streak of nihilism, but it was also pretty funny. It was a sign that part of the movement was breaking away from the straight, the purely political."

After FSM ran its course in early 1965, a radical in Berkeley had nothing to do, and Rubin acknowledged that he contemplated, among other alternatives, going to law school or even returning to journalism. But the Vietnam War rescued him from ennui, and by early spring he was busy organizing the Berkeley teach-in. Its spectacular success earned him his first press notices, in one of which he described the teach-in as "fun, politics and ideas together, an antidote to the vulgarized main culture of the society around it." The fusing of politics with fun was a notion Rubin promoted widely in the ensuing years, and in 1968 brought exultantly to Chicago.

After the teach-in, Rubin joined with other Berkeley militants to found the Vietnam Day Committee. Several times in August 1965, VDC brought hundreds of protesters to the Berkeley railroad tracks to block trains carrying troops to Vietnam. With each protest, police cleared the tracks more vigorously. "The troop train demonstrations are the thing I'm most proud of," Rubin told me. "As far as I'm concerned, they saved the world." Whether or not they did, they set an example of confrontation with the police that the antiwar movement emulated, and expanded over the years.

On October 16, 1965, the VDC staged a march from Berkeley to the Oakland Army Terminal, which halted at the city line before a phalanx of Oakland policemen. Rubin was among the leaders who urged that the fifteen thousand demonstrators surge forward, whatever the risks. Outvoted, he called the retreat to Berkeley a "funeral march," but VDC protests that fall continued. Rubin's next escapade was to spill a container of blood on the car of General Maxwell

427

Taylor, Johnson's military adviser, for which he served thirty days, his first jail term. By the end of 1965, he was an antiwar celebrity, known nationwide for his imagination and daring.

What distinguished Rubin from so many activists at the time, explained in part by his newspaper background, was his grasp of media manipulation. Rubin understood that a bottomless bank account could not buy the services that television, if properly exploited, would furnish free. Though it was often said that he was a media creation, which was true, he himself directed the media in the creative process.

"It was a conscious thing," he said to me of his media manipulation, "and I guess it came from an intuitive understanding. You know, stopping troop trains, a little violence, students and police clashing on the railroad tracks. The media loved it.

"They exaggerated the event on television, and then the papers exaggerated it some more. The people who read it or saw it exaggerated it even more when they talked about it to others. The process was like a riot, with thousands of people transmitting emotions from one to another, and the emotions growing. They created myths, saying, 'Wow, that's exciting!' Everybody wanted to do what we were doing in Berkeley, and from that the movement grew."

In 1966, Rubin became manager of Robert Scheer's antiwar campaign for Congress but quit before the election, protesting that Scheer had abandoned radical principles in order to win. A year later, Rubin himself filed for mayor of Berkeley, on a platform in support of Black Power, the legalization of pot and opposition to the war. Then, like Scheer, acquiring a vision of victory, he put on a coat and tie and launched a serious campaign. Rubin took 22 percent of the vote, and won four student precincts.

Between the two election campaigns, Rubin had to answer a subpoena to appear in Washington before the House Un-American Activities Committee. He rejected the conventional legal advice to plead the Fifth Amendment and remain silent. Instead, he entered the hearing room wearing the uniform of a Revolutionary War soldier, which he had rented at a Berkeley costume shop for $25. It was a stunt, but it was also a political statement, counterculture style, designed to make a mockery of HUAC's stuffed shirts. The committee was too stunned even to retaliate, and Rubin won television coverage and page one attention throughout the country.

428

In 1967, Rubin was twenty-eight, experimenting increasingly with drugs, and living more or less in the style of a hippie. Across San Francisco Bay from Berkeley, Haight-Ashbury in San Francisco was the capital of the hippie world, indifferent to the radical politics of Berkeley. The hippie program was "Tune in, turn on, drop out." Rubin had no quarrel with the "Tune in" or the "turn on" parts, but wanted to transform the "drop out" mandate into a positive revolutionary commitment.

Rubin reasoned that, with both hippies and radicals in rebellion against American values, they should make common cause. At "be-ins" in San Francisco's Golden Gate Park and New York's Polo Grounds, he made speeches calling for the two to form new communities, where they could work together to change America. Though he got little response, he would not give the idea up.

In the fall of 1967 in New York, David Dellinger of the National Mobilization Committee to End the War in Vietnam invited Rubin, the acknowledged master of the theatrics of dissent, to direct a major demonstration that was being planned for the weekend of October 21 in Washington. Norman Mailer, in *The Armies of the Night*, wrote that inviting Rubin "was in effect to call upon the most militant, unpredictable, creative—and therefore dangerous—hippie-oriented leader available on the New Left." Rubin, a bit depressed after his election defeat, was delighted by the offer. On arriving in New York, he vetoed the rather bland demonstration planned for the Capitol, which he foresaw as another well-mannered, nonviolent event the government could simply shrug off. He substituted for it a militant march on the Pentagon.

Once installed in New York, Rubin encountered Abbie Hoffman, thirty-year-old luminary of a hippie clan that lived on the Lower East Side and called itself the Diggers. Hoffman, with sharp Semitic features and curly black hair, had first come to New York to do supportive work for SNCC. Gradually, he grew apart from SNCC and evolved a revolutionary philosophy based on merriment and frivolity. Though easily the zaniest of the rebels of the 1960s, Hoffman was by no means the least serious.

"I was once in the New Left but I outgrew it," Hoffman wrote in his whimsical autobiographical tract on revolution.* ". . . I don't like the concept of a movement built on sacrifice, dedication, responsibility, anger, frustration and guilt . . . You want to have more fun, you want to get laid more, you want to turn on with your friends, you want an outlet for your creativity . . ." Behind Hoffman's endless capers was a sense of purpose. Rubin found in him the model he had been seeking of political and cultural synthesis.

"When I first got to New York," Rubin said to me, "I heard someone talking about this Abbie Hoffman who thinks it's more important to burn dollar bills than draft cards. I said to myself, 'Perfect, of course, dollar bills is the issue,† not draft cards.' What an imagination, what weird and absurd ways of looking at things! I knew I had to meet this guy.

"He was probably the best known hippie on the Lower East Side. When I met him, he had flowers in his hair, had just gotten married, and he was just a trip. I immediately saw him as an incredible inspiration."

Rubin found much truth in Hoffman's contention that the SDS people were pompous and pretentious. While planning for the October demonstration, the SDS militants announced their intention to attack and occupy the Pentagon. Hoffman talked instead of exorcising the Pentagon's evil spirits and of levitating the building three hundred feet into the air. He also said he would threaten to release a make-believe gas he called LACE, which on contact created an irresistible sexual urge. Rubin, as project director, had to remain on good terms with all the factions participating in the demonstration, but as the weeks passed he moved further from the grim rebelliousness of SDS to the saucy politics of Abbie Hoffman.

As Rubin expected, the Pentagon did not rise three hundred feet in the air, and the SDS militants dominated the protest with their quasi-violence. But, under Hoffman's influence, a mischievous impudence that was almost good-natured appeared for the first time in an antiwar demonstration. Hoffman's hippies put flowers in the gun barrels of the soldiers, which disoriented these men more than the fury of the militants. Nonetheless, Rubin considered the massive disorder at the Pentagon a measure of the demonstration's

---

* *Revolution for the Hell of It*, written under the pseudonym Free.
† In *Howl*, Ginsberg had a line about the best minds of his generation "who cowered in unshaven rooms in underwear, burning their money in wastebaskets . . ."

success. He himself was arrested during the last hours of the week-end, and spent thirty days in jail. Also arrested, Abbie paid a $10 fine and went home.

After the Pentagon march, Rubin decided to remain in New York rather than return to Berkeley, and he and Hoffman became fast friends. Abbie with his wife Anita, Jerry with his girl friend Nancy, spent most of their nights together, turned on, Rubin said, fanta-sizing new stunts to captivate the media and advance the revolu-tion. "We figured we could create a new myth," Rubin said, "of the dope-taking, freedom-loving, politically committed activist. Abbie and I began living it." So successful were they at being noticed together that they began to lose their individual identities. It was common to have Jerry mistaken for Abbie, and Abbie for Jerry, and for the world to use their two names almost interchangeably.

Rubin remembered that around Christmas, 1967, while Abbie and Anita were taking a vacation in the Caribbean, he hit on the idea of repeating the triumph of the Pentagon at the Democratic National Convention the next summer. He was so excited, he said, that he phoned Hoffman, who immediately perceived how perfect the setting was for guerrilla theater. "He said we'll get the thirty most important people in Greenwich Village and issue a call to have thousands of people come to Chicago," Rubin remembered. "We'll take the convention over. We'll make it our convention. We'll be in the streets, and the people will be with us." When Hoffman came back, Rubin said, the two of them were bursting with ideas, and agreed to set up an organization to carry out the project.

On New Year's Eve, at a party in Hoffman's apartment, the new organization acquired a name and, with it, a character. "We started putting the elements together," Rubin said, "youth, international, an all-over-the-world party that could run a great festival." He credited Paul Krassner, editor of a satirical underground magazine called *The Realist* with being the first to hit on the combination. "Yip, yippie, hippie, oh, God, it was perfect," he recalled. "Hippie to yippie, yippie to hippie. Suddenly, that was it: Youth Interna-tional Party—Y.I.P.—YIP—YIPPIE!"

Rubin and Hoffman began immediately to disseminate the mes-sage and, within a few weeks, the name was circulating throughout the underground press. A month later it began to appear in the

431

"straight" press. The message was that the Yippies were mobilizing, and going to Chicago.

Martin Luther King, too, had been making plans for 1968, hoping to channel some of the splenetic, aimless energy within the black community. The riots in the summer of 1967 had been catastrophic, and in Detroit, King himself endorsed the use of federal troops in the ghetto. Stokely Carmichael seemed to be everywhere stirring up trouble, including Cuba and North Vietnam, and his successor as SNCC chairman, H. Rap Brown, was openly preaching guerrilla warfare. King's antiwar crusade had failed to unite blacks in a single purpose. Even Bayard Rustin, old pacifist that he was, held firm to the position that blacks had to continue currying the favor of the Johnson Administration.

But the government's support of civil rights continued to erode in 1967. Though Johnson resubmitted the open housing and equal employment bills he had proposed the year before, he no longer pressed seriously for their enactment, and Congress passed nothing. The federal antipoverty program, which had shown positive results in the creation of independent black institutions, lost backers because it threatened local politicians. The House even voted down a small appropriation for rodent control in the slums, with Southerners crowing that they had beaten a "civil rats bill."

In November of 1967, King went off with three other SCLC ministers to serve five days in jail on a charge dating back to the Birmingham protests, and the four used the time to consider ways to harness the furies of the ghetto into a purposeful, militant and nonviolent campaign. The idea they came up with was a Poor People's March on Washington, envisaged as a means for the poor themselves to bring their case to the federal government. They saw the March as an interracial coalition, which would unite blacks with Indians, Mexican-Americans and even the white poor. They contemplated a highly disciplined program of civil disobedience, in which the poor would show that they, too, could exercise political power.

In December 1967, King presented this idea at the annual SCLC conference in Atlanta. He proposed that the Poor People's March take place the following April, and he talked of tactics ranging from boycotts and strikes to massive disruption that would close down the city. It was a more radical Martin Luther King than anyone had heard before. But King had established a remarkable record of doing what he said and, even in these times of exploding rhetoric, he had to be taken seriously.

I went down to Atlanta in January 1968, on a magazine assignment, to interview King. I found him in SCLC's storefront headquarters on Auburn Avenue, a decaying thoroughfare of bars, poolrooms and restaurants in the heart of the ghetto. The SCLC offices, partitioned with thin plywood, were crowded. Young people, mostly black, wandered in and out, exchanging greetings like "Hey, man," and "How you doin', brother?"

King was in an interior sanctum, where the atmosphere was calm. A bare bulb hanging overhead provided a dim light. Books filled the shelves on the walls, and spilled out of open cartons on the floor. Filing cabinets crowded the corners, leaving little space for King's ancient wooden desk. King, clad in shirt-sleeves and a tie, seemed to me preoccupied as he spoke.

King said he and his SCLC associates were laying plans to "dislocate" the city of Washington by legitimate nonviolent protest, which would be "disruptive without being destructive." The protests, he said, would begin with traditional mass marches and would grow to sit-ins in federal offices, in Congress and in the streets. Depending on how the government responded, he said, the protesters might even immobilize the city, by blocking air and train traffic and by stopping local transportation.

King told me he planned to begin the protest with three thousand people, two hundred from each of the nation's fifteen worst ghettos. The participants would receive three months of training in nonviolence in their local communities, then descend on Washington on foot. When they arrived, they would build tent cities, he said, and prepare for the "waves of the nation's poor and disinherited" who would follow. King said their objective would be represented by the slogan "Jobs or Income," which the government could readily satisfy with a massive WPA-type program.

"We have found throughout our experience that timid supplication for justice will not solve the problem," King told me. "We have got to confront the power structure massively. We can't live with another summer like the last. This is a desperate plea. I want to

433

give the nation the opportunity to respond. This is a means to channel the inchoate rage of the ghetto into a creative force.

"Gandhi did it this way, and so can we. Our power will be in numbers and in keeping at this until we succeed. We'll accept scorn and ridicule, jail, or worse. Our power will be in our ability to maintain discipline. The more nonviolent we are, the more we will arouse the conscience of the nation."

It was classic Martin Luther King, Jr., trying new tactics but unchanged since Montgomery a dozen years before in his belief in the efficacy of nonviolent direct action. King did not dismiss the prospect of an intensified white backlash, but he said he would overcome it, as he had in Birmingham and Selma.

"They may try to run us out, like they did with the bonus marchers.* The army may try to run us out . . . But if we go to jail, we'll stay there indefinitely, without putting up bail."

King did not deny that from 1955 to 1965 blacks had made more progress than in the previous three hundred years of American history. But this very progress had aroused in them a taste for real equality.

"These years changed the psyche of the Negro," King said. "They gave the Negro a new sense of dignity and self-respect. They broke down the edifice of segregation in the South. But they did little to penetrate the lot of the millions of Negroes in the ghettos . . . It didn't cost anything to integrate lunch counters. Now we are talking about something that will cost billions and billions of dollars."

King was planning for the Poor People's March when the sanitation workers in Memphis, almost all of them black, went on strike against the city over a demand for union recognition. SCLC's Memphis affiliate, led by Reverend James Lawson, mobilized the entire black community to their support. Walter Reuther, as well as other high officials of the AFL-CIO, went to Memphis as a gesture of labor solidarity. Five hundred white unionists marched with the

---

* A gathering of fifteen thousand World War I veterans who marched to Washington in 1932 to demand relief from the Depression. After spending some months camped out, their presence an embarrassment to the government, they were dispersed by the army on orders of President Hoover.

blacks. Roy Wilkins and Bayard Rustin also appeared, reviving memories of the classic civil rights demonstrations. But the issue was no longer segregation, and even the old leadership perceived the strike, with its economic implications, as one of the new issues crucial to the movement.

King, as usual, was expected to be the linchpin that held diverse participants together but, in one critical way, Memphis was different from the earlier campaigns. SCLC had not organized it, and it bore the marks of indiscipline. At mass meetings, young blacks shouted "Black Power!," and spoke of guns and fighting. Black drunks lined the route of the mass marches. Rocks and bottles were thrown at the police.

On March 28, King addressed a crowd preparing for a downtown march, which ended not long after it began in an orgy of broken glass, looting and burning. That night the National Guard was called in, but not before a black teenager was killed. King was consumed by frustration, and talked of retreat, of meditation and of a Gandhian "fast until death" unless all black Americans forswore violence.

Death did intrude upon him at Memphis, but in a quite different way. King had long felt that it pursued him. As early as 1964, he said that "I must face the fact, as all others in positions of leadership must do, that America is an extremely sick nation and that something could happen to me at any time." His SCLC associates recalled that, in the months before Memphis, he was often despondent, and dwelt heavily upon the decline of the movement, and upon his own inadequacies as leader. In February 1968, he told his congregation in Atlanta that he had been thinking of his death and his funeral, and that he wanted to be remembered as a man who gave his life serving others.

In Memphis on April 3, King delivered a touching, melancholy speech, in which he said, "Like anybody, I would like to live a long life. Longevity has its place. But I'm not concerned with that now. I just want to do God's will. And He's allowed me to go up to the mountain. And I've looked over, and I've seen the promised land. I may not be there with you, but I want you to know that we as a people will get to the promised land."

The next evening, as he stood on the balcony outside his motel room, King was shot dead by a white assassin.

435

Within minutes after the announcement of King's death, crowds began to gather at Fourteenth and U Streets, the heart of Washington's black ghetto. The capital had not had a riot. Many believed that, because so many blacks had well-paying jobs with the government, it never would. When King was killed, there were ghetto uprisings in Boston, Detroit, Chicago, Philadelphia, San Francisco, Toledo, Pittsburgh. But the biggest of the week was in Washington.

Stokely Carmichael was in the ghetto when the riot started. After leaving the chairmanship of SNCC the year before, he returned to Washington, where he had started his career as a militant. Organizing with his usual energy, he succeeded in bringing the leading black organizations under a radical umbrella called the Black United Front, with which even King had had to deal when he was in town. Carmichael told me he had remained on warm terms with King, and looked forward to the Poor People's March, because he was sure it would somehow spark a Washington uprising. Yet it was Carmichael, when the rioting began, who was seen racing from one cluster of angry blacks to the next, urging people to go home.

For the three days that followed King's death, the riot raged, corresponding to a pattern of looting and burning that had become familiar since Watts. An incendiary stench filled the air, as miles of the Fourteenth Street corridor were reduced to a ghostly rubble. What the omnipresent TV crews transmitted to the world was a picture of blacks, whatever their grief over King, conducting themselves once more as if they were at a festival. Again, National Guardsmen stepped in to quell the frenzy and mop up the last pockets of disorder.

Carmichael, watched closely by police and FBI, pleaded with rioters up and down the street to give the police no pretext for shooting. But he also took the platform on the Howard campus, itself in the central ghetto, to deliver an extravagantly antiwhite speech. Most of the time, however, Carmichael's whereabouts was a mystery. Anonymous militants boasted of fire-bombing white businesses, but no evidence was ever produced that he was among them. As in Watts, the authorities concluded that there had been no conspiracy, and Carmichael emerged from the ruins free of blame.

Yet, when I talked to Carmichael many years later, he said he

436

had worked throughout those three days to keep the riot alive. He said he was sure the FBI had killed King, and would have killed him, too, if it could have done so with impunity. He wanted Washington to riot, he recalled, to show unmistakably that blacks would not stand for the assassination of their leaders without exacting a heavy price. As he explained it, the rioting to him was a form of self-defense.

"So when King died," Carmichael told me, his voice growing excited, "I said, 'Retaliate quick. The people are ready for it. Push 'em. So they'll know if they want to get another one of us that this is what they got coming for 'em.' "

I might have taken Carmichael's words as paranoia, except that he had worked for years in the rural South, where the FBI consistently showed its animosity toward the civil rights movement. J. Edgar Hoover, the FBI director, had waged a personal, almost psychopathic, vendetta against King. In a congressional investigation in 1978 into King's murder, the FBI's conduct was found, in many instances, to have been quite inconsistent with its law enforcement responsibilities. The FBI may have had no role whatever in King's death, but Carmichael was not irrational in being suspicious of it.

Nonetheless, the Washington riot was in a sense a disappointment to Carmichael. He had come North to organize for revolution, which he was convinced would start in the nation's black ghettos. The rampage in Washington looked like a revolutionary step forward. But the ghetto uprisings, which had begun in the blossoming period of civil rights, ended in the era of the movement's desiccation. When Watts exploded in 1965, the hope for change was still buoyant. Three years later King was dead, and what remained of hope was buried with him. Washington was the last of the great ghetto riots of the 1960s.

Though King was dead, the Poor People's March surged forward on its own momentum. Bayard Rustin had opposed it from the start. He had warned King that the ghetto kids who had been invited were unlike the middle-class blacks who had been the backbone of the movement, and could not be counted on for nonviolence. He warned also of the danger of losing control, as King did when he

437

wound up associating himself with Black Power during the Meredith March. Ralph Abernathy has speculated that King, after Johnson's withdrawal, would have canceled the March, to avoid embarrassing the Democrats in their 1968 election campaign. But Abernathy, who inherited the presidency of SCLC, decided that the March had to go on, precisely because King was dead. Abernathy was determined to continue the Poor People's March to show the world that the movement remained a powerful force, even without Martin Luther King.

Abernathy, though trusted friend and adviser to King, sadly lacked King's skills, however. After much negotiation, the government granted him a permit for fifteen acres in the park beside the Lincoln Memorial, where three thousand people could camp. The permit was good for a month. But when Abernathy drove in the first stake on May 13, less than six weeks after King's death, he vowed that the marchers would remain "until the Congress of the United States and the leaders of the various departments of our government decide that they are going to do something about the plight of the poor . . ." It was a threatening statement and Abernathy, speaking while the ashes of the riot were still warm, did not endear himself by it to nervous Washingtonians.

Resurrection City, as the encampment was called, was a disaster, though not all the fault was Abernathy's and SCLC's. Rain began to fall soon after the first wave of marchers moved in, and it continued relentlessly. The mud, ankle-deep for weeks, frustrated plans for construction of decent plywood dwellings, prevented trash from being picked up, kept sewer, water and electrical lines from being laid. Moreover, the preoccupation with physical survival diverted all attention from political questions, and kept the encampment shrouded in gloom. Almost no one attended the nightly revival meetings, which had been a standard feature of civil rights campaigns since Montgomery.

Abernathy and his staff made matters worse by spending their nights in a motel miles away, forswearing leadership, generating resentment. They never closed the cultural gap with the Indian and Mexican-American groups that had joined the campaign, and the squabbling among them was endless. Far from the massive demonstrations Abernathy had advertised, the daily fare he provided for weeks was a ragged march to some government agency,

the presentation of an exaggerated list of demands, some singing
and speech-making and a return march to the camp.

The high point of the campaign was to have been Solidarity Day,
which Bayard Rustin had agreed to organize along the lines of the
March on Washington of 1963. But when Abernathy rejected Rustin's condition that demands on the government be limited and
attainable, Rustin quit. Solidarity Day, which took place on June
19, was nonetheless the biggest success of the campaign, attracting
more than fifty thousand people. But it was inevitably compared
with Rustin's earlier March, of which it was only a pale reminder.

Perhaps worst of all, Abernathy and the SCLC staff failed to
maintain in the campaign the level of dignity which King had im-
parted to the movement. The ghetto recruits, making a mockery of
Christian nonviolence, turned Resurrection City into a den of
thievery, assault and rape. Serving as marshals, they harassed visitors and abused the press. In response to the conditions in the
camp, population dropped from twenty-six hundred on May 26 to
five hundred ten days later. On June 24, the Washington police
entered Resurrection City and cleared out the stragglers. Scarcely
anyone protested.

In such ignominy the work of Martin Luther King, Jr., came to an
end. King himself had set for the Poor People's March a goal that
was probably unattainable, and the lesser men who succeeded him
could only have done more poorly than he. The squalor of Resurrection City served as fodder for white backlash. But, in perspective, it was only the debris of a heroic cycle of American history
which began on a bus in Montgomery in 1955 and ended on a motel
balcony in Memphis in 1968. King was dead, and Americans were
exhausted, disenchanted and uncertain of the future.

Robert Kennedy made much of Martin Luther King's funeral,
Eugene McCarthy did not. The difference was not a measure of
which of the two cared more, but of how they saw themselves in
relation to events. Kennedy felt that if he was to share with the
nation in its moments of exultation, then he had to share with it in
the moments of agony. His family sent an airplane to Memphis to
bring King's body back to Atlanta, and he marched five miles under
the grueling sun in the funeral cortege. McCarthy resented emo-

439

tion, high or low, as an obstacle to the rational consideration of public questions. He remained inconspicuous at Atlanta, in part because he believed that to do otherwise would be gross political showmanship, in part because he did not want to add to the frenzy which already gripped the nation.

Kennedy and McCarthy were no longer alone in the presidential race. After Johnson's withdrawal, Hubert Humphrey loomed behind, the choice of the president, the party bosses and the organizational regulars. Humphrey represented loyalty and orthodoxy, and he sought the nomination from within the party structure. He chose to run in no primaries. But Kennedy and McCarthy, being dissidents, had to turn to the people.

Politically, there was little to distinguish between the two. Save for nuances, they agreed on the Vietnam War, civil rights, economics, urban affairs, even national security and foreign policy. What separated them was personality, a conception of the presidency, a style of campaigning—and a profound mutual aversion.

Kennedy had no appreciation for McCarthy's subtle ecclesiastical mind. He found McCarthy vain, insincere and lazy. He was forced to admire McCarthy for taking up the challenge which he himself had shunned, but he had contempt for the lackadaisical way in which McCarthy pursued it.

For McCarthy, there was no ambivalence. He had had little use for Jack Kennedy, who he felt had bought the presidency in 1960, and even less for Bobby, whom he considered the creation of family myth and family money. He was contemptuous of Kennedy's refusal to enter the race early, and unforgiving of his decision to enter it late.

Of the two, Kennedy made a far greater effort to keep the bridges open between them, both before and after Johnson's withdrawal. He had reason to, since he perceived his position as morally weaker, and he wanted ultimately to win over those who had stayed with McCarthy in principle. On a number of occasions, he made friendly overtures to McCarthy, aimed at keeping the antiwar movement from suicidal division. In every instance, however, McCarthy summarily turned away.

It was not a pleasant campaign. The country was in a foul mood not only from King's murder, the ghetto riots, the Poor People's fiasco—and relentless failure in Vietnam. There was also a new round of campus ferocity, most spectacularly at Columbia in New York, where the SDS chapter led demonstrations that lasted for weeks, required the police to clear buildings, left dozens injured and sent the academic world into shock. Aggravating the sense of disorder were rising crime rates, which many Americans felt as a personal threat. The daily headlines and nightly TV fare conveyed a morbid feeling that blood was being spilled everywhere, no more in Vietnam than at home.

For Richard Nixon, the sense of national disarray was a political asset. The leading contender for the Republican nomination, he enjoyed the challenger's luxury of being able to blame incumbents for whatever was amiss. But having started his career as a Red-baiter in the 1940s, he was an old hand at appealing to insecurity, and his theme now was called "law and order." He denounced the Supreme Court for being soft on criminals, and the Administration for tolerating "rampant lawlessness." Critics charged that such attacks were meant as an incitement to backlash and a veil for racism, but Nixon's arguments found among Americans an appreciative audience.

Of the two Democratic campaigners, only Kennedy played the "law and order" game. In blue-collar neighborhoods he pointed out that, having been attorney general, he *knew* how to enforce the law. There was a paradox in the Kennedy candidacy: he had a genuine concern for the disinherited of society, he dined with Tom Hayden and he somehow embodied the "new politics" of the 1960s. And yet the old politicians who had supported his brother ran his campaign, and the white working classes who were most susceptible to backlash delivered him their votes.

A Gallup poll suggested that Kennedy's support was the product of a personal loyalty, of a mystique that no one could quite explain but that was without relation to issues. It was a bizarre and improbable coalition that Kennedy put together, and McCarthy argued that ultimately it would all have gone to him, along with the middle classes who were frightened by Kennedy's passion. McCarthy may in fact have been right, but he was unwilling, even after Kennedy was dead, to extend himself enough to prove it.

In the last month of the contest, Kennedy was increasingly fervent, McCarthy increasingly factious. On May 7, Kennedy won a plurality in the Indiana primary, and a week later he received a majority in Nebraska. But, on May 28, McCarthy took Oregon after a campaign in which Kennedy's zealous style was said to have frightened voters away.

Neck and neck the two came for the June 4 primary into California, which was to determine which of them would be the preeminent challenger to Hubert Humphrey. Both men were at their best. Kennedy drew huge, cheering crowds but McCarthy remained persistently at his heels.

Kennedy emerged the victor, by a very small plurality, and before a ballroom of jubilant supporters just before midnight, he declared, "On to Chicago, and let's win." At that moment, he surely considered the nomination attainable, for unlike McCarthy he was tough and wily enough to have matched Humphrey card for card in the back rooms of the Democratic party. But as he left the auditorium he was shot, and on June 6 he died.

McCarthy seemed to lose interest in the campaign after Kennedy's death. He continued to campaign, and drew enthusiastic crowds wherever he went. With Humphrey undeviatingly faithful to the Johnson line, McCarthy remained the only hope for ending the war. But Kennedy's death seemed to deprive McCarthy of his reason for running, and more than once he let slip that Humphrey, his fellow Minnesotan, would not make such a bad president.

McCarthy won a big primary victory in New York on June 18, and the public opinion polls regularly showed him running stronger than Humphrey against Nixon. But, instead of seeking momentum from this evidence, he appeared burdened by it, and reverted to his earlier passivity. Though he traveled dutifully during the summer, he characteristically offered rather than argued for his candidacy in talking to uncommitted delegates. Whatever McCarthy may have felt inside, this appearance of indifference left the delegates cold.

After the murder, McCarthy made no serious overtures to the Kennedy people. Virtually the last thing Kennedy had done was direct a phone call to Al Lowenstein, through whom he had hoped to make contact with McCarthy. But McCarthy, after the shooting, could barely bring himself to pay a courtesy call at the hospital and, after Kennedy died, he delivered no tribute. McCarthy made no real effort to reestablish the antiwar, anti-Johnson coalition which might have salvaged his prospects. Few knew it for certain and

442

many who sensed it continued to hope, but McCarthy had finished off his own candidacy well before the Democrats convened.

Al Lowenstein made a final effort to rescue the antiwar enterprise he had started. On June 29 he called Kennedy and McCarthy volunteers together in Chicago and proposed forming a "Coalition for an Open Convention." He argued that much of Humphrey's delegate strength was weak, which it was, and that it would erode before a united antiwar candidacy. Then he made the rounds, in his usual tireless way, to stimulate, at least at the lower levels of the two organizations, some pressure on the decision-makers.

But McCarthy continued to look on Lowenstein with mistrust, and the Kennedy people, discouraged by McCarthy's rebuffs, were already turning to such possible alternatives as George McGovern and Ted Kennedy, the last of the Kennedy brothers. On the eve of the convention, McCarthy vetoed a huge antiwar rally at Soldier Field that Lowenstein had proposed. Still, until the convention opened, Lowenstein, characteristically frenzied, collared delegates in McCarthy's behalf. Apart from a few diehards who threatened weakly to walk out and form a third party, however, the McCarthy supporters within the convention seemed resigned to having their votes recorded as nothing but symbolic protest.

Despite McCarthy, thousands of his volunteers showed up in Chicago, ready to perform any service for their cause. Having challenged the Johnson juggernaut and defeated it, they were furious that it was rolling toward them once again. They had appealed to the people with an antiwar commitment and driven Johnson from office. Now Johnson was forcing the party to nominate a prowar candidate who had not stood in a single primary. Incredulous at what had befallen them, McCarthy's volunteers still hoped for a miracle. Instead, what they encountered in Chicago was frustration, and violence.

In January of 1968 Jerry Rubin, along with his pal Abbie Hoffman, established a Yippie office on Fourteenth Street in New York to plan for Chicago. They envisaged a "Festival of Life," to contrast with what they described as the "Convention of Death," where they expected, at the time, that the Democrats would renominate Johnson and endorse the Vietnam War.

443

Rubin and Hoffman set out to recruit forty rock bands, to serve as the focus for hundreds of thousands of young protesters. They did not agree on everything. Rubin wanted more politics in the festival, Hoffman less, and their friendship showed signs of the strain. But they did agree on a "nude-in" on a Lake Michigan beach, workshops on LSD and draft resistance, poetry sessions and forums of radical intellectuals for the consideration of ideas on the creation of a new society.

"Abbie and I worked out of our homes, called each other in the morning and met in the office. It was like two energy centers," Rubin recalled. "And we held insane meetings on Fourteenth Street, where there'd be a couple of hundred people, and they'd end up in fights and craziness and madness. Everybody was bursting out, whatever they wanted to be and whoever they were. Everybody was really asserting themselves. It was a wonderful, exciting, creative, weird and . . . dangerous period."

In February, Rubin went to Chicago and enlisted Abe Peck, leader of a hippie group centered around *The Seed*, an underground newspaper, to be the local Yippie organizer. Then, in March, he and Hoffman met in Chicago with Tom Hayden and Rennie Davis, who were working for the National Mobilization Committee to End the War in Vietnam, the coalition that had staged the Pentagon March. Rubin had once asked Hayden to organize for the Yippies in New York, but Hayden preferred the Mobe, which was more clearly political. Now the Yippies and the Mobe were conferring to see if they could profitably work together.

Tom Hayden and Rennie Davis, both twenty-eight, were now elder statesmen of the New Left, founders of SDS who had been pushed aside by a new generation of radicals. Before the antiwar movement, both had spent years at community organizing. Hayden, with an instinct for being at the center of events, had been among the first militants to visit North Vietnam, and had had his passport lifted by the State Department for it. He was in the Newark riot, and suspected for a time of being an instigator of it. In the fall of 1967, he and Davis attended an international conference of radical students in Bratislava, Czechoslovakia, and then went to Hanoi together. They returned on the day of the Pentagon March, flew to Washington, and went directly to the demonstration to speak.

Hayden had now evolved a global view of student radicalism. He

444

told me that he and Davis returned from Bratislava convinced that the campuses were the new centers of revolution. "A new international was formed without a Comintern," he said, "without a bureaucracy, reaching outside and inside of parties, all the way around the world, to students in France, West Germany, Cuba, Venezuela, Quebec. Vietnam was the internationalizing force, and SDS was the inspiration." His experience seemed to confirm C. Wright Mills's observation that young intellectuals had emerged as the "historic agency of change." Hayden said campus radicalism had invalidated the lessons of 1917, which held that a revolution needed a conscious vanguard.

The new revolutionaries, Hayden said, would probe to find the "weak points" in the social structure, and keep the pressure on these points until the system shattered. One example of this strategy was Columbia, where he had himself played a crucial role in the SDS uprising in April. Paraphrasing Castro's theorist Ché Guevara, Hayden had written in *Ramparts* that revolutionary strategy required "Two, Three, Many Columbias." * He was thrilled by a series of student revolts in Europe in 1968. The most dramatic of them, in Paris in May, had been New Left in style, consciously modeled after Berkeley and Columbia. Hayden was convinced by now that the system was trembling under student blows. As he and Davis laid plans for the Chicago demonstrations, he added the Democratic convention to the list of "weak points" in the structure, and he told himself that an event of revolutionary magnitude was impending.

Hayden and Davis, having conceived of a Chicago protest immediately after the Pentagon March, had proposed that SDS take the leadership. But the SDS national office, still shy of leading, said the time was not right. According to SDS calculations, Hayden said, "either we were leading demonstrators into Chicago to be co-opted by McCarthy or Kennedy when they won the nomination, in which case we would be reformist, or else we were leading them into repression, into a premature confrontation which would somehow destroy the movement. Either way, we couldn't win."

Hayden sneered at the notion of waiting for the perfect revolutionary moment, and had no qualms about forming a united front, if

* Ché's formula for bringing down the capitalist world was "Two, Three, Many Vietnams."

445

it served the purposes of radicals, with liberals or reformers. Revolution, he told me, could not be defined "by ideas without putting them into practice or by tactics independent of the situation." A man of action, he was persuaded that Chicago was the right moment so, dismissing SDS's reservations, he turned for support to the Mobe.

Dave Dellinger, chairman of the New Mobilization, had already begun thinking of Chicago, too, when Davis contacted him to say that he and Hayden had a proposal to present. Dellinger was having trouble keeping his broad coalition together, largely because liberals had become increasingly apprehensive about the violent turn that demonstrations were taking. Deeply committed himself to nonviolence, Dellinger was suspicious of Davis, and even more so of Hayden. Nonetheless, after Davis made an impressive presentation at a meeting in New York, Dellinger appointed him the Mobe's Chicago coordinator, and named Hayden as his associate.

In February 1968, Davis opened a Chicago office. On the weekend of March 22, the Mobe sponsored a meeting at Lake Villa, north of Chicago, to discuss strategy for the convention week. About two hundred representatives of several dozen organizations were present, among them liberal antiwar groups, blacks, Yippies and SDS.

Hayden and Davis presented a paper which proposed three days of "sustained, organized protest," the object of which would be to "delegitimate" the Democratic party. They urged heavy organizing in the spring and summer to bring demonstrators to the city, and a buildup of community organizing in the fall to sustain the antiwar momentum after the convention. They promised that the planning for the demonstration would be "nonviolent and legal," but they noted that they could not be responsible if the events during the week turned out otherwise.

The statement satisfied neither liberals, who smelled disingenuousness, nor radicals, who called it a sellout. After the presentation, the delegates embarked on a round of speeches, followed by a number of indecisive resolutions. But the meeting never came to a decision on mounting a unified protest. The outcome was a defeat for Hayden and Davis, and a blow to the Mobe.

Jerry Rubin and his Yippie friends, finding the meeting insufferably dull, gave it a dose of their own treatment. Abbie Hoffman

446

announced that critical to the Yippie revolutionary program was the abolition of pay toilets. The liberals did not know what to make of him. The SDS delegates, insisting that revolution was a serious matter, said the Yippies' frivolous attitude was misleading to the people.

In the middle of the crucial vote on mass action, a band of Yippies burst into the meeting room and tossed posters into the air. "Our slogan was 'Abandon the Creeping Meatball, Come to Chicago,' " Rubin told me, explaining that this translated into an appeal for aggressive street action. He said he told the meeting that, whatever the self-important people on the left decided, the Yippies would go to Chicago on their own, for revolution and for fun.

After Lyndon Johnson's withdrawal as a candidate on March 31, 1968, many potential protesters, convinced that either Kennedy or McCarthy would consummate their antiwar work, had canceled their plans to go to Chicago. When Chicago's ghettos rioted a few days later, after King's murder, and Mayor Richard Daley ordered his police to "shoot to kill," many blacks understood that they would be risking their lives to demonstrate against the war at the Democratic convention in August. Three weeks after King's death, Daley's cops clubbed down middle-class peace marchers at a protest in downtown Chicago. The message seemed to be that Daley's mailed fist would fall indiscriminately on demonstrators, and whites as well as blacks wondered whether marching in Chicago would be worth the potential cost.

Sensing this loss of interest, the Yippies in New York, like the New Mobilization in Chicago, worked listlessly throughout the spring. Rubin said he even drafted a statement canceling the Yippie protest, but withheld its release pending the results of the California primary. "Some Yippies had hidden fantasies of Bobby Kennedy smoking pot in the White House," Rubin wrote in *Do It!* This observation conveyed something of the message Kennedy transmitted to radicals in his last months. Rubin told me the demonstrations would never have come off had Kennedy not been killed.

But, in an epigram Rubin attributed to Abbie Hoffman, the California primary got "the fastest recount in history." In one of the more tasteless lines in *Do It!*, Rubin extolled the rejuvenation of

447

the Yippie program in Chicago by proclaiming "Sirhan Sirhan is a yippie." A young Palestinian studying in the United States, Sirhan was tried, convicted and imprisoned for the murder. Only after Kennedy's death did real frenzy begin pouring into the organization of the protest, both in Chicago and New York.

Part of the Yippie planning consisted of needling Mayor Daley. Rubin and Hoffman proclaimed their intention of putting LSD in the water supply, and having thousands of young people run naked through the streets. They published a list of demands that included, in addition to ending the war, the legalization of marijuana, the disarming of the police, the abolition of money and, as an afterthought, a note that, "We believe that people should fuck all the time, anytime, whomever they want . . ." The mayor, never known for a sense of humor, was not amused.

Eccentric as they were, the Yippies were just serious enough to cause worry. In February, they had staged a destructive raid on the Stony Brook campus of New York's State University and, in March, an impromptu "party" in Grand Central Station, where five thousand hippies cavorted and fifty arrests were made. Unlike the Mobe, they issued no pious disclaimers about violence. Rubin, particularly, exulted publicly over the prospect of bloodshed.

Though they could not touch the Yippies in New York, Daley's cops periodically raided the Chicago Yippies, arresting twenty-five at one party, thirty at another. The Chicago Yippies were not just angry at the city but annoyed with Rubin and Hoffman. They pointed out that, after the convention, the New Yorkers could go home, while they would have to remain. Their reaction to the harassment, as the mayor hoped it would be, was to contemplate pulling out entirely of the political action in August.

At the New Mobilization, where Davis and Hayden were planning, there was also a growing apprehension. Dellinger clashed repeatedly with his two organizers, saying they signaled an ambivalence about violence. Both replied, with some truth, that this ambivalence kept them in touch with the militants. But Hayden had often said the revolution would ultimately spill blood, and Davis, beneath a more benign exterior, seemed to veil a comparable fury.

Furthermore, both were publicly identified with SDS, in which they had deep roots, and SDS spokesmen were publicly boasting that their forces would go to Chicago to perform audacious revolutionary deeds. It was difficult for anyone to grasp the nuance that SDS had actually repudiated the work Hayden and Davis were doing for the Mobe, and that SDS had refused to endorse the Chicago demonstration. What people knew was that Hayden was the most celebrated student radical of his time, and the organization with which his name was associated threatened violence. Since neither he nor Davis had explicitly disassociated the Mobe from the threats, the Chicago authorities proceeded to treat SDS and the Mobe as indistinguishable.

Under Davis, the Mobe organized with great diligence. Davis arranged for housing in local churches, representation by the National Lawyers Guild, treatment by the Medical Committee for Human Rights. He provided for "movement centers," in church basements and vacant stores, from which individual delegations, in "do–your–own–thing" fashion, could run whatever kind of protest suited them.

Daley's strategy to counter this planning was to refuse to grant the Mobe any municipal permits. Davis had filed in mid-June for permits for two parades, and for the use of ten parks for rallies. Having calculated that he had indoor sleeping facilities for only thirty thousand demonstrators, he also asked for the use of six areas, including downtown Lincoln Park, for outdoor sleeping space for seventy thousand more.

Negotiations dragged on between Davis and David Stahl, an assistant to Daley, for eight or nine weeks. The city would not act even after Washington sent out Roger Wilkins, director of the Community Relations Service, to seek a solution. A week before the convention, Mobe lawyers filed a suit in Federal court but, after several days of hearings, Judge William Lynch dismissed it. Mobe people found it funny that Daley's negotiator was named Stahl, his judge named Lynch.* Funny or not, in the end, the city granted only one permit, for a daytime rally in Grant Park on the day that Humphrey was to be nominated.

The Yippies were even less successful than the Mobe with the Chicago authorities. Their approach was to request suspension of the 11:00 P.M. curfew in the city parks so they could have places to sleep. They asked also for waiver of narcotics regulations and per-

---

* David Stahl was, for a time, a Daley favorite. Judge William ("Billy") Lynch was Daley's boyhood friend and former law partner.

449

mission to sleep on the municipal beaches. When they received no answers they filed a suit, but dropped it when the Mobe suit was dismissed. In the last days before the convention, the Chicago authorities responded to the Mobe and the Yippies by installing fresh signs in the parks warning that the laws and curfews would be strictly enforced.

As summer approached, veteran Daley-watchers were mystified. Mayor of Chicago since 1955, Daley had mastered a technique of giving small gifts to avoid large struggles for power. During the end-the-slums demonstrations in 1966, Daley had outmaneuvered Martin Luther King by "killing him with kindness." Daley was generous with his favors. His political machine traditionally absorbed dissidents rather than have to subdue them. Though he was no stranger to ruthlessness, Daley preferred to use gratitude to keep his machine in power, and he made his influence felt on virtually every street in the city.

Those who were convinced that Daley would ultimately give way on the permits had not calculated, however, on the mayor's loathing for young white radicals. They were outsiders, not constituents, and he owed them no courtesies. They were ingrates, punks, parasites. They offended his sense of morality, they did not fight according to the rules, they publicly ridiculed him. Privately he shared their objections to the war, and had told Lyndon Johnson as much. But he would not let a bunch of brats create havoc within the Democratic party or the city of Chicago, institutions he loved.

Chicago was not a city with a natural tolerance for nonconformists. Its huge white working class, much of it only a generation away from Europe, extolled religion and hard work. Its blacks, however disaffected in their ghettos, saw hippies and radicals as just spoiled, overprivileged white kids. Its police, never seriously inhibited by libertarian niceties, dreamed of reprisals against the ne'er-do-wells who had the nerve to call them pigs. Only a few liberals, concerned about civil liberties and the war, worried about Daley's intentions, and their influence in the city was negligible.

Aware that public opinion was with him, Daley also knew he had the federal government's support. He ordered Chicago's twelve thousand cops to work twelve-hour shifts. He held five thousand National Guardsmen and six thousand Army troops in reserve. He deployed hundreds of FBI and Secret Service agents, along with

450

state and county police forces, for special assignments. Daley was determined to show that Chicago knew how to preserve order, and he anticipated that America would applaud him.

Daley's strategy of intimidation succeeded. The masses that the Yippies and the National Mobe had beckoned to Chicago never came. After Kennedy's death, when preparations for the protest began anew, colleges were already on vacation, and students were unavailable to organize. Not only Eugene McCarthy but Al Lowenstein, furthermore, told supporters to stay away. The Chicago Yippies, to the dismay of Jerry Rubin and the New York Yippies, announced that the Festival of Life threatened to become a "festival of blood," and plans to attend should be canceled. Most significant of all, the thousands upon thousands of unaffiliated people who had packed antiwar demonstrations for years—people of goodwill who thought nothing of jumping into buses to cross the country to protest—these people were scared, and decided to stay home.

In the end, only about five thousand demonstrators came from out-of-town, to be joined by perhaps an equal number from around Chicago. Roughly half were undaunted McCarthy backers. Almost all the rest were countercultural and political radicals, nearly every one white. Most arrived with an awareness of the risk, prepared for physical confrontation. Some were even eager for it.

Jerry Rubin hitchhiked to Chicago in the third week of August 1968, a few days before the Democratic convention opened, and linked up with Abbie Hoffman and a half-dozen other Yippies for a flurry of last-minute preparations. Shortly after Rubin's arrival, a seventeen-year-old American Indian named Jerome Johnson, dressed as a hippie, was killed by police gunfire near Lincoln Park, where the Festival of Life was to be held. Rubin said the incident cast a pall over the Yippies' organizational activities.

Soon, Rubin and Hoffman were barely talking. "There had always been a natural competitiveness between us," Rubin told me, "and the tensions of all those months were getting to us." The dispute, reflecting their ongoing differences over politics versus fun, crystallized in a pig named Pigasus, the Yippie candidate for president. They had agreed to release the pig, as a way of ridiculing the system, in Chicago's Civic Center Plaza.

451

"Abbie and I fought over what kind of pig to deliver," Rubin said. "He already had a pig, a cute little pig. I wanted a really ugly pig, that was obnoxious and horrible. So I went out into the fields south of Chicago and for twenty-five dollars found a pig that was six months old and weighed two hundred pounds. It was really a battle between us for self-definition."

Rubin, winning the battle, released his pig near the plaza's celebrated Picasso statue on Friday, August 23. In front of television cameras, the police chased and captured the pig, and turned it over to the Chicago Humane Society. Rubin and five other Yippies were arrested, and were jailed briefly before getting out on bail. The Yippies, Rubin said, considered the stunt a major score for their side.

On Saturday afternoon, two days before the official opening of the convention, some two thousand people assembled in Lincoln Park for a prelude to the Festival of Life. A large proportion were sightseers, and more than a few were undercover cops. Clusters of young men and women in long hair played guitars and bongo drums, and the atmosphere was cordial. Yippie leaders passed out information from tables on where to go for medical aid, workshops, free food and beds for the night.

Not yet ready for confrontation, Rubin and Hoffman issued a statement during the day advising observance of the 11:00 P.M. curfew. "The cops want to turn our parks into graveyards," they said, and at the curfew hour the police's clearing operations began. The several hundred youths that remained in the park left with little resistance, and some lusty jeering. But, on the nearby streets to which they had been driven, the first skirmishes of the week took place, and the police made eleven arrests.*

On Sunday afternoon, when the festival formally began, only a few thousand people, and a single rock band, had gathered. Jerry Rubin admitted he was disappointed, even "paranoid" at the small

---

* The account of the violence in Chicago is taken largely from the "Walker Report," a study prepared under the direction of Daniel Walker, a Chicago attorney and later governor of Illinois, for the National Commission on the Causes and Prevention of Violence. It should not be confused with the Kerner Commission, which studied the ghetto riots. The Walker Report, officially entitled *Rights in Conflict: The Violent Confrontation of Demonstrators and Police in the Parks and Streets in Chicago During the Week of the Democratic National Convention*, stirred much controversy when it was published in December 1968 because of its critical treatment of police conduct, but its facts were never seriously disputed.

turnout. Much of the crowd again consisted of tourists, enjoying a few Sunday hours in the park. In the center of one of the circles was Allen Ginsberg, now an elder statesman of the counterculture, who would be around Chicago all week. Ginsberg chanted his deep bass "om-m-m, om-m-m," a Buddhist mantra meant to convey a sense of calm.

A bit incongruously, fifty or seventy-five motorcyclists, white toughs from the working class, were also in the park. Though social outsiders, and cop-haters, they had little else in common with the Yippies. To most of the Yippies, the presence of the bikers was half-frightening, half-thrilling.

One of them, a tall blond man in his thirties, attached himself to Rubin and, late in the day, volunteered to serve as his bodyguard. Bob Pierson was his name. Wearing a black T-shirt and a helmet, he remained at Rubin's side for most of the next few tumultuous days. Then, having battled shoulder to shoulder with the protesters, Pierson removed his disguise and revealed his identity as a Chicago cop. He later served as the chief witness against Rubin on a charge of incitement to riot.*

"Abbie and I had this crazy idea," Rubin told me, "that the white working class would join us, and when this guy volunteered to be my bodyguard I thought, 'Damn, I've got a genuine biker who's been radicalized.'† I took it as a real compliment. It didn't even dawn on me that he was a cop. We were seduced by our own macho fantasies."

The atmosphere in Lincoln Park on Sunday began turning ugly after the tourists left, when police ordered the Yippies to remove a flatbed truck that served as a rock band's stage. One youth blocked the truck's route, while others screamed, "Kill the Pigs" and "Fuck the Pigs." Rubin's contention that the inciters may have been cops is not implausible, but there were plenty of willing followers. Demonstrators surged into police lines, and the police struck back with clubs. The fighting subsided after a few arrests, but tension was high throughout the evening and rose as the curfew approached.

---

* Pierson held the title of investigator, state's attorney's police, Cook County, Illinois. He told his own story in the December 1968 issue of *Official Detective Stories*. It was headlined: "Exclusive! Behind the Yippies' Plan to Wreck the Democratic Convention."

† Remember Allen Ginsberg's line in *Howl* about "saintly motorcyclists," a group that somehow enchanted the counterculture.

About 10:30 a police car cruised slowly through the park, its loudspeakers warning everyone, including newsmen, to clear out at once. When the police began their sweep a short while later, about a thousand demonstrators remained. As the two forces made contact, some of the cops were heard to yell, "Kill the Commies" and "Get out of the park, you motherfuckers!" In many cases the demonstrators resisted, singly or in clusters, and sometimes they grouped to counterattack. They taunted the police with cries of, "Pigs, Pigs, Pigs," and worse. The cops swung out with a fine indifference at demonstrators, male or female, and news reporters. Shortly after midnight, with the help of tear gas, most of the crowd was finally driven from the park.

The Democratic National Convention officially opened on Monday, August 26, and trouble in Lincoln Park began that afternoon. Tom Hayden was arrested then under circumstances that seemed contrived by the police to separate him from his following. Rennie Davis, who had been standing near Hayden, drew together a crowd of five hundred or so, and set off on a peaceful protest march to police headquarters. After winding through downtown Chicago, Davis's column filed into Grant Park, a mile-long stretch that ran between Michigan Avenue and Lake Michigan, directly in front of the Hilton Hotel.

The Hilton was where Humphrey and McCarthy both had their working headquarters. The plenary sessions of the convention were being held at the International Amphitheatre, near the old stockyards four miles to the south, but the Hilton was the downtown focus of the convention proceedings. Inside Grant Park, within view of the Hilton, Dave Dellinger was making a speech before an orderly crowd as Davis arrived. Trouble started when police pulled down several young men in his audience from an equestrian statue, where they had planted Viet Cong flags. The cops then did some clubbing and the demonstators some stoning. But as night fell, and Davis's marchers drifted back to Lincoln Park three miles to the north, Grant Park and the streets around the Hilton were quiet.

Lincoln Park, site of Rubin's Festival of Life, was not quiet, however. In the darkness, protesters began constructing barricades of

454

picnic tables and trash bins, anticipating battle. Over the course of several hours, mobs in hippie dress made sorties from the park, and clashed with the police in adjacent neighborhoods. By midnight they had filtered back, and a crowd of two or three thousand now waited nervously.

Half an hour after midnight, the sweep began. The police lobbed smoke and tear gas bombs, and received a hail of bricks and bottles in return. Then the police attacked, and demonstrators ran in every direction, through the park and into the streets, shouting obscenities, stopping to fling rocks. The cops, using language no less obscene, swung their clubs at any moving figure. Hundreds of protesters were beaten, along with some bystanders and newsmen. It was 2:00 A.M. before calm descended and the last of the participants limped off to tend their wounds.

Jerry Rubin had been laid out during Monday's events by a "bad trip," product of some high-powered drug administered anonymously—he suspected by the police—in Lincoln Park. On Tuesday he was on his feet, and in the afternoon he excited the crowd with a harangue on racism and police brutality. But Rubin readily conceded that his speeches had little impact on events.

"I had no street leadership function," he said, "and I don't know anyone who did. We had figured on running through the streets. But the people were not ours to control."

Rubin was described to me by one of his Yippie friends as a "middle hero," always at the point of confrontation, never one of the first to leave, but not among the most aggressive, not among the chargers of the police. That kind of leadership always seemed to be seized by some unidentified figure, from SDS or a bikers' gang or the Mobe or from none of them. Bob Pierson, the police informer, wrote that he was as zealous as anyone in urging the crowds forward. These faceless people, not the better known figures of the radical movement, provided the leadership for the chaos around Lincoln Park, by surging to the front ranks and locking themselves angrily in combat.

Meanwhile, the Democratic delegates had arrived. Tainted by war, assassination, urban riots and a foreboding of defeat, their reunion had none of the élan of earlier Democratic conventions.

The McCarthy people felt swindled, the Humphrey people were an object of contempt. Daley's suffocating security arrangements made matters worse. So did indignation at Johnson, who in disgrace continued to exercise an iron hand over proceedings. It was a final straw that the cops, so busy drawing blood at Lincoln Park, could not stop troublemakers from setting off stink bombs that constantly permeated the Hilton.

The cops treated the demonstrators in Grant Park, across from the Hilton, more respectfully than they did the Yippies in Lincoln Park. The Grant Park protests were political rather than counter-cultural, and they were dominated by neatly dressed McCarthy supporters, who seemed as contemptuous as the cops of the beaded longhairs. On Tuesday night, when the crowd swelled to three thousand or four thousand with Yippies fleeing from the embattled north, Grant Park became as rowdy as Lincoln, and the police found themselves targets not only of stones but of bags of excrement and cans of urine. Nonetheless, a police commander announced at 1:30 A.M. that, as long as the Hilton remained safe, the curfew would not be enforced.

Meanwhile, feelings of tension grew in expectation of the convention's climax on Wednesday night. The last possibility of surprise, a presidential draft of Ted Kennedy, had by now vanished. Wednesday's script, written by Johnson in Washington, contained a rejection of the peace plank, which would at least have been consolation to the antiwar delegates, and the nomination and selection of Hubert Humphrey, who represented a major endorsement of the war. Wednesday night was the moment proclaimed by both the Yippies and the Mobe for making their principal political statement of the week, a wrathful march to the Amphitheatre.

But the authorities would have nothing of such a march. The Secret Service, responsible for security around the Amphitheatre, said it would be too dangerous. The city administration now had the National Guard on the street as reinforcements. The orders of the Chicago police were to turn back any march south from the Hilton, however peaceful, by whatever force was necessary.

In full knowledge of the orders, Dave Dellinger announced in Grant Park that a line of march to the Amphitheatre would form at four thirty that afternoon. Some ten thousand people had already come to the park to participate in the rally, for which Rennie Davis had obtained the only permit of the week. A battalion of tired, irascible cops watched over them. As they waited for the march to begin, the demonstrators were aroused by speaker after speaker denouncing the Democrats' betrayal.

About four o'clock, a young man climbed a flagpole adjacent to the bandstand and grabbed at the American flag. The gesture, less provocative than many that week, suddenly ignited the police, who lunged forward, nightsticks swinging. They arrested the climber, then retreated through a rain of bricks, cans, plastic bags said to be filled with paint and urine, eggs, tomatoes and parts of park benches.

From the stage, Dellinger pleaded for a restoration of order. Davis, backed by a squad of the Mobe's marshals, circulated through the park, trying to calm the crowd. Suddenly, Davis was struck from behind by a policeman's baton and came up covered with blood. For the next twenty minutes bedlam reigned, with cops attacking indiscriminately and demonstrators fighting back with frenzy. When the battle stopped, Dellinger took the microphone and called for a march to the Amphitheatre that would be dignified and nonviolent. His call was greeted with raucous jeers.

Tightly arrayed, a bristling column of five thousand or six thousand marchers set out southward, but it was stopped before it even crossed the boundaries of the park. "On orders of the Chicago Police Department," a uniformed commander announced, "there will be no march today." The marchers then sat down, and waited impatiently while Dellinger negotiated.

Meanwhile, a second crowd of two thousand, most of them McCarthy "straights," had assembled in front of the Hilton. Allen Ginsberg was among them, helping them to retain their calm by chanting "om-m-m, om-m-m." The police, by refusing to let Dellinger's column wander off toward the Amphitheatre, made it inevitable that the two crowds would attempt to merge for a huge demonstration at the hotel.

Dellinger's column began breaking up about 6:30, scattering as individuals or as groups. The police and the National Guard tried to block the exits from the park but they were too thinly deployed. They tried tear gas, which drifted mischievously back on the lake breezes into the Hilton, where it infiltrated the air-conditioning system and brought tears to the eyes even of Hubert Humphrey.

Shortly after seven, a large crowd of demonstrators found a totally unguarded exit several blocks north of the hotel, and poured out of the park onto Michigan Avenue.

By coincidence, the crowd ran into a mule train brought to Chicago by Reverend Ralph Abernathy as the symbol of the Poor People's campaign. The mule train, with a valid permit, was parading around the Loop. Caught in the swell, it was a curiosity of the civil rights era, and a reminder of earlier, more good-natured Democratic conventions. The crowd rushed past the mule train, barely noticing. By seven thirty, most of the Grant Park demonstrators had made their way out of the enclosure and were swarming toward the Hilton.

By nightfall, some five thousand demonstrators, of every age and style, were massed at the intersection of Michigan Avenue and Balbo, the northeast corner of the hotel. Though the crowd was leaderless, its unarticulated intention, understood by the police, was to storm the hotel, where Humphrey was deliberating inside, and then to continue south to the Amphitheatre, where the party was preparing his coronation. The intersection was brightly lit, thanks to the television crews who had set the stage for the performers. "The whole world is watching," the crowd chanted gleefully, waiting for some signal to begin.

The signal was the contact made by the pressing crowd with the nightsticks of the police defenders. While a police legion on Michigan Avenue tried to hold its ground against the advance, a flanking force raced toward the crowd from the Balbo side. Both contingents were making arrests, throwing demonstrators roughly into vans, when a deluge of missiles of every kind descended on them. That was the point at which the cops lost control.

Sticks flailing, swarms of them waded into the throng, shouting obscenities that rivaled the cries of the Yippies. Gripped by frenzy the police clubbed men and women, young and old, newsmen and bystanders, straights and hippies—but especially hippies. Those who stood fast were bashed; those who ran were chased. Discipline vanished, as officers who tried to restrain their men were disregarded. The Walker Commission later spoke of a police riot. It was the most violent night of a violent week, and the cameras captured it in detail.

"We wanted exactly what happened," said Jerry Rubin, reminisc-

458

ing with pleasure. "We wanted the tear gas to get so heavy that the reality was tear gas. We wanted to create a situation in which the Chicago police and the Daley administration and the federal government and the United States would self-destruct. We wanted to show that America wasn't a democracy, that the convention wasn't politics. The message of the week was of an America ruled by force. That was a big victory.

"Everything that happened was both intentional and inadvertent. Everything was by accident, nothing happened as we planned. But it was all planned. Everybody played out their karma. It was all perfect. After the convention was over the question was not what had gone on inside but why did the Chicago police go crazy, and what's wrong with America?"

Even to the delegates, what went on inside seemed trivial. The Johnson script was being played as written. A speech seconding Humphrey's nomination was being pronounced when the film of the riot at the Hilton appeared on television screens throughout the hall. To those inside, the Amphitheatre felt like a fortress, beyond whose walls there was a raging war.

When Allard Lowenstein, who had worked to the end to draft Ted Kennedy, saw the film, he rushed angrily to a microphone. A bona fide delegate from New York, he tried to move for a recess of the convention. But the chair pointedly ignored him.

A few minutes later Senator Abraham Ribicoff of Connecticut provided the only good TV drama of the proceedings. Taking the podium, he looked straight at Daley, who was seated directly in front of him, and calmly pronounced a condemnation of the "Gestapo tactics on the streets of Chicago." The camera panned on Daley, who reddened and muttered, "You Jew son of a bitch." *

Just before midnight the script came to an end, with Humphrey duly nominated and McCarthy a distant second. After the proceedings closed, Lowenstein told a television interviewer that "This convention elected Richard Nixon president of the United States tonight . . . I never thought it would happen." About 3:00 A.M., some six hundred delegates carrying lighted candles—apparently coaxed by Lowenstein from the storehouse of a Chicago synagogue

---

* The phrase was attributed to Daley by lip-readers, since his words were inaudible. Some maintained that he prefaced them with, "Fuck you." Daley denied saying anything of the kind.

459

—held their own march along Michigan Avenue to the Hilton. It was meant as a kind of requiem for a lost cause.

Jerry Rubin, along with Dave Dellinger, Tom Hayden and Rennie Davis, tried to rouse the crowd in Grant Park to one more march to the Amphitheatre on Thursday, when the Democrats finished the last items on their agenda. But a dozen busloads of demonstrators had already left for home, and more left as the hours passed. The police primed themselves for a final assault, but the spark had died and, on the last afternoon, about two thousand people were content to stand around, listening to speeches and folk songs.

Late in the day, Senator McCarthy crossed over from the Hilton and addressed the crowd as the "government of the people in exile." There were a few small battles in the evening, one between the police and a group led by Abbie Hoffman, another between the National Guard, using tear gas, and a larger group led by Dick Gregory, the black activist and comedian. A huge mass of litter remained to be cleaned up in the parks. But, by Thursday night, the drama of Chicago was over.

The police delivered a single encore during a good-bye party in one of McCarthy's work suites on the fifteenth floor of the Hilton. The McCarthy quarters had served throughout the week as a first aid station for demonstrators. The police claimed, in addition, that objects were thrown at them from its windows. At 5:00 A.M. Friday cops burst in unannounced, maintaining that missiles were again being dropped, and began to beat partygoers. The incident ended quickly, but its gratuitous violence seemed to sum up the week's brutal insanity.

Yet, for all the violence, no one was killed in Chicago, nor was there even a record of a serious injury. According to the official reports, 192 policemen were treated during the week, most of them for bruises from stones or bottles. For the demonstrators the records were much less exact, since only a few were treated at hospitals. Most of those who were hurt went to the temporary facilities manned by mobile medical teams. The Medical Committee for Human Rights, the most active group, reported attending to 425 injured, plus 400 more who were given first aid for Mace or tear gas.

For all the anger at Chicago, there is no record that firearms were ever used, either by police or demonstrators. Obviously the police were instructed not to use their weapons, in spite of the "shoot to kill" orders that Daley issued after the ghetto riots in April. Whatever the reason—publicity or politics or racial discrimination—the police chose to treat the white rioters in the Loop differently from the black rioters on the West Side a few months before. When the results were in it became clear that, compared to earlier civil disorders of the 1960s, Chicago was a rather tenderhearted affair. For all the savagery, both sides had abided by relatively benign rules of conduct.

The police also reported that 668 were arrested during the week. Among them was Jerry Rubin, who was ultimately imprisoned for sixty-six days on the testimony of Bob Pierson, the underground cop. Rubin and the other organizers went home satisfied, however, that they had "radicalized" thousands of McCarthy supporters at Chicago, as well as many thousands more who they were convinced had been won over by what had appeared on television.

What Rubin and Hayden understood less clearly was that they had outraged millions who would no longer look with indifference, much less with favor, on student protest. Events would show that the pendulum swung away from the revolution, perhaps even from the antiwar movement, after Chicago. A shift in public perception of student disorder would, in the remaining years of the decade, serve as the sanction for increasingly tough enforcement of "law and order" in the country. In the long run, Rubin and Hayden would have to face the consequences of Chicago: they had lost, and Daley had won.

The biggest loser at Chicago, however, was Hubert Humphrey, the man who had so publicly craved the presidency. Quintessential liberal of his time, he was skewered by Johnson and lacked the strength to wrench free. If he had been against the war, he was too weak to say it; if he had been against the beatings, he was too weak to stop them. As presidential candidate, one day he criticized the Chicago police, the next he defended the Chicago mayor. In the end, his irresolution defeated him, and discredited liberalism itself.

The denouement of the Chicago drama was the realization of the

461

fears which had haunted many who had sympathized with the Dump Johnson campaign. Not only did the campaign fail to nominate a liberal peace candidate, it elected a conservative war president. The Democrats revealed at Chicago they were so deeply riven that they could not manage their own affairs, much less the nation's. The voters showed they recognized as much by election day and, in January, Richard Nixon entered the White House.

THE
CONCLUSION

XIII
JAMES MELLEN:
The Days of Rage

1969

"When we started saying, after Chicago, that the violent revolution is here and now, it enthralled a lot of people. In many ways, I misunderstood it. One of the things that enthralled them was the opportunity to go out and do something existential, like James Dean. The political effectiveness of an act was less important than the demonstration of one's own character. Obviously, we had struck a meaningful chord by saying that the fighting is going on in the world, and we are part of it, we are fighting, too."

FOR STUDENT RADICALISM, and particularly for SDS, 1969 promised to be a vintage year. Chicago had changed the premises of the radical movement, and many believed that the revolution was at hand. In spite of itself, SDS had emerged as a revolutionary vanguard.

After Chicago, the number of campus chapters of SDS passed three hundred and the figures on membership, though never accurately calculated, reached into the tens of thousands. With its new prosperity, SDS sent dozens of organizers into the field, working in colleges and junior colleges, and even in some high schools. SDS also organized at military bases, welcoming servicemen to SDS coffeehouses, encouraging desertions and resistance to the war.

In the year after Chicago, the country took serious note of what was happening. *Life* and *Newsweek* ran major articles on campus radicalism, focusing on SDS. *Fortune* published a poll showing that opinion on American campuses, especially among student leaders, was much further left than had generally been believed. *Reader's Digest*, in an article entitled "SDS: Engineers of Campus Chaos," expressed a fear that SDS was succeeding in the subversion of American society.

In Washington, Director J. Edgar Hoover of the FBI declared, with some accuracy, that SDS's aim was "to smash first our educational system, then our economic system, then, finally, our government itself," and he instituted a secret program of surveillance of

467

the New Left. The House Un-American Activities Committee sub-poenaed Tom Hayden and Rennie Davis to testify on the role of SDS in Chicago. And when Spiro Agnew, Richard Nixon's running mate, asked an audience of a thousand students at Towson State College in Maryland how many belonged to SDS, two-thirds raised their hands. "I know you'd like to overthrow the government," Agnew responded, "but on November fifth, we'll put a man in office who'll take this country forward without you."

Jim Mellen, a full-time revolutionary, had been among the SDS leaders who opposed massive participation in the protests in Chi-cago. He went to Chicago himself, he said, out of curiosity, to see how young American radicals would conduct themselves under stress. He fought in the streets and was beaten up. Unlike many in SDS, Mellen had no fondness for violence itself, but he considered it occasionally necessary to promote revolution. He had not favored confrontation with the police in Chicago because he believed that radicals, to succeed, had to acquire self-confidence, had to believe the revolution possible, had to feel strong. He had reasoned that, inevitably, the protesters would leave the convention demonstra-tions feeling defeated and demoralized.

"Well, I couldn't have been more wrong," he told me. "What we did there made a lot of people feel *very* strong. Chicago really mobilized them."

Mellen said he learned at Chicago that young people in America were tough enough to withstand the hatred and brutality of the police. He said it was only their courage that transformed Chicago into a significant political event. Chicago convinced him, he said, that the radical movement was ready for revolution.

"I came away from Chicago believing that the young people's movement had crystallized," he said, "and was prepared for a vio-lent assault on the institutions of state power."

The increasingly militant protests of the ensuing academic year seemed to confirm Mellen's assessment. On nearly three hundred campuses, in every part of the country, demonstrations were staged. A third of the nation's college students were said to have been involved. One in five of the protests was accompanied by bombs, fires or destruction of property, one in two by strikes, sit-ins or some other form of institutional disruption.

At San Francisco State, black students sparked a campus-wide strike which lasted more than four months, and led to more than seven hundred arrests, a hundred injuries, a dozen fire bombings and the presence of hundreds of policemen on the campus daily. At Cornell a building was seized by black students brandishing rifles and wearing bandoliers. At Santa Barbara a bomb at the faculty club killed a custodian, and in a burst of gunfire at Berkeley— always Berkeley—the decade's first killing was recorded of a white in a campus demonstration.

Jim Mellen said the first half of 1969 was the most exciting, optimistic period he lived through as a revolutionary. Tom Hayden's prediction that the Democratic national convention would prove to be one of the "weak points" in the political structure seemed to be vindicated. Revolutionaries had only to direct the popular fervor aroused by Chicago into the proper channels, it seemed, and the state would fall.

Mellen said he was convinced that by early 1969, SDS had the strategy, as well as the ideology, it had sought for so long in order to realize its goals. Even spontaneous events seemed to be feeding into SDS's designs.

Then, in midyear, Mellen and his SDS associates established a militant cadre called the Weathermen, which was to take the revolution from the campus to the entire society. In place of the "do-your-own-thing" revolutionaries of the early 1960s, the Weathermen were to be disciplined and tough. In the fall, a year after the Democratic National Convention, they returned to Chicago to take on Mayor Daley's police in a second round. Called the Days of Rage, this was protest no longer, but a calculated revolutionary act. SDS had passed into a new phase, as the Weathermen marched through Chicago in jackboots and helmets, spouting Marxist slogans, carrying clubs and pipes.

The Days of Rage were a fiasco but, by then, the rocket of student revolution was burning out, and in precipitous descent. "I hadn't seen the incipient collapse and internal failure that were developing," Mellen said to me. The year that began with such promise ended in catastrophe. And, when it was over, all but the most hard-bitten dogmatists understood that what had been taken as signs of revolution had always been illusion.

469

James Mellen was born in a suburb of Los Angeles in 1935. Abandoned by his father, he was raised by his mother alone, on her modest income as a drugstore clerk. His home, he said, was without intellectual, much less political, stimulation. After high school, Mellen gravitated into junior college, then to UCLA to study business. He dropped out before graduation and, for the next few years, roamed California's Central Valley selling portrait photography on what he called "rip-off" terms.

Mellen said he did not drop out of school for reasons of ideology, a practice which became fashionable in the mid-1960s, but because he was demoralized by the prospect of a business career. He wandered about in search of himself, he said, and in the small towns where he bedded down he spent hours in the public library, trying to catch up on his education. He came to admire Steinbeck and Hemingway, he said, but the writer who moved him most was Jack Kerouac. As a Kerouac disciple, he became intrigued by San Francisco, and in 1959 he decided to go there to live among the beatniks.

"I had had a very straight childhood," Mellen told me, "and their exhibitionism offended me. I didn't have the quality of existential expression they had, the outraged howling and costumes and beards. Nonetheless, what the beatniks were saying about the hollowness of American life, the deadliness of a career and a house in the suburbs, the need to try and develop a fuller sense of one's person, and the poetry and music that they were into, that all excited me. They were mostly drifters, but I was as alienated as they were and, though I was only half in half out, being part of them gave me a sense of security."

In San Francisco, Mellen became involved in the early stirrings of the student movement. In the spring of 1960 the anti-HUAC demonstration—which aroused Tom Hayden in Ann Arbor and Jerry Rubin in Cincinnati—caught his attention. Indifferent to it at first, Mellen said he became impressed by the strength of the students who implacably faced police batons. Before long he was picketing the HUAC hearings himself.

"My viewpoint was basically liberal then," Mellen said. "My argument against HUAC was that it violated civil liberties and misused the Constitution. Before I became one myself, I favored defeating the Communists, but by coming up with better solutions to problems than theirs, not by oppressing them."

470

Mellen had by then enrolled in San Francisco State for some courses in literature and history. He began reading C. Wright Mills, and slipped easily into the left-wing campus milieu which had spread from Berkeley around San Francisco Bay.

"Before Mills, I hadn't even thought of what an intellectual was," Mellen said. "Then Mills opened me to the idea that the intellectual had an obligation to spread a critique of society, and influence the political process. There was nothing revolutionary about him, especially in his early work, but Mills gave me the idea that the society we lived in was not what they told us it was in the 1950s, and that we had an obligation to do something about it."

At San Francisco State he suddenly became a passionate student, Mellen said. Though he had never considered an academic career, he did so well in his work that professors encouraged him to go to graduate school. Mellen said he took the graduate record exam, did brilliantly, and to his surprise came away with a three-year fellowship to study for a Ph.D. at the University of Iowa.

I found Jim Mellen back in Berkeley, living in a small house not far from where the Free Speech Movement had triggered the radical student movement many years before. Solidly built, he was making a living as a carpenter, specializing in solar heating systems. His odyssey had brought him to the gates of revolution and back, but in Mellen there still beat a radical's heart. He answered my questions neither pompously nor apologetically, but with the patience of a caring professor.

His transformation had taken place in Iowa City, a pretty dull place, Mellen said, except for a few Marxists around the university who had exciting ideas. He began by studying with them, he recalled, and then joined the Socialist Discussion Club, which he helped turn from discussion to activism. He led picketing at Woolworth's in support of the sit-ins, a campus-wide protest of Kennedy's position in the Cuban missile crisis and a demonstration against racism within the university. Such activism created a sensation on the campus, Mellen remembered, though it was all very tame compared with what was to come later.

Meanwhile, he had acquired an interest in the underdeveloped world, and particularly in the Cuban revolution. He admired Castro and Ché Guevara, he said, and followed closely their step-by-step conversion of Cuba into a socialist state. By the time he finished at

471

Iowa in 1964, Mellen said, Fidel and Ché were fully committed Marxists, and so was he.

"The notions I developed then, which are with me today," Mellen said, "is that the masses of workers in the advanced industrial countries are held in thrall by better living conditions, and by bureaucratic institutions which are supposed to represent their interests. So they continue to find themselves fighting for special privileges for themselves, and uniting with the imperialists to keep the rest of the world in its place.

"In sixty-five, Lin Piao wrote his famous article analyzing the Chinese revolution,* making a worldwide analogy with the Chinese experience. He said that in China the revolutionaries first had to control the countryside, to isolate and then cut off the cities. He argued that the Third World was like the countryside, and the revolution would spread like wildfire, and that the imperialist centers were like the cities, and would be the last to fall.

"When I read that, I realized that this was the way I had been thinking all along. Revolution to me then was the Cuban revolution, the African revolutions, the Chinese revolution. That was it, Third World revolutions. Even then I thought, God, we Americans may be the last holdout. We may be the fascist center with all the rest of the world liberated. But I never thought then there was a prospect of organizing our own people."

After he finished at Iowa, Mellen moved to New York and took a job teaching foreign affairs at Drew, a small college in nearby Morristown, New Jersey. He also became involved with the Progressive Labor party, a group of some six hundred pro-Chinese Marxists who had left the Communist party at the time of the Sino-Soviet split in 1960. Known as PLP and, later, just PL, it had sponsored the extralegal tours that many young radicals, including Jerry Rubin, took to Cuba in 1963 and 1964. Mellen never joined PL, and later became its bitter enemy. But, sympathetic to its Maoist bent, he worked closely with its members. It was his first experience with organized Communism.

"I had difficulties with the Communists, much as I was opposed

* The article in English was called "Long Live the Victory of the People's War," published by the New China News Agency, September 3, 1965.

to ideological anti-Communism," he said. "I considered myself more Marxist than they, and longed for a movement with more revolutionary thinking. But, mostly, I couldn't see myself in a tightly organized, highly disciplined organization like theirs. PLP was run by so-called 'democratic centralist' leadership and, when my friends tried to recruit me, I realized I was offended by its Stalinism, its elitism and its manipulation."

Instead, Mellen joined the May 2nd Movement, a front formed by PLP in 1964 to agitate on campuses against the Vietnam War. Mellen favored M-2-M* over PL itself, because of its looser organization. M-2-M, furthermore, provided campus support for Cuba as well as China and, he said, "we saw our job as building a base among students for a Third World revolution here in the United States." Mellen gave talks for M-2-M at colleges around New York, and performed such other chores as stuffing envelopes and handing out leaflets on street corners.

In the spring of 1965 Mellen, along with some friends from PL and M-2-M, founded the Free University of New York. The idea grew out of SNCC's "freedom schools," which the Free Speech Movement in Berkeley had adapted the previous fall to a university setting. Students had begun talking by then not just of reformed but of *new* universities to explore the questions neglected on other campuses. The counterculture had combined with radicalism to persuade students that, having created an "alternative life-style," they needed their own unique institutions too. The underground press, one of them, was already thriving. SDS assisted local chapters in establishing free universities, and both the Communist party and Progressive Labor encouraged members to get involved. By the fall there were free universities in Berkeley, Chicago and Gainesville, Florida. The Free University of New York, of which Mellen was secretary-treasurer, opened in Greenwich Village with eight hundred students and fifty teachers, all unpaid.

In its catalog for 1965, FUNY listed such courses—at a tuition of $8 each—as Marxist Geography, Life in Mainland China Today, Poetry and Revolution, and Art and Communism. Mellen also remembered courses in "radical Egyptology and sex and other funny things." He himself taught Imperialism in Latin America and The

---

* As the movement grew older, it grew increasingly fond of jargon such as this.

473

Instruments of Imperialism, in which he said he analyzed such questions as the interconnections between the State Department and the big corporations.

"It was a serious intellectual undertaking in many ways, and people learned a lot," Mellen remembered. "But it was also a three-ring circus with all kinds of things going on, movies being shown, speakers making speeches, places to sign your name to petitions, places to organize a demonstration, and also crazy things like hippies coming to play rock music.

"At the time I was mainly interested in classical music, and they were telling me that I ought to be serious about the Beatles and Bob Dylan and the Rolling Stones, and that rock music was politically redemptive. I had a hard time believing it."

That fall, the free universities were news, and major publications like *Life* and *The New York Times* came to Mellen for interviews. The publicity, he said, brought him an invitation to speak at a teach-in at Rutgers, where Professor Eugene Genovese, a highly regarded historian, had gone on record in April as saying, "I am a Marxist and a Socialist, [and . . .] I do not fear or regret the impending Viet Cong victory in Vietnam. I welcome it." Since Rutgers is the state university, conservatives responded by demanding Genovese's dismissal and, in the gubernatorial campaign that summer, his fate became the central issue. Mellen stepped into the controversy by declaring at the teach-in that every professor in New Jersey should repeat Genovese's statement, and thereby signify a willingness to share his fate.

"It was an all-night teach-in, and I didn't speak until six A.M.," he recollected with some bemusement. "An AP stringer was there, and he slept most of the night. But he woke up while I was talking and wrote down what I said. When I got home about seven o'clock, my phone was ringing off the hook, and every newspaper and radio station in the region was calling me up. I guess I was naive, but I didn't think anyone cared what I said.

"Well, it just caused a furor. The local newspaper in Morristown ran big pictures of me across the front page, headlined 'Red Professor at Drew.' The college came under terrible pressure. I was charged with staging the whole thing but, in fact, I blundered into it. I think Drew tried to keep from having to cave in and can me but big contributions were involved. So, of course, they fired me."

For a while, Mellen said, he enjoyed his role as the "fired professor." *The New York Times* wrote an editorial in his support, and the American Civil Liberties Union demanded his reinstatement. William Kunstler, the famous civil rights lawyer, offered to represent him in court. Campuses everywhere summoned him to make speeches. He became something of a hero to those he esteemed most, Mellen said, the antiwar activists.

Then the speaking invitations stopped coming, and by early 1966 frustration set in. He got to work finishing his doctoral dissertation and began looking for a job. But no college wanted a troublemaking radical instructor with a Midwestern Ph.D. About that time, the Free University began to disintegrate, with PL complaining the program was not serious enough, and students dropping out, and money running short. Though he continued to teach there, his involvement waned. Finally, Mellen remembered, he broke up with a woman he had been living with, which left him more despondent than ever.

Then, in February 1966, Progressive Labor decided to disband the May 2nd Movement. M-2-M had done its job in conveying an "anti-imperialist perspective" to the student movement, PL said, particularly to SDS. In reality PL, without explicitly repudiating its allegiance to Chinese Communism, was reasserting the strategic priority of Marxist orthodoxy, which exalted proletarian revolution. To outsiders the distinction may have seemed like doctrinal hairsplitting, but to Marxists the debate was deadly serious.

PL also objected to M-2-M's increasing identification with the New Left, and its life-style of blue jeans and drugs, long hair and sexual freedom. PL's position, expressed sternly during the quarrels at the Free University, was that revolutionaries had to blend in with the proletariat and reject offensive life-styles that would conflict with their mission.

Jim Mellen, as well as most other M-2-M people, did not like PL's decision, which challenged both the way they lived and the way they thought about revolution. PL, in spite of its Maoist label, was Old Left and orthodox. M-2-M, despite its Marxist zealotry, was New Left and unorthodox. Mellen fought PL at M-2-M meetings, as he would fight it later in SDS. But, not being a member, he had little influence. In retrospect, it is apparent that in the M-2-M radicals lay the germs of the Weathermen, he said, and that the break forecast the savage struggle between PL and the Weathermen which three years later devastated SDS.

In fact, the PL leadership decided it had more to gain by enrolling its members in SDS than in perpetuating M-2-M as a front organization. M-2-M had only a few hundred members; SDS had thousands. PL had an established ideology; SDS was still in search of one. The PL leadership reasoned that within SDS were many young radicals who were tired of the search, and would willingly adopt its rigorous, disciplined brand of Marxism. To Progressive Labor, SDS looked like a succulent target for expanding its influence as a revolutionary instrument. In early 1966, PL moved in on SDS, bidding ultimately to take over.

Jim Mellen, at this point, did not take SDS seriously. Much as he objected to PL's Stalinism, he had no sympathy for SDS's participatory democracy, which he considered too soft to sustain a revolution. He found SDS's structure flabby and its tolerant spirit too liberal.

But SDS was proud of its loose organization, its nonauthoritarian style of leadership, its "nonexclusionism" that welcomed anyone into its ranks. SDS never gave serious thought to keeping PL people out, either at the national or the chapter level. So when PL's infiltration began in 1966 SDS had no defense against it.

Meanwhile, Jim Mellen was without a job, a girl or an organizational attachment. So he sent an inquiry to Conor Cruise O'Brien, the Irish writer and diplomat, who had been involved briefly with the Free University and had become vice-chancellor of the University of Ghana. O'Brien forwarded his inquiry to a professor at the University of Dar es Salaam in Tanzania. Shortly afterward, the professor came to New York, interviewed Mellen and offered him a four-year teaching contract. In the fall of 1966 Mellen, astonished by his good luck, set off for Africa.

Mellen said he wound up with two teaching posts, one at the university, where he helped groom the ruling elite, the other at a civil service academy, set up to train agricultural extension workers, water commissioners, community development officers and the like. He was uncomfortable at the university, he said, with its British-style colonial structure. But at the academy, he said, "these

476

were guys trying to develop a socialist policy in a very backward country. They were ready to hear about the political ideas of the Chinese revolution." It was, he said, one of the most rewarding teaching jobs he ever had.

"I also learned a lot about Africa, and about Third World revolution," Mellen told me. "I arrived thinking that a person from the metropolis with some special skills could be a help. After a while, I began to see that it's very difficult for white people to give much assistance to African revolution. Consciousness of one's blackness, of the need for black people to unite, is essential to revolutionary development. In many ways, the medium is the message. You try to teach people a black self-reliance, and you're white. That's a serious contradiction, and I found it discouraging."

As his sense of usefulness in Tanzania diminished, Mellen said, he became aware from cascading news reports of the new dynamism of the antiwar movement at home. He understood that much of it was the product of student concern about the draft, and adult worries about economic and social instability. But part, he calculated, had to come from a recognition by Americans that the United States had no business meddling in Third World revolutions, including Vietnam. That was a big change, Mellen said, so he decided to return home after finishing half of his four-year contract, to devote full-time to promoting Third World revolution in America.

"In Africa," Mellen said, "I sensed a massive mobilization of opinion against the United States. It gave me a feeling I didn't have when I was a tiny minority at home, within a monolithic political system. It gave me strength and heart and courage. Everyone, meanwhile, was reading the papers and asking, 'What's happening in the United States?' When I arrived back, I felt like a spokesman for a massively expressed point of view from around the world."

Mellen landed on April 4, 1968, the day of Martin Luther King's assassination. In the ghetto riots of the succeeding days, the image he saw was of America's Third World colonies rising up. The next week he went to Washington to tour the smoldering streets, which he perceived as a revolutionary battlefield.

Later in April, Mellen joined the student uprising at Columbia. He was encouraged that SDS had triggered the protest not over

477

student gripes but over the university's treatment of the black community in nearby Harlem. He saw an eloquent and aggressive new leader named Mark Rudd. Columbia students had an anti-imperialist perspective and a zest for militant self-defense, Mellen observed, which he took as the first signs of real revolution.

"It was like 1905, the beginning of the end," he said. "But it was still only blacks and the students, who were upper-middle-class types. What had to be done was to make a bridge to the rest of the population. That's the question I put my mind to, how do we spread beyond this?"

Mellen then bought a car with money he had saved in Africa, acquired names from his radical friends in New York, and set out to cover America. He felt a need to make up for two years of absence from the political scene, he said. He drove from town to town, looking up people whom he could visit, and in a few months he'd had two hundred or more long conversations on the prospects for revolutionary action.

"When it was over," he told me, "I said I think SDS is where it's at. Before I left for Africa I had argued that SDS would never become a revolutionary organization. But when I got back, SDS had changed. It was nothing like sixty-five and sixty-six. I saw pockets in SDS all over the country, like at Columbia, with a very radical analysis.

"SDS was open to new ideas, and new radicals were being created by the dozens every day. Some of my M-2-M friends were already working in SDS, and others looked into it because I was going around saying SDS is where it's at. I argued that SDS could be transformed into a revolutionary organization. I decided the thing for me to do was to get into the center of it."

Mellen had no trouble recognizing that the center was in the campus chapters, not the national headquarters in Chicago. He called the national officers "know-nothings," who gave pep talks to the chapters and arranged conferences, but conveyed no sense of purpose. Yet, as the campuses became increasingly radical, a recognition grew within SDS that it could not become a revolutionary organization without some central ideological commitment, equal to its chapters' penchant for action.

The "Port Huron Statement," SDS's first tentative step into radicalism, long since seemed outdated as a revolutionary document.

478

Several times over the years, SDS thinkers presented other papers for discussion, but from them no New Left ideology emerged. For years student militants had argued that action was the first priority, and that ideology would somehow develop out of it. But now SDS had a following that seemed on the verge of making revolution, and the time for an ideology was growing short.

Marxism, of course, offered a ready-made program. For most of the decade, SDS people had sneered at it, as being Old Left. Now, having found nothing better, many were going back for another look. But Marxism presented some problems, not the least of which, in the SDS context, was that there existed two bitterly competing forms, and two bitterly competing factions.

Progressive Labor, though it began as pro-Chinese in the Sino-Soviet struggle, had turned sharply back to Old Left orthodoxy. By a peculiarly Bolshevik intellectual process, PL managed to promote a Soviet-style proletarian revolution, along with a rigorous Stalinism, without ever renouncing its allegiance to Mao. Whatever the ideological paradox, PL was getting recruits, largely among young students who seemed to find comfort in strong authority. PL had built strongholds in university communities in Boston, Chicago and New York, and had tough and united caucuses in major SDS chapters throughout the country. PL regarded the Third World Marxism professed by Mellen and his friends as an unconscionable heresy.

Mellen's Third World faction was much more loosely organized than PL. Third World Marxism, in the values it shared with the civil rights movement, as well as in its rejection of authoritarianism, was much closer than PL to SDS's historical traditions. It was an adaptation of Marxism that seemed to correspond to the world of the 1960s, and it was congenial to the overall New Left outlook. A majority of SDS certainly favored Mellen's over PL's brand of Marxism, but in factional rivalry, Progressive Labor's discipline gave it an important tactical advantage.

Jim Mellen finished his cross-country tour in Ann Arbor, Michigan, convinced his task was to commit SDS to Third World Marxism. In Ann Arbor, he found a small SDS unit called the Radical Education Project, which had been established as a kind of think tank for New Left ideas. Over the years it had produced many papers, and few ideas. Mellen said that when he arrived one of the old hands lamented that the Project was going downhill, because the Marxists were taking over. He promptly moved in, Mellen noted with a smile, and helped the Marxists finish the job.

Over the next year, Mellen covered Midwestern campuses, sponsored either by the Radical Education Project or by SDS itself, talking about Cuba, China, the uprising at Columbia, Africa, American imperialism. Besides lectures, he led debates and seminars, and showed films, usually to SDS chapters, sometimes to larger audiences. He made useful contacts, he said, and may even have converted a few students to his Third World analysis.

Mellen also worked to put together a group of "radical anti-imperialists," which was another name for the Third World Marxists, to take over the national office. One of his allies was Mark Rudd, who had led the uprising at Columbia. Another was Bernardine Dohrn, a twenty-five-year-old graduate of the University of Chicago Law School, who had started at Columbia as a lawyer for the demonstrators and ended up on the barricades. Brilliant, eloquent and pretty, she would become the most celebrated member of the Weathermen and, ultimately, a legend in the annals of student radicalism.

At the SDS national convention in June 1968, Mellen's group succeeded in electing Dohrn interorganizational secretary, one of SDS's three national offices. "I consider myself a revolutionary Communist," she announced solemnly after her election. *The New York Times* duly reported her comment, which no doubt shocked most of its readership. Dohrn brought two other anti-imperialists, Gerry Long and John Jacobs, to Chicago to work with her. These three became the "central nexus for our ideas," Mellen said. They aimed to make the national office, for the first time, into a powerful instrument of SDS policy.

Though he had opposed SDS sponsorship of the Chicago protests in August, Mellen was quick to admit that he had been mistaken. He acknowledged that, without Jerry Rubin and the Yippies, there would probably have been no confrontation. Even though the triumph did not truly belong to SDS, he said, the end result was transmission of a message of hope to friends of Third World revolution, both in America and abroad.

But on the streets of Chicago, Jim Mellen encountered a problem, which would ultimately compel him to leave SDS. The problem was that he did not like to fight. Mellen was thirty-three years old in 1968, among a band of men and women in their early twenties. He was an intellectual, and a theoretician of revolution, at a time when the others hungered less for thought than action. Though badly beaten by young thugs who singled him out for his long hair, he had engaged in little of the street fighting in Chicago. His reticence contrasted with the exultation felt by so many of the others at hand-to-hand combat with the police, and with the growing insistence within SDS that the measure of a revolutionary was physical courage. Mellen said he understood fighting for a revolutionary goal, but not for the love of fighting.

"When we started saying, after Chicago, that the violent revolution is here and now," Mellen remembered, "it enthralled a lot of people. In many ways, I misunderstood it. One of the things that enthralled them was the opportunity to go out and do something existential, like James Dean. The political effectiveness of an act was less important than the demonstration of one's own character. Obviously, we had struck a meaningful chord by saying that the fighting is going on in the world, and we are part of it, we are fighting, too."

Mellen said the sudden zest for fighting appeared chiefly among the children of upper-middle-class families, who felt alienated, unreal and manipulated, and whose only encounter in the home environment with work was as an intellectual activity. The attitude Mellen perceived was no doubt also a product of the counterculture, which defined revolution as an act of internal purification, the proof of which had become a black eye or bloody nose. His own upbringing, Mellen said, was lower-middle-class, an environment which had plenty of physical reality and few ideas. He said he never felt the need of violence to prove his courage or his worth.

"I was better prepared intellectually than physically for violent revolution," Mellen said. "I sometimes wish I had done a better job in the violence we participated in, at least to hold up my end. Chicago was a learning experience for me, where I experimented to see how close I could get to the violence without finking out. But I had too much fear that if I bashed a cop I might not hit him well enough and he'd turn around and hit me back.

"Besides that, I was all the time trying to figure out what we could do that was effective, and I certainly didn't include getting my head bloodied or spending a lot of time in jail. That turned out

481

to be a real difference between me and some of the other leaders in the Weathermen. How many stitches you had, and how many felony indictments, became a badge of value. It's true that people kept saying, 'Why wasn't he ever arrested?' and 'Why wasn't he ever beaten up?' I know why. Because I tried *not* to get arrested, and I tried *not* to get bashed. I would run the other way."

When Mellen returned from the Chicago protests to Ann Arbor in September 1968, he met Bill Ayers and Diana Oughton. In their mid-twenties, both attractive and from wealthy families, they lived together and worked as teachers in a progressive school. Marginally associated with SDS for a few years, they had lined up with the radical anti-imperialists and fought on the streets of Chicago in August. After their first encounter, the three agreed to join forces to take over the SDS chapter at Michigan. The objective of Mellen, Oughton and Ayers was to make it into a regional headquarters for the promotion of Third World Marxism.

SDS history at Michigan went back to Tom Hayden and Al Haber and, through thick and thin, the chapter had been a cornerstone of the organization. But SDS at Michigan was not action-oriented. It deemphasized demonstrations in favor of an educational program to develop a broad radical base. The Mellen-Ayers-Oughton faction, arguing that this strategy had patently failed, disrupted meetings for several weeks in succession and, very quickly, reduced the chapter to paralysis. Without much of a fight, the regulars withdrew, leaving the intruders in command.

Mellen now had the campus base he wanted. The Third Worlders, in addition, had a foot in the national office in Chicago through Bernardine Dohrn, and controlled the New York region through the power of Mark Rudd in the Columbia chapter. Mellen could now talk accurately of a "radical anti-imperialist axis" within SDS.

If Mellen wanted his "radical anti-imperialist axis" to transform SDS into an instrument of revolution, however, he had first to win it away from his rivals, Progressive Labor. Since Chicago, the struggle between the two had become more acerbic. No one talked any longer of reconciling the concepts of Third World and proletarian revolution. The difference, once abstract, now extended into the life beat of the movement.

Whatever Jim Mellen's personal reservations, the Third World-ers argued for student street action. They said it would weaken the rear of the industrial powers in the anti-imperialist struggle. PL objected to street action, contending that it was the play of spoiled kids, and would generate counterrevolution among the workers. The Third Worlders saw racism as the core of the revolution, and the white industrial proletariat as the worst offenders. PL dis-missed racism as a diversion from the class struggle, and saw class struggle as the only permissible definition of revolution.

"They accused us of being against the workers," Mellen said. "It's true that I didn't feel under much obligation to support Amer-ican white workers who wanted to make fifteen times, instead of twelve times, as much as other workers of the world. But I never felt we were against the workers.

"The thing is, the white working class was not feeling like a revolution, and there *was* a youth rebellion going on, and we were trying to direct it into socialism. They said the industrial workers would build socialism, but the PL people weren't the children of industrial workers. They didn't even know any industrial workers. They continued in their hollow insistence on the dictatorship of the proletariat, when no proletariat supported them. I could under-stand their sense of moral righteousness, but I could never under-stand their patent unreality."

PL and the Third Worlders even disagreed on the Vietnam War, which had become the very heart of the revolution. PL was cool to the cause of North Vietnam, which it saw as a tool of Soviet "revi-sionism." The Third Worlders exalted North Vietnam, considered it the revolutionary vanguard, and praised its struggle as the spear-head of a worldwide anticapitalist uprising.

Mellen's faction felt strong enough to challenge Progressive Labor directly at a national SDS meeting in December 1968. The challenge was presented in the form of a policy paper called "To-ward a Revolutionary Youth Movement"—nicknamed RYM, pro-nounced "rim." Written in an arcane Marxist language which the Port Huron framers would have laughed at, the paper was virtually incomprehensible to outsiders, but the initiated could decipher it as an endorsement of Third World strategy. When a majority voted to support it, Mellen and his people claimed a big victory.

Nonetheless, the factional competition intensified. On the cam-

483

puses, both sides played rough, stacking meetings, stuffing ballot boxes, tearing up each other's literature to win allegiance of the chapters. Off the campuses, the Third Worlders went to high schools, to coax adolescent rebels into anti-imperialist socialism. Arguing that antiauthoritarianism was counterrevolutionary, PL people instead went to factories, to organize alliances between workers and students. Each side heaped the other with calumny, "antiworker" being the favorite oath of the one, "antiblack" the favorite of the other.

Mellen told me, barely controlling his anger, that PL even circulated a rumor that he was a CIA agent. Though his friends dismissed it, the cloud of doubt was never fully dissipated. He said he learned, some years later, that some PL friends of M-2-M days had started the rumor, knowing it to be false. But to charge a revolutionary with being an enemy agent was the foulest of blows, and an index of how seriously both sides took the struggle over SDS.

"But whatever the ideology, I think why we were at each other's throats," Mellen said, "had to do with the nature of Marxist-Leninist organizations. We were afraid of them because they were so tightly disciplined. They thought Lenin said that you had to get an organization and control it absolutely from the top, and never allow in a new idea, and always condemn anybody who disagrees with you as an enemy of the revolution. I think I know what Lenin is about, too, and I don't think they bore any resemblance to Lenin. They could have gone their way and we could have gone ours. Sure, we didn't want them to take over. But it wasn't necessary for us to kill SDS in the process."

The irony was that Mellen's people reacted to PL by copying it. Forgotten were the days of the "Port Huron Statement," when SDS said, "We have no sure formulas, no closed theories." The good-natured, easygoing ways of early SDS might inevitably have disappeared anyway, with the gravitation to violence, the spread of Marxism, the repression of the state. Nonetheless, a feeling of civil war within SDS hastened the demise. In girding for a showdown, Mellen's people adopted concepts, once so alien to SDS, of cadre, discipline, austerity, security. In response to the struggle, PL's adversaries transformed themselves into its mirror image.

484

During the first half of 1969, Mellen and his ten or eleven closest companions knitted themselves into a leadership cadre which in due course became the Weathermen. Bernardine Dohrn was among them, along with Bill Ayers and Mark Rudd. They traveled a great deal, to influence campus militants to adopt their brand of politics. By midyear, Mellen said, they had built a following of some six hundred or seven hundred activists.

The leadership cadre established major units at Ann Arbor and East Lansing in Michigan, Mellen said, and at Columbia in New York. Though efforts to organize the West Coast failed, reliable groups were founded in Chicago and New England. They also formed a sizable unit at Kent State in Ohio, a fact which would be of dramatic importance before the curtain came down on the 1960s.

Mellen recalled that he met with the others every week or so, at some point central to them all, for intense analysis of their work. Increasingly, they felt themselves besieged by the government. They were alarmed by warnings from Nixon, FBI Director Hoover and Attorney General John Mitchell. They were shaken by the federal indictments against eight leaders of the 1968 Chicago demonstrations.* They knew they were sometimes followed, and that their phones were tapped. They chose their meeting places more for security than for convenience. The intimidation, Mellen said, gave them a feeling of solidarity, drew them closer together and elicited in them a new conspiratorial view of their work.

"As I look back on it, I think it's amazing that we were never really suspicious of each other," Mellen said. In the collective houses where campus militants now often lived, he said, there might be doubts about someone who had recently wandered in off the street, but the confidence within the top two hundred or so Third Worlders, and especially within the dozen of the leadership cadre, was complete. "Even with the rumor that PL was spreading," Mellen said, "no one ever said a single word about my being

* The "Chicago Eight" were Jerry Rubin and Abbie Hoffman of the Yippies, Dave Dellinger, Tom Hayden and Rennie Davis of the Mobilization, Bobby Seale of the Black Panthers, and two lesser known activists, John Froines and Lee Weiner. After the trial began in October 1969, Seale's case was severed from that of the others, and the defendants became known as the "Chicago Seven." They were acquitted of the major charge of conspiracy, but Rubin, Hoffman, Dellinger, Hayden and Davis were convicted on a lesser count. All the convictions, however, were overturned on appeal in 1972, on the grounds of legal error.

485

an agent. Even now they might call me a bastard, but no one would ever say, 'You turned us in.' "

Mellen took time off in the spring of 1969 to collaborate with Bill Ayers on a paper designed, in part, to answer PL's charges that Third Worlders were antilabor. They tried meeting PL halfway by proposing transformation of SDS "from a student movement to a working-class youth movement," and they offered a plan for an SDS summer program to organize city youth. But they also argued that the movement for "black liberation"—once called "civil rights"—remained the true path to understanding imperialism, class oppression and the "need for armed struggle as the only road to revolution."

For some time, the Third World faction had been seeking to reestablish SDS's ties with black radicals, severed by SNCC after its move to Black Power. Mellen reasoned that the Third Worlders needed such ties to legitimize their anti-imperialist posture. Over PL's objection, they courted the Black Panther party, which the Third Worlders now took to be the vanguard of revolution in America.

Founded three years before in Oakland, the Panthers were revolutionary black nationalists who openly, even belligerently, carried arms. In May 1967, thirty of them brandished rifles on the steps of the state capitol at Sacramento, an act for which Bobby Seale, one of the Panther founders, was jailed for six months. A few months later Huey P. Newton, Seale's cofounder, was imprisoned after a fatal shoot-out with the Oakland police, and "Free Huey" became a rallying cry of radicals around the country. In 1968, the Panthers took the lead in the tumultuous student strike in San Francisco State, which many considered Third World in character. Clad in black leather jackets and berets, the Panthers cultivated the symbolism of violence, which Mellen's faction much admired.

For the Panthers, no less than for SDS, the alliance presented internal problems. Stokely Carmichael and Jim Forman had become Panthers after SNCC disintegrated, but both quit the party when the leadership insisted over their objections upon making common cause with SDS whites.

In March of 1969, Jim Mellen persuaded SDS to endorse the Panther alliance, over complaints by the PL faction that it would threaten working-class solidarity. When the alliance was sealed anyway, Mellen said he became convinced the road to revolution was wide open. He did not acknowledge that what was more probable was a schism within SDS.

That was the moment Mellen remembered feeling most exuberant. He even looked forward to running for the SDS national leadership. Then, suddenly, the deep-seated misgivings he felt over the course his radical anti-imperialist faction was taking began to emerge. His optimism vanished, and he acquired a burdensome feeling of self-doubt. Within a few weeks his status had changed, and by the time of the crucial SDS convention in June, Mellen had surrendered the leadership of the Third Worlders to others in his group.

"I was moody with them a lot," Mellen told me. "Under situations of stress, I sometimes get heavy-handed and a couple of times during this period, like when they attacked things I had written, I got angry. A lot of it was unconscious to me at first, but now I think I understand why. They were moving in another direction. They wanted me to take much more extreme positions than I could go along with. I didn't think they were wise, and our differences got worse as time went on."

SDS met for the most momentous of its annual conventions in Chicago's gloomy Coliseum on June 18, 1969. It took hours for the security check, as the staff scrutinized credentials to exclude cops, and frisked bodies to keep out weapons, tape recorders, cameras and dope. Inside, the delegates found a stuffy auditorium crowded with display tables, from which SDS factions, along with Yippies, anarchists, Wobblies and assorted Socialists hawked their respective ideologies.

Of the fifteen hundred delegates, PL had the allegiance of about a third, the Third Worlders of somewhat more. Several hundred delegates were unaffiliated, but a third faction under Mike Klonsky, a twenty-five-year-old Californian who was the SDS national secretary, probably held the balance. Ideologically, Klonsky's people had a little of the proletariat and a little of the Third World in them, and they were on speaking terms with both camps. But they objected to PL's Stalinist style of leadership, and in a showdown would probably have sided with the Third Worlders.

487

The Third Worlders had once again prepared a paper, which they circulated among the delegates. It was a sixteen-thousand-word restatement of their position, with little except tone to distinguish it from earlier documents. Mellen, who had made only a small contribution to it, said he was troubled by its defiant rhetoric. It was entitled, "You Don't Need a Weatherman to Know Which Way the Wind Blows," a line from a Bob Dylan song. The title was an inside joke, meant to offend PL, which disapproved of rock music as part of the counterculture. It would also give a new name to the Third Worlders in SDS. They would henceforth be known as the Weathermen.*

The convention proceedings got off to a contentious start, and then degenerated into Marxist burlesque. PL moved to exclude the "capitalist press," a move which carried by a three-to-two margin. The PL people then won two more minor procedural motions, which was less a measure of its power than its organization. The Third Worlders counterattacked. Whipping out copies of Mao's little red book, fifty of them arose and, mocking PL, began to chant, "Mao, Mao, Mao Tse-tung, Dare to Struggle, Dare to Win." Another inside joke, but it signaled that the battle was joined.

If the convention's first session was bewildering, the second was lunatic. Dominating the agenda, the Third Worlders presented Rufus ("Chaka") Walls, Minister of Information of the Illinois Black Panther party. Walls sneered at PL as "armchair Marxists" who claimed to be the vanguard of the revolution but had not yet shot rubber bands. The Third Worlders were delighted with his performance.

Then Walls, without prior hint, digressed onto the subject of women's liberation. For a year or so, women's liberation had been an increasingly sensitive issue within SDS. PL scoffed at it as being, like racism, a diversion from the class struggle, while the Third Worlders were generally sympathetic. As the delegates listened with disbelief, Walls declared, "We believe in freedom of

---

* The original Weathermen are generally thought of as the eleven, most of them from Mellen's original Third World group, whose names were attached to the paper. In addition to Mellen himself, they were Bernardine Dohrn, Bill Ayers and Mark Rudd, the best known, John Jacobs and Gerry Long, who worked with Dohrn at the national office, Terry Robbins, who worked with Mellen and Ayers at Ann Arbor, and Jeff Jones, Karen Ashley, Howard Machtinger and Steve Tappis. Jacobs, once of PL himself, had done the major drafting.

love. We believe in pussy power." Seizing the initiative, some PL leaders shouted, "Fight male chauvinism," and the PL ranks repeated the chorus, filling the auditorium with their chant. Obviously upset, Walls retorted angrily over the din, "Superman was a punk because he never tried to fuck Lois Lane." That was signal enough, and from every corner of the hall came the cry, "Fight male chauvinism. Fight male chauvinism." The Third World leadership reeled in disarray.

For the next twenty-four hours, the Third Worlders and PL danced wrathfully around each other on the convention floor, exchanging accusations and resolutions. Then late in the Friday night session, June 20, a Panther delegation appeared at the front door. "We had security guards everywhere but the Panthers wouldn't submit to a search," Mellen recalled. "Our guards were confused, because we were supposed to be simpatico with them. But they just knocked our guards out of the way and busted through." Under the circumstances, the convention agreed to give the Panthers the floor.

The Panther delegation came not to apologize but to attack. Its spokesman declared that if the SDS–Panther alliance was to be preserved, the convention would have to expel Progressive Labor. Mellen was sitting backstage with Mike Klonsky during the Panther presentation, and he recognized at once that the Panther demands corresponded precisely with the objective of Bernardine Dohrn and the Weatherman firebrands. In fact, some SDS people suspected that Dohrn had cooked up the whole scenario with the Panthers.

"As soon as this Panther finished," Mellen recalled, "I heard Mark Rudd get up and say, 'Right! We should do it. Let's split the organization right now. All those who want to expel PL should move to the next room.'

"I didn't want to split the organization. A lot of PL's people were only recently recruited and could easily have been won over to us if we tried. A lot were middling between PL's politics and ours, and a lot didn't know which side they were on. I didn't want to lose them. I didn't want PL to control SDS, but I thought it would be suicidal to split.

"I grabbed Klonsky and I said, 'Is this what you want?' and he said, 'No!' And I grabbed a couple of other people and I said, 'What are we going to do?' We tried to figure out how to get up on the stage and stop the movement to split. And then I looked around and all our people had started out the door."

Within the Coliseum, adjacent to the auditorium, was an old sports arena, which was where the Weathermen headed. Mellen said that, at this point, he performed his responsibilities as head of the Michigan-Ohio delegation, and scurried about getting people to join the walkout. According to estimates, somewhat less than half the delegates made the journey next door.

Inside the Weatherman caucus, Mellen said, he grabbed a megaphone and made a speech pleading against the split, but he was greeted with silence. The cheers, he said, went to those who called for PL's expulsion. Well past midnight, after several hours of talk, the caucus broke up. Most of the delegates went back to where they were staying, Mellen said, while he and the rest of the leadership made the rounds, trying to persuade the uncommitted to their respective points of view.

"At about three in the morning, we had a Weatherbureau meeting," Mellen recalled. The leadership group naturally called itself the Weatherbureau, savoring the double pun, one alluding to meteorology, the second to the *politbureau* of Communist party fame. "I was completely overwhelmed there. Not a person in the group wanted to keep the organization together except me. The meeting lasted until ten in the morning, when we had to go back to the caucus again."

Though the Weathermen deliberated all day, the result was foreordained. About six in the evening, Bernardine Dohrn, dressed in scruffy jeans and a faded men's shirt, delivered the climactic speech. "I didn't agree with her," Mellen remarked, "but it was a brilliant speech, and it really galvanized people." Dohrn declared that SDS had a tradition spawned by black student sit-ins in the South and energized by the guerrillas of Vietnam and Cuba. PL's old-fashioned Marxist ideology violated that tradition, she declared, and had to be stamped out. Concluding her advocacy of division, she delivered the line which became famous in radical annals. "We are not a caucus," she declared. "We are SDS."

Near midnight, Bernardine Dohrn led her followers back into the auditorium. While the Weatherman leaders stood belligerently at her side, she shouted from the platform that PL had been expelled

490

because it was racist, anti-Communist and reactionary. "Shame! Shame! Shame!" the PL people shouted back at her on cue.

Dohrn then stormed out of the room, followed by a column of some eight hundred sympathizers chanting, "Ho, Ho, Ho Chi Minh, Dare to Struggle, Dare to Win." PL's partisans shouted back with slogans invoking Mao Tse-tung, their own hero in the SDS pantheon. For a moment the arena seemed poised at the edge of a free-for-all, but both sides drew away from fisticuffs. When Dohrn and the Weatherman contingent had departed, Progressive Labor had possession of the battlefield, leaving unsettled the question of which faction had been expelled. The Weathermen, however, had the keys to the office, the mailing lists and all the records. Insisting they were the *real* SDS, the Weathermen were now on their own.

The next day, the Weathermen assembled in a church next to the SDS national headquarters to elect their officers and begin rebuilding. Mellen said that, as he saw it, the first priority was to heal a breach between themselves and the third SDS faction under Mike Klonsky. The Weatherbureau had only to make a place on its slate of candidates for one of Klonsky's group, Mellen said. It would have required little compromise of ideology, and united the anti-PL people in the struggle against PL for the campus chapters.

"Instead," Mellen told me, "the Weatherbureau people, not including me, said, 'We got rid of PL yesterday, and we're going to get rid of the Running Dogs* today.' " The Weatherbureau proposed a slate of hard-core insiders, Mark Rudd for national secretary, Bill Ayers and Jeff Jones for the other two offices. The slate won without opposition.

By now, Mellen said, he was feeling demoralized, and more alienated than ever. When the meeting broke up, the Weatherbureau people proposed staying in Chicago for another few days, to talk and, if necessary, to defend the office from storming by PL. "And I said no, fuck you," Mellen recalled. "As far as I'm concerned, I'm not part of this leadership group anymore. I'm going back to Michigan and go to work."

---

* A name of ridicule attached some months earlier by Mellen's faction to Klonsky's faction. It was actually a translation from the Chinese, used by Maoists against their "revisionist" enemies.

Mellen returned not to Ann Arbor but to Detroit, to direct the summer program which he and Bill Ayers had proposed and SDS had endorsed the previous spring. It was a program for organizing white working-class youth in industrial cities. Though he had left the Weatherbureau, Mellen was still leader of the Michigan region, and he had recruited fifty people as full-time Weatherman cadre.

The people in the Detroit program, young middle-class whites just out of the university, lived together in five SDS "collectives," Mellen said. They did some karate training and a great deal of reading. He recalled assigning them Malraux's *Man's Fate*, to get them to focus on the terrorist who lost sight of the revolution in his insane pursuit of emotional gratification. But he admitted he did not succeed in weakening their attraction to mindless violence. After countless sessions of criticism and self-criticism, he said, they remained unshakably attached to the belief that physical courage was the key to creating a new, nonbourgeois character.

"Sex and drugs also became very important at this time," Mellen remembered. "There had always been a lot of both but, until then, it was accompanied by hilarity and great fun. The rest of society was regarded as backward for not enjoying it. Then sex and drugs acquired a political quality, like you showed your leadership in violence by expressing yourself sexually, or by how much LSD you could take and not freak out.

"In those days we used the expression 'Do It,'* which meant seize the initiative, take strong and spontaneous action. There was an esteem for people who could 'Do It' with sex and drugs and violence, and a feeling that all the sensual pleasure in them was somehow connected."

"One time in our house, Bill [Ayers] and Jeff [Jones] said, let's seize the initiative and have an orgy," Mellen remembered, "and so they took off all their clothes. Twenty other people did, too, and lay down on mattresses on the floor. And they all did it, because they were supposed to, for the revolution."

That summer, the Weathermen were struck by the momentum of the women's movement, Mellen recalled, and a consensus was reached in the collectives that women were justified in complaining of exploitation. Much of the fault lay with monogamy, it was

* The title of Jerry Rubin's book.

492

said, which put women in an inferior position, deprived them of their potential and left the revolution without their leadership talents. Romantic love, privacy and even heterosexuality were extremely middle class, it was decided, and thus counterrevolutionary. So, for the sake of the revolution, the Weathermen abolished monogamy, even among married couples, and replaced it by various arbitrary sexual arrangements.

Mellen said the breakdown of relationships actually liberated many women, making them more creative and dynamic than before. On the other hand, the sexual anarchy was very disturbing to others, and diminished their usefulness. In a remarkable autobiography called *With the Weathermen,* Susan Stern, a dedicated SDS member from Seattle, described in detail the pains taken by collectives to establish a "line" to assure equality to women. And yet, with the exception of Bernardine Dohrn, SDS remained dominated by men. Neither the radical restructuring of sexual relationships nor a variety of noble resolutions succeeded in SDS in ending inequality between the sexes.

Nor were the Weathermen successful in the summer of 1969 in their program to convert working-class youths to the revolution. His own group in Detroit, Mellen said, recognized quickly that no conversions would be made through talk. So they developed "weird and strange" techniques, he said, based on a theory that direct and traumatic confrontation would force people to make an honest, and therefore revolutionary, choice.

He and his organizers went to rock concerts and drive-ins, to create disruptions to call attention to themselves. He recalled going once into the University of Detroit cafeteria, climbing on a table with a bullhorn, and starting a debate that first drew two or three hundred participants, then continued before an audience of a thousand or so in an auditorium, where local television filmed the event for the evening news. Once nine Weatherwomen invaded a classroom at Macomb County Community College, he said, started talking about women's liberation, disposed of two combative men with karate, and finally got "busted" by the cops on charges of disorderly conduct.

"A lot of motorcycle-gang types and toughs hung around out at Metro Beach," Mellen said, recounting the most bizarre episode of the summer, "and they all imagined they hated Commies. What

493

they hated more were soft, condescending intellectuals from Ann Arbor, and whenever our people went out, singly or in small groups, they would get brutalized. Some of the Weather people fancied that the way you established grounds for comradeship was to fight, so one day they decided to go out there and take a stand.

"They handed out their red leaflets as fast as they could, then went back to the center of the beach, where they had planted a big SDS flag. People gathered around, there was a lot of shouting and eventually fists started to fly. There was a terrible, terrible fight. One of our people got hit so hard he bounced off the ground and a lung collapsed. Several of the women had bloody noses and teeth knocked out. It was amazing how proud they were. The fight was fought to a standstill, and eventually the police came and scattered everybody."

Mellen said the papers were full of the incident, the whole city was talking about it and, even if no motorcycle riders were converted, his people acquired a new respect. "It's funny," Mellen noted, "you start out being against the war and in favor of world revolution, and you wind up in a fistfight on a beach with a motorcycle gangster wearing a Nazi insignia around his neck." The Weathermen enjoyed it, Mellen said, but even sympathizers wondered whether this was serious political action, or decadence.

Whichever it was, under Mellen's leadership the Michigan region, shattered by the effects of the SDS schism, had by fall been rebuilt into a solid organization. Programs based on the Detroit model, meanwhile, were operating in ten or twelve other regions, Mellen said, and the cadre of committed Weathermen grew around the country to seven or eight hundred.* But no triumph could be repeated and, to keep getting attention, each one had to be followed by something more dramatic. Mellen acknowledged that the process was exhausting.

The spectacular that the Weathermen decided upon to climax the summer skirmishes was a return to Chicago, for a rematch with Mayor Daley's police. They called the event the "National Action" but, thanks to the newspapers, it went down in history as the "Days of Rage." The date was set to correspond with the opening of the

* Sale thinks the figure should be only about a third as high.

conspiracy trial of the Chicago Eight, the second week of October 1969.

Mellen's Michigan group, like the other regional organizations, was assigned to recruit willing bodies to participate. The Weatherbureau spoke of bringing thousands to Chicago, mostly the working-class kids who had been the target of the summer's organizing efforts. The Weathermen talked of mounting demonstrations bigger than those at the Democratic convention the year before.

Mellen had by now rejoined the Weatherbureau, on the strength of his commanding position in Michigan, but his relations with his old comrades remained uncomfortable. Klonsky's faction, still unreconciled, announced it would hold a rival, peaceful demonstration in Chicago the same weekend. Mellen said he pleaded at the Weatherbureau meetings against purposeless violence, but anyone who favored moderation simply could not be heard. No one stood up to support him.

"Nobody knew at first what we would do in Chicago," Mellen said. "I imagined it would be like 1968, only with more people. I thought we would raise hell in a general way, resist when attacked, and try not to be driven out of town.

"But, as time went by, more of the stuff coming out of the Chicago office, and repeated among the people I was working with in Detroit, said we were going there to attack, to conduct a guerrilla raid on the city of Chicago. At first I thought the meaning was symbolic, that we were going to break glass and paint slogans on the walls. But more and more people began to see it as an all-out assault on the police and the National Guard. They began to say it was going to be a bloody stand-up battle, and some of us were going to be killed."

Mellen said he told the Weatherbureau people that, wherever he went in the Michigan region, he found young militants, and even working-class kids, who were willing to participate in an "action" in Chicago. But he said they were not ready to expose themselves to a massacre. Nonetheless, the Weatherbureau went on talking about doing something outrageously bloody, on a massive scale. There was even talk now, he said, about going underground afterward in "victory."

On a chilly Wednesday evening, October 8, the revolutionaries assembled in Lincoln Park, where the 1968 protests had begun.

Almost all of them wore helmets, many carried clubs and a few had gas masks swinging around their necks. Men and women alike wore combat boots, jeans and padded clothing. A rally had been scheduled to honor Ché Guevara and Nguyen Van Troi,* martyrs of the anti-imperialist struggle. It was to be followed by a Weatherman assault, the plans of which were a tight secret.

At about eight thirty a column of briskly marching Weatherman shock troops arrived at the park, chanting, "Ho, Ho, Ho Chi Minh." At nine, Bernardine Dohrn delivered a fiery address through a bullhorn about the need for revolutionary sacrifice. At ten, Tom Hayden, representing the Chicago Eight, spoke briefly in praise of the new militancy. At a signal at ten thirty, about three hundred people burst out of the park in execution of the plan.

Though police were long before alerted by the Weatherman publicity, they assumed the trouble would begin at curfew time, as it had in 1968. Dozens of plainclothesmen bumped shoulders with people in the park, but the main police force had been stationed well to the north. When the Weatherman column began moving southward, virtually no policemen were in position to stop it.

Racing through the streets, oblivious to traffic, the Weathermen broke up into assault groups as they reached the business section. There they took out clubs and chains, and smashed the windows of shops and parked cars. When the police vans finally caught up, cops spilled out and engaged the rebels in nasty battles at a dozen intersections. Before long a thousand uniformed men and hundreds of plainclothesmen were roaming the streets in search of demonstrators. Less fastidious than in 1968, they fired their revolvers when they chose, and even struck some bodies with cars. Within an hour, the rampage had been brought under control. Six Weathermen had been hit with buckshot, and sixty-eight were arrested.

Mellen said he was unable to get away from Detroit in time for the first night's action. Many of his people were on probation, and it took most of the first day to sneak them out from under the noses of the police and the FBI. En route, he said, the group in the car heard interviews of Chicago cops, who expressed grudging admiration for the courage of the rebels. The Weathermen took these

* Guevara had recently been killed in Bolivia. Nguyen Van Troi was a Vietnamese who was tried and executed for attempting to assassinate Secretary of Defense Robert McNamara during a visit to the battle area.

words as a big victory, he said, but to him the number of wounded and arrested made it look like a defeat.

"We were hoping to find fifteen or twenty thousand people when we got there," he said. "What happened was that a lot of people had rooted us on, and then didn't come themselves. We didn't have any working-class kids. We had ourselves, the Weatherman cadres, and almost nobody else. We didn't have even a thousand people there. We failed abysmally."

On the second day, Bernardine Dohrn's Women's Militia, in charge of the action, announced with bravado that "thousands of women will destroy the armed forces induction center." The rendezvous was at the General Logan statue in Grant Park, where considerable blood had flowed the year before. But not more than seventy women—"some of them pretty, most of them scared," said the *Chicago Tribune*—showed up.

After Dohrn gave one of her inspiring speeches, they started marching, and were stopped at the edge of the park by a phalanx of cops. Dohrn charged, was thrown to the ground and, with eleven others, was arrested and taken away. The remaining women were invited to take off their helmets and leave quietly. "Some intelligent police officer, rather than some idiot who just wanted to beat up Commies, publicly humiliated them," Mellen commented. Helmets in hand, the women accepted the offer and meekly marched into a subway station and vanished.

Later in the day, Klonsky's faction held its counterrally at the federal building, where Fred Hampton, chairman of the Illinois Black Panthers, addressed a small crowd. The Weathermen had never repaired their alliance with the Panthers after the fiasco at the Coliseum. Since then the Panthers had, in fact, turned to a "united front" strategy, and had taken to berating the Weathermen for offending liberals and other potential friends. Hampton was particularly harsh that day on the Weathermen's fondness for violence, which he called "anarchistic, opportunistic, adventuristic" and, in a linguistic masterpiece, "Custeristic." Abrogating the Panther–SDS alliance, he left the Weathermen with their Third World ideology intact but, once again, without Third World allies.

That night, the Weatherbureau had scheduled a "wargasm" in Lincoln Park but, in consideration of its heavy reverses, it summoned two hundred or so members of the Weatherman cadre to a

497

strategy session instead. Trying to make the best of a bad situation, the Weatherbureau canceled events for the remainder of the week, and instructed its followers to spend Friday afternoon scouting the streets of downtown Chicago in preparation for a major assault on Saturday.

"I actually chaired that meeting," Mellen said, "because I knew I wasn't going to have anything to say. We had an understanding in the leadership that if you disagreed with an accepted position, you either had to speak in favor or remain silent. I felt that solidarity was important and I never argued with our people in public, so nobody outside knew about our differences. But I thought the National Action was fucked up, and I didn't see how to get out of it. I was like a zombie."

On Friday, while the Weatherbureau was meeting with the New York collective in a church hall, Mellen heard shouting and fighting, and raced to the back to find some Weathermen beating up a police spy. He pulled them off and told them to clear the church at once. "Beating up a cop was really dumb," Mellen said. He was convinced that the police, provoked by the incident, would be murderous at the downtown demonstration the next day.

The demonstrators began to assemble in Haymarket Square at noon on Saturday, around the pedestal of a venerated policeman's monument, which had mysteriously been blown up four days before. The Weathermen's plans called for a rally and parade, for which the city administration, shifting from the strategy of 1968, had actually granted a permit.

About twelve fifteen, a squad of plainsclothesmen mingling with the crowd abruptly targeted five Weathermen leaders and attacked them with clubs. After a brief but vicious fight the five—Mark Rudd among them—were arrested and taken away. By then the crowd of demonstrators surpassed three hundred, including about a hundred Weathermen who had been arrested earlier and released on bail. The crowd listened to several short speeches, then moved out along a parade route to which the police had given approval.

"Blue-helmeted police were lined up shoulder to shoulder along the entire route," Mellen remembered. "It was clear we couldn't get out of line without their banging us in the head. But we couldn't just walk through meekly and go home. The defeat would have been too much for a militant organization to sustain. I didn't favor

498

another kamikaze attack, and most people agreed that we had too many casualties already. But I did go along with the leadership that we had to do something audacious."

Mellen said a decision had been reached within the Weatherbureau to break through the police lines. By rotation, his turn came that day to be tactical leader, and he sent someone ahead to scout out where the police ranks were thinnest. His own Michigan delegation, which was the toughest and most reliable, lined up directly behind him. The New York group under Ted Gold agreed to bring up the rear, and push hard when the police line was broken. Going through last, Mellen said, the New Yorkers would take the worst beating.

"By the time the column got a few blocks, we had several hundred cops following us," Mellen said. "We were scared shitless. But when we got to the designated spot, bang, we turned and went. All the leaders had a bodyguard for the day, and mine was really good. He ran right ahead of me, holding my wrist. The first thing he did was to give an elbow to the plainclothesman standing there at the intersection and send him sprawling.

"We went right through and took off running down the side street. Our people came up right behind us. Since we were in the front, we had the greatest opportunity to survive."

The Weathermen had once again caught the police napping but, as the lead ranks raced off, cops in riot gear closed in from all sides on those who remained behind. "The New York people were creamed," Mellen said, "utterly creamed. And Teddy was creamed worse than anyone." The Weathermen who escaped raced eastward, breaking off in different directions at intersections to elude squads of police. Up and down the pavement fights broke out, with much punching and clubbing but no shooting. Some demonstrators attacked cops, others concentrated on smashing store windows. But most ran as fast as they could.

"I never did get pinched," Mellen recalled. "When we got down the street a little way I found myself in a normal Saturday shopping day in the Loop. I still had my helmet on, so I took it off and dropped it into a trash can.

"I strolled around a little bit to see what was going on, but I knew the police had my picture and I ought to get out of sight. I walked into a cafeteria, bought a cup of coffee, sat down by the

499

window and watched the National Guard patrolling the streets. I feel bad sometimes about the suffering we caused people who followed us blindly. But I never got caught."

When the coast was clear, Mellen said, he left for a secret rendezvous at a point the Weatherbureau had previously fixed. It was a remote cabin in an Illinois state park. None of those who made it there that day was followed, but several members were delayed, some by a day or so in jail, and behind one of the stragglers came the police. On flimsy pretexts two people were arrested, and all were taken off to the police station. But no charges were placed, Mellen said, and everyone was promptly released.

The session in the cabin was tumultuous, Mellen recalled, both before and after the arrests. The quarrels over how to get the organization back together were severe. His own proposal was for the Weatherbureau to submit itself to general political criticism from within the collectives, but no one would hear of that. Instead, a decision was reached to reorganize the regions, and Mellen was given an assignment in Boston. Leaving Michigan deprived him of his political base and rendered him, the Weatherbureau's only internal critic, totally powerless.

By now it was clear to everyone that, whatever the Weatherbureau's power over a small cadre of followers, SDS as a national organization was dead. Campus demonstrations continued throughout the fall of 1969, many of them led by SDS chapters. But no effort was made from within SDS to coordinate them into a nation-wide effort, and before long the SDS designation, and sometimes the chapters themselves, faded away. PL tried to pick up some of the pieces, and so did Klonsky's faction, but with no success. The Weathermen, obsessed with tightening their cadres for the revolution, no longer even tried.

In the fall of 1969, the antiwar movement once again gathered a mass of protesters, this time to appeal to President Nixon. Sam Brown, former student coordinator of the Dump Johnson campaign, was the key organizer of the Vietnam Moratorium, a campus-oriented liberal coalition. Dave Dellinger, the Mobe's chairman, reorganized his coalition into the *New* Mobilization to End the War in Vietnam, which still had a wide radical fringe. On October 15, the two conducted a series of protests together around the country, and drew hundreds of thousands to the streets once more. On November 15, New Mobe–Moratorium held the largest antiwar march ever in Washington, with a crowd of 250,000 people.* But Nixon appeared no more moved by protest than Johnson had been.

Bill Ayers was at the head of a three-thousand-member Weatherman contingent at the November 15 demonstration. The night before the march they attacked the South Vietnamese embassy and, in an atmosphere charged with tear gas, smashed windows throughout downtown Washington. Late the next day, Jim Mellen and Ted Gold led several thousand Weathermen in a spectacular assault upon the Justice Department. The attacks produced 150 arrests and brought SDS's name momentarily back into the news. But, in a parody of Dylan's weatherman line,† the chic one-liner on campus now seemed to be, "You don't need a rectal thermometer to know who the assholes are." SDS's final lunges brought no new converts to radicalism.

The Weathermen came together for a final public meeting at the end of December 1969, in a black ghetto in Flint, Michigan, one of the few places where they could still rent space. About two hundred people were there, most of them veterans of Chicago and a dozen other furious street campaigns. The Weatherbureau called the meeting the National *War* Council. An enormous cardboard machine gun hung from the ceiling, and from the rafters fluttered banners picturing Ché, Ho, Fidel and Malcolm X.

A whole wall, however, was dedicated to Fred Hampton, the Illinois Panther leader who had publicly repudiated the Weathermen during the Days of Rage. A few weeks before, Hampton was shot to death in his bed by the Chicago police, in a calculated act of assassination. In life a tormentor, Hampton was restored in death to the Weatherman pantheon.

Hampton's murder confirmed to the Weathermen the existence of "white skin privilege," of which they now spoke often, and with much self-contempt. The Chicago cops, at their worst, had brutally

---

* Some responsible estimates were as high as 500,000.
† "You Don't Need a Weatherman to Know Which Way the Wind Blows."

smashed heads during the Weathermen protests, but they had never tried to kill. It was apparent that, like police forces elsewhere in the country, they applied far harsher retribution on black than on white revolutionaries. The Weatherbureau proclaimed its guilt feelings over this distinction, and the guilt helped drive it to ever wilder extremes.

The Weathermen now saw themselves as a merciless army of avengers. During the Days of Rage, they had been rejected on the one hand by the white working-class youths, whom they had hoped would be their link to the masses, and on the other by the Black Panthers, who were to be their link to the Third World. But their isolation only seemed to convince them that they were the truest of the revolutionaries.

The leaders of the Weathermen no longer said with modesty, "Let the people decide." Instead, they proposed to "fight the people," in a war that would wipe out the special privileges of "honkies." They talked no more of organizing a mass movement of the young. Instead, the leaders debated strategies of terrorism, vandalism, even barbarism to bring down a decadent state.

The most ferocious speech at Flint was once again delivered by Bernardine Dohrn, whose ideas had by now become a caricature of ideology. Dohrn eulogized Charles Manson, leader of a sex-and-drug cult which had, to no apparent purpose, recently murdered Sharon Tate, a Hollywood actress, and several of her friends. In some circles, the murders were taken as a kind of quintessential countercultural statement, and Manson became a diabolic hero. "Dig it, first they killed those pigs,"* Dohrn cried, "then they ate dinner in the same room with them, then they even shoved a fork into the victim's stomach! Wild!" For a desperate Dohrn, revolutionary virtue had taken a bizarre turn, indeed.†

"What happened at Flint was a primitive tribalistic ceremony," Mellen said. "Instead of debate we had karate practice. People gave confession on how they had not fought hard enough, how they lacked courage. And the leadership gave speeches on practicing strategic sabotage. One of the Weatherbureau members proposed

---

* "Pigs," in Weatherman talk, had now come to mean enemy, or at least any enemy with white skin.

† Mellen insisted that Dohrn was being sarcastic. I know of no other eyewitness, however, who did not think she was serious.

bombing the Strategic Air Command base outside Dayton, Ohio to knock out an H-bomb. It was weird."

The Weathermen had by now persuaded themselves that, by going underground, they would be acting in the grand tradition of the Viet Cong, the Tupamaros, the Fidelistas. The Weatherbureau decided to break the collectives up into cells or, as the Latin-American guerrillas called them, "focos." It announced, in capital letters, that its objective was MAKING WAR on the state. The Weathermen reassured themselves with reminders that Cuba's Castro and North Vietnam's General Giap, too, had begun with only a handful of followers.

In February 1970, the Weathermen began to slip out of sight. Some were awaiting trial on charges that had been brought over the Days of Rage; others had pending indictments that dated from well before. Among the first to disappear underground were Bernardine Dohrn, Mark Rudd and Bill Ayers. Four others of the original eleven Weathermen followed them. Before long, an estimated hundred of the Weatherman cadre were living clandestinely.

Jim Mellen was not among them.

"I was reluctant to quit. I couldn't give in," Mellen said to me. "I had to keep fighting. But what finally happened was I got sick. A lot of times in the last couple of months I got sick, demoralized with migraine headaches, and I just went to pieces.

"Then, in secret meetings of the Weatherbureau, the decision was made to do a 'consolidation.' We had catchy names for everything. The 'consolidation' was to get rid of all the people in the organization that didn't measure up, who couldn't 'do it.' My usefulness was long since used up. So when the decision was made to 'consolidate' down to a small group, I wasn't in it.

"Within a few days after Flint I left them. I have never seen nor heard from any of them since."

By whatever historic standard, the Weathermen were not very successful revolutionaries during the decade after they went underground. On March 6, 1970, in the first weeks of their exile, a homemade bomb accidentally exploded in a brick town house on West Eleventh Street in New York. Two Weatherwomen fled from the debris, one partially clothed, the other naked. Diana Oughton, who had been Bill Ayers's girl when Jim Mellen arrived in Ann Arbor, was killed. So was Ted Gold, whom Mellen had met at

503

Columbia, and with whom he had fought on the streets of Chicago and Washington. The third victim, so decimated that it was some days before his body could be identified, was Terry Robbins, who had been SDS director in Ohio and Mellen's partner in organizing the Middle West.

The tragedy on West Eleventh Street was the most dramatic episode in a pattern of Weatherman bombings which extended sporadically for a year or so. As fugitives, the Weathermen were excellent, and the FBI failed dismally in its prolonged search for them. But, apart from an occasional statement from the underground, nothing much was heard of them again.* They believed they were the vanguard of a great revolution. Instead, their role in history was to mark the end of a movement.

---

* Many of the Weathermen have remained under federal indictment since going underground. A few have surfaced voluntarily. Mark Rudd gave himself up to authorities in September 1977. In January 1978, having pleaded guilty to charges dating from the Days of Rage, he was fined $2000 and placed on two years probation by a Chicago court. At this writing, Bernardine Dohrn and Bill Ayers are among those still underground.

XIV
ALAN CANFORA:
The Days of Death

1970

"When I got to the Commons, the Guard was stretched out all along the ruins of the ROTC building. One Guardsman at the end of the troop says to me, 'Hey, boy, what's that you're carrying there? And I said, 'Just a couple of flags.' And he answered, "We're going to make you eat those flags today.' So I kind of mouthed off to him. 'Just don't get too close, motherfucker,' I said, 'or I'm going to stick them down your throat.' It was an arrogant remark. I didn't like being threatened, but I figured as long as I kept my distance there wouldn't be any problem."

T

HE 1960S ENDED in a small town in Ohio called Kent. It happened on May 4, 1970, in the bright sunshine, just after midday, at a campus demonstration which was like so many others except that, in thirteen crackling seconds of gunfire, four students were killed and nine were wounded. What passion remained of the 1960s was extinguished in the fusillade.

The Kent State University killings came when the country's involvement with great issues at home and abroad was already in retreat. In the years after 1960, Americans had been riding an ever-rising emotional wave, wrestling with evil of many different orders. In those years Americans generally sanctioned protest, as an expression of the nation's social conscience. Then, in 1968, the wave reached its crest, when student discontent culminated in Chicago, black discontent in the Washington ghetto. By then, most Americans had had enough of fire in the streets. The willingness to be aroused by injustice gave way to apathy, even surliness. The country wanted a period of repose.

Richard Nixon sensed as much. When he asked Americans to lower their voices, his words found willing listeners. Though known as a contentious man, he conveyed in his first years in office a desire to realize a campaign commitment to bring the country back together. Strategically he sought to isolate dissenters, but he tended to speak of them in sorrowful rather than angry terms, la-

507

menting "old standards violated, old values discarded." He invented the concept of the "silent majority," to reassure the country that its essence was not protest but a solid, quiet conformity.

By the time Nixon took office the civil rights movement, the noblest cause of the 1960s, had been reduced to a handful of angry nationalists, threatening mayhem, muttering invective. The Nixon Administration was not overtly racist. It simply made clear that the federal government could no longer be counted on to promote the cause of racial equality. Under Nixon, the last hopes of the movement collapsed and, in the summer of 1969, for the first time since Watts, there was not even a ghetto riot.

The antiwar movement, too, had lost its edge. Demoralized at what it had wrought after defeating Johnson, it watched suspiciously as Nixon proclaimed a doctrine of gradual withdrawal from Vietnam and began bringing combat forces home. In October of 1969, the movement held nationwide rallies, and announced it would repeat them monthly until the war was over. In November, it filled Pennsylvania Avenue while Nixon, spending his Saturday afternoon like other Americans of the "silent majority," watched a football game on television. After that, no more demonstrations were held, and the war went on.

Student opposition to the war remained overwhelming, but a drop in the draft calls brought a corresponding decline in the level of outrage. Student radicalism, discredited by the factionalism of SDS, appeared itself to have waned. On April 20, 1970, Nixon stated over television that he would withdraw 150,000 additional American soldiers from Vietnam the following year. From the available signs, 1970 promised to bring the quietest spring on the campuses since FSM overran Berkeley.

Only ten days later, Nixon changed all that. On April 30, he announced that, to clean out enemy sanctuaries, American forces had invaded Cambodia. He was unwilling, he declared, to have "America become a second-rate power and to see this nation accept the first defeat in its proud 190-year history." He argued that he was sending troops deeper into Indochina only to get them out faster, but students took his words as sophistry, interpreting the invasion as the biggest escalation yet of the Vietnam War.

The next morning, anticipating trouble at the colleges, Nixon spoke extemporaneously of "these bums, you know, blowing up the campuses," who in reality were "the luckiest people in the world." The president, who had conducted himself circumspectly during his sixteen months in office, now seemed to give way to what his adversaries saw as the *real* Nixon. The assault on Cambodia was the kind of incident that had been often predicted of him, and widely feared. By nightfall, protests against the invasion had broken out spontaneously on hundreds of campuses throughout the land.

When it started Friday night, the rioting at Kent State was much like the rioting elsewhere. But Kent's few policemen were unable to contain the disorder of several thousand students, and on Saturday the Ohio National Guard arrived. Neither the officers nor the men of the Guard had much patience with the demonstrators, and tensions swelled. At a rally on Monday, a Guard contingent turned its rifles into a crowd at football-field distance and fired. Of the four students who died, two were demonstrators. The other two were coming from class and were on their way to lunch.

The fusillade at Kent was the climax of a thousand confrontations during the 1960s. It seemed to signal, without notice, that the rules of the game had changed. In the succeeding days, the fury of campus protest rose to an unprecedented level but, by the close of the spring term, this energy was spent. The campus demonstrations that had distinguished the 1960s from the rest of American history came to an end. Students were not willing to pay the penalty of Kent State to rebel.

Students were not alone in sensing that the country, while shocked, was not remorseful over the killings. For Nixon, the lesson was that "when dissent turns to violence it invites trouble." The dominant reaction of public opinion seemed to be that "they had it coming to them." The sanction for social protest which characterized the 1960s had finally been withdrawn. The country's concern with whatever injustice had evoked demonstrations had given way to an intolerance of demonstrations themselves.

The 1960s were over.

Alan Canfora, a twenty-one-year-old junior, was one of the students wounded at Kent State. When he was struck by a bullet in the wrist, he was 225 feet away from the Guardsmen, much farther than

509

he could throw a rock. He told me he was convinced he would have been killed had he not scurried behind a tree as soon as the firing began.

Canfora never claimed to have been a bystander at the demonstration. Radicalized by the war, he carried a black flag which he waved defiantly, while taunting the Guardsmen with antiwar slogans and obscenities. But he committed no capital crime nor, as the photographic evidence confirms, did he present a threat to anyone. In fact, it is hard to think of any crime at all that the students who were shot that day might have committed, unless disrespect for authority be an offense.

Canfora was born and raised in Barberton, a small industrial city about a half-hour's drive from Kent. His father was a factory worker who had been active in trade unionism. Canfora said his father, whom he admired, sometimes called himself a radical. But he was really a liberal, Canfora said, which was embarrassing, since son often joined other radical students to challenge father by shouting, "Combat Liberalism." His father, after holding several union offices, was elected to the Barberton city council in 1964, then was defeated in 1971 when he stood up for his son in the aftermath of the Kent State killings.*

"My father raised me to believe that the Democratic party was the answer to everything," Canfora said, "and that the worst Democrat was better than the best Republican. I can remember, when I was seven, pulling for Adlai Stevenson and, when I was eleven, I worked for John Kennedy. Not many kids in Barberton at that time were politically minded, but I always was, because my father always talked about politics."

Alan Canfora and I talked in his apartment above a garage in Barberton, not far from where his parents lived. Slim, of medium size and with reddish hair, he spoke comfortably of his Italian, Catholic, working-class upbringing. In the mid-1970s, when I interviewed him, Canfora worked part-time in a factory, and had returned to Kent State for an M.A. in library science. Canfora still

---

* After losing a second time in 1973, Canfora won back his seat in 1975. Then, after identifying himself with Alan's efforts to stop Kent State from erecting a building on the site of the killings, he was unseated in a 1977 recall election. The entire family—father, mother and four children—were arrested protesting the construction.

considered himself a radical, and looked ahead to a lifetime of promoting radical ideas. But his first priority at that time was the ongoing court battle to remedy the wrongs done to the Kent State victims.*

Canfora said he had begun thinking about Vietnam when he graduated from high school in 1967, and saw most of his friends go off to the Army. His own decision was to enroll in Wadsworth, a nearby branch of Kent State, which drew students from the working-class families of the region. Most of these students were conservative, like their parents, though he was not alone in being disturbed by the moral issues of the war. If he had then been drafted, however, he would surely have served, he said.

In the fall of 1968, Canfora transferred to the main campus of the university at Kent. With more than twenty thousand students, Kent State was twenty-fourth nationally in campus population. Open to any graduate of an accredited Ohio high school, it enrolled students with a wide range of abilities, and its academic record suffered from the diversity. But this problem was common to public universities in America, of which Kent State was more or less typical.

In his lengthy study of the killings,† the novelist James Michener estimated that fifteen thousand of Kent's students considered themselves liberals, a third that number conservatives. He calculated there were five hundred or so radicals, of which sixty or seventy were "hard-core operators." Other categories, he said, were jocks and grinds, straights and freaks, Greeks from the Greek-letter fraternities and non-Greeks, whites and blacks. Of the blacks, he said, several hundred were "very angry."

Canfora, who arrived at Kent as a liberal, started the fall term in 1968 working with the campus Young Democrats on the Humphrey campaign, notwithstanding his misgivings about the war. One night in October, he said, he and Tom Grace, his roommate and best friend, drove with a caravan of Young Democrats to the University of Akron, where Richard Nixon was speaking. The Young Demo-

* A suit was brought by the survivors of the four who were killed at Kent State, along with those most seriously wounded, against Governor James Rhodes, the state adjutant general's office, and twenty-six Guardsmen. The plaintiffs lost in a trial in 1975, but a retrial was ordered on appeal. The second trial began in December 1978. In January 1979, after intense negotiations, the state agreed to an out-of-court settlement, in which it paid the victims a total of $675,000 and, for the first time, publicly expressed responsibility and regret for the killings.

† *Kent State*, researched immediately after the killings and published in 1971.

crats' plan, he said, was to heckle Nixon for refusing to engage Humphrey in debate.

"In the top bleachers was a section of SDS people from Kent, maybe two hundred of them," Canfora recalled. "Tom and I had heard about SDS, and seen things about them in the newspapers. They weren't yelling 'Debate Humphrey.' They were yelling antiwar slogans and 'Ho, Ho, Ho Chi Minh, NLF is gonna win.'

"Tom and I looked around at the liberal guys pulling for Humphrey. I remember thinking, 'Maybe we should just go up with the SDS people. They seem to have the right sentiments.' The Democrats appeared kind of wishy-washy to us, so we walked away from them, and went up and sat in the very top row.

"Some pretty heavy heckling followed, which Nixon's people tried to shout down. Then, at one point, Nixon said something ridiculous, and an SDS guy yelled, 'You asshole.' So the police came up and threw him out. We all walked out after him, everybody with their fists in the air. Tom and I rode back to Kent with SDS, and stuck with them for the rest of the year."

The SDS contingent at Kent State was led by a charismatic pair, sometimes referred to jokingly as "Fidel" and "Ché." One was Rick Erickson, tall with flowing hair, son of a former mayor of Akron, a star athlete in high school. The other was Howie Emmer, short and muscular, son of immigrants, an excellent speaker with a great command of SDS dialectics. These two, and their followers, gave SDS at Kent State the most effective radical leadership in the Middle West.

Luminaries from SDS headquarters supplemented their influence. Bernardine Dohrn was in and out, along with Bill Ayers. Mark Rudd drew an audience of a thousand in October 1968, and came close to blows with Erickson over whose group would get the collection when the hat was passed. The most regular visitors were the SDS regional coordinators, Terry Robbins and Jim Mellen, whom Alan Canfora often saw on campus.

In November SDS, still exultant over Chicago, touched off the first demonstration of the 1968 school year. The university had granted permission to the police department of Oakland, California, to recruit trainees at Kent State's Law Enforcement School. This was the police force that was brutally embroiled with the Black Panthers, and a few weeks earlier Huey Newton had been sentenced to prison on what radicals called political charges. "Free Huey" was on everyone's lips when the Oakland recruiters arrived, to be greeted by a mass sit-in at the student placement office.

"I was coming back from classes, and instinctively thought this was a worthwhile cause, so I took part," Canfora remembered. "When word came out the next day of impending arrests for the sit-in, the Black United Students voted to leave the campus in protest. Of about six hundred black students at Kent, all but a dozen or so, very dramatically, took their suitcases, marched to their cars and drove off. They stayed away for about three days, until the administration gave in to their no-arrest demand. It was very humiliating for the administration."

Then, in January, Canfora and Tom Grace joined a 50-member SDS contingent that went to Washington for the "counterinaugural," a demonstration scheduled to coincide with Nixon's swearing-in ceremonies. Some 10,000 protesters participated in the event, which had been organized by Dave Dellinger and Rennie Davis. It was Canfora's first major radical action, and he recalled that the Ohio people, 250 strong, were assigned to a black church, where they were fed peanut butter and jelly sandwiches and spent the nights on a cold floor in sleeping bags.

The day before Nixon was sworn in, Canfora marched in the "counterinaugural" parade from the White House to the Capitol, the reverse route of the inaugural parade. According to the *Washington Post*, six thousand marched, including "Yippies, hippies, clergymen, housewives, Democrats, Socialists, students and drifters . . . mostly young, mostly white . . . in a wild assortment of clothes, masks and body paint, carrying everything from billowing banners to symbolic coffins and toy machine guns." Several times demonstrators clashed with the police, who did some heavy clubbing. Of the twenty-two whom the *Post* reported were arrested, Canfora said three or four were from Kent State.

"That day had a pretty big effect on me," Canfora remembered, "seeing that it wasn't just the people at Kent State who were against the war, against Nixon, against the system in the country. I saw thousands and thousands of people from across the country thinking along the same lines as me.

"These people weren't willing to just stand around and give the peace sign. They had an understanding of what was going on, and they knew the situation was so drastically wrong and so serious that they had to shake the system to its foundations to get some changes. These people were determined to take militant action, and they did. It really affected me."

That night, Canfora listened to antiwar speeches and rock music in a crowded circus tent on the Washington Monument grounds, then went to a mass meeting at the St. Stephen's Church on Sixteenth Street. There Dave Dellinger, the moderate, debated the militant Mark Rudd over the tactics for the next day's protest. Canfora said Dellinger made a more logical case, but that Rudd's arguments corresponded more closely to the frame of mind of the audience.

The debate continued within the Ohio delegation the next morning after breakfast. Canfora said Howie Emmer and Terry Robbins both delivered "eloquent raps." But Rick Erickson, Kent's most dynamic leader, carried the day for militancy.

With police permission, the demonstrators gathered in Franklin Park, several blocks north of Nixon's parade route. At noon the militants, many wearing helmets, goggles and gas masks, started streaming toward Pennsylvania Avenue. The *Post* reported that they congregated at selected street corners with police consent, then began pelting the presidential procession with mud balls and empty bottles.

"When Nixon came by," Canfora said, "he was looking out the window and he's waving and all of a sudden he realized he'd come up on our section, and he turned away, and started waving to the other side. But people by the thousands were screaming, real loud, and he definitely saw us. I've often thought back to that day, like when he called students 'bums,' and I remember he had quite an introduction to the way we felt." *

Canfora said the crowd, spontaneously, then proceeded to go on a rampage through downtown Washington. Demonstrators threw

* The *Post* wrote the next day: "At 2:57 p.m., the Nixon limousine passed. It was showered with a dozen to two dozen missiles—sticks, stones, empty drink cans and what appeared to be cherry bombs, none of which exploded. A heavy stick struck a paratrooper in the head. Companions helped him from the scene. Secret Service agents, their faces anxious, hovered around the slow-moving presidential car. Agents on the running-boards batted down several of the missiles. The black limousine slowed momentarily, then sped up past the jeering crowd. Mr. Nixon's back was turned to the demonstrators. He waved to the spectators on the south (other) side of the Avenue."

bricks at police cars and through store windows, overturned trash barrels and assaulted policemen. Using clubs more sparingly than in Chicago, police kept the demonstrators away from the White House, inflicting relatively few injuries. No shots were fired, eighty-five were arrested and night had fallen before the last clusters of demonstrators got tired and went home.

In the spring of 1969, SDS was riding high in the Middle West, and Jim Mellen was its chief theoretician. Organizational efforts were achieving great success, and Midwestern radicals were embracing Mellen's anti-imperialist brand of Marxism. To Mellen, the prospects for student-led revolution seemed good, and nowhere better than at Kent State.

Canfora said the first time he met Mellen was at a study-group meeting in the basement recreation room of somebody's off-campus house. He and Tom Grace attended all the SDS functions now, he said, films and slide shows and lectures and what-have-you. Both were increasingly impressed with the view SDS took of the world.

"So we went to this meeting where Jim Mellen was talking," Canfora said, "and we thought it would be just another SDS meeting about the general political situation. But the first thing Mellen said after he was introduced was, 'Well, we have to really get down to the serious business of developing a Young Communist movement in this country.'

"Now Tom and I had just freshly gotten off our liberal trip. We knew that the system was screwed up, that the Democrats weren't the answer, we knew that the war and racism were wrong, but we didn't see that Marxism provided any answer. So when he said that, I looked at Tom and Tom looked at me and we thought, Oh, oh, what are we doing here? So at the earliest opportunity, during some pause in the meeting, we made up a convenient excuse and we went up the stairs and out the door."

Canfora said that both he and Grace had been raised on anti-Communism and that, as a result of the "brainwashing," they pulled away reflexively from involvement with Communists.

"For a week or two," he said, "we figured that if this is what SDS is all about, then we're not going to have anything to do with it. We went through a brief period where we were kind of confused, and

515

we didn't know what we should think. We realized there might be some Communists in SDS. In fact, on the back of the membership card it said SDS is a student organization comprised of Democrats, Communists, Republicans, Socialists, the whole spectrum. Then we remembered that SDS was the only group on campus that was coming out with any concrete analysis of things, especially the war, and they weren't afraid of action.

"As time went on, SDS brought down more and more of an analysis with class perspective, and they really pointed the brunt of their attacks at the ruling class. Gradually we became very sympathetic to those kinds of ideas. You might say we even started in the winter and spring of 1969 to consider ourselves to be socialists."

That spring, SDS made Kent State its major target in the Middle West. As Mellen's regional office saw it, this was a campus that had all the necessary attributes to be a part of the revolutionary vanguard. It had an excellent leadership cadre, its student body was essentially working class, its blacks possessed a Third World consciousness. SDS called its campaign at Kent the Spring Offensive, and planned an intensive indoctrination program to enhance "revolutionary awareness," to be followed by a major confrontation with the university administration.

SDS scheduled the confrontation for April 8, 1969. Erickson and Emmer presided over a campus rally, and read a list of "nonnegotiable" demands. Then they led 250 marchers to the administration building, which was guarded by the police. After a dean refused to admit more than a three-student delegation, the crowd lunged for the doors, and a brawl ensued. Erickson and Emmer were arrested and immediately suspended. At the same time, SDS was summarily forbidden to operate on the campus any longer.

For a few days SDS managed to keep the campus in disequilibrium. Radicals had fistfights with Greeks, and the State Highway Patrol was called to keep order. SDS demanded that the suspension of its leaders be reconsidered at an open hearing. When the administration announced there would be a hearing, but it would be closed, SDS adopted the battle cry, "Open it up or shut it down."

Jim Mellen showed up on campus for the hearing, on April 16, and delivered what he said was the best speech of his life. He stood on an upturned fifty-gallon drum, and shouted through a bullhorn to a crowd of several hundred. The phrases have often been pub-

516

lished since, in anthologies of 1960s radicalism. Mellen told me he felt good as he got into the rhythm of the speech, and heard the cheers.

"We're no longer asking you to come and make a revolution," he proclaimed. "We're telling you that the revolution has begun, and the only choice you have to make is which side you're on. And we're also telling you that if you get in the way of that revolution, it's going to run right over you."

After he finished, two hundred SDS supporters reassembled in front of the Music and Speech Building, where the hearing was taking place. Several hundred jocks guarded the doors. The crowd attacked, and exchanged black eyes and bloody noses with the defenders, then broke it off when a side door was found open and unguarded. The two hundred raced up to the third floor and burst into the hearing room, stopping the proceedings. The state police arrived a few minutes later, and blocked the third-floor corridor at both ends, trapping everyone inside.

"That was about three o'clock in the afternoon," Canfora remembered. "We were there for about four or five hours. We had a bullhorn, and were talking to people outside. Some of them were throwing food up to us. There was a pretty good feeling of solidarity, inside and outside.

"I was up there with my sister.* She wasn't much interested in politics but, much to my surprise, she was there that day. My father was a council member then, and he always told us, 'Don't get in trouble with the SDS or it's going to make me look bad in the election.' We were both worried about what our parents would think.

"Then a professor came along with a key to an elevator that wasn't guarded. The hallway wasn't straight, so the elevator wasn't visible from the two ends, where the police were. Several elevator loads got out, and Mellen was in one of them. My sister and I were in a classroom taking part in a political discussion. I looked out and saw a bunch of people getting on the elevator, so I said, 'Hey, let's get out of here.' We were in the last load to get out. It felt great, the fresh air, the people cheering us. We just went back to our dorms."

Canfora estimated that more than a hundred people escaped via

* Canfora's sister Roseanna, better known as "Chic," was a year younger, and a year behind him at Kent State.

the elevator. The rest were captured and fifty-eight were booked, including Erickson and Emmer. They were among four tried on various charges, and sent for a term in the county jail. All were released on April 29, 1970, the day before Nixon announced the invasion of Cambodia.

As for the Spring Offensive, SDS knew that the price had been heavy. Some of its supporters had been suspended, eleven faced criminal charges and bail had tied up a substantial amount of its cash. Hundreds of students had regularly shown up for the big demonstrations, but the SDS indoctrination sessions had drawn only thirty or forty. It would have been hard to claim that the Spring Offensive had brought the revolution closer.

Canfora said he experienced some disillusion because the people who were the most fiery in advocating militancy were often nowhere to be seen when the heads were being beaten. He said he was also annoyed by SDS's bickering, omen of what was revealed later to be a profound organizational schism. Factions, he said, attacked one another more zestfully than the college administration.

Yet SDS undoubtedly succeeded in forcing students to take a stand. For the remainder of the semester, thousands of liberal students demonstrated against the banning of SDS. More important, thousands had become aware of the war, which they might otherwise have comfortably ignored.

"When the invasion of Cambodia happened," Canfora said, "you had thousands and thousands of students who took part in the demonstration at Kent State. They would not have responded without the work that SDS did in the 1968–69 school year. I think it's safe to say it was only then that a very large number of people came to understand what was going on."

SDS people contacted Canfora during the summer of 1969, while Jim Mellen was trying to organize working-class kids in Detroit, and invited him to join a Weatherman collective. He was holding a temporary job in a factory in Barberton, he said, making boilers for steam generators. Joining SDS's revolutionary cadre, he said, did not even tempt him.

"They came down to Barberton," he said, "and talked about karate and self-defense. And they passed out leaflets at park dances calling for youth to fight for Communism. The kids of Barberton didn't know where these people were coming from. They used to pick up the stuff and laugh.

"I was somewhat sympathetic to the SDS goal, but I knew that wasn't the way to pursue the political struggle. There was a lot of anarchism in what those people were saying and doing, which I understand better now than I did then. But I knew instinctively that it wasn't the way to go. I couldn't see having a handful of people going off the deep end, doing some suicidal action, winding up either hurt or arrested."

In the fall, after the summer in the factory, Canfora returned to Kent, but he said his heart was not really in academic work. He had switched majors several times, was bored with his courses and felt uncertain about his future. He would have dropped out of school, he said, but for the slight protection his student status gave him against the draft. He said he had already made up his mind that if drafted he would flee the country.

At the start of the school year he, Tom Grace and three other friends left the dorms and took an apartment in town, several blocks from the campus. They read a great deal of Socialist literature, he said, to develop their powers of scientific analysis. He said they did not even know about the Days of Rage until they read about them in the newspaper. But they did go to Washington in mid-November 1969, for the weekend of demonstrations known as the Moratorium.

In the calendar of events published by the *Washington Post* on the opening day of the weekend, the following notice appeared under the heading for Friday, November 14, 1969: "8:30 p.m.—Revolutionary Contingent in Solidarity with the Vietnamese People—made up of SDS chapters, Youth Against Fascism, Mad Dogs, Crazies, Weathermen—will rally at Dupont Circle." Of the 250,000 who marched in the Moratorium, an estimated 2000 to 3000 accepted the invitation conveyed by the *Post* for Friday night.

Canfora went to Dupont Circle that night, but not because it was a Weatherman action. He said he had little interest in the Weathermen. He knew there was to be a march on the South Vietnamese embassy, he said, "and it was something constructive to do." The march would challenge the legitimacy of the Saigon government, he said, and show his solidarity with the Vietnamese people.

"It was a chilly night," he remembered. "People had red flags

519

and helmets, and there were some fiery speeches in Dupont Circle. Then we formed up and started on Massachusetts Avenue toward the embassy. We stayed pretty strong, pretty together. The people were chanting traditional slogans, 'Ho, Ho, Ho Chi Minh, NLF is Gonna' Win,' and 'One, Two, Three, Four, We Don't Want Your Fucking War.' We used them at Kent.

"Then we reached a barricade, and the police were there with riot guns and clubs. People just marched right up against them, and I think some tried to get through. They repelled us there with large quantities of tear gas, so people started to run back toward Dupont Circle and re-form there. Tear gas was as high as the buildings.

"Then people started trashing out windows. I remember the windows of the Riggs National Bank got completely trashed out, and a lot of high-class stores along the avenue. There was quite a bit of looting. Police cars got trashed in, too, and a lot of police got hit by objects. People all over were getting their heads beat in by police clubs. It was really like guerrilla warfare going on in the streets."

The main march the next day, in chilling autumn cold, was peaceful and dignified, and apparently quite futile. Herbert C. Klein, Nixon's spokesman, said the quarter-million or more who took to the street to end the war were a small number compared to those who stayed at home to support the president's policy of gradual withdrawal. Nixon, in watching a football game on television, signaled that he had sealed himself off from public protest. His reaction made the Moratorium look like a meaningless gesture.

Equally discouraging was the public perception of the event. The violence generated by the Weathermen, good film for TV news, dominated the bystanders' impression of the day. Attorney General John Mitchell said he had been reminded of the Russian Revolution, and less partisan observers were no less dismayed. Millions identified the Moratorium not with the solemn procession down Pennsylvania Avenue but with the destructiveness of a few thousand militants. Increasingly, that was how the country now perceived the antiwar movement.

Yet it is worth distinguishing Alan Canfora's militance from that of, say, Tom Hayden or Jerry Rubin or Jim Mellen. These three had made revolutionary commitments before Vietnam became a public issue, and they used the war as an instrument to advance these aims. Though Canfora may have been en route to being a revolutionary, his militance was directed at the war itself. Like many others at Dupont Circle the Friday night of the Moratorium, he was there because he considered the war so evil that, to end it, he could justify any level of disruption. Many Americans who were not at Dupont Circle concurred with that view.

Revolutionaries or not, however, the antiwar firebrands made good enemies for Nixon. On the one hand, the majority of the antiwar movement, still essentially liberal, feared that the militants would cast such discredit on the efforts to end the war that they would actually prolong it. On the other, many conservatives who had no moral objection to the war—and that may have included Nixon himself—were so appalled by the social disarray which the militants represented that, for stability's sake, they adopted antiwar positions. Both groups approved of Nixon's efforts to isolate, even to suppress, the militants.

By the end of the 1960s, only the militants would have denied that the war, which retained almost no constituency, was coming to an end. National debate was limited to the means and terms for getting out of Vietnam. The antiwar militants had undoubtedly accelerated the debate, provoking the conscience of some and the dismay of others. But their practices had placed a barrier between themselves and their sympathizers, and they became increasingly vulnerable to the repression of the state.

Trashing was not all that offended the straight world. The counterculture spoke more blatantly than ever of revolution, to be achieved not by fighting cops on the streets but by grooving at rock concerts, and getting turned on by sex and dope in scruffy pads. The modesty, even the sense of privacy, that was once convention had given way to defiant nudity and much more. "Let's make love, not war," was one of the touching slogans the counterculture presented to the times. Less tender was the observation of Janis Joplin, one of the rock idols of the late 1960s, a passionate performer known for her own relentless highs. "My music isn't supposed to make you riot," she once said. "It's supposed to make you fuck." Its partisans argued that the counterculture was riding a supple but irresistible current to authentic social values, called a "new consciousness." Many Americans were offended by them, however, and found them even more threatening than Marxism.

Alan Canfora, with many of the New Left radicals, had an attrac-

tion to the counterculture, mixed with some reserve. Unlike Jerry
Rubin, he was not equally committed to both camps but, if he had
a foot in political radicalism, he certainly had a toe in the counterculture. He was the first kid in Barberton to grow long hair, he said.
He was devoted to rock music, he experimented with marijuana
and he was even busted once.

But, on the whole, Canfora's private life was traditional. He
shared an apartment with other men, and brought his girl friend
home to meet his parents. He did not consider personal hygiene
bourgeois. He did not favor bizarre clothes or junk jewelry or the
other public extravagancies of the freaks. He was, if anything, even
a trifle antagonistic to the counterculture, whose notions, he believed, were a distraction from the imperatives of radical politics.

In fact, by the end of the decade, the two communities—which
Rubin had tried vainly to unite under the Yippie banner in 1968—
seemed to be drawing apart. *Screw*, one of the underground's most
single-minded papers, treated New Left politics with the contempt
it had once reserved for straights. *Rolling Stone*, the most successful
of the underground establishment, learned that its readership had
turned off politics when half its edition on the trial of the Chicago
Eight was returned unsold. Increasingly the counterculture took the
view that street protest was a waste of time, and that its own practices, by example, would ultimately win the society over.

In countercultural terms, the most revolutionary event of the
1960s took place in a pasture in upstate New York on the weekend
of August 16, 1969. It was the great Woodstock rock festival, for
which no less than four hundred thousand young people showed
up. Rock music was still the special language of the counterculture,
the aspect to which militants were most attracted, the vehicle for
extolling love, drugs and radical social ideas. Amid brutal heat and
torrents of rain, the most celebrated rock groups of the day played
at the festival engulfed in waves of generosity and affection. No
one had expected such a human sea, and pot smoking and nudity
were as common as hot dogs at the ball parks of the straight world.

The weekend was a spectacular success. It was the counterculture at its best—sweet and undemanding and sharing—and its
apologists took to calling this segment of America the Woodstock
Nation, harbinger of a better world. But most Americans were much
less enthusiastic. What they saw was not the spiritual richness but

the public lovemaking and pot smoking, and they did not like it. Woodstock probably made many more enemies than friends for the counterculture, and for the rebellious young.

Four months later, before three hundred thousand people at a stock-car raceway in Altamont, California, the image of the Woodstock Nation collapsed. The Rolling Stones, rock superstars whose strongly sexual performances invariably emitted signals of violence, held a promotion concert to which all were invited. As security guards, they hired a band of Hell's Angels, black-clad motorcyclists who had become famous as terrorists of California's open road.

The atmosphere, far from loving, was sordid, and what had been a "high" in upstate New York became a "bad trip" in northern California. "The crowd had been ugly, selfish, territorialistic, throughout the day," an observer wrote. "People held their space. They made no room for anyone. It was a gray day, and the California hills were bare, cold and dead." * Before it was over, the Angels had beaten a black man to death on the stage, and three others had been killed in squalid incidents of drugs and brutality. No one would ever again be able to say that the Woodstock Nation was the wave of a better, gentler future.

In December 1969, the same month as Altamont, the Los Angeles police arrested Charlie Manson and his "family" for the murder of Sharon Tate and her friends. Manson, a thirty-four-year-old ex-convict, had once been a familiar figure in San Francisco's Haight-Ashbury, a would-be rock singer who took drugs and chattered about revolution. He seemed to exercise special powers of enchantment, particularly over young women who had crossed over into the counterculture, and in 1968 he led them on their murderous rampage. Bernardine Dohrn was not alone in adulating him. Jerry Rubin said he fell in love with Manson's "cherub face and sparkling eyes" when he saw him on television. A Los Angeles underground paper named Manson Man of the Year. This eerie hero worship was frightening proof even to many of its sympathizers that the counterculture had gone astray.

---

* Greil Marcus, "The Apocalypse at Altamont," in *The Sixties*.

Oblivious to this shifting opinion in the country, Canfora and his friends went circuit riding to demonstrations in the early months of 1970. They protested in behalf of the Chicago Seven on one occasion at the Cook County Courthouse in Chicago. On another, they picketed a meeting in Cleveland of AT&T stockholders, to protest corporate profits from the war.

They went to a rally of two thousand students on the Kent State campus on April 10 to hear Jerry Rubin. That was when Rubin made the celebrated statement that, "Unless you're prepared to kill your parents, you're not ready to change this country. Our parents are our first oppressors." Rubin told me, in our talk many years later, that he meant the statement metaphorically, to urge students to free themselves from parental domination.* But the newspaper accounts of the rally did not include Rubin's explanation.

The campus was rather indifferent to Rubin. Nor did it get very excited a few days later at an antiwar rally sponsored by the Student Mobilization Committee. The committee was the campus branch of the New Mobe, which was trying vainly to resuscitate antiwar protests nationally. Canfora remembered the rally for another reason.

"It was the day I found out about my friend getting killed in Vietnam," he said. "His name was Bill Caldwell, and I had known him since the fifth grade. I went to high school with him, played with him on the baseball team, shot pool with him. His brother George was one of my roommates at Kent.

"After high school, Bill got drafted and didn't know whether to go in or go to Canada. He thought about being a conscientious objector, but he went in. Then, when he got his orders to go to Vietnam, he came back home on leave. That was the summer of sixty-nine, and he was torn. Should he go to Canada, should he go to Vietnam? He really didn't know what to do. Finally the attitude he took was that he'd take his chances and hope everything turned out for the best. It didn't."

Canfora said that all the guys in the apartment were awakened by a phone call at 7:00 A.M. on April 14. It was George's sister calling to say that Bill was dead. Later in the day, Canfora said they all went to the rally, even George. They felt that the war had been brought right home, and they were pretty serious about ending it.

* In *Do It!* Rubin wrote, "Kids should steal money from their parents, because that is true liberation from the money ethic: true family." He told me he meant the kill-your-parents statement in the same way, as a friendly metaphor for liberation.

Bill Caldwell's body was returned from Vietnam in a coffin, Canfora said, and the funeral was held on April 27. He and his friends drove back to Barberton for it. An Army officer had accompanied the coffin and stood at attention during the burial ceremony.

"We all had strong feelings of disdain for this guy," Canfora recalled, "because he was the living representative of the military, which directly caused our friend's death. We felt the U.S. Army should not even be at the funeral. A lot of us were disgusted that the Army would show up."

Three days later, Nixon announced the invasion of Cambodia. Canfora remembered that he was sitting with his friends around the television set in the apartment in Kent. No one was prepared for the announcement, he said, but all recognized its seriousness at once. Vietnam had been bad enough all those years, and now it was Cambodia. And after Cambodia, they reasoned angrily, it would be Laos, Thailand, and maybe the People's Republic of China. Canfora said they all feared the invasion would mean World War III.

Though the campus had been quiet for a year, Canfora said, they had no doubt from the moment they heard Nixon that nothing could stop the students at Kent State from taking to the streets.

The precedent for killings during campus demonstrations of the 1960s was not established at Kent State. On February 8, 1968, police fired into a crowd at South Carolina State, a small college for blacks in Orangeburg. Three young men were killed.

The country hardly noticed the "Orangeburg massacre." It seemed to be just another skirmish in the long history of violence between whites and blacks in the South. In an era of ghetto riots, the shooting of blacks had become commonplace. The victims, being black, were of small interest to the majority. Whatever the explanation, the Orangeburg killings took place within a racial framework, and seemed to have little in common with the killings at Kent.

The People's Park killing in 1968 at Berkeley, however, was another matter. The victim was white, and he was shot by police while students were rampaging through the streets to protest an action of the campus administration. Except that confrontations between rebels and authority had become more severe, and more violent, little had changed in Berkeley since the days of FSM.

525

Berkeley, as usual, set the stage for what happened elsewhere, but now the country seemed to take less notice. Berkeley was always having disruptions, and even killing was hardly a shock. Furthermore Berkeley—unlike Kent State—was not an ordinary campus, with average American students, in the nation's heartland. Americans expected disturbances at Berkeley as they did, for other reasons, at Orangeburg. But Berkeley, having cut the pattern to start campus rebellions in the 1960s, now cut the pattern for their end.

Just a few minutes' walk down Telegraph Avenue from the spot where the Free Speech Movement started was a three-acre plot which, in the early 1960s, was a jumble of bookstores, coffee shops and old houses favored for lodging by radicals and freaks. The university considered it a rats' nest of trouble. The local police kept the neighborhood off-balance with drug busts and sweeps. Then, in 1968, the university and the city decided to tear the buildings down, to make way for urban renewal.

For nearly a year the land remained vacant, an eyesore of concrete remnants, mudholes, garbage and broken glass. Then, in the early spring of 1969, a loose association of neighbors, students and nonstudents agreed on a plan for renovation. On Sunday, April 20, with private donations and volunteer labor, they cleared the land and built People's Park. In the succeeding weeks, children played on its swings and slides, and on weekends as many as three thousand people would come daily to picnic or take the sun, plant shrubs and flowers, putter in a common vegetable garden.

At 5:00 A.M. on May 15, without notice, some two hundred policemen from the City of Berkeley, the County of Alameda and the campus force arrived to reassert the university's rights of ownership. The cops wore flak jackets, and carried tear gas launchers, shotguns and rifles. They were followed by a construction crew, equipped with gas masks, which by midafternoon had surrounded the plot with an eight-foot-high chain link fence.

As soon as word got out that "the pigs are ripping off the park," students headed for the campus and, by noon, three thousand had assembled at Sproul Plaza. Radicals and freaks were in a minority, observers said. Most of the crowd was straight, and within it were pom-pom girls, jocks and Greeks. At about twelve thirty, people began surging down Telegraph Avenue, chanting, throwing stones, shattering store windows. As they approached the park, the police charged with their clubs, then laid down a barrage of tear gas. About one o'clock, they started firing shotguns.

The students, accustomed to nightsticks and tear gas, were incredulous at the shooting. It was a violation of the rules of combat, observed for half a decade by both sides. James Rector, a twenty-six-year-old visitor from San Jose who was standing on the roof of a two-story building from which stones were thrown, was blasted in the side by buckshot and died. Some thirty persons in all were wounded by gunfire, thirteen seriously. No specific incidents had provoked the shift to firearms, nor were any policemen seriously injured. The cops just seemed fed up.

Governor Ronald Reagan's gibes reflected the new mood. People's Park, he said, had served as an "excuse for a riot." Denying police excess, he declared, "Once the dogs of war are unleashed, you must expect things will happen." * If anything, he said, the university's "liberal" administration was to blame. "The police didn't kill the young man," he said. "He was killed by the first college administrator who said some time ago it was all right to break the laws in the name of dissent." To the governor's taunts, the "liberal" administration raised no protest.

The student body, straights more prominently than freaks, demonstrated heavily throughout the succeeding week. At a campus referendum fifteen thousand students voted, the greatest number ever, and 85 percent supported the restoration of People's Park. But no official action was taken to fix responsibility for the killing, nor was the tactic of crowd control by shotgun fire officially repudiated. The university tried to shift responsibility for the violence to campus radicals. Clearly, the students were alone.

The People's Park episode seemed to be evidence that public sympathy for student protest was exhausted. The absence of a popular outcry had left authorities free to administer virtually any lesson they chose. People's Park might have been taken as a warning to white students that revolution was no longer to be treated as a gentlemen's game.† A year later, crackling M-1 rifles would confirm the lesson at Kent State.

* Compare to Nixon's statement after Kent State: "When dissent turns to violence it invites tragedy."

† Mark Rudd, for one, did not believe it, even after People's Park. "We estimate that the pigs probably will not fire into crowds, although they have done it at Berkeley," he was quoted as saying. "But they won't fire into white crowds."

"It was a Friday night in Kent, the day after Nixon's speech," said Alan Canfora, speaking of May 1, 1970, "and we were planning on going downtown, which we did practically every Friday night, to have a few beers and relax. There's this one section of town called the Strip, where there are a lot of bars, and people always gathered. We were still in my apartment about nine o'clock when we got a phone call from someone who said, 'Hey, something is going to happen down here. Tensions are really building.' So we went down right away."

Actually, the signs of unrest had started on Thursday, within hours of Nixon's speech, when small groups of students circulated through town chanting antiwar slogans, and spray-painting the sides of buildings. At noon on Friday, three hundred students met for a ceremony at the Victory Bell, center of the campus, and amid fervid rhetoric buried a copy of the Constitution. At three in the afternoon, the Black United Students held a rally of their own. By then, however, many of the students had left for the weekend and, with only fifty people in attendance, the blacks' rally fizzled.

Some college administrators were apprehensive at the release that week of Rick Erickson and Howie Emmer, the SDS leaders who had been jailed after the campus disorders of 1969. But there is no evidence that either was involved in the events of the subsequent days. The college paid no attention to the announcement of another rally scheduled at the Victory Bell on Monday at noon, when the students would be back on campus. The administrators thus neglected to take any precautions for what, predictably, could be a troublesome event.

Canfora, like most Kent State students, normally went home on Friday nights, but he often returned to the campus to spend the weekend with his friends. He remembered eating a spaghetti dinner with his parents on Friday evening, before making the half-hour drive from Barberton back to Kent. He and his friends were sitting around the apartment watching television when the call came from the Strip. It was beautiful spring weather, Canfora remembered, and by the time his group arrived, the sidewalks of the Strip were already alive with people. Most were Kent State

528

students, some were from nearby colleges and a few were bikers who roared their motorcycles up and down the street.

"People were coming in and out of bars, and we joined them in chanting antiwar slogans," he said. "People seemed to be more political than usual, but a lot were just whooping it up, like any spring night.

"Pretty soon a police car came by and some adventurous soul threw a beer glass at it. The police car just took off. Then a second police car came by, and two or three students standing on the sidewalk threw more glasses. That car sped away, too. Then no police cars came back, and the people out on the street were feeling pretty good.

"By now the street was filled, and the atmosphere was very political. Someone made a bonfire in the middle of the street, and pretty soon it was raging. Then some students cried, 'Let's move,' and in a few minutes maybe five hundred or a thousand people were marching down the street. As they went, they trashed the windows of the banks and loan companies, the East Ohio Gas Company, the Ohio Edison Company, the business establishments that were representative of the ruling class. There were also some drunks and anarchists, who broke windows in a hardware store and a shoe store, and there was some looting."

Meanwhile, the Kent police force asked for help from neighboring communities and the county sheriff's office. Around midnight Kent assembled its full twenty-two-man complement and at 12:30, dressed in riot gear and reinforced by sheriff's deputies, the city's policemen confronted the mob and ordered immediate dispersal. For the next several hours there was the usual exchange of rocks and tear gas, and about 2:30 A.M. the last of the crowd straggled off to bed. Injuries were few, and fourteen were arrested. At first the city said damages were $50,000 but eventually it reduced the estimate by three-fourths.

"I think it's important to note," Canfora said, "that, though some in Kent saw these actions only as violent and destructive, the students looked at them in political and historical perspective. We heard on the news that actions like these were happening across the country. The damage they did was insignificant compared to the death and destruction in Indochina during any one day. The

529

way we saw it, these kinds of actions had to be taken to bring the war to a close. Nothing else was working."

Indeed, within hours of Nixon's speech, the protests at Kent were overshadowed by those at Oberlin in Ohio, at Rutgers and Princeton in New Jersey and at many other colleges. Ohio State, centerpiece of Ohio's public university system, had already had several days of rioting that week, which was quelled after a curfew was imposed and the National Guard summoned. Even Ohio's little Miami University had rioted, and the state was nervous.

On Saturday, Mayor LeRoy Satrom of Kent, who had closed the bars on Friday night, issued an emergency proclamation. During the course of Friday evening, Satrom had phoned the office of Governor James Rhodes, who was in the midst of an election campaign, and announced that he thought SDS was then in command of the disorder. Rhodes's office promised to alert the National Guard. Satrom's proclamation the next morning established a dawn-to-dusk curfew in the city, plus a curfew which began only at 1:00 A.M. on the campus. The proclamation was of questionable legality but, what was worse, the difference in the curfew hours between campus and town virtually assured trouble that night on the college grounds.

Canfora said the word was passed throughout the day of an action at the ROTC building after dark. By then some fifteen hundred students, with nowhere else to go, had congregated on the campus. Most were straights. A few wore the beads and headbands favored by the radicals. It was a hot night, and the mood was angry rather than frolicsome. Students threw rocks and firecrackers, shouted slogans and spray-painted peace signs and obscenities on buildings and sidewalks.

"ROTC was a hated institution on campus," Canfora said, "and when people would walk by they would say, 'Some day this building is going to go.' It was an old army barracks, built around World War Two, and it was going to be torn down anyway. Then someone that night trashed the windows, and the police didn't come, so that was the signal.

"One guy who looked pretty straight walked up, broke out a window and lit a corner of the curtain. People were cheering and whooping it up, but the fire went out. Then some people threw flares on the roof. Some other people got rags and dipped them in

530

the tank of a motorcycle which was near the corner of the building. That did it.

"The building started to burn pretty good, and the fire department came, but they had no police protection. Some people in the crowd, since there were no police around, ran up and took their hoses away. Some turned the water on the firemen, some cut holes in the hose. Then hundreds of people unrolled the hoses and dragged them across the campus. Everybody was cheering. People wanted the building to burn as a demonstration of their outrage about the invasion of Cambodia."

When the police finally arrived after nine o'clock, they laid down a barrage of tear gas to defend the firemen, but they were too late to save the building. Finally the crowd, feeling exultant, broke up. A few skirmished with the police. One group set fire to a storage shed, but another put out the blaze. Several hundred, in violation of the curfew, swarmed toward town. Canfora said he headed to a friend's room back at the dorms.

The National Guard began rolling into town about that time, under a hail of bottles and stones thrown at them by the students parading off-campus. The units reaching Kent had already been on duty for several days, patrolling under tense conditions during a strike in Akron. The Guardsmen were tired, and anxious to go home. They were, for the most part, young whites from the working class, like the students at Kent. Many served in the Guard because, like their adversaries that night, they did not want to go to Vietnam. But they did not have the privilege of attending college, and they were in no mood to take guff from some spoiled kids who did.

The Guard officers had been ordered by the governor—another order of dubious legality—to supersede civilian authority at Kent. The men were in full battle gear, carrying M-1 rifles designed not for riots but for battle. Though the Guardsmen knew of the standing orders to use minimum force in civil disturbances, they were used to having civilians flee at the first show of arms, particularly when bayonets were bared. They were not prepared to face student resistance.

The Guardsmen reached the campus as the last students were leaving the embers of the ROTC building. Nonetheless, the soldiers fixed their bayonets and advanced. Their attitude, noticeably harsher than that of the police, was epitomized by their com-

531

mander, General Sylvester T. Corso, who was seen flinging a rock at retreating students, shouting, "If these goddamn kids can throw rocks, I can, too." Some Guardsmen chased students, and inflicted minor stab wounds with their bayonets.

At midnight, some faculty members negotiated an agreement with several Guard officers at the dorms to permit students who lived off-campus to go home. Canfora, still inside, said he and his roommates decided to return to the apartment. On the way back, some Guardsmen summoned him from the other side of the street.

"They had a big armored personnel carrier," he said. "It looked like a tank. I started up a conversation with one of them, since I knew some guys in the National Guard. I asked him where he was from. He took the butt of his gun and hit me on the chest with it. Then he told me to get back over with the others. I knew we were headed for trouble right then."

Others sensed trouble, too. On Sunday morning Ronald J. Kane, the county prosecutor, recommended closing the campus and sending the students home. A student body scattered over Ohio would be unable to riot. Based on that reasoning, 135 American colleges had closed their campuses that weekend. But the Kent State administration, all weekend long, took no initiative, allowing all the crucial decisions to be made by the politicians or the Guard, with little regard for the students' safety.

Governor Rhodes, in this instance, issued the instructions. Rhodes, at that moment, was presenting himself as the "law and order" candidate in the Republican senatorial primary. The vote was on Tuesday.* On Sunday he showed up at Kent and, before noon, held a press conference.

"We have to keep this university open at all costs," he declared. "To close it down would be to play into the hands of all the dissident elements that are trying to do just that." Rhodes made no mention of student safety. On the contrary, he spoke of protest leaders who were "worse than the Brown Shirts and Communist element and also the night riders and vigilantes. They're the worst type we harbor in America."

Rhodes conveyed the same signal as Nixon, who had already referred to rioting students as "bums." The implication of both seemed to be that student demonstrators were fair game.

"We thought what Rhodes said was kind of funny, but danger-

* He lost.

ous," Canfora said. "Students were not harming any individuals. They were committing some acts of property damage, because they were irate about the war. We wondered how the National Guard took what Rhodes said, like, did they take it to heart?"

On Sunday, Guard units pitched tents all over the Kent State campus, and appropriated the gym. The students felt that the campus was occupied territory, and resented it. But the sun was shining and tensions seemed to abate over the course of the afternoon. According to some accounts, there was even some casual fraternizing between Guardsmen and students.

Canfora remembered it differently. "A lot of the Guards were making wise remarks to the women," he said, "and uncalled-for comments toward guys wearing bell-bottom pants or flashy clothes, or with long hair. They were very antagonistic." Nonetheless, the daylight hours were uneventful, and contentiousness rose only after night fell.

By eight o'clock, several hundred students had gathered at the Victory Bell, apparently spoiling to break the curfew again. At nine o'clock, in a sudden change of orders, a curfew was clamped on the campus, but hundreds of students had already marched off together. Overhead, a Guard helicopter shining a searchlight on the formless parade added an ominous quality to the scene. At Kent's principal intersection the students stopped, and blocked traffic with a mass sit-in.

A spokesman for the students said the protesters would move if they were allowed to present a list of grievances to the college president. A lesser campus functionary took responsibility for refusing the request, but the crowd thought it was still negotiating when a tear gas canister exploded in its midst. Convinced it had been betrayed, the crowd scattered, with Guardsmen giving chase in every direction.

The next hour or so was bedlam. On campus, Guardsmen chased students indoors, using their bayonets. Inevitably, a sniper was rumored to be present, which intensified anxiety. Downtown, students pelted Guardsmen with rocks, or struck them with clubs. Girls fought as hard as boys, and shouted the same obscenities. Guardsmen swung with their rifle butts and bayonets, and fired more tear gas. Meanwhile, the helicopter roared overhead, conveying intimations of a Vietnam battle zone.

When the battling ended on Sunday at midnight, a half-dozen or

so students had stab wounds, and an equal number of Guardsmen had stone bruises. More important, the level of mutual hostility had reached an explosive point. Students were primed to
provoke, Guardsmen to retaliate. The elements were in place for
catastrophe.

On Monday morning, with the campus population back to its
normal level, the students prepared their official rally to protest the
Cambodian invasion. The intent of the rally was peaceful, and they
were certain that it was legal. The governor had not declared a state
of emergency, or martial law. The mayor's proclamation did not
forbid campus assembly. The university had imposed no ban. Only
the Guard, with no lawful standing to act on its own, considered
the demonstration prohibited. As the students gathered around the
Victory Bell, Guardsmen made preparations to disperse them.

Of the various Guard units preparing for the encounter, the critical one was to be Troop G of the 107th Armored Cavalry Regiment.
Troop G had been pelted with rocks when it rolled into Kent on
Saturday, and several of its men had been injured. On Sunday, its
eighteen members had gone off duty at 6:00 P.M. but, even before
they ate their supper, they were sent back for riot duty. They retired at 1:00 A.M., only to be up again at four to relieve another unit
on watch. On Monday morning, as they looked over the growing
crowd, the men of Troop G were not in good humor.

Alan Canfora said he was not very cheerful himself. Many students who had been absent over the weekend were demonstrating.
Many who had never demonstrated before wanted to protest Cambodia. Many others were spurred on by antagonism to the Guard.
But his own girlfriend, scared by what had happened the night
before, would not join him, Canfora said, and he was feeling irritated.

Before he left the apartment, Canfora recalled, he and his friends
made some flags, as they often did, to bring to the rally. The flags
were black, he said, because that was the only material around. But
to avoid being taken for anarchists, he said, they sprayed Kent on
them in light paint.

"When I got to the Commons, the Guard was stretched out all
along the ruins of the ROTC building," he recalled. "One Guards-

534

man at the end of the troop says to me, 'Hey, boy, what's that you're carrying there?' And I said, 'Just a couple of flags.' And he answered, 'We're going to make you eat those flags today.'

"So I kind of mouthed off to him. 'Just don't get too close, motherfucker,' I said, 'or I'm going to stick them down your throat.' It was an arrogant remark. I didn't like being threatened, but I figured as long as I kept my distance there wouldn't be any problem."

In the thousands of photos that were taken that day, Canfora, wearing a red headband, was often seen at the head of the crowd, taunting the Guard, waving his flag. In a photo published in *Life*, he was about 150 feet from the nearest Guardsman. No photograph showed him any closer, and he has sworn to me that most of the time he was much farther away.

As for the crowd, estimates varied of the numbers that swarmed around the Victory Bell as noon approached. Canfora calculated 1500, which is a widely accepted figure. Michener's estimate was 1100. The field commander of the Guard, curiously, put the number at only 800. But the Guardsmen, clustered at the ruins of the ROTC building several hundred yards below, saw the crowd swelling rapidly as classes broke for lunch. They saw several thousand other students, most of them spectators, congregated on the terraces of nearby buildings. They calculated they were outnumbered by tenfold or more, by those they now considered the enemy.

At 11:50 a National Guard jeep carrying a campus policeman drove up to the edge of the crowd. With two Guardsmen perched on the rear seat, the jeep slowly circled the demonstrators, while the officer shouted through a bullhorn, "This assembly is unlawful. This crowd must disperse immediately. This is an order."

The students, feeling the solidarity of nationwide protest, greeted the announcement with such endearing slogans as "Pigs Off Campus," as well as the more traditional antiwar obscenities. Canfora remembered that "some people were even chanting 'Sieg Heil.'" The jeep retreated in a chorus of jeers and a shower of stones.

On the field below, the order was passed to the Guardsmen to load their weapons and put on their gas masks. At a minute before noon, the field commander gave the crucial order: "Prepare to move out and disperse this mob."

Buckling on the gas masks protracted the distance between

Guardsmen and foe. Heavy and uncomfortable, the masks also narrowed vision and distorted hearing. They made the Guardsmen sweat, and they evoked a self-image of plodding Frankenstein monsters, the objects of mockery. To the students, nimble-footed and casually clad, the masks made the Guardsmen look like robots. The masks seemed to erode the last shred of sympathy between the adversaries.

Laying down a barrage of tear gas, the Guardsmen stepped off from the ROTC ruins, Troop G in the center, Company A on its right and Company C on its left, 113 men in all. To reach their objective, they had to mount a rise known as "Blanket Hill." As they advanced, the students retreated—throwing stones, shouting obscenities, flinging back empty canisters of gas—their ranks growing larger with people leaving classes for the midday break.

Later, Guardsmen would claim they had been struck often, not only by stones but more damaging projectiles. In fact, the number of hits probably was few. Of the photographs taken that day, the bulk showed the crowd much too distant to hit the Guardsmen. Occasionally some bold student would approach fairly near but, out of discretion if not fear, the moat was never breached.

Michener cited one firebrand who met the description of Alan Canfora. "One young man, with extremely long hair held in place by a beaded band," Michener wrote, "displayed a large black flag at the end of a pole, and with extreme bravado waved it at critical moments at the troops, almost in their faces, retreating to eight or ten yards at other times." Canfora acknowledged that Michener's player was he, but he said there were no beads on his headband, and he was not nearly so close to the Guard any time that day.

"Whenever the Guard came near us we backed away," Canfora said. "We didn't make any kind of stand. In other demonstrations, we got right up close to the police and even fought with them. But the Guard had already stabbed people with bayonets, and nobody was foolish enough to stand there. In fact, I didn't see a single Guardsman get hit by a rock. Some Guardsmen picked up rocks and threw them back at the students, but those rocks fell short, too, because of the distance."

As the Guard advanced, the students backed toward Taylor Hall, at the center of three buildings set side by side, with about twenty yards between them. The students passed through the two openings between the buildings, then dispersed to the right and left.

536

While Company C followed a pack going the one way, Troop G and Company A pursued students going the other. At a concrete sculpture called the Pagoda, Troop G and Company A stopped to regain their bearings. Then, inexplicably, they chose to descend the other side of the hill to a practice football field, where they immediately found themselves hemmed in by a chain link fence.

When the Guardsmen turned, seventy-six of them in all, they found their rear covered by the fence, and students ringing the crest of the hill they had just marched down. Rocks were being thrown in their direction, and a particularly militant contingent, of which Alan Canfora was a member, taunted them from an asphalt-covered parking lot to the right. In a sense, the two units were besieged, but they were not in danger, and there was no sign whatever of the snipers they later cited to defend their actions. Mainly the men felt hot and angry, and humiliated at having walked into a trap of their own making.

At 12:10 P.M., sixteen members of Troop G knelt in unison and aimed their rifles at the students in the parking lot. "The brazen young man with the black flag," Michener wrote, "ran close and waved it before the silent rifles, daring the Guardsmen to fire." The men did not then fire.

"In the photos, you can see at least three Guardsmen with their guns aimed right at me," said Canfora. "I thought to myself at the time that there was a possibility that they might wound some people, kill some people. But I thought they would not be so foolish to shoot. There was no reason for them to fire. No one was threatening their lives.

"I thought then my life might be in danger. But I thought that across the country other people felt the same way as I did, and took the same risks to fight against the war. So I decided that the possibility was not enough to make me just turn around and walk away and go hide someplace."

A few minutes after they rose from the firing position, the men of Troop G, plus a few other Guardsmen, huddled together on the football field. No one had ever revealed what they said in the huddle. But subsequent events suggest strongly that the men of Troop G must have reached a decision among themselves to deal with their antagonists.

At 12:18, the Guardsmen began their undignified retreat. Regrouped, they were ordered to march back over the hill to the original point of deployment at the ROTC ruins. Troop G was on the right flank, its men in a tight V formation.

"As they started moving up the hill," Canfora said, "the most militant, the most active and most vocal of the students were still in the parking lot. We were moving parallel to them, at a distance of about three hundred feet. We kept an eye on them, trying to anticipate what they would do when they reached the top."

As they advanced, the men of Troop G kept glancing to the right. The official explanation was that they were looking out for flying rocks, or a sniper. But Company A's men, at their side, looked neither right nor left. Canfora said they appeared to be picking out targets, and some of the most scrupulous investigators of the Kent State killings concur.

"I'm absolutely convinced that they fired at me on purpose," Canfora said. "I was down there on the practice field denouncing the National Guard. I was very vocal, shouting a lot of antiwar slogans. I shouted some obscenities at the Guardsmen. I was very visible.

"As they went up the hill, I think they kept their eye on several other people, too. I include Joe Lewis and Tom Grace, my roommate. I include Jeffrey Miller, who was very active that day. He threw some rocks, and in the pictures you can see Miller right down in the front ranks, raising his middle finger. I think Allison Krause was shot on purpose, and Robbie Stamps perhaps, and Dean Kahler. He admits throwing a rock or two. He's a tall guy, about six feet three. He was very visible, very vocal. I think certain people in the group were definitely shot on purpose."

When Troop G reached the Pagoda on the top of the hill, its members stopped simultaneously, turned together, raised their weapons and fired in unison. No proof was ever established that an order was given. But the men of Troop G could not have acted with such synchronism in the absence of an order, or of prearrangement. The firing lasted thirteen seconds.

"There was maybe one tree in that entire line of fire in the parking lot," Canfora recalled, "and I had just moved past it, maybe five or six feet. I heard the guns go off, and I thought to myself, surely they must be firing blanks, because there was no reason for them to be firing. It was broad daylight. Nobody was doing anything deserving to be killed.

538

"Then I thought, even though they're only firing blanks, I'm going to make it behind this tree. So I took a couple of real quick steps and, as I swung around, my right wrist was protruding and I was hit. Another student was standing behind the same tree. I knelt on the ground, about two feet behind him.

"Ten feet to my right was Tom Grace. He and I had gone through this political metamorphosis together. I hadn't seen him since earlier in the day but, by some coincidence, he was right near me when the shooting began. He was right out in the line of fire, lying flat. He was in extreme pain, because a bullet had passed through his left ankle, and shattered quite a few bones. He still walks with a limp. He started to get up to grab his foot. Though I still thought it was only buckshot, I yelled at him to keep his head down. To this day, he credits me with saving his life.

"I could have sworn the shooting lasted thirty seconds or a minute. As soon as it stopped, there was a moment of silence. After that, you could hear a lot of screams of pain and a lot of screams of people horror-stricken and anguished."

Of the four students who were mortally wounded, Jeffrey Miller and Allison Krause had been demonstrators. They were killed at a distance from the Guardsmen of 265 and 343 feet respectively, far greater than either could throw a stone. William Schroeder and Sandra Scheuer, both passersby, were nearly four hundred feet away.

Nine other students were struck and left with wounds. They ranged from minor, like Alan Canfora's, to permanent paralysis of the lower body, suffered by Dean Kahler. The most distant victim was Donald MacKenzie, shot through the back of the neck at 730 feet—nearly two and one-half football fields away—as he ran from the firing.

Nixon's initial reaction was to yield nothing to the student protest over Cambodia. The first White House statement was the callous observation that "when dissent turns to violence it invites tragedy." But in the days after Kent State, some 450 colleges were closed or on strike, and emotions remained high. A Harris poll found that 80 percent of American campuses experienced protests after Kent State, that 75 percent of the students approved of them, that 58 percent participated in them. On May 7, Nixon met with eight college presidents, who warned that only prompt withdrawal from Cambodia was likely to avert permanent alienation of the student generation.

The next day Nixon told a press conference that he understood how deeply students felt, and that he was concerned about their protests. "They are trying to say they want peace," Nixon stated. "They are trying to say they want to stop the killing. They are trying to say that they want to end the draft. They are trying to say that we ought to get out of Vietnam. I agree with everything that they are trying to accomplish." Nixon defended his decision to strike into Cambodia, but restated a commitment to get all Americans out by the end of June.

Most students, and many other Americans, considered his statements cynical, and on the weekend after Kent State some seventy-five thousand descended on Washington, including huge delegations from Yale, Brandeis, North Carolina and Haverford. At dawn on Saturday morning, an insomniac Nixon drove to the Lincoln Memorial to chat with some of these students. Though the conversations were stilted and uncomfortable, they were his way of reaching out a hand to close the gap with the young.

But an ominous incident had occurred the day before in New York, where Mayor John Lindsay, a persistent war critic, had ordered the flag on City Hall to half-staff to honor the Kent State victims. Several hundred students from New York University and Hunter College had chosen the morning for a protest march through the Wall Street district. At the lunch hour some two hundred construction workers, wearing their hard hats, attacked the students with fists and lead pipes and, while policemen looked on indifferently, gave them a good beating. The workers then set off for City Hall, where they raised the flag to full-staff.

Three days later two thousand "hardhats," more formally organized, paraded through Wall Street in support of Nixon, patriotism and the war. They were showered with ticker tape. More such demonstrations followed, and hardhats became popular heroes. *Time* said "the rebellion of the hardhats seemed only the surface of a resentment that doubtless runs deep across the nation," and *Newsweek* ran a poll that showed a majority supported the President on Cambodia. The poll also revealed that, of the Americans

540

responding, nearly six out of seven blamed demonstrating students, rather than the National Guard, for the deaths at Kent State.*

A month later Nixon appointed former Governor William Scranton of Pennsylvania to head an inquiry into campus unrest. Its mandate included Jackson State, a black college in Mississippi where two students were killed by police, though not in the course of a war protest. These two deaths, but for Kent, would probably have been forgotten, like those at Orangeburg in 1968. The Jackson State inquiry was a formality, since there was no doubt that the chief concern of the Nixon Administration, and the country, was Kent State.

Though the commission performed conscientiously, it failed, even with subpoena powers, to get a single Ohio Guardsman to testify at its hearings. The evasion seriously undermined the inquiry. Still, the commission concluded that the Guard shared in the blame, along with students and even the President of the United States, whom it urged to show greater leadership in reconciliation. Most important, the Scranton Commission concluded that the killings at Kent were "unnecessary, unwarranted and inexcusable." Nixon intimated his displeasure with the report by discreet silence, but Vice President Agnew denounced it as "pablum for permissiveness," and other Administration officials similarly complained.

In Ohio, the official response was even less balanced. The state initiated a legal inquiry only in August, under threat of competition from the county, but well before a grand jury was empaneled the attorney general rejected any indictments against Guardsmen. Instead the grand jury brought twenty-five indictments, several of them felonies, against demonstrators.

Alan Canfora was charged with second-degree riot, a misdemeanor, which was dropped with the charges against the others in December 1971, after a long legal battle. "We were on the defensive trying to clear ourselves all this time," Canfora said, "rather than going on the offensive to expose the nature of the murders." Ohio's law enforcement establishment, however, had no intention of letting the victims, dead or alive, take the offensive.†

---

* Specifically, 58 percent blamed the students, 11 percent the National Guard and 31 percent had no opinion.

† The state finally reversed its position in 1979, when it became apparent that Canfora and other survivors were determined not to let the issue die. In consenting to the out-of-court settlement, the judge cited "the incalculable benefit" to Ohio "in finally closing this chapter in our state's history." See footnote, p. 511.

The FBI investigated the shootings, too, and a report of its findings said, "The shootings were not necessary and not in order . . . No Guardsmen were hurt by flying rocks or projectiles and none was in danger of his life . . . One Guardsman fired at a student who was making an obscene gesture." In a more complete report later in the year the FBI said, "We have reason to believe that the claim by the Guard that their lives were endangered by the students was fabricated subsequent to the event." Though the FBI statement covered a range of federal violations, the Justice Department did not convene a grand jury to request indictments.*

According to the evidence, the country clearly had little desire, and the people of Ohio even less, to exact punishment for the killings at Kent State. On the contrary, in the weeks and months that followed, popular outrage was directed not against the killers but against the victims.

Michener cited the deluge of letters to the local newspapers. He took testimony on conversations in the streets, and in bars and supermarkets. He spoke to young people who returned to college after visits with their parents. To an astonishing degree, he concluded, students had become an object of hatred.

This hatred came out not simply in objection to student politics, or to student protest in the name of politics. It was directed, perhaps more than anything, at students' countercultural habits, from the long hair and blue jeans that everyone saw in public to the sexual freedom that so many fantasized about in private.

Considerable research into public attitudes followed the Kent State killings and, again and again, the assertion that emerged was that the students deserved what they got. To a large proportion of Americans, perhaps to a majority, the National Guard performed an act at Kent State that was not reprehensible but praiseworthy. In many instances, Americans seemed to be seized by a feeling almost of relief that the act had been done at last.

The Scranton Commission, which published its findings in the fall of 1970, was not optimistic about prospects for the immediate

* The *Washington Post* on May 5, 1978, reported that NBC News had possession of a memo from John Ehrlichman, Nixon's assistant, which attributed the decision rejecting indictment to the President himself. In 1974, after Nixon resigned, the Justice Department did convene a grand jury, which took extensive testimony and indicted eight Guardsmen. A federal judge later dismissed the charges.

542

future. It stated that America had been generally successful in finding common values within a diverse culture but that "we are now
in grave danger of losing what is common among us through growing intolerance of opposing views on issues and of diversity itself."
Acknowledging that a new culture had emerged among students
in the 1960s, the Commission added with alarm that this culture
tended to be self-righteous, impatient with democratic processes
and resistant to civil restraint. It concluded that prospects for social
tranquility were very gloomy.

The Scranton Commission's alarm was misplaced, however, for
the 1960s, as suddenly as they began at Greensboro, ended at Kent
State. That is not to say that the counterculture vanished, or that
radicalism died. Blue jeans and rock music lived on, adopted by
the majority culture. Jim Mellen remained a fervent Third Worlder,
and Alan Canfora agitated faithfully to keep the memory of the Kent
State victims alive. There was even an antiwar protest or two in the
early 1970s. But as an era when masses of people, most of them
young, regularly took to the streets to challenge the practices of
society, the 1960s ended with a thirteen-second fusillade in a small
Ohio town.

The decade ended because the civil rights movement, which was
responsible for its conception, no longer contributed the seed to
enrich it. It ended because antiwar protest, discredited at Chicago,
never regained popular approval. It ended because a consensus
was reached that the country had blundered in entering the war,
and because Americans accepted the government's assurances that
only time was needed until the last soldiers came home. The 1960s
ended because a society can function at a feverish emotional pitch
for only so long, and Americans, after ten years of it, were tired.

At Kent State, the country seemed to announce that whoever
among the young felt deeply enough to continue the practices of
the 1960s had to be ready to die for them. On these terms, radicalism turned out to have a less committed following than had once
been believed. Few were ready to die, and so the decade reached
its end.

EPILOGUE

THE 1960S ENDED as they began, abruptly. It was as if the country suddenly went into sedation, its passions, removed from the streets, taken home and locked in a closet. Our ideas became timid, our leaders drab, our concerns self-centered. Lecturing on college campuses in the early 1970s, I regularly heard the question, usually posed with nostalgia, "Where did the 1960s go?" The triumph of the 1970s was so quick and thorough that many were led to wonder whether the 1960s had been real or an illusion, an integral part of American history or an aberration never to recur.

Students of the 1970s, both black and white, went back to their books. Though their hair was still disheveled, and they never returned to coats and ties, they were as conscientious as the students of the 1950s in doing their academic chores. If the killings at Kent placed the seal on student protest, the collapse of the assumption of permanent prosperity was followed by the return of the old ways. By the early 1970s, the country had once again experienced recession. Jobs were scarce, and inflation was puzzlingly persistent. America's young, who had taken for granted—as did every generation before them—that they would live at a higher standard than their parents, began to worry whether they could even keep up. They were forced to recognize that if they were to *succeed*, they would, like their parents before them, have to work very hard at it.

And yet, like rock music and marijuana, the spirit of the 1960s hung on, in many ways. Among them was the new view of the individual in relation to society. The rights which the 1960s asserted the 1970s seem to have entrenched.

Blacks, whatever their economic disadvantages, were never freer to pursue the lives of their choice, and so were women, homosexuals and other minorities. In the spirit of the 1960s, even the handicapped, prisoners, and union members insisted upon, and won, a wide range of new rights. Americans, furthermore, participated more directly than before in every level of government, including selection of the president, and even acquired the legal authority to

547

have the FBI turn over the files it had kept on them. In the 1970s, the drive for personal freedom led to the abolition of the draft, access by women to legal abortions, social acceptance of unmarrieds living together, the proliferation of bizarre religious and semireligious cults.

There was a reaction to the 1960s, but more to its practices than its spirit. In fact the 1970s has drawn quite perversely on the 1960s' spirit to reach very different ends. The exaltation of personal freedom, once directed against racism and a militant foreign policy, became the vehicle for an abandonment of social responsibility. The society retreated significantly from politics, and from concern for the distress of others. In the "do-your-own-thing" spirit, there was a growing resistance to taxes and social regulation, to restraints upon consumption and gain, to traditional notions of public service. A set of ideas which began in the 1960s as a protest against the stodginess and conformity of the 1950s has served in the 1970s, I think, to fuel a national propensity to self-indulgence.

In defense of the decade, I think it is fair to say that, Watergate apart, the pervasive issues of the 1970s have not had the same clear-cut moral cogency as the issues of the 1960s. Jim Crow gave way to the more subtle questions of busing and affirmative action, the Vietnam War to the more technical problems of the decline of the dollar and the energy shortage. Even had the ardor of the 1960s been undiminished, it is not easy to envisage crowds taking to the streets to express emotions over issues where the line is fuzzy between good and evil, or where there is no line at all.

In time, new issues will surely emerge. And even if the old issues remain around awhile, unresolved, they may together create a crisis in which government appears unable to make and enforce decisions, and is stripped of popular confidence. Though current signs may be deceptive, there are plenty of them. The country's sense that it is in responsible hands has declined steadily through four administrations, from the mid-1960s to the end of the 1970s. The feeling of popular frustration which was basic to the 1960s seemed once again on the rise as the 1980s approached.

THERE IS, of course, nothing sacred, much less scientific, about a ten-year cycle in the national temperament. But with some accu-

548

racy we characterize the 1950s as stuffy, the 1960s as turbulent and the 1970s as placid, so historical precedent seems to presage in the 1980s another dramatic shift. I would be loath to speculate on its nature, but, if we learned nothing else from the 1960s, it must be that, contrary to what Americans once believed, we as a people possess no magic which spares us the pain of social disorder. This book is by no means meant as prophecy. But the lesson of America in the 1960s, I think, is that the country, given the provocation, could once again turn away from its political institutions and take its controversies into the streets.

Washington
June 1979

GLOSSARY

ACLU—American Civil Liberties Union
ADA—Americans for Democratic Action
CIA—Central Intelligence Agency
CORE—Congress of Racial Equality
ERAP—Economic Research and Action Project
FEPC—Fair Employment Practices Commission
FOR—Fellowship of Reconciliation
FSM—Free Speech Movement
FUNY—Free University of New York
HUAC—House Un-American Activities Committee
LAPD—Los Angeles Police Department
LID—League for Industrial Democracy
M-2-M—May 2nd Movement
MIA—Montgomery Improvement Association
NAACP—National Association for the Advancement of Colored People
NAG—Non-Violent Action Group
NLF—National Liberation Front
NSA—National Student Association
PLP—Progressive Labor Party (or PL—Progressive Labor)
SCFIW—Student Committee for the Improvement of Watts
SCLC—Southern Christian Leadership Conference
SDS—Students for a Democratic Society
SLID—Student League for Industrial Democracy
SNCC—Student Non-Violent Coordinating Committee
VDC—Vietnam Day Committee
VEP—Voter Education Project

551

BIBLIOGRAPHICAL NOTE

THOUGH THE LITERATURE of the 1960s is vast, it is disappointing both in quality and scope. There are good accounts of the politics of the successive administrations, but they tend to treat the social disorder of the period as little more than a distraction. The literature is heavy on memoirs, largely the work of young activists, but only Martin Luther King's series of volumes and James Forman's *The Making of Black Revolutionaries* cover extended involvement in the events of the decade. Very few efforts at synthesis have been attempted. The most helpful to me were Thomas Brooks's *Walls Come Tumbling Down*, Kirkpatrick Sale's *SDS* and Thomas Powers's *The War at Home*.

Though some good material has been published on the Mississippi Summer, and the events at Berkeley, Watts, Selma, Columbia and Kent State, there is very little that is readily available on such important episodes as the sit-ins, the Freedom Ride, the March on Washington and the Birmingham demonstration. Virtually no research was available on the seminal years of the civil rights movement, from 1957 to 1960. I could not find a complete text of the "Port Huron Statement" in print, and I was lucky to obtain an old mimeographed version. The literature on the Chicago riot of 1968, spectacular as it was, is surprisingly thin, and I found only a single volume of reprinted articles and documents on the Weathermen.

As often as not, I had to go back for information to what had been published during the period. I relied heavily, as one might imagine, on *The New York Times* and the *Washington Post*. John Seigenthaler, now the editor, was kind enough to send me the *Tennessean*'s file on the Nashville sit-in of 1960. *Congressional Quarterly* was a faithful companion, particularly in putting matters into their proper political context. The magazines that were most regularly useful to me were *Life, Ramparts* and the *Nation*.

The inadequacy of the literature forced me to turn early in my

553

research to personal interviews, from which the organization of the book emerged. Although a few people I had wanted to interview had vanished, of those I found, no one refused to talk to me, and answer my questions patiently and courteously. To them I am indebted, since without them this book would not have been possible.

Besides the people whose names head the respective chapters, I conducted interviews of some length with the following: Stew Alpert, Arnold Aronson, Julian Bond, Heather Booth, Paul Booth, Wiley Branton, Sam Brown, Tom Cottle, Rennie Davis, Ivanhoe Donaldson, Curtis Gans, Todd Gitlin, Edith Green, Jack Greenberg, Lawrence Guyot, Al Haber, David Horowitz, Paul Jacobs, Tom Kahn, Andrew Kopkind, James Lawson, Larry McMurtry, Harry McPherson, Burke Marshall, Diane Nash, Frances Fox Piven, R. Sargent Shriver, Richard Townsend, Roy Wilkins, Dagmar Wilson, Adam Yarmolinsky, Andrew Young, Dorothy Zellner and Robert Zellner. In addition, I was able to draw upon interviews of Mayor Richard Daley, Martin Luther King, Jr., Thurgood Marshall, Dr. Benjamin Spock and others which I conducted during the 1960s in connection with magazine articles.

I am also indebted to a long list of people to whom I was able to address specific questions, or who helped me in some other important way. I benefited particularly from the wisdom of Alan Barth. At the risk of forgetting some, I would also like to note with appreciation Mayor Ivan Allen, Jr., Richard Archer, Leonard Boudin, Paul Bullock, Bo Burlingham, Richard Buxbaum, Clayborne Carson, Jr., Paul Cobb, Stephen Cohen, Peter Collier, Jack Conway, Cortland Cox, G. William Domhoff, Douglas Dowd, Richard Flacks, Harold Fleming, James Forman, Albert Gollin, Sanford Gottleib, Genie Grohman, Seymour Hersh, Siegfried Hesse, Norman Hill, David Hoeh, Harold Horowitz, Rachelle Horowitz, Marvin Kalb, Mary King, Jerry Lewis, Gene Lichtenstein, Stanley Lubman, August Meier, Stanley Newman, Robert Pitofsky, Stephen S. Rosenfeld, Richard Rubenstein, Elliott Rudwick, Kirkpatrick Sale, Robert Scheer, Paul Schrade, Lawrence Speiser, David Stahl, Gregory Stone, William L. Taylor, Edith Wilkie, Roger Wilkins, Harold Willens, Hosea Williams, David Wise and Harris Wofford.

I have special thanks for Mary Allen and the staff of the Cleveland Park Branch of the Washington, D.C., Public Library, who were so indulgent of my needs, and Mary Davis, who graciously served as my channel to the Library of Congress. I note with appreciation the generosity of the Kettering Foundation, which allowed me to do this research while writing *The Citizen Poor of the 1960's.* I would also like to thank the staff of the Moorland-Spingarn Research Center at Howard University for making its excellent collection of civil rights materials available to me. From it, I was able to draw from taped interviews of Ella Baker, Edward Brown, Dion Diamond, Charles McDew, Clarence Mitchell and others. My own materials, including the tapes and transcripts, will be filed at the Center, where they will be generally accessible.

I want to thank Sheila Clarke, who worked so hard on the materials that went into this book. I would like to express special appreciation to Robert Lescher, my friend and literary agent, who encouraged me through the years that this work was in progress, then gave so generously of his time and talent in editing the manuscript. I am also grateful to Judith Viorst, in-house reader, inspiration and wife.

BIBLIOGRAPHY

ALI, TARIQ, ed. *The New Revolutionaries*. New York: William Morrow, 1969.

ALLEN, IVAN, JR., with Paul Hemphill. *Mayor: Notes on the Sixties*. New York: Simon & Schuster, 1971.

ALTBACH, PHILIP G. *Student Politics in America*. New York: McGraw-Hill, 1974.

ANDERSON, JERVIS. *A. Philip Randolph*. New York: Harcourt Brace Jovanovich, 1972.

APTHEKER, BETTINA. *The Academic Rebellion in the United States*. Secaucus, N.J.: Citadel, 1972.

AVORN, JERRY L., and members of the staff of the Columbia *Daily Spectator*. *Up Against the Ivy Wall, A History of the Columbia Crisis*. New York: Atheneum, 1968.

BALL, GORDON, ed. *Allen Ginsberg Journals, Early Fifties, Early Sixties*. New York: Grove Press, 1977.

BATES, DAISY. *The Long Shadow of Little Rock*. New York: David McKay, 1962.

BELFRAGE, SALLY. *Freedom Summer*. New York: Viking Press, 1965.

BENNETT, LERONE, JR. *What Manner of Man*. Chicago: Johnson, 1968.

BOECKMAN, CHARLES. *And the Beat Goes On*. Washington, D.C.: Luce, 1972.

BOYLE, KAY. *The Long Walk at San Francisco State*. New York: Grove Press, 1970.

BROOKS, THOMAS R. *Walls Come Tumbling Down*. Englewood Cliffs, N.J.: Prentice-Hall, 1974.

BROWN, EDMUND G. ("PAT"). *Reagan and Reality*. New York: Praeger, 1970.

BULLOCK, PAUL. *Watts: The Aftermath*. New York: Grove Press, 1969.

BURROUGHS, WILLIAM S. *Naked Lunch*. New York: Grove Press, 1959.

CARMICHAEL, STOKELY. *Stokely Speaks*. New York: Random House, 1971.

———, and HAMILTON, CHARLES V. *Black Power: The Politics of Liberation in America*. New York: Vintage, 1967.

CARSON, CLAYBORNE, JR. "Toward Freedom and Community: The Evolution of Ideas in the Student Non-Violent Coordinating Committee, 1960–1966." Ph.D. dissertation, University of California, 1975.

557

CHESTER, LEWIS; HODGSON, GODFREY; and PAGE, BRUCE. *An American Melodrama, The Presidential Campaign of 1968.* New York: Viking, 1969.

The Civil Rights Act of 1964. Washington, D.C.: Bureau of National Affairs, 1964.

CLEAVER, ELDRIDGE. *Soul on Ice.* New York: Dell, 1968.

COHEN, JERRY, and MURPHY, WILLIAM S. *Burn, Baby, Burn!* New York: Dutton, 1966.

COHEN, MICHAEL, and HALE, DENNIS, eds. *The New Student Left.* Boston: Beacon Press, 1966.

COLES, ROBERT. *Farewell to the South.* Boston: Little Brown, 1972.

CONOT, ROBERT. *Rivers of Blood, Years of Darkness.* New York: Bantam, 1967.

COOK, BRUCE. *The Beat Generation.* New York: Scribners, 1971.

CRANSTON, MAURICE, ed. *Prophetic Politics.* New York: Simon & Schuster, 1970.

DALTON, DAVID. *James Dean: The Mutant King.* New York: Dell, 1974.

DAVIDSON, SARA. *Loose Change.* Garden City, N.Y.: Doubleday, 1977.

DAVIES, PETER. *The Truth About Kent State.* New York: Farrar, Straus & Giroux, 1973.

DELLINGER, DAVE. *More Power Than We Know: The People's Movement Toward Democracy.* New York: Doubleday, 1975.

DOS PASSOS, JOHN. *Mid-Century.* Boston: Houghton Mifflin, 1960.

DRAPER, HAL. *Berkeley: The New Student Revolt.* New York: Grove Press, 1965.

DU BOIS, W. E. B. *The Souls of Black Folk.* New York: Fawcett, 1961.

EHRLICH, JOHN, and EHRLICH, SUSAN, eds. *Student Power, Participation and Revolution.* New York: Association Press, 1970.

EHRLICH, J. W. *Howl of the Censor.* San Carlo, Calif.: Nourse, 1961.

EISEN, JONATHAN, ed. *The Age of Rock.* New York: Random House, 1969.

EICHEL, LAWRENCE E., et al. *The Harvard Strike.* Boston: Houghton Mifflin, 1970.

ENGLISH, DAVID, and the staff of the *London Daily Express. Divided They Stand.* Englewood Cliffs, N.J.: Prentice-Hall, 1969.

ESZTERHAS, JOE, and ROBERTS, MICHAEL D. *Thirteen Seconds.* New York: Dodd, Mead, 1970.

EVANS, ROWLAND, JR., and NOVAK, ROBERT D. *Lyndon B. Johnson: The Exercise of Power.* New York: New American Library, 1966.

———. *Nixon in the White House.* New York: Random House, 1971.

FAGER, CHARLES E. *Selma, 1965.* New York: Scribners, 1974.

———. *Uncertain Resurrection: The Poor People's Washington Campaign.* Grand Rapids: Eerdmans, 1969.

FERBER, MICHAEL, and LYND, STAUGHTON. *The Resistance.* Boston: Beacon Press, 1971.

FEUER, LEWIS S. *The Conflict of Generations.* New York: Basic Books, 1969.

FLACKS, RICHARD. *Youth and Social Change.* Chicago: Markham, 1972.

BIBLIOGRAPHY

FOGELSON, ROBERT M., ed. *The Los Angeles Riots.* New York: Arno Press, 1969.

FONER, PHILIP S., ed. *The Black Panthers Speak.* Philadelphia: Lippincott, 1970.

FORMAN, JAMES. *The Making of Black Revolutionaries.* New York: Macmillan, 1972.

———. *Sammy Younge, Jr.* New York: Grove, 1968.

FOSTER, JULIAN, and LONG, DURWARD, eds. *Protest! Student Activism in America.* New York: William Morrow, 1970.

"Four Days of Rage: The Power Play That Failed." *Chicago Tribune,* November 23, 1969.

FRADY, MARSHALL. *Wallace.* New York: World, 1970.

FRAZIER, E. FRANKLIN. *The Negro Church in America.* New York: Schocken, 1963.

———. *Negro Youth at the Crossways.* New York: Schocken, 1967.

———. *On Race Relations.* Chicago: University of Chicago Press, 1968.

FREE (ABBIE HOFFMAN). *Revolution for the Hell of It.* New York: Dial, 1968.

FRIEDAN, BETTY. *The Feminine Mystique.* New York: Dell, 1963.

GARDNER, DAVID. *The California Oath Controversy.* Berkeley: University of California Press, 1967.

GARFINKEL, HERBERT. *When Negroes March.* Glencoe, Ill.: The Free Press, 1959.

GARROW, DAVID J. *Protest at Selma.* New Haven, Conn.: Yale University Press, 1978.

GENOVESE, EUGENE. *Roll, Jordan, Roll: The World the Slaves Made.* New York: Pantheon, 1974.

GEYLIN, PHILIP. *Lyndon B. Johnson and the World.* New York: Praeger, 1966.

GILBERT, BEN W., and the staff of the *Washington Post. Ten Blocks from the White House.* New York: Praeger, 1968.

GINSBERG, ALLEN. *Allen Verbatim.* Edited by Gordon Ball. New York: McGraw-Hill, 1974.

———. *Howl and Other Poems.* San Francisco: City Lights Books, 1956.

GLAZER, NATHAN. *Remembering the Answers.* New York: Basic Books, 1970.

GLEASON, BILL. *Daley of Chicago.* New York: Simon & Schuster, 1970.

GOLDMAN, ARTHUR. *Freakshow.* New York: Atheneum, 1971.

GOLDMAN, ERIC. *The Tragedy of Lyndon Johnson.* New York: Knopf, 1968.

GOOD, PAUL. *The Trouble I've Seen.* Washington, D.C.: Howard University Press, 1975.

GOODMAN, EZRA. *The Fifty Year Decline and Fall of Hollywood.* New York: Simon & Schuster, 1961.

GOULDEN, JOSEPH C. *Meany.* New York: Atheneum, 1972.

GRIER, WILLIAM H., and COBBS, PRICE M. *Black Rage.* New York: Basic Books, 1968.

GUTHMAN, EDWIN. *We Band of Brothers.* New York: Harper & Row, 1971.

559

HALBERSTAM, DAVID. *The Best and the Brightest.* Greenwich, Conn.: Fawcett, 1971.
———. *The Unfinished Odyssey of Robert Kennedy.* New York: Random House, 1969.
HANEY, ROBERT W. *Comstockery in America.* Boston: Beacon Press, 1960.
Hard-Core Unemployment and Poverty in Los Angeles. Washington, D.C.: U.S. Department of Commerce, Government Printing Office, 1965.
HASKINS, JAMES. *Profiles in Black Power.* Garden City, N.Y.: Doubleday, 1972.
HAYDEN, TOM. *Rebellion and Repression.* Cleveland: World, 1969.
———. *Trial.* New York: Holt, Rinehart & Winston, 1970.
HEDGEMAN, ANNA ARNOLD. *The Trumpet Sounds.* New York: Holt, Rinehart & Winston, 1964.
HEIRICH, MAX. *The Beginning: Berkeley 1964.* New York: Columbia University Press, 1968.
HEMPHILL, PAUL. *The Nashville Sound.* New York: Simon & Schuster, 1970.
HODGSON, GODFREY. *America in Our Time.* New York: Doubleday, 1976.
HOEH, DAVID C. "The Biography of a Campaign: McCarthy in New Hampshire." Unpublished, 1975.
HOLT, LEN. *An Act of Conscience.* Boston: Beacon Press, 1965.
———. *The Summer that Didn't End.* New York: William Morrow, 1965.
HOROWITZ, DAVID. *Student.* New York: Ballantine, 1962.
HOROWITZ, IRVING LOUIS, ed. *The New Sociology.* New York: Oxford, 1964.
HUGHES, LANGSTON. *Fight for Freedom.* New York: Norton, 1962.
———. HUGHES, LANGSTON, ed. *New Negro Poets.* Bloomington: Indiana University Press, 1964.
HUIE, WILLIAM BRADFORD. *3 Lives for Mississippi.* New York: New American Library, 1968.
HUMPHREY, HUBERT H. *The Education of a Public Man.* New York: Doubleday, 1976.
JACOBS, HAROLD, ed. *Weathermen.* Berkeley: Ramparts Press, 1970.
JACOBS, PAUL. *Prelude to Riot.* New York: Random House, 1967.
———, and LANDAU, SAUL. *The New Radicals.* New York: Vintage, 1966.
JOHNSON, LYNDON B. *The Vantage Point.* New York: Holt, Rinehart & Winston, 1971.
JOSEPH, PETER. *Good Times: An Oral History of America in the Nineteen Sixties.* New York: Charterhouse, 1973.
KAHN, ROGER. *The Battle for Morningside Heights.* New York: William Morrow, 1970.
KATOPE, CHRISTOPHER G., and ZOLBROD, PAUL G. *Beyond Berkeley.* Cleveland: World, 1966.
KEESING'S RESEARCH REPORTS. *Race Relations in the USA, 1954–1968.* New York: Scribners, 1970.
KELMAN, STEVEN. *Push Comes to Shove.* Boston: Houghton Mifflin, 1970.

KENISTON, KENNETH. *The Uncommitted.* New York: Harcourt, Brace and World, 1965.

KEROUAC, JACK. *On The Road.* New York: Viking, 1957.

KERR, CLARK. *The Uses of the University.* Cambridge, Mass.: Harvard University Press, 1964.

KILLIAN, LEWIS M. *The Impossible Revolution.* New York: Random House, 1968.

KING, CORETTA SCOTT. *My Life with Martin Luther King, Jr.* New York: Avon, 1969.

KING, MARTIN LUTHER. *Stride Toward Freedom.* New York: Harper & Row, 1958.

———. *Where Do We Go From Here? Chaos or Community.* New York: Harper & Row, 1967.

———. *Why We Can't Wait.* New York: Harper & Row, 1963.

KLEIN, ALEXANDER, ed. *Natural Enemies.* Philadelphia: Lippincott, 1969.

KOPKIND, ANDREW, ed. *Thoughts of Young Radicals.* Washington, D.C.: The New Republic, 1966.

KRAMER, JANE. *Allen Ginsberg in America.* New York: Random House, 1968.

KUNEN, JAMES SIMON. *The Strawberry Statement.* New York: Random House, 1968.

LANDAU, SAUL. "The Last Six Months of C. Wright Mills." *Ramparts,* August 1965.

LARNER, JEREMY. *Nobody Knows.* New York: Macmillan, 1969.

LAUTER, PAUL, and HOWE, FLORENCE. *The Conspiracy of the Young.* Cleveland: World, 1970.

LEAMER, LAURENCE. *The Paper Revolutionaries.* New York: Simon & Schuster, 1972.

LEVINE, MARYL, and NAISBITT, JOHN. *Right On!* New York: Bantam, 1970.

LEWIS, DAVID L. *King: A Critical Biography.* New York: Praeger, 1970.

LINCOLN, C. ERIC. *The Black Muslims in America.* Boston: Beacon Press, 1961, 1973.

———. *The Sounds of the Struggle.* New York: Morrow, 1967.

LIPSET, SEYMOUR MARTIN, and ALTBACH, PHILIP G., eds. *Students in Revolt.* Boston: Houghton Mifflin, 1969.

———, and WOLIN, SHELDON S., eds. *The Berkeley Student Revolt.* Garden City: Doubleday, 1965.

LOMAX, LOUIS. *When the Word Is Given.* Cleveland: World, 1963.

LOUIS, DEBBIE. *And We Are Not Saved.* New York: Doubleday, 1970.

LUCE, PHILLIP ABBOTT. *The New Left.* New York: David McKay, 1966.

LUKAS, J. ANTHONY. *Don't Shoot—We Are Your Children!* New York: Random House, 1971.

LYND, ALICE, ed. *We Won't Go, Personal Accounts of War Objectors.* Boston: Beacon Press, 1968.

LYND, STAUGHTON, ed. *Nonviolence in America: A Documentary History.* Indianapolis: Bobbs-Merrill, 1966.

561

———, and HAYDEN, TOM. *The Other Side.* New York: New American Library, 1966.

McCARTHY, EUGENE. *The Year of the People.* New York: Doubleday, 1969.

McMURTRY, LARRY. *In a Narrow Grave.* New York: Simon & Schuster, 1968.

MAILER, NORMAN. *The Armies of the Night.* New York: New American Library, 1968.

———. *Some Honorable Men, Political Conventions 1960–1972.* Boston: Little Brown, 1976.

MEHNERT, KLAUS. *Twilight of the Young.* New York: Holt, Rinehart & Winston, 1967.

MEIER, AUGUST, and RUDWICK, ELLIOTT. *CORE: A Study in the Civil Rights Movement, 1942–1968.* New York: Oxford, 1973.

———. *From Plantation to Ghetto.* 3d ed. New York: Hill & Wang, 1976.

MENASHE, LOUIS, and RADOSH, RONALD, eds. *Teach-ins: USA.* New York: Praeger, 1967.

MERRILL, THOMAS F. *Allen Ginsberg.* New York: Twayne, 1969.

MICHENER, JAMES A. *Kent State: What Happened and Why.* New York: Random House, 1971.

MILLER, WILLIAM ROBERT. *Martin Luther King, Jr.* New York: Weybright and Talley, 1968.

MILLS, C. WRIGHT. *The Power Elite.* New York: Oxford, 1959.

MITFORD, JESSICA. *The Trial of Dr. Spock.* New York: Knopf, 1969.

MOYNIHAN, DANIEL P. *Maximum Feasible Misunderstanding.* New York: The Free Press, 1969.

MURPHY, TERRENCE J. *Censorship: Government and Obscenity.* Baltimore: Helicon, 1963.

MUSE, BENJAMIN. *Ten Years of Prelude.* New York: Viking, 1964.

MYRDAL, GUNNAR. *An American Dilemma.* New York: Harper & Row, 1944.

NAVASKY, VICTOR. *Kennedy Justice.* New York: Atheneum, 1971.

NEARY, JOHN. *Julian Bond.* New York: William Morrow, 1971.

NELSON, JACK, and BASS, JACK. *The Orangeburg Massacre.* New York: World, 1970.

NEWFIELD, JACK. *A Prophetic Minority.* New York: New American Library, 1966.

———. *Robert Kennedy: A Memoir.* New York: Dutton, 1969.

OBERDORFER, DON. *Tet!* New York: Doubleday, 1971.

O'BRIEN, JAMES. "A History of the New Left, 1960–1968." Unpublished manuscript, 1968.

OBST, LYNDA R., ed. *The Sixties.* New York: Rolling Stone Press, 1976.

O'NEILL, WILLIAM L. *Coming Apart.* Chicago: Quadrangle, 1971.

OPPENHEIMER, MARTIN, and LAKEY, GEORGE. *A Manual for Direct Action.* Chicago: Quadrangle, 1964.

ORRICK, WILLIAM H., JR. *Shut It Down! A College in Crisis: San Francisco*

State College, October 1968–April 1969. A Report to the National Commission on the Causes and Prevention of Violence. Washington, 1969.

PAUL, JAMES C. N., and SCHWARTZ, MURRAY L. *Federal Censorship*. New York: Free Press of Glencoe, 1961.

PECK, JAMES. *Underdogs Vs. Upperdogs*. Canterbury, N.H.: Greenleaf Books, 1969.

PETERSON, RICHARD E., and BILORUSKY, JOHN A. *May 1970: The Campus Aftermath of Cambodia and Kent State*. Berkeley: The Carnegie Commission on Higher Education, 1971.

PORAMBO, RON. *No Cause for Indictment: An Autopsy of Newark*. New York: Holt, Rinehart & Winston, 1971.

POTTER, PAUL. *A Name for Ourselves*. Boston: Little, Brown, 1971.

POWERS, THOMAS. *Diana: The Making of a Terrorist*. Boston: Houghton Mifflin, 1971.

———. *The War at Home: Vietnam and the American People, 1964–1968*. New York: Grossman, 1973.

RAINES, HOWELL. *My Soul Is Rested*. New York: Putnam, 1977.

RAKOVE, MILTON. *Don't Make No Waves...Don't Back No Losers*. Bloomington: Indiana University Press, 1975.

RAPOPORT, ROGER, and KIRSHBAUM, LAURENCE J. *Is The Library Burning?* New York: Random House, 1969.

REICH, CHARLES. *The Greening of America*. New York: Random House, 1970.

REMBAR, CHARLES. *The End of Obscenity*. New York: Random House, 1968.

Report of the National Advisory Commission on Civil Disorders. New York: Bantam, 1968.

The Report of the President's Commission on Campus Unrest. New York: Arno Press, 1970.

Rights in Conflict: The Violent Confrontation of Demonstrators and Police in the Parks and Streets of Chicago During the Week of the Democratic National Convention (The Walker Report). New York: Bantam, 1968.

Riots in the City—An Addendum to the McCone Commission Report. Los Angeles: National Association of Social Workers, 1967.

ROSSMAN, MICHAEL. *The Wedding Within the War*. New York: Doubleday, 1971.

ROSZAK, THEODORE. *The Making of a Counter Culture*. New York: Doubleday, 1969.

ROYKO, MIKE. *Boss, Richard J. Daley of Chicago*. New York: Dutton, 1971.

RUBIN, JERRY. *Do It! Scenarios of the Revolution*. New York: Ballantine, 1970.

———. *Growing (Up) at 37*. New York: Warner, 1976.

———. *We Are Everywhere*. New York: Harper & Row, 1971.

RUSTIN, BAYARD. *Down the Line*. Chicago: Quadrangle, 1971.

SAFIRE, WILLIAM. *Before the Fall*. New York: Doubleday, 1975.

SALE, KIRKPATRICK. *SDS*. New York: Random House, 1973.

SAUNDERS, DORIS E., ed. *The Day They Marched*. Chicago: Johnson, 1963.

SCHEER, ROBERT. "The People's Park." *Ramparts* magazine, August, 1969.

SCHELL, JONATHAN. *Time of Illusion*. New York: Knopf, 1975.

SCHLESINGER, ARTHUR, JR. *A Thousand Days*. Boston: Houghton Mifflin, 1965.

SCHULTZ, JOHN. *Motion Will be Denied: A New Report on the Chicago Conspiracy Trial*. New York: William Morrow, 1972.

SEALE, BOBBY. *Seize the Time*. New York: Random House, 1970.

SELLERS, CLEVELAND. *The River of No Return*. New York: William Morrow, 1973.

SHANNON, WILLIAM V. *The Heir Apparent*. New York: Macmillan, 1967.

SHULBERG, BUDD. *From the Ashes: Voices of Watts*. Cleveland: Meridian, 1969.

SILBERMAN, CHARLES E. *Crisis in Black and White*. New York: Random House, 1964.

SKOLNICK, JEROME H. *The Politics of Protest*. New York: Simon & Schuster, 1969.

SOBEL, LESTER A., ed. *Civil Rights, 1960–3*. New York: Facts on File, 1964.

SORENSEN, THEODORE C. *Kennedy*. New York: Harper & Row, 1965.

SPENDER, STEPHEN. *The Year of the Young Rebels*. New York: Random House, 1969.

STERN, SUSAN. *With the Weathermen*. Garden City, N.Y.: Doubleday, 1975.

STEVENSON, JANET. *The Montgomery Bus Boycott*. New York: Watts, 1971.

STONE, I. F. *The Killings at Kent State*. New York: New York Review, 1971.

STOUT, RICHARD T. *People*. New York: Harper & Row, 1970.

STROUT, CUSHING, and GROSSVOGEL, DAVID I., eds. *Divided We Stand: Reflections on the Crisis at Cornell*. New York: Doubleday, 1970.

"Students Protest." *The Annals of the American Academy of Political and Social Science*. May 1971.

SUGARMAN, TRACY. *Stranger at the Gates: A Summer in Mississippi*. New York: Hill & Wang, 1966.

SUTHERLAND, ELIZABETH, ed. *Letters from Mississippi*. New York: McGraw-Hill, 1965.

TAYLOR, WILLIAM L. *Hanging Together*. New York: Simon & Schuster, 1971.

TEODORI, MASSIMO, ed. *The New Left: A Documentary History*. Indianapolis: Bobbs-Merrill, 1969.

TERKEL, STUDS. *Hard Times*. New York: Pantheon, 1970.

TYTELL, JOHN. *Naked Angels: The Lives and Literature of the Beat Generation*. New York: McGraw-Hill, 1976.

Violence in the City—An End or a Beginning. A Report by the Governor's Commission on the Los Angeles Riots, 1965.

VIORST, MILTON. *The Citizen Poor of the 1960's.* Dayton: Kettering Foundation, 1977.

———. *Fall From Grace.* New York: New American Library, 1968.

———. *Hustlers and Heroes.* New York: Simon & Schuster, 1971.

VON HOFFMAN, NICHOLAS. *We Are the People Our Parents Warned Us Against.* Chicago: Quadrangle, 1968.

WALLENSTEIN, IMMANUEL, and STARR, PAUL, eds. *The University Crisis Reader.* 2 vols. New York: Random House, 1971.

WARREN, ROBERT PENN. *Who Speaks for the Negro?* New York: Random House, 1965.

WARSHAW, STEVEN. *The Trouble in Berkeley.* Berkeley, Calif.: Diablo Press, 1965.

WATTENBERG, BEN J. *The Real America.* Garden City, N.Y.: Doubleday, 1974.

WATTERS, PAT, and CLEGHORN, REESE. *Climbing Jacob's Ladder.* New York: Harcourt, Brace, 1967.

WHITE, THEODORE H. *The Making of the President: 1960.* New York: Atheneum, 1961.

———. *The Making of the President: 1964.* New York: Atheneum, 1965.

———. *The Making of the President: 1968.* New York: Atheneum, 1969.

WILHOIT, FRANCIS M. *The Politics of Massive Resistance.* New York: Braziller, 1973.

WITCOVER, JULES. *The Resurrection of Richard Nixon.* New York: Putnam, 1970.

WOLFF, MILES. *Lunch at the Five and Ten.* New York: Stein & Day, 1970.

WOLIN, SHELDON S., and SCHAAR, JOHN H. *The Berkeley Rebellion and Beyond.* New York: New York Review, 1970.

Writers at Work: The Paris Review Interviews. 3d ser. New York: Viking, 1967.

ZINN, HOWARD. *SNCC: The New Abolitionists.* Boston: Beacon Press, 1964.

———. *The Southern Mystique.* New York: Knopf, 1964.

PICTURE CREDITS

Index

567

Jacobs, John, 480, 488n
Japan, 163, 187, 207, 304, 388
Japanese-Americans, 296
jazz, 61, 68, 79
Jews:
    blacks and, 322, 333, 378, 412
    in student movement, 164, 296
jobs, 322, 547
    discrimination in, 50, 204, 205,
        283
    Emancipation March for, 216–17
    federal, for blacks, 129, 139–40,
        205, 206
    FEPC and, 205, 206
    March on Washington and, 216–
        217, 226, 228, 230–31, 346
Johnson, Jerome, 451
Johnson, Lyndon B., 191, 230, 236,
        310
    assets of, 384
    civil rights issues and, 235, 238,
        239–40, 254, 255–56, 321,
        328–29, 330, 362, 372, 379,
        395, 432
    credibility gap created by, 384–
        385
    Kerner Commission established
        by, 337
    in 1960 convention, 238–39
    in 1964 convention, 254, 255,
        262, 263, 264–65, 266, 267,
        269, 358, 392–93
    1968 convention and, 456, 459
    political background of, 238
    on Selma demonstrations, 328–
        329
    Vietnam War and, 306, 347, 363,
        383–86, 389, 393, 394, 397,
        400, 402–3, 404, 406–11,
        414–20, 450
    in withdrawal from 1968
        election, 419, 440, 443, 447
Jones, James Edward, 340
Jones, Jeff, 488n, 491, 492
Joplin, Janis, 521
Journey of Reconciliation (1947),
        137–38, 140, 141, 156
Justice Department, U.S., 132, 146,
        501, 542
    Birmingham campaign and, 218,
        221–22

Civil Rights Division of, 181–82
    Freedom Rides and, 147, 148,
        152, 214–15
    voter registration campaigns and,
        246, 247–48, 257–58, 354

Kahler, Dean, 538, 539
Kahn, Tom, 216–17
Kane, Ronald J., 532
Kazan, Elia, 81
Keats, John, 70
Kennedy, Edward (Ted), 443, 456,
        459
Kennedy, John F., 127–28, 129–30,
        132–33, 139–40, 146, 400,
        440
    assassination of, 199, 230, 235,
        239–40, 255, 282, 384
    Birmingham campaign and, 218,
        219, 220, 221
    civil rights bill of, see civil rights
        bill (1963)
    Freedom Ride and, 148, 153
    March on Washington and, 222,
        225–26, 230
    in 1960 convention, 238–39, 250,
        262
    students and, 171–72, 173, 174,
        175, 276, 282
Kennedy, Robert, 133, 140, 239,
        439, 440
    assassination of, 423, 442, 447,
        448, 451
    Birmingham campaign and, 219,
        223
    Freedom Rides and, 146–48, 151,
        152, 153, 155, 157–58, 214,
        242
    as presidential candidate, 417–
        418, 420, 440, 441–42, 446,
        447
    Vietnam War and, 404, 409–10
    voter registration and, 241–42,
        243, 248, 354
Kent State (Michener), 511n, 536,
        537, 542
Kent State University, 13, 170, 485,
        508–9, 511–13, 515–18,
        524–43
    Black United Students at, 513,
        528

577